From Signs to Design

From Signs to Design

Environmental Process and Reform
in Early Renaissance Rome

Charles Burroughs

The MIT Press
Cambridge, Massachusetts
London, England

This book was set in Trump Mediaeval by Asco Trade Typesetting Ltd, Hong Kong, and printed and bound in the United States of America.

Library of Congress Cataloging-in-Publication Data

Burroughs, Charles.
   From signs to design : environmental process and reform in early
Renaissance Rome / Charles Burroughs.
      p. cm.
   Includes bibliographical references.
   ISBN 0-262-02298-2
      1. Architecture, Renaissance—Italy—Rome.   2. City planning—
Italy—Rome—History—15th century.   3. Rome (Italy)—Buildings,
structures, etc.   4. Urbanization—Italy—Rome—History.   I. Title.
NA1120.B87   1990
307.76′0945′63209024—dc20   89-13768
                                                                        CIP

For Christine

Contents

Preface

This book examines some seven years in the life of a single city and its hinterland. Such restriction of attention, however, provides the basis for a different kind of expansiveness. The theme of the journey is central in the discussions. Sometimes the territory traversed is literal: the text explores the urban quarters, processional and utilitarian thoroughfares, shrines and secular institutions, markets, harbors, and hinterland of early Renaissance Rome. And I have sought to follow within this social and topographical context the tracks of certain individuals whose activity and social or professional relations seemed of particular importance for an understanding of continuities and changes in the physical environment.

Discussions of the life of Rome at any particular time are almost inevitably colored by the sense of the development and fate of the city as imperial, papal, or national capital; teleology—again, a metaphor of journey—seeps into the most resolutely social historical or anthropological writing. Any account of the era of Nicholas V can fall easily victim to the teleological temptation, setting Nicholas's achievements or at least ambitions in the context of long-term processes that they seem to anticipate. This is especially the case in discussions of architecture and urbanism, terms that themselves, of course, tend to be irredeemably colored by teleological suggestions.

There are many reasons, nevertheless, for seeing the era of Nicholas as pregnant, as it were, with important transformations, as a time of experimentation out of which certain crucial trends would take their form. The sense of a watershed, of symptomatic processes, is immanent in the following discussions, underpinning whatever claim they have to more general interest. The vernacular world of Rome, then, which I seek to evoke and analyze, becomes the background noise of human activity and interaction and environmental process against which new processes and patterns assert themselves, however gradually. Dimly the profile of a societal journey, history itself, becomes apparent, signposted by the marks inscribed on the walls, in the streets, or even in the very fabric and structure of the city and the wider environment. Such marks, indeed, are a particular focus of this book.

To some readers the tapestry of intersecting itineraries—both specific routes and, more generally, life paths—followed around and through fifteenth-century Rome may seem less respectably academic than Joycean in character. Indeed, *Ulysses* has served in some respects as a model. It is hard, for example, to think of a better evocation of the ceremonial use of a city than James Joyce's account of the funeral of Paddy Dignam (as long as public ceremony is not seen as exhausted in the agendas of the power centers of a society). No author has so tellingly described the multiple intersections, relationships, and encounters that constitute the fabric of urban life, intersections that involve even inanimate elements, notably the river (one thinks of the celebrated encounter of a bar of lemon-scented soap with the River Liffey); the river, too, in my account of the city of the Tiber eventually emerges as a major protagonist. As in Joyce's work, the same themes, characters, and places reappear at different points in my discussions, though viewed in a different light and in relationship to different contexts. There is even a suitably daedalic candidate for a leading role in a Joycean Rome of c. 1450 in the bookish but resourceful Francesco del Borgo, student of Archimedes and careful observer, one presumes, of the administrative structures and public works projects with which he was connected as he laid the foundations for an apparently quite stellar later career as architect.

Joyce's epic is distinguished not least by its contrastive and often parodic deployment of discursive and rhetorical modes, some lifted from the milieu of Dublin itself and its habits and fashions, others from the literary tradition variously celebrated and manhandled throughout. The present book is made up of a set of diverse soundings into a determinate historical situation, but also into modes of analysis and (re)presentation. As such it crystallizes or even (as in the introduction) rehearses my own itinerary through the challenges and temptations of the many intellectual positions and methodologies that compete for the soul of an architectural historian. The introduction is intended as a brief and inevitably allusive account of these positions, including those explicitly or implicitly exemplified in the remarkably diverse and original tradition of scholarship on the Nicholan era itself. For an account of Roman topographical, social, and institutional structures, readers should begin rather with chapter 1, which is intended to be introductory in a more concrete, social historical sense.

Architectural history stands at present exposed between the methodological rigor of the social sciences, the powerful interpretive instruments and models of the recent school of cultural studies, the mastery and tactful explication of archival sources of widely differing type of the traditional historical disciplines, and the concern for problems of signification and representation of a newly prominent current in art historical and especially literary studies. This is, in my view, salutary, and I have to confess impatience with the positivist slant and narrowly defined scope of much recent Anglo-American and German architectural historical scholarship, while recognizing some truly remarkable achievements, not least in the study of the architecture and built environment of Rome itself. Indeed, much of my own discussion is ultimately grounded in empirical or even empiricist inquiry, and I have chosen to use the resulting data to elaborate a highly complex and conflicted societal model in conscious contrast with the relatively reductive models employed, albeit with impressive trenchancy and rigor, in certain recent studies of the period. In particular, I have been concerned to essay reconstructions at least of aspects of the symbolic environment of mid-fifteenth-century Romans, an enterprise that, needless to say, has required the synthesizing and perhaps forced deployment of a wide range of evidence.

I have already implicitly begun to register my acknowledgments. This book has been long in the making and its own journey to publication has been marked by various interruptions and changes of locale and climate, both physical and intellectual. It has both the strength and weaknesses of being written in relative isolation, at a distance from contemporary Rome and its archives, libraries, and human resources; though in two quite brief research campaigns in the 1970s I undertook, as far as I was able, to work through the extant documentation of all types produced in Rome and its hinterland in the restricted period under study, my research proceeded independently of impressive archival and social historical studies, to a great extent carried out as a cooperative and coherent endeavor, that are radically changing the parameters of work on the late medieval and early Renaissance city. At least, this book gives English-speaking readers some idea of the remarkable work carried out in the last decade and a half, notably by Italian and French scholars, on the institutional and economic structures of the city and region. My debt to this work is evident enough in the chapters that follow.

On the other hand, I have been fortunate enough to come into close contact with vital currents of scholarship of great interest, though at first sight little common ground. As an undergraduate at Oxford I came across the prosopographical reconstruction of careers of administrators and other important figures in the Roman Empire, a historiographical program that has challenged long-held assumptions about the nature and homogeneity of systems of power relations. At the Warburg Institute I encountered studies of remarkable concreteness and sophistication of the formation and transformation of discursive patterns, intellectual models, and institutional formations underlying the cultural shifts of the Renaissance. Two extended sojourns at the British School at Rome (for which I thank the Leverhume Trust and the British School itself) familiarized me with the tradition of the archaeological study of a whole region pioneered in the British School's South Etruria project. At the University of California, Berkeley, I became acquainted with leading practitioners of the North American school concerned with the study of vernacular building and the cultural landscape, a highly cross-disciplinary enterprise that has brought together geographical, anthropological, and a variety of historical perspectives. Finally, at the State University of New York at Binghamton I found myself challenged, like it or not, by an intense debate among exponents of various theoretical positions in the spectrum conveniently designated as poststructuralist, and between them and scholars referring social science models to long-term historical processes.

In specific terms I should first honor the dead: Russell Meiggs, my tutor at Balliol, set a standard of historiographical fastidiousness that I shall never reach; Frances Yates of the Warburg Institute was a model of academic originality notably in the linking of mental process and spatial order; John Ward-Perkins of the British School at Rome and protagonist of the South Etruria project never suspected, I am sure, that I might, with whatever result, follow his lead (and, further back, that of Thomas Ashby); and Wolfgang Braunfels (whom I met only once) provided with his magnificent books on the shaping of urban environments an indelible influence and inspiration.

Among the many friends and colleagues who have variously helped along the way I should like to single out Robert Adam, Michael Baxandall, Zeynep Celik,

David Chambers, Ted Goodman, Richard Ingersoll (who introduced me to Victor Turner's ideas), Preminda Jacob (who introduced me to the work of Michel de Certeau), Paolo Polledri, David Thomas (who taught me something about how neighborhoods and other local allegiances work), and C. W. Westfall, author of a remarkable book that addressed some of the same material in a very different way.I owe a special debt to colleagues at Binghamton—Barbara Abouel-Haj, Donald Preziosi, Tony King, George McKee, Norman and Yedida Stillman, John Tagg, Richard Trexler, and Jean Wilson—for their intellectual inspiration and their support in a difficult period. I am grateful to Randy Mack and Henry Millon for the opportunity to present drafts of chapters to learned and critical audiences. And I received indispensable assistance from the staffs of the Archivi di Stato in Rome, Venice, Florence, Siena, and Milan and from those of the Archivio Comunale of Fabriano, the Archivio Capitolino at Rome, and, of course, the Archivio Segreto Vaticano. My gratitude goes also to the staffs of the Vatican Library, the Avery Library of Columbia University, the Warburg Institute, the British Library, the British School at Rome, the Hertziana, the Cornell University Libraries, the New York Public Research Library, and the University Library of SUNY Binghamton. The maps were prepared by Richard Zobel and Ashley Wisner, outstanding architects in the making. At MIT Press my thanks go to Mark Rakatansky who signed me up, Roger Conover who has been consistently supportive, and Matthew Abbate, prince of editors, who has saved me from many an error and brought order to a luxuriating abundance of footnotes.

Finally, the journey which has issued in this book was not only mine; I dedicate the book to the one whose support and patience made the journey possible, and with whom I have come to know at first hand a succession of cities and neighborhoods as the image of the distant but vivid place evoked in the following pages developed in my mind.

From Signs to Design

Introduction

All human societies occupy, utilize, and invest meaning in territory. The physical setting of settlement and husbandry, whether or not it undergoes extensive physical change through human agency, becomes a repository of symbols—or rather a privileged matrix and even medium of symbolization—through which patterns of belief, authority, and social structure are realized (not merely reflected).[1] This is not, needless to say, simply a matter of the operations of artifice on nature, of transformations of natural substance into cultural products, for no landscape is a clean slate. Even as new demographic, sociocultural, religious, or political phenomena assert themselves within and through their physical setting, the latter bears the marks of earlier human activity and settlement or, more often, that of surviving but politically and otherwise subject population groups. On occasion this receives expression in the myths of a culture's origins: in Virgil's epic of the foundation of Rome, for instance, Aeneas is guided by providence to a land that is already ancient, where the ruined vestiges of past civilizations constitute a shadowy prophecy of the grandeur of the cities of Aeneas's descendants, if not also, on a subtextual level, of their ultimate and inevitable decay (*Aeneid* VIII). The appropriation, indeed naturalization, of such earlier or concomitant human presence, assimilated to the geographical and ecological substratum of a dominant social formation, is a familiar aspect of the ideological underpinnings of civilizations, not least in the western world since the Renaissance.[2]

In many cultures, especially those founded on Greco-Roman precedent, the built environment is a preeminent constituent of the physical setting. The environment is marked and ordered through monumental architecture and through planned settlement forms, often relating territory and the patterns of human life to cosmological conceptions and geometrical schemata, though not in general, at least overtly, to traces of earlier patterns of spatial order and symbolization on the land (Müller 1961; Rykwert 1976). In such cases, there is much to justify the scholarly focus, prevalent among architectural historians, on buildings and places privileged by a given society through the disproportionate allocation of available resources (sometimes resulting in a damaging degree of immobilization of societal capital). Nevertheless, the process of exclusion implicit in any tradition of monumental architecture, the contrast established with the world of vernacular building and everyday activity, implies that the former can only be properly studied in the context of the vernacular, its excluded yet essential context and frame. Paradoxically, moreover, the excluded substratum remains central to the monumental traditions of western architecture, not least in the Renaissance, through the insistent grounding of the latter in idealized abstractions of the natural order, considered as including the societal order and its physical expression. Examples reviewed in later chapters are the paradigmatic role of Leone Battista Alberti's conception of the traditional household in his social and architectural thought, for all his occasional criticism of aspects of the medieval urban environment, or Leonardo Bruni's emphasis on the no less ideal than natural concentricity of the city of Florence as a synthesis of human agency and geomorphic circumstance.

Such general issues are addressed in this book not on the level of abstract speculation, but through the reconstruction of the milieu of a particularly crucial environmental initiative, that of Nicholas V, though it has proved necessary to reexamine with due skepticism the very conception of a contrast of milieu and initiative in this case, and the viability of each term. In addition, I have provisionally drawn attention to visual codes and systems of communication operative in the social and cultural practices and the environmental formations concerned. An inevitable weakness in the procedure followed is that although the social and environmental hypotheses hazarded below indeed concern a vernacular world in contrast to that of the papal court or aristocratic households, the discussion largely concentrates on a relatively small social elite, the patriciate of Rome. This elite can legitimately be defined in class terms through its institutional affiliations and its dominant role in local administrative and ritual structures, which in turn depended on the possession and active exploitation of wealth; it is clearly distinct from—and doubtless saw itself as distinct from—less affluent population groups on whom the available documentation, at least for the brief time period with which this study is concerned, sheds far less light. Whatever is understood, however, under the descriptions "the Roman population" or "the city"—in the ideologically charged discourse of the fifteenth century, of course, the covert real referent is generally the patriciate—there is still great heuristic value in the discussion of the changing relations between the city and the papal regime, itself far from a self-evident concept. And central in this history is the evolving conception of an exclusionary monumental architecture and urbanism with far-reaching implications for the development of the built environment in the city and region of Rome and even, on the other hand, for its historiography.

There still exist in modern Rome certain winding alleys or narrow courts where it is possible to get an impression, however fragmentary, of the city of the early Renaissance. Here and there, among the barrage of stronger competing stimuli, there are even architectural elements and inscriptions that recall the patronage of Nicholas V. The great setpieces of the Renaissance and baroque city—the elaborate piazzas enlivened with spirited, occasionally witty ornament, the serried palaces flanking elegant streets aligned with distant monuments, the domed and becolumned churches entering into complex relationships with each other and with the urban fabric and spaces among which they rise—all these familiar images of a grandiloquent urbanism distance us, indeed, from the shabby and shrunken Rome of the fifteenth century. Yet this very grandiloquence is grounded in the ideas and, less clearly, in actual projects conceived in Nicholas's pontificate, which inaugurated a process of urban transformation that would continue for some three centuries and provide models for emulation throughout Europe and beyond.

The transformation of Rome occurred under conditions that led inevitably to the construction of numerous buildings of conspicuous size and ostentation. The erection of impressive private palaces, especially, was encouraged by the prevalent ideological or even propagandistic aspect of architectural patronage in a city where signs of status, power, or wealth often, if not typically, indicated a desired rather than actual state of affairs. From the pontificate of Sixtus IV, moreover, building legislation, designed to accelerate the acquisition of blocks of property and the erection of fewer but grander residences on particular sites, served the interests of the elite at the same time as, no doubt, it strained the finances of many a palace builder, impelled—perhaps compelled—to lock up capital in the interests of an *ornatus* envisioned by the rulers of the city.[3]

On the other hand, in many recent discussions of Roman urbanism attention has been focused not on the great setpieces, but rather on the urban fabric in general, or at least on the subtlety and contextual responsiveness with which the setpieces were often inserted into their respective settings.[4] Clearly, such contextualism was in many cases a result of unintended, if not unwanted, circumstances beyond the control of a building patron and the coercive stratagems at his disposal. On the other hand, it is surely the case that the remarkable cohesiveness of the Roman urban environment—first disturbed, from a late-twentieth-century viewpoint, by the interventions designed to transform the city of the popes into the capital of a modern nation-state—is also the product of innumerable decisions and negotiations made by builders and architects concerned, on some level, to establish relations of scale, form, material, and character between the new and the old, between building and setting, even when, as so often, an element of conscious rivalry colored these relationships.

In any history of Rome or indeed of western urbanism that adopts this perspective, the pontificate of Nicholas V must surely occupy an important place. This brief but eventful period (1447–55) constitutes a particularly significant field for the study of the dialectic of formal urban design and incremental development in a major city. Though concentrated in space and time, moreover, it is associated, in a paradigmatic or even causal relationship, with important long-term shifts, notably the passage from the concern with urban utility, order, and ornament of the Italian city-states to the emblematic formalism and projective spatial organization characteristic of absolutist planning, if not of early modern nation-states in general. This is, of course, a highly schematic historical claim, though similar explanatory schemata are implicit in many discussions of Nicholas's pontificate. In such cases, history and historiography merge, for an undeniable schematizing and simplifying tendency is apparent in the cultural milieu of Nicholan Rome itself, and has indeed caught the attention of several major scholars of the period, not least as it is exemplified in the hierarchical certainties of the doctrine of papal supremacy or in the crystallization of urban process described and celebrated in contemporary panegyric.

No account of Nicholas's pontificate, then, can shrink from historiographical discussion. On the other hand, the present work marks an attempt to reach an understanding of the concrete conditions of the formulation of the fateful schemata, whether political or urbanistic, that haunt the history of the Renaissance and early modern city, by giving an account of the complexities and resistances of mid-fifteenth-century Roman society and its environment. It builds, of course, on the work on Nicholan Rome of such scholars as Magnuson (1958), Westfall (1974a), and Spezzaferro (1973), whose synthesizing account of the interrelationships of social historical process and urban development has proved especially valuable.[5]

Only to a limited degree, however, is this book conceived as a social history. Through its complexity of cultural meaning, its varied and shifting ideological character, and its very reflexivity, our object of inquiry, the city of Rome in the early Renaissance (as throughout its history at least as a papal capital), challenges and often eludes the methods and models of social historical explanation, for all the remarkable results of certain, largely quite recent, researches into aspects of the social and institutional history of the period. If any aspect of the historical environment of Rome is emblematic of the perils confronting social historians it is the phenomenon of Pasquino, though certainly this belongs to a slightly later period than that discussed here. Pasquino was the name given to the most celebrated and perennial of the speaking statues of Rome (fig. 1), a mutilated block that stood from the early sixteenth century at a prominent position on the main processional route through Rome. On the statue and its base were affixed lampoons purporting to be utterances of Pasquino himself, who with his counterparts, notably Marforio, appeared as characters in satirical comedies that mocked the papal government and its agents.[6] These voices marked not only a projection of discourse onto the stones of the city, but also a collapsing of the topography and the social and political relations of Rome into a symbolic and theatral space. Such convergences should not be regarded as novel or eccentric, however, for though Pasquino represented a current of alterity and even resistance within Rome, he provided a distorting—but perhaps not therefore less revelatory—mirror of the official city enunciated and affirmed through a plethora of evocative, symbol-laden, and ideologically charged signs and codes arrayed throughout the urban environment.

This affirmation occurs most conspicuously and accessibly, of course, in the multitude of texts that document the symbolic values and structures of the city and the ideal or even utopic conceptions to which they are frequently related. The sacred topography of medieval Rome, for instance, often imitated in other cities, received permanent expression in the Roman liturgy, the pilgrims' handbooks, or the chronicles of papal history. The almost constant architectural and urbanistic campaigns of Renaissance and later Rome might echo and sometimes generate a proliferation of texts, from administrative orders and statutory ordinances (whose history, of course, reaches far back into the medieval period) to doctrinal tracts, literary celebrations, antiquarian and historical studies, or accounts of public ceremonial and spectacle. And the idea of a building as a kind of text, as assimilable in its commemorative aspect to writing (though more durable), is already current in the fifteenth century.[7] In the transitional period between medieval and Renaissance Rome, then, in which the pontificate of Nicholas V is an especially significant episode, the relation of city and text is a crucial issue.

The physical city itself, moreover, is invaded by texts—inscriptions affixed to or inscribed on facades, public monuments, and other more conspicuous surfaces, or in the relatively intimate spaces of the courtyards and porticoes of private residences. Such inscriptions are of varying origin, purpose, character, and relation to nontextual elements such as statuary. Many, needless to say, are *spolia*, fragments of antiquity torn from their original setting and remounted according to the concerns and desires of successive populations of the city (Esch 1969); others, though contemporary with the buildings they mark, revive the forms and style of ancient epigraphy, a fashion prevalent from the early Renaissance, if not before (Petrucci 1980; Kajanto 1982). Inscriptions undergo actual or apparent reinscription; texts and images enter new contexts of meaning. In a broader sense, however, such reinscription is not merely a matter of specific physical operations and interventions, but of the general transformation of the contexts themselves. For the most established symbolic values in the Roman environment—obvious examples are the great pilgrimage shrines associated with fundamental religious observances and ritual practice—nevertheless received new complexities and shades of meaning in response to and as part of changing political circumstances and ideological representations.

Against a background of the constant reordering and realignment of symbolic values, the fate of *spolia*, a designation generally reserved for the objects subjected to a medieval practice of naive architectural and environmental montage, appears typical of Rome at almost any stage of its history. Indeed, beyond the more familiar examples of *spolia*, the broken remnants of ancient artifice tacked up on or incorporated into a wall, the category can be extended to the city's setpieces, the Renaissance Campidoglio, the baroque Piazza San Pietro or, had it been realized, the Nicholan Leonine City. For these are essentially— and not seldom with a touch of pathos—fragments, pieces of a heroic but never attained or even attainable urban order, a condition that was to be given an extraordinary visual expression by Giambattista Piranesi (fig. 2; see Tafuri 1976, 13–19). And their fragmentary condition reveals the much-admired coherence of the city (of which the currently privileged document, somewhat ironically, is the famous plan of Rome of Piranesi's contemporary, G. B. Nolli) as a matter of displacements and discontinuities, only perhaps accentuated by the manifold strategies of combinatory and contrastive linking.

My emphasis on mutability and complexity is intended in part to redress the balance; the ideal conceptions of Rome that underly or motivate so many operations within the physical city are grounded in a pervasive if by no means unchanging sense of the city as a physical and symbolic totality. Christian believers saw and perhaps still see Rome as in essence a spatiotemporal system of liturgically linked holy places and memorials of the operations of providence at the center of power and its transmission. Humanists turned their attention to the ancient city and, for all their awareness of a history of successive and often violent transformations, typically envisaged it as a spectacle of a timeless and integral magnificence. The systematic study of the ancient city was inaugurated in the mid-quattrocento by Flavio Biondo, whose first major work was composed not long before Nicholas's accession, and who was concerned not only with the elucidation of topographical features of the ancient city, but also with the identification of phases of development through which it had passed (Weiss 1969, 66–89).

The patient tabulator Biondo did not, however, provide concepts to structure his readers' comprehension and imaginative experience of the principles of ancient Roman architecture and urbanism, as a synchronic system. For the latter we may turn to Biondo's contemporary and sometime colleague in papal service, Leon Battista Alberti, in full cognizance of the snares and quagmires awaiting the unwary interpreter picking a way through Alberti's prose, marked by ambiguities, ironies, and varying degrees of rejection of the ethical and even political compromises necessary in the world of action, or even of that world itself. In his architectural treatise, in which the "real" Alberti generally remains concealed (as if in ambush) within a relatively impassive and public discursive formation, both rhetorical and technical, we meet at the same time and in barely resolved tension a conception of the city as process and also as a bounded and structured totality. I will frequently have occasion to return to the role of Alberti as observer, theorist, and possible instigator of urbanistic or architectural projects in the period of Nicholas V; and I will seek to reveal and set in context some of the conceptual discordances that fissure the calm and authoritative progress of his discussions of architecture, society, and the city.

Alberti's reflections on architecture and urbanism provide an archive of building types and spatial formations and relations culminating in the city itself or, more accurately, the city region. Of course the technical advances and epistemological shift implicit in the Albertian visualization of the city did not constitute a complete break from medieval symbolic concerns, although the primary symbolic connotations of Renaissance images of cities inhere often in the mode of representation, in the trace of rationalizing and ordering techniques, rather than in the sign or signs offered to the eye.[8] The familiar medieval type of city representation as hieroglyph, as conceptual construct and unified symbol, an example of which is the celebrated image of Rome in the form of a lion (fig. 36), intersected and mingled in interesting ways with types of imagery grounded in very different cultural and intellectual premises. In a society as given to archaizing practices and forms as papal Rome, such mingling was almost inevitable and of particularly enlivening importance in various forms of cultural production; certainly it will intermittently complicate the discussions here.

Alberti's technical writings, including those on the visual arts, are ultimately subordinate to and instrumental for the ethical and social concerns fundamental in his literary production. Theory and practice, text and city, become terms of a utopic projection into the phenomenal world of human interests and desires, though this is certainly not without the often ironic sense of the difficulties and complexities involved, and may even be undermined by the savage pessimism that courses through Alberti's literary production. Central in the

De re aedificatoria, nevertheless, is a conception of an ideal urban environment that can mold human behavior, while itself determined in important respects by the society that inhabits it. This aspect of Alberti's meditations on the theme of the city is of particular importance in the historiography of Nicholan Rome, to which I now turn.

In the study that can be seen as inaugurating the tradition of scholarship on Nicholas V as a patron of architecture and pioneer of urban planning, that of Georg Dehio first published in 1880, the argument is already developed around a confrontation of texts. One of these is a somewhat restrictive and tendentious selection of passages from Alberti's treatise, an often expressly normative and idealizing work, and exclusively so in Dehio's reading. Dehio's other text is the famous account of Nicholas's transformation of Rome and the Vatican that appears in the biography of Nicholas written by Giannozzo Manetti in 1455 or shortly thereafter; it is therefore roughly contemporary with Alberti's treatise, written partly before and partly during Nicholas's pontificate.[9] Dehio accepts the Manettian text as a document of actual achievement, and the Albertian passages as a record of conceptions or even designs for new urban monuments and spaces on which the pope's interventions were based. The ascription to Alberti of general authorship of the Nicholan projects has subsequently remained standard, though within typically broader and richer frameworks of argument and documentation (the great and salutary exception is Tafuri 1987).

The texts considered by Dehio are clearly far removed, given their idealizing and prescriptive quality, from the world of the craftsmen and laborers at work on the construction sites of mid-quattrocento Rome, though Alberti occasionally mentions conversations with craftsmen in whose skills and lore he was interested.[10] Dehio's choice of a documentary basis for his discussion, then, is in sharp contrast to the work of his contemporary, Eugène Müntz, whose remarkably wide-ranging archival studies of urban development and papal patronage throughout the quattrocento are still of fundamental value. Though Müntz made extensive use of literary, second-level sources, including those employed by Dehio, he concentrated on documents produced in the very process of urban change and artistic and architectural patronage. In particular, Müntz combed the ledgers of the ecclesiastical and papal officials concerned, even if only intermittently or indirectly, with the production of the physical setting of papal ceremonial and the operations of the papal court. Although Müntz's art historical emphasis, broad though it was, led to the exclusion from his work of documents of central importance to the understanding of the administrative structures and institutional frameworks through which papal patronage operated, at least in Nicholan Rome, his work laid the foundation for various studies contrasting often exaggerated and encomiastic contemporary claims for papal achievement in the restoration and beautification of Rome, on the one hand, and the more modest documented reality, on the other.[11]

Müntz can also be criticized for the all too exclusive focus on papal patronage as the crucial factor in the development of the city. This has been made good by a largely recent and continuing series of investigations in the archives of city institutions, or in the records of notaries serving often quite diverse strata of the urban population (see Brezzi and Lee 1984). Such documents are rarely of direct art or even architectural historical importance, but they are indispensable for an understanding of the social and institutional milieu within which more conspicuous and ambitious projects, increasingly associated with papal and curial interests, were realized. And there now exists a brilliant account, grounded in research in notarial archives, of the late medieval urban environment of Rome (Broise and Maire-Vigueur 1983); this is fundamental to my own discussion.

Unfortunately, the chronicles and diaries extant from the period are hardly numerous or informative enough—in contrast, say, to the *ricordanze* obsessively kept by contemporary Florentine businessmen—to provide direct documentation for a study of the mentalities or *genre de vie* of late medieval Rome,[12] though I will occasionally and tentatively attempt such an approach on the basis of such fragmentary and indirect evidence as exists, or at least of which I am aware. In any case, the variety and wealth of noncurial archival sources invite, or even oblige, readings of the urban environment and society of early Renaissance Rome that do not filter images of the city through all too exclusively official papal lenses. In this, I follow the lead especially of A. M. Corbo's pioneering study (1969) of nonpapal sources of patronage and investment in the built environment of early quattrocento Rome, as well as, more generally, the methodological example of Fergus Millar and Martin Warnke.[13]

Archival studies of late medieval Rome tend to be based on particular types of document, followed through a relatively lengthy time period, as is appropriate in social or economic historical research. My investigations, in contrast, depend on appeals to highly heterogeneous sources and explanatory models, insofar as these seem relevant to the understanding of the brief period delimited by Nicholas's accession and death. I have sought to do justice to the range and variety of sources that have been the subject of recent archival research, in addition to those reviewed in my own extensive and broad-based survey of archival documents produced in Rome during Nicholas's pontificate.

Nevertheless, though my account aims in some respects for a synchronic understanding of Nicholan Rome, it is ultimately concerned with radical historical shifts, with a particularly intense diachronicity. As such it is related less to the archival investigation of relatively slow shifts in the social history of Rome, for all the use that is made of these, than to attempts, notably that of C. W. Westfall (1974a), to elucidate the place of Nicholas's pontificate in the history of conscious urban design—for generally, of course, Nicholas is assigned a place of honor in the Valhalla of important urbanists—and in the context of the development of cultural instruments of authority and government. At its most extreme, as in the book published in 1927 by the later National Socialist, Kleo Pleyer (author of *Das Volk im Feld* of 1943), such an approach can lead to cynicism about the relationship of raison d'etat and cultural formations, religious doctrine, and intellectual activity; a much more moderate but fundamentally similar approach is taken by Toews (1968). Westfall, on the other hand, has no doubt about the good faith of Nicholas and his advisers; indeed, it is perhaps a signal defect of an extraordinary account of the intellectual, institutional, and iconological frameworks of Nicholas's policies that Westfall takes at face value declarations of policy, without appeal to a category of ideology.

In his highly original and important book, Westfall makes relatively restricted use of archival sources, implicitly assuming, like many scholars of the period, the exhaustiveness of Müntz's publication of documentary sources. On the other hand, Westfall's discussion marks a remarkable amplification of the textual material introduced into the discussion of Nicholas's achievement and programs. He weaves together expository sections from Nicholas's major bulls and other papal documents, from declarations of papal supremacy in contemporary theological and political writings, from humanist reflections on the nature and transformational quality of human agency or *virtù*, and from statutory and discursive texts pertinent to the physical development of Rome itself, especially that of Manetti to which he devotes a full and excellent discussion. The communality of ideas and attitudes represented by such texts, as these appear in the mirror of a highly idealizing account, establishes the object of study as a kind of super-text, a ghostly and relatively timeless articulation of the various cultural productions of the time. This is not opposed to the city; rather the latter, defined through the language of government and administrative regulation, is absorbed into the super-text, or at least forms a largely passive substratum on which the super-text can be inscribed.

The methodological basis for Westfall's textualization of the city is explicit and of great interest. He derives his inspiration from the Augustinian doctrine of the interpretation of the world of things as a system of signs revelatory of divine truth and order.[14] It is a methodological approach that finds its correlate, if not its paradigm, in the period under study itself. For Augustinianism, as Battisti (1960), who has also employed an Augustinian approach to iconological interpretation, has emphasized, formed an important current in the intellectual and ideological history of early Renaissance Rome (Golzio and Zander 1968, 135–144), while the refoundation and elaboration under Sixtus IV of the great Augustinian churches of S. Agostino and S. Maria del Popolo was to have a significant and surely not entirely unforeseen impact on the topographical development of the city (Bentivoglio and Valtieri 1976, 15–22).

The coherence of Westfall's super-text depends, in specific terms, on the interpretation of a famous passage in Manetti's panegyric of Nicholas V that surely represents Nicholas's own views, at least at the end of his life. The pope himself, on his deathbed, provides an interpretation or rather a justification of his own building programs; he appeals to the rhetorical and illocutionary function of architecture:

Hear—he said—O venerable fathers, hear the reasons and consider the causes by which we were led to our campaign of building and architecture. . . . We want you to know and fully understand that there were two principal reasons for our buildings. For only those who have grasped the origin and development of the Roman Church through the mastery of texts can fully understand the extent and character of its authority. As for the multitudes who are ignorant of letters and have absolutely no apprehension of them, they may often hear wise and erudite men preach on the nature and importance of these matters, and may seem to accept what they hear as truths and certainties. But this acceptance, supported as it is on weak and feeble foundations, gradually slips away until, in many cases, it is reduced to nothing, unless such people are moved by certain extraordinary sights. Now, when beliefs . . . founded on the teachings of learned men are constantly, even daily, confirmed and corroborated by the spectacle of great buildings—think of them as perpetual monuments or eternal testimonies, as if made by God Himself—then they are permanently impressed on those . . . who see such buildings. In this way belief is preserved and increased, and if this happens as I have described, then people experience a special kind of devotion that establishes and consolidates their belief.[15]

The second reason cited by Manetti for Nicholas's building campaigns concerns fortifications, which met an obvious need in a time of great anxiety following the fall of Constantinople to the Turks; my focus here, however, is on Nicholas's first reason.

In his deathbed speech as reported by Manetti, then, Nicholas directly assimilates the role of buildings to that of texts; the former have for the unlettered a similar role in the establishment and reinforcement of the faith as scripture has for the learned. For all the restriction in Manetti's text of the paratextual efficacy of buildings to lay populations (we should probably not read a social hierarchy into Manetti's category, since relatively few people outside the Church had mastery of Latin), its historical importance is beyond doubt; it reflects and promotes a clear awarenesss of the ideological role of architecture as a particularly conspicuous and permanent mode of didactic and exhortatory communication, while it indicates a capacity on the part of building patrons to understand architectural patronage as an instrument or perhaps rather an aspect of government and social control.

For Westfall this self-consciousness is integral to the humanist conception of planned operations in the phenomenal world, as formulated with particular trenchancy in studies, notably those of Alberti, in the visual arts and related disciplines. In addition, Alberti's architectural writings provide a coherent and ordered system of types, motifs, and combinatory patterns through and in which a society can articulate its higher goals. In a sense, accordingly, Westfall's discussion of Manetti's and Alberti's connection to the projects undertaken by Nicholas V and its intellectual background is a restatement, on a level of far higher complexity and sophistication, of Dehio's direct confrontation of texts. Curiously, the intellectualist bias in Westfall's account leads him to neglect a central concern of Alberti himself and a crucial theme in early Renaissance culture, the development of artificial perspective, though earlier scholars had sought, perhaps too mechanistically, to relate mid-quattrocento urbanistic projects to the new techniques of the organization of space and objects within it, and to the implications of this as they were beginning to be worked out by Alberti and others.[16] In a climate of discussion affected notably by Michel Foucault's work and responses to it, it is clearly vital to consider the epistemological shifts heralded if not instituted by the diffusion of perspectival constructions of "reality."

Though various points of disagreement will emerge, the present book depends heavily on Westfall's presentation of officially articulated policy and its doctrinal background in Nicholas's pontificate, though in my view Westfall's account fully applies only in a final phase that he does not distinguish, since he clings to a conception of Nicholas's pontificate as homogeneous and internally consistent. Accordingly I do not extensively address the vital question, well discussed by Westfall and others, of the formulation of doctrines of papal supremacy under Nicholas, largely by Cardinal Torquemada, the formidable Dominican theologian whose development of images for the edification of the unlearned in the context of charitable activity at his convent, S. Maria sopra Minerva (Golzio and Zander 1968, 140, 279), requires further study, especially in view of its relation with Nicholas's concerns. Nor will I discuss, except in passing, the vexed question of the building campaigns at the Vatican and the elucidation of Manetti's problematic account of these.

The focus of my discussion, rather, is the city itself and the evidence in a brief period of significant transformations. Many of these, certainly, are clearly evident only when tracked over far longer periods, though some at least can be specifically associated with decisions made and initiatives undertaken during Nicholas's pontificate. In particular, I am concerned with the apparent realization in mid-quattrocento Rome of novel conceptions of physical and social space. But I have chosen to look away from the usually privileged case, the Borgo scheme, partly since it remained unrealized and may well never have been realizable, and partly since drastic interventions in the physical substance of a city, such as those described in the Manettian account of the Borgo scheme, were by no means the only or even most obvious way to undertake the reordering and reinterpretation of an urban environment. After all, the emphasis in Nicholas's account of the purpose of his buildings on their rhetorical or communicative function distracts attention from their physical substance to features, which might be quite incidental, conveying meaning. Moreover, I have expanded the subject of the argument from the physical fabric of Rome itself to the wider region, as variously defined and understood, as a site of elements that might carry meaning and inform developments in the cities. In other words, I mount a critique of the very notion of urbanism as a central categorical framework for discussion, and instead consider the interplay and connections of signs and codes within diverse topographical and metaphoric spaces.

The Augustinianism that marks the work of Westfall and Battisti sets a theory of signs at the center of the discussion. Rome—or at least those parts of the city most affected by papal patronage—becomes a constellation of elements that encourage a hermeneutic transfer of attention from their physical presence to ulterior meanings. In the light of Augustinian doctrine the phenomenal world is constituted as an always potential system of traces of divine providence, in which things can be read as signs and signs—including words and other textual elements—also qualify as things. The notion of the textualization of the city, then, can be seen as a more modern correlate of the medieval and Renaissance notion of the world as book or text; Rome, clearly, with its universal implications and importance for people of the period with which we are concerned, may be regarded as a privileged world within a world, a text within a text, which is also—in the endless recession of Augustinian hermeneusis—a privileged and vivid sign or set of signs for that world or text.

The question of the sign is at the heart of the present discussion also, but I generally do not attempt to penetrate beyond the level of appearances to a shadow world of theological correlates of the actual city and its places. Rather my concern is with the surfaces of the city, and what may be or may arguably have been attached to or inscribed on them. Inevitably a semiological study of the mid-fifteenth-century physical environment must also take account of Renaissance methods and even principles of design associated with the production of surfaces or objects as articulated wholes (culminating, we might say, in unified architectural compositions) with particular kinds of sign value; these considerations apply especially, of course, to privileged buildings. Such cases invite iconographical investigation, as practiced, notably, by Battisti and Westfall. My own strategy, on the other hand, has been to subsume the discussion of major architectural monuments in that of the general environment as a matrix of repeated and often quite trivial and everyday signs whose interest lies less in what they stand for or connote, or even in what they singly denote, than in the patterns of information that they constitute. In Augustinian terms, perhaps, I focus on signs as things rather than things as signs, while the signs of particular interest in my discussion are those that function through their relational links to other signs and systems of signs arrayed within the fabric of the city, rather than through connections to transcendent levels of knowledge and doctrine.

My discussion of the urban environment, on the other hand, concentrates on signs in the sense of elements, whether objects or images, originally conceived as signs—elements, for example, that constituted heraldic insignia or property markers evidencing specific human intentionality. There is, of course, a deeper level of semiological analysis in terms of which the environment supplies information about the unconscious desires and apprehensions of a culture, in terms, say, of the "thick description" of Clifford Geertz (1973). I have hazarded this mode of analysis only rarely, at junctures when it seemed to follow naturally from a more primary level of attention to and analysis of environmental signs, as defined above.

The emphasis on the sign function of elements within the urban environment raises, needless to say, serious problems of evidentiality. The sources for the physical fabric of Rome in the fifteenth century are fragmentary in the extreme; even scantier and generally impossible to quantify is the evidence for the visual aspect of the city. Inevitably, therefore, the discussion proceeds by means of hypotheses constructed on the basis of evidence of disparate character and reliability. The undertaking is important, however, since it provides at least a model of the matrix within which Nicholas V's extensive and often-noted insertion of signs (coats of arms, abbreviated inscriptions, occasional lengthier celebratory texts) into the fabric of the city occurred.

In contrast with the practice of earlier regimes in Rome, the array of Nicholan signs in the city constitutes in its scale, consistency, and sophistication a qualitatively distinct operation within the informational patterns ordering the urban environment for its users. Above all, we seem to be confronted by a conscious concern to rewrite the city, whose Aurelianic walls, church facades, public buildings, and fountains provided surfaces for the inscription of a cohesive urban text. It is even probable that Nicholas's restorations were in part carried out with the goal of the constitution of appropriate architectural frames and surface finish for such inscription. An especially conspicuous case is that of the Castel S. Angelo, which was of particular symbolic importance to Nicholas; this received, as Manetti emphatically records, a coat of white plaster, the function of which may well have been the provision of a homogeneous ground against which the many Nicholan heraldic or epigraphic elements could be prominently displayed.[17]

At this point the question arises of the relationship of Nicholas's almost obsessive signage to vernacular practice. Signage applied to private buildings in an urban context has been especially richly documented, for example, in the case of the small provincial town of Ascoli Piceno, with its many surviving residential buildings from the fifteenth and sixteenth centuries (Castelli 1975); in Rome itself, of course, the available sample of minor domestic architecture of the period is relatively scanty. It is clear, in any case, that the use of informational signage of various types on the exterior of houses, as also, a fortiori, of churches and other more public buildings, was a major feature of the late medieval and early Renaissance urban environment,[18] which thereby became intelligible and familiar to its residents and other users. This is an aspect of the late medieval city that has been gravely neglected, though it is surely of the first importance in assessing the architectural developments of the period.

The evidence that I will present suggests that Nicholas's practice in this regard was an expansion of an existing and widespread use of exterior surfaces of residential and nonresidential property for informational display. I will further maintain that the Nicholan array of signs depended for its vivacity, its very intelligibility, on the co-presence of the manifold other signage marking the urban environment, and ordering it in diverse ways according to the roles and needs of groups within the population at any time. The physical evidence alone, certainly, hardly allows such a conclusion, and the argument will necessarily turn elsewhere, notably to a consideration of Nicholas's urban policies throughout much of his pontificate, and their implications for the nature and scope of urban interventions planned or even executed during that time. In my view, the good relations—or even collaboration—between Pope Nicholas and the local elite, at least up to the Porcarian conspiracy of 1453, were such as to warrant their expression or even commemoration within the city. And I will later note examples of the juxtaposition of papal and communal arms, or those of a major local confraternity, as evidence for the deliberate manifestation of the association of papal and local interests, especially in sites of particular significance for the people of Rome.

The array of signs requires—and this was perhaps partly the point—minimal actual intervention in the physical fabric of the city. But Nicholas's pontificate has become associated, through the arguments and assumptions of generations of scholars of the history of urbanism, with the radical physical reordering of an urban fabric, on the level of planning if not of actual intervention. It is clear that, long before 1453, certain physical changes did occur in Rome, some of which at least can be set in the context of a consistent pattern of urban development that occurred under the aegis of the pope and was controlledby his household officials in close contact with magistrates and other officials of the commune, in pursuit of goals that could, to some degree, be shared by the different parties involved.

Such changes in the physical environment, however, were quite distinct in character from the utopic program described or proposed by Manetti; they amounted to a clarification of existing realities and their reinterpretation in terms of papal concerns and ideology. Nevertheless, this clarification did not— indeed could not—proceed without the appeal to certain conceptual models of spatial organization. In particular these involved the geometrical abstraction inherent in perspectival construction; besides this, however, and merging in some way with it, I would emphasize the operation of an idea of the organization of terrain through convergent axes focusing attention on a conspicuous site or marker, an idea that I will argue was derived from the perceived order of existing spatial constructs, notably the wider territory of the city region. For the symbolic landscape (to use a concept developed notably in the remarkable study of Cosgrove [1984]) of late medieval Italy was structured in large part through the interrelationships on a regional scale of major centers of economic and ritual activity and social intercourse (cities, villages, markets, pilgrimage churches, sites of industrial and agricultural production, bathing establishments, and villas) and the highways and waterways that connected them; the perceived order of such wider structures of geography and human activity provided a basis, or even a model, for the conception of a clarified and reorganized urban space, a conception that I will argue emerges from a close reading of contemporary authors, notably Alberti and Flavio Biondo. Urban space, in other words, reflected regional space, at least in this crucial period of the passage in the consciousness and practice of contemporaries—here I refer in particular to the analysis of the development of legal codes relating to urban-territorial relations conducted by Chittolini (1979)—from an idea of Italy as a peninsula of discrete communalities to one of wider territorial constructs. And it is significant that the conception of Italy as a balanced system of interrelated states finds its earliest formalized expression in the Peace of Lodi of 1454, negotiated largely through Nicholas V's diplomatic initiatives.

Whatever the sources of the spatial concepts involved, however, a further step was taken in mid-quattrocento Rome: the spatial models for urban reorganization underwent a degree of crystallization, embarking on their celebrated career as elements of a recurrent vocabulary of urbanism and spatial organization in a variety of contexts. As we meet them in the Manettian Borgo scheme, devices such as the trident of converging streets or the central marker in a regularized piazza are presented as a priori motifs of an urban ordering that largely abstracts from the existing urban fabric if it heeds it at all. Some degree of abstraction was clearly already evident in actual Nicholan projects discussed at length in later chapters; I will argue, further, that in the course of Nicholas's pontificate the device of topographical order itself came to acquire particular semantic value that canceled out or obscured the values of the existing fabric except those of direct pertinence to the newly imposed categories of environmental symbolism. In brief, under Nicholas we follow the movement from the reorganization and enhancement of the existing fabric by means of signs and minor physical changes toward a holistic and schematic concept of urban transformation that itself came to constitute a privileged, indeed imperious sign, though the latter stage appears fully realized only in the pages of Manetti.

The contrast between the city as a matrix of signs and as itself a privileged sign is now of particular importance in view of the recent deployment by Manfredo Tafuri (1987) of the term "resignification" in connection specifically with Nicholas V's policies in and toward Rome. I would emphasize that in Tafuri's discussion resignification applies to the city as a whole, the city itself as transfigured sign; the concern of Nicholas V with neighborhoods outside the Leonine City, accordingly, is construed as evidence for a concern with the reform of the city as an entity, though certainly a polycentric one. The physical city becomes, as it were, the signifier for a signified that is sought exclusively in a consistent political agenda, which Tafuri, following Prodi (1982), locates in the turn to a caesaro-papist absolutism and which, in agreement with Westfall (1974a), he finds present from the beginning of the pontificate. Architecture, the potentially complicating modality of the articulation of political programs in and through an urban environment, is denied any separate, constitutive role ("there is nothing architectural in the pope's 'plan'; everything is clearly aimed at the foundation of a new type of government"), while the very term "urbanism" is rejected as a flagrant anachronism.

Nicholas's tactful handling of the Roman patriciate is dismissed by Tafuri, insofar as he is aware of the evidence for it, as a temporary expedient appropriate to particular circumstances: this Machiavellian position, reached from the left by Tafuri, is remarkably similar in principle to that reached from the right by Pleyer (or even Westfall, whose insistence on Nicholas's alliance with the commune is challenged by Tafuri as inconsistent with Westfall's own general presentation of the evidence). Consistently, Tafuri neglects entirely the ritual aspect of the city: all is subsumed in the overriding political signified.

Tafuri privileges, moreover, the evidence of official texts, here following not only Westfall but also studies such as those of Laura Onofri (1979), in which papal rhetoric is analyzed in the context of neoplatonist humanist discourse. The trap here is that disclosed, though in a somewhat different context, by Jerrold Siegel (1966), of reading humanist texts at face value, without due attention to the institutional and professional contexts within which the new humanist culture was developed and promoted, or to the Ciceronian absorption of philosophy into rhetoric, or indeed to the value ascribed to the erudite and ingenious deployment of classical allusions and quotations in the service of conventional content. Siegel's position, developed in a celebrated polemic with Hans Baron (1968b), anticipates certain familiar thrusts of poststructuralist criticism, as adopted for instance in the discussion of Renaissance writing by Richard Waswo (1987), in that it challenges the generally implicit imputation of transparency to Renaissance texts. In the particular context of Nicholas V's Rome, it is pertinent to note O'Malley's account (1979, esp. 78f.) of the triumph of epideictic rhetoric at the papal court, that is, of a type of rhetorical practice that foregrounds "vision and contemplation" or, more generally, strategies and modes of representation and communication in the elaboration of often familiar material. In O'Malley's view, Nicholas's pontificate marks a crucial stage in the development of this phenomenon.

In any case, the focus in Tafuri's account, like that of Westfall, on official discourse obscures the economic and administrative processes occurring within the city. In this way a highly unified picture of Nicholas's policies and programs is established, though with numerous and significant caveats and qualifications, to be then set in contrast with a powerful and brilliant reading of Alberti's intellectual and ideological position that detaches the latter totally—except possibly as dissimulator—from the policies of a pope presented as an enlightened but opportunistic autocrat steeped in neoplatonist conceptions of monarchic rule. Tafuri, indeed, moves Alberti firmly into the ambit of the rebel Stefano Porcari (there is probably some truth in this, though the question is extremely complex), in spite of evidence, detailed in the following chapters, for Alberti's close association with individuals and groups within or close to the papal court, as well as with those alienated from it.

The transformations within Nicholan Rome occurred, certainly, in the context of particular political shifts, which involved among other things the marshaling and instrumentalization of cultural formations in the service of centralized authority. In itself, of course, this was not new; what gives the period of Nicholas V its particular fascination and importance is the degree of self-consciousness, as evidenced especially in Nicholas's deathbed speech, with which cultural instruments of policy could be articulated and deployed. But this self-consciousness developed, in my view, out of the practices of administration and the various processes of mediation that distinguished the intersections, on different levels, of papal policy and the city and its populations, with all the independence, stubbornness, and guile the latter might display in their dealings with bearers of authority and prestige in their environment. It is, indeed, the emphasis on practice and the quite generally diffused and available skills and dispositions developed in and through practice that distinguishes the present approach to and articulation of the historical issues under review from those of its predecessors.

The discussion of administrative practice enables two major themes of the book to be brought into relation, the discussion of the functioning of signs in the urban environment, on the one hand, and the question of patronage, on the other. Much previous discussion of Nicholas's achievements as "urbanist" depends on a highly ideal notion of patronage, implying the direct and uncomplicated transmission of commands from thinkers to makers, a process in which the artists occupy an intermediate position as involved in both intellectual and manual labor, while certain privileged artists function as translators of lofty notions, even of a theological kind, into appropriate material form. It is undeniable that cases of such translation occurred, though these were by no means unproblematical, as I will stress in a discussion of the frescoes in Nicholas's private chapel. Most notably, this model of cultural practice is fundamental in Manetti's account of Nicholas's building programs, in which a central theme is Bernardo Rossellino's activity as the pope's executive architect and designer of the major buildings. On the other hand, the authorial role ascribed to Rossellino (and clearly related to Alberti's famous conception of the architect) corresponds to that of the humanist writer, of Manetti himself. Even at the beginning of the literature dedicated to Nicholas's place in history, then, the object and mode of representation tend to converge.

The reality of the Nicholan construction programs and urban interventions, as I will argue on the basis of extensive prosopographical researches documented below, was different indeed from the image presented by Manetti. A picture emerges of variable and often apparently ad hoc procedures. There were no clear-cut avenues of command, rather a fluid situation in which men of versatility and diplomatic skill could assert themselves in the realization of certain papal objectives, both specific and general, while often meeting the interests of other centers of influence in the city, notably of course the social formations to which they themselves belonged. The variety and complexity of the processes through which urban and regional shifts came about correspond to the complexity of the environment, especially as defined as a symbolic system or group of systems, among which and on which these operated. In the ideal, utopic space elaborated in the Manettian account, on the other hand, both the process and the product of Nicholan urbanism appear characterized by a comparable simplification.

The question of patronage can be directly related to the model of the city as a symbolic space. The neo-Augustinian notion of the city as a super-text, especially, implies the presence of an author who may write or rewrite (in) that text. Authority is conflated with authoriality, and invests the notion of patronage, not least on the scale claimed for Nicholas by Manetti, with a particular charge; the bibliophile pope's support of humanist writing and his commissions for building campaigns in some of the most hallowed sites of ancient Rome, both pagan and Christian, appear in this way as converging aspects of a unified activity. But the Manettian model of the metaphorically rewritten city of Nicholas V and even the literal rewriting of the city undertaken in such texts as those of Manetti and Alberti are vulnerable to a fracturing and decomposition that encroach on the most ideal accounts of or proposals for a reorganization of urban space. Alberti's carefully wrought literary edifice, in particular, is grounded, however nervously and with whatever defiant caveats, in the solid treatise of Vitruvius with its imperial dedication and its rejection of contemporary experimentation; nevertheless it lends itself to a process of excavation and desedimentation, and in the process opens out to illuminate many of the shifts in the social use and physical configuration of urban environments that constitute major themes of the present work.

Any process of formalization and clarification within an urban context is likely to entail some degree of impoverishment of the existing symbolic landscape, reducing the city or its prominent sites to a stage for the manifestation of relatively univocal and readily intelligible ideological values. It is a process typically identified with all forms of Renaissance urbanism or architectural design, one that invited the familiar Ruskinian critique of Renaissance classicism in the built environment that still echoes in the current climate of attacks on twentieth-century modernism and its precursors.[19] In the Rome of Nicholas V, however, the strategies of the papal regime and the tactics of the leading groups in Roman society (to use the categories of Michel de Certeau [1984]) often merged—or, at least, the former appropriated the latter—though certainly the weight of papal authority made itself increasingly evident as the fifteenth century progressed or, indeed, in the last years of Nicholas V himself.

But if Nicholas's architectural patronage is perhaps indelibly associated with an architectural monumentality redolent of absolutist certainties, I will argue that evidence embedded in the imagery and subject matter of his private chapel indicates that Nicholas at very least understood the reasons for unease in the face of the monumental transformation of the built environment. Indeed, a central image of the major narrative cycle of the chapel is a telling example of a tactic of the disadvantaged confronted with overriding power (fig. 21): the saint—he is, of course, the Roman deacon Lawrence—identifies the poor of Rome as the wealth of the Church. And in the light of St. Stephen's attack on the Temple, the architectural backgrounds of Fra Angelico's frescoes, usually assumed to be paradigms of Nicholas's projected transformation of Rome, acquire a distinct ambivalence.

Rome under Nicholas, in conclusion, was not an arena of unilateral patronage and the coherent spatial and figural expression of ideological values. Rather, it was a setting for the play of signs and codes associated with different elements within the complex stratigraphy of the city, and of interventions that accented certain aspects of this complex situation, or gave it new directions.

I have used theatral metaphors advisedly: the Renaissance city is often characterized or even defined as a place of political and ritual spectacle, through which the processions of the great moved slowly to the applause of the populace, though sometimes accompanied by violence and disorder (Zorzi 1977; Trexler 1980).[20] The grand ceremonies, however, were but special events in an environment infused with everyday theatricality. The streets and squares—and in Nicholan Rome, we presume, the many private porticoes discussed below—served as frames for the more or less formalized or ritualized acts of ordinary hospitality, exchange, reconciliation, or hostility, sometimes orchestrated by lawyers or other officials. And the statues and buildings of the city, themselves often endowed with magic qualities, as detailed at great length in the medieval pilgrim guides, entered into a constant drama of presences. The city itself, of course, may be regarded as the greatest of all these presences, an interlocutor in an environmental discourse within which the most diverse desires and concerns could find expression.

This discourse of the urban environment, with all its speaking stones and inscribed surfaces, finds in Nicholan Rome an especially intense and originary milieu. The many tensions and contradictions characterizing the social processes and the development of the physical fabric of the city constitute central elements of this discourse, at least until the final act. It is entirely in keeping with the enthusiasm that the historical individual is known to have had for elaborate ceremonial and liturgy that Nicholas's last mortal appearance should have orchestrated a largely fictive image of his pontificate. On his deathbed, surrounded by his cardinals in appropriate attitudes of grief (perhaps feigned in the many cases of those who hoped to benefit from the change of pontiff, or even to assume the See of St. Peter themselves), Nicholas conjured up the vision of a new Jerusalem realized on earth as a splendid and efficacious setting for the assertion of the Church's prerogatives to its vacillating faithful and its enemies alike. With this dramatic gesture—and the selection of the able publicist Manetti to record it—the curtain was closed across the complex developments in which, certainly, the projects and attitudes described by Manetti were grounded. The course of subsequent Roman urbanism was thereby set, and a model of city development adumbrated that would lie behind so many of the splendors and miseries of the western tradition of urbanistic and architectural monumentalism.

City and Pope: The Problematicity of Patronage

We begin with a paradox, as is appropriate in the discussion of a complex and transitional historical conjuncture, one distinguished by the co-presence of various, sometimes contradictory, tendencies and circumstances. On the one hand, the reputation of Pope Nicholas V as one of the most important and influential patrons of building and proponents of the transformation of urban space stands unchallenged; recent scholarship has not dissented from the assessments of such qualified observers among Nicholas's own contemporaries as Aeneas Sylvius Piccolomini (Pius II) or Pier Candido Decembrio, who remarked with admiration and astonishment on Nicholas's "insatiable thirst for building."[1] On the other hand, this reputation rests, to a remarkable extent, on images. For Nicholas's pontificate was framed by visual and literary manifestations of ideas of architectural magnificence grounded in the ancient traditions and symbols of pagan and especially Christian Rome, and in the new aesthetic and intellectual currents emanating, in 1447–55, largely from Medicean Florence. Both Nicholas's accession and his death provided occasions for the production of ambitious but fictive architectures, important less in themselves than as revelatory of and instrumental for deeper ideological and political concerns, which naturally presented themselves to contemporaries in theological terms.

Nicholas formally acceded to the throne of St. Peter on March 19, 1447. As tradition demanded, the new pope was crowned at the Vatican, then rode in procession through the streets of the city whose spiritual shepherd and temporal lord he now was.[2] The coronation procession, the *possesso*, wound from the Vatican to the Lateran; it joined, accordingly, the two most sacred sites of Roman Christianity, whose status and sacrality had recently been celebrated by artistic production of the highest quality and prestige. Nicholas's predecessors, Martin V and Eugenius IV, had recruited the leading artists of the day to execute frescoes in the two great basilicas at either end of the Via del Papa, the route of the *possesso* and the ceremonial axis of late medieval Rome (map 2). At the Lateran, Gentile da Fabriano had been succeeded by Pisanello, who worked there until 1432 (Golzio and Zander 1968, 201–205),[3] while at the Vatican Fra Angelico, in Rome since 1445, was in 1447 still at work in the choir chapel of St. Peter's and in the so-called Chapel of the Sacrament in the Vatican palace. It is likely that Fra Angelico was among those who witnessed Nicholas's coronation as the latest successor of St. Peter, the saint whose life formed the subject of his lost frescoes in the apse of the Vatican basilica, at a short distance from St. Peter's tomb and the place where Nicholas received St. Peter's crown.[4]

One of Nicholas's earliest artistic commissions was that given to Fra Angelico, at the very latest by February 1448, for the decoration of his private chapel. A prominent, if not insistent, element of the chapel's decoration is the series of grand architectural settings that give an aulic and *all'antica* air to the narrative cycles that have pride of place in the small room, and in which the artist represented Nicholas himself in the guise of a third-century pope (fig. 16). This crucial visual document has received remarkably scant attention from students of Nicholas's pontificate and patronage; its critical fortunes certainly stand in marked contrast to those of a celebrated literary account of Nicholas's life and achievements composed shortly after his death on March 17, 1455.

Giannozzo Manetti's panegyric of Nicholas V, with its extended account of the pope's building programs, has long constituted an almost obligatory starting point for the discussions of Nicholas's architectural patronage and his general impact on the city. It is a particularly compelling if in several respects obscure document; it appears to have exerted a significant influence on later builder popes and certainly provided Vasari with the basis for his account of Nicholas's achievements as patron of the arts. It includes what purports to be a report of the "testament" vouchsafed by Nicholas to the eminent prelates present at his deathbed, spelling out the reasons for his large-scale building campaigns. Manetti's text has, in general, the air of an official publication, and it is plausible to assume that the dying pope entrusted to Manetti, who of all his secretaries had the highest gifts and renown as a scholar and master of epideictic discourse, the task of presenting his case for the benefit of posterity. It was a necessary undertaking: in 1453 Rome had been shaken by the attempted coup of Stefano Porcari in Rome, an event that profoundly affected Nicholas's morale, and by the terrible news of the fall of Constantinople to the Turks, which immediately sparked criticism of the pope's alleged negligence in meeting the threat from the East. Indeed, Nicholas's achievements in various spheres were now overshadowed, or even placed in question.

Manetti succeeded only too well in his justificatory endeavor. The impression he gives is that of an internally consistent and successful pontificate, in which monumental architecture was a major medium of the expression of principles present from the outset. The description of the transformation of the Leonine City (the district around the Vatican) and indeed of the city of Rome itself—or at least its major churches, public buildings, and defenses—is especially well known. Though many of the projects celebrated by Manetti were begun or even in some cases completed under Nicholas, many more were not only not realized but were in any case of doubtful feasibility. More significant and compelling than his description of any particular project, however, is Manetti's image of a coherent and unified program of restoration and construction, of a reborn city finally worthy in its physical appearance of its sanctity and splendid history. And this, whatever elements of truth it may encompass, is a myth. It is, we may say, a dream of Rome, no less than the images of the third-century city visualized by Fra Angelico on the walls of Nicholas's chapel, and it is not inappropriate that it should occur in a text giving particular emphasis to the dreams and visions that punctuated Nicholas's career and allowed anticipatory insight into his promised greatness (Onofri 1979, 50–56).

Manetti betrays little understanding of the realities of mid-quattrocento Rome. His text reflects changes in papal policy and concerns that accompanied the increasing isolation and melancholy of the pope, stricken by painful illnesses,[5] in the wake of the twin tragedies of 1453. Of particular significance in any discussion of the architectural history of Nicholas's pontificate is the model of patronage implicit in Manetti's account of the building campaigns. He emphasizes the importance of his fellow Florentine Bernardo Rossellino, the sculptor and architect, within the building office of Nicholas V. According to Manetti, Rossellino was to Nicholas V and his projects for the rebuilding of the Vatican palace and basilica what Hiram of Tyre had been to King Solomon and the erection of the Temple of Jerusalem and Solomon's palace. There is no doubt that Rossellino, who arrived in Rome in 1451, played an important role in the building projects at the Vatican (where he was one of two men with the title *ingegniere del palazzo*), though it is impossible, given the state of the evidence, to be precise about the nature of that role (Mack 1982; Westfall 1974a, 180–183). On the other hand, Manetti's account of Rossellino's role as a technical expert with the skill and authority to translate into material reality the ideas enunciated by a wise pope amounts, once again, to the production of a highly efficacious myth. For the process of the origination and transmission of ideas was by no means as simple as Manetti suggests (or as described by many modern scholars), nor was the physical and social matrix within which building took place as passive. And Nicholas's cultural program, if so it can be called, was far from unified, though some things were constant, like the pope's penchant for precious materials and elaborate display, at least where these conferred splendor and dignity on high ritual and papal ceremonial (Peti 1981).

Correction of the image of Nicholan Rome provided by Manetti must necessarily involve close-grained discussion of the social and economic realities of the city and its hinterland, and of the means by which Nicholas—or at least his administration—sought to affect and direct the status quo. I will be concerned with both questions, relying heavily on the impressive recent scholarship on the social and institutional history of late medieval Rome. None of the scholars who have studied the workings of the fifteenth-century city, however, have yet assembled the evidence for the particular achievement of Nicholas V and his staff in arriving at a comprehension and redefinition of the administrative and fiscal structures with which they necessarily operated. This is all the more remarkable in view of the importance of the pontificate of Nicholas V as a watershed—the term is Paolo Prodi's—in the development of early modern political or administrative structures in Italy (Prodi 1982, esp. 91, 110, drawing on Westfall 1974a). Of particular significance, then, are the manifold activities and crucial responsibilities of Nicholas's major associate, Nello da Bologna, whom no previous scholar of Nicholan Rome, from Dehio to Westfall, has so much as mentioned.[6]

Nello da Bologna's ascendancy in Nicholas's administration was confirmed, at the very latest, by the success of the Jubilee of 1449–50, which turned into an extended celebration of revived papal authority in the Church and of victory over the conciliarists. For by the end of 1449 the Council of Basel had formally dissolved itself, its chief adherents had declared their allegiance to Nicholas V, and the last of the antipopes, Felix V, had resigned. The Jubilee, then, marked the achievement of unity in the Church, news of which had already led to euphoric demonstrations in the streets of Rome (Pastor 1949, 43). The city had to be made ready to receive pilgrims from all parts of western Christendom who would act out through their prayers, processions, and reverence of often ideologically charged relics the harmony that Nicholas could claim to have brought to the Church.

Overall responsibility for the preparations for the Jubilee, especially for the supply of grain and other necessities to the city, was given to Nello; he must also have been involved with the restoration campaign on the station churches of Rome, the shrines at which the liturgy directed that the faithful should pray, which must have begun soon after Nicholas's accession. From 1450 Nello emerges from the documents as the director of a papal staff effective and authoritative enough not only to run the various building and procurement programs set in motion or appropriated by Nicholas, but also to invade and even absorb vital sectors of the traditional communal and curial administrations. Most remarkably, Nello's assertion of papal prerogative apparently occurred without alienating the often powerful individuals or groups concerned; not the least among Nello's qualities was certainly his tact. Indeed, his importance may have lain not so much in the range and character of his responsibilities as in his capacity to mediate between the pope, the officials of the Curia, and a host of local magistrates, entrepreneurs, merchants, and lords. Nello's effectiveness, in other words, depended on a profound knowledge of the pertinent people and institutions in Rome and the wider region; he must, for instance, have been familiar with the world of the brickyards and building sites of the city, that of the harbor of Rome with its quays, warehouses, and buffalo teams, that of the Tuscan bankers and dealers in luxury commodities, and that of the corridors and inner chambers of the papal palace. His knowledge, moreover, of local people must have been supplemented by sensitivity toward their interests and aspirations. This kind of responsiveness to local realities, especially though not exclusively apparent in Nello, underlay the urban policies and interventions of much of Nicholas's pontificate, in marked contrast with Manetti's picture of the period. This discrepancy, however, was partly a matter of the character of the city itself and the varying experiences it called forth.

Late medieval Rome presented itself in manifold and only occasionally intersecting ways to those who lived or sojourned within it (Guidoni 1983; Broise and Maire-Vigueur 1983; Krautheimer 1980, esp. 289–326). Of course, this was true to a degree of any major city, where the experience of one class or social group was necessarily distinct from that of others. Nevertheless, Rome was a special case, a place of unresolvable contrasts. It was a holy city of shrines, its buildings founded in terrain bathed in the blood of martyrs; it was an agglomeration of broken remnants of a glorious, if pagan, imperial past; and it was the site of a relatively recent and temporarily successful struggle for communal autonomy and the ascendancy of new and dynamic groups within the population. It was the city of the concord of the apostles (Pietri 1961), but also of the seemingly incessant and often violent rivalries of powerful clans and factions. Its ancient glories attracted and fascinated visitors, who were only too prone to note with a critical eye the confusing topography of the modern city and its relatively primitive stage of economic development and cultural sophistication. Many wondered at and were offended by the ruinous condition and rough aspect of much of the built environment, for even the palaces of the powerful and wealthy—prelates and aristocrats alike—could not bear comparison with their counterparts in most contemporary cities of importance (Partner 1972, 4–7, 96–97; Mazzocco 1975). The sacred shrines themselves, especially before Nicholas's restoration campaigns, showed only too clearly the marks of neglect and of the difficulties that had afflicted the city. In its disrepair the city had become an assembly of signs of sacrality guaranteed by relics and holy legend, but lacking manifest presence and the power to move and teach. It was to be many years before the major shrines and sites of Rome received an appropriate and coherent physical expression, consistent with the concerns of a more visualistic age; Nicholas's pontificate, of course, was crucial in the development of this attitude.

The city's population was varied and shifting. At times—notably in 1449–50—pilgrims flooded the city, their numbers fluctuating as religious festivals came and went and in response to such factors as the security of the city and the pilgrimage roads, the presence and virulence of disease, and the availability of bread, lodging, and other necessities. The staffs of important households and the officials and employees of the Curia itself included relatively few long-term residents of the city, especially as the succession of popes frequently entailed the shifting of favor from one nationality to another, and service at the Court of Rome was, we may presume, an excellent stepping stone to an ecclesiastical or administrative career in a man's homeland. It is likely that the sheer artificiality of the society of Rome, where men greatly outnumbered women, may have been a major factor in the experience of many foreigners and immigrants, many of whom held quite humble positions in the Curia or in prelates' households or practiced various trades, and were accordingly not in holy orders.

The local population itself doubtless included a sizable migratory element, moving with the seasons or as economic or epidemiological conditions dictated between the city and the hills of Lazio or even beyond. As in any medieval city, immigration was an important if not necessary factor in the maintenance of population levels (Comba, Piccinni, and Pinto 1984), while the economy of Rome, in particular, was marked by a preponderant pastoral sector (Maire-Vigueur 1976). The various edicts and regulations concerning the activities of butchers, tanners, and kindred trades in Rome remind us that in the winter the flocks and herds descended from remote mountain pastures to winter in the environs of Rome, or even within the walls of the city. With the flocks, of course, came the men who tended and guarded them, while others, no less migratory, made hay and otherwise tended the *casali*, landholdings in the agricultural belt that extended for some twenty kilometers around the city (Broise and Maire-Vigueur 1983; Coste 1976). Demographically, then, Roman society must have been fluid and heterogeneous, and we may well see the urgency with which, in the course of the Renaissance, confraternity and guild churches were founded and reconstructed, an attempt to establish stable and visible centers of solidarity within a highly unstable milieu (Guidoni 1983, 328–330). Similarly, the organizations of numerous ethnic and national groups played an important part in the religious life, the social fabric, and the development of the environment of Renaissance Rome (Brunel 1981).

The citizenry—and here I refer, needless to say, to the elites whose activities have left the clearest traces in the documents—were organized in institutional structures that intersected in various ways with the administrative structures of the Curia, or with the household staffs of popes or other important prelates. Guilds were of relatively limited importance, at least by the fifteenth century, when the society of the *bovattieri*—the leading guild, reflecting the economic importance of pastoralism—had lost much of the influence it had enjoyed in the heady days of the fourteenth-century commune (Gennaro 1967a; Guidoni 1983, 330). Scant evidence exists for guild membership or even leadership on the part of mid-fifteenth-century Romans whose prominence in other institutions can be readily documented. Among such institutions were the various communal magistracies, including those at *rione* or ward level that apparently functioned as a necessary stepping stone to the more prestigious city-wide offices, such as that of the *maestri di strada*, the magistrates responsible for the physical environment of the city, which has received particular attention from scholars (Westfall 1974a, 78–84; Guidoni 1983, 330–332).

Confraternities were especially important in Rome, perhaps occupying something of the place of guilds in the Tuscan cities; one, the Society of the Raccomandati Ymaginis sanctissimi Salvatoris (henceforth referred to as the Confraternity of the Salvatore), boasted several popes and other high-ranking prelates among the brothers and played an extraordinarily significant role in fifteenth-century Roman society (Partner 1972, 102–106). But any discussion of the social, administrative, and institutional structures of Rome requires caution; office-holding often did not confer, but rather ratified and reflected standing and authority in the city or, increasingly, papal support, so that the conspicuous or innovative occupation of an office may well need to be explained by reference to factors outside the statutory scope of the office itself.

Several of the men (we are dealing, again, with a masculine world) whose activity and impact on their milieu I shall attempt to trace operated often not so much within institutional frameworks as in the interstices of administrative and institutional structures. To this extent, Nello da Bologna was typical. Flexibility and versatility were crucial qualities, rather than specialized knowledge or even personal affiliations, though these were of course important. In several cases the potential importance or even character of an office was determined by the individual career, a phenomenon that Allan Ceen's discussion of the activity of Latino Manetti has made clear with regard to the magistracy of the *maestri di strada* in the sixteenth century (Ceen 1977, esp. 97). In seeking to understand the pontificate of Nicholas V, therefore, I shall follow the careers of several individuals, both citizens and immigrants, through various official designations and spheres of activity. The resulting picture will unavoidably be one of great complexity and heterogeneity.

No less complex than the social structure of Rome was its topography. It is often asserted that Rome is a city of many and distinct centers (Westfall 1974a, 69–70), though their spatial relationship may possibly have been perceived by medieval Romans as constituting an overriding symbolic schema (Guidoni 1972, 3–32). The political and judicial center of the commune was located on the Campidoglio (fig. 3; map 2), itself peripheral to the major inhabited area of the late medieval city; the major markets were also, for the most part, in that vicinity. The center of papal Rome, of course, became established in the course of the fifteenth century at the Vatican. Westfall and others have argued the importance of Nicholas V in this process; certainly the overriding importance of the Vatican is clearly articulated in the pages of Manetti, who is in this case, as usual, only partly right. Throughout the medieval period a keen rivalry had existed between the clergy of the two great basilicas of the city, the Vatican and the Lateran; indeed Nicholas's two immediate predecessors gave particular attention to the latter, especially Martin V Colonna, whose family allegiance precluded a close association with the Vatican, overshadowed as it was by the nearby stronghold of the Colonnas' great rivals, the Orsini, at Monte Giordano (Westfall 1974a, 6–7; Guidoni 1983, 329–330, 348–349).

The question of Nicholas's relations with the Lateran clergy and the confraternity headquartered there is of considerable importance. Distant from the main populated areas of the city, whose cathedral it was, the Lateran (map 2) provided a privileged arena for the traditional expressions of social cohesiveness and—in the context of these—the occasional demonstrations of public concerns in a less formal, even downright riotous, manner. The great procession of the Assumption, in particular, the major ritual event of the Roman political calendar, started here. Here stood structures of crucial importance in the religious and social life of the city, notably the ancient basilica itself and the rambling bulk of the adjoining papal palace, which included the chapel known for its plethora of relics as the Sancta Sanctorum, a magnet for pilgrims and a center of communal reverence and social activity. Here, finally, stood the Lateran Hospital, the greatest charitable institution of the city (fig. 37).

These buildings and others surrounded and informally demarcated an expansive space, the Campo, marked at its approximate center by prominent symbolic markers, the bronze wolf, the equestrian statue of "Constantine" (the history of the removal of these and other markers to the Campidoglio is well known), and a large and spreading elm tree (Herklotz 1985). The tree constituted a "roland," defined by John Stilgoe as the objectified essence of its surrounding territory, especially as defined through legally formulated tabus (Stilgoe 1982, 18–19). Its status as such was given conspicuous expression not long before Nicholas's accession by the execution of especially notorious malefactors, one hanged from the elm, the others mutilated and burned at the stake nearby. The story is related in the fifteenth-century chronicle of Stefano Infessura:[7] the men, one canon and two *beneficiati* of the Lateran, had taken precious stones from the reliquaries containing the heads of SS. Peter and Paul, preserved in the Lateran basilica, and had sought to find buyers for them in the markets of the city; their punishment has the air of an act of violent expiation visited on their bodies on the part of and for the sake of the whole community of Rome (Foucault 1979, esp. 47–59; Ragon 1983, 181–191).

Such a wealth of local and specifically communal resonances as we have found at the Lateran might well induce the popes to lavish attention on sites where the expression and symbolization through architectural or other means of their own wider agendas could be achieved; after all, the popes of the Renaissance claimed, with varying degrees of urgency, a central role in the political affairs of Italy or even Europe. Nicholas V was a pioneer of such a strategy; his development of the Vatican as the representative focus of papal authority and sacrality on a continental scale allowed the retention of the Lateran as a primarily local center, where papal policies toward the city could be manifested by subtle additions to or alterations of the familiar physical environment and its various ritual uses. The Lateran was not neglected by Nicholas; I will argue, instead, that it received real and symbolic attention of a kind that perhaps inevitably failed to impress a nonlocal observer like Manetti, especially in the conditions after 1453.

There is a case, moreover, for regarding Nicholas's better- known concern for the Campidoglio as closely related to that for the Lateran. At the Campidoglio extensive building campaigns involving both the Senator's Palace and the Palace of the Conservatori were carried out under Nicholas, and one of the leading craftsmen available to the pope, Paolo Romano, was committed to the project (Corbo 1966; Westfall 1974a, 94–100). It is significant that particular attention was given to the rear of the Senator's Palace (fig. 3), that is, to the facade that faced not toward the Vatican, the traditionally accepted focus of Nicholas's patronage, but toward the Lateran. This facade, which is still conspicuously marked with Nicholas's insignia, was framed to the northeast by a tower that guards the point at which the Via Maggiore leaves the floor of the Forum to ascend the steps that rise, aligned with the Capitoline obelisk, to the plateau of the Campidoglio (fig. 39). The other corner of the facade of the Senator's Palace facing the Forum, if it perhaps does not strictly constitute a tower, was at least built up in such a way as to suggest a tower, as is indicated in certain contemporary views or descriptions.[8]

The Senator's Palace now faced in two directions, pulling together visually and symbolically the distant poles of the city and proclaiming the interpenetration of papal authority and communal institutions. The building campaign at the Campidoglio, therefore, manifested a concern, paramount in other Nicholan projects, not only with the condition of specific monuments or sites, but also with the topographical relationships between them, and with the routes or even visual axes that concretely expressed these relationships. The character of Rome as a dispersed, many-centered city was recognized but then transcended by Nicholas's interventions. This was not new; the ceremonial emphasis on and architectural regularization or even elaboration of routes connecting urban foci, instituting a relational centeredness in a dispersed spatial matrix, occurred in other cities and was perhaps even typical.[9] It was the case, certainly, with the Via de' Calzaioli in Florence, which was formalized as a privileged connector between the cathedral complex and the seat of secular government, and led from both to the major market at the Mercato Vecchio (Braunfels 1979, 119f.).

Such axial centrality was provided in Rome by the Via del Papa, the route of the *possesso*, for all its irregularity (maps 1, 2). On its way from the Vatican to the Lateran, of course, it passed the municipal palaces of the Campidoglio and the major market of the city, which was located until 1477 in the vicinity of these. The *possesso* involved the ritual interaction of the pope and Roman society, including the nobles who marched with the procession, the poor who fought for the coins flung down at prescribed places, and the Jews who came forward with their sacred books and whose interpretation of the Law was rejected by the pope. It is likely that the opportunity was taken by the leaders of the municipal government to bring to the pope's attention as he traversed the Campidoglio the concerns of the city or at least of their class; the procession of the Assumption certainly brought together the pope and the city magistrates drawn up at the rear of the Campidoglio, and there is evidence that the opportunities for the expression of civic agendas were taken by elements of the city population present in the procession.[10]

Part of the route of the *possesso* had particular significance in the political topography of the city, though less so than it had had in the fourteenth century. The section of the Via del Papa that ran between the Lateran and the Campidoglio was known in late medieval parlance as the Via Maggiore or Sacra, indicating the status of the street (figs. 4, 37, 38).[11] To a degree it followed the course of the ancient Via Sacra through the Forum, but the medieval Via Sacra continued toward the Lateran, circumventing the Colosseum, whose symbolic, even emblematic, significance to medieval and postmedieval Rome is well known (Di Macco 1977). The Roman commune of the fourteenth century had sought to encourage settlement along the Via Maggiore between the Colosseum and the Lateran, a project that may stand as a conspicuous example of the frequent political associations of Roman topography and the buildings and signs that marked and defined it. In this case the region extending south and east of the Campidoglio in an approximate arc from the river toward the Quirinal Hill was punctuated by the fortified headquarters of baronial clans, the feudal overlords who controlled vast territories in the vicinity of Rome and the more distant mountains; a district at the edge of the high ground of the Quirinal and Viminal hills was even known as the Campo Torrecchiano (the spelling varies considerably), the place of towers, one of which was the Torre dei Conti that still stands (fig. 38).[12]

The barons had occupied and transformed into castles such prominent landmarks as the Colosseum or the Theater of Marcellus; by the fourteenth century, however, their power in the city was being energetically and largely successfully opposed by the emergent urban patriciate, whose power bases lay in the densely populated quarters on the other side of the Capitoline Hill. The gradual expulsion of the clan of the Annibaldi from the Colosseum and the assertion of communal claims to the building are symptomatic of an important shift in Roman politics and topography alike, though other clans, like the Savelli at the Theater of Marcellus, proved more difficult to dislodge.[13] Against this background, the concern shown by Nicholas V for the Lateran and institutions and social groups associated with it is of particular significance, not least in view of the apparent paradigmatic importance for Nicholas's own urban policies of the communal project of bringing demographic and economic revival to the Via Maggiore and its environs.

The question of Nicholas's policy toward the Lateran is closely connected with the fortunes of the Roman citizenry during his pontificate. An important theme of this book is the close relations, amounting even to collaboration, between Nicholas, his staff, and the urban patriciate. In subsequent discussions several members of the urban elite will step forward as individuals involved in concrete historical situations and nexuses of relationships; here we are concerned with their typicality in terms of class, neighborhood, and kinship (the approximate location of clan compounds in Rome is indicated in map 2). In a series of important studies, Jean-Claude Maire-Vigueur and other scholars have analyzed the development in the fourteenth century of an economically and politically ascendant class, associated with the guild of the *bovattieri* and engaged in the exploitation of the agricultural hinterland of Rome (Maire-Vigueur 1974, 1976; Gennaro 1967A; Coste 1976). Maire-Vigueur's more recent study (authored with Henri Broise) of the city itself as a residential habitat, however, has tended to emphasize the degree of physical and even social fragmentation; the urban environment and the habits of mind of the people are marked less by class loyalties and cohesion than by the mutually reinforcing values of kinship and neighborhood (Broise and Maire-Vigueur 1983). Analysis of marriage patterns, the primary evidence adduced, indicates that while social endogamy remains the preeminent concern of patrician families, this is typically secured by marriage alliances conducted within limited topographical areas; topographical exogamy occurs, in general, only when no appropriate matches are available within the neighborhood, as is the case, especially, with the relatively small and topographically scattered baronial aristocracy. Against this background, the physical configuration of Rome appears as a loose collage of clan compounds comprising residential units inhabited by related nuclear families and clustered around shared open spaces and such communally owned and used built elements as towers, wells, and storage facilities, which may have been placed also at the disposal of unrelated, socially inferior inhabitants of the wider neighborhood. The aspect of these compounds is markedly affected by rural models, once again revealing the importance of the agricultural and pastoral economy of the Roman hinterland in the lives of the patrician elite.

This model of social and environmental fragmentation is somewhat mitigated by the communal character of religious life. Maire-Vigueur and Broise emphasize the preference of patrician families to associate themselves with a relatively restricted number of churches of city-wide status and importance, rather than with more local churches that might not only be located in the immediate vicinity of a family compound, but even incorporated within it, as occurred in certain other medieval Italian cities, notably Genoa. Communality, then, albeit often charged with undertones of clan rivalry manifested in the occupation and embellishment of space within the major churches, is expressed at the level of ritual and symbolic practice, but finds little corresponding expression in terms of the ordering of the physical urban environment as a whole.

Accordingly, Maire-Vigueur and Broise associate the tendency to unification and regularization, which they find typical of the Renaissance and implicit in mid-fifteenth-century statutes, with external stimuli and pressures. On the other hand, their own account of consistency in the configuration and even appearance of the various clan compounds suggests that a certain degree of homogeneity was consciously upheld as a desired characteristic of privileged compounds within the city. In particular, the most dynamic part of the late medieval city, the north-central sector including the Rioni Ponte and Parione (maps 1 and 2) where new patterns of property holding and exploitation are apparent, is marked especially, in their view, by immigration and the influence of the nearby Vatican, though they also note the involvement of local patricians in the developing economy of the area. My reading of the evidence from the period of Nicholas's pontificate, however, suggests that the projects and reforms that seem to reflect a new attitude to urban space required and received the support of at least some key elements of the local social elite and other, less well documented groups. Much of the Roman citizenry, indeed, rather than withdrawing to a position of discontented passivity, took an active role in such reordering of their environment as occurred throughout all but the final phase of Nicholas's pontificate.

Maire-Vigueur and Broise give little attention in their discussion of the urban habitat to the corporate institutions that cut across neighborhood and rional loyalties, forming an important horizontally structuring element in Roman society. The most prominent of these was the commune itself, which provided for ambitious patricians a *cursus honorum* rising from rional to city-wide office, in this way formally relating different spheres of institutional involvement, as also of individual experience. C. W. Westfall has correctly stressed Nicholas's policy of upholding the authority and functions of the commune, though he overstates the case through a characteristic reliance on declarations of policy rather than evidence for implementation (Westfall 1974a, esp. 74–84). In fact, the evidence reviewed in chapter 4 indicates a series of encroachments and appropriations under the surface of the traditional communal structures, and I would suggest that Nicholas's support for the commune was primarily a matter of support for and reliance on the class that provided the personnel who served in communal offices and that, after generations of such service, had accumulated invaluable experience and expertise; the papal lists of office-holders make very clear the range of responsibilities with which local patricians were invested in diverse sectors of the papal administration in the city and the adjacent provinces alike.

The other type of city-wide institution relatively neglected in Maire-Vigueur and Broise's discussion is the great confraternities of the city, though they note, somewhat in passing, their involvement in the property market of Rome.[14] The most important confraternity was that of the Salvatore;[15] indeed, it is indicative of its status that Nicholas himself was a member, as were other important personages. Papal membership, however, was not a formality, and it is no surprise, for instance, to find Eugenius IV, who faced and fled from a popular uprising in Rome, among popes who did not belong (Egidi 1914, 456). The charitable activities of the confraternity were centered at the Lateran; it administered the great hospital on the Campo Laterano, as well as a smaller hospital attached to the Colosseum.[16] The two hospitals stood at the boundaries of the district around the Via Maggiore that the commune had been concerned to develop; it did so by investing the confraternity with administrative and judicial authority over the area and by providing incentives for settlement. The pertinent statutes remained in force throughout the fifteenth century,[17] supplying the model for an urban development project that occurred early in Nicholas's pontificate and was appropriated if not initiated by him. The role of the confraternity in Nicholan Rome, therefore, is of crucial importance to an understanding of the pope's program of urban improvement, at least in the early years.

The Confraternity of the Salvatore was founded to institutionalize reverence for a precious and celebrated icon representing Christ; this was kept in a costly shrine in the palatine chapel of the Lateran, the Sancta Sanctorum.[18] According to Giovanni Rucellai, the Florentine merchant who visited Rome during the Jubilee of 1449–50, Nicholas was the first pope in more than a hundred years to have mass said in the chapel, where only the pope had this privilege, and where, according to legend, St. Peter himself had once celebrated mass.[19] Surrounded by relics, the icon had itself the character of a relic, for an ancient tradition claimed that it was of miraculous provenance; it was *aceropita*, produced by no human hand.[20] But Nicholas's concern for the chapel and the icon was politically self-serving, in view of the major role of the icon in the religious life both of the confraternity and of the Roman people as a whole. In particular, it was the centerpiece of the procession of the Assumption, during which it was carried in triumph past the Colosseum and the Campidoglio to S. Maria Maggiore.[21] During the procession the icon made a series of ritual pauses to receive anointment of basil water; the first occurred in front of the major portal of the hospital complex, which looked over an informal space opening off the Campo Laterano defined by buildings of the hospital and the triumphal arch motif of the Arco di Basile (actually part of an aqueduct), at the opening of the Via Maggiore proper. The ceremony brought the divinely fabricated image of Christ, the center of the confraternity's religious practice and guarantor of its cohesiveness and status, to the place most evocative of its charitable role in the city and marked by its emblems. Here at least once a year, then, the assembled brethren and the chief officials of the confraternity, the *guardiani*, doubtless gave ritual expression to the place of the confraternity in Roman social and religious life; there are no eyewitness accounts of the ceremonies known to me, but they were perhaps too regular and familiar to warrant description.

The list of the *guardiani* of the fifteenth century (Marangoni 1747, 316–318) is a roll call of the leading figures in the Roman patriciate of the period; it indicates clearly that the supremacy of the confraternity in Roman society was unchallenged. But if the confraternity was especially associated with and represented the interests of a particular urban class, it was by no means exclusive, at least for a while (Marangoni 1747, 286f; Egidi 1908, 311–320; Egidi 1914, 451–458; Pavan 1984). During the pontificate of Nicholas V all restrictions on the number of brothers were lifted (in 1452) and membership increased considerably (Egidi 1914, 451); it is possible that Nicholas himself exerted some influence on the passing of this resolution, though pressure from newly prosperous elements of the citizenry and the financial needs of the confraternity itself may well have been factors. In particular, the Lateran hospital underwent a large-scale program of expansion in the fifteenth century and enjoyed generous support, for instance, from Everso di Anguillara, a leading representative of the barons based in the surrounding territory, ally of the Colonna, and resolute opponent of papal domination in the third quarter of the century; the confraternity's net was indeed cast wide (Sora 1907, 72–76; Egidi 1908, 435).[22]

Apart from occasional large donations, like that of Count Everso, and revenues from rents, the standard mechanism by which income was generated for the confraternity and its hospitals consisted of a regular and formalized system of donations in which most of the churches of the city and much of the population were implicated. In return for donations the confraternity provided a service: it guaranteed the performance of annual masses for the soul of each donor on a date and in the church, usually the place of burial, of his or her choice. Most donations were testamentary bequests, though those made *inter vivos* were not uncommon. The secretary of the confraternity kept a record, the *liber anniversariorum*, of the donors' names, their gifts, the churches chosen for burial, and the persons, usually executors, who transferred the gifts to the officials of the confraternity. Many gifts took the form of property, which had then to be administered and in most cases sold by the officials; the volume of transactions in which the confraternity was involved indicates its probable major impact on the property market of the city (Egidi 1914, 153–160).[23]

The great majority of donations, of whatever kind, were of the value of 50 to 100 florins; the sums mentioned are usually multiples of 50, more rarely 25. Gifts, especially testamentary bequests, were expressed in money terms and in round figures, probably more for accounting convenience than to indicate the availability of the stated value in cash. Indeed, the variety of equivalents resorted to, sometimes in installments, to make up the cash value of a gift illustrates the shortage of cash that was a constant feature of economic life at Rome in this period.[24] In such a situation, the availability of credit becomes crucial for the development of economic activity; the complaint that after the conspiracy of Porcari credit dried up (as reported by the Sienese envoy Bartolomeo de Lagazzara, February 14, 1453 [Pastor 1949, 238 n.3]; note the general remarks of Spufford 1988, 347, on the increasing problem of scarcity of credit in fifteenth-century Europe) suggests that it had been readily available previously, doubtless due to the infusions of capital during the Jubilee and the relative security of Rome under Nicholas. The increased flow of cash through the local economy and the ease of credit would have enabled the confraternity to realize more easily the property and commodities that continually accrued to it, and perhaps to assess their monetary value more accurately.

Prosperity alone, however, was not responsible for the availability of credit; the events of 1453 affected not the objective amount of cash in the local economy, but the mood of confidence brought about by the conciliatory policies of Nicholas V and, no doubt, by the enlivening effect of his architectural and other patronage, especially his many, often small-scale building projects scattered through the city. And we may be sure that subtle fluctuations in the economic situation and prospects of the city were apparent to the officials of the Confraternity of the Salvatore, who over years of assessing and disposing of property and major commodities had gained perhaps unrivaled insight into economic trends. The support of the local elite for Nicholas, then, however assertive his financial administration, was surely based on a clear-sighted understanding—indeed, the expert assessment—of the significance of his pontificate to the material interests of the economically dominant citizenry.

Though donations of property preponderate in the *liber anniversariorum* of the confraternity, we note also the frequent mention of furnishings (*mobilia*), wine and other agricultural or horticultural produce, and industrial products. There are occasional gifts of building materials such as timber, ropes, and even windows (Egidi 1908, 388, 391). The high value—and, consequently, the probable scarcity—of furnishings in relation to basic housing is striking; many houses are valued in the 50 to 100 florin range, while a quilt (*cultrum*) might be valued at 25 florins and a bed at about the same.[25] Houses and *vigne* are the major forms of property appearing in the ledgers, the latter indicating the importance of small-scale viticulture and horticulture in the life of quattrocento Romans. The expansive landholdings known as *casali* that lay beyond the suburban belt of *vigne* rarely find mention, on the other hand, nor do their products; this may perhaps reflect the growing desirability of urban property in the fifteenth century. The majority of houses donated to the confraternity were sold off, though the latter, like other similar institutions, possessed its own extensive property holdings, which were recorded in a *liber stabilium* (Egidi 1908, 392). The high rate of conversion of property into money doubtless reflects the high running expenses of the hospitals and, perhaps, the almsgiving expected of any wealthy institution, especially under Nicholas V.[26] There is evidence, however, that institutions preferred to hold rural rather than urban property, for the latter was often in poor condition and the returns low (Broise and Maire-Vigueur 1983, 107, 112f.). Private owners, on the other hand, had noneconomic reasons for holding onto urban property; Maire-Vigueur and Broise have noted the consolidation through property ownership of a family's position in a neighborhood, while houses, in particular, often appear as pledges in marriage agreements, when a family's wealth and status were most closely scrutinized (ibid., 116–120).[27]

The most conspicuous changes in the fabric of Rome in the mid-fifteenth century, however, were due not to the activity of institutions, but to men whose financial means and cultural horizons belonged to a wider world than the city of Rome. The contemporary emphasis on the wealth and magnificence especially of the French cardinals, however, should not lead us to neglect the importance of local men among the leading patrons of residential architecture. Such individuals, who combined high rank and authority within the Church with strong local and familial loyalties, include Pope Martin V and Cardinals Prospero Colonna, Giordano and Latino Orsini, and Domenico and Angelo Capranica. In the case of the Capranica, especially, we can follow the gradual acquisition over many years of an extensive rural estate, at the same time as the famous urban palace was under construction.[28] The two projects are surely related; both appear to project feudal or perhaps rather feudalizing authority, as is borne out in the case of the palace by certain quasi-public uses of the building and, as we shall see, by its architectural characteristics.

Portico and Tower: Built Form, Social Function, and Meaning
The Palazzo Capranica, with its tower and guelph windows (fig. 4), still gives an impression of the simple but powerful and orderly architecture in vogue in Rome and environs in the mid-fifteenth century.[29] The most conspicuous example was perhaps the new wing of Nicholas V in the Vatican palace, which was significantly adopted as a model for the slightly later palace built by the Caetani, one of the baronial clans of the Campagna, at their stronghold at Sermoneta.[30] The date of the Palazzo Capranica cannot be exactly determined; the *bifore* (double arched windows divided by a colonnette) on the right of the facade suggest the incorporation of earlier structures into a gradually evolving project, while a *terminus ante quem* for the completion is the death of Domenico Capranica in 1459.[31] Subsequent building was carried out by Domenico's brother Angelo, but this involved only the structure behind the palace proper that was intended to house the college founded by Domenico.

The Capranica palace is distinguished by elements that were surely readily decoded by a population adept at reading a physical environment in which, for all its complexity, architecture served as both a medium and frame for signification. The high, massive tower of the palace was one such element, as were the battering of the prominent buttresses, the sham rustication of the basement story, and the guelph windows (fig. 4). The latter are of particular interest: their crossed stone mullions recall—and perhaps alluded to—the rectilinear tracery prominent in the late gothic residential architecture of France and other northern lands. Guelph windows quickly became naturalized in Roman palace architecture of the quattrocento, and even infiltrated the generally classicizing taste of the early sixteenth century; no doubt their feudal and chivalrous associations were congenial and appropriate in the particular social conditions of Renaissance Rome. Certainly, they appear in the Nicholan wing of the Vatican palace (it is not certain that they are original) and were perhaps used by his builders at the Castel S. Angelo, as some early representations suggest (fig. 32).

It is noteworthy that guelph windows—and other window types that came into fashion at the same time—could be used as a conspicuous field for inscriptions (fig. 5); in other words, they could literally become lexical elements in a text constituted by the various kinds of signs arrayed in the public domain of the city. In addition, inscribed windows can serve as examples of the combination of different modes of encoding the built environment, a not infrequent practice, since the window type itself carried significance.[32]

Guelph windows became, perhaps already by the pontificate of Nicholas V, a basic element of a conservative but flexible Roman palace architecture that proved remarkably resistant to influences from more sophisticated centers of architectural production, for all the foreign provenance of the leading craftsmen in the *cantieri* of Rome. Both the provincialism and the extensive diffusion of this style, if so it can be called, are well illustrated by the case of the extensive addition made in 1447 to a house in the Rione Trevi; the contract specifies that the structure is to be built and fitted out with elaborate woodwork on the model of the residence of Cardinal Colonna, which stood nearby. In 1462 the agent of the court of Mantua, commissioned to find appropriate lodging for the young Cardinal Gonzaga, reported that Cardinal Colonna was one of those "che stano male de casa."[33] Though we have no direct evidence for the appearance of either building at this time, we may presume that they were consistent with the general fashion in the city. The sturdy architectural tradition of fifteenth-century Rome has been well studied by Pietro Tomei and others, who have drawn attention, for instance, to the characteristic preference in Rome for the octagonal brick pier, ubiquitous in the grander architectural projects (fig. 6), over the *all'antica* column long established in Florence.[34] This conservatism does not seem to be a matter of mere aesthetics, still less of cultural backwardness, concepts that hardly provide an explanation of the phenomenon. Rather, I would suggest that Roman residential buildings of the fifteenth century reflected a concern with the legibility of the urban environment in a time of change and challenge to traditional assumptions.

We should not be surprised, accordingly, if quattrocento Romans were slow to adopt the motif of the formal, interior courtyard, though by midcentury this had become accepted as a crucial element of an up-to-date palace in Florence and elsewhere. As the century progressed, however, the courtyard invaded and established itself in Roman palace architecture in a process that could be described, albeit with some simplification, as the transfer of a motif, the portico, from the exterior to the interior, so that it was no longer visible, still less intelligible, to beholders in the public domain. Certainly, the Roman early Renaissance courtyard long remained more loosely designed, or at least arranged, than its Florentine counterpart: the former tended to be informal, with multistoried porticoes sometimes arrayed only on two sides of a relatively expansive, often markedly oblong area; the courtyards of the more prominent Florentine palaces, on the other hand, opposed matching interior facades across a cubic volume defined and dissected by colonnaded bays suggesting an underlying tight geometrical matrix.[35] In both cases, albeit more clearly in

Florence, the Renaissance courtyard appears as an element of conscious planning and design, rather than a mere void more or less surrounded by buildings. It may suggest an idealized urban space—or even a substitute for urban space—in the spirit of Alberti's conception of the courtyard of a house as the counterpart on the domestic scale of the forum on the larger scale of the classical city (Alberti 1966a, 1:339 [V.ii]); such analogical correspondences may be corroborated by synecdochic references to emblematic elements in the city, as in the allusion to the nearby Colosseum in the mighty arcades of the Palazzo S. Marco (Palazzo Venezia), built in the 1460s (fig. 7). For all such celebratory metaphors, however, the courtyard was incontrovertibly a private space, charged with signs of ownership and organized for private needs; on the other hand, it served for those who penetrated the outer periphery of the building as a mediating point on the route from the public domain of the streets to the intimacy of the chambers of the master or mistress of the house.

In Florence the ascendancy of the Renaissance palace type seems correlated—though the situation is still far from clear—with the decline of the loggia, a representative arcaded structure used for the festivities and/or business of a particular family but open to the inquiring and perhaps envious view of the neighborhood (Kent 1977, 244). In Rome, on the other hand, the wave of palace construction of the quattrocento apparently coincides with the disappearance of the porticoes that had been a characteristic element and mediatory zone of the larger houses of late medieval Rome. These porticoes, though evidently more widely distributed than the Florentine loggias and perhaps never freestanding as some of the latter were, nevertheless seem to have served many of the same functions (Krautheimer 1982, 294f.; Broise and Maire-Vigueur 1983, 152f.). And it is significant that facade porticoes are absent from Roman Renaissance palaces, with the obvious exception of the Palazzo Massimo alle Colonne, where the motif has clear emblematic or even heraldic significance, in terms of the concern of the patrons to commemorate the continuity of their occupation of the site through the incorporation into the palace of certain archaizing features (fig. 8; Wurm 1965, 145f.). The courtyard, then, comes to prominence at the expense of a functionally similar element in both Florence and Rome; this is clearly primarily a social rather than architectural phenomenon. Indeed, the adoption of the interior courtyard is one of the elements that signal the shift in attitudes, brilliantly analyzed by Maire-Vigueur and Broise, toward the use of public space and the relationship of this to the private sphere of the house.[36]

The course of this development and its implications in fifteenth-century Rome have been obscured partly, no doubt, by the scattered and fragmentary nature of the evidence, but also by the attention given to urbanistic measures taken by Sixtus IV and to a celebrated anecdote involving that pope. The contemporary chronicler Infessura relates that after a cavalcade through the streets of Rome on the occasion of the state visit of King Ferrante of Naples in 1475, the king remarked to the pope that he would never be master of Rome until the porticoes and other obstacles to movement through or surveillance of the narrow streets were removed. According to Infessura, the pope followed this advice and ordered the porticoes to be removed and the streets widened (Magnuson 1958, 37–40; Tomei 1942, 20–22; Broise and Maire-Vigueur 1983, 146f.).

Unfortunately for Infessura's account, late medieval porticoes are still visible, though they have generally been filled in, in many parts of Rome (Tomei 1942, 21); a conspicuous example is the portico of the Casa Bonadies (fig. 9) in the present Via del Banco di Santo Spirito, which the pope must have passed every time he left the Vatican by way of the Ponte S. Angelo. Sixtus's documented action against the illicit occupation of public space by private structures did no more than observe the letter of the statutes of Rome, which in turn were typical of the regulatory environment as it had existed for centuries in most Italian cities (Braunfels 1979, 102–104); there is no need to ascribe to Sixtus opposition to porticoes as such, at least in cases where no legal objections to their survival existed. Clearly, the circumstances of the decline of the late medieval Roman portico must be sought elsewhere; in particular, the model of administrative fiat implied in Infessura's narrative should yield to one of gradual and profound social transformations with important environmental and even psychological implications. For nothing less seems to be involved than an increasingly hierarchical stratification of Roman society, a corresponding ordering of architectural expression, and a concern with privacy on the part of those who could afford it.

As so often, the documentary evidence pertinent in this case is illuminated by the theoretical remarks and keen observations of Alberti. The palace courtyard, of course, is a theme discussed at length in the De re aedificatoria, where it is most memorably presented in the context of the palace appropriate for important figures in the government of a city; in the nature of their office, such men receive a stream of visitors, whose servants and followers need a place where they can kick their heels during their masters' audience in the inner chambers (Alberti 1966a, 1:345 [IV.ii]). Alberti also notes that palaces officially implicated in the conduct of the city's affairs need to be conspicuously placed. Otherwise, however, he recommends the siting of houses on secondary streets that do not give access except to a limited neighborhood; he cites with approval the notoriously tortuous urban fabric of Islamic cities.[37] This arrangement, in Alberti's view, provides relief from the congestion of the major thoroughfares of the city and makes it easier for the house to be so designed that it receives good natural light (ibid., 309 [IV.vi]).

These recommendations are consistent with the passage elsewhere in the treatise in which Alberti advises that urban houses should have as much as possible the characteristics of suburban residences, which in turn combine the best of city and country living and allow more expansive and flexible architectural solutions than are possible on typically confined urban plots. Alberti (1966a, 1:433–437 [V.vi]) further recommends that urban houses should be associated with shops, though these for obvious economic reasons need to occupy more conspicuous locations; we may imagine an Albertian neighborhood, then, as comprising relatively humble buildings linking the main thoroughfare with more quiet and protected alleys (Alberti is explicit about the concern for security), which lead down to the residences of more affluent citizens who prefer to lead their lives out of the public eye. It is a neighborhood defined by a hierarchy of increasingly private spaces, parallel—in terms of Alberti's familiar analogy of the house as small city—to the hierarchy of rooms and other spaces within a house; in both cases the various thresholds marking passage through a sequence of spaces receive architectural expression appropriate to their importance in the ritual of entry and to their place in the overall organism whose articulation they emphasize.

Alberti here hints at a process of privatization, one of which he approves, though elsewhere he expresses approval of the facade portico as a mediating element between the private and public worlds (Alberti 1966a, 2:803 [IX.vi]). Significantly, however, he is defensive: the portico, he says, should be for the benefit of the community, the public domain, as a whole, and not just for that of slaves.[38] In spite of the literary reference the implication is clear: porticoes had become associated with low-status activities and individuals. If so, the medieval portico was losing its function, its very identity, as a stage for ceremonies and festivities of various kinds. The process is extremely difficult to track, for all its importance in the transformation of attitudes to urban space. Light may be shed, however, by apparent shifts in one of the most conspicuous and better documented functions of the portico, that as a setting for legal cases involving arbitration.

The importance of arbitration in late medieval Roman society can be gauged from the insistence of the Confraternity of the Salvatore that the inhabitants of the Via Maggiore, placed under the jurisdiction of the officials of the confraternity, should go for arbitration only to the latter (Adinolfi 1857, 143). In practice, an arbitration constituted a typical occasion for the involvement of high-ranking figures—prelates, aristocrats, even the occasional ambassador—in the affairs of more humble citizens and for the visits of the latter to the houses of their social superiors (Corbo 1984, 61f.). The population must have been extremely litigious: notarial protocols are full of cases of disputes adjudicated by a third party acceptable, presumably, to both parties. In many cases, the social distance of the arbitrator or arbitrators from the disputants ensured his or their objectivity and—perhaps more importantly—enjoyment of the respect of all concerned. In the more usual cases where no grand personage was involved the distance of the arbitrator from the disputants was physically expressed. The arbitrator was seated—"sedens pro tribunali" is the formula of the documents—as if in contrast with the other participants, who presumably stood throughout the proceedings. Often a prominent and permanent raised seat or bench, sometimes on a stone base, was used by the arbitrator; a typical case was that of 1451 carried out by arbitrators "sedentes pro tribunali in quodam podio in pietro sito in porticali" in the house of the notary concerned, which seems to have been provided with the appropriate furniture for such transactions.[39] In contrast, Cardinal Domenico Capranica himself was involved in April 1448 in a case of arbitration transacted in the hall of his palace, and then solemnly ratified in the nearby church of S. Maria in Aquiro. Subsequently the principals returned to the palace, where they did obeisance before the cardinal and gave pledges of their good behavior in future.[40]

The use of porticoes for such transactions, the success of which clearly depended and was thought to depend on the prestige and authority invested in an enthroned arbitrator, may have contributed to the loss of status of the portico—or even the street itself—as an accepted arena at least for formalized social interaction. Customary legal ritual, involved in the life of the streets, perhaps required at least the potential attendance of the whole neighborhood in witness; M.-L. Lombardo, indeed, has stressed the theatral character of arbitration proceedings (Lombardo 1984, 308f.), while Broise and Maire-Vigueur (1983), 152f., have noted the general use of porticoes for legal transactions. Such ritual was now perhaps giving way to more courtly practices framed in an exclusive architectural setting sufficient to impress Romans, however provincial it may have seemed in Florentine eyes. The suggestion of Westfall (1974a, 152–156), then, that loggias and porticoes were typically used or even designed as theatral spaces, if it is true, may well link the humanist fashion for *all'antica* dramatic entertainment to the rituals of everyday life.[41] And it is significant that Alberti himself noted the ancient predilection for porticoes in the form of a theater; though he expressly refers to a formal condition, his words, here and elsewhere, surely reflect the central role of porticoes in the urban environment as places of spectacle, of enacted and encoded meaning alike.[42]

A well-documented case of the interiorization of legal activity is that of the house of Pietro Mellini, who was in many respects a typical Roman patrician, if perhaps unusually adept at securing social and professional connections in mid-fifteenth- century Rome. Mellini lived in the environs of the Piazza Navona in a neighborhood long associated with his family; his house was a short walk from the palace of Cardinal Ludovico Trevisan, the chamberlain, whose role in the development of Rome, especially the environs of his palace, in the years before Nicholas V's accession is discussed in a later chapter. Mellini clearly enjoyed the cardinal's support, which doubtless contributed to his success: in his legal practice he could boast of several prominent clients, including the chapter of St. Peter's, while he was also a leading member of the Confraternity of the Salvatore, serving as *guardianus* in 1452.[43] Before October 1451 several notarial transactions are recorded as having taken place in Mellini's house with no further indication of locale; after that date we find that similar transactions occurred in a "studium novum" in the house.[44] The documents suggest that Mellini had a private study, a *studiolo*, constructed in 1451, possibly on the model of the obviously far more elaborate *studiolo* that Nicholas had recently had built in the Vatican palace and decorated by Fra Angelico. There is some evidence that Mellini's *studiolo*, like that of Nicholas, was part of a more extensive construction campaign. In any case, after Mellini's death his widow presented to her husband's confraternity, as part of her donation to pay for anniversary masses for his soul in the neighborhood church of S. Agnese, three marble windows "ad cruces" (i.e., guelph windows; Egidi 1908, 478). Evidently Mellini had at some time ordered a number of these fashionable windows to bring his house up to date, but his widow was less convinced of the importance of this.[45]

Though Mellini's *studiolo* is the only documented case of such a room privately constructed in Rome during Nicholas's pontificate, it is unlikely that it was an anomaly in the social and professional circles to which Mellini belonged. Others in the same position surely felt the need for a functionally defined and private space in which to conduct business. If so, it is noteworthy that the withdrawal from the public domain and the elaboration of private space that Mellini seems to exemplify did not entail an abandonment of public space; on the contrary, Mellini's class—and probably Mellini himself—supported the aestheticization of the public domain that occurred, or was at least envisaged, in the early Renaissance, not least, as we will see, in Mellini's own quarter of the city.

Social and professional functions migrated, then, perhaps undergoing transformations en route, from the facade portico to various interior spaces, of which the new courtyard type was to be the most conspicuous. Documentary evidence for the exact functions of any of these spaces is fragmentary, and any discussion of these is necessarily speculative. Even rarer is direct evidence for the physical appearance of porticoes in the fifteenth-century city. Nevertheless, we can relate the questions of function and aspect alike to the conspicuous assertion in the urban environment of property rights on the part of owners and/or residents of buildings, concerned to identify and convey information about their buildings and, doubtless in many cases, themselves. This is an aspect of the late medieval visual environment almost completely neglected by scholars, even though, for instance, the otherwise excellent and exhaustive Maire-Vigueur and Broise attend to the visual properties of the urban fabric of the time.

We know that Rome, like most medieval cities, was a veritable forest of signs attached to or painted on house facades; these took the place of house numbers in a more rationally ordered age, for their primary purpose was simply to identify buildings in a relatively circumscribed area, like a parish, within which further information as to topographical relationships or architectural aspect would be unnecessary. The extensive property holdings of the chapter of St. Peter's, for instance, which were located throughout the city, were marked off from their neighbors by a relatively small number of sign types that recurred from parish to parish, or even street to street. There is no way of knowing what form these signs took or what difference the presence of a portico might have made to the method of display adopted; we can perhaps assume that the portico, where it existed, was often used for the display of house signs, since it provided shelter from the elements and by reason of its distance—however small and symbolic—from the frequent turbulence of the street.[46]

The signs used by property owners like the chapter of St. Peter's to identify their houses necessarily gave no information about the inhabitants, though it is not unlikely that tenants, especially those who effectively rebuilt their houses as a condition of their lease, added their own signs to those of the landlord. At the highest social level, of course, the dynastic aspirations of patrician families were often identified with and sustained by a building marked with appropriate signs of family status and continuity, kinship relations, and political and military exploits; Gnoli (1938, 16) noted the commemoration of marriage alliances through the display of coats of arms in porticoes in Rome as late as the early sixteenth century. Goldthwaite (1980, 86–88), on the other hand, in a discussion of Florentine palace facades in the quattrocento, has emphasized the variety as well as the frequency of signs asserting ownership. I would distinguish three types, which may well have occurred in Rome also and have been diffused beyond the grander palaces to "bourgeois" buildings. The most favored means was the simple mounting of a coat of arms or a similar heraldic item; more subtly, heraldic elements might be integrated into the decoration of a facade or another part of a house. These two types of display occur together, for instance, on the facade of the Rucellai palace (fig. 10) and probably originally on the adjacent loggia, where their sign value was periodically reinforced by family rituals and festivities framed in an architecture carrying theatrical connotations.

On a third level, the sign value of the Rucellai palace, as of Renaissance palace architecture in general, is conveyed by the configuration of the palace as a whole, especially by means of the architectonic or textural handling of the facade through such devices as rustication or the explicit or suggested presence of one or more classical orders (Preyer 1981). This is clearly no longer a matter of heraldry, but rather of emblematic resonances, alluding to the patron's sociopolitical and cultural horizons or his professed ethical values. While the specific design solution of the Rucellai facade remained an anomaly in Florentine palace architecture, it may represent a tendency for cultured or merely pretentious members of the elite to reject the blatant display of heraldic insignia (see Sinding-Larsen 1975, 191f.; Damisch 1979, 18–25), preferring the integration of these, perhaps wittily incorporated into *all'antica* ornamental motifs, into an articulated surface, or even resorting to nonarchitectural, nonheraldic *all'antica* identifying elements, like the portrait bust placed on his house by a prominent quattrocento humanist, Matteo Palmieri (Burroughs 1983).

Even if native Romans failed to indulge in such practices by the mid-fifteenth century, the affluent Florentine community in Rome doubtless transferred to their temporary place of residence the customs followed at home, all the more as the houses of many Florentines in Rome doubled as business premises and as such required distinguishing marks for the orientation of clients. Some of the Florentine residents of the Rome of Nicholas V, moreover, had close connections with the new artistic and architectural fashions: Roberto Martelli, for instance, for many years the director of the branch of the Medici bank in Rome (De Roover 1963, 198, 211, 217), was a connoisseur of such artists as Donatello (Wackernagel 1981, 249), while Tommaso Spinelli, banker to the commune of Rome under Nicholas, built a palace in Florence in the 1450s that still carries *sgraffito* decoration alluding to the surname and patronymic of its owner, whose architectural projects in Rome have unfortunately disappeared without trace.

Spinelli played an important role (detailed in chapter 3) in the reordering of the main thoroughfare of the Florentine quarter of Rome, the district immediately facing the Castel S. Angelo across the river. The campaign of improvement in this district involved and presumably benefited a range of groups and interests, the Florentine bankers prominent in the area, some of their Roman neighbors, the magistrates of the commune, and the papal staff. A piazza was created at the bridge approach, and the street leading into Rome was cleared of obstructions, paved, and perhaps regularized. It is possible, further, that cosmetic or even architectural improvements were made to the facades fronting the spruced-up street and piazza. No doubt the merchants and bankers of the area, whatever their origin, mounted on their premises signs advertising their presence; as commercial rivals they may have been concerned to give their houses a strongly individualizing physical appearance. On the other hand, the documents relating to the urbanistic improvements in the area suggest a degree of cohesiveness among the various participants whose payments toward the costs of the project are recorded. Certainly a strong sense of community underlay the nearly contemporary establishment of the Florentine confraternity of S. Giovanni Battista at a nearby church; this occurred in 1448, though Florentines had been resident in the area for many years and could easily have taken this step much earlier (Maroni-Lumbroso and Martini 1963, 165).[47]

It is possible, then, that the urbanistic improvements undertaken in the district known as Ponte under Nicholas V extended to the scale of the street or even neighborhood the third kind of sign value distinguished above with regard to single facades. The area may have received something of the visual cohesiveness and the orderly and dignified ambiance of the Tuscan cities, recently transformed, as noted by Alberti (1966a, 2:698 [VIII.v]), by the extensive rebuilding in stone of formerly wooden structures. This had surely produced a more unified, even homogeneous aspect, though Alberti does not make this point explicitly; on the other hand, he elsewhere recommends restraint in house design, at least in an urban setting, and the subordination of individual display to the overall effect (ibid., 778–785 [IX.i]; cf. 1:401 [V.xiv]; 2:789 [IX.ii]). If such an effect was achieved in Ponte, Alberti's involvement may be suspected; after all, he was a familiar figure in the area and was closely associated with some of its more prominent residents, notably Tommaso Spinelli; his role in the Nicholan intervention in Ponte, however indirect, cannot be doubted.

The evidence allows little more than speculation about the appearance of Ponte at this time; all the more important, then, though difficult to interpret, is the available information about a proposed rebuilding of the district immediately across the river. The ideal enclave in the Borgo, described by Manetti, boasts regular, straight thoroughfares fronted by uniform structures, the model of which, at least in part, seems to be the actual fabric of Ponte. Manetti's streets, moreover, were to be lined by colonnaded porticoes that recalled the ancient pilgrims' way to the Vatican but surely also echoed the architectural features of the Via del Papa across the bridge, where the entrance of the street is still marked by the conspicuous portico of the Casa Bonadies (fig. 9), the mansion of a prominent local family with close links to Nicholas and his court (Giovannoni 1935, 34; Tomei 1942, 263; Magnuson 1958, 46). This portico, with its lavish use of *spolia*, is a rare example in this area of the survival of quattrocento architecture, though it is impossible to be precise about its date of construction. It is likely, in any case, that it represents a familiar building type in Ponte in this period.

The unifying function of the porticoes of the Manettian Borgo is clear: they are to shelter and afford dignity to a commercial area set aside for the purveyors of various commodities. The central street in particular was to be reserved for goldsmiths and similar high-status trades (Magnuson 1958, 353; cf. Westfall 1974a, 111f.). The resulting functional uniformity would doubtless have been disturbed, had the Borgo scheme ever been built, by the signage and other means adopted by the craftsmen, surrounded by rivals, to draw attention to their own wares; such discordance would have been disguised, however, by the continuous porticoes constituting the armature, the dominant visual element, of the ideal curial enclave envisaged in Manetti's text. Formally, indeed, the porticoes are consistent with the grand buildings to which they were to lead; with these they form an ensemble emblematic of the ideological claims of the early Renaissance papacy, perhaps symbolizing the projection of the latter's authority in the temporal realm. The porticoes of the Borgo scheme, then, are double-coded, and their monumentality is moderated by a canny sense of the advantages of combining commercial and representative functions.

If Manetti's scheme was never realized, it is perhaps partly because his emphasis on porticoes in the streetscape coincided with their definitive fall from favor in Rome. Like the facade portico, the tower suffered a marked decline in the fifteenth century in Rome as a requisite element of the residences of leading families. The tower was a more tenacious motif, however, and long continued to punctuate the skyline, even rising from occasional major late-quattrocento buildings. A tower even appears, albeit in residual form, to mark the corner of the Cancelleria and support the patron's arms, relating the bulk of the palace to the Via de' Pellegrini and the hub of activity at the Campo de' Fiori (fig. 11). Only in the late sixteenth century did a reconstructed and newly emphatic portal eclipse the tower motif and redefine the relationship of palace and urban context. None of these towered private residences of the Renaissance sported a portico, except as an element of an enclosed courtyard.

We must be careful, accordingly, not to associate too closely the portico and tower as standard elements of a coherent repertoire of forms at the disposal of medieval Roman palace builders. Towers were doubtless always rarer than porticoes, and more exclusively associated with aristocratic families. In addition, there is evidence that a tower, rising from the clustered houses of a baronial or patrician clan, served a particular function as signifier, indicating the social status enjoyed by that clan in the neighborhood and beyond. Maire-Vigueur and Broise have noted that towers in such compounds tended to remain communal property, even after other elements of a patrimony had been divided up among the units comprising the clan. Though the French scholars offer no explanation of this phenomenon, it must surely reflect the tower's value as a marker of the clan's solidarity and continuity, as well as its probable function as a carrier of heraldic insignia and some of the related material often also displayed, as I have suggested, in porticoes.

The decline of the tower in the fifteenth century can be better documented than that of the portico: Broise and Maire-Vigueur (1983), 124, have noted cases of the relatively late formation of clan compounds in which no tower was erected, presumably though the clans concerned had the resources to do so and were the social equals, at least, of clans who had towers. On the other hand, many patrician families appear to have built or at least restored their towers in this period, among them the upwardly mobile Mellini, whose impressive tower still stands in the Via dell'Anima; this appears to have marked specifically the actual or claimed rise of the Mellini out of a "bourgeois" patrician stratum through intermarriage with the Cybo family of Pope Innocent VIII (Tomei 1942, 270, cf. 51).[48] It is likely, however, that Alberti (1966a, 2:699 [VIII.v]) was not alone in voicing opposition to towers as elements of domestic architecture. His strictures are especially worthy of note as he rarely mounts a direct attack on a specific aspect of the contemporary built environment; though he carefully pushes the phenomenon into the past ("about two hundred years ago"), this fits the case of Tuscany better than that of Rome where some towers continued to be built even in the fifteenth century.In any case, a tinge of snobbishness may lurk in the background, for Alberti observes that, in his words, hardly a single head of family could do without a tower. The result, in his view, was the transformation of cities throughout Italy into "forests of towers." (He was anticipated by Biondo, c. 1443; see Hay and Law 1989, 210). The problem, evidently, was that the diffusion of the fashion to diverse strata of the population had led to visual and social confusion.[49]

The image of the city as a forest, whether or not transmitted by Alberti, was later to play a fateful role in the articulation of attitudes toward the traditional city—one thinks of the paradigm of the emparked forest in the mid-eighteenth-century meditations of the Abbé Laugier on the reform of the city (Laugier 1977, 128f.)—preparing the way ultimately for the disruption of its scale and the destruction of its fabric. Alberti, like Laugier, was concerned with the city as a site of meaning: the ancient building types and urban ornaments—the triumphal arches and the like—that he privileges as models for development have the effect of clarifying the environmental expression of social and political realities, albeit through the projection of or allusion to heroic narratives and other fictions naturalizing the divisions within society.[50] The Albertian emphasis on the clarification, in this sense, of the codes of the city brings the discussion back to Nicholas V and the interventions carried out during his pontificate in the city and the wider region, understood less as physical environments than as spaces of signification in which rebuilding was, to a degree, but a conspicuous form of recoding.

The Forest of Signs
At first sight, the Manettian Borgo qualifies as a paradigm for a space of signification, abstracted, as it is, from the wider urban environment and framed by

colonnades and by boundaries marked and symbolized by the Castel S. Angelo and the monumental entrances foreseen for the Vatican palace and basilica. In the light of its unitary and schematic character, however, and of its absolute dependence on the ideological and economic requirements of the resurgent papacy, it appears less as a space within which signifiers might be marshaled (as I sought to interpret it above) than as itself a signifier.

It is not accidental, accordingly, that Manetti's description allows no clear and detailed visualization of the Borgo project, in which major elements remain subject to dispute (Westfall 1974a, 104f.). This is not a matter of the problems faced by a layman, however rhetorically adept, in giving literary shape to difficult and in part technical information supposedly vouchsafed to him by Alberti or some other putative designer or designers; the details simply do not matter. The Borgo as envisaged in Manetti's text is no city or part of a city; instead, it stands (in) for the city or rather for an already schematized conception of the city.

There is no doubt that an urban vision like the Manettian Borgo arose against the background of the process of reduction and rationalization characteristic of much fifteenth-century Italian architecture, not least that associated with Brunelleschi and his influence. More immediately, however, it constitutes an abstraction from and topographical concentration of an earlier program through which Nicholas and his advisers introduced into the urban environment a pattern of signs expressive of papal concerns and claims. These signs, in my view, depended for their efficacy on the constant, if fluid, background of elements fraught with associations and symbolism, marking on the surfaces of the city the various histories of Rome and its people; they did not require a *tabula rasa* such as that presupposed by the Borgo scheme. Alberti's metaphor of the city as forest is useful here, especially in view of the essential sign value embodied by the towers to which he explicitly refers, implying a reaction against both social and semiotic ataraxia. In this light, then, Nicholas's program of reordering the city as a legible space may be represented as a policy of clearing the underbrush, improving the rides, and attaching markers to prominent trees and rocks, but not of destroying and remaking the forest.

Especially significant in this respect is the extensive campaign of construction at the Campidoglio undertaken by Nicholas early in his pontificate (Magnuson 1958, 31f; Westfall 1974a, 92–97; von Moos 1974, 91–94); the new buildings and the papal insignia conspicuously affixed to them associated Nicholas's pontificate with this crucial arena of the political life and symbolism of Rome. In his attention to the Campidoglio, indeed, Nicholas anticipated that of later popes—such as Sixtus IV, Leo X, Paul III, and Sixtus V—also notable for their sophisticated understanding and manipulation of the role of signs in the public realm of Rome. Like them, Nicholas both accommodated and appropriated the powerful associations of the Campidoglio; his building program there involved major work on the Senator's Palace and the Palazzo de' Conservatori, of which the latter was fronted by a prominent portico, while the former received its high tower facing the Forum and marking the ascent from the Via Maggiore (figs. 3, 39). Both tower and portico, of course, are typical features of late medieval public buildings; as such they are combined in the slightly later Palazzo Comunale of Pienza, which seems to represent the conscious resumption of a traditional and familiar type. On the Campidoglio, on the other hand, they may have recalled equally strongly the traditional features of the houses of the dominant classes of Rome, at a time when they were beginning to seem rather passé—perhaps too familiar—for residential architecture; as such they perhaps contrasted with the fashionable guelph windows installed under Nicholas in both Capitoline palaces. Though the pope probably initiated and certainly took charge of the project, the resulting buildings echoed the domestic environment of the Roman patriciate, the political class of the city; at the same time, moreover, the relationship of these municipal palaces to the city as a whole is comparable, in terms of the familiar and fundamental analogy of house and city, to that of a patrician compound to the neighborhood visually dominated by its tower.[51]

The tower and portico of the Campidoglio, like those of patrician dwellings, were privileged sites for the display of signs. Under Nicholas, however, the whole city became the matrix of an extensive and coherent system of signs (figs. 12, 30). Many buildings still carry the insignia of the pope and occasionally also abbreviated inscriptions proclaiming Nicholas's part in their restoration or reconstruction (fig. 14);[52] a few contemporary images provide a visual impression of the effect, as in the cassone panel showing the coronation of Emperor Frederick III outside the Vatican palace marked with the papal arms (fig. 12).

The insignia themselves are restrained in form and uniform in character; they are clearly classical in inspiration, and as such constitute publicly displayed examples of the reform of letters, the paradigmatic role of which in humanist culture is the subject of an important discussion by E. H. Gombrich (1976). The space of the city, then, is organized through the insistent recapitulation of standard, individually laconic elements, the crossed keys and the inscribed letters, which recall—or even revive—the late ancient, early Christian city, which, as we have seen, was also given visible form on the walls of Nicholas's chapel, though with very different means. The effectiveness of such restrained signs in a complex urban environment may perhaps be doubted; we must bear in mind, however, that Nicholas's signs predated the variety and particularism asserted in the urban environment through the later fifteenth-century enthusiasm for *sgraffito* ornament (examples in Pericoli Ridolfini 1960, 54, 59, 68; general discussion in Giovannoni 1935, 38; Tomei 1942, 264), elaborate rustication, or extensive epigraphic or sculptural display, in short for the individual facade as itself an especially emphatic, even ostentatious sign.

Nicholas's inscriptions were no doubt especially prominent on ecclesiastical buildings, notably the station churches restored by or for him (his arms appear on the keystone of S. Teodoro, for example; see also fig. 14). They were particularly associated, however, with ancient buildings that retained important roles in the Christian city, like the Pantheon (generally referred to in the fifteenth century as S. Maria ad Martyres or in vernacular parlance as S. Maria Rotonda), the Aurelianic walls, or the bridges, all of which received attention from Nicholas's builders and were marked with his insignia.

An especially interesting case is that of the ancient diaconate of S. Teodoro, originally constructed among the extensive granaries that flanked the Palatine in late antiquity (fig. 15; map 2; see Urban 1961, 205; Borsi 1975, 40f.). Nicholas's attention to this rather small and out of the way church, which underwent two successive restoration campaigns, may reflect his concern for the history of the diaconate as an institution rooted in the concern for the welfare of the Christian population of the city and the provision of food, an aspect of the diaconal office prominently illustrated, for instance, in Fra Angelico's frescoes in Nicholas's private chapel. The church, moreover, occupied a site that overlooked the area linking the Campidoglio and the bridges that carried the routes between the Capitoline and other markets and the harbor and distribution centers of Trastevere.[53] Its very location, therefore, draws attention to the interweaving of economic, political, and religious life at Rome.

No doubt it was of importance also that S. Teodoro was a circular structure, one of no fewer than four circular churches whose restoration and embellishment seem to have been particularly close to Nicholas's heart, and which were marked with his insignia (the others are S. Maria Rotonda, S. Stefano Rotondo, and S. Maria della Febbre; the use of insignia also associated the pope visibly with the oval Colosseum, which though not a church had evident sacral connotations). These structures functioned, in my view, as privileged sites for the association of Nicholas's programs and aspirations with the city of Rome both in its historical dimension, given the connotations of imperial grandeur and/or the achievements of the early church that adhere to the buildings, and in its socio-spatial dimension, since they stand in disparate and widely distant areas of the city. They were to be joined, moreover, by a domed *tribuna* projected for St. Peter's basilica, whose formal configuration related to the city as a unified field of signs, rather than, as Manetti's account may suggest, primarily to the artificial environment of the Leonine City and Borgo (Urban 1961, 267; Urban 1963, esp. 125; Borsi 1975, 41–50).

Perhaps the only structure in Rome where the visual quality of a major Nicholan restoration campaign survives is S. Stefano Rotondo, a church that certainly underwent important changes after the fifteenth century but was never subjected to the total transformation to which more topographically central and fashionable churches were subjected (figs. 13, 37). At S. Stefano, significantly, the circular character of the building was emphasized through the demolition, condemned by Francesco di Giorgio, of circumferential elements (Borsi 1975, 41–50; Urban 1961, 267). It was believed to be a building of great and even pre-Christian antiquity, and it was dedicated to a deacon saint particularly revered by Nicholas. It was also remote enough from major populated areas to be suitable for the establishment of an austere, reforming order of monks, and close enough to the Lateran to provide a moderating influence, or even surveillance, over the sometimes turbulent conditions there.[54] There are many reasons, therefore, for Nicholas's concern for the church, in which the restrained character of the new sculptural and architectural details, notably the double doorway and the papal insignia placed on the building (fig. 14), echo that of the ancient architecture, at least as restored by Nicholas's builders.

For all the radical transformation of the urban fabric of Rome since 1455, then, there is evidence to indicate the scale and consistency of Nicholas's program of inscribing his mark within the city. Perhaps no later pope until Sixtus V approached this conception of the city as a set of surfaces carrying diverse and often particularistic signs that could be brought to order by the superimposition in visually and symbolically prominent locations of signs referring to the sacrality and authority of the Church and the pope. Nicholas's arms as pope, moreover, were not those of his family, but the crossed keys of the See of St. Peter; the claim to universalism is clear. Under Nicholas the informational multiplicity of the late medieval city was reduced, at least in terms of a reading of the urban environment as a whole, to a condition of duality: the insistent repetition of Nicholas's arms and the cipher of his abbreviated title constituted a simple but ubiquitous code distinct from the complex background. This double coding, however, was not the mere suppression of a rich variety of signs by a dominant code; rather, the impact of Nicholas's insignia depended on the co-presence of all the other signs, of whatever function and visual character, though they certainly now receded into the background.

Just as the man Tommaso Parentucelli disappeared into the office of pope, whose insignia he took for his own and whose external signs—vestments, liturgies, even architecture—he emphasized, so now the signs of papal rule over Rome were identified with and even merged into the urban text, the existing matrix of signifiers, though as a uniform and prevalent element. On the level of concrete activity, on the other hand, a correlate to the somewhat abstract play of signs exists, in my view, in the complex mechanisms through which different elements of the papal and communal administrative structures interacted with the social and institutional hierarchies and economic realities of Rome. I will argue that the evidence precludes a conception of the pope as a controlling and unified source of power, whatever the language, in any case largely formulaic, of his edicts.[55] During the greater part of Nicholas's pontificate, at least, the decisions and initiatives affecting the city grew out of an interplay of concerns and interests mediated and no doubt to an extent formed by Nello da Bologna and his staff. The diffusion of Nicholas's insignia among a wide range of buildings and places echoes and announces, then, not a centralization and homogenization of power relations (in the manner, say, of Sixtus V's deployment of urban signs), but a set of sites of often diversely operating contact and interaction, which cannot simply be dismissed as appropriation. We might speak here as much of fragmentation as of condensation of authority.

The coextension of Nicholas's signs with those of and in the city is not materially limited, still less invalidated, by the establishment of enclaves particularly associated with the pope's presence and the performance of the ceremonies and rituals that defined and expressed his official persona. At least until shortly before Nicholas's death, the development of residences at the Vatican and S.

Maria Maggiore (in the quarters of the Orsini and Colonna respectively) may be regarded as connecting the pope to the topographical and attitudinal extremes of the city, in view of the crucial micropolitical authority that the two major baronial clans had come to exert. With the changing atmosphere of Nicholas's pontificate, however, the signifying function especially of the Vatican and its fortified perimeter and thresholds also changed. And along with the various attitudinal and political shifts came a concern to go beyond the organization of signs and the reinterpretation of the city to the reconstitution of the latter, emblematically represented in the Borgo of Manetti's panegyric, as a passive body subject to unilateral operations and physically restructured, or at least restructurable, according to the requirements of the exercise and display of authority. The political instrumentality of this reform of urban space was naturalized, as is clear from Manetti's text, by recourse to theology and scripture; I will argue, nevertheless, that scriptural authority for the earlier and radically different practices of Nicholas's pontificate not only existed, but was subtly expressed at the very center of the pope's private space, his chapel. Here, indeed, patient archaeology can lay bare the fissures within the carefully constructed and maintained edifice of Nicholas's pontificate.

Manetti's account of Nicholas's architectural patronage, finally, is a doubtless partial crystallization of a momentous development in attitudes toward the physical fabric of Rome, and of ideas about the city in general. The urbanism of Nicholas's pontificate grew out of a complex texture of urban projects and interventions marked by the complicity of important elements of the local population. It reflected the subtle transformations of the urban and social environment, but its development can be adequately clarified only by looking beyond the urban milieu itself to paradigms, prominently that of Albertian perspective, arising in other areas of experience. Until the profound change in the political climate of Rome during Nicholas's pontificate, such paradigms fostered the clarification of urban space; thereafter they came to contribute to the development of an urbanism abstracted from the city itself, and opening the latter to the projection of a unilateral and ideologically charged ordering principle, or rather desire. It is an urbanism grounded centrally and fatally in nonurban realities, for all its characteristic and surely only superficially Albertian appropriation of the architectural trappings and the functional and spatial elements of the ancient city. The urban forest, with its jagged towers breaking the skyline of an environment no longer legible, gives way to an unequivocally legible city as an ordered and ordering totality; the real city, damned now as a confusion of signs, yields to the invented city of authorial desire and design.

Interior Architectures: Discordance and Resolution in the Frescoes of Nicholas's Private Chapel

Cults of Saints and Cult of History

Shortly before his death in 1447, Pope Eugenius IV summoned the eminent Dominican painter Fra Angelico to execute frescoes in a new palace chapel in the Vatican and in the choir of St. Peter's basilica. On his accession, Nicholas V took advantage of Fra Angelico's presence in Rome to commission from him two further projects, in addition to the completion of those of Eugenius. Both of Nicholas's commissions were for small and intimate spaces, a *studiolo* and a chapel, both situated in his private apartment in the Vatican palace. No trace of Fra Angelico's work has survived except in the private chapel (fig. 16), which remains in an excellent state of preservation, though its altarpiece has been lost, minor architectural changes have been made, and the frescoes themselves have suffered extensive retouching. Gilbert has securely dated the frescoes to 1448–50; they constitute, then, one of Nicholas's earliest artistic commissions. Both the date and the site indicate the importance of the project to Nicholas, who may well have been involved directly with not only the choice of subject matter, but also the development of the imagery. It is remarkable, however, that few scholars of Nicholas's pontificate or even of his patronage have devoted a more than summary discussion to the frescoes as a whole, at least as carrying meaning, though certain aspects have been singled out for attention (Gilbert 1975; Pope-Hennessy 1974, 29–33; Greco 1980; cf. Westfall 1974a, 132).

Collaboration between the artist and the pope is especially probable in view of the unusual qualifications and status of the former. Fra Angelico held a position of some eminence in his order and was clearly a respected figure in ecclesiastical circles in Florence, where his name was put forward in deliberations about the selection of a new archbishop for the city (Gilbert 1975, 249 n.14). Much of his energy in the years before he left for Rome had gone to the production of a celebrated series of paintings, including the altarpiece for the high altar, at the reformed Dominican priory of S. Marco, established and largely rebuilt by Cosimo de' Medici, who maintained a spartan cell in the priory for his own use (Orlandi 1964, esp. 85–89, 114–116). Relations between Nicholas V and Cosimo were close after the former's accession, as they undoubtedly had been for years. In particular, Tommaso Parentucelli, the future Nicholas V, had prepared a list of books recommended for purchase for a monastic library, and it seems that this list was used as a guide in the acquisition of books for the fine library, designed by Michelozzo, that Cosimo erected at S. Marco (Pastor 1949, 22, 33). The acquaintance of the two men, then, went back to a time when Parentucelli, whose rise through the ecclesiastical hierarchy was rapid and unexpected, had little prospect of rising to the heights he was eventually to reach (Vespasiano da Bisticci 1970, 1:38; Manetti 1734, c.912).

As its original appellation suggests, Nicholas's chapel is a very constricted space; with the exception of the altar wall, all the available surface is frescoed.[1] Three walls carry representations of the deeds and martyrdom of Saints Stephen and Lawrence; the two cycles begin on the window wall, to the right of the altar, and continue around the room. Figures of the Fathers of the Church appear in tabernacles forming margins to the narrative cycles, and the Evangelists occupy the vault. The cycles of the two saints run horizontally in superimposed zones; the St. Stephen cycle occupies the upper zone, which comprises three lunettes formed by the springing of the vault, and is therefore smaller and differently shaped from the zone of the cycle of St. Lawrence beneath. As we will see, the odd shape of the pictorial fields of the St. Stephen cycle suggested to the artist at least one unusual and significant compositional expedient.

The frescoes of the chapel are clearly of the greatest importance in the analysis and assessment of Fra Angelico's development and achievement as an artist. Though they remain somewhat controversial, most scholars agree that the paintings are distinguished by monumentality of a kind, or at least a degree, unprecedented in Fra Angelico's work. Attention has been focused in particular on the elaborate and assertive architectural settings, both interior and exterior, that are a feature of the paintings and seem to reflect the artist's experience of Rome. They have elicited remarkably divergent critical assessments on the part of modern scholars. Some find the backgrounds intrusive and badly integrated into the overall composition; others credit Fra Angelico with a successful late development of his expressive means.[2] Both views have some merit; I will combine them, in a sense, and argue that the artist's success in at least one scene depends on the viewer's recognition of the discontinuity of foreground and setting.

The magnificent fictive architecture of the frescoes has inevitably caught the eye of architectural historians. There have been lengthy discussions of the relationship between the architectural backgrounds and actual ecclesiastical building and restoration projects in quattrocento Rome, notably and most controversially the Nicholan project, as reported with whatever degree of accuracy by Manetti, for St. Peter's.[3] Such discussions have remained tendentious and inconclusive; they share the fatal flaw of indifference to the compositional and iconographical context for which the architectural settings were manifestly designed, but from which they have been regularly detached by scholars. In my view, these settings are of crucial importance for our understanding of the frescoes' meaning; the iconography of the chapel, moreover, though it may seem at first sight straightforward, is remarkably problematic, and intended to be so. And much of the interest of the chapel and its decorative program, as far as it can be elucidated, lies in the status of architecture itself—not the specific architecture represented in the frescoes—as a central subject and theme of Fra Angelico's paintings.

It is easy to assent to the general proposition that the fictive architecture of the chapel was paradigmatic in character. Clearly Nicholas and his advisors must have begun very soon after his accession to give thought to the preparations necessary for the Jubilee of 1449–50, especially the campaign of restoration on the station churches of the city, in anticipation of the influx of pilgrims (Pastor 1949, 169f). Ideas about ecclesiastical architecture in general and about the restoration urgently needed by St. Peter's basilica in particular must have been in the air in Nicholas's early years. And the two basilican projects of Brunelleschi in Florence were now, after the architect's death, finally so far advanced that their eventual character and aspect could be grasped, even by laymen; they may well have exerted considerable influence on ideas about ecclesiastical architecture current in Rome in midcentury.

Nicholas himself, moreover, was not only a patron, but also an amateur, of architecture. This was no new enthusiasm: as a young man in the service of Cardinal Albergati he had played an evidently important role in the reconstruction of the bishop's palace in Bologna.[4] Perhaps exemplary of his activity as pope is the report of Nicholas's visit to the shrine of St. Francis at Assisi; he subjected the great building to a close and exhaustive scrutiny, such as might be expected of a building professional, even making recommendations for its restoration.[5] His architectural patronage, however, must be set in the context of the apparently programmatic acquisition of luxury goods that were likely, far more than the buildings within which they were used or displayed, to determine the character of the physical environment in which the pope appeared, especially, but not exclusively, on high ceremonial occasions. The ledgers kept by the pope's officials, indeed, record a flow of precious materials, vestments, liturgical vessels, and the like into the Vatican; the effect of these clearly reinforced that of the tapestries, stained glass, and wall paintings, which also find frequent mention (Müntz 1878, 77–79, 166–188).[6] Writing soon after Nicholas's death, Manetti dwells at length on this aspect of the pope's patronage, associating it with a concern to heighten the impact of papal ceremonial on those who experienced it; by so doing, Nicholas greatly exceeded the usage of his predecessors. Manetti enumerates in almost obsessive detail the range of precious stones employed to concentrate attention and reverence on the pope's own vestments, notably the miter, as the resplendent focus of an image on earth, in Manetti's words, of the Church triumphant.[7]

In such magnificence, no doubt, the pope's liturgical policy and his aesthetic preferences met and merged. Both were surely expressed in Fra Angelico's paintings in the chapel, in the rich and elaborate draperies and accoutrements of the figures, the traceried windows of the sacred buildings, and the often noted and sometimes criticized polychromy of the architecture itself (Pope-Hennessy 1974, 32). On the other hand, this richness and elaboration are combined with relatively austere architectural forms recalling the buildings of the early Church, as imagined in the fifteenth century. Fra Angelico's fictive architectures are no neutral backgrounds; his and Nicholas's contemporaries were surely attentive to the potential connotations of architectural settings in depictions of sacred narrative.[8] In this case, moreover, the settings of narrative were made to conform to the historical period of the scenes enacted within them, exemplifying the formal reintegration of figure and setting that Panofsky (1964a, 1:163–173) established as a central element of the artistic achievement of the early Renaissance (Panofsky hails Mantegna as the hero of the process, but it is likely that the author of the Eremitani frescoes learned from Fra Angelico's work in Rome). At the same time, both figures and settings expressed Nicholas's concern for the moral and organizational aspects of the early church, a concern reflected not least in the reverence that he showed to the two saints whose example attended his daily devotions, and who as deacons in Jerusalem and Rome played crucial roles in the institutional establishment of the early Church.[9]

Nicholas's particular veneration for Saints Stephen and Lawrence can be readily documented. The two deacon saints are known to have featured prominently in the lost decoration of his *studiolo*, which was evidently located in a room adjoining the chapel, or at least in the same suite,[10] while Nicholas saw to the restoration of the major churches in Rome dedicated to each saint. The evidence suggests that the extensive restoration of S. Stefano Rotondo on the Caelian Hill took place before 1451, or at least was well advanced by the time of the Jubilee; the concentric layout of the church and its fine architectural ornament perhaps linked it in Nicholas's eyes to early Christian precedents, notably the Constantinian church of the Anastasis in Jerusalem.[11] Nicholas also restored, if only through intermediaries, the church of S. Lorenzo fuori le Mura, which was always counted among the seven great pilgrimage basilicas of the city.[12] This was the traditional burial place of St. Lawrence himself, who had lived and died in Rome, as also of St. Stephen, whose body had been miraculously discovered in Palestine, transported by way of Constantinople and Ancona to Rome, and placed in the tomb of St. Lawrence, his fellow deacon and martyr (Valentini and Zucchetti 1953, 9; cf. Jouvel 1977, 272; Kirschbaum and Braunfels 1968–72, 7: c.374). Great excitement was caused in 1447 by the discovery of two well-preserved corpses at S. Lorenzo; their appearance and clothing suggested an identification with Saints Stephen and Lawrence (one showed unmistakable marks of scorching, recalling St. Lawrence's death by roasting on the gridiron). Nicholas appointed a commission to investigate the matter; predictably, perhaps, the identification was quickly ratified (Sollerio et al. 1735, 496). Doubtless the discovery of the tomb and the results of the commission's inquiry were conspicuously celebrated in Rome; these were indeed excellent omens at the beginning of a pontificate, especially in the dangerous and unsettled conditions confronting Nicholas and in view of his own lack of the prestige conferred by high birth or even lengthy tenure of high ecclesiastical office.

It is all the more likely, then, that the emphasis on St. Lawrence, at least, evinced a concern to observe, or rather to appropriate, religious tradition. The palace chapel of the Lateran, the celebrated Sancta Sanctorum with its collection of relics of holy individuals crucially associated with the establishment of Christian Rome, was dedicated to St. Lawrence, and Nicholas himself was a member of the Confraternity of the Salvatore whose cult centered on the icon of Christ in the chapel.[13] On the other hand, Nicholas finally resolved the age-old rivalry of the Lateran and the Vatican in the latter's favor, and did so, as the evidence indicates, from the beginning of his pontificate (Westfall 1974a,

5–7, 19–21). The veneration of St. Lawrence at the Vatican under Nicholas, accordingly, may represent the deliberate and consistent bestowal on the Vatican of prestige and even sacrality hitherto associated with the Lateran. It is true, of course, that Fra Angelico's frescoes of the lives of Saints Stephen and Lawrence were painted in Nicholas's private quarters, but these may have been reasonably accessible; in any case, the discovery of the saints' tomb would have given Nicholas ample opportunity to give public expression to his devotion to St. Lawrence through ritual and liturgy. It is of note, too, that S. Stefano Rotondo is located in the vicinity of the Lateran (map 2). The cult of both saints, then, was emphasized at both ends of the ceremonial axis traversing papal Rome. At the Lateran, Nicholas associated himself with ancient cults intimately bound up with the religious and social customs of the Roman patriciate, as we have seen, while at the Vatican he gave to the same cults a particular, even a personal, emphasis.

In a more tangible way Nicholas's position in both a Roman and an Italian context was strengthened by his Florentine connections, notably his close association with the Medici, who profited greatly from his pontificate. I have noted the apparent formal echoes, albeit of a general kind, of the Florentine basilica dedicated to St. Lawrence in the basilican architecture painted in Nicholas's chapel. Cosimo de' Medici's assumption in 1442 of the patronage of the S. Lorenzo project, which was thereby transformed from an ostensibly parochial to an overtly dynastic undertaking, was to be marked after his death by the installation of his tomb beneath the crossing (Paatz and Paatz 1955, 495); this placement corresponds to that of the tomb of St. Peter in the Vatican basilica on which, in turn, the general architectural configuration of S. Lorenzo was based. (Both churches are oriented with their altars to the west). It is likely that Cosimo's choice of a burial place had already been made; it may well have been a condition of his decision to shoulder the expenses of a highly ambitious building campaign (Battisti 1981; Hyman 1975). In any case, Nicholas's publicly expressed reverence for St. Lawrence may well have seemed to contemporaries as, among other things, a veiled homage to Cosimo. Indeed St. Stephen, traditionally associated with St. Lawrence, also had Medicean connections. One of the most important shrines of St. Stephen in central Italy was the major church of Prato (Marchini 1957), a small but prosperous city close to Florence and long subject to its more powerful neighbor. From 1451 the archpriest of this church was Cosimo's illegitimate son, Carlo, who had already been provost designate for some time. Carlo de' Medici, who was something of an art aficionado, commissioned an extensive cycle of the life and legends of St. Stephen for the *cappella maggiore* of the church; the commission, originally offered to but declined by Fra Angelico, was executed by Filippo Lippi (fig. 23; see Borsook 1975).[14]

If such Florentine associations were indeed suggested by Fra Angelico's frescoes in Nicholas's chapel, they did not detract from the far more important association of both saints with Rome, however contorted this may have been in the case of St. Stephen. Both saints, moreover, were important figures in the early history of the office of the diaconate (Krautheimer 1980, 77, 110f.), and in their capacity as deacons they had been responsible for the material as well as the moral welfare of their congregations. This aspect of both saints' activity is given marked emphasis in the frescoes in Nicholas's chapel; Lawrence, in particular, is shown distributing largesse to the poor of Rome (fig. 21). As a brother of the Confraternity of the Salvatore, Nicholas belonged to one of the major charitable institutions of the city, and as pope, possibly continuing policies with which he had been associated in his capacity as a clerk of the *penitentiaria* under Eugenius IV, Nicholas was committed to a program of alms provision.[15] Thus he soon identified his pontificate, together with the office of the *penitentiaria*, with the hospital of the Maddalena, near the Pantheon; at the Vatican he founded the great papal almshouse, where food and wine were regularly distributed to considerable numbers of indigent people (Pastor 1949, 20); and he encouraged others to be generous to the unfortunate (Platina 1913, 338).[16] Almsgiving and a general concern for the welfare of vulnerable elements of the population, then, played an important part in Nicholas's political strategy toward the city, and linked him and his cardinals (whose office descended from that of the first deacons; Moroni 1843, 19:274) with the example of Saints Stephen and Lawrence.

Nicholas's devotion to the two deacon saints, however, had a more personal aspect. Both saints were associated, especially through their popular cults, with activities and interests close to Nicholas's heart. Lawrence's responsibilities as deacon included care of the sacred books; quite naturally he became the patron saint of librarians (Kirschbaum and Braunfels 1968–72, 7: c.374f.). It is true that Fra Angelico does not show Lawrence himself holding a book in any of the five scenes in which he appears in the chapel (the demands of the narrative may have precluded this). In the scene of the ordination of the saint, on the other hand, in which the officiating pope bears the features of Nicholas V himself, the central figure between the pope and Lawrence conspicuously holds a partly opened book in which he seems to point to a particular passage; he wears the dalmatic of a deacon (fig. 17). The following scene, in addition, shows Roman soldiers, representing the detachment of troops despatched to arrest Pope Sixtus II, beating at the door of an apparently claustral building, to the alarm of one of the clerics within (fig. 18). Above the door appears a tympanum containing a relief bust of Christ in the act of giving the benediction with one hand, and holding an open book in the other; it is a conventional motif, needless to say, but it is the only figural sculpture represented in the sacred architecture of the frescoes. Books, finally, are prominently depicted as attributes of the Fathers and Evangelists in the vault and between the narrative fields.

Stephen, through a somewhat ironical association of the instruments of his martyrdom, the stones, was revered as a patron saint of builders (ibid., 8: c.396). We have already noted the elaborate architectural backgrounds or settings of many of the fresco scenes, in which Nicholas's own enthusiasm for architecture is surely reflected. The clearest evidence for Nicholas's close concern with the themes of the frescoes is his own entry, as noted above, into the story of Lawrence as Pope Sixtus II. Both episodes in which he appears are set within architectural settings that it is tempting to connect with Brunelleschi's paleo-Christian revival at S. Lorenzo in Florence. These Florentine resonances, beyond their political and economic implications, perhaps carried an element of autobiography, recalling Nicholas's own early career in Florence as an impecunious tutor in patrician households and his identification with Florentine humanism (Greco 1980, 46 n.15).

Nicholas, indeed, was above all a man of letters, a passionate bibliophile deeply interested in the reconstitution of the culture of the ancient world through the discovery and translation of texts of various types. His election raised the expectations of those who sought to live by the pen and inkhorn and by their skill in the arts of exposition and discourse; literary offerings soon flowed into the Vatican. Nicholas did not, on the whole, disappoint the hopes placed in his patronage, though he took care not to accept dedications indiscriminately; on one occasion he hurled a proferred manuscript into the fireplace (Miglio 1975, 93f.). He sent agents far and wide to search libraries for previously unknown texts, and he rewarded generously a number of humanists who carried out translations, often solicited, of Greek authors. His literary patronage reveals a particular interest in the Greek Fathers and in the historians of antiquity, both pagan and Christian (Stinger 1977, 157–159, 223f.; Stinger 1985, 228f., 391 n.164). The prominence of the translators of and commentators on the histories of pagan antiquity, however, has overshadowed Nicholas's concern with the history of the early Church; a Valla or a Perotti, needless to say, repay study better than an Antonio Agli or a Jacopo Zeno.[17]

Writing and Painting: Questions of Translation and Expression in the Frescoes of Fra Angelico

The scenes from the lives of Saints Stephen and Lawrence painted by Fra Angelico in Nicholas's private chapel echo, therefore, an important strand in the pope's intellectual interests and literary patronage. All the more suggestive, then, are the allusions to textuality present in the frescoes. Indeed, the theme of the chapel might be regarded as the descent of the Word from the Evangelists writing in the vault, through the interpretations of the Fathers, to the world of action and history represented by the deacon saints;[18] such a descent was perhaps paralleled on the altarpiece by the movement of the body of Christ from the cross to the world of his mourning followers beneath, and to the altar that must have served as a dado to the composition. In any case, we might expect to find in the imagery of the chapel reflections of the pope's concern for historical truth and for the effective and elegantly composed transmission of that truth; these were concerns, we might add, that he surely shared with Fra Angelico himself. One of the two narrative cycles, that of St. Stephen, was based on scriptural text, as were the lost cycles painted elsewhere for Nicholas and Eugenius. Fra Angelico's activity as painter to Nicholas V must have coincided broadly with the inception of the pope's program to prepare a new translation of the Bible from the original texts, a task that was given to Giannozzo Manetti, the leading Hebraist among contemporary humanists. Both men were concerned, in different ways, with the translation and adequate expression of the history of revelation, or of history as revelation, though Manetti's achievement in this regard was slight compared with that of the artist.[19]

The cycles of Saints Stephen and Lawrence evince scrupulous attention to the respective textual sources. This is conspicuously the case with the Stephen cycle, based on an important but brief scriptural passage (Acts of the Apostles 6:8–7:50). Stephen was a popular saint throughout late medieval Europe, not least in Rome, and extant representations of his life are not rare. For many adherents of his cult, the passage in Acts provided meager fare, and the basic narrative soon became the core of a hagiographic tradition replete with quaint legends of Stephen's childhood and posthumous miracles.[20] There is no trace of such material in Nicholas's chapel, though it is prominent, for instance, in the nearly contemporary cycle in S. Stefano, Prato (Kirschbaum and Braunfels 1968–72, 8: c.400).

If Fra Angelico remained faithful to his primary textual sources, he was confronted necessarily with the challenge of creating a convincing and appropriate visual environment for the actions of his protagonists from the spare indications contained in the relatively laconic sources. The elaborate architectural settings, of course, are not even suggested by the pertinent texts, while the presence of architectural paradigms in hagiographic narrative involving, in the view of some scholars, a direct relationship with actual projects, seems without obvious recent precedent. On the other hand, the insertion into paintings of elements referring to the patron's interests and person is familiar, and from this point of view the architectural backgrounds of the frescoes may be regarded as functionally similar, for example, to the representation of Pope Sixtus II as Nicholas V, emphasizing the latter's concern for the theme of the frescoes through his own physical presence in them. Such donor or patron portraits are frequent, needless to say, in fifteenth-century art, and were clearly not regarded as disturbing the primary communicative and religious functions even of altarpieces. We may suppose, then, that the architectural settings of the frescoes, like the portraits of the pope, were regarded as legitimate elements of the inevitable process of enrichment and elaboration that accompanied the translation of narrative from a textual to a visual medium.

The question may gain in complexity, however, once we examine the relationship of the Stephen cycle, at least, and its textual source. Fra Angelico's narrative follows closely the elements of the saint's story enumerated in Acts: we see Stephen ordained (fig. 20), performing his duties as deacon and minister, disputing before his judges (fig. 19), and expelled from the city and put to death by stoning (fig. 22). But the essential content of the story as related in Acts is not reducible to straightforward narrative. This content, which has been the subject of considerable discussion on the part of modern biblical commentators and theologians (Simon 1951; Klijn 1957–58; Cullman 1958–59), is conveyed not by the actions of the protagonists, but by means of the speech made by Stephen at his trial. The extreme and provocative character of this speech, which supplies the immediate occasion for the saint's martyrdom, is vividly conveyed by the artist, who shows the effect on its audience through facial expression and gesture (in general, Fra Angelico makes telling use of hand gestures in the Stephen cycle). Whatever the virtues, however, of the artist's description of the event, it inevitably falls short of exposition of the matter that has elicited the frowns and the agitated play of hands of the listening judges (fig. 19).

We might conclude, then, that Fra Angelico here came up against the limits of his medium. On the other hand, the presence of elaborate fictive architectures recalls views expressed in Manetti's account, usually accepted as veridical (Westfall 1974a, 18f., 129f.), of the pope's deathbed speech. Nicholas asserts the primacy of verbal communication, especially as enshrined in texts, and stresses the importance of a historical understanding of a principle for full assent to it to occur. On the other hand, he notes the communicative, even didactic, power of monumental and permanent architecture, at least over the minds of the unlearned. The passage dates from 1455 but may well reflect a conception of the value of monumental buildings already held by Nicholas in 1448–50, however greatly the scope and character of his building projects were to change in the meantime.[21] Accordingly it is plausible a priori to search for meanings conveyed by or associated with the architectural settings of the frescoes, for if Nicholas restricted the efficacy of monumental buildings to the common people, he had no such reservations about magnificent ritual and liturgy, as noted above; in this case, the polychromy of the architecture and the splendor of the vestments and other accoutrements coincide, invalidating distinctions between kinds of efficacy. A potential strategy for uncovering more or less covert meaning might involve the Panofskian category of disguised symbolism. This, however, was developed to elucidate artworks very different from those of Nicholas's chapel; moreover it presupposes the formal coherence and unity of scenes in which specific elements of symbolic import are naturalized within a plausible world in which the mundane and the miraculous may occur simultaneously without strain (Panofsky 1964a, 1:140–144). The absence of such unity in the Fra Angelico frescoes is a crux in my argument.

The final and most crucial passage of Stephen's diatribe before his judges contrasts the Solomonic temple and the tabernacle, condemning the building of the former as an act of impiety no less profoundly wicked than the erection and veneration of the Golden Calf. God does not dwell, Stephen insists, in houses made by human hand. The tabernacle itself, of course, was produced by human agency, but it escapes Stephen's condemnation because it was made according to a God-given model vouchsafed to Moses (Acts 7:44–50). Stephen's lengthy disquisition on the tabernacle implies the belief that all essential revelations occurred during the period before the Jews arrived in Canaan, when it served, in other words, as a portable shrine for a still nomadic people (Cullman 1958–59, 166; Klijn 1957–58, 291; Simon 1951; 130–132). Stephen's position is not without authority elsewhere in scripture, and his attack on the temple is echoed to a degree in other passages in the New Testament, even in utterances attributed to Christ Himself (e.g., Isaiah 46:1–2; John 2:19–22).[22] Nevertheless, the vehemence and extremism of Stephen's outburst and, in particular, his unqualified equation of the temple with the most notorious of idols are without parallel in scripture (Simon 1951, 127), though similar views are expressed in a recently discovered scroll, the "Manual of Discipline," recording writings of a fanatical Jewish sect (Klijn 1957–58, 31).

The temple, as is well known, served as a model, however interpreted, for medieval church builders, and the biblical account of the construction of Solomon's temple was an important part of the liturgy for the consecration of a church (Stookey 1969, 35–38; Sauer 1924, 107). Stephen's attack on the localization of the sacred and—worse—its enshrinement in monumental architecture constitutes an explicit attack on the Jewish temple, and as such scandalized his hearers, but its place in Christian scripture surely suggests that Christian monumental architecture would be no less vulnerable to his strictures. This indicates the pertinence, for instance, of a fresh consideration of passages in which Alberti, perhaps with traditional sumptuary regulations in mind, pleads for restraint in religious architecture (Alberti 1966a, 2:609 [VII.x]). Stephen's opposition of Solomon and David, moreover, recalls Alberti's opposition of the tyrant and the king and the built environments associated with the rule of each (ibid., 1:333 [V.i]).[23] Indeed, Alberti's rejection of excessive monumentality and elaboration in both sacred and profane architecture culminates in his opposition of virtue and building. Even though Alberti nowhere condemns sacred architecture as such, this irreconcilable clash of categories, which Alberti is careful to ascribe to men of remote antiquity (ibid., 2:779 [IX.i]),[24] can surely be regarded as a secular ethical version of Stephen's point of view. It is even perhaps a veiled critique of architectural patronage and attitudes such as those of Nicholas V himself, whom Manetti was to describe as the "new Solomon" in a passage that, while it might provide a generally appropriate scriptural paradigm for the building campaigns, especially at St. Peter's, was unlikely to mollify sterner observers of Nicholan Rome (Magnuson 1958, 360–362).

The magnificent basilicas depicted in Fra Angelico's frescoes in Nicholas's chapel certainly constitute examples of architectural monumentality. In view of the content of Stephen's speech, which alone makes the narrative of his final hours intelligible and important, an inconsistency, if not an outright contradiction, arises between the substance of the St. Stephen cycle and the elaborate mise-en-scène provided for it by Fra Angelico. On the assumption that both the pope and the artist, the future prior of the Dominican abbey at Fiesole, knew their scripture very well, we may suppose that this inconsistency did not at least go unnoticed. We are confronted, accordingly, with the paradox that one of the most renowned and enthusiastic of architectural patrons in the history of the Church approved and possibly initiated the conspicuous celebration of that enthusiasm on the walls of his private chapel, a celebration that at the same time alluded to doubts about the justifiability and prospects for divine acceptability of his own or any monumental sacred architecture.

The objection might arise here that the primitive, paleo-Christian character of the basilicas represented in the frescoes might itself be regarded as emblematic of a concern with authenticity of worship, ritual, and architecture that can confidently be associated with Nicholas. His early reverence for the shrine of S. Pudenziana, which was of great importance in the history of the early

Christian community in Rome, is characteristic. One of the scenes of the St. Stephen cycle, moreover, asserts the familiar identification of Rome as the new Jerusalem. The consecration of Stephen as deacon is depicted as occurring within an expansive basilica; the representation of the crossing of the basilica and the recession of the far transept are perspectively and compositionally more complex than the interior architectural setting of any of the other scenes of the cycle (fig. 20). The officiating priest, shown in the act of passing the Host to the kneeling Stephen, is St. Peter himself, identifiable both through his traditional physical characteristics and, more crucially, through the echoes of the Vatican basilica in this fictive setting. In addition, St. Peter is shown standing in front of and as close as possible to the high altar and is framed within the columns of the ciborium raised over the altar; he is associated, in other words, with the most conspicuous marker of his own place of burial. It might be objected that the conspicuous spiral columns of the altar of St. Peter's, traditionally considered relics of the Temple of Jerusalem, are not indicated here (Shearman 1972, 56f.); it is possible, however, that the artist was concerned to allude to the pre-Constantinian *martyrium*, the tomb itself that, in the case of St. Peter's, forms both literally and figuratively a cornerstone. A closer thematic relationship arises, therefore, between St. Peter as the first pope in his basilica and the figure of Nicholas himself, representing the pope of the St. Lawrence narrative, in the setting of a similar basilican architecture. In particular, Nicholas's political concerns, notably in terms of his response to the waning challenge of Basel and his assertion of papal supremacy, are clearly of relevance here.[25]

These considerations mitigate but do not entirely satisfy the uncomfortable, even subversive, demands of the St. Stephen narrative and its contrast of content and setting. After all, the position taken by Stephen, though certainly extreme, is related to a general current of attacks on the Jewish temple in the New Testament. Such attacks tend to be formulated as demands for the spiritualization of the temple, as in the metaphor of the latter as the congregation of the faithful. As such, pure and whole, it is contrasted with false and decadent institutionalized religion, a contrast that need not be associated only with currents of radical reformist ideas, such as those that carried the Reformation itself, but can also be linked, for instance, with the conception of the community of believers as the true temple familiar in Pauline theology, to which I will return.

I have hitherto concentrated attention on the St. Stephen cycle; it is important to note, however, that thematic correspondences of relevance for the argument link the two narrative cycles of Nicholas's chapel. Once again, in the case of the St. Lawrence cycle, it is the iconological resonances of the settings rather than the overt matter of the frescoes that concern us. The story of Lawrence is familiar (Kirschbaum and Braunfels 1968–72, 7: c.374): in a period of terrible persecution of Christians, Pope Sixtus II, knowing his own arrest and martyrdom to be imminent, consigned to Lawrence the treasures of the Church. Lawrence then distributed the treasures to the poor of Rome; though an important aspect of the primitive diaconate was the concern with the material welfare of the congregation, this was perhaps an excessively zealous interpretation of the requirements of the office. In time Lawrence too was arrested by the Roman prefect, who demanded the treasure. Lawrence then provoked his own particularly unpleasant martyrdom on the gridiron by gesturing to the Christian community with the words "These are the treasures of the Church."

The distribution of the treasure is the subject of one of Fra Angelico's most striking and controversial images (fig. 21). The recipients of the treasure are represented as a group of clearly disadvantaged individuals, distinguished by marks of poverty and physical disability. The saint and the people are shown not so much in as in front of a basilican interior. The composition has been criticized as discordant, with the implication that the artist unsuccessfully sought to achieve in this painting a putative compositional coherence. The contrast, however, between the clear integration elsewhere in the frescoes of figures and setting, foreground and background, indicates that the discordance in this case—and it seems to me that the critics of the painting have drawn attention to a real and important aspect of it—may have iconological significance (Pope-Hennessy 1974, 19, 32, 66).[26]

In the scene of St. Lawrence's distribution of the treasure the relationship of figures and setting is in fact far from simple. From one point of view the figures appear in a friezelike zone in front of a flat plane parallel with the picture surface; beyond this zone and distinct from it opens a somewhat stark and unpopulated colonnaded nave receding sharply toward a high, narrow apse. The separation of the zones, however, is not absolute, for the figure of the saint is set within and is formally related to the strongly vertical apse; indeed, the fact that the base of the apse is concealed behind the saint's upper body confers a marked element of ambiguity on the scene. In other words, the painting seems to generate a play of perspectival and pictorial relationships.

The figures of the poor, moreover, are not strung out in a single plane; rather they are assembled to either side of the saint in an echelon arrangement that produces an echo of the basilican architecture behind them. This is an image, then, not only of the congregation as the wealth of the Church, but also as the Church itself. If so, Fra Angelico found a way to give visible expression to resistant material, while recalling a familiar tradition of metaphorical allusion inherent in at least certain currents of medieval theology and even liturgy. In particular, the late medieval theologian Durandus, whose writings were to prove especially influential in matters of architectural aesthetics and symbolism and whose major work, the *Rationale divinorum officiorum*, went through no fewer than forty-three printings in the fifteenth century, asserted that the saints form the "living stones" of the mystical Church; indeed, Durandus's book is a veritable compendium of scriptural and patristic references to the idea of the metaphorical equivalence of the congregation of the faithful and the church building (Sauer 1924, 28–37, 98–116).[27] But Durandus, not surprisingly, ignored the point of view expressed by Stephen; for Durandus the temple succeeds the tabernacle, as the triumphant succeeds the militant Church (ibid., 107 n.2, noting the frequency of this formulation in medieval texts).

Manetti does not mention the tabernacle; rather he establishes at great length and with extensive biblical quotations the paradigmatic value of Solomon's temple for Nicholas's basilica, and of Solomon's activity as "architect" for that of Nicholas. For all Manetti's praise of the temple, however, he nowhere claims that it corresponded to a divine prototype. This is exactly what he does assert of the other paradigm cited as operative in the design of Nicholas's basilica, the ark of Noah. Much has been made of Manetti's insistence on the microcosmic quality of the ark, the correspondence of its form and proportions to those of a human body lying on the ground with arms outstretched (Magnuson 1958, 206–210; Westfall 1974a, 120–123).[28] The comparison of a church with the microcosm, however, was not uncommon; Manetti himself, as Westfall points out, had earlier introduced the notion in a discussion (1436) of the cathedral of Florence (Westfall 1974a, 120). The ark, on the other hand, had particular significance in the conditions of 1455 when Manetti wrote his text; as a powerful salvational symbol it was clearly relevant at a time when, following the fall of Constantinople, the fortifications raised by Nicholas around the Vatican had become emblematic of the embattled state of Christendom.[29] It is all the more striking, then, when Manetti's discussion of the microcosm and the ark precedes—as if forming only a preliminary for—the discussion of the Solomonic temple (or rather of Solomon's complex of palace and basilica). Yet the explicit reference to the divine model that inspired the ark and, though only at second remove, Nicholas's basilica points to the absence in Manetti's account of the tabernacle, an absence that the plethora of references to great monuments of antiquity cannot assuage.

The wonders of the ancient world as listed by Manetti provide examples of magnificence equaled or surpassed by Nicholas;[30] they recall Manetti's passage on Nicholas's concern to employ precious materials and goods, as we have noted, to create an image of the Church triumphant "in hac militante." For a mid-quattrocento humanist, no doubt, such magnificence, with its emphatically rhetorical and didactic character, required *all'antica* forms and sources, which are in this case curiously allied with biblical material, as in the juxtaposition of Solomon's architect Hiram and Philo, the architect of the ancient Athenian arsenal (Magnuson 1958, 360). Though Manetti's text is justificatory, as we have noted, it is clear that certain kinds of reservations about Nicholas's achievement are not addressed (Miglio 1975, 105 n.55). Manetti's suggestion, if only by juxtaposition, of a classicizing Solomonic temple (a familiar later motif) makes for a coherent and compelling culmination of the account of the revived city of Rome and the rebuilt Leonine City that he presents. Doubts that Nicholas and others may have harbored about the legitimacy of the building campaigns were submerged in the celebratory text as effectively as the various projects and policies that antedated Manetti's arrival in the Curia and that no longer seemed relevant, if indeed Manetti even knew of them, to the image of a new Solomon that he assiduously set out to create.

There are slight but insistent traces of evidence for antihumanist attitude toward pagan monumental buildings in mid-fifteenth-century Rome; some are of particular interest in the context of Fra Angelico's frescoes. In the church of S. Lorenzo fuori le Mura, whose importance as the burial place of both St. Lawrence and St. Stephen has been noted, an image was preserved of Lawrence and Pope Sixtus II in the act of destroying a temple of Mars (Kirschbaum and Braunfels 1968–72, 7: c.377; Wilpert 1929, 620 and fig. 22).[31] Such antipathy to the architectural monuments of antiquity was not unknown in the fifteenth century; Poggio Bracciolini, for instance, in a letter of about 1445 to a fellow humanist complained of stupid people—presumably of rank and importance at Rome, or Poggio would not have cared about their opinions—who believed that the grand buildings of ancient Rome could only have been constructed by demons (Battisti 1962, 405 n.149). Poggio, who scoured the city in his search for classical inscriptions for his *sylloge* (Weiss 1969, 63–65, 147), may well have known the relief at S. Lorenzo; in any case, it was presumably the association of the temple with demons that provoked its demolition by Lawrence and the pope. This legend, if indeed it was current in the Rome of Nicholas V, may have colored the associations of St. Lawrence and his cult at the time. It is especially remarkable, then, that one of the most significant building operations actually undertaken by Nicholas, the restoration of the early Christian rotunda of S. Maria della Febbre (fig. 31), involved a building believed in the Renaissance to have been built as a temple to a pagan deity, in this case Apollo (Burroughs 1982a). Nicholas's redemption of this supposedly originally pagan structure contrasts markedly with the implacable action attributed to St. Lawrence and the very pope who appears endowed with Nicholas V's features in Fra Angelico's frescoes in the latter's chapel.

As in the St. Stephen cycle, then, if somewhat less clearly, the relationship of narrative content and classicizing setting in the Lawrence cycle is fraught with ambiguity. In the scene of the distribution of the treasure, I have noted the coincidence of a sharp distinction of foreground and background with an equally conspicuous formal correspondence—as it were, a formal rhyme—between the figures in the foreground and the basilican architecture beyond; this is at the same time a compositional and discompositional device. Insofar as this formal disparity reverberates on the level of iconology, two alternative readings are possible. One would interpret the basilica, understood as standing for the institution of the Church, as an entirely appropriate frame for and expression of communal worship. The other, on the other hand, might seek meaning in the division of setting and narrative, and in a thematic correspondence of the Lawrence cycle with the subversive implications of the story of Stephen. Both readings are grounded in architectural metaphors that invade the physical volume of the chapel itself, which, through its decorative program, forms a spatialized metaphor of the relationship of authority and action, or of hierarchy and community. The effect of Stephen's latent but inescapable condemnation of the temple, however, is to hollow out the architectural metaphors of community; the idea of the congregation as an ecclesiastical edifice or as the wealth of the Church tends, in other words, to exalt the congregation at the expense of the terms of comparison.

The Rehabilitation of the City

The beholder/reader in Nicholas's chapel is not trapped in this bleak impasse; the frescoes themselves offer a way out. Once again, vital cues are provided by details of the paintings that seem, at first glance, merely to be further evidence of Fra Angelico's narrative skill and vivacity. The culminating scene of the St. Stephen cycle is the martyrdom; Stephen kneels in prayer while the stones fly (fig. 22). It is a standard episode in cycles of the saint's life (though it is often not the final episode), and is not uncommon as the subject of an independent painting (Kirschbaum and Braunfels 1968–72, 8: cc.396–400). The penultimate scene of the cycle, adjacent to that of Stephen's death, is less frequent, though certainly not unprecedented. It represents the expulsion of the saint from the city and is based on a single phrase of the Vulgate: "eicientes eum extra civitatem" (Acts 7:58). Nevertheless, the scene as painted occupies as much space as the martyrdom itself.[32] The apparent emphasis on the expulsion of Stephen makes sense in terms of the consistent organization of the fresco fields and in terms of the demands of the narrative, in that it makes possible the vivid expression of the impact of Stephen's words on his hearers, two of whom already grasp stones; the saint's martyrdom appears as a direct consequence of his speech.

The scene also gives visual emphasis, however, to the localization of the execution on a piece of ground outside Jerusalem that is clearly contrasted with the enclosed and built-up space within the city. The wall of the city, curving around the expulsion scene to break off at the center, forms the towered boundary of the two scenes, so that formal and narrative function coincide. In its architectonic quality the wall contrasts with the rounded hills in the background of the execution scene, though these curve upward and inward from left to right, thus echoing the curve of the wall; again, contrast and correspondence coexist.

In the scene of the expulsion, St. Stephen turns back, irresolute and reluctant, coerced by his tormentors; in the execution scene, on the other hand, he determinedly turns his face away from the city, from the Jerusalem of the "stiffnecked and uncircumcised in spirit" (Acts 7:51). The composition of the scene is remarkable; the saint is placed at the extreme right of the painted surface, with his back turned toward the other figures and to the whole lunette. This arrangement contrasts markedly with the compositional schema employed in most representations of the martyrdom from the fourteenth to sixteenth centuries, such as Filippo Lippi's nearly contemporary version at Prato (fig. 23). This schema sets the saint at or near the center, kneeling in a frontal pose with the executioners around him, and looking up to the vision of heaven opening in the sky. (Kirschbaum and Braunfels 1968–72, 8: c.401).[33] Such a composition, clearly focused on the major figure, may even have constituted in 1448 the standard version; in any case, Fra Angelico's compositional demotion of the saint, made to undergo his last agony in a cramped corner of the fresco field, surely requires comment.

In the painting as it has survived, having undergone various campaigns of restoration, there is no visible trace of a further standard element of the martyrdom scene, the vision of Christ in glory at the right hand of God the Father; indeed, there is little room for such a vision. If Fra Angelico left the vision out of his composition he was merely following the text (Acts 7:55, 56), which mentions the vision as occurring at the end of Stephen's speech, such that, presumably, it confers divine approval on the saint's assertions, not least those concerning the temple. Versions of the scene that showed the vision at the moment of death were derived, however, from no less a source than a sermon of St. Augustine, during which, as the text makes clear, Augustine used an image of Stephen's martyrdom as a visual aid; the implication is that Augustine's image included the vision.[34] We may expect, then, that a representation of the vision once appeared in Fra Angelico's scene of the trial of Stephen (fig. 19), and indeed traces of this were discovered during a modern restoration, though they are not visible in the painting as it now exists (Redig de Campos 1950, 338; Fallani 1955, 21).

In the scene of his martyrdom, the kneeling saint is compositionally clearly demarcated from his executioners and from the wall that both frames and metonymically stands for the city of Jerusalem. This distance is emphasized by the pose of the saint, who faces away from the city in an attitude of concentration and prayer.[35] His head is unbowed and his eyes are open (fig. 24), a detail that might conceivably be owed to a later repainting, though there is no reason to suppose this. It is an important detail, for if the saint's eyes are open the beholder is invited to consider what it is that the saint sees. We have established that this was not the vision mentioned in Acts, the possibility of which is anyway excluded by the composition. The emphatically peripheral placement of the saint suggests that we should direct attention to the picture surface to the right of the lunette under discussion, on the hypothesis that the figure of the martyred Stephen acts as a link between his own cycle—and perhaps that of St. Lawrence—and imagery that is spatially and iconographically distinct.[36]

The wall to the right of the final scene of the narrative cycles is the altar wall; it originally carried a painting, also by Fra Angelico, of the Deposition from the Cross. This painting has disappeared without trace, and nothing is known of it except its subject and author; these are transmitted to us by Vasari, who can be believed in this case as he provided the painting that replaced Fra Angelico's altarpiece.[37] It is likely, however, that the Deposition painted for Nicholas V was modeled on or developed from one of Fra Angelico's most celebrated and beautiful paintings, the *Deposition from the Cross* painted in the early 1440s for the sacristy of S. Trinita in Florence (fig. 25).[38] The speed with which Fra Angelico and his equipe worked on the commissions for Nicholas (Gilbert 1975, 262f.) suggests that, where possible and appropriate, new compositions were not worked out, while Nicholas may have had personal reasons for recalling the S. Trinita painting in his own private chapel.

The sacristy of S. Trinita served also as the private chapel of the Strozzi family, whose leading member in the early quattrocento was Palla Strozzi, in whose household Nicholas had lived as a young man. Palla Strozzi was exiled from Florence in the wake of Cosimo de' Medici's assumption of power in 1434, but there can be little doubt that so major a commission as the altarpiece for the family chapel was not decided on and awarded without the long-range involvement of Palla, whose status as an art patron is well known. Nicholas himself spent much time in Florence in the 1440s, first as a participant in the Council of Union and subsequently during a diplomatic mission (Pastor 1949, 15–18); he surely knew the altarpiece painted by Fra Angelico for a chapel with which he was certainly familiar. The probable echoes, then, of the S. Trinita *Deposition* in Nicholas's own chapel may have constituted a subtle homage to Palla Strozzi and his family, alongside the echoes of Medici patronage in the narrative cycles. Indeed, though Palla himself remained in exile, the Strozzi commission of a major altarpiece from Fra Angelico, which can hardly have escaped the notice of the Medici with whom the painter had been closely associated, may well represent an early stage in the rapprochement of the Medici with the Strozzi and their allies, including the Rucellai, that is celebrated in the ornament of the family palace of the latter (fig. 10).[39] If so, the desire for such a reconciliation of his various Florentine friends may be a theme of Nicholas's chapel.

Prominent in the background of Fra Angelico's *Deposition* is a luminous image of the city of Jerusalem, its towers bathed in the intense light of an evening sun, casting strong shadows. There is, of course, no direct evidence that such a landscape feature appeared in the background of Fra Angelico's altarpiece for Nicholas's chapel. The theme of landscape is largely absent from the frescoes of the chapel; most of the scenes, after all, occur in architectural interiors or in spaces bounded by city buildings. The single exception is the scene of St. Stephen's martyrdom, where the horrible event takes place against an expansive background of gentle green hills studded with villages and cypress groves (fig. 22). It would be a matter, at least, of artistic consistency if a similar landscape appeared beyond Golgotha in the adjacent altarpiece. And a representation of the Deposition with a landscape background would almost certainly have included an image of the city outside whose walls the Crucifixion occurred.[40]

It is significant, further, that Stephen's death as protomartyr was a type (in the technical medieval sense) of that of Christ: such a typological relationship would have been emphasized by the correspondence of landscape settings. Stephen's last words echo those of Christ, while the importance of Stephen's vision, as pointed out by St. Augustine and others, is that he was the first since Adam's transgression to see the heavens opened, thanks to the redemption of humanity through Christ. Stephen, then, like Christ, is a second Adam; indeed, it is possible that the general resemblance of the scene of his expulsion from Jerusalem to that of Adam from Paradise might not be accidental.[41] Both Christ and Stephen, of course, died outside the walls of Jerusalem, which frequently appears in paintings of the martyrdom of both.[42] The specifically Christlike aspect of Stephen, then, would make it particularly appropriate that he should gaze in his last moments on the exemplary martyrdom of Christ himself. And Stephen was one of the original deacons of the church, whose ministry to the faithful necessarily included a marked liturgical component; in

Nicholas's chapel he looks toward the body of Christ symbolically and liturgically present in the Host of the Eucharist, and visually present in the central figure of the altarpiece.[43]

I have stressed the implications of an architecturally elaborate and monumental temple especially in the St. Stephen cycle. The theme of the temple is closely linked to that of the city; both the city of Jerusalem and the temple, which it contains, may symbolize worldliness and wickedness, or celestial purity and communality. Just as the introduction of the Solomonic temple into consecration rites and other liturgical contexts is often accompanied by reference to Ezekiel's vision of a celestial temple, so the earthly Jerusalem receives its transcendent correlate in the apocalyptic heavenly city of the Book of Revelation. At the climax of this text (Revelation 21:2–5), moreover, the Holy City itself is identified as the tabernacle (Stookey 1969, 36). In late medieval Italy, Rome and other cities, while they might be denounced for their Babylonian sinfulness, might also serve as images of the heavenly Jerusalem, a theme to which we will return. In Nicholas's chapel, the ambivalence in the motif of the temple is present also in that of the city: both Jerusalem and its successor and type, Rome, are emblematic places of corruption and wickedness that achieve redemption through the blood of martyrs and the worship of the faithful. The theme of the refoundation of Rome through the apostles Peter and Paul is familiar, and echoes the refoundation of Jerusalem by Christ (Pietri 1961, 272; Krinsky 1970, 12). Saints Lawrence and Stephen, moreover, played a crucial role in the glorification and redemption of their respective cities: in the words of Leo the Great "Rome has become as famous thanks to Lawrence as Jerusalem had been glorified by Stephen" (Jouvel 1977, 272; Pietri 1961, 303). The city of Stephen's martyrdom—the city to which he turns his back—may well have been contrasted in Nicholas's chapel with the redeemed city of the altarpiece. It is probable, at any rate, that the city that appears in the background of the S. Trinita *Deposition* is represented as in a state of redemption (fig. 25).

Stephen's story intersects, of course, with that of a further leading figure in the history of the early Church, the apostle Paul, protagonist of the text on which the visual narrative is based. In his earlier life as Saul, the persecutor of Christians, St. Paul appears in the scene of Stephen's martyrdom holding the robes of the men who stone Stephen, as the narrative demands (fig. 22). Stern and bearded, Saul stands to the left of the scene, his back to the city wall.[44] At first sight, no reference appears to be intended to Saul's dramatic later conversion, still less to his emergence as a crucial interpreter of Christ's message who would dwell in his writings especially on the idea of the Church as the congregation of the faithful, united by love. The employment of architectural metaphor is insistent: "Ye are built upon the foundation of the apostles and prophets, Jesus Christ himself being the chief corner stone, in whom all the building fitly framed together groweth unto a holy temple in the Lord, in whom ye are also builded together for an habitation of God through the spirit" (Ephesians 2:19–20; cf. 1 Peter 2:5, and Sauer 1924, 101, 103f., noting patristic use of the same concepts). The stiff, upright pose of Saul in Fra Angelico's painting rhymes conspicuously with the strongly vertical motif of the wall of Jerusalem, against which the future apostle is set. Such a compositional rhyme of a human figure with an architectural motif is paralleled, as argued above, in the depiction of the consignment by St. Lawrence of the treasures of the Church to the poor (fig. 21), in which the pose of the saint is echoed in the apsidal element beyond. In this case, the rhyme may assert a parallelism of the city and Saul/Paul; the conversion of the latter and the transformation of the former are each present *in potentia*.[45] Beyond the confrontation, then, of Saul and Stephen as protagonists of simple narrative, the martyrdom scene as painted by Fra Angelico invites reflection on the relationship of Stephen's intransigent position and Pauline theology with its intrinsic appeal to architectural metaphor.

A final, seemingly incidental detail of the St. Stephen cycle may be of significance here. The stoning of Stephen begins, as Fra Angelico depicts it, within the walls of the city; in the expulsion scene, the two more prominent figures among the saint's enraged enemies already grasp stones (fig. 22). This may be merely a device to heighten dramatic intensity, along with the violent gestures and facial grimaces of the men; on the other hand, it does not seem likely that dramatic concerns alone prompted the theologically sophisticated artist to depart, however subtly, from the scriptural text, in which the expulsion from the city and the stoning constitute separate, successive episodes. The stones in Fra Angelico's narrative are picked up in Jerusalem; they are part of the unredeemed city itself. Nevertheless, they become instruments of divine providence as manifested in the martyrdom of St. Stephen, the conversion of St. Paul, and the history of the early Church in general. Like the city, like St. Paul, the stones undergo transformation; their metaphoricity depends equally on historical occurrence and varying semantic values. St. Augustine's meditations on the death of St. Stephen are of particular pertinence here, not least for the elaborate wordplay involving "stone" and related concepts: the executioners are hard like the stones they handle; they hurl their own counterparts at Stephen; Stephen is stoned with rocks and dies for the Rock, which is Christ (Migne 1844–64, 38: c.1437). It is a crucial episode for Augustine; we have noted that he enhances its importance by associating with it the saint's vision of the heavens opening. He emphasizes in his commentary the metaphoricity of the concept "stone" in the Bible, not only in the story of Stephen. I have noted St. Paul's image of Christ as the cornerstone; it is important, further, that this is the stone rejected by the builders (1 Corinthians 3:10–11), and which can thus be taken as a model for the kind of transformational quality inherent in the stones of Stephen's martyrdom, especially in terms of an Augustinian interpretation.

Nicholas V must have known of Augustine's sermon on St. Stephen; St. Augustine, certainly, appears with the other Fathers of the Church frescoed in the chapel. The story of Stephen, then, may have served as a focus around which to develop discussions of the value or even justifiability of elaborate building programs and ceremonial, and Fra Angelico's paintings may be seen as echoing, if not rather contributing to, such discussions. But beneath any intellectual level on which the frescoes may have operated, they are surely charged with an expiatory urgency, a concern to defuse the challenge menacing the monumental architecture of Nicholan Rome.

If indeed a critical or even expiatory subtext lurks within the grand imagery of Nicholas's chapel, it may not have gone unremarked or without influence on subsequent work at the Vatican. Nicholas's chapel continued to serve its original function. Julius II, in particular, preserved it carefully, inserting a new entrance to improve its accessibility (Valentini and Zucchetti 1953, 507; Mostra 1955, 135). It was, in fact, the only element of the papal apartment on the second floor of the palace not transformed by Julius and his successor Leo X. The campaign of decoration, from 1508 under the direction of Raphael, began in the Stanza della Segnatura, where the first wall to be frescoed was that carrying the scene of the Exaltation of the Host, usually known as the *Disputa* (fig. 26). It is not novel to see in Raphael's work in this room, especially in the *Disputa*, echoes of the decoration of Nicholas's chapel. It is doubtless relevant that Raphael was interested in early Christian forms, such as were prominent, as we have noted, in Fra Angelico's frescoes (Wickhoff 1893, 64).[46] It has even been suggested by scholars from Passavant (1872), 87, and Pastor (1950), 574, to Pfeiffer (1975), 65, that Raphael paid homage to Fra Angelico by representing him in the *Disputa* as the aged friar to the far left of the painting (fig. 27), opposite the area of the *School of Athens* in which Raphael's own self-portrait appears on the extreme right (fig. 28). If so, he is placed in close and surely significant proximity to an especially archaizing passage, the scene of Pope Gregory IX consigning the decretals to a jurist.[47] Framed in an impressive apse, apparently within an expansive, monumental architecture, Gregory bears the beard and features of Julius II (fig. 29). The echoes of Nicholas's appearances as Sixtus II in Fra Angelico's St. Lawrence cycle are surely unmistakable (figs. 17, 18).

Near the old friar in the *Disputa* stands an animated group of disputants often identified as heretics, and certainly contrasted with an angelic figure who calmly points toward the Host on the altar at the center of the painting, as if to assert that here and not in texts, still less in quibbling about texts, is the truth to be found. The leader of the disputants is a bald old man who closely resembles the geometrician (variously identified as Euclid or Archimedes) directly across the room in the *School of Athens*, whom Vasari's informants identified as Bramante.[48] This seems to be incorrect, but may have arisen for good reason. Behind the old heresiarch is a large building under construction, apparently contrasted with a rock formation to the far right of the fresco that has the air of an ancient ruin, and around which no activity is visible. Various attempts have been made to elucidate the two motifs;[49] a complicating factor is that they are known to have been added in the course of work on the composition (Shearman 1965, 158f.). Whatever iconographical interpretations might be made, the building on the left can hardly not have been associated by contemporaries with the huge and controversial building campaigns in progress a short distance away, the reconstruction of St. Peter's and the expansion of the Vatican palace, both inaugurated by Nicholas V.

The basilica project was, of course, celebrated in the magnificent ideal architecture depicted in the *School of Athens*, across the room from the *Disputa*. Though Raphael had originally planned to set the figures of the *Disputa* in a fictive architectural frame, receding into space, he soon adopted an apsidal compositional motif constituted by the figures themselves; he or Julius, in other words, rejected a literal architectural setting for a metaphorical one (Freedberg 1979, 55). But the contrast of literal and metaphorical architectures remains in the Stanza, since the grand vaults of the *School of Athens*, peopled by pagan philosophers, confront the saints who may be described metaphorically, in Pauline or Augustinian terms, as the stones of the Church.[50] The motif of construction in the *Disputa* might naturally, then, be associated with an especially controversial architect or, if the identification of the old "heretic" with Bramante is discounted, at least with concerns about the legitimacy of monumental building.

The metaphorical, mystical architecture of the *Disputa* suggests further connections with Nicholas's chapel. There is a marked correspondence of *dramatis personae*, granted the obvious greater richness of Raphael's fresco. In the upper zone of the *Disputa* Saints Stephen and Lawrence flank the central nimbus; Stephen, doubtless in an allusion to his celestial vision, turns his gaze to heaven, while Lawrence gestures toward the scene below. As befits his diaconal office, then, Lawrence mediates between the levels of the fresco.[51] Prominent beneath are the Fathers of the Church; whereas in Nicholas's chapel these function as framing devices, here they assume a more active role. The Evangelists, *pace* Vasari, are corporeally absent from the *Disputa*, though they are emphatically introduced into the painting by the device of their open books, displayed by cherubim; in Nicholas's chapel they occupy the vault. In the chapel, then, the deacons are protagonists, the Fathers intermediaries; in the *Disputa*, the roles are reversed. In both cases doctrine is transmitted downward into the human sphere, though the Stanza differs from the chapel in the philosophical cast of its imagery; in the place of the Evangelists of the chapel vault, indeed, are set personifications of abstract entities of no immediate Christian character.

The most telling correspondence between Raphael's painting and Nicholas's chapel involves the subject of the latter's lost altarpiece. This represented, as we have seen, the Deposition from the Cross; in its position above the transubstantiated Host on the altar, the mystical body of Christ, it surely drew attention to his physical body sacrificed for humanity. In the *Disputa* as in the chapel the eucharistic theme is paramount (Freedberg 1979, 54f.; Pfeiffer 1975, esp. 50–53), though the Stanza did not contain an altar apart from the painted one carrying the Host at the center of the *Disputa*, adored by a fictive assembly. In both cases, moreover, the theme of a metaphorical architecture, of the congregation of the faithful as the constituent elements of the great mystical building that is the Church, seems to be present.

The construction site of the *Disputa* hardly elaborates and enriches the central core of meaning of Raphael's painting, as it should according to Gombrich's theory of the iconographical function of subsidiary imagery in classical works of art, especially in the case of the Stanza. Gombrich was concerned, of course, to cut down the proliferation of iconographical readings applied to incidental details of a painting; his is a critical position of much value (Gombrich 1978).[52] Nevertheless, the detail of the mysterious building—or rather building process—in the background of the *Disputa*, if indeed it is taken as an allusion to the work at St. Peter's, injects a discordant note into the fresco, and still more into the room, with its celebration of monumental architecture. Perhaps, then, Julius understood the relevance to his own projects of the themes of the chapel in which he daily prayed, and whose decoration he manifestly valued highly. If so, like Nicholas, he may have appreciated the potentially hubristic aspect of his own architectural patronage, which was probably consciously modeled on that of Nicholas, especially as transmitted by Manetti.[53] Certainly, there were those in Julian Rome—perhaps echoing Nicholas's critics—who were only too willing to characterize the mania for building as sinful luxury, and to attack in particular the project to rebuild St. Peter's.[54] Beyond his own anxieties and the recurrent moralistic censure of luxury, however, Julius may have been concerned with the need to appease potential divine disapproval. I would suggest, then, that Julius had Raphael introduce into the pope's private study—in the fresco that most resembled a devotional painting and gave to the Stanza the semblance of a devotional space—a subtle but subversive subtext, both confessional and expiatory in character, leading back to the imaged debate in the chapel of Julius's great predecessor and paradigm.

Beyond the theological ideas and issues stated or alluded to in the frescoes of Fra Angelico or Raphael lurks the matter of their popes' political agendas. The pontificate of Nicholas V, as we have seen, has plausibly been characterized as a watershed in the development of the papacy into a recognizable state in the modern sense. Nicholas's own policies toward the subject cities and territories were coherent yet flexible; he clearly preferred to work through intermediaries as long as the sovereignty and overriding interests of the Church were accepted and observed. No doubt this was partly a matter of the limited coercive power available to Nicholas, but his evident concern to work with and through existing political and administrative structures was surely more than mere expediency. The temporal power of the papacy itself was certainly controversial; the challenge of the conciliarists was not yet forgotten, and so stern a critic of papal pretensions as Lorenzo Valla was established in Rome, enjoying the patronage of Nicholas himself. The assertions of papal supremacy in tracts produced by prominent clerics associated with Nicholas's court and even the language of some of Nicholas's own bulls cannot, accordingly, be taken as a direct reflection of a homogeneous set of policies.In the sixteenth century, certainly, the general issue of the temple and that of the temporal domain of the popes were regarded as indissolubly linked (Prodi 1982, 46f.),[55] and it is likely that Nicholas's sensitivity to the political issue was grounded in theological considerations. In this way, then, the enclosed and private world of Nicholas's chapel resonated with the complex larger world, with the political processes acted out in the streets and squares, the public halls and audience chambers, and occasionally in the armed camps and battlefields of Italy.

3 Far and Near Perspectives: Urban Ordering and
Neighborhood Change in Nicholan Rome

The Gaze of the Sign: Reflections on the Angel of the Castel S. Angelo

In the winter of 1452–53 a bronze statue of the archangel St. Michael was placed atop the Castel S. Angelo (Borgatti 1930, 204; Westfall 1974a, 100; Müntz 1878, 153). The angel commemorated the name of the castle, the legends associated with it, and perhaps aspects of its function and symbolic character. In particular, it marked the transformation of one of the most conspicuous extant monuments of ancient Rome into, literally, a bulwark of the Church. The history of the building is well known (Weil 1974; D'Onofrio 1978; Krautheimer 1980, 268f.); it was erected by the Emperor Hadrian as a mausoleum of great size and magnificence for himself and his successors, dominating the bend of the river and the Campus Martius, the monumental zone of the city, beyond. An impressive bridge, now the Ponte S. Angelo, linked the mausoleum and the Campus Martius, and carried a processional route across the Tiber to the tomb and shrine of the deified Hadrian. With the collapse of Roman central power and the assaults of tribal invaders, the mausoleum served as a convenient strongpoint, and its smashed statues as projectiles. It guarded, thenceforth, not only those who sheltered within it in times of danger, but also, more importantly, the shrine at the Vatican of St. Peter, whose cult replaced that of Hadrian as the goal of the processional route through the Campus Martius. The castle's association with St. Michael, indeed, may well be connected with its function as a fortified bridgehead, reflecting the archangel's traditional character as guardian of gates and entrances (Réau 1956, 50, 52; Kirschbaum and Braunfels 1968–72, 255–266; Schmidt 1967).

The castle had already exchanged its funerary function for that of a strongpoint in 590. In that year Pope Gregory the Great, in a time of pestilence and military threat, led an expiatory procession (or so the legend has it) toward the Vatican (fig. 30). At the approach to the Castel S. Angelo, the procession halted, frozen in place by a vision of the archangel high over the castle. St. Michael was seen to sheathe his sword, and the pestilence ceased. In the fourteenth century the miracle was repeated, and the cult of the archangel and its association with the castle were confirmed (Weil 1974, 25; Burroughs 1982a, esp. 114f.). Nicholas V's pontificate, no less than that of Gregory, was darkened by the plague endemic in Rome and by the ambitions and threats of powerful rulers and warlords. The raising of the bronze angel on the castle, however, celebrated—certainly by coincidence—the brief period of confidence, prosperity, and security following the successful Jubilee of 1449–50, but irredeemably cut short by the catastrophes of 1453. It commemorated the once-repeated miracle, and must have seemed to promise its always potential further repetition to a people whose need was urgent. The angel completed and concentrated an extensive space reordered during Nicholas's pontificate, a space that provided a potential setting for the reenactment of the salvational rituals. In this way it reflected and manifested certain of Nicholas's most central preoccupations: his punctilious concern with liturgy and elaborate ritual, his passion for architectural and environmental improvements, and his skillful commitment to tactful social control.

The angel marked a boundary. The traveler crossing the Ponte S. Angelo, at least until the late sixteenth century, left the city of Rome, understood as a formal administrative entity, and entered the Leonine City, which was subject to direct, unmediated papal rule. Before reaching the Vatican basilica and palace, the traveler passed through the area of settlement known as the Borgo, which in the mid-fifteenth century was in particularly lamentable condition (Westfall 1974a, 107); I have already referred to the unrealized project for its transformation described by Manetti. Under Nicholas the Vatican entered a distinct phase of its history, for it now became definitively the primary residence of the popes. From the outset, Nicholas was deeply concerned for the security of the city, the Vatican, and his own person. The extensive construction campaigns on the walls of the Leonine City, well documented from 1451, probably began earlier; in particular, the Castel S. Angelo, which had quite recently served the Orsini barons as a strongpoint from which to control the surrounding area, was rapidly and thoroughly integrated into the defenses of the Leonine City (Westfall 1974a, 108–111, 143–145). The cylindrical mass of the building was surrounded by a square perimeter wall reinforced at three of its four corners by circular towers; the emblematic and perhaps paradisial geometry of the resultant defended space, in its symmetry and regularity, doubtless enhanced the sacrality conferred by the association with St. Michael.[1]

The entrance of the castle was greatly strengthened. New walls ran forward to a gatehouse on the bridge, which, with two stout, square towers, constricted the path leading from the bridge toward the Vatican, forcing it to pass through the outer defenses of the castle before it issued into the open space, the glacis, that separated the castle from the first houses of the Borgo (Westfall 1974a, 108; Esch 1969, 144f.). Beyond the houses, no doubt, towered the wall that guarded the papal enclave and that by the end of Nicholas's pontificate, in Manetti's words, was such as to deny access, if the pope so willed, to all but the birds of the air (Manetti 1734, c.932). The character of the Leonine City, apparently as foreseen from the beginning of Nicholas's pontificate, as a physically and psychologically separate and distinct place, was enhanced by the function of the angel as a conspicuous sign, a kind of punctuation mark interrupting the continuity of the visual environment and drawing attention to the heavily fortified threshold over which it was poised. In legal terms the Borgo was not part of Rome; indeed it was not to be formally incorporated into the city until the pontificate of Sixtus V.

The bronze angel of the castle was by no means the only angel emblazoned within the city, though its distinctive setting and symbolic implications were unmatched. It is useful to compare the function as sign of Nicholas's angel with that of its more humble counterparts displayed in the streets of Rome.

These angels, along with a host of other images, served as property markers in the fashion to which I have already drawn attention; they were perhaps especially associated with the Vatican chapter (Pecchiai 1952, 25–48), an especially important owner of real estate in the city, particularly the northern quarters. The function of such house signs was purely denotative, though we may be sure that to those familiar with a particular street or neighborhood a painted sign might carry a wealth of associations and convey various kinds of information. Like an angel used as a property marker, the archangel of the Castel S. Angelo gave notice of a bounded space beyond a clearly delimited threshold, a space protected and defined by a series of legal, customary, and even religious stipulations.

Nicholas's angel, clearly, was far more than a marker. Unlike most house signs, it was not an arbitrary sign, for it manifested and stood for the name and legendary associations of the castle. The question of the significance of the angel, however, is far from simple; indeed, the evidence indicates that the meaning and implications of the angel were never univocal or stable, but were affected or even generated by the various associational contexts in which the angel was set. Most obviously, the meaning of the angel was tinged by the defensive function, the embattled appearance, and the sheer size of the Castel S. Angelo beneath it. While it designated the castle, in the manner of a large label, it also referred beyond itself and its own immediate position in the city to the space and buildings enclosed by Nicholas's walls; it communicated to travelers approaching from Rome some apprehension of the place, the Leonine City and Vatican, that they were about to enter. For many pilgrims, in particular, the angel must have marked the final stage of their progress toward the long-desired shrine of the Prince of Apostles and the seat of St. Peter's current successor. In short, the angel symbolized the function of the bridge and castle, whose central axis it marked, as a narrow but major threshold into a privileged site and source of religious, temporal, and judicial authority.

This aspect of the angel has been emphasized by scholars; for Westfall, in particular, it is a symbol of papal justice, confronting, across the roofs of the city, the center of communal justice—and symbols of such justice—at the Campidoglio (Westfall 1974a, 100f.). St. Michael, however, traditionally not only kept evil from holy places, but also guided souls through the thresholds of existence. I have referred to the early sympathy shown by Nicholas for the interests of the local population, and to the post-1453 change of policy and atmosphere; the angel, perhaps commissioned no later than 1450, must be elucidated in this light. The evidence suggests that Nicholas, while welcoming the physical security guaranteed by the improved defenses of the Leonine City, was concerned to abate the sense of alien power that these may well have engendered in the Roman populace. Mindful of the unpopularity of his predecessor, Eugenius IV, and its untoward result, Nicholas adopted symbolic measures to counter the inevitable associations of the massive and threatening complex at the head of the Ponte S. Angelo, enlisting the angel as a device to aid the interpretation of the castle less as an awesome barrier than as a threshold through which the reverent and obedient would be welcome to pass.

At the southern flank of the basilica stood the chapel of S. Maria della Febbre, on which Nicholas lavished particular attention (fig. 31). The cult of the Madonna of the Plague, centered on an icon housed in this building, clearly was closely linked to the angel's role in actual or potential rituals of expiation and liberation from pestilence; indeed, an image of the angel was perhaps displayed on the exterior of the chapel.[2] The existence of this cult at the Vatican surely gave to the route from the city and through the Borgo a distinct popular resonance, beyond its more obvious ceremonial and triumphal associations (Burroughs 1982a, 112f.). The latter were reinforced especially by the vestiges of ancient pomp along the route—the remains of triumphal arches, elaborate bridges, a pyramidal *meta*, and the like (Nash 1968, 2:59–61, 193–195). Conspicuous among such monuments, even culminating the sequence, was the Vatican obelisk, which was surmounted by an orb containing, according to a famous legend, the ashes of Julius Caesar; it stood immediately adjacent to the chapel of S. Maria della Febbre, perhaps functioning as a terminal marker for supplicants making their way toward the miracle-working shrine, or at least carrying some of the popular resonance of the chapel itself. If so, the proposal reported by Manetti of transferring the obelisk to the center of the projected great piazza in front of the Vatican basilica and palace is revealed as ideologically highly charged, for it stripped the obelisk of its association with a major popular cult and ascribed to it a far simpler and more authoritarian meaning.

This reading of the angel—to say nothing of the obelisk—necessarily presupposes my conception of Nicholas's pontificate as distinguished by sensitivity to local interests and by a concern to maintain an accord or even an authentic cooperation with at least the leading segment of Roman society. It was a policy that, as I have noted, did not survive the hammer blows of 1453, the fall of Constantinople to the Turks and, briefly preceding it, the discovery and suppression of the conspiracy of Stefano Porcari against the pope. The two events seem at first sight entirely dissimilar, except in terms of their impact on the mood of the city and Nicholas himself. There is an important link, nevertheless: the disaster in the East aroused, or perhaps merely brought to the surface, a wave of criticism of Nicholas's expenditure on books and buildings, which now seemed irrelevant to the challenges confronting Western Christendom (Miglio 1975, 105 n.55; Pastor 1949, 238f., 273f.). This is now most evident through the justificatory literature, notably Manetti's panegyric, that sprang up to counter it; humanist publicists were doubtless concerned to fend off criticism of the new humanist culture itself, of which Nicholas was the first representative to ascend the throne of St. Peter. Porcari too, of course, had been a representative of humanist culture, and had perhaps for this reason enjoyed remarkably lenient treatment by Nicholas after earlier seditious behavior (Pastor 1949, 222–224). Nicholas did not abandon his humanist concerns; rather, Manetti in 1455 was to give these particular emphasis, presenting them as a consistent program encompassing the different aspects of the pope's patronage, notably the buildings. Nicholas's career, even his life, became in Manetti's account a progressive working out of themes and motifs present from early on; in particular Manetti draws attention to signs of divine intervention, the dreams and visions that punctuated Nicholas's life from his early childhood (Manetti 1734, c.910; Onofri 1979, 51). The watershed of 1453 was ignored.

That there was a watershed, however, is beyond doubt. It was given symbolic expression by Nicholas himself through the decision to execute Porcari not at the gallows at the Campidoglio, where several of his fellow conspirators met their end, but by hanging from the battlements of the Castel S. Angelo. The black-clad figure of Porcari dangled for two days from the central tower of the castle watched by crowds gathered, to judge from extant eyewitness accounts, in the new open space across the river, created *inter alia* as a place in which to commemorate and reenact angelic and papal mercy.[3] The meaning of the angel was surely now radically revised and redefined; now indeed it was a symbol of retributive justice, blocking the entrance to the Leonine City no less firmly than that other angel that with its fiery sword barred the gate of Paradise. Policies had shifted and symbols shifted accordingly; the marks of papal supremacy, already fundamental for Nicholas's conduct of policy as leader of the Church in the face of conciliarism or of particularism among the subject princes in the ecclesiastical territories, were now inscribed in the fabric of the city (Burroughs 1982a, 123).

The angel of the Castel S. Angelo, then, traversed profound changes of meaning in the course of Nicholas's pontificate. In the discussion so far, however, the referential function of the angel as sign has been presented as unidirectional, in the manner of a signpost indicating the presence beyond itself of places whose names are inscribed upon it; similarly, the angel preceded and pointed the way to the buildings of the Vatican. This does not, however, exhaust the sign function of the angel, for unlike conventional signs it referred in two directions, both beyond itself to its rear and in the direction of its gaze and gesture. It faced toward the city of Rome and the winding and irregular streets along which travelers passed on their way to the Vatican; as an anthropomorphic image it addressed such travelers, as is suggested in Renaissance representations of the angel and its viewfield (e.g., fig. 30). The angel's gaze engaged the gaze of those who caught sight of it from the streets below, establishing an always potential relationship with the occupants of the intricate and sinuous urban fabric of which the angel was a symbolic, transcendent beholder.[4]

To a degree, this is a highly primitive phenomenon. Nicholas's angel resembles in its dual referentiality apotropaic figures such as the gorgons mounted in the pediments of early Greek temples both to mark the identity or at least type of the building at their back and to affect through the projection of some magical field the area through which the temple was approached (Rodenwaldt 1939, 18–43, 135–138). As such, it belongs in a long history of images of St. Michael and other angels set up to guard the entrance of churches, or imagined as performing the same function for cities, for the Heavenly Jerusalem, or even Paradise (Reau 1956, 50, 52; Kirschbaum and Braunfels 1968–72, 256–266).[5] In this case, however, the primitive, even atavistic quality of the angel is combined with a remarkably modern aspect, in that the full efficacy of the angel seems to depend on the new practice and theory of one-point perspective. Displayed to the high angelic gaze, the city revealed itself caught and organized within a cone of vision anchored at the castle; the major streets, meander as they might (though Nicholas saw to the improvement and perhaps partial regularization of the initial section of the Via del Papa, on the axis of which the angel stood), constituted the convergent lines of the cone. The geometrical organization of visual perception, by the mid-quattrocento familiar to intellectuals in Rome, here doubled as the rational, albeit ideal, ordering of urban space, a space imbued with theatral character, since the angel was the potential focus of worshipers seeking deliverance from the plague through the reenactment of ancient ritual.

I suggest, further, that the convergence of visual and urban axes in the viewfield of the angel took on a panoptic character, involving the potentially unceasing but initially benign surveillance of an urban structure now symbolically comprehended by as well as subordinate to an all-seeing and all-knowing authority. It is a model expressed (in tactile rather than visual terms) in Alberti's image of the ideal *paterfamilias,* maintaining unremitting surveillance over his house and everyone in it, as a spider at the center of a net, attentive to the slightest movement of the strands that radiate from him. Alberti's tactile model, needless to say, presupposes a kind of instant and error-free communication not subject to the contaminations only too easily suffered by speech, especially in the urban milieu, marked by situational rhetoric, intrigues, and ethical compromises, with which Alberti contrasts the way of life of his rural and autarkic *paterfamilias.* Yet the *De re aedificatoria* represents, to a degree, a merger (or at least the examination of the possibility of such a merger) of the ideal vision of the *Della Famiglia,* by way of the familiar analogy of household and city, with a systematically developed array of architectural and urbanistic motifs as especially efficacious devices of social edification and control.[6]

The apparently simple act of raising a figure of St. Michael on the Castel S. Angelo thus carried complex and far-reaching resonances. There is concrete evidence that tends to corroborate this hypothesis. Knowledge of perspective in contemporary Rome can be assumed: Alberti, the pioneering theorist of the subject, was almost certainly implicated in the reorganization of the space opened up by demolitions in 1450–52 around the southern end of the Ponte S. Angelo and the nearby church of S. Celso; certainly, he moved in the milieu of men who played a leading role in this project. By now, of course, he had done the groundwork for the first true plan of Rome (it is difficult to believe that, having progressed so far, he did not follow his own directions to produce such a plan); he had reduced the city to quantifiable order in relation to a single viewpoint on the Campidoglio, which was perhaps chosen not only for its excellent views over the city, but also for its political associations, whether ancient or communal (Gadol 1969, 168–195; Vagnetti 1969, 1974). Certainly, the centrality of the Campidoglio entailed the peripherality of the papal centers of the Vatican and Lateran. Alberti's viewpoint on the Campidoglio and that of the angel above the Castel S. Angelo, accordingly, were topographically and ideologically distinct, but both could be understood as foci of convergent axes (the Campidoglio as that of the great long-distance ancient roads, to which I will return). In both cases, then, we find anticipations, on an ideal level, of the physical arrangement of convergent axes in line with a privileged nodal point that was to be such a crucial phenomenon in the subsequent history of the street system of papal Rome.[7]

The privileged view from the Castel S. Angelo was not reserved exclusively to the symbolic beholder, the angel. As we noted, the Castel S. Angelo was a particular object of Nicholas's attention early in his pontificate; a month, indeed, after his accession in March 1447 his closest collaborator, Nello da Bologna, carried out an inventory of the building and its contents.[8] Substantial construction at the castle is documented by Jubilee year (1449–50); apparently the inventory of 1447 had involved the review of the restorations and improvements considered necessary or desirable at the castle (Müntz 1878, 151–154; Borgatti 1930, 157–163).[9] Contemporaries were particularly impressed by a fine papal apartment created by Nicholas's builders within the castle, presumably at or near the summit.[10] In view of the pope's well-known taste for sumptuous furnishings and precious objects, we may assume that the apartment deserved the praise of those who saw it, though there is no extant evidence of its appearance. In any case, it is likely that Nicholas's concern was not—or not only—to provide himself with a safe refuge in time of danger, but to create well-appointed, comfortable, and airy residential quarters, fit to be shown to eminent visitors and, not least, commanding a fine view over the city, perhaps through great guelph windows like those represented in the miniature of Niccolò Polani of 1459 (fig. 32). Such a view encompassed much of Rome, with the papal palace at S. Maria Maggiore in the distance, from which the pope could enjoy the view over the city in the opposite direction.[11] Nicholas's probable viewpoint, then, was all but identical with that of the angel; we may accordingly transfer to the pope much of our discussion of the significance of the gaze of the angel, the bronze statue that he perhaps commissioned to stand in, in some sense, for himself. Not for nothing were Nicholas's arms prominently displayed on the central tower of the castle, in line with the angel (fig. 30).

Soon after its installation the angel presided directly over a physically reordered space. Extensive demolition in 1451–53 created an arrangement of street and piazza aligned with the Castel S. Angelo and the angel, along an axis constricted and emphasized by twin octagonal chapels erected by Nicholas at the southern bridgehead in commemoration of the many pilgrims who lost their lives in an accident on the bridge in 1450. (The chapels were replaced by the extant statues of Saints Peter and Paul in the early sixteenth century.) A secondary focus was provided by the porticoed facade of the restored church of S. Celso, which faced over the piazza toward the river and the castle. The reform of this space cannot be understood without reference to the statue of the angel and the miracle whose renewed occurrence it promised. Indeed, the approach to the castle surely now constituted a perspectively ordered theatral setting (Burroughs 1982a), in which the procession of Pope Gregory could be imagined as acted out (as perhaps it was) along the axis receding between the flanking chapels and culminating in the angel; the urban environment, in other words, became a place of ritual drama enacted either through the performance of human actors or, in their absence, through the play of sightlines, panoptic and supplicant respectively, from and to the angel.[12]

The redevelopment of the area adjacent to the Ponte S. Angelo and the symbolism associated with it form the necessary context for the discussion of the famous 1452 edition of the statutes of the *maestri di strada*. These were the communal magistrates with responsibility for the maintenance of public spaces, thoroughfares, and facilities, though in the context of the general absorption of city government into the papal administration; so significant an act as the publication of new statutes, if not necessarily initiated by the pope and his staff, must have at very least accorded with papal interests. The 1452 edition of the statutes was the first issued in Italian rather than Latin, a choice of language that underlined the programmatic nature of the document, which established clear and accessible guidelines for the activity of the magistrates concerned. Some authors have represented the 1452 statutes, accordingly, as a direct instrument of papal policies imposed on the communal milieu (Westfall 1974a, 81–84). The evidence indicates a more ambiguous situation.

The most conspicuous provision of the new statutes, certainly in the view of modern scholars, was the distinction of three principal streets for which especially punctilious upkeep was mandated (Re 1920, 99 no. 32, 101 no. 39). One of these was the tortuous but ceremonially crucial route of the *possesso*, the Via del Papa, part of which, the so-called Canale di Ponte, was undergoing improvement at the time that the new statutes were issued; this was the main street of the Florentine bankers' quarter that debouched into the new piazza at the Ponte S. Angelo and S. Celso (map 2). The other two streets also traversed the funnel-shaped area of Rome within the Tiber bend, joining the Canale di Ponte from opposite sides not far from the bridge. One was the Via Retta, which owed its straight course and its name to the fact that, alone of the three streets, it followed an ancient street line; it connected the district of Ponte with the important church and market of S. Maria Rotonda (Pantheon) and with the Via Lata, the main route into Rome from the north. The third, the Via Mercatoria (an important stretch of it became known, as it still is, as the Via del Pellegrino), connected Ponte with the markets of the Campo de' Fiori, Piazza Giudea (or dei Giudei), and S. Angelo in Pescheria, and with the port and markets of Trastevere (map 2).[13]

The three principal streets of the 1452 statutes, then, converged in the area of the Canale di Ponte, providing a first, if approximate, example of the crow's-foot motif that, by way of the Manettian Borgo scheme, was to become an almost indispensable element of the vocabulary of Renaissance and absolutist spatial organization. The panoptic viewfield of the angel thereby acquired legal status and administrative implications. It is true, of course, that all three streets were already familiar and well-established elements of the topography of the city. Nevertheless, there were many other possible candidates for the status of principal street and for especially careful maintenance; the statutory institution of the crow's foot, therefore, must be regarded as an act of abstraction and formalization determined by ideological and political considerations connected, especially, with the new ascendancy of the Vatican. The Castel S.

Angelo, then, as magnificent propylon of the Vatican and, as it were, as its urbanistic proxy, came to dominate the meeting point of a coherent set of links with major sites of Rome. The topographically peripheral status of the Vatican was thereby overcome, and a new symbolic centering inscribed in the fabric of the city. Implicit and fundamental in this centering, however, was an over-laying of topographical, ideological, and visualistic aspects that accounts for the generalizable and paradigmatic quality of the motif, as prominent in the layout of Versailles, Hampton Court, or St. Petersburg as in the northern quarters of Rome or occasional small towns in Lazio, like Bagnaia.

The publication of the 1452 statutes of the *maestri di strada* was a call to action. In the case of the three principal streets, direct papal intervention was out of the question; improvement was to be secured through the confirmation and extension of the responsibilities and powers of the *maestri di strada*, as also, in my view, through paradigmatic development projects like that involving the Canale di Ponte. Even this, of course, was the result not of papal fiat but of a meeting of various interests. As I have noted, the costs were carried by the owners of properties abutting on the street, many of them Tuscans who had a clear interest in bringing their Roman neighborhood up to the standards of urbanistic maintenance and hygiene prevalent in their own cities.[14] The idea of the improvement project may even have arisen among the Tuscan merchants and bankers, though if so it was soon appropriated by the pope and his administration and incorporated into a more ambitious and complex undertaking.

The coherence of the improvement campaign in the area of the Canale di Ponte and the pertinent clauses of the 1452 statutes of the *maestri di strada* can be documented. In the first place, Nicholas's urban policies and interventions were developed and monitored through a central office, that of Nello da Bologna. Nicholas's staff, moreover, proved particularly adept at enlisting the support and cooperation of leading local patricians. One of these men, Massimo de' Massimi, played a major role both in the Canale di Ponte project and in the preparation of the 1452 statutes. A prominent resident of the Via del Papa and an important figure in rional and communal politics, Massimo was a lawyer whose status in his profession is indicated by his role in revising or even drafting the statutes of the Roman guild of notaries.[15] In 1451–52 he served as one of the two *maestri di strada*; his term of office culminated with the publication of the new statutes (Tommasini 1887, 207).[16] Since nothing is known of Massimo's partner in office, it is likely that he concentrated his attention on abusive occupation of public space and other routine business. Massimo, on the other hand, was a protégé of the chamberlain, Cardinal Ludovico Trevisan, whose involvement with the urbanistic measures of Eugenius's pontificate is discussed below. Unlike other associates of the chamberlain, Massimo was clearly able to maintain close relations with Nello da Bologna and his staff, and it is even possible that his selection as *maestro di strada* at a particularly crucial conjuncture occurred with support or pressure from the pope's men.[17]

Massimo's role in the development of the Canale di Ponte area was to act as notary for the property purchases, some of which may well have been compulsory, that preceded or possibly, in some cases, succeeded the extensive demolition carried out to form the new piazza (Burroughs 1982a). He was certainly already acquainted with the individual who, more than any other, may be plausibly identified as the chief promoter of a more commodious place of business for the Florentine colony. This was Tommaso Spinelli, doyen of the Tuscan community, formerly banker to the Camera Apostolica and now to the commune of Rome. Spinelli's architectural patronage in Florence and his interest in the 1450s in a specifically Albertian current of design have been documented by Saalman (1966) and Mack (1983);[18] it is probable, moreover, that Alberti was his client, at least in Rome, for legal transactions involving Alberti took place in Spinelli's premises in Ponte, though Spinelli himself is not named in the documents.[19] Spinelli's bank fronted on the Canale di Ponte, as seems clear from Spinelli's prominent contribution to the funding for the improvement of that street; at the same time he was advancing considerable sums for the construction work on St. Peter's basilica and S. Maria della Febbre.[20] The prosopographical evidence, then, indicates a close relationship between the various projects affecting the Canale di Ponte area; these in turn, as we will see, were linked to significant developments elsewhere in the city.

Along the Papal Way: Continuity and Change in the Development of Rome under Nicholas V

The angel of the Castel S. Angelo, if I am right, presided over a largely notional reordering of urban space, involving little physical transformation of the actual fabric of the city. This reordering, moreover, resulted not from unilateral papal ordinances, but from the careful meshing of papal and local initiatives and interests. In both respects, the measures that I have discussed were typical of urban development under Nicholas, as I will document below. Even sharper, then, appears the contrast with the most famous urbanistic project associated with Nicholas, the Borgo scheme described by Manetti. I have already noted this ideal evocation of a residential and commercial enclave functionally and ideologically correlated with the grander structures of the adjacent Vatican; it has been the subject of penetrating discussions, notably by Westfall (1974a), and there is no need for lengthy comment here. It is, of course, a major document in the history of urban design; perhaps its most striking provision is that for three main streets connecting the glacis in front of the Castel S. Angelo respectively with the Vatican palace, basilica, and the ancient street to the south of the basilica that led past S. Maria della Febbre and the obelisk. This configuration, underscoring the character of the reformed Borgo as an appropriate approach to the Vatican, recalls or—to use a term introduced by Spezzaferro, to the implications of which I will return—mirrors the triadic arrangement of thoroughfares instituted in the 1452 statutes of the *maestri di strada* across the river.

The version of this motif in the Borgo scheme, however, has undergone an evident process of abstraction and formalization, although echoes of the urban reality across the Ponte S. Angelo are still perceptible. Spezzaferro has noted, in particular, the relationship of the central street of the Borgo scheme and the stretch of the Via del Papa; the former is both a formalized version and a continuation of the other, while it shares its ceremonial and perhaps commercial character as a privileged site for high-status trades and businesses (Spezzaferro 1973, 36). The focus of the central street of the Borgo was to be the obelisk, moved from its original position next to S. Maria della Febbre to mark the center of the great piazza projected in front of the basilica and palace, into which all three streets were to debouch. The obelisk, relaying the new central axis of the Borgo into the basilica, was to be raised on figures of the four evangelists, symbols of scriptural authority connected by the upward-pointing shaft of the obelisk with the divine source of all authority above, and by the axis of the papal coronation procession with the foundation stone of the Church and of papal temporal and spiritual power, the tomb of St. Peter beneath the high altar of the basilica.[21]

Giannozzo Manetti, in whose panegyric of Nicholas V the account of the replanned Borgo appears, has entered the discussion already on several occasions. His first appearance in the Rome of Nicholas V was at the beginning, for he was chosen to join the Florentine delegation sent to congratulate the newly elected Nicholas in 1447. Manetti delivered the address on behalf of his city, to the admiration of the pope and his other hearers. In a few years, however, he became politically a *persona non grata* in Florence, and in 1454 abandoned his native city and was made welcome in Rome by Nicholas, who had already enrolled him among his secretaries.[22] This is important: Manetti's arrival in Rome and his immersion into the world of the papal court coincided with the change of mood occasioned by the events of 1453; it coincided also, then, with the shift in Nicholas's policies toward the city and its population. The description of the replanned Borgo belongs fully in this milieu; though it is regularly hailed as a key document in the history of conscious urban planning, it involves or at least implies a rejection of the actual city, the disorderly and sometimes dangerous environment beyond the Ponte S. Angelo. Certainly Manetti lists the major building projects undertaken or supported by Nicholas in the city proper, including secular projects along with the restoration of churches. But the possibility of a rationally ordered space, in which ceremonial, economic, residential, and ideological functions can merge, is limited to the Borgo and to a project predicated on the complete removal of the existing fabric.

If so, Manetti's text rehearses, if somewhat covertly, a familiar theme of humanist literature produced in the milieu of the papal court, that of disdain for contemporary Rome and its population. This waspish attitude was not unwarranted in some respects, though Rome could boast an impressive current of humanist scholarship and patronage. But humanism in Rome, especially as exemplified by an individual like Stefano Porcari, could and did easily acquire a political or even radical tinge. Utopian visions of the forms and trappings of ancient Roman authority might merge with a more practical interest in the restoration to the Roman commune of some of its quite recent power, the shell of which—the magistracies and public ceremony—was still maintained. A current of Ghibellinism bubbled under the surface, occasionally breaking into the open. Nicholas and his advisers were well aware of this, and at times when the public expression or even eruption of Ghibelline sentiment seemed especially likely, as during the visit to Rome of Emperor Frederick III, they took steps to counter it (Pastor 1949, 147–149).

Porcari's support, the extent of which is not clear (Nicholas was careful to limit his response, severe though it was, to the ringleaders), was based mainly in disaffected members of the Roman patriciate. Some humanists were implicated, or at least behaved as if they might plausibly be regarded as suspects.[23] Others, notably Alberti, hurried to compose accounts of the uprising and its suppression that left no doubt—and this was perhaps the point—of their authors' loyalty to the pope and opposition to the principles espoused by Porcari. But long before the Porcari affair, Nicholas had shown distinct coolness to a group of humanists associated especially with Cardinal Prospero Colonna and with the future Pope Paul II, Cardinal Pietro Barbo. I will return to Colonna's circle in a later chapter; the comparison of Nicholas's and Paul II's urban measures and policies, on the other hand, is of particular value for the understanding of the former.

Cardinal Pietro Barbo demonstrated his alliance with the Colonna clan and his sympathetic attitude toward the Roman commune through the foundation, about 1455 (perhaps significantly about the time of Nicholas's death), of an impressive palace in the environs of the Colonna palaces and the Campidoglio. After his accession, Paul greatly expanded his palace, the present Palazzo Venezia, and transferred some of the festivities of the Roman carnival to the nearby piazza and section of the Via Lata, subsequently known, for the carnival races associated with it, as the Via del Corso. In this way, as is often noted, Paul expressed a concern to identify papal authority with the traditional structures of the city, though perhaps rather on the level of spectacle and ritual than actual delegation of real power (Frommel 1982; Frommel 1984, esp. 162; Westfall 1974a, 66; Spezzaferro 1973, 37f.).

Paul's removal of the center of papal power, at least on the level of symbolism, almost to the opposite edge of the Roman *abitato* from the Vatican seems to represent a clear, if temporary, abandonment of the emphasis placed by Nicholas and most Renaissance popes on the residential, official, and religious enclave of the Leonine City. It was not enough of an enclave for Paul, however, who sought to remove himself from the sphere of influence of the Orsini clan, whose headquarters at Monte Giordano dominated the Via del Papa at a point not far from the Ponte S. Angelo and the Banchi district.[24] Whereas Nicholas had at least given the impression of rising above the factional conflicts endemic in Rome, especially those between the Orsini and Colonna, Paul made clear his alliance with one faction, that more closely identified with the commune. The conspicuous echoes in the architecture of Paul's palace of the Colosseum, a building of particular symbolic value both for the Roman patriciate and the Colonna faction, as I have noted, may well have carried, therefore, specific ideological value (fig. 7).

There are, nevertheless, instructive parallels between the two pontificates. The intricacies of humanist culture in Rome and its not infrequent political implications are evident in the challenge that each pope had to face from conspiracy, or at least opposition, on the part of certain humanists. Unlike Nicholas, whose humanist credentials were never challenged, Paul was the object of withering scorn directed by humanists especially at his passion for small and precious objets d'art, over which, according to his detractors, he obsessively gloated (Dunston 1973; Palermino 1980). Yet Paul's activities as collector and his aesthetic tastes seem—and perhaps seemed to Paul himself—not unlike those of Nicholas (Weiss 1958; Weiss 1969, 186–188). It is noteworthy that Paul, with more commitment than any other of Nicholas's successors until Julius II, continued Nicholas's construction project at the west end of St. Peter's basilica (Westfall 1974a, 116). Paul's palace, including both its Albertian and non-Albertian elements, owed little or nothing to non-Roman architectural models, and may have been deliberately designed in a tradition of local palace architecture that included the Vatican palace as expanded by Nicholas. Indeed, if Frommel has correctly identified the architect of the Palazzo Venezia as Francesco del Borgo, Paul chose a man who had come to prominence and doubtless gained important experience and expertise as the assistant to Nello da Bologna, Nicholas's head of staff; his role in this capacity was largely administrative, as far as the documents indicate, but it is likely that he was involved with Nicholas's building projects, especially as these were Nello's ultimate responsibility. It is likely, further, that Paul took some of his concern for public symbolism, whether expressed in architecture, ritual, or the unedifying spectacle of the carnival festivities, from the example of Nicholas, though with a more populist tinge than Nicholas would probably have ever countenanced.

A final and especially striking parallel between the two popes is the association of each with particular Roman neighborhoods. Paul, both as cardinal and pope, favored the area between the Campidoglio and the Via Lata. Nicholas, on the other hand, is usually represented as associated with the Borgo, thanks to Manetti's text. The records of the major property owner in the Borgo, the Chapter of St. Peter's, however, contain no hint of investment or economic vitality in the area, as might be expected in response to such grandiose visions as those transmitted by Manetti. Instead, the picture of the Borgo that the property records give us is of an area of ruinous hovels inhabited, when habitable, by tenants of low status and, in many cases, foreign origin. There is no trace of goldsmiths or the other prestigious businesses located by Manetti in the central street of his utopic enclave. Still less is there evidence in the "district of the papal court," as Manetti called it, of the settlement of leading figures in Nicholas's administration or other high-ranking prelates or officials who owed their advancement to the pope and would accordingly have been vulnerable to papal pressure to contribute to the improvement of a district identified with him. In other words, there was no anticipation of the tactic employed in 1459–64 by Pius II to bring high-ranking residents to Pienza, a kind of up-country Borgo where the major buildings were designed by another architect closely identified with Nicholas, Bernardo Rossellino. Though it is possible that under Nicholas the availability of building materials and skilled labor for private commissions may have been limited by the volume of papal and public projects, yet there is evidence for small-scale development in Rome, though not in the Borgo (Spezzaferro 1973, 36; Burroughs 1982a). The inescapable conclusion is that Manetti's account of the replanned and rebuilt Borgo arose out of concerns and conditions at the papal court only in the very last phase of Nicholas's life; for an understanding of Nicholas's actual impact on the city we must look elsewhere.

If we locate the residences of Nicholas's closest associates, a clear topographical pattern emerges. We find them settled, above all, in the Rioni Ponte and Parione on or near the Via del Papa (map 1), in other words in the quarter of Tuscan settlement in which urbanistic improvements were undertaken under Nicholas. They were close to the Orsini strongpoint at Monte Giordano; Paul's strictures about Orsini influence at the Vatican were evidently not without foundation. They were not particularly close to the papal palatial complex at the Vatican; rather, their pattern of settlement continued a process of development and demographic growth that can be shown to have been present in Ponte and Parione from the later fourteenth century (see chapter 1 above).

Nicholas affirmed and contributed to this process: in 1447, for instance, he issued edicts (bandi) controlling commercial activity in Ponte. In particular, these edicts sought to halt the dumping in the streets of offal and other waste products of tanning and other trades concerned with the butchering and processing of animals; such materials were now to be disposed of in the river downstream of the main populated area of the city. No doubt Nicholas was responding to the interests of the leading inhabitants of Ponte, perhaps especially the Tuscan bankers with whom his relations were close; it is likely also that the pope was following an agenda of his own, that of concentrating industrial activity in the area of Ripa (map 1; fig. 49), in conjunction with an apparently consistent campaign to improve harbor and warehousing facilities there (Re 1928, 93 no. 2.i; Romano 1941, 5). In any case, the effect of such measures, if implemented, would have been to liberate at least the better-policed thoroughfares of Ponte from noisome, low-status trades; they may have helped bring about, therefore, something of the hierarchy of streets that was formalized in the 1452 statutes of the maestri di strada. Whatever the success of Nicholas's edicts, the long-term transformation of the district is evident from the etymology given in the sixteenth century to the name Scortecchiara, a district of Ponte, as derived from scortum as meaning "prostitute," rather than from its original meaning, "hide": this was doubtless an unanticipated corollary of Nicholas's urban policy (Gnoli 1939, 294; Spezzaferro 1973, 24).

It was perhaps with Nicholas's assent or even support, then, that a group of close associates and collaborators settled in Ponte and Parione. Among them were Niccolò Amidani, Nicholas's vice-chamberlain and governor of Rome; Francesco della Zecca, the master of the mint; Giacomo Calvi, the soldano or chief law-enforcement officer, who was based at the Tor di Nona; and in all probability Pietro de' Nobili da Noceto, Nicholas's secretary a secretis, whose purchase of a large property on the Via del Papa (it was later transformed into the grand Palazzo del Governo Vecchio by Stefano Nardini) is undated, but should surely be associated with the apogee of his career.[25] All these men lived within easy reach of Monte Giordano, site of the residence of Latino Orsini, canon of St. Peter's and one of the first group of cardinals created by Nicholas, in 1448 (Katterbach 1931, 25). No doubt in conjunction with Nicholas's urban policies, Latino set about refounding S. Salvatore in Lauro, the major church on the Via Retta and close to his palace, where he had perhaps already begun the important building and decoration campaign still evident in the fabric.[26]

But if the district was overlooked by Monte Giordano on one side, on the other it was dominated by the Tor di Nona, not far from the edge of the piazza created at the Ponte S. Angelo in 1451–53 and presided over by the *soldano* Calvi, who was also a *familiaris* of the pope and a *scriptor*, and by the Castel S. Angelo, from 1447 placed in the charge of Giacomo de' Nobili, probably a brother of Pietro da Noceto.[27] Papal and traditional local centers of authority faced each other, then, across the roofs of the quarter, apparently in amity; indeed Amidani and Pietro da Noceto may have acted as conduits of local concerns back to the inner circle around the pope. On the other hand, early in 1453 certain of Stefano Porcari's allies hoped to win Latino Orsini to their cause, though in vain. Since Latino, like Pietro da Noceto, was strongly pro-Venetian (in 1451 Pietro da Noceto even applied for membership in the Venetian Maggior Consiglio), the shift at this time of Nicholas's close ally Cosimo de' Medici from a pro-Venetian to a pro-Milanese alignment may have prompted the conspirator most familiar with the Orsini quarter, Massimo de' Massimi's brother Giacomo, to appeal to Latino, who, like Porcari, was a leading representative of Roman humanism.[28] And there is much irony in the sale by Giacomo of a house at Monte Giordano to none other than the *soldano* to raise money to buy arms for Porcari.[29]

The development of Ponte may even have been aided by direct subventions on Nicholas's part. Platina, in a near-contemporary account, emphasized the pope's charitable activity, notably that directed at those, evidently not entirely without means, who would otherwise not be able to build their own houses (Platina 1913, 338; see also Pastor 1949, 20; Spezzaferro 1973, 18). Indeed, Platina expressly states that Nicholas aided distressed gentlefolk, and though he does not indicate the nature of this aid, it is likely that it consisted of dowry grants, which would naturally encourage household formation and consequently building. There is little direct evidence of such a program; the one documented recipient was a Porcarian conspirator (mentioned because of his ingratitude), while a possible case involves a family resident in Ponte.[30]

If there was consciously manipulated development in Ponte and Parione under Nicholas, it must be seen as merely a continuation of the longer-term process. Early foci of development were doubtless the palaces in Parione of the powerful cardinals Giordano Orsini, who however retained his association with Monte Giordano, and Francesco Condulmer, the Venetian aristocrat and vicechancellor under Eugenius IV, who established himself in a palace, which became a landmark in early Renaissance Rome, above the ruins of the Theater of Pompey at the edge of the Campo de' Fiori.[31] The crucial example, however, as set by the chamberlain, Cardinal Ludovico Trevisan, whose residence adjoined his titular church of S. Lorenzo in Damaso; it was situated, then, between and close to two of the principal streets identified in the 1452 statutes, the Via del Papa and the Via Mercatoria (del Pellegrino).

After the brutal but slickly stage-managed elimination of Cardinal Vitelleschi in 1440, Cardinal Trevisan inherited Vitelleschi's role as effective ruler of the lands of the Church, and continued his program of reducing recalcitrant communities and lords to obedience.[32] He showed particular concern for the condition of Rome, appointing officials whose authority must have overlapped with that of the communal officials with responsibility for the maintenance of public order and the upkeep of the urban environment. On July 31, 1441, Alessandro Schiacchi, a citizen of Rome, was created "murorum et ceterorum edificiorum publicorum custos sive officialis," a post with precedent in the pontificate of Martin V, though not in the context of consistent urban improvements. Schiacchi's salary, set at 4 florins a month, was doubled at the time of the celebrations of carnival and the Assumption of the Virgin; this perhaps allowed him to hire constables and ensure the decent condition of the spaces used in the festivities (Paschini 1939, 137).[33]

At the very beginning of Nicholas's pontificate we find a further official apparently combining responsibility for public order and for the physical upkeep of the urban environment. This was Antonio Pio da Carpi, *commissarius in alma urbe*, whose salary included an allowance for a constable. In 1444, however, he had received 200 florins for restoration work on the walls and *rocca* of Ceprano (ASR, M 830, fols. 85v, 166r; Corbo 1969, 163). It is likely, then, that Antonio's role in Rome too involved some administration of building projects, and that his activity under Nicholas merely continued that for the chamberlain; certainly, he does not reappear in Nicholan ledgers after 1448, while there is no mention at all of Schiacchi or his post. Nicholas may have sought to separate the policing of the city, which he left as much as possible to communal officials, as Westfall (1974a), 76, has rightly emphasized, from urbanistic measures.[34] Nevertheless, as we will see, he set beside the communal officials concerned with the physical environment a group of his own officials, whose roles may have been developed out of those exercised by the chamberlain's appointees; in either case, no regular pattern of appointment can be discerned.

The regulatory environment within which the chamberlain's own officials and those of the commune alike operated was of particular concern to Cardinal Trevisan. By 1446 at latest he and the commune had agreed on a series of important provisions of urbanistic significance, some of which clearly anticipated those issued under Nicholas.[35] In particular , the principal streets of the city, perhaps now for the first time officially designated as such, were to be kept clear of bulky traffic. Heavy wagons served certain trades rather than others, of course, and it is likely that such a regulation had, if implemented, a marked effect on the commercial and other character of the streets concerned (they are not, as in 1452, identified in topographical terms), perhaps contributing to an ongoing process of hierarchical gradation. The activity of butchers was to be especially carefully supervised; they could set up their stalls only in certain locations traditionally used by their trade, and they were to keep those areas clean. Commercial activity in general was affected by the chamberlain's reform, which can in part be independently verified, of important public spaces, like the Piazza Giudea and the Piazza della Rotonda; these, significantly, were all sites of major markets. Three of the piazzas named were situated on the Via Mercatoria, while the Piazza della Rotonda was effectively on the Via Retta (map 2); the connection with the formalized geometry of the 1452 statutes is clear.

The Campo de' Fiori served at the time as the city's horse market; it was referred to as such in most vernacular documents (Gnoli 1939, 165; Egidi 1908, 326), while the more pretentious and surely less accurate reference to a field of flowers was typical of documents written in Latin (Sora 1907, 117 n.13). It is likely that the Campo was paved for the first time during Eugenius's pontificate; if so, the residence in the environs of the piazza of important prelates must have been a contributory factor (Castagnoli et al. 1958, 358). It is especially probable that the chamberlain, the parish of whose *titulus* ran up to the Campo,[36] was directly involved with this project. It is possible that in other respects too the Campo was undergoing a degree of upgrading. By the mid-fifteenth century the activities of local bankers on or near the piazza can be documented, though these may, of course, have been ancillary to the horse coping that went on there.[37] There is evidence, further, that the later association of the area with hostelries (commemorated in the present name Via del Pellegrino of the section of the Via Mercatoria between the Campo and Ponte) can be traced back to this period.[38]

Speculation on the chamberlain's concern for the Campo de' Fiori gives way to firm evidence in the case of the piazza that extended in front of the Pantheon. Since the latter, a major shrine of the Virgin, was known as S. Maria Rotonda, the open space associated with it was known as the Piazza della Rotonda. The chamberlain apparently visited the piazza in person; his inspection led to the institution of regulations governing the setting up of stalls and benches in the piazza. In particular, some "most squalid shops" were removed from the portico of the venerable building itself; the piazza was paved, as was the street leading "to the Campo Marzio," presumably connecting the piazza with the Via Retta (the present Via delle Coppelle) and the church and hospital of the Maddalena.[39] Flavio Biondo, who informs us of the measures taken, draws attention to the restoration of the Pantheon itself, giving the credit, naturally enough, to the pope (Eugenius IV), though the involvement of the chamberlain was probably crucial (Valentini and Zucchetti 1953, 313).[40] It is important further, however, to record the crucial part played in the restoration campaign by a prominent patrician, later active on behalf of Nicholas's administration, Lorenzo Altieri, who was buried in S. Maria Rotonda.[41]

At the Pantheon, then, the regulation of economic activity occurred alongside and even as a corollary of the restoration of a major architectural monument of ancient Rome. While we may regard the improvements as motivated in part at least by a spirit of antiquarian enthusiasm—this is the implication of Biondo's text—it is more pertinent to note the evident aesthetic aspect of the chamberlain's urbanistic measures, all of which seem intended to promote the production of a better-ordered and more salubrious urban environment, in which functional, economic, and social hierarchies were clearly expressed. Given the focus of the chamberlain's measures, it is clear that a high degree of continuity marked policies affecting Ponte and Parione from the last years of Eugenius IV through the pontificate of Nicholas V. On the other hand, the city fabric, even if it was already understood as a system of interlocking elements, was evidently not yet regarded as reducible to formal schemata; this step was to be taken under Nicholas.

Cardinal Trevisan remained in office as chamberlain under Nicholas, but his activities were severely circumscribed (see chapter 4 below). In 1452 he received permission from the pope to reform S. Lorenzo in Damaso and its dependent churches in Rome; it is likely that this reform, like that of SS. Apostoli discussed below, involved inspection and repair of the physical fabric of the building (ASV, RV 422, fol. 301r). No work is documented on the adjoining palace, though it is probable that the cardinal's interest in the improvement of his country seat at Albano, which is well documented, carried over to his city palace. On the other hand, his preoccupation with his rural retreat was perhaps, to a degree, a compensation for his lost role in the politics of urban administration and reform, in which he was succeeded by men closer to Nicholas and raised to prominence by him. Nevertheless, there is evidence that the chamberlain maintained good relations with these individuals, while some of his earlier protégés, notably Massimo de' Massimi, continued to play an important role in Nicholan Rome. Massimo, who was a parishioner of S. Lorenzo in Damaso, may well have needed support in high places when his brother Giacomo was revealed as a member of the Porcarian conspiracy; significantly, his own career does not seem to have suffered.[42]

In 1451 Francesco Orsini, the leading secular scion of his clan and prefect of the city, founded a palace fronting on the Via del Papa at the point where it broadened to become the Piazza di Parione; it faced, therefore, the property of the Massimi family across the square (Magnuson 1958, 241; Golzio and Zander 1969, 116). Orsini's choice of site for his palace is of great interest; it was some distance from the Orsini enclave at Monte Giordano, but there seems no reason to connect Francesco's move with the precedent set by his uncle, Cardinal Giordano, whose palace was on the corner of the Via del Papa and Via Monterone (Adinolfi 1865, 90) but who had died in 1438. The stimulus for the creation of a fine new palace may have come from the recent award by Nicholas to Latino Orsini, Francesco's nephew, of a red hat; I have already noted the construction undertaken at Monte Giordano by Latino, who now probably began the process of transforming the fortresslike complex into an appropriate center for intellectual and cultural activities of a humanist cast.

At the rear of Francesco Orsini's palace lay the Piazza Navona. The history of this famous open space as a grand, open-air *salone* is usually taken as commencing with the transfer to the square of the main market of Rome under Sixtus IV, soon after the Jubilee of 1475 (Castagnoli et al. 1958, 359; Spezzaferro 1973, 41–44; Infessura 1890, 83). The decision to move the market was implemented, if not initiated, by Cardinal Guillaume d'Estouteville, whose crucial role in the urbanistic projects and reforms under Sixtus recalls that of Cardinal Ludovico Trevisan under Eugenius, though with the experience of Nicholas V's pontificate as a crucial additional factor. Sixtus's emphasis on the Piazza Navona must be seen, as is often noted, in the context of the repair of the Ponte Sisto and the consequent establishment in the *abitato* of a new axis, cutting across and linking the three principal streets identified in 1452.

It is possible that such a transverse link was anticipated in Nicholas's pontificate. Sometime between 1447 and 1450 Cardinal d'Estouteville moved from a palace on the Piazza di Parione, where he had been a near neighbor of the Massimi and the site developed by Francesco Orsini, to one at S. Apollinare (map 2). His occupation of a palace on the Via del Papa in Parione may have been a response to the topographical pull of the chamberlain's palace at the nearby S. Lorenzo in Damaso; d'Estouteville's move to the other end of the Piazza Navona, to the environs of the Via Retta, one of the principal streets of 1452 and connecting with the church of S. Salvatore in Lauro, may be regarded as a paradigmatic maneuver within the context of Nicholas's urban policies.[43] The same is perhaps true of the location of Orsini's palace at the other end of the square. If so, there was evidently already a concern to foster a route leading from the Via Retta at S. Apollinare through the Piazza Navona, across the Piazza di Parione, as far as the Campo de' Fiori and the Via Mercatoria.

Such a clarification or even rethinking of the topography of the *abitato* would certainly have benefited elements of the local patriciate and may well have been carried out with their support or even pressure. Two important families occupied extensive property in the vicinity of the Piazza Navona, the Mellini on the side toward Monte Giordano and the Muti on the other side. The leading representative of the Mellini at midcentury was the prominent notary Pietro. By the 1440s he was evidently a member of the inner circle around the chamberlain, while in 1438 and 1469 he is known to have been involved in the reforms of the city statutes carried out in those years; it is a reasonable assumption, then, that he had a hand, along with his neighbor and professional colleague Massimo de' Massimi, in the preparation of the 1452 statutes that promised to have an important and beneficial effect on his own quarter.[44] Indeed, apart from the regulations concerning the maintenance of the major streets to either end of the Piazza Navona, a clause stipulated that the piazza itself should be kept free of refuse and, as Re has emphasized, that the remains of the ancient "theater" (i.e., the Stadium of Domitian) should be preserved.[45] Re saw this clause as formalizing the preservation of an important ancient monument for reasons of humanist antiquarianism. As with the Pantheon, however, other motives were probably also involved; in this case, certainly, the upgrading of the piazza would have improved the setting of Mellini's palace, in which significant new construction can be documented about this time.

Across the piazza, to the east, were the houses of the Muti family, some of whom were especially closely allied with Nicholas's administration. In 1453 a younger member of the family purchased a house fronting onto the Piazza

Navona, while a general concentration of Muti property in and associations with the piazza and the adjoining section of the Via del Papa can be followed in the documents.[46] The presence of such important clans in the vicinity of the piazza implies that, even before the impetus of the 1452 statutes, attention was given to the upkeep of the piazza. Giovanni Rucellai, indeed, visited the piazza in 1450 and was impressed by it; he mentions the jousts held there, and notes the correspondence of the piazza both in form and function to its ancient counterpart, the Circus Maximus (Rucellai 1960, 76). We can be sure that many of the residents of the quarter introduced in this chapter were present at the festivities witnessed by Rucellai, and that decorations on the houses and in the streets and squares celebrated the solidarity of the quarter's elite.

The Rioni Ponte and Parione were, in sum, the site of extensive development, especially in the vicinity of the Via del Papa and the other major streets, resulting from a complex interweaving of private initiatives and papal or at least official inducements and directives. It was a process of long duration, to which at first sight Nicholas's accession made little difference. Certainly, Nicholas's openness to communal sensitivities and local concerns owed much, as Westfall has emphasized, to the agreement reached in Eugenius's last years between the papal administration and the commune. Nicholas's confirmation of this agreement—Westfall calls it a concordat—is a further indication of the continuity between his and Eugenius's pontificates, and we may regard the 1452 statutes of the *maestri di strada* as representing a crystallization of earlier concerns and initiatives (Westfall 1974a, 73 n.26, 74). On the other hand, I would tentatively assert that Nicholas's pontificate saw the development of a concern not merely with the functioning of the city, but also—even primarily—with the clarification and simplification of topographical pattern and symbolic values; this sets off Nicholas's urbanism, even in his earlier years, from that of his predecessors.

A generally ignored project from the very beginning of Nicholas's pontificate may stand as an example of the change, albeit still embryonic, to which I refer. In 1447 Nicholas established a public fountain at the church and hospice of the Maddalena.[47] This project should doubtless be connected to the economic importance of the nearby market of the Piazza della Rotonda and the restoration under way at the Pantheon; it may also be regarded as a conspicuous, even emblematic example of Nicholas's consistent charitable concerns; and some political connotations may have adhered to the fountain in view of its proximity to the grand palace, then under construction, of the powerful Roman prelate Cardinal Domenico Capranica (map 2; fig. 4).

Ritually, however, the fountain should be related to the shrine of the Magdalene at S. Celso, where important relics of the saint were preserved (Burroughs 1982a, 98); Nicholas was later, of course, to show particular favor to the church, while one of the two octagonal chapels erected at the head of the Ponte S. Angelo in 1451 was dedicated to the Magdalene, presumably because of and to draw attention to the cult at S. Celso. The Magdalene was associated especially with penitence, while Nicholas's concern with the sacrament of penance and its emphasis in his Jubilee bull have been stressed by Westfall (1974a), 22–25; it is also of note that Domenico Capranica was the grand penitentiary in 1450 (Pastor 1949, 75 n.2), and that Nicholas himself showed particular favor to the office of the penitentiary and its personnel (Göller 1911, 71 no. 4; cf. note 47 above).

Penitence, of course, was a major motive for pilgrimage, and it is therefore significant that both the Maddalena and S. Celso marked points on the Via Retta/Canale di Ponte axis that connected the Leonine City with the Via Lata, the main road into Rome from the north. I have already noted Latino Orsini's refoundation, probably connected with his promotion to the cardinalate in 1448, of the church of S. Salvatore in Lauro on the Via Retta; this was surely related to if not part of Nicholas's campaign of church restoration at this time. In view of its site between S. Celso and the Maddalena along an axis privileged under Nicholas, I would suggest that this church of the Savior was related both topographically and thematically, as a shrine of redemption, with two shrines associated with penitence.

St. Mary Magdalene herself, finally, was identified at the time with Mary of Bethany, sister of Martha, who anointed Christ's feet with precious oil, incurring Martha's criticism for not serving Christ in a more active and useful way (Gnoli 1934, 298; Celletti 1966, 1078). The washing and anointing of feet, performed by Christ himself, was imitated as a symbolic gesture by popes and others; the waters of the fountain of the Maddalena, given the associations of the cult, may have acquired corresponding resonances. Certainly, references to streams of divine mercy, no doubt a familiar image, occur in Nicholas's Jubilee bull (Westfall 1974a, 23), and we may well regard Nicholas as a pioneer not only in the conspicuous provision of water to the city, but also in the ascription to it of symbolic value and ideological overtones, thereby anticipating the later development of the Roman monumental fountain, the *mostra d'acqua*.

The fountain of the Maddalena, then, is an early case of Nicholas's employment of interconnected signs of diverse but related symbolic value. On the other hand, his early concern with the Maddalena had deeper, even personal, significance. In 1447 he explicitly associated penitence with the support of ecclesiastical, charitable, and even public works projects, implying that his emphasis on building in Rome and elsewhere could readily be given a religious, even sacramental justification.[48] At the Maddalena, however, Nicholas may have undertaken a kind of anticipatory expiation, not unlike that which I have sought to discover in the contemporary frescoes of his private chapel. He may have expected criticism both of his humanist program of literary and architectural patronage, and of his concern with the external trappings of religious ceremonial, from buildings and their furnishings to precious vestments, liturgical vessels and instruments, incense and oil. As far as these were concerned, Nicholas was himself open to the chiding suffered by the Magdalene— or her double—in the well-known story, and though Christ defended Mary of Bethany, the issue remained, as we have seen, and left its mark in the fabric of Nicholan Rome.

The Politics of Neighborhood Development: The Case of Trevi

In 1453 began the history of that most celebrated of aqueous monuments, the Trevi Fountain (map 2). The conduits of the Acqua Vergine were restored and a new outlet built, the appearance of which is known from an early woodcut (fig. 33; see Spezzaferro 1973, 16 n.5, 17; Westfall 1974a, 106). It was quite simple, certainly in contrast to its elaborate successors, and it carried the arms of Nicholas V and an inscription dating the project and ascribing the credit for it to the pope. Though further restoration occurred under Sixtus IV, the physical structure of the outlet was apparently left essentially unchanged until the major rebuilding carried out in the seventeenth century (Pinto 1986, 28–37). Nicholas's project has attracted the attention of scholars for two main reasons, the probable involvement of Alberti in the restoration of the only ancient aqueduct that still supplied water to the city, and the concern apparent in the siting of the fountain to encourage settlement in an area distant from the river, the major source of water in late medieval Rome, and peripheral to the *abitato* as it existed at mid-quattrocento.

As with other Nicholan projects, we must be careful not to neglect the degree of continuity with at least the more recent past. In his *De varietate fortunae* (published in 1448 with a dedication to Nicholas, but started as early as 1431), Poggio Bracciolini noted that the Acqua Vergine was the only functioning ancient aqueduct (Valentini and Zucchetti 1953, 235), while a clause of the 1452 statutes of the *maestri di strada* enjoins those officals to inspect the aqueduct regularly and to see to its upkeep.[49] The survival of the aqueduct was largely due to the fact that its channels ran underground as it neared the city, and so were less susceptible to hostile action on the part of forces besieging the city and ravaging its environs. It is likely, then, that water was available from the aqueduct in the Trevi area before 1453; certainly, though Trevi was not one of the more densely populated *rioni*, it was far from depopulated, not least perhaps because of the proximity of the Colonna palace and the consequent probable attractiveness of the area to immigrants from rural areas controlled by the Colonna. Further, the sums dispensed by Nicholas on the project indicate a campaign of repair rather than elaborate reconstruction; after all, the major focus of the pope's concerns in 1453 was the ambitious building project at the Vatican (Müntz 1978, 139).[50]

The repair, however minor, of the aqueduct doubtless resonated with contemporary antiquarian interests. Any humanist, especially if at all concerned with questions of technology and public administration in ancient Rome, will have been familiar with the text of Frontinus's treatise on aqueducts, a major manuscript of which was discovered at Monte Cassino by Poggio (Valentini and Zucchetti 1953, 237f.; Weiss 1969, 64). Alberti's interest in ancient hydraulic engineering is clear from the pages of the *De re aedificatoria*, as is his apparent technical expertise. Of particular relevance is the discussion of the technical problems associated with subterranean conduits; this may well reflect studies carried out on the Acqua Vergine in connection with a restoration project (Alberti 1966a, 2:924–933 [X.vii]). Elsewhere, moreover, Alberti notes the use of surveying instruments to trace the course of an evidently subterranean aqueduct (ibid., 922–925).[51] If these references circumstantially link Alberti with Nicholas's project, the design of the outlet is surely such as to exclude Alberti from any involvement with its design; it corresponds fully, however, to the simple and dignified *all'antica* aspect of the inscriptions placed by Nicholas on buildings restored by him throughout Rome.

If it is correct to ascribe urbanistic significance to the Nicholan aqueduct project (Spezzaferro 1973, 17; Castagnoli et al. 1958, 351), this was surely linked with a contemporary restoration campaign at the nearby church of SS. Apostoli, one of the most important churches of Rome. In 1453 extensive work was carried out on the roof of the church; the project cost over twice as much as the work on the aqueduct, at least according to the figures entered in the papal ledger of that year (Müntz 1878, 134, 140).[52] Since all building projects under Nicholas were coordinated and administered by Nello da Bologna and his staff, there is an a priori presumption that two contemporary projects in close topographical proximity were connected; this seems corroborated by the implications of the date of the projects and the probable involvement of prominent residents of the quarter.

The church of SS. Apostoli was held *in commendam* by the Greek prelate and intellectual Cardinal Bessarion. Bessarion had been created cardinal in 1439; SS. Apostoli was his original *titulus* (Coccia 1973, esp. 378–382; L. Labowsky in *DBI* 9 [1967]: 686–696).After his promotion to cardinal bishop of Tuscolo in 1449, Bessarion retained SS. Apostoli, while the adjacent palace continued to serve as his residence in Rome (Magnuson 1958, 312f.). In 1446 he had convened a council of the Basilian order, the Greek monastic order to which he belonged, in the church; this led to the publication of a compendium of the rule of St. Basil, largely written by Bessarion himself. In 1450 SS. Apostoli served as the chief site for the festivities celebrating the canonization of S. Bernardino of Siena, the great preacher and proponent of observant Franciscanism (Della Tuccia 1872, 214); Bessarion had been a member of the commission appointed by Nicholas to investigate the life and posthumous miracles of the saint prior to his canonization, an event to which Nicholas attached the greatest importance (Arasse 1977, 277).[53] It is interesting that Nicholas also appointed Bessarion to the commission set up to investigate and identify the putative remains of another saint revered by Nicholas, St. Lawrence (Möhler 1923, 260). It appears, then, that the relationship between the pope and the cardinal was close; this was perhaps publicly displayed during the ceremonies at SS. Apostoli in 1450.

Also in 1450 Nicholas appointed Bessarion as the papal legate in Bologna. This was a mission of the utmost importance and difficulty, for Bologna was one of the chief cities of the papal states, had long suffered from internal factionalism, and was especially dear to Nicholas, its former bishop. Then to Bessarion's other responsibilities Nicholas added the surveillance of Stefano Porcari, whose increasingly fiery rhetoric Nicholas attempted to defuse by sending him to a comfortable and dignified exile in Bologna. As it turned out, Porcari was able to give Bessarion the slip, with fatal results, but otherwise the cardinal proved an able administrator in Bologna, where he pacified the warring factions, largely through reliance on the strongest of the factions, that of Sante Bentivoglio. In addition, he devoted considerable attention to the revival of the ancient and famous university of Bologna; the latter's statutes were issued in a new edition, buildings were restored and expanded, and professors appointed, among them Bessarion's own close associate and head of household, Niccolò Perotti (*DBI* 9:686–696).[54]

Though kept busy and far from Rome by the various responsibilities entrusted to him by Nicholas, Bessarion did not neglect SS. Apostoli. By 1454 he had carried out a reform of the clergy of the church, as is described in detail in a document of that year that also includes a history of the building and its major cults, those of the apostles St. Philip and St. James. The author, Gerardo Maffei da Volterra, emphasizes (incorrectly) the Constantinian origin of the church and its status as one of the leading pilgrimage basilicas of the city. Maffei, who served as Bessarion's vicar at SS. Apostoli during the cardinal's absence, must have been involved also in the physical restoration of the church that occurred in 1453; as so often in Nicholan Rome, architectural restoration and moral reform went hand in hand.[55]

Even if Maffei was wrong about the foundation of the church, which he evidently assimilated to Constantine's church of the Apostles in Constantinople, SS. Apostoli was an ancient and important church;[56] clearly, by 1453 it was also in need of major repairs. The question arises why these repairs, if not also the reform of the clergy, waited until 1453, when so many of the churches of the city had received well-publicized restoration in preparation for the Jubilee of 1449–50. A detailed account of architectural projects by then undertaken by Nicholas, including church restorations, is contained for example in the encomium of the pope produced in 1451–52 by Michele Canensi (Miglio 1975, 230f.); had work been carried out on SS. Apostoli, we might expect to find explicit mention made of it here.[57]

The question of the date of the work at SS. Apostoli may be connected, however, to the similar question of the date of the provision of water—or rather the conspicuous commemoration of that provision—at the Piazza di Trevi, a short distance from the church. Both projects would surely have been regarded, whatever the truth of the matter, by contemporary Romans as examples of an understanding or even alliance between the pope and the most important resident of the area, Cardinal Prospero Colonna, whose palace adjoined that of Bessarion on the Piazza SS. Apostoli. Indeed, the last pope to bestow favor on SS. Apostoli was Prospero's kinsman, Martin V, whose support of his own family and of people and places associated with them almost inevitably elicited the vehement reaction of Eugenius IV, who set in motion a terrible campaign against the Colonna and their allies.[58] Nicholas pursued a policy of balance in his relations with the Colonna and Orsini alike, and in the early years of his pontificate he restored to Prospero and his clan first the properties and rights stripped from them by Eugenius, and subseqently the particular right to fortify their strongholds, which had been largely destroyed by Eugenius's troops (Tomassetti 1979, 3:602f.).[59] It is true that Nicholas's emphasis on the Vatican, as Paul observed, placed him somewhat within the topographical sphere of the Orsini; on the other hand, Nicholas matched this emphasis, to a degree, with attention to the papal residence at S. Maria Maggiore and a further residence at S. Pudenziana (map 2; fig. 35), to which I will return. There seems, therefore, prima facie every reason to expect a public demonstration of the reconciliation between the papacy and the Colonna in the period of the bulls issued by Nicholas on their behalf, and in any case by the opening of the Jubilee of 1449–50.

The key to the problem may lie in the source of the money used to pay for the restoration work on SS. Apostoli. As the papal accounts make clear, the very considerable amount of 600 ducats was made available for this purpose; the pope's apparent generosity, however, cost him and his treasury nothing, for the entire sum constituted the proceeds of a sale of a house that had belonged to one Angelo di Masso, executed in 1453 as a leading fellow conspirator of Stefano Porcari. The house, in turn, was sold to Antonio Colonna, Prince of Salerno, who was Prospero's brother; the effective benefactor of SS. Apostoli, then, was Antonio Colonna, whose purchase of Angelo's house can hardly have occurred as a simple transaction on the open market. Indeed, among the responsibilities entrusted to Nello da Bologna by Nicholas was the disposal of property confiscated from the Porcarian conspirators.[60] In this case, the disposal of the house was perhaps a particularly delicate matter, for it had some notoriety as the site, according to some accounts, of Porcari's discovery; he was found hiding in a chest on which some of the ladies of the house were sitting (Pastor 1949, 228). Moreover, Angelo di Masso himself was rumored to be an illegitimate son of Pope Martin V, and so a close relative and presumed ally of Prospero and Antonio Colonna (ibid., 512).[61]

The house itself, as the documents show, was large and rambling, indicating the wealth of the original owner, as well perhaps as the truth of the rumors about his parentage. It stood in the Rione Trevi, apparently in the vicinity of the Piazza Colonna; if the work of 1453 on the Acqua Vergine indeed fostered the development of the neighborhood, Antonio Colonna's investment may well have turned out, whether or not it was entirely voluntary, as a very successful one. More importantly, however, the transfer of ownership of the house, like the work on the aqueduct and the church, looks—and must in 1453 have looked—like a clear indication of a rapprochement of the pope and the Colonna, or, in other words, like an expression on the part of the pope of his gratitude to the Colonna for loyalty during the Porcari affair, and of his expectation of their future cooperation. For though Nicholas let the arms of the commune appear alongside the papal arms on the fountain of the Piazza di Trevi (fig. 33), yet he perhaps had already determined to set a greater distance between his administration and the Roman patriciate; if so, he would have been well advised to foster other alliances.

Alberti's probable involvement with the restoration of the Acqua Vergine now comes to acquire distinct political overtones. For this may well have been, or at least been begun as, a Colonna project, perhaps before 1453; it is possibly significant that the church of S. Maria in Via, not far from the Piazza di Trevi and boasting a cult of the Virgin centered on a miracle-working flow of water, became a parish church in 1452 (Armellini 1881–82, 119). This may have been in response to actual or expected population increase generated by the improvement of the water supply to the area. The workman in charge of the aqueduct project was a certain Pietro da Colonna, who is otherwise not mentioned in the papal ledgers. His name implies that he hailed from the homonymous stronghold of the Colonna clan in the Alban Hills (map 3); he was, accordingly, probably a Colonna retainer, and may well have been involved in building projects known to have been undertaken by Cardinal Prospero in Rome (see note 50). It is likely, then, that Nicholas's subvention paid for the completion of the project and for the commemorative fountain, a characteristic introduction of a new sign into the urban matrix to mark a project absorbed into and adapted by papal urban policy and architectural patronage.

Alberti's connections in the Colonna quarter were by no means, however, only with Prospero Colonna, though these were important. Gerardo Maffei, Bessarion's vicar at SS. Apostoli, was also implicated in the creation of the Piazza S. Celso; in addition, he served as Alberti's lawyer in the two pieces of legal business transacted, as I have noted, in Spinelli's premises in Ponte. He represents, then, a further link between Alberti and the improvement project in the area of the Canale di Ponte. Maffei's activity no doubt brought him into contact not only with the ubiquitous Nello da Bologna, but also with Nello's assistant, Francesco del Borgo, whose probable role as the designer of the Palazzo Venezia for Cardinal Pietro Barbo (later Paul II) I have noted (Frommel 1984, 129–138). Pietro Barbo, in turn, was allied with the strongly philo-Venetian Bessarion, two of whose *servitores* appeared with Alberti and Gerardo Maffei in Spinelli's bank in April 1450 to be sworn in as witnesses of the appointment of a procurator to look after Alberti's affairs in Rome during his impending absence; one of them was an *accolitus* of the pope and a native of Volterra, the small Tuscan town that was also the home of Gerardo Maffei (Parronchi 1972, 231).[62] And to complete this picture of alliances and movement between the circle of Bessarion and Pietro Barbo at one end of the *abitato* and that of Spinelli and perhaps Nello at the other, I note the confluence of intellectual interests between Francesco del Borgo, with his fine Archimedes manuscript; Niccolò Perotti, Bessarion's right-hand man, who was deeply interested in ancient methods of surveying and representing topographical features, and who took delivery in 1469 of a splendid illuminated manuscript of Ptolemy, prepared in the workshop of Vespasiano da Bisticci, and including important city views (including one of Rome) by Piero del Massaio;[63] and Alberti, whose studies both of aspects of ancient engineering and of surveying and cartography I have mentioned.

We find Alberti, then, deeply implicated with two evidently related cases of urban development at either end not only of the topographical structure of the city but also of its political spectrum, since the Canale di Ponte was clearly in the Orsini sphere, for all its associations with Tuscan bankers, and the Piazza SS. Apostoli and Trevi in that of the Colonna. We find also, moreover, that Gerardo Maffei, Nello da Bologna, and Francesco del Borgo also moved with apparent ease between the two milieus. But the relatively late date of Nicholas's association with the developments in and near Trevi suggests that this required a marked shift in his policies, at least in terms of the kinds of public perception that he hoped to create. It raises questions, further, about Alberti's career and affiliations under Nicholas that may affect the interpretation and even the dating of his great treatise on architecture.

Roma caput
Attamen ipsa

Aeternum qui se aut
Bullam esse sequi ex

Ecce quam bonum et
quam iocundum
habitare fratres
in Vnum

Lurcones scurra nebu
lones Vobis ego

Che fate qui a torno buffoni
Non conoscete la vera effigie mia
Io son pasquin cvl molesche dio vi dia
vi possa venir i strangogliani

ANT. LAFRERI FORMIS ROMAE ꝏ D L

1. The statue of "Pasquino," with attached
lampoons and slogans. The statue still
stands in a small piazza on the Via del Papa,
close to the Piazza Navona. Engraving by
Nicholas Beatrizet from the *Speculum
Romanae Magnificentiae*, an atlas of prints,
of which several slightly diverse exemplars
exist, assembled in the sixteenth century by
the dealer and publisher Antonio Lafréri.
Courtesy of Avery Architectural and Fine
Arts Library, Columbia University in the
City of New York (Duke of Crawford's *Speculum Romanae Magnificentiae*, no. 449).

Map 1. City of Rome showing ward boundaries (Rioni), high ground, and major thoroughfares.

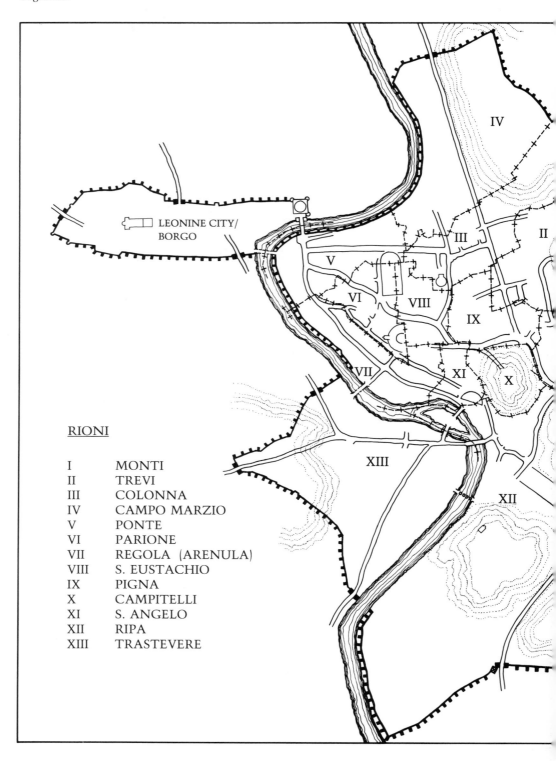

LEONINE CITY/
BORGO

IV

III

II

V

VI

VIII

IX

VII

XI

X

XIII

XII

RIONI

I	MONTI
II	TREVI
III	COLONNA
IV	CAMPO MARZIO
V	PONTE
VI	PARIONE
VII	REGOLA (ARENULA)
VIII	S. EUSTACHIO
IX	PIGNA
X	CAMPITELLI
XI	S. ANGELO
XII	RIPA
XIII	TRASTEVERE

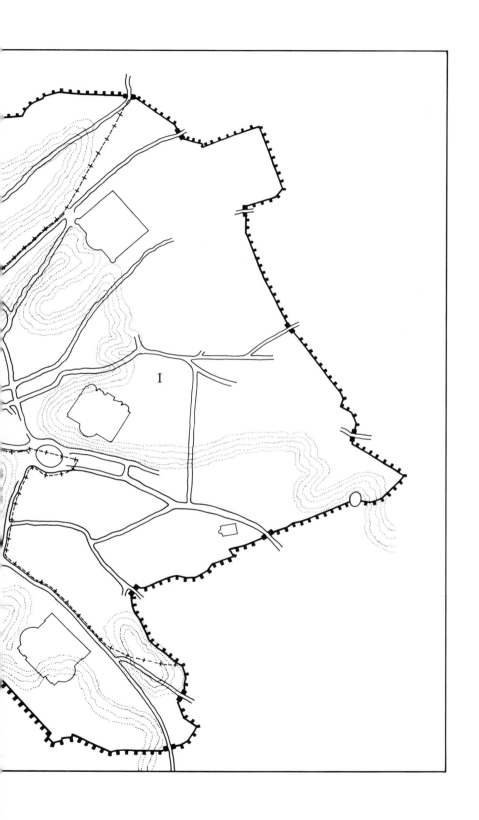

Map 2. City of Rome in the fifteenth century indicating major shrines, thoroughfares, aristocratic and curial palaces, and patrician compounds.

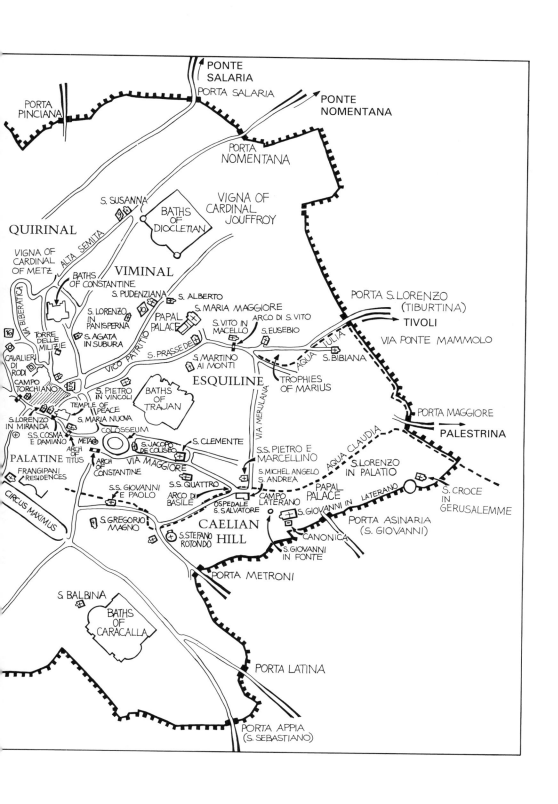

2. Giambattista Piranesi, map of ancient
Rome, modeled on the ancient marble plan
of the city and imitating its fragmentary
condition. From his *Antichità Romane*, vol.
1 (Rome, 1756), fig. 2. Courtesy of Avery
Architectural and Fine Arts Library, Columbia University in the City of New York.

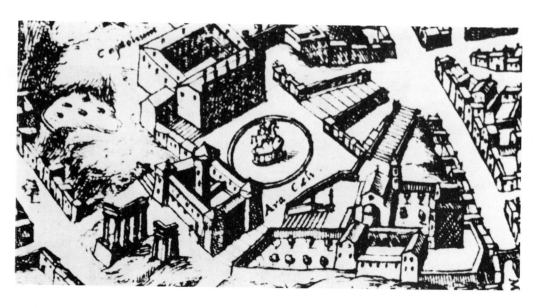

3. The Campidoglio in 1577. Detail of
Etienne Dupérac, *View of Rome*, 1577. Reproduced by permission of the British Library (BL. Maps 23805[8]).

4. The Palazzo Capranica in the late
nineteenth century, facade on the Piazza di
S. Maria in Aquiro. Reproduced by permission of Alinari/Art Resource.

5. Palazzo Venezia (originally Palazzo S.
Marco), Rome, detail: inscribed guelph windows of piano nobile. Reproduced by permission of the Conway Library, Courtauld
Institute of Art, London.

6. Palazzetto Venezia, courtyard, c. 1465,
detail. Octagonal piers, favored in fifteenth-
century Rome, are used here in a conspicuously extravagant building (note the
ornate and varied capitals), perhaps constituting a vernacular order in contrast to the
monumental classicism of the main courtyard (see fig. 7). Reproduced by permission
of Alinari/Art Resource.

7. Palazzo Venezia (originally Palazzo S. Marco), courtyard, detail. The massive arcading and superimposed orders quote the Colosseum. Reproduced by permission of Alinari/Art Resource. (*Below.*)

8. Palazzo Massimo alle Colonne, Rome, 1534, facade. The doric columns of the portico combine an allusion to the traditional Roman street portico (cf. fig. 9) with Vitruvian and emblematic resonances characteristic of the visual culture of the early-sixteenth-century elite of Rome. The curve of the facade marks the line of the Via del Papa. Reproduced by permission of Alinari/Art Resource. (*Opposite, top.*)

9. Casa Bonadies, Via del Banco di Snato Spirito, detail. The portico of this late medieval patrician house combines *spolia* (fragments of ancient entablature) and fine early or mid-quattrocento capitals. The house marks the western edge of the medieval Canale di Ponte, widened under Julius II. The lions' heads suggest the public display of communalist sympathies, in spite of the proximity to the Castel S. Angelo. Photo author.

10. Palazzo Rucellai, Florence, facade with detail of window. Ornament of various kinds is adjusted to the overall architectural effect: the windows, classicizing *bifore* of medieval type, are ornamented with the Medicean emblem of triple rings; more prominent are the Rucellai arms on a sculpted shield and the sail emblem of the patron. Among more general references to ancient Rome, the superimposed orders allude to the Colosseum. Reproduced by permission of Alinari/Art Resource.

11. Palazzo della Cancelleria, facade and southwest corner. The palace is seen from the direction of the Campo de' Fiori with the Via de' Pellegrini to the left. The corner is marked by a vestigial tower and the patron's arms. Reproduced by permission of Alinari/Art Resource.

12. Scenes from the visit to Rome (1452) of Emperor Frederick III on a mid-fifteenth-century Florentine cassone panel. From the left, in succession, Nicholas V crowns Frederick in front of St. Peter's (note the papal arms on the palace portal); the pope and emperor ride in procession through the Borgo, the pope enframed in the columns of S. Maria in Traspontina; the emperor dubs knights on the Ponte S. Angelo. Courtesy of Worcester Art Museum, Worcester, Massachusetts.

13. S. Stefano Rotondo (S. Stefano sul Celio). The circular aspect of this fifth-century church was enhanced under Nicholas V by the demolition of an outer ambulatory. Reproduced by permission of Alinari/Art Resource.

14. S. Stefano Rotondo, details. Outer portal with inscribed insignia and initials of Nicholas V (*opposite, bottom*). Double portal between vestibule and nave with Nicholan inscription recording the restoration of the church (*below*). Courtesy of the Istituto Centrale per il Catalogo e la Documentazione, Rome.

15. Marten van Heemskerck, Panorama of
Rome from the Campidoglio, c. 1535. The
Colosseum and Forum are to the left, with
the Lateran in the background; the small,
cylindrical church of S. Teodoro, the hospital of S. Maria della Consolazione, and the
Palatine hill appear in the center; further to
the right are S. Anastasia, the arch of Janus,
and S. Giorgio in Velabro. Courtesy of the
Kupferstichkabinett, Staatliche Museen,
Preussischer Kulturbesitz, Berlin.

16. Chapel of Nicholas V, Vatican palace:
general view. Reproduced by permission of
Alinari/Art Resource.

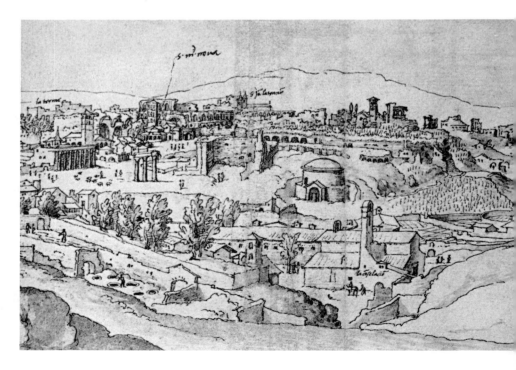

18. Fra Angelico, *Pope Sixtus II Consigns the Treasure of the Church to St. Lawrence*, Chapel of Nicholas V, Vatican palace. Reproduced by permission of Alinari/Art Resource.

19. Fra Angelico, *St. Stephen Preaching,*
Trial of St. Stephen, Chapel of Nicholas V,
Vatican palace. Reproduced by permission
of Alinari/Art Resource.

21. Fra Angelico, *St. Lawrence Distributes Treasure to the Poor of Rome*, Chapel of Nicholas V, Vatican palace. Reproduced by permission of Alinari/Art Resource.

22. Fra Angelico, *Expulsion of St. Stephen from Jerusalem, Martyrdom of St. Stephen*, Chapel of Nicholas V, Vatican palace. Reproduced by permission of Alinari/Art Resource.

23. Filippo Lippi, *Martyrdom of St. Stephen*, Prato cathedral (formerly Abbey of S. Stefano). The scene is painted on two walls meeting at the right rear corner of the choir chapel. The men casting stones seem physically to surround the figure of the kneeling saint and the action invades the beholder's space. Courtesy of Soprintendenza per i Beni Artistici e Storici, Florence.

24. Fra Angelico, *Martyrdom of St. Stephen*, detail. Reproduced by permission of Alinari/Art Resource.

25. Fra Angelico, *The Deposition from the Cross*, S. Marco Museum, Florence. Reproduced by permission of Alinari/Art Resource.

26. Raphael, *Disputa*, Stanza della Segnatura, Vatican palace. Reproduced by permission of Alinari/Art Resource.

27. Raphael, *Disputa*, detail of left corner. Reproduced by permission of Alinari/Art Resource.

28. Raphael, *School of Athens*, Stanza della
Segnatura, Vatican palace. Reproduced by
permission of Alinari/Art Resource.

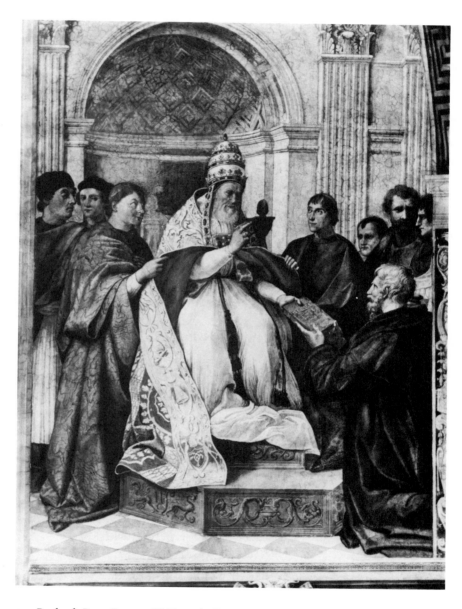

29. Raphael, *Pope Gregory IX Gives the De-cretals to a Jurist*, Stanza della Segnatura, Vatican palace. Reproduced by permission of Alinari/Art Resource.

30. The apparition of the archangel Michael
to Pope Gregory the Great at the Castel S.
Angelo. Note the insignia of Nicholas V
prominent on the castle. Miniature from the
Sforza Book of Hours, c. 1490. Courtesy
British Library Manuscript Division (Add.
Ms., fol. 236r).

31. S. Maria della Febbre and the Vatican obelisk: drawing by Giovanni Antonio Dosio (Ehrle and Egger 1911, no. 39). Courtesy of Avery Architectural and Fine Arts Library, Columbia University in the City of New York.

MCC
CC·
LVI
III
ADI
P·
OT
VB
RI
O

LORIOSE

tem dei su

curfu cum in

natur ex fid

stabilitate fe

nunc expect

quo adufq

in indicium

ra per excell

ultima & p

pere ad æ in

missionem debuta eius deos suos preferunt filii

32. Rome as the Heavenly Jerusalem, miniature by Niccolò Polani in a manuscript (1459) of St. Augustine, *City of God*. To the left the Castel S. Angelo, with large guelph windows and one of Nicholas's circular towers in the foreground, is flanked by the Pantheon and helicoidal towers emblematic of Rome. The Borgo and Vatican basilica, on the right, are marked by slender towers. Towered baronial strongholds loom in the background, but communal buildings are absent (cf. fig. 43). Note the suggestion of the landscape setting of Rome. Courtesy Bibliothèque Ste.-Geneviève, Paris (Cod. 218, fol. 2r).

33. The Trevi Fountain as built under Nicholas V. The unusually lengthy inscription is surmounted by the arms of the pope and the commune; the lion heads of the central outlet may also refer to the heraldic beast of the medieval commune. Woodcut from Federico Franzini, *Descrittione di Roma antica e moderna* (Rome 1643), 744. Courtesy of Avery Architectural and Fine Arts Library, Columbia University in the City of New York.

FABRIANO.
Lieu de l'Etat de L'EGLISE il est
Dans la Marche d'Ancone

Se vend
A AMSTERDAM
Chez PIERRE MORTIER
Avec Privilege

J. BLAEU Excud.

34. Fabriano in the seventeenth century. The triangular Piazza Maggiore, centered on a monumental fountain, is in the center with S. Francesco and the papal palace to the left; the cathedral and the large Ospedale di S. Maria del Buon Gesù, with its courtyard and fountain, are to the right. At the foot of the Piazza Maggiore appears the Palazzo del Podestà through which a vaulted passage leads to the market square and the industrial quarters clustered around the river. From Joan Blaeu, *Nieuw vermeerded en verbeterd groot stedeboek van geheel Italie* (4 vols., s'Graavenhage 1724), vol. 2, De Kerkelyke Staat, fig. 27. (First edition, in three volumes, Amsterdam 1663.) Courtesy of Map Division, The New York Public Library, Astor, Lenox and Tilden Foundations.

35. The quarter of Monti in a sixteenth-century panorama (1562) attributed to Giovanni Antonio Dosio. The Campidoglio and Forum are at top center; beginning at the Forum the Via Subura runs past the churches of S. Pietro in Vincoli and S. Prassede through the Arco di S. Vito to the Porta Maggiore at lower left. At the center appears S. Maria Maggiore with the L-shaped papal palace; behind it, at the foot of the hill, are the Vicus Patritius and S. Pudenziana. The Column of Trajan and the Piazza SS. Apostoli mark the edge of the *abitato* at top right; above them on the Quirinal hill are the Baths of Constantine and the "Tower of Maecenas." Courtesy of the Royal Institute of British Architects, British Architectural Library, Drawings Collection (Palladio VII/7).

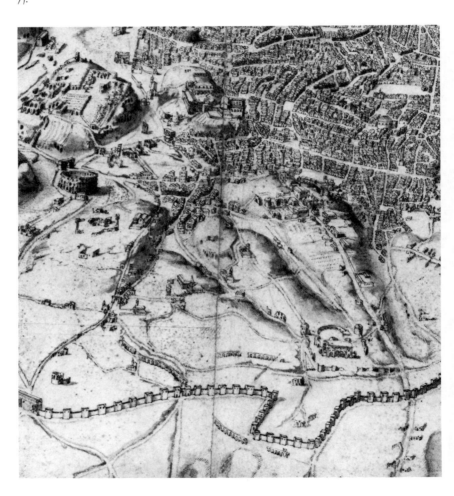

36. Rome in the form of a lion: miniature
in a thirteenth-century vernacular manuscript of the *Liber ystoriarum Romanorum*.
Courtesy of the Handschriftenabteilung,
Staats- und Universitätsbibliothek Hamburg (Cod. 151 in scrin., fol. 107v).

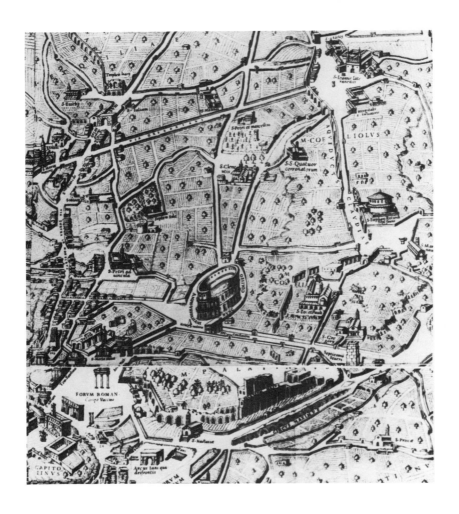

37. Monti and the Forum area in the *Great View of Rome* by Mario Cartaro (1576). The Campo Laterano is at upper left with the Sancta Sanctorum in the background and the hospital facing the basilica across the square; S. Stefano Rotondo and SS. Giovanni e Paolo are on the high ground to the right (Caelian hill). The Via Maggiore runs from the Campo Laterano past the church of S. Clemente to the Colosseum; the route then passes through the arches of Titus and Septimius Severus to the Campidoglio. To the left the Via Subura runs from the Forum and the towers of the Campo Turclani toward S. Prassede, S. Maria Maggiore, and the Arco di S. Vito. Beyond the arch are the Trofei di Mario and S. Eusebio. Courtesy of the Biblioteca Apostolica Vaticana (Cod. Barberini X.l.20–23).

38. Panoramic view of the Forum by Martin van Heemskerck (c. 1535). The view is taken from the rear of the Senator's Palace. At the extreme left the reclining statue of Marforio faces the arch of Septimius Severus; beyond and partly concealed by the arch appear the gable of S. Adriano and the towers of the Campo Turclani; to the right, beyond ruined temples, appear the Colosseum, the bell tower of S. Maria Nuova, and the arch of Titus incorporated into medieval fortifications. Courtesy of the Kupferstichkabinett, Staatliche Museen, Preussischer Kulturbesitz, Berlin.

39. The Senator's Palace from the Forum in
a view by Marten van Heemskerck (c. 1535).
Restoration has exposed elements of the
facade of the ancient Tabularium, but a tower built by Nicholas V still marks the corner
on the right. Next to this the Via Sacra, having passed through the half-buried arch of
Septimius Severus, ascends the Capitoline
steps. Atop the hill to the right sits the
church of S. Maria in Aracoeli beyond the
obelisk and palm tree. Courtesy of the Kupferstichkabinett, Staatliche Museen, Preussischer Kulturbesitz, Berlin.

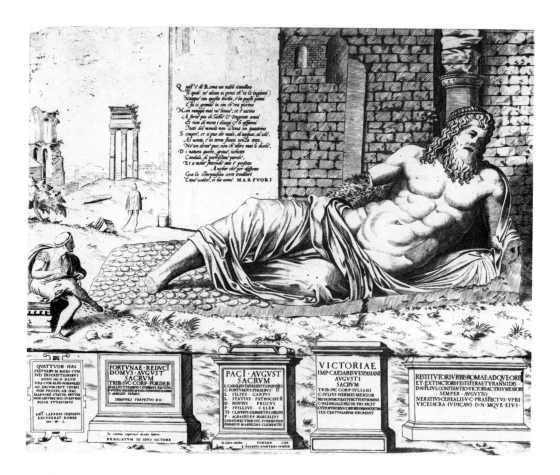

40. The statue of "Marforio," engraved by Nicholas Beatrizet. The statue is shown in its original position (the position it had until 1585) near the arch of Septimius Severus, as the inscription notes. Courtesy of Avery Architectural and Fine Arts Library, Columbia University in the City of New York (Duke of Crawford's *Speculum Romanae Magnificentiae*, no. 443).

41. Panorama of Rome from the Quirinal hill by Martin van Heemskerck (c. 1535). The city is framed between the "Frontispiece of Nero" on the right and the Torre Milizie on the left. The Campidoglio appears slightly to the right of the latter, and the Vatican to the left of the former. The Palazzo S. Marco (left center) and the Pantheon dominate the *abitato*. Courtesy of the Kupferstichkabinett, Staatliche Museen, Preussischer Kulturbesitz, Berlin.

fulli Roma

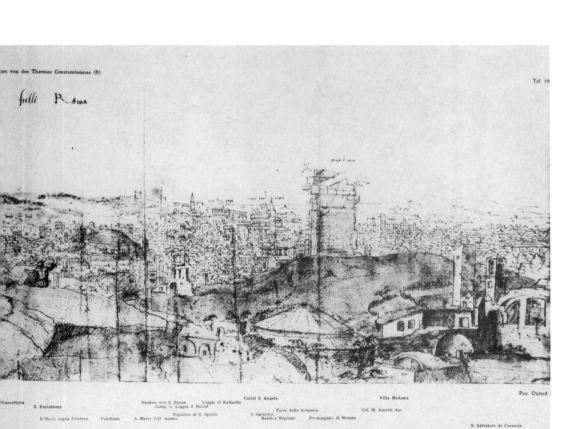

plays d sua

Cancelleria		Neubau von S. Pietro	Loggie di Raffaello	Castel S. Angelo		Villa Madama	
	S. Pantaleone	Camp. u. Loggia d Bened			Torre della Scimmia	Col. M. Aurelii Ant	
	S. Maria sopra Minerva	Pantheon	S. Maria dell' Anima	Ospedale di S. Spirito	S. Agostino	Frontispizio di Nerone	
					Basilica Neptuni		S. Salvatore de Cornutis

— Thermae Constantinianae —   — Thermae Constantinianae —

42. Sassetta, *The Wish of the Young St. Francis to Become a Soldier.* The image of the Church militant, represented by its walls and carrying banners marked with the cross, floats in the sky. Courtesy of the National Gallery, London.

NTEREA.C
GOTHOR\
one agentium fe
impetu magne
useuersionem e
torumqz cultore
paganos uocam
gionem referre c
usa amarius der
re ceperunt. Vi
z elo domus der
phemias uel erre
dei scribere institui. Quod opus per aliquot annos

43. Rome as the Heavenly Jerusalem in a
miniature (1456) by Giacomo da Fabriano
from a manuscript of St. Augustine, *City of
God*. Courtesy of the Biblioteca Apostolica
Vaticana (Cod. Reg. Lat. 1882, fol. 2r).

44. Antonio Averlino (Filarete), plan of the ideal city of Sforzinda, from his architectural treatise of c. 1461. Reproduced by permission of Yale University Press from *A Treatise on Architecture* (translated with an introduction and notes by John R. Spencer), vol. 2, fol. 43r. © 1965 Yale University Press.

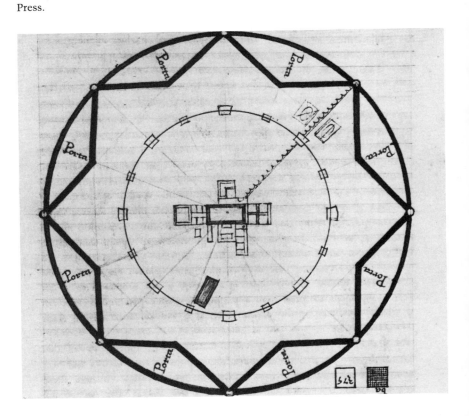

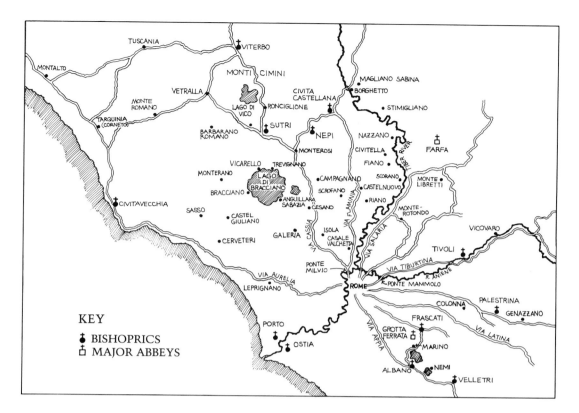

Map 3. The ecclesiastical province of the
Patrimonium sancti Petri and adjoining
areas of the papal states.

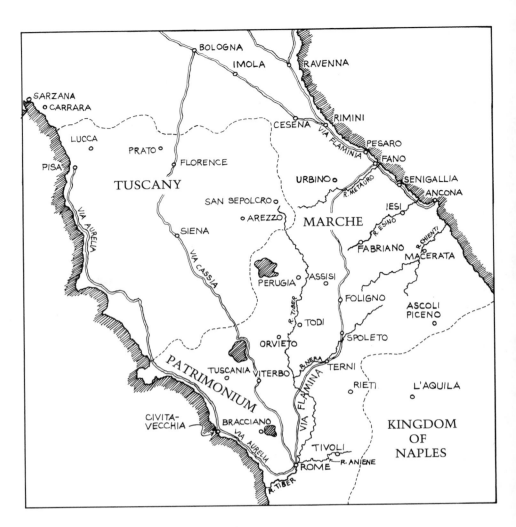

Map 4. Central Italy and the northern papal states.

45. Arch of Augustus, Rimini. The inscription, which refers to the restoration of the great routes of Italy, is clearly visible, as are the remains of the towers to either side of the arch and the medieval crenellations above. Reproduced by permission of Alinari/Art Resource. (*Opposite, top.*)

46. Facade of the Tempio Malatestiano
(church of S. Francesco), Rimini. The frieze
around the base repeats the elephant
emblem of Sigismondo; the date 1450
appears in the great inscription recording
the refoundation of the building by Sigismondo. Reproduced by permission of
Alinari/Art Resource.

47. Piero della Francesca, *Sigismondo Malatesta Reveres St. Sigismund*. Fresco, Chapel of the Relics (formerly sacristy of adjacent Chapel of St. Sigismund), Tempio Malatestiano, Rimini. The Rocca of Rimini (Castel Sismondo) appears in a circular frame to the right, above Sigismondo's dogs. Reproduced by permission of Alinari/Art Resource.

48. Marble elephants and medallion of Sigismondo from the Tempio Malatestiano. Two pairs of dark marble elephants support the piers flanking the entrance of the Chapel of St. Sigismund, in close proximity to the tomb of Sigismondo. Reproduced by permission of Alinari/Art Resource.

49. The Ripa Grande and surrounding districts from the *Great View of Rome* by Mario Cartaro (1576). The harbor of Ripa Grande, with clustered ships, appears at center. Below it the church of S. Francesco a Ripa stands in open territory (this detail was surely inaccurate) near the Porta Portese. S. Maria in Trastevere appears at lower left, the island and the theater of Marcellus at center left. The Ponte S. Maria, to the right of the island, is shown in operation, not long before the cataclysm that transformed it into the modern Ponte Rotto. Courtesy of the Biblioteca Apostolica Vaticana (Cod. Barberini X.l.20–23).

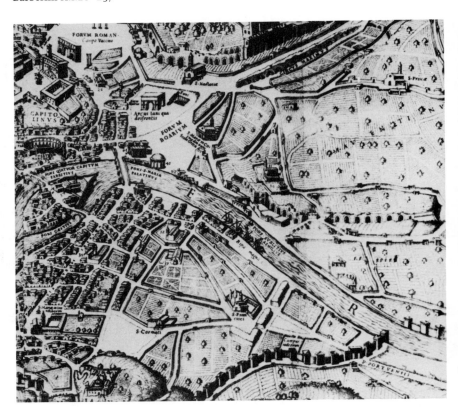

Middlemen: Lines of Contact, Mutual Advantage, and Command

The Spider in the Web: Nello da Bologna and the Household Administration

Nicholas V's pontificate marks an important phase in the process of domestication (the term is Arnold Esch's) of the Roman population, and the absorption of its municipal institutions into an absolutist or at least protoabsolutist framework (Esch 1971, 2). This is the long view: close study of Nicholan Rome reveals a remarkable predominance of ad hoc expedients, involving both papal officials and members of the local political class, whose crucial role in the government of the city and region and in the furtherance of papal policies, certainly until 1453, I have already had occasion to note. And there is a conspicuous heterogeneity in terms of background, official position, and professional or social status among the individuals who came to mediate between the pope and his closest advisers and the various groups affected by different aspects of papal rule or policy, or implicated in their implementation. Such evidence as exists of steps taken toward the formalization or institutionalization of administrative patterns indicates that these were partial and hesitant at best, as was perhaps inevitable in view of the necessarily temporary nature of the regime. This is particularly the case in the sphere of Nicholas's building campaigns, whose disparate personnel will be studied at length later in this chapter.

On the other hand, it is clear that for the most part Nicholas's administrative corps functioned well: the Jubilee was or at least could be claimed to be a success; a wide range of restoration and construction projects were carried out, though more were commenced than completed; and the city population remained largely acquiescent as not only its institutions but also its physical environment began to carry the stamp of new and ultimately implacable political realities and social relations. From 1450, at latest, almost every aspect of papal rule in the city itself and its hinterland was in the hands of a single individual, who managed the various responsibilities allotted to him and the personnel under his command with great skill and resourcefulness. This was Nello di Bartolomeo da Bologna, whose crucial role in Nicholas's pontificate has escaped all previous students of the period, in spite of the fact that Nello constituted, as Nicholas recognized, the chief and irreplaceable intermediary between the ambitions and ideas of the pope and their realization, not least in the sphere of the building campaigns.[1] To borrow, once again, Alberti's metaphor of the successful head of a household (Alberti 1969, 263), Nello was established spiderlike at the center of radiating lines of communication that reached into widely divergent spheres of operation and policy; his was a reactive yet, at the same time and increasingly, a controlling role.

Nello's invisibility to modern scholars may reflect the historical individual's capacity to blend into his surroundings, for he largely escaped the notice of contemporary chroniclers also. In diplomatic correspondence emanating from the Rome of Nicholas V I have found no mention of him, at least in the reports of the greater powers of the peninsula. On the other hand, such correspondence concentrates on matters of direct political importance, to the exclusion, for instance, even of Nicholas's building programs (whatever the political significance ascribed to these by modern authors).[2] Nor do contemporary humanists seem to have found Nello worthy of mention.[3]

Even the name, Nello, is a measure of the inconspicuousness of the man, for Nello is a diminutive of Antonello, itself a diminutive of Antonio. Invariably, however, he is designated simply as Nello, or in Latin—pehaps more surprisingly in view of the greater formality of the contexts in which that language was used—as Nellus. The obscurity extends to his career before 1447, by when he clearly enjoyed the pope's confidence and had presumably done so for many years. It is likely that the acquaintance between the two men began in Nello's hometown, Bologna, where Tommaso Parentucelli, the future Nicholas V, served in Cardinal Albergati's household and later became bishop of the city, albeit for a short period; indeed, Nicholas's close association with Albergati and his role in the administration of the cardinal's household can surely be regarded as fundamental for his own later practice as pope, presiding over complex and overlapping spheres variously amenable to diverse administrative and political strategies and devices.[4]

There is nevertheless a single document that allows Nello to step forward, however briefly, from the shadows. The context is the Jubilee of 1449–50 and the problem, which it was Nello's responsibility to solve, that of ensuring an adequate supply of grain to Rome during Jubilee year, a matter of concern at any time but especially when throngs of pilgrims were anticipated. One of the merchants on whom Nello relied for shipments of grain was a certain Giovanni di Iuzzo, a prominent citizen of Viterbo, who vaunted his association with Nello in the account he wrote of his life and times (Ciampi 1872, 65 n.5):

There was a man with the pope, who was called Nello da Bologna, the commissioner general. He and I did business together. He was an old man, wise, and he had the reputation of being a second father Abraham.

The passage gives an impression of patriarchal dignity and remoteness, as also of the respect that Nello inspired in those who had dealings with him. Yet it is perhaps also significant that the writer seems unable to assume knowledge of Nello's identity and position on the part of his readers.

The titles and offices assigned to Nello are legion, indicating the gradual development and official recognition of his role. This may have been connected to his evidently relatively humble origin: no surname is ever recorded, for instance. He is apostrophized often enough in the documents as "nobilis vir," but this seems to reflect his position at court rather than his general social standing. Only once is the epithet *magnificus* used of him, and that by a member of his own staff (Caetani 1930, 18 no. 2111). He was evidently not a lawyer or the holder of an academic degree; rather his background must have been in commerce. If so, it gave him skills and experience that proved immensely valuable in Nicholan Rome.

Nello first appears in the official record as the pope's *factor*; it is neither a specific nor a prestigious title.[5] Perhaps to confer general authority on Nello in the implementation of the varied tasks that were assigned to him, he soon received honorific titles. Shortly after the beginning of Nicholas's pontificate Nello must have been made a member of the college of *servientes armorum* (gendarmes); his admission to the college is not documented, but his resignation and replacement by an obscure Torinese *condottiere*, Domenico da Carmagnola, occurred on February 28, 1448 (ASV, RV 435, fol. 81r). There is no evidence that Nello had any connection with military matters, or that this was expected of the *servientes armorum*; indeed, some years later another individual closely involved with the building programs, Niccolò da Fabriano, received the same honor (ibid. 430, fol. 188r). In the same year Nello received the more exclusive and presumably prestigious honorary appointment as shieldbearer of the pope and was granted a salary of 25 ducats a month (ibid. 409, fol. 5v [April 22, 1449]).[6] From the beginning, of course, he appears as a papal *familiaris*, and he seems to have controlled the papal household, the *res familiaris*, from the time of Nicholas's election;[7] no doubt he had previously served as head of household for the then Cardinal Parentucelli. His later duties and responsibilities, then, probably grew from his role in a private household; the spider spun an increasingly extensive and variegated web.

In the month of Nicholas's accession, as preparations were being made for the coronation, Nello appears in the records as in charge of purchasing. This activity brought him into close contact with the representatives in Rome of the major Florentine banking firms, which also dealt in luxury commodities. He bought, for example, a large quantity of cloth from (or through) the Medici company; in this case he was responsible not only for handling the transaction, but also for the distribution of the cloth to the appropriate recipients (ASR, M 830, fol. 5r). His attendance at Nicholas's coronation is attested, since he was among those who received lengths of cloth, free of charge, for the occasion (ibid., fol. 20r). He had not been present, though this is hardly a surprise, at Eugenius's funeral (see the list in Bourgin 1904, 216).

The reconstruction of Nello's activities and position in Nicholas's early years, however, is complicated by the effective loss of the ledgers kept by Nello (the so-called volumes of the Tesoreria Segreta) up to 1450.[8] The purchase for the pope of precious materials and exquisite artifacts, whether for liturgical or personal use, continued to be part of Nello's domain throughout.[9] He also oversaw the acquisition of the fine wines that Nicholas enjoyed, perhaps more than he should (ASR, M 830, fol. 108r). Nello was instrumental, then, in creating the aestheticized, indeed somewhat precious environment in which the pope preferred to live and carry out the duties of his office, whether as priest or ruler. Nello saw to the purchase of tapestries for the papal apartments, for example, and brought northern weavers to Rome to establish a workshop in the palace (Pastor 1949, 191). And he must have had dealings with the most celebrated craftsman to work for Nicholas, the painter Fra Angelico, for in October 1449 Roberto Martelli of the Medici bank was recompensed for a very expensive order of ultramarine that Nello had purchased to be used in the magnificent frescoes executed by Fra Angelico in the pope's private chapel (ASR, M 830, fol. 127v).

It is not clear when Nello began to be involved with the pope's building campaigns. It is probable that some repair work was done in the basilicas used in the ceremonies of the coronation and along the processional way between them, while some temporary structures may also have been required; if so, Nello was perhaps in charge. Shortly after the coronation Nello was charged to survey the Castel S. Angelo, and he produced an inventory of the castle's contents (Zippel 1912, 175f.). Nicholas's concern with the castle soon led to an extensive building campaign, involving the creation of relatively sumptuous papal apartments, among other things. But Nello may not have been implicated in this; certainly the large payments of 1449 and 1450 (the latter to the contractor, Beltramo da Varese, who was later to be closely involved with the Vatican projects under Nello's supervision) were handled by the pope's private secretary Pietro da Noceto, an old hand in the papal court, and the funds were supplied by the chamberlain.[10] It is possible, however, that Pietro's involvement was a temporary expedient since Nello, as we will see, was absent from Rome at the time, and Pietro's own brother was castellan of the Castel S. Angelo.[11]

The chamberlain, Cardinal Ludovico Trevisan, had been centrally involved with urbanistic reform and restoration projects in the later years of Eugenius's pontificate and perhaps continued to occupy a similar role in the period between Nicholas's accession and the Jubilee, when there was an urgent need for extensive, widely ranging, but perhaps architecturally unambitious restoration on the churches and public buildings of the city. After 1450 at latest, on the other hand, the chamberlain became a marginal figure, while Pietro da Noceto's attention was focused on the political affairs of the peninsula and the pope's initiatives for peace and a united front against the Turks. By then Nello was firmly in charge of the papal administration in Rome, though it was only now, for the first time, that his position even in the papal household was formally spelled out.

So far the discussion has concentrated on Nello's activities on the expenditure side of the balance sheet. Soon after Nicholas's accession, however, Nello began to assume supervisory responsibilities for various sources of revenue, notably taxes and tolls generated by the major economic activities of the city and region, some of which had been long absorbed into the papal administration, while others remained, at least on paper, under communal control. On September 14, 1448, he and an associate were sworn in as chief officials of the *dogana di bestiame* of the city and the province of Campagna Marittima (ASV, RV 407, fol. 234v). This was already a papal office (Partner 1958, 118); it oversaw the administration and taxing of the herds and flocks that wintered in the environs of Rome, after descending from the mountains of Campagna Marittima. From 1448, indeed, Nello annually purchased winter pasturage for the animals from the Vatican chapter (BAV, ACSP, Censuali 7 [1454], fol. 20r; and see chapter 6).

By 1449 Nello was also implicated in the importation of grain into the city (ASV, IE 416, fol. 1r; ibid. 417, fol. 3v; and see chapter 7), and in 1450 he was

appointed director of the perhaps newly instituted offices, known in the vernacular as the *abbondanza* and *grascia*, that ensured the flow of victuals into the
city and saw that the papal government derived both political and economic
benefits from this (ASV, RV 433, fol. 92r; cf. Esch 1981, 20, and Ait 1981, 97,
who do not seem aware of this document). In the next few years Nello became
deeply involved with the tax offices (*dogane*) both of the harbor of Rome (the
ripa grande) and that of the province to the north of Rome, the Patrimonium
sancti Petri, where the winter pasturage for transhumant animals was a particularly important source of revenue. Nello himself, usually paired with an
associate, took direct charge simultaneously of several *dogane*, which in the
early fifteenth century had been generally farmed by private businessmen
though that of the Patrimonium had already under Martin V been entrusted to
a papal official, presumably because of its vital economic importance (Partner
1958, 118–123). It is unlikely that Nello purchased these offices, and even if he
did it is clear that effectively he acted as a papal official, taking as his partners
men with specific knowledge of the areas concerned and, no doubt, the ability
to buy into the partnership. In this role Nello acted as a crucial intermediary
between the papal household and administration and the economically prominent sections of Roman society; it was a sensitive position, as the revenues
concerned had traditionally accrued to the Roman commune, while Nello was
clearly also invading administrative territory once occupied, at least in Eugenius's later years, by the chamberlain, the head of the permanent ecclesiastical
bureaucracy. The reports of strife between Nicholas V and the chamberlain,
Cardinal Ludovico Trevisan, then, are likely to be true (see, e.g., Paschini 1938,
65f.).

As Nello's involvement with and expertise in the local administrative and
fiscal systems developed, so his position became formalized. In 1449 he received his first appointment to an official position (whatever his actual responsibilities, he was not yet formally head of the papal household).[12] In a bull
issued at Fabriano on September 26, 1449, Nicholas made Nello *nuntius, provisor et commissarius generalis* for the duration of the Jubilee (ASV, RV 433,
fol. 49v). This appointment can have done no more than recognize the status
quo; indeed, Nello had already appeared with the title of *commissarius*,
though in a Marchigian rather than a Roman context.[13] The evidence suggests
that in the summers of 1449 and 1450, when Nicholas traveled into the hill
country of the March of Ancona (map 4) to avoid the plague, Nello made more
extensive journeys in the same general area reviewing the economic condition
of territories that had suffered much in the recent unsettled period but were
potentially rich sources of income for the pope and of victuals for the capital.
Various appointments indicate Nicholas's concern for the area, none more so
than that of his own brother, Cardinal Filippo Calandrini, as legate of the
March in 1450. A number of administrators—and one builder—seem to have
proved their mettle in the administration of the province, before being transferred to Rome.[14]

In 1450 *commissarius* becomes Nello's standard title.[15] His position had become established through his efforts on behalf of the provisioning of the city

for the Jubilee. Contemporary accounts of the pilgrimage of holy year marvel at the numbers of pilgrims who poured into Rome; we can assume that existing supply and distribution systems were strained to the limit, and that administrative innovations might be in order. Indeed, there is evidence, though not quite unbiased, that there were for a time fears that the city would not be adequately provisioned. The Viterbese grain merchant Giovanni di Iuzzo gives a trenchant account of the difficulties experienced in a period that "came in plentiful and went out in famine."

The said pope proclaimed the Jubilee . . . and built up the grain stocks. And he couldn't find men to take part in this, indeed many of his contractors failed to bring grain to Rome. The pope was very upset about this, but then I was brought before him, through the good offices of my friend Nello. I took the job, and the pope, seeing what I was doing, wanted me to have funds at my disposal, and gave me a commission. So I sent by sea about 70 ships laden with grain and a large quantity by river too, since when there was bad weather at sea I resorted to the river. In the end, thank the Lord, we received great honor (Ciampi 1872, 56 n.6).

Though it is difficult to accept Giovanni's image of himself as a *deus ex machina* suddenly flooding the granaries of the city when the pope and Nello were in despair, he does not perhaps misrepresent the gravity of the situation that Nello, through the cooperation of merchants like Giovanni, was able to bring to a successful outcome, as was no doubt recognized in a quittance or financial absolution of 1451.[16]

It is noteworthy that Nello did not formally become director of the *abbondanza* until May 23, 1450, some months after his appointment as commissioner for the Jubilee; evidently further powers and perhaps a better-worked-out administrative structure were required. It was not just a matter of adequate supplies; the mere rumor of scarcity might inflate grain prices and encourage practices like hoarding and price gouging, which were likely to occur anyway in a time of sharply increased demand. Certainly the bakers of Rome were caught raising their prices above officially sanctioned limits, and Nello took action against them.[17] For all its problems, however, the Jubilee was successful; this success was vital to the long-term political and ecclesiastical ambitions of the pope, while the revenues from the Jubilee provided the material base for the ambitious building campaigns that followed. It was certainly the base for Nello's authority in those years.

The year following the Jubilee saw a further formalization and confirmation of Nello's position: a bull of July 23, 1451, appointed him *commissarius generalis negotiorumque gestor*, a far more resounding title than that of mere papal *factor*, as he had been not long before.[18] The appointment was presumably delayed until July to allow time for Nello to return to Rome from an extensive purchasing expedition to Tuscany that saw him engaged in business with several Florentine mercantile houses, including that of Giovanni Rucellai.[19] The responsibilities mentioned in the July document include the supervision of construction and restoration work at churches and other sacred sites in Rome and throughout the papal territories, as well as the collection of revenues owed to the church by means of which such projects might be financed.

The preamble makes clear that Nello was already discharging the duties enumerated in the bull, though the only earlier documents cited are those that retrospectively approved past conduct, rather than creating a context for future action.

The bull states that Nello had been in charge of the "fundacio, constructio et reparacio" of ecclesiastical buildings from the beginning of Nicholas's pontificate. Further, the moneys said to have been collected or spent by Nello are referred to as the property of the apostolic chamber; the papal household and some at least of the operations of the financial office of the Church are thus effectively represented as merged. There is no mention of the Jubilee, perhaps since it was a temporary event, while the operations cited in the document are institutionalized and constant operations and responsibilities. It is highly unlikely, however, that Nello's fiscal control of so many aspects of the economic life of Rome and the papal states developed as rapidly or encountered as little resistance as the bull suggests. In particular, it is hardly plausible that the chamberlain was prevailed upon to step aside so soon. And the organization of the restoration campaigns of Nicholas's early years doubtless left much to be desired, in view of the difficulties inherent in the allocation of material resources and personnel to different projects. Yet in this document a surely idealized image is projected of calm, coherent, and centralized administration. The parallels, indeed, between the 1451 document and Manetti's equally retrospective and even more idealizing account of the pope's building programs in 1455 are striking; in the former case, however, there was still time for the image to guide action.

From 1451, perhaps now that his position had been clarified, Nello was able to delegate many responsibilities. At the harbor Francesco del Borgo was a capable deputy. Payments to building contractors and other tasks at the Vatican could be handled by men such as Gottifredo de Waya.[20] Early in 1452 the Sienese Luca di Niccolò Amadei, *scutifer et familiaris* of the pope (he held, significantly, the honorific title that Nello himself had held since 1448), was appointed to a position that corresponded, in many respects, to that given to Nello in the previous year. For Luca Amadei (his surname does not appear in this document, but is known from other sources)[21] received charge of the papal household as well as of the building work on the Vatican palace and associated projects (ASV, RV 433, fol. 218v [January 23, 1452]. It is now Luca's name, not Nello's, that appears on the title page of the great ledger of papal revenues and expenditures in the year 1452, though we can be sure that Nello kept a close eye on his protégé as on Francesco del Borgo's activities at the *ripa grande*. Luca's accounting skills as well as a less easily quantifiable talent for diplomacy were tested in 1454 when he was appointed treasurer of the Patrimonium S. Petri (ASV, RV 434, fol. 71v [ay 28, 1454], at a time of serious and increasing unrest in that province. The evidence suggests that he had been groomed to succeed Nello, at least in the day-to-day administration of the financial affairs of the papal court and the Vatican building office, but that the gravity of the situation in the Patrimonium, a territory for which Nello had shown particular concern, diverted his career.

Luca Amadei's provenance is of great interest. He was prominent enough in his hometown of Siena for the news of his arrival there following Nicholas's death to be reported by the Venetian ambassador, who noted the particular esteem Amadei had enjoyed at the papal court (Pastor 1949, 532 no. 27). It was even rumored that, in the period of depression following the Porcarian conspiracy early in 1453, the pope considered a plan to transfer the papal court to Siena. Amadei, who had been in Rome at least since 1448, must have been implicated in the formulation of such a plan, if it existed (Pastor 1958, 583 n.4). He would surely have been working under Nello, who entertained particularly close relations with Siena, and exchanged dispatches with the Sienese government. Indeed by October 22, 1448 (perhaps in response to an oral communication from Amadei), Nello was signing himself *Nellus civis senensis* in letters to Siena (ASS, Concistoro 1962, e.g. nos. 13, 21, 99), though the first reference to a formal grant of citizenship is in a letter of November 22, 1450. I have been able to find no explanation of why the Bolognese Nello should have become so closely associated with Siena; given Nello's prominence in Nicholas's building campaigns, however, the possibility must be entertained that the model for the concerted program of urban improvements in Rome was not Renaissance Florence, increasingly slipping under the control of a single man or at least party, but late medieval Siena, with its more open, if somewhat less than harmonious, political system and its remarkably flexible yet effective management and improvement of urban open spaces and other public amenities and facilities.[22]

Nello da Bologna's visit to Florence in 1451 was made possible by the recent Jubilee and the resultant healthy state of the papal coffers. Already in 1450 an upsurge in construction activity seems to have been under way, and new ideas about the prospective transformation of the city may have been in the air. When Nello left Rome in the spring of 1451, the decision had surely been made to recruit for the pope's building office more experienced and sophisticated designers than were available in Rome. By the end of the year Bernardo Rossellino had come to Rome as "ingegnere del palazzo" (he was one of two men, both Florentines, who had this title). It is likely that Nello contacted him, perhaps through Rucellai, in Florence, and even that the contract that he and Nello signed, mentioned in a document of the following year, was entered into in that city.[23]

In 1452 the project began with which Nicholas's name is particularly associated, the erection of a new *tribuna* or east end and crossing for the Vatican basilica.[24] The contract, which included not only the work on the basilica proper but also that on the adjacent chapel of S. Maria della Febbre, was given to Beltramo da Varese, whose large equipe had already been hard at work in 1451 on the fortifications of the Leonine City. The initial payment to Beltramo was registered in the ledger on June 16; it amounted to 2,000 ducats and was to cover the period until September 23. The money was advanced by Tommaso Spinelli, here acting not in his official capacity as banker to the commune, but as private merchant and financier "di corte." No doubt, however, Spinelli was repaid out of funds generated by the communal revenues that he administered.

Obviously Spinelli and Nello, who were both deeply implicated in the fiscal structures of the city and in the papal building projects alike, must have known each other and collaborated in both areas of operation.[25]

Spinelli and Nello doubtless also played important roles, given their respective official responsibilities, in the rebuilding of the municipal palaces of the Campidoglio. The effective rebuilding of the Palazzo dei Conservatori and the restoration and expansion of the Senator's Palace (fig. 3), to which towers were added, were in the hands of Beltramo da Varese, though fine stonework was executed by Paolo Romano, who had also worked at the Ponte S. Angelo; these correspondences reveal, then, a characteristic intersection of city and papal projects both at the level of workshop production and at that of administration. Though the palaces on the Campidoglio would doubtless have been restored in any case, the plans were certainly accelerated and perhaps elaborated in anticipation of the visit of Emperor Frederick III in 1452 (as is explicitly stated in Nello's quittance of 1453; Appendix, no. 4). Nello was placed in charge of the preparations for the visit; he had to find accommodations for the extensive entourage with which Frederick was traveling, and he also oversaw a number of construction and restoration projects, of which the work on the Campidoglio had pride of place.[26]

The list of structures restored or rebuilt "in adventu imperatoris" includes, besides the two municipal palaces, the churches of the city, the walls, and the gates. Projects in Ostia and several towns in the Patrimonium are also mentioned; these seem to be connected with the need to provide for security in the region, as much for the passage of foodstuffs as for that of the royal traveler and his entourage. Security in the city itself was also, as contemporaries noted, very much on the minds of Nicholas and his staff in connection with the emperor's visit, since it was feared that it might provoke demonstrations of the antipapal, Ghibelline sentiment that was still quite common among the townspeople. But the list of structures restored in Rome, though it includes the walls and gates that both defended the city and provided it with a particularly impressive testimonial of its ancient size and power, does not include the Castel S. Angelo or the Vatican palace, buildings evocative of specifically papal power within the city, and where work was continuing. Instead of a concern with mere security, then, the list reveals a desire to impress the eminent visitor with the spectacle of a great city recovering from its long period of squalor.

It was not only the buildings of Rome that were expected to impress the emperor; they formed the setting for elaborate public ceremonial. It is recorded that the city magistrates, especially the senator, made a brave show as they rode out to meet the emperor, no doubt passing along a route appropriately selected and prepared for the occasion (Infessura 1890, 50–52; Platina 1913, 334). Stefano Infessura, the witness concerned, was fiercely pro-commune and neglected to mention the inconvenient fact that the vestments of the magistrates and even of some of the leading citizens in attendance who did not hold office at the time were paid for by the Church, as directed by Nello. The pope's concern, indeed, was perhaps not only to show the emperor a city but also a city government in blooming condition, or at least to show the latter as such to itself. This may be reflected in the decision to lodge the emperor's younger brother Albrecht, one of the young men knighted on the Ponte S. Angelo, in the private house of a Roman citizen, rather than in a papal palace (see note 26). And the emperor himself spent the night before his ceremonial entry into the city at the *vigna* on Monte Mario of Tommaso Spinelli (Dykmans 1968; Burroughs 1982a), a setting that, like the Ponte S. Angelo, brought together the communal and papal worlds of Rome, in both of which both the host, Spinelli, and the documented organizer of the affair, Nello da Bologna, were deeply implicated. It also placed Spinelli firmly in Nello's debt, for that Florentine burgher was surely greatly honored to be able to entertain so glamorous and highborn a guest.

The senator who rode out, richly caparisoned, to meet Frederick and his company was Niccolò Porcinari, a jurist from Aquila (the senator, the chief judicial official of the city of Rome, was by statute a foreigner).[27] He had studied in Siena, where he had come to know a fellow student whom he was to meet again in 1452 when he appeared in Rome in the entourage of the emperor; this was Aeneas Sylvius Piccolomini, who was serving as the emperor's private secretary. For many reasons, perhaps including the Sienese connection, Nello and Porcinari were known to each other, and they must have collaborated; indeed, there is direct evidence for contact, if not collaboration, between the two in the December after the emperor's departure from Rome, when Nello and Porcinari were appointed by the commune of Sezze, a small town in the hills east of Rome, to settle a dispute between the town and the aristocrat Onorato Caetani concerning a case of horse rustling allegedly carried out by some of the men of Sezze at Caetani's expense (Caetani 1930, 75 no. 2369). I will return to Nello's administrative concerns in this often wild and remote terrain; for now the visit of Nello and Porcinari to Sezze and, doubtless, to the seat of Caetani at Sermoneta serves to illustrate the working relationship of the two men.

Porcinari had recently been involved in a case of far more obvious seriousness and political resonances: on September 18, 1451, he had ruled in favor of Cardinal Prospero Colonna, who had been accused of subverting certain servants of Aldo and Grato Conti, representatives of one of the old baronial families of the Campagna, to poison their masters (Tomassetti 1979, 3:631; *DBI* 28:346). A confession had been extorted under torture from the unfortunate defendants, but Porcinari overruled this evidence and cleared the cardinal from all suspicion. It was later rumored that Porcinari, though no longer senator, was among the intended victims of the Porcarians (Paschini 1940, 181), perhaps for his conduct in the Colonna case. Clearly, if the cardinal had been found guilty, the arts of peace, in Manetti's phrase, that Nicholas exercised in Rome might soon have proved futile, and the conflict between the Colonna faction and its opponents that was to bedevil Roman life in the pontificates of Paul II and Sixtus IV might already have broken out. We may suspect that Nello took close interest in the conduct of the case, and was not without some influence on its outcome.

Nello's many and varied responsibilities, especially in the area of finance, are fully documented in two quittances issued on his behalf on February 20, 1453 and January 12, 1454 (Appendix, nos. 4, 5; the latter document largely recapitulates, with a few omissions, the contents of the first). The second document refers to Nello as *commissarius generalis*, the title he had formally received without time limit in 1451; the earlier document, curiously, uses only the uninformative titles *familiaris* and *scutifer*. The documents retrospectively approve all Nello's activities in the pope's service up to the date of issue, and provide him with immunity from any potential claims or legal actions against him arising from those activities. The 1453 quittance was issued, surely not coincidentally, shortly after the suppression of the conspiracy of Stefano Porcari. It confirms Nello's operations and those of his subordinates on three major occasions: the Jubilee, the emperor's visit, and the Porcarian conspiracy and its aftermath. Nello's role in the suppression of the conspiracy and in the framing of an appropriate response may have been controversial; if so, this may provide a clue to the apparent concern apparent in the 1453 quittance to play down that role, as well as Nello's official capacity at that time.

For all the coyness about Nello's title, the 1453 document leaves no doubt about his part in the events that transpired in Rome after Porcari's detection barely more than a month before. Nello receives credit "for uncovering the plot and conspiracy of the late Stefano Porcari [he had been executed by this time], and for the confiscation of the property of Stefano himself and his accomplices and its disposal whether by sale or gift or any other kind of concession." This is explicit enough. Yet the quite numerous sources for the conspiracy, the letters and memoranda in which both Romans and non-Romans report the sensational affair of Porcari's attempted coup and its detection, invariably ignore Nello's role in the events of January 1453. One contemporary account mentions Nello, but in the most garbled way possible, asserting that "Nello di Bartolomeo, a Roman citizen, revealed to the chamberlain that Messer Stefano had returned to Rome" (Tommasini 1880, 107 n.6); he then, presumably, receded into the gloom from which he had inexplicably and temporarily emerged.

Nevertheless, one contemporary observer was able to give a reasonably accurate account of the affair: in a letter from Rome the obscure Novarese Stefano Caccia wrote that Porcari, after his capture shortly before dawn, was taken to the Vatican palace and led into the room of the "noble Nello" where he was detained for some time.[28] Here he seems to have undergone a preliminary interrogation and to have made a full confession. Only then did Nello and others, whom Caccia does not identify by name, go to the pope to announce that Porcari had been captured and was under guard in the palace. The news inspired the pope to some philosophical reflections on the power of Fortune in human affairs, whereupon the others asked him what they should do with Porcari. According to Caccia, the pope responded only that "they should do what they thought fit." It is not clear who Caccia's informant was, but his picture of the pope's household corresponds to that indicated by the documents of Nello's activity. The suspicion arises, indeed, that the true story of the Porcari affair was suppressed in order to keep from the pope's subjects and from the many diplomatic representatives in the listening post that was Rome the impression of a pope seriously out of touch with the course of events and the activities of his own staff.

There was perhaps a further reason for minimizing Nello's role in the affair, which is connected with his activity, as registered in the quittances, in connection with the restoration of churches. At first sight this may seem an uncontroversial operation, merely continuing the practice of Nicholas's early years or the period of Cardinal Trevisan's ascendancy under Eugenius. There is evidence, however, that suggests that a particular campaign to improve ecclesiastical buildings was in process in 1451–52. This involved a certain Michele da Prato, who held the salaried office of *procurator fiscalis* under both Eugenius and Nicholas. His chief function was to visit communities whose readiness to pay taxes owed to the Church left something to be desired; in 1450, for instance, he appeared at Gualdi as the pope's *commissarius*. Since Gualdi was one of the subject towns where Nicholas is recorded as having building work carried out, it can be supposed that Michele was involved in the collection of revenues to be used for such a purpose, as well as perhaps in the disbursement of moneys to contractors, craftsmen, and others.[29]

Michele had an eye for architecture: in the fall of 1453 he was sent on a mission to Sermoneta from which he sent a report that noted that new construction work at the residence of the lord of the place, Onorato Caetani, made the latter resemble the new palace built by Nicholas at the Vatican (*DBI* 1:204; cf. Caetani 1930, nos. 589, 1042). In the difficult last year of Nicholas's pontificate, as unrest broke out in the Patrimonium, Michele was sent to Viterbo (map 3) to investigate the circumstances of the murder of the leading citizen of the town, Princivalle Gatti; in spite of his experience he seems to have lacked the requisite diplomatic skills, and returned to Rome having accomplished nothing (Pinzi 1887–1913, 4:159).

Michele da Prato's only commission in Rome itself, at least under Nicholas, was given to him in April 1452, soon after the emperor's visit. He was made procurator of all the churches of Rome, of whatever type, with the goal of regaining all illegally alienated property.[30] The principle, of course, was by no means new; Cardinal d'Estouteville, for example, had been charged in 1448 to proceed against those who held property illegally alienated from the basilica of S. Lorenzo fuori le Mura (ASV, RV 408, fol. 61v), and Nello himself was involved in the campaign to restore the possessions of the abbey of S. Paolo fuori le Mura.[31] The scope of Michele's commission, however, seems to have exceeded at least recent precedent. Not surprisingly he was not expected to act alone, but was to collaborate with the *vicar in spiritualibus*, Berardo Eroli, the bishop of Spoleto and from June 1451, at latest, effectively vice-chancellor.[32]

Such a campaign to reform the finances of the city's churches must be connected with Nello's particular charge to restore them in advance of the emperor's visit, and may reflect difficulties encountered by Nello in financing the necessary construction. On the one hand, Nello may have been concerned—

possibly for political reasons—to use general papal revenues as little as possible, relying instead on the income of the churches and other ecclesiastical institutions themselves; on the other hand, the illegally alienated property that Michele was charged to recover had presumably passed into the hands of members of the Roman socioeconomic elite. If so, the latter may well have considered that they had acquired the property in question, doubtless mostly real estate, by due process, and resented pressure on the part of the pope's officials to surrender their rights to it. It was the kind of issue that lent itself to exploitation by radical adventurers such as Porcari, though I have discovered no evidence that Michele da Prato and Bishop Eroli were successful in their task. In any case it is noteworthy that the Porcarian conspiracy was followed by signs of a rapprochement between Nicholas and the Colonna and their partisans, the traditionally Ghibelline element in Roman politics, though relations with the Roman elite in general became markedly cooler.

Nello's position, in the meantime, was greatly strengthened. Certainly his quittance of 1454 (see Appendix, no. 5) emphatically recognizes his control of the internal affairs of the papal government and enumerates projects that he had been supervising, some of which were not mentioned in the document of the previous year. The projects are the Vatican palace, the *tribuna*, the walls both of the city and the *civitas Leonina*, the Acqua Vergine and its outlet, the palace of the *conservatores*, the Ponte Milvio, many private and public "structuras et opera," the purchase of precious stones, and the purchase for demolition of houses and shops in the vicinity of the Ponte S. Angelo and the related project of erecting chapels on the bridge. The emphasis here is quite distinct from that of the earlier document (Appendix, no. 4), which listed projects that involved or at least could be claimed to involve the cooperation of the papacy and the commune, bringing benefits to both. In the 1454 document, strictly papal projects preponderate; indeed, the otherwise baffling inclusion of the purchase of precious stones in a list of construction projects serves to place in relief the papal character of the latter. On the other hand, the 1454 list refers to the categories of "private and public projects": the distinction here, in my view, is not that between papal and communal projects (a distinction that was becoming increasingly anachronistic), but rather that between projects carried out directly by contractors hired and administered by Nello and his staff, and subventions given to private individuals to improve their own property, as was claimed by Platina (1913), 338.

The St. Peter's project (the *tribuna*), begun in 1452, is not mentioned in the 1453 quittance, though it is in that of 1454. It is not clear what the significance of this is, but it is perhaps relevant that in January 1452 Luca Amadei was put in charge of the office of the *fabbrica* of St. Peter's. On September 20 of that year Amadei received a quittance, though this referred to his activity in the preceding year rather than the Vatican project (ASV, DC 27, fol. 22r).[33] It is noteworthy that Nello received no quittance in 1452, though he had received one in 1451 and was, as we have seen, to receive quittances both in 1453 and 1454. It seems, then, that Nello, having set an administrative structure in place, withdrew from direct control in 1452, but that he was soon recalled to his former role, perhaps in view of the importance and even controversiality of the projects concerned.

In 1452, indeed, Nello's attention was somewhat removed from Rome. In October 1451 he was put in charge of the *dogana di bestiame* of Campagna Marittima and the Roman district; thus he was concerned with the affairs of the territories to the south and southeast of Rome and in particular with the functioning of the transhumance system that was the mainstay of their economy. We have seen him arbitrating in a dispute about rustled cattle in 1452 at the town of Sezze. At the same time he was in contact with prominent figures of the region, like the chamberlain's protégé Onorato Caetani, lord of Sermoneta. Caetani sent Nello a gift of trout sometime before September 1452,[34] perhaps as a gesture of gratefulness to Nello for arranging the visit of Frederick III and his knights, on their way south from Rome to Naples, to Sermoneta, where the Italians present were amazed at the appetite of the flower of German chivalry for Caetani's wine (Caetani 1926, 35 no. 865). Finally, new statutes were issued in 1452 governing the transhumance system of Rome and the adjacent provinces (De Cupis 1911, 555 doc. 1); clearly this was Nello's doing.[35] He was, of course, by no means completely removed from the conduct of affairs in Rome, where he retained overall responsibility for the building works. He surely oversaw, then, also in 1452, the revision of the statutes of the Roman *maestri di strada*. By the end of 1452 Nello's direct involvement with the provincial economy of Campagna Marittima was no longer needed, or more pressing concerns had arisen in the city. In any case in 1453 Nello's activity was once again concentrated on Rome, while Michele da Prato was dispatched to Campagna.

In 1453 and into 1454 Nello exercised close control over the building works; indeed he seems to have presided over a kind of tribunal that settled cases of fraud or negligence. In 1454, for instance, two of Beltramo da Varese's men were brought before Nello and charged with building a length of wall without mortar; they were fined 20 ducats, which were paid by the contractor.[36] But in the same year Nello's attention was diverted from the building campaigns to the Christian response to the Turkish advance, which had already enveloped Constantinople and now threatened Italy itself. A new tax on clerics was imposed to raise money for ships and armaments; the tax was administered by Nello, who is referred to on the title page of the ledger for 1454 as "depositario," the only occasion this term, familiar from the world of papal finance, is used of him. The ledger itself was kept by Francesco del Borgo, while the distribution of the revenues was administered by the Lucchese Gaspare Pellegrini, who was clearly a capable professional, having recently held—and perhaps continuing to hold—important posts in the financial administration of the March, the province governed by Nicholas's brother.[37]

By the end of 1454 Nello was dead. His death, on December 28, was recorded in the register of benefactors of the Vatican basilica, to which he bequeathed four chasubles of purple cloth (Muntz 1878, 148 n.3). Fittingly he is identified in the register simply as "Nellus de Bononia, familiaris domini nostri"; all his many titles have fallen away except the one he held throughout Nicholas's pontificate, which, more than any other, emphasized his loyalty and indispensability to the pope. With him died his central controlling position in Rome; his responsibilities were divided up, and his assistant Francesco del Borgo inherited the supervision of at least some of the construction projects.[38]

In contrast to the case of Francesco del Borgo, there is no evidence to suggest that Nello was directly involved with the design of buildings, though it is clear that he possessed considerable expertise in the organizational and financial aspects of construction, and he must have played a role in decisions pertaining to the architectural character of various projects. There is evidence that Nello shared the pope's aesthetic tastes; he bought, for instance, from a senior colleague four engraved silver plates specifically for private use (ASR, TS 1451, fol. 78v). Indeed, since Nicholas was increasingly affected by melancholy and by painful ailments in his latter years and cut himself off from all but his closest associates, as diplomats ruefully noted,[39] it is likely that Nello acted, on the basis of long and intimate knowledge of the pope, as the latter's proxy in various areas of policy. There can now be no doubt of the ideological and persuasive dimension of Nicholas's patronage, a dimension crystallized, with whatever distortions, in the language of Manetti's biography. In this framework, Nello may take his place as the pope's chief minister of internal affairs, with special responsibility for the use of architecture and environmental interventions as an arm of general policy in the city and region, but also as a space for the meeting of a range of concerns and interests for which Nello evidently possessed remarkable sensitivity and responsiveness.

Contractors and Builders: The Local Men

Nello da Bologna and his assistant Francesco del Borgo supervised the activity of a number of contractors and craftsmen, whose names appear in the documents assembled by Müntz and in that author's discussion of the structure of the building campaigns under Nicholas in which he draws attention, in particular, to the prominence of entrepreneurial middlemen (Müntz 1878, 122f.). More recently C. R. Mack has studied the distribution of craftsmen among Nicholas's various projects, their ethnic background, and the remuneration allotted to the salaried employees (Mack 1983, 66f.). Neither Mack nor Müntz—nor, to my knowledge, any other scholar of the period—has paid due attention to the sheer diversity and heterogeneity of the personnel, not so much in terms of place of origin (though this varied considerably), as in terms of official standing and connections outside the world of the building sites. This is of interest for understanding the development both of the building campaigns themselves and of their administrative framework.

The major craftsmen and contractors, for all their diversity, can be divided into two main groups, those who appear in papal documents before Nicholas's accession in 1447 and those who received papal commissions only thereafter. These two groups also correspond, in broad terms, to those who hailed from Rome itself and the surrounding region and those who came from farther afield. Very full lists of craftsmen and contractors employed in Rome during Eugenius's pontificate have been published by Corbo (1969): only two of the men prominent in those lists hold onto their position under Nicholas. This is surprising, as the scale of Nicholas's projects must have been such as to strain the available resources and to generate work for all the available *maestri*.

It is possible that such turnover of personnel is more apparent than real. There are immense lacunae in the documentation, at least for the earlier part of Nicholas's pontificate, and it is not possible to associate craftsmen with all the projects known to have been undertaken under Nicholas. On the other hand, plague was virulent in Rome in the summers of 1449 and 1450, at a time when the building operations were kept going (Manetti 1734, c.928); many of those working on the building sites must have succumbed. Further, the particularly large-scale enterprises that distinguished Nicholas's architectural patronage from his predecessors' were entrusted to entrepreneurs capable of advancing funds and with access (presumably often through ownership) to brickworks, quarries, kilns, transport facilities, and a qualified and reliable labor force. Some independent craftsmen active before 1447 may have disappeared into larger units. The most significant such enterprise under Nicholas, however, that of Beltramo da Varese, was not present in Eugenian Rome. Rather, the building world under Eugenius was dominated by a certain Duccio, who headed an enterprise of the type later controlled by Beltramo: it is possible that Duccio's position was such that he could inhibit the development of rival firms. Nevertheless, Duccio himself disappears completely from the building records after 1447, nor does his equipe seem to have survived under another name (Corbo 1969, 43).

There is more evidence about the strange circumstances in which a better-known craftsman proved unable to survive the succession of popes, though he not only possessed a level of technical skill and artistic ability unparalleled in Rome at the time but must also, as a sculptor and caster, have disposed of a well-organized workshop as well as a foundry and other elaborate workshop facilities. In a letter of February 7, 1447, to the Florentine ambassador in Rome, the government of Florence mentioned calumnies circulating in Rome against their compatriot Filarete, as a result of which the latter had undergone imprisonment and even torture (Milanesi 1901, 93; Golzio and Zander 1968, 320). He had been freed from prison at the pope's behest but was still barred from working in Rome; this was especially distressing to him as he had undertaken an important commission that he could now no longer complete. The Florentine government pleaded that Filarete be allowed to remain in Rome to finish this project. The bizarre charge against Filarete was serious enough; he stood accused of the theft of the head of St. John the Baptist, though it seems that the pope, at least, was unwilling to believe this. Nevertheless, Filarete's Roman career was over, though other Florentine bronze masters worked for Nicholas V.

Much later, in the famous treatise that he wrote at the Milanese court, Filarete was to allude to intrigues to which he had fallen victim, though he suggests they were personally motivated (Golzio and Zander 1968, 320). In this case, on the other hand, the involvement of a relic of the patron saint of Florence suggests that anti-Florentine feeling fueled the accusation. A possibly comparable instance was the appearance of the eminent Florentine banker and merchant Antonio Pazzi before the court of the *conservatores* of Rome sometime in the spring of 1447 on the charge of illegally procuring porphyry from holy places, or at least receiving it from those who had (Milanesi 1901, 91). This practice was no doubt far from unknown in Rome, as Eugenius's bull of 1436 indicates (Theiner 1882, 3:338 no. 261). It is possible, then, that the arrest of Pazzi, whose bank was one of those serving the papal court, reflected deep undercurrents in the city, such as might most readily rise to the surface in a time of transition like the interregnum between two popes.

As we have seen, Nello's authority in the city expanded from his base in the papal household. Many of the major figures involved in the building campaigns were members of the household and vaunted titles such as *familiaris* or, less frequently, *continuus commensalis*; sometimes they are simply referred to in the accounts as *nostri*. It is not clear what the precise significance of such status was in the context of the building campaigns; to some extent it distinguishes those who received a fixed salary from those who received payment on the basis of the volume of the work performed and the expenses incurred. But this was not a hard and fast rule, as will become clear. In general, the large-scale entrepreneurs tended to be independent of the household, which presumably performed some of the organizational functions of the entrepreneurs; skilled craftsmen, especially those who worked with precious metals, which were typically purchased not by the artists but by papal officials or the *depositarius* (the Florentine banker Roberto Martelli), tended to be *familiares*. It is noteworthy that of the many Lombards active in Nicholas's service (Mack 1983, 66, lists nine, mostly men of some standing), none seems to have been a member of the household; Lombards, indeed, were especially prominent in the independent building sector.

A small but remarkable group consisted of craftsmen or entrepreneurs who were also clerics. As individuals they appear to have had little in common, and probably did not regard themselves as a distinct group (as, for example, the Lombards surely did, given the traditional strength of the building trades and guilds in Lombardy). Some were papal *familiares*, though one who executed a particularly important commission, the work on the angel of the Castel S. Angelo, was a member of the household of Cardinal Domenico Capranica and was probably responsible for some of the finer work on the cardinal's palace (ASR, TS 1453, fol. 69r). Most of the cleric craftsmen who worked for Nicholas V were of local origin; an exception to this—and exceptional in many other ways—was the Dominican friar and painter, Fra Angelico.

Continuity between the building world of Eugenian and Nicholan Rome is represented by two major survivors of the former. They are contrasting figures, having little more in common than local origin, one coming from Rome itself and the other from the Roman hinterland. The Roman, Antonio Paciuri, was a large-scale producer of building materials, mostly bricks and mortar, and clearly was able to expand his business greatly under Nicholas. He also appears as a contractor on public works projects that required solid workmanship, though hardly architectural finesse, such as a salt warehouse at Ostia, lengths of wall along the river, and a portion of the fortifications of the Leonine City (this was in 1454, evidence of increasing use of his services even in Nello's last year).[40] He was a man of high standing in the Roman patriciate, and held high office in the city; he was, indeed, a key figure in the intersection between urban interests—or at least the interests of a certain class—and those of the papal court and associated institutions.

Of far greater importance than Paciuri at the beginning of Nicholas's pontificate, though his star as a builder later waned, was Antonello di Giovanni, usually known as Antonello d'Albano, after his hometown in the hills southeast of Rome (map 3). It was almost certainly he who appears as a *muratore* in the records of building projects under Eugenius (Corbo 1969, esp. 230f.). The evidence suggests that he was a builder and contractor from the time of Nicholas's accession, and he may have played a crucial role in the wave of restoration activity initiated in the short period between 1447 and the Jubilee. In 1447–49, for example, his connection with no fewer than three projects can be documented. Already on June 20, 1447, he received a large payment for work done at S. Maria Maggiore on behalf of the chapter (Müntz 1879, 316); it was evidently a project begun under Eugenius. The document, which is in Latin, gives Antonello's name as "Antonius Johannis de Albano": it is instructive to compare the standard latinization of Nello's name as "Nellus." Antonello's work at S. Maria Maggiore was contemporaneous with work at S. Eusebio and was followed, at latest by 1450, by work at S. Pietro in Vincoli (ASR, TS 1450, fol. 2r and passim), both in the same general area of the city (map 2; fig. 35).

Antonello's third project of 1447 took him far from the Esquiline hill: he was paid for work in connection with the windows of the Vatican basilica (Müntz 1878, 135), an aspect of the building that Nicholas, with his love of the effects of colored glass, is known to have been especially interested in. It is not clear what Antonello did; no documents have come to light that constitute direct evidence that he continued in this role, and in 1447, accordingly, he perhaps merely reinforced the windows of a notoriously unstable building.

The payment to Antonello was registered in a "bastardello delle finestre di Sto. Pietro," a ledger devoted specifically to the windows of the basilica. The ledger itself is lost, but it still provides ghostly evidence of the importance of stained glass in this as in most major late medieval sacred buildings, an importance that in this context is even evident in the organization of projects involving glass. On the whole the projects of Nicholas V, however diverse in scale and character they may have been, followed a vertical principle of organization: contractors or officials were set in charge of topographically distinct projects in which work of different kinds and level of skill was carried out. In a larger project various intermediaries might be appointed, and the project itself might be sectioned up and distributed to contractors working independently, if not in rivalry.

Work on windows, on the other hand, which presumably involved mainly the production and assembly of the painted glass, rather than the preparation of the apertures that would contain them, was organized horizontally: a single individual was responsible for such work throughout the city. This was the

Benedictine monk Francesco Barone, priest of the Roman church of S. Salvatore, who had in 1446 been employed on the windows of Orvieto cathedral (Müntz 1878, 134).[41] If, as is likely, he was summoned to Rome in 1447, perhaps to work on the stained glass windows known to have been installed in Nicholas's *studiolo* and no doubt elsewhere, he must have collaborated with Fra Angelico. Indeed the Dominican's position may have been similar: he may have been the general supervisor of painting projects, at least at the Vatican, in the same way that Barone oversaw work on windows.

At the time that Antonello appeared in the accounts in connection with the windows of St. Peter's, he was a *beneficiatus* of the basilica (BAV, ACSP, Censuali 5 [1447], fol. 18r). He belonged, then, to the inferior of two categories of persons who made up the chapter of St. Peter's; the other more senior category was that of the canons. Regularly two *beneficiati* were elected as *camerarii*, and these officials, together with three canons, formed a committee responsible for the preparation of a ledger recording the expenditure and revenues of the chapter, mostly from rents. In 1447 Antonello was one of the *camerarii* and found himself as the colleague of two canons, Niccolò de Leis (or de Leys) and Antonio Margani, both of whom were of some importance in the building programs of Nicholas V. De Leis was a clerk of the *camera apostolica* and on occasion stood in for the chamberlain (ASV, RV 435, fol. 47r): on May 22, 1447, he received from the papal staff reimbursement for money that he had disbursed on carpentry, mainly scaffolding, in the apse chapel (*cappella maggiore*) of the Vatican basilica (ASV, IE 414, fol. 77r). The scaffolding in question can only be that used by Fra Angelico for the decoration of the chapel of St. Peter, as it was called. This project had been begun by Eugenius; its interruption and the temporary dismantling of the scaffolding were probably due to the needs of Nicholas's coronation ceremony. In any case Nicholas clearly saw quickly to the resumption of work on the frescoes, which are known to have illustrated the life of St. Peter (Gilbert 1975, 256, 265 n.81). Evidently de Leis acted as a papal intermediary, and his role in regard to Fra Angelico can be compared with that of Antonello in regard to Barone, who was perhaps already in charge of the glass for St. Peter's in 1447.

In the early years of Nicholas's pontificate Antonello clearly benefited from support in high places, receiving certain most desirable benefices. By 1448 he was a canon of Tivoli; the pope confirmed his succession to a vacant benefice in a manner that apparently did not accord with precedent and met with the opposition of the other canons (ASV, RV 407, fol. 241r). But Nicholas may have had his own reasons for placing the energetic Antonello in Tivoli; in 1451, by which time Antonello had moved on, Nicholas ruled that the Tivoli canons should distribute their revenues more equally and that they should be more conscientious in the performance of their duties, especially liturgical ones (ibid: 415, fol. 206v). The document reveals, or at least asserts, that the senior canons had traditionally laid claim to the fatter benefices over which the chapter had jurisdiction, and suggests that this had occasioned the contention of 1448. Antonello, then, was perhaps installed in the Tivoli chapter to monitor reform from the inside. If so, he may have acted in concert with Niccolò de

Leis, who had by 1447 drawn up an inventory of the property of the Vatican chapter in Tivoli (BAV, ACSP, Censuali 5 [1447], fol. 51r). Accordingly Antonello, as *camerarius* of the Vatican chapter at the time and colleague of de Leis, was surely associated with one of the many attempts made by the chapter during Nicholas's pontificate—and doubtless with his support—to identify and recuperate alienated property of the chapter in the Roman hinterland.[42]

In 1447 Antonello himself invested in property: for nearly 60 ducats he bought a house in the parish of S. Niccolò de' Calcarari, which he had rented at least since 1439, when he spent some 20 ducats in repairing it. The value of Antonello's repairs was assessed in 1439 by the *camerarii* of the chapter, the owner of the house until 1447.[43] This was doubtless one of the major functions of these officials, and it may be presumed that Antonello's expertise in building was especially valuable to the chapter during his term as *camerarius*; no other member of the chapter appears to have had similar skills and business interests. Antonello's house, like many of those owned by the chapter, was identified by an image of the sword-wielding archangel. It stood in a district associated, as the name of the parish church, S. Niccolò de' Calcarari (map 2), suggests, with the building trades, especially with the production of mortar from marble burnt in the many limekilns (Marchetti-Longhi 1919, 401f.). No documents have come to light of Antonello's ownership of such facilities, but it is likely that he was involved in the most conspicuous economic activity of his neighborhood.

Antonello's purchase of his house occurred at the time of a campaign to regain alienated property; evidently the chapter was concerned to recover larger-scale rural properties, while the sale of urban houses to men such as Antonello and Paciuri, who would then restore them, perhaps promised the improvement of neighborhoods in which other of the chapter's properties stood. In 1447 many of the urban properties sold by the chapter (including Antonello's house) went to raise funds for the purchase of the estate of S. Pietro in Formis, near Velletri (map 3), with its ruined castle. This had been a stronghold of the Savelli, an aristocratic clan allied with the Colonna, until wrested from them by Cardinal Vitelleschi during the war waged under Eugenius IV against the Colonna and their partisans. The castle was badly damaged in the fighting and was then largely demolished by the people of Velletri, anxious for revenge on their former tyrants and taking advantage, no doubt, of a convenient supply of building stone. On June 11, 1448, Nicholas confirmed the chapter's purchase of the estate for 9,000 ducats. The Savelli were not yet satisfied, however, and lawsuits continued for some years.[44]

Finally in March 1452 Antonio Margani, the sacristan of St. Peter's, was paid for his services in connection with the case, which he had apparently brought to resolution. Margani, whose relative Pietro Margani was involved with the construction of the chapels on the Ponte S. Angelo and the restoration of the bridge, was a Vatican canon and had been a colleague of Antonello in 1447.[45] He must have had legal expertise as well as administrative skills, both of which seem to have benefited the chapter's estate planning, if not also some of the papal building campaigns.

In August 1450 Nicholas formally promoted Antonello to the rank of canon of St. Peter's, in succession to a papal acolyte and *abbreviator* (ASV, RV 412, fol. 179r). Already on February 7, 1450, however, Antonello is referred to as canon in an entry in Nello's ledger recording Antonello's receipt of 50 ducats for winter pasturage owned by the chapter (ASR, TS 1450, fol. 77v). The evidence suggests that, as here, Antonello regularly acted as an intermediary between the chapter and the papal staff (ibid., fol. 39r; ASR, M 830, fol. 261r). Both his new position in the Vatican chapter and his standing with Nello and his colleagues presumably lay behind his application, granted by Nicholas in January 28, 1451, to "repair, adorn, and extend" a house in the atrium or "paradise" of the basilica (*Collectio bullarum brevium* 2:133). The house at the sign of the archangel reverted to the chapter and in 1452 was let to a leather merchant (BAV, ACSP, Censuali 6 [1452], fol. 13v [November 13, 1452]); Antonello's new residence was altogether more conspicuous and prestigious.

The best known of Antonello's colleagues in the Vatican chapter was the datary and humanist Mafeo Vegio, author of a Christian thirteenth book of the *Aeneid*, among other things. In a passage written after Nicholas's death, Vegio lamented the condition of the buildings in the vicinity of the basilica, including some inhabited by canons, though he seemed satisfied with his own accommodation; his account is perhaps colored by his concern to emphasize the ruinous state of early Christian monuments in the area, to which he was the first to draw attention (Valentini and Zucchetti 1953, 387). According to the testimony of contemporary observers, indeed, the canons' quarters were the only residential element of the Leonine City where work was actually carried out. Niccola della Tuccia, a Viterbese chronicler with access to good sources of information in Rome, even compared the work on the canons' quarters with that on the Vatican palace and the Castel S. Angelo (della Tuccia 1852, 210; cf. Miglio 1975, 230).

Antonello's apparently private undertaking must be set, therefore, in a wider context, and in 1453 another canon, the protonotary Giorgio Cesarini, received permission to restore his quarters, which were of particular importance for the visual aspect of the outer facade of the atrium as seen from the piazza, since they were located "at the head of the piazza, next to the steps [i.e., those leading up to the entrance into the atrium] and the house of the arch-priest" (ASV, RV 430, fol. 80r). In addition, a large consignment of bricks delivered by Paciuri in late 1452 to the chapter may well have been for construction work on the canons' housing (BAV, ACSP, Censuali 5 [1447], fol. 48r). The evidence suggests that in a somewhat piecemeal fashion and largely through individual investment the chapter improved its quarters and, in the process, the surroundings of the basilica. They continued thereby the action taken by Nicholas in the first month of his pontificate to improve the aspect of the atrium of St. Peter's: several shops were demolished at that time, one of them under the famous mosaic of the *navicella* (ibid., fol. 8v). This was no religiously or ideologically motivated expulsion of money lenders from the temple, however; other shops in the atrium were not touched, including at least one in ruinous condition (ibid., Censuali 6 [1450], fol. 39r).

Antonello's standing with the pope is clear from his role in the nomination of one Cristoforo Santi, a *beneficiatus* of the Vatican chapter, to a canonicate and prebend in S. Maria in Aquiro in January 1451; Santi asserts that he is a *familiaris* of Antonello, who is in turn a *familiaris* and *continuus commensalis* of the pope (ASV, RV 413, fol. 251v [January 21, 1451]). Nicholas appointed a three-man committee, which included Antonio Margani, to see that Santi gained possession of his rights. In the following year, moreover, Antonello appears as a member of a similar committee charged with investing one Domenico Salviati with the *primiceriatus* of S. Maria Domne Rosa (ibid. 422, fol. 70r).[46] Antonello's colleagues on this occasion were Abbot Angelo of S. Anastasio alle Tre Fontane, whose connection with building operations under the chamberlain I have noted elsewhere, and Giorgio Cesarini, who was a figure of great importance in Nicholas's pontificate, as is evidenced by the prominent location of his house overlooking the Borgo from the steps of St. Peter's (as vicar and procurator general of Cardinal Bessarion in 1454 [ASR, CNC 482, fol. 291r] he was perhaps implicated in building projects, described in chapter 3, in the Trevi area). The houses of Giorgio Cesarini's family, an important patrician clan, stood in or near the district known as the Calcarario where Antonello had long been resident (Müntz 1878, 83; Lanciani 1902, 2:134). At least one of the family, however, was a leading resident of Ponte (*caporione* in 1448 and *conservator* in the following year); this was Giacomo Cesarini who had played an official role at Nicholas's coronation and was to be involved with street improvement under Paul II (Tommasini 1887, 205f.; ASV, RV 435, fol. 80r; Müntz 1879, 97).[47]

The apogee of Antonello's career came in 1452 with his appointment as *altarista* of the Vatican basilica in succession to Lorenzo Santi (*Collectio bullarum brevium* 2:109), who had been appointed soon after Nicholas's accession and with whom Antonello entertained relations of mutual dependence. The altarist had responsibility for the collection and distribution of alms given by pilgrims in the basilica; in the fourteenth century this office had been associated with that of guardian of the Vatican palace, concerned with the physical upkeep of the papal residence and its grounds (Moroni 1840–79, 1:282; Ehrle and Egger 1935, 55; Amadei 1969, 50). Certainly in 1335 the altarist was commissioned to survey the structural condition of the basilica.[48] It is possible, then, that Antonello's appointment involved a return to an earlier practice, for the *cura palatii* had hitherto evidently been in the hands of Nello as head of household (which, of course, included Antonello as *familiaris*; indeed, he handled the transfer of funds collected in St. Peter's from Santi to Nello at least in 1450; ASR, TS 1450, fol. 4v). Santi's appointment as altarist occurred in the same year, 1447, as that of Antonio Fatati as vicar and canon of the basilica, with a brief to reform the latter both spiritually and temporally.[49] Such reform must have involved restoration of the basilica, which would have required the use of funds given by pilgrims; if so, the two appointments were closely related.

Santi certainly knew men involved in construction and urban improvement under Nicholas; the 1439 will of Paolo della Valle of the powerful family of the Via del Papa vividly illuminates Santi's position in Roman society (Adinolfi

1865, 132 no. 9). Santi, identified as a Vatican canon, appears as a witness, alongside the contractor Frate Cola, whose career is discussed below, and Massimo de' Massimi, the prominent lawyer who played an important role in the preparation of the 1452 statutes of the *maestri di strada*. Santi was also an executor of the will; as such he found himself in the company of Domenico Porcari and Battista Leni, whose close involvement with the Medici bank and hence with Nicholas's pontificate I note elsewhere. Both these men were neighbors and no doubt allies of Giorgio Cesarini; Santi, on the other hand, had worked for Giorgio's uncle, the great prelate Cardinal Giuliano Cesarini. The chronicler Michele Canensi noted that members of the cardinal's household enjoyed the favor of the new pope; the case of Santi bears out his assertion (Miglio 1975, 217). It is possible, indeed, that Antonello too had been associated with Cardinal Cesarini—certainly he had ties in the appropriate neighborhood—and by 1447 was closely linked both to Giorgio Cesarini and Lorenzo Santi.

After 1452 there are few references to Antonello in the records. He does not appear in a list of canons who were present to approve the sale of a house belonging to the chapter in December 1453 (ASV, RV 430, fol. 265r), though it is the kind of transaction that might have required his particular expertise. It is possible that Antonello fell foul of the scrutiny to which the chapter was subjected by a committee of bishops appointed in 1452 to review and reform lapses in the performance of the divine cult in the basilica (ibid. 419, fol. 147r); he may, more probably, have lost the pope's confidence when the vault of S. Teodoro, which he raised in 1451, collapsed and had to be rebuilt, this time by Pietro da Varese (Urban 1961, 205; Müntz 1878, 145).[50] In any case, he survived, and in March 1455 an inventory of the treasury of the basilica noted that a chalice was in the possession of *dominus Antonellus*; he had perhaps borrowed it in order to say mass more impressively in a church entrusted to his care (Müntz and Frothingham 1883, 91). He was prominent in the building campaigns of Paul II; indeed he is named as the supervisor of the papal building works (Zippel 1904, 48 n.2).[51] Paul also made him a leading figure in his campaign to relieve distress among the well-born but economically vulnerable elements in the Roman population; Canensi relates that it was Antonello who in a ceremony in St. Peter's handed over a hundred gold pieces to an impoverished noblewoman to serve as her dowry (ibid., 138). It is probable that here, as in other ways, Paul modeled his policies on those of Nicholas, in whose caritative program Antonello perhaps played a leading role.

The careers of Antonello or of Giorgio Cesarini direct attention again, with some urgency, to the Borgo, for they indicate that the personnel for a thoroughgoing reconstruction of the Borgo—men, moreover, with a personal stake in such a project in a neighborhood in which they themselves resided—were available to Nicholas; indeed, the question now becomes not so much why Nicholas envisaged such a project at the end of his life, but why existing initiatives tending toward the improvement of the Borgo were not backed by papal authority and funds, as were not dissimilar initiatives in the city. Part of the answer may lie in the character of the chapter itself, in which prominent local families were heavily represented, as we have seen; it is possible that, as at the Lateran, Nicholas left powerful local interests in control of areas traditionally subject to them. For much if not most of the property in the Borgo, of course, was owned by the Vatican chapter, and any papal program of improvement might encounter suspicion on the part of the chapter that its rights and revenues in the area might be adversely affected.

Antonello's activity under Nicholas is comparable to some extent to that of a third local builder of importance in Nicholas's pontificate, a man usually identified in the documents simply as Frate Cola. His full name, Fra Niccolò Jacobelli da Cori "ordinis mendicatorum," occurs in the earliest reference to him that has come to light, the 1439 will of Paolo della Valle (Adinolfi 1865, 132 no. 9); here he appears not only as a witness, along with Lorenzo Santi, but also as a beneficiary of Paolo's will.[52] It is not clear what his connection with della Valle was; the latter, a medical doctor, had been chancellor of the commune and certainly could have afforded to use Cola's services as builder in his large palace complex on the Via del Papa.[53] On the other hand, Cola may well have been a neighbor; the will states that he had left Cori and come to Rome as "unus de pauperibus," and elsewhere it includes among the beneficiaries a settlement of friars (*fratres mendicantes*) located behind della Valle's house.

Cola's first appearance in connection with a building campaign reveals him as the architect of a structure that may have been relatively large and conspicuous, though it has now completely disappeared. He was responsible for the quarters built for the Lateran chapter during Eugenius's pontificate, even though the turbulent history of the Lateran as well as other contemporary troubles interrupted work on the building, the inception of which can most plausibly be dated to before Eugenius's flight from Rome in 1434.[54] Since Cola does not appear in the documents collected by Corbo (1969) illustrating building activity under Eugenius IV, it is reasonable to assume that he was employed by the Lateran chapter rather then the pope, though the latter may well have subsidized the project. Under Nicholas, Cola was put in charge of a project of particular concern to the pope, the restoration of S. Stefano Rotondo, though he was soon replaced by Rossellino (Müntz 1879, 317). Cola appears in Nello's ledger of 1450 alongside Beltramo da Varese, who was then working on the Castel S. Angelo. It is extraordinary to find a friar—*unus ex pauperibus* as he is termed in della Valle's will—classed with the greatest entrepreneur in the construction sector under Nicholas. Contractors generally had to be prepared to supply materials and labor in advance of payment, while many owned or leased facilities for the production and storage of materials; presumably the mendicant Cola drew on institutional funds and facilities, perhaps even belonging to the Cistercian order with which, through his office as *bullator*, he was associated as a *conversus*.

After 1450 Cola is not directly mentioned again in connection with building activity under Nicholas, though his documented activity as a builder was to be resumed long after the latter's death. It is possible that he could not match the skills and expertise at Nicholas's disposal after Rossellino's arrival in late 1451, or simply that he merely had other duties to attend to. Sometime in 1450 he was appointed *bullator*; indeed in the papal accounts thereafter he is normally referred to as Frate Cola Bolatore (Müntz 1879, 317). The *bullatores* were a small college of officials, at this time rarely exceeding three or four active members, who prepared the leaden seals and attached them to papal bulls (Baumgarten 1907, passim). Since excellent opportunities for alteration of the documents that passed through their hands obviously presented themselves, the *bullatores* were supposed to be illiterate, at least in Latin. They were often laymen, therefore, and of low rank. Although expected to be celibate, their conduct was frequently lax; much of the evidence for the college in the fifteenth century comes from papal dispensations granting the right to make wills in which children could be provided for (ibid., 337–341).

Such leniency may reflect the close proximity to the pope that they enjoyed, as was necessary for the discharge of their duties. However small the retinue that accompanied the pope on visitations and during the summers spent in retreat from the heat, dust, and mosquitoes of Rome, at least one *bullator* was present to enable papal business to coninue without interruption: this was the case, for instance, during Nicholas's extensive travels in the summers of 1449 and 1450. Nicholas's appointment of a trusted architect was to have a famous sixteenth-century parallel: Julius II appointed Bramante to the office, and other artists of the period were nominated.[55] This suggests that the particular expertise and background of such men was of concern especially to those popes interested in artistic patronage. We may guess, therefore, that the *bullator* Frate Cola played a crucial advisory and mediatory role at the papal court, both through his knowledge of the construction industry and through his connections with leading figures of local society.

Such suggestions, unfortunately, are beyond proof. All that is known about Cola's activity in Nicholas's later years is that he took two adjacent houses in the Borgo S. Spirito in August 23, 1453; according to the conditions spelled out in the papal letter that enabled him to do this, he was to thoroughly repair the property and to pay the remarkably low rent of two ducats per annum (Baumgarten 1907, 33). It is perhaps significant that the apparently celibate Cola took over an extensive residence in the Borgo while his probable predecessor in office, who had sired a large illegitimate family, resided in doubtless cramped quarters in the Vatican palace.[56] Cola's move to the Borgo S. Spirito may reflect papal pressure, though it is perhaps more likely that the administration of the hospital was interested in the improvement of the immediate environs of their building. In any case, Cola's influence on the measures for the Borgo described by Manetti looks likely.

Like Antonello, Cola does not reappear in the building accounts until the pontificate of Paul II, when he was commissioned to work on the roof of S. Maria in Aracoeli (Müntz 1879, 87). He was also concerned with the erection of new quarters for the exercise of his office (Baumgarten 1907, 344–346). These stood near the palace of Paul II, the Palazzo Venezia, on which Cola also worked, occasionally in collaboration with Antonello (Zippel 1904, 42 n.2; Gottlob 1889, 307). After Paul's death in 1471 Cola and a Florentine, as former supervisors of construction at the palace, were summoned to present accounts of work done during their terms of office. It was Cola's last task, for he died the following year (Baumgarten 1907, 350).

Frate Cola's career, like those of Antonello d'Albano and Paciuri, illustrates the extent to which Nicholas's campaigns, far from constituting a foreign element transplanted onto the aged body of medieval Rome, were deeply involved with local initiatives, experience, and skills, though this is not to deny the innovatory nature of Nicholas's pontificate in this respect. The sheer diversity of these three careers, extended and confirmed by the forms of patronage offered by the pope or his officials, is most striking. Coherence or even homogeneity was secured at the level of account keeping and supervision through the operations of Nello and his staff, yet at the level of the actual work processes and organizational structures in the *cantieri* relatively little standardization can be observed.

In the three cases in review, indeed, building was by no means an exclusive activity, let alone profession. All three men had skills, contacts, experience, and status that could be exploited as need arose in various contexts. In the unpredictable atmosphere of fifteenth-century Rome, with the frequent succession of pontiffs and consequent changes in patronage as in other areas of policy, such versatility was essential for survival and for the preservation of position in Roman society. These objective conditions and the natural responses to them might well inhibit the development by local men of consistent careers or professional status in the sector of construction and architectural design. In contrast immigrant—or perhaps rather migrant—craftsmen and contractors had less time to adapt to specifically Roman conditions and might, if the wind changed, take their pickings and be off to exploit their newly gained or enhanced expertise and reputation, if such they had, in another place and at another patron's expense. Such professionals, who applied their technical, organizational, and sometimes design skills where work was to be had, also played a major role in the building campaigns of Nicholas V.

Contractors and Builders: The Immigrants
Wherever in fifteenth-century Italy there were bricks to be laid, stones to be cut, and cement to be mixed, migrant Lombard craftsmen provided an often conspicuous component of the work force. The traditional skills of these men and their readiness to travel long distances in search of work were greatly valued, not least in Rome. Nor were large and wealthy cities alone in this respect. Lombards traditionally formed an important element of the labor force of Viterbo (Pinzi 1887–1913, 4:21), while they appear also in small towns of purely local significance such as Vitorchiano in the Patrimonium (Aleandri 1911, 102–105) and Matelica in the March of Ancona (Touring Club Italiano 1962, 259; the Palazzo Ottoni in Matelica was built in 1452 by builders from Lugano). On the other hand, they were able to penetrate into cities with strong local building traditions and skilled manpower, like Venice or Florence.

Expansion in the building trades in Rome naturally accompanied the growth of prosperity and economic activity that followed the definitive return of the popes to Rome and the various attempts of the latter to restore the city's decaying buildings. Under Martin V and Eugenius IV immigrant workers were prominent in the labor force employed on the major building projects. Lombards, however, were but one of several national groups represented; many of the less skilled workers were of transalpine origin, while the highly skilled men were often Tuscans. The latter were associated especially with fine stonecutting and woodworking; Lombard expertise in the crafts of construction as such was perhaps unrivaled, though their concentration on craft activity perhaps inhibited the development of architects among them and left the field open for others, especially the Tuscans (Corbo 1969; Bertolotti 1861; Battisti 1959). On the other hand, the general built environment in central Italy in the quattrocento may have been deeply affected by Lombard design procedures and even stylistic preferences, even if these were of no great sophistication.

In the many building projects of Nicholan Rome the Lombard contribution, though considerable, was far from predominant. Müntz was struck, however, by the crucial role played by one especially large and well-organized Lombard equipe, that headed by Beltramo di Martino da Varese (Müntz 1878, 104; Golzio and Zander 1968, 512f.). Some measure of Beltramo's importance can be given by the major projects on which he worked—the Castel S. Angelo, the Campidoglio, the *tribuna* of St. Peter's, S. Maria della Febbre, the Ripa Grande, the fortifications of the Leonine City, S. Teodoro, and S. Maria Maggiore. Outside Rome he worked on the castle at Orvieto. In addition to the manpower at his disposal, he had access, presumably through ownership, to considerable capital assets: quarries, limekilns, wagons, and barges. He occupied an effectively supervisory role beyond his own equipe, for on at least two occasions he served on a committee charged to investigate completed buildings to check that contracted tasks had in fact been carried out.

Beltramo's services to the pope went beyond the merely professional, and his firm evidently enjoyed direct papal favor, probably mediated through Pietro da Noceto, the pope's compatriot and private secretary. In 1451 the Lombard master Benedetto Beltrami da Compione, who may have been one of Beltramo's sons, worked on the chapel of the family of Nicholas's stepfather in the cathedral of Sarzana, Nicholas's hometown (Sforza 1884, 248).It is likely, then, that Beltramo's prominence in the building trades in Nicholan Rome, where his position was established already by 1450, resulted from contact with Nicholas and his circle outside Rome before 1447, for there is no trace of involvement on his part in the extensively documented campaigns of Eugenius IV, nor is there evidence to connect him, like Frate Cola, with nonpapal sources of patronage before 1447. References to him after Nicholas's death are few and uncertain; clearly his prominence in the building trades in Rome coincided with Nicholas's pontificate, though he was never received into the papal household. Nor, finally, has evidence come to light of the location and nature of his residence, workshops, or other premises, extensive though these must have been.

In 1450 Beltramo was remunerated handsomely for his work on the Castel S. Angelo (ASR, M 830, fol. 152v), a project of great importance to Nicholas. The documents of 1450 do not connect this project with Nello and his staff but rather with Pietro da Noceto, who conveyed the money to Beltramo and perhaps had some supervisory responsibility. Beltramo, then, was undoubtedly one of the *praefecti* mentioned by Manetti as presiding over the building activity that continued throughout the hot and plague-stricken summers of the Jubilee, to Manetti's evident approval. Manetti's source for such activity was perhaps his fellow-secretary Pietro da Noceto (Manetti himself moved to Rome some years later), who may have helped Beltramo to his prominent position in the Vatican *cantiere* in and after 1452. Indeed, Beltramo's highly organized equipe may have provided a model for the Vatican building operation or, at least, for Manetti's account of it as a coherently structured operation under the direction of a single individual; Manetti himself, needless to say, advanced classical and biblical paradigms (Magnuson 1958, 360).

Beltramo's work on the Castel S. Angelo may have enabled him to build up his equipe and capital assets. In any case, by the end of 1450 Beltramo was branching out into other projects, notably the often quite small-scale projects along the river that could be supplied by water in the same way as the *cantiere* at the Castel S. Angelo. It is highly unlikely that Beltramo could have undertaken such projects if the work at the castle was not already largely complete. The work on the river installations, of course, brought Beltramo into close contact with Nello, whose control of the *dogana* of Ripa and associated construction has been mentioned. Indeed, though the work at the castle does not appear in Nello's ledger for 1450 (it is entered in that kept by the chamberlain), the work along the river is recorded in detail. Closer to the castle, Beltramo worked on the restoration of the river wall above the Ponte S. Angelo and on that of the Tor di Nona (map 2), referred to in the documents as the tower of the *soldano*, the chief security official in Rome (ASR, TS 1450, fol. 159v). The *soldano* at the time was a Lombard, the rich Milanese Giacomo Calvi, who received other signal favors from Nicholas.[57] Both Calvi and Beltramo appear as *procuratores* for Lombard clerics needing mediators with the ecclesiastical financial administration.[58] Beltramo thus enhanced his standing in his native country, to which he doubtless expected to return some day. And it is probable that he benefited from the generally pro-Milanese policies of Nicholas V; already in April 1447 the vice-chancellor Francesco Condulmer was writing to his native Venice that the Milanese lobby in Rome was especially powerful and that the pope was *infestatus* by supporters of the duke of Milan (Archivio di Stato, Venice, Deliberazioni del Senato 17, fol. 124v). Indeed, the Cremonese Niccolò Amidani was rising rapidly in Nicholas's administration; after serving as de facto vice-chamberlain probably from 1448, he was appointed governor of Rome during the absence of the pope in summer 1449 and finally received permanent appointment as vice-chamberlain and governor of the city in January 1453.[59]

In 1451, according to Stefano Infessura (1890), 3f., Nicholas restored the buildings of the Campidoglio; Infessura, as the *scribasenatus* or chancellor of the Roman municipality later in the century, was in a position to know, and indeed his assertion is corroborated by the archival evidence. A particular impetus for the reconstruction of the municipal palaces on the Campidoglio, which Giovanni Rucellai in 1450 described as partly in ruins (Rucellai 1960,

76), must have been given by the impending visit of Frederick III. This occurred early in 1452, and the Campidoglio served as the scene for ceremonies of welcome on the part of the officials of the commune. Beltramo's equipe was centrally involved in the work on the Campidoglio, especially that on the Senator's Palace. Here in 1452 and 1453 extensive operations are documented as carried out by the nephew of Beltramo, Pietro di Giovanni, who, though normally identified as a stonecutter, was now evidently acting as his uncle's representative in a major construction campaign; indeed Beltramo, whose particular concerns were now elsewhere, had to undertake formally to guarantee Pietro's work (Müntz 1878, 150).[60] Much of Pietro's task involved the rear of the Senator's Palace, including the tower that flanks the route up to the Campidoglio from the Forum (fig. 3), adjacent to the office where in the fifteenth century the sale of salt, an important papal monopoly, took place.

Between 1449 and 1451 Beltramo had at least one project outside Rome: in 1451 he received payment for work on the castle at Orvieto (map 4; ASR, TS 1451, fol. 37v). He may have been connected with another major project in that city, for in 1450 a Pietro di Giovanni da Como, a stonecutter described in the documents as a good and skilled artisan, was at work in the cathedral, where considerable construction took place at this time (Müntz 1878, 89; Battisti 1959, 56; Golzio and Zander 1968, 545). There is little doubt that Pietro da Como is the nephew who later found himself in charge of operations at the Campidoglio, presumably on the basis of his experience in Orvieto. Beltramo's role in Orvieto was not without risk; the people of the city protested vehemently against the establishment of a castle in their unruly town (della Tuccia 1852, 210), where Stefano Porcari had taken advantage of his term of office as *podestà* to muddy the waters (Pleyer 1927, 51; Toews 1968, 278); evidently the pope was concerned to leave no doubt of the absolute subjection of the town to the rule of the Church. It is not surprising, then, to find the supervision of the building operations and perhaps the control of the town entrusted to the Paduan *condottiere* Antonio de Rido (ASR, CDG 1449–51, fol. 80r; ASR, M 830, fols. 15v, 18r, etc.), who had under Eugenius IV held the position of castellan of the Castel S. Angelo (Zippel 1912, 175).

If, as is likely, Beltramo had been associated with the Orvieto project from the beginning (i.e., at latest from 1449), he may have worked for Antonio at the Castel S. Angelo on the small-scale restoration carried out there under Eugenius; the connection with Antonio may explain Beltramo's appearance at Orvieto and at no other provincial site. Beltramo may even also have worked at the Lateran, where Antonio's relative Pietro de Rido played an important role in the 1440s as the spokesman of the reformed canons. The reformed Lateran chapter was made up largely of northern Italians (Pietro de Rido was from Padua), among them many Lombards (Widloecher 1929, 375); the Lateran *cantiere* was perhaps a natural entry point for a Lombard master into the competitive construction sector of Rome.

In 1452 Beltramo was no longer occupied at Orvieto, nor were the operations there directly entrusted to Nello's supervision. Indeed, already in late 1451 a further Lombard, Simone da Pavia, who does not otherwise appear in the records of building projects under Nicholas, though he was a *familiaris* and *scu-tifer*, was in charge of the work on the castle (ASV, RV 419, fol. 176v); in 1455 yet another Lombard, Orlando Maffei, received payment as builder of the palace and castle of Orvieto (Aleandri 1911, 107). At the cathedral work continued independently; in September 1451 the chapter succeeded in attracting to Orvieto no less a personage than the *capomaestro* of Siena cathedral, Antonio Federighi (Müntz 1878, 102; Milanesi 1854, 266 no. 187). Given his Sienese connections and his responsibility for affairs in the Patrimonium, Nello da Bologna may well have had a hand in this appointment, as also in the recruitment of Pietro da Como for the cathedral building office; the presence of these men at Orvieto may indicate the concern of Nicholas and his representatives to placate the Orvietani by supplying highly skilled craftsmen to work on a project of central importance to the townspeople.

In 1452 Beltramo was assigned to tasks of far greater significance than construction in a provincial town. In this year began the work on the *tribuna* of St. Peter's and the adjacent chapel of S. Maria della Febbre (fig. 31); whatever the authorship of this project there is no doubt that the construction process was firmly in the hands of Beltramo (Müntz 1878, 122–124; Mack 1983, 66), who may himself, needless to say, have had some imput in the design of a project that, as has often been pointed out, bears little resemblance to the more advanced ideas of the leading Florentine masters (Urban 1963, 150–154).

Beltramo had worked in the Leonine City already in 1451 when he was in charge of considerable construction on the perimeter wall in the area of the Porta Pertusa (ASR, TS 1451, fols. 106v–107v), a gate to the west of the basilica that marked the threshold of a spur of the Via Cassia (Poggio referred to it once as the Porta Cassia), perhaps coincidentally the road that linked Rome with the Patrimonium and such towns as Orvieto and Siena (maps 3, 4). The project continued until 1454, when a lock and keys were provided for a postern gate in the "muro di Porta Pertusa" (ASR, SMP 1454, fol. 71v).[61] Manetti in 1455 was to describe the improvement of the fortifications of Rome as one of the five main areas of construction under Nicholas. After the Jubilee at least, the emphasis seems to have been on the defenses of the Vatican (apart from the restoration of existing fortifications, the perimeter of the Leonine City was greatly expanded; Westfall 1974a, 107–109, 143–148), a project in which it is clear that Beltramo played a major role.

On June 16, 1452, Nello da Bologna and Beltramo da Varese signed an agreement (*patti*), and Beltramo received the handsome sum of 2,000 ducats, advanced by the bank of Tommaso Spinelli (Müntz 1878, 122f.). The substance of the agreement is unfortunately not given in the extant documents, though it is clear that Nello and Beltramo had negotiated the schedule and cost of work on the *tribuna* and the chapel of S. Maria della Febbre; doubtless the basic design of each building had also been determined and agreed to. In the same month Beltramo signed as guarantor for his nephew's activity at the Campidoglio; clearly Nello was concerned to monopolize Beltramo's services at the Vatican. Though the disbursements for the *tribuna* and S. Maria della Febbre are not distinguished in the accounts, the funding came from different banks, that for the *tribuna* from Spinelli, and that for S. Maria della Febbre from the firm of the Spannocchi and Mirabelli (ibid.).[62] The chapel with the adjacent obelisk stood on the southern flank of the basilica, where it was skirted by the route that led through the Borgo, past the basilica, and out through the Porta Pertusa to the Via Cassia. In a way, then, Beltramo's work on fortifications and that on the chapel were related, especially if these construction projects can be set in the context of papal concern with the economic development and political security of the area traversed by the Cassia, a rural sector with its apex at the Vatican.

The early phase of work on the *tribuna* was plagued by difficulties. The first task facing Beltramo and his men was the demolition of certain venerable structures located to the rear of the apse of the Constantinian St. Peter's. Information about the buildings concerned is contained in a text written by one of the Vatican canons, the datary Mafeo Vegio, who shortly before or, more probably, shortly after Nicholas's death recorded his investigations of the early Christian monuments swept away to make room for Nicholas's *tribuna* (Vignati 1959, 58). Vegio, whose own quarters were in a nearby ancient structure converted for use by the chapter, is silent about the pope's building projects, though he laments not only the ruinous condition of the early Christian structures in the area but also of the canons' quarters, for all the improvements carried out on the latter under Nicholas (Valentini and Zucchetti 1953, 387). There can be little doubt that he regarded with disfavor the operations of Beltramo and his men, which he perhaps saw as diverting resources from more useful projects that might also be less destructive of antiquities and sacred sites. It is not clear how representative Vegio's views were either of the Vatican canons or of the pietistic current of humanism to which he belonged; in the atmosphere in Rome after the fall of Constantinople it is likely that they were.

Progress on the work on the foundations of the *tribuna* was impeded less by criticism than by the discovery of certain tombs (ASR, TS 1452, fols. 14v, 27r [July 2, 1452]); Nicholas paid the workmen who found the tombs a small reward, which he could well afford to do since the tombs contained a considerable amount of gold (Bertolotti 1861, 16). In the following year, however, work was evidently proceeding on a large scale: at the end of 1453 18,000 ducats are recorded as the sum of the amounts paid to Beltramo for projects at the Vatican, the *tribuna*, S. Maria della Febbre, and the wall at the Porta Pertusa (ASR, TS 1453, fol. 33r).[63] On the same page is recorded the relatively paltry sum of 1,000 ducats paid to Rossellino for work at S. Stefano Rotondo (where the basic restoration work and, probably, the roofing had already been carried out by Frate Cola); it is hard to see why, if Rossellino was indeed the design architect both at the *tribuna* and S. Stefano, the accounting procedures were so different in each case. This does not rule the Florentine sculptor-architect out as designer of the *tribuna*, especially as he was drawing a salary as "ingegnere del palazzo," but it draws attention to the lack of direct archival evidence for such an assumption and to the abstract quality of the argument, most cogently advanced by Westfall (1974a, 35–62, esp. 59), that the Nicholan building projects, especially those at the Vatican, should be investigated in the light of the familiar Albertian distinction between ideation and realization of a building project.

We have noted the coherent pattern of attention given by Nicholas to centrally planned structures, culminating, of course, in the projected crossing of St. Peter's. Beltramo and his equipe were involved with at least three of these. At S. Maria della Febbre, originally an early Christian mausoleum, a new vault was erected, while at about the same time a similar project is documented at a venerable diaconal church, that of S. Teodoro in the lee of the Palatine (map 2; fig. 15). Here Antonello d'Albano had already sought to vault the relatively small building, but his vault had collapsed, and Beltramo's nephew Pietro, fresh from his achievments at the nearby Campidoglio, was called in to try his hand; his vault, with the arms of Nicholas V in the keystone, survives to this day (Urban 1961, 205; Fasolo 1941, 112f.). Pietro had probably also been implicated in the work at S. Maria della Febbre, in his capacity as *scalpellino*, as the maker of the carved marble windows that Beltramo installed there.

The sums recorded as paid to Beltramo for the *tribuna* do not constitute the total amount spent on this project. Other, much smaller payments also went toward it, and the manner of their payment allows some insight into the organization of the Beltramo equipe at the time of its greatest success. The records quite often mention supervisory foremen (*soprastanti*) working under Beltramo, usually with responsibility for particular parts of a project and, presumably, charge of a particular group of men. These foremen might be more or less independent: the men who received a reward for finding tombs at the back of St. Peter's, as noted above, are described as having their own "compagnia"; nevertheless, their reward was transferred to them by a man described as Beltramo's assistant. The amount of the reward, on the other hand, was determined not by Beltramo, but by Nello.

Certain foremen found themselves answering both to Beltramo and Nello; a certain Giuliano Vergorella, for instance, received a salary of three ducats a month from the papal treasury, while Beltramo was responsible for his maintenance (Müntz 1878, 85). He is perhaps to be identified with the Giuliano di Ser Ruberto who is recorded as "soprastante nostro a la trebuna di S. Pietro" on March 19, 1453, implying that his position was higher than Beltramo's other foremen, and that he took orders from persons higher than Beltramo (the epithet *nostro* is normally used of members of the household). It is noteworthy that Giuliano di Ser Ruberto was neither a Lombard nor a Florentine but a Roman, a citizen of the Rione Ponte who enjoyed sufficient standing in the city to be elected to the highest communal magistracy in 1449 (Tommasini 1887, 205). It is not clear what the significance of this might be: Giuliano's position at least on the margin of Beltramo's equipe may represent a process of Romanization undergone by the latter, or he could simply have been a competent and well-connected craftsman and contractor whom Beltramo found it convenient to hire.[64]

Whether or not Vergorella should be identified with Giuliano di Ser Ruberto, he may perhaps have been a confidante rather of Nello than Beltramo, and his role in the Vatican *cantiere* may have been related to a concern on the part of

Nello to assume closer control of the project. Nello may have had good reason for such a step. With the expansion of Beltramo's equipe that must have accompanied the development of the Vatican projects, Beltramo's ability to supervise the various operations carried out by his men suffered. Inevitably he came to rely on foremen, as we have seen. They were not always dependable; in 1453 two of his men were caught building a wall without mortar (ASR, SMP 1453, fol. 75r), probably that of the Porta Pertusa, which was relatively remote. The culprits are not named in the papal ledger; they were identified at first as *garzoni* of Beltramo, but this was corrected to *maestri*, as if to emphasize their independent status and diminish Beltramo's culpability for their act of dereliction. He was not the only contractor to suffer from the actions of unscrupulous subordinates; the same occurred, at about the same time, to the Roman contractor Giuliano di Ser Ruberto, indicating that some of his activity at least was independent of Beltramo (ASR, SMP 1454, fol. 4v).

In Nicholas's last years Beltramo's activity as supplier and probably as producer of building materials seems to have grown relative to that as contractor. In Nello's ledger of 1453 several references appear to consignments for which Beltramo is paid, including large quantities of bricks and mortar; these suggest that Beltramo operated his own kilns. In September 1454 he was paid for no fewer than 133 wagon loads of stone brought downriver mainly in his own boat and, after unloading, carried to the *tribuna* on wagons some of which belonged to Beltramo and some to the papal household (Müntz 1878, 109).[65] Since a Pietro Lombardo who was involved with quarrying activities in the area of the Roman forum (ASR, TS 1452, fol. 218r) should probably be identified as Beltramo's nephew, it is likely that Beltramo owned or leased his own quarries. The growing evidence of Beltramo's penetration into the local building economy corroborates the suggestion advanced above of the Romanization of his equipe and his operations, which by the end of Nicholas's pontificate must have been quite similar to those of the Roman contractor and supplier Antonio Paciuri. In 1455 Pietro di Giovanni left Rome for Naples to join the band of sculptors in the employ of King Alfonso (Battisti 1959, 56); there is no evidence that Beltramo accompanied his nephew, and he was perhaps able by now to survive in Rome without papal commissions.

Nicholas V's reliance on Beltramo went beyond the latter's primary professional role. In the account of the suppression of the Porcarian conspiracy written by the Viterbese chronicler Niccola della Tuccia, Beltramo features prominently in the attack made by papal forces on the house of Stefano Porcari soon after the news of the planned coup had first broken: Beltramo and the captain of the pope's bodyguard, Sbrandellato da Narni, went there at the head of a band of some 200 armed men (della Tuccia 1852, 232). Among the latter, we may assume, were some tough laborers from Beltramo's building teams. Della Tuccia's account states that the pope himself sent Beltramo and the others to attack Porcari's house; in view of Stefano Caccia's assertion that the pope learned of the conspiracy only after Porcari's capture (see note 28), it is far more probable that it was Nello who involved Beltramo in an operation whose outcome was by no means yet certain. Nello obviously knew Beltramo well and could rely on his loyalty and strength of character.

Neither Caccia nor any other contemporary observer, however, mentions the ragtag army prominent in della Tuccia's account; instead the scene is dominated by familiar figures of authority, like the chamberlain, the governor of the city, or Cardinal Capranica. The governor, Niccolò Amidani, must have been involved early on, and indeed Pietro de Godis reported that he was the first high official, along with Domenico Capranica, to receive intelligence of the impending coup (Lehnerdt 1907, 58).[66] This is consistent with della Tuccia's account, for Amidani's fellow Lombard Beltramo would surely have been careful to alert him as soon as possible, probably at his quarters in the palace of the mint; if so, it was there that Amidani joined the papal force on its way from the Vatican to the house of Stefano Porcari in the Rione Pigna. After the condemnation and execution of Porcari, the latter's house was destroyed in the traditional manner (ibid., 67); it was perhaps another commission that Nello, who was charged with the disposal of the conspirators' property, gave to Beltramo.

If della Tuccia's mention of Beltramo occasions surprise, his emphasis on the role of Sbrandellato da Narni, captain of the papal guard, though unique to della Tuccia's account of the conspiracy, conforms to what Sbrandellato's official activities would have been on such an occasion.[67] Nor is there any reason for della Tuccia to invent Beltramo's role in the events; he does not mention him otherwise. Della Tuccia, therefore, must have had access to information not accessible to or not used by other writers. In view of the relatively low social status of the protagonists in his account, della Tuccia's informants must be sought, as it were, below stairs. Della Tuccia lived in Viterbo, far from the rumors and gossip of the papal court, but there was one individual in particular who provided a link between the two. The *scriptor* and papal secretary Pietro Lunense combined his services to the pope, on whose behalf he occasionally went on missions to towns in the papal states (e.g., ASV, IE 414, fol. 97v), with the office of chancellor of the commune of Viterbo. For though Pietro, like Nicholas himself, was of Ligurian origin, he had settled in Viterbo and taken Viterbese citizenship (Pinzi 1887–1913, 4:66). He too is mentioned by della Tuccia, but by no other chronicler, in connection with the Porcarian conspiracy: the conspirators planned to seize not only Pietro da Noceto, brother of the castellan of the Castel S. Angelo, but also "Messer Pier Lunense, cognato del detto." It is plausible, then, that della Tuccia's source was Pietro Lunense or someone close to him; in addition, some connection to the Lombards in the employ of Nicholas can be assumed, on the part either of della Tuccia or his source in Rome. Pietro Lunense can be suspected here too, since he was himself a building patron; his house in Viterbo was reconstructed sometime in the mid-fifteenth century in a remarkably up-to-date style.[68] It must have been in reasonable condition in the spring of 1448, for when the pope's mother and sister visited Viterbo at that time, they were received and entertained by Pietro in his house, after passing in procession through the city (Pinzi 1887–1913, 4:65). Later expenditure on improvements to the property can be documented:

a bull of June 1, 1451, granted tax immunities to Pietro to aid construction work at the house. Unfortunately the names of the craftsmen involved are not known; they may well have been—in a demonstration of Nicholas's favor toward Pietro—members of Beltramo's extensive equipe.

Better documented are major building schemes of a public nature in Viterbo. On June 4, 1447, a contractor undertook to carry out repairs on city hall, the *palazzo dei priori*, partly because it was unsuitable for winter use and had caused illness among members of the city government; it was also found architecturally lacking ("male ornatum"), and it was surely in part for this reason that a loggia was built in the fountain court. Nicholas also confirmed Eugenius's edict that income from fines should be committed to repairs at the official residence of the *podestà* (ibid., 59f.).

The most important project in Viterbo in Nicholas's pontificate was the construction of new baths. The pope suffered from gout, and when the commune of Viterbo invited him to spend the summer of 1448 in their city, it was no doubt intended that he should avail himself of the existing bathing facilities. The pope stayed in Rome but sent his mother and sister, who visited at least three of the Viterbese baths, as della Tuccia relates. This visit doubtless provided the impetus for a campaign of construction, the results of which received high praise; della Tuccia gives an extended description of the new baths, emphasizing the variety and luxury of the rooms, with their chimneys and fine windows (della Tuccia 1852, 247). Manetti, too, praised the "plura ac diversa habitacula," though he doubtless had higher standards of luxury than the provincial della Tuccia (Manetti 1734, c.929). The complex, known as the Baths of the Crusade (were the revenues from it pledged to the fund for the crusade against the Turks administered by Nello?), was ready by 1454, for in that year at latest Nicholas V, whose gout attacks had meanwhile intensified, came to undergo the treatment there (Ciampi 1872, 235; Pastor 1958, 426).[69]

Vasari attributed the design of the baths, as of so much else, to Rossellino (Müntz 1878, 164); the contractor, certainly, was a Lombard, Stefano di Beltramo. The baths project was not among those supervised by Nello; it was financed from the provincial treasury and supervised, presumably, by its officials. Nor was Stefano di Beltramo a son of Beltramo da Varese, for he came from Lugano (ibid., 164), though it is possible that he had been at least professionally adopted by the leading Lombard contractor of the day.[70] In any case, it is likely that the Lombard builders in Rome and Viterbo were in contact, and that stories of Beltramo's role in the events of January 1453 spread to the builders of the "bagno della cruciata" who in turn may even have been the builders also of the house of Pietro Lunense. Unfortunately, the baths complex has completely disappeared, and no assessment of its architectural character is possible.

With the death of Nicholas V and the winding up of the majority of his projects, Beltramo disappears from view. The cutback began before the pope's death, however, as resources were diverted to the crusade and the pope's morale deteriorated. A letter of January 20, 1454, sent to Nicodemo Tranchedini by his successors in Francesco Sforza's legation in Rome states that no fewer than 150 builders had been dismissed from the pope's employ (ASM, ASD 41, no. 28); Beltramo himself is not mentioned, but some of his men must have been involved. The documents indicate that Beltramo worked for Pius II on the Castel S. Angelo, and for Paul II on the Trevi aqueduct and fountain (Borgatti 1930, 1178; Müntz 1878, 124); significantly perhaps these were projects on which Beltramo's earlier involvement under Nicholas is certain. The work in Trevi under Nicholas must have brought Alberti and Beltramo into contact, and may have been a factor in the involvement of Alberti in the Vatican *cantiere*. For Beltramo, however, the abandonment of Nicholas's *tribuna* project marked the conclusion of the triumphal phase of his career. Apart from very occasional commissions in Rome after Nicholas's death, the last we hear of Beltramo is as contractor at minor and remote *castelli*, distant indeed from the shrine of the prince of the apostles.[71]

An important aspect of Beltramo's role under Nicholas was evidently his representative status as a leading figure not only in the community of Lombard builders and laborers, many of whom he employed, but of the Lombard community itself. And this, as we have seen, may have involved him on occasion as a conduit of information between Rome and other centers where Lombards were employed. Such connections with particular places or regions were of importance for many of the more prominent figures in the building campaigns: it is almost as if they provided an alternative, informal diplomatic corps. My final example of a prominent craftsman in Nicholas's employ is a further case of this phenomenon.

Niccolò di Lorenzo da Fabriano was the only immigrant craftsman whose transfer to Rome and the occasion for it can be reconstructed, and he is interesting not so much for his evident professional skills as for the vicissitudes of his career and the variety of his activities. Niccolò owed his employment by the pope to the fortunate circumstance of Nicholas's visits to his hometown, Fabriano. This middle-sized town (fig. 34), situated in the heart of the mountainous province of the March of Ancona (map 4), was and still is famous for its paper industry (Gasparinetti 1943); in the later medieval period the production of paper and other industrial activities brought Fabriano a fair degree of prosperity, creating the conditions for the emergence of a Sienese-influenced school of painting, of which Gentile da Fabriano was the leading representative (Bertolotti 1885).

By the middle of the quattrocento, the level of artistic production had fallen with the general economic decline caused by intermittent warfare and by the domination and exploitation of Francesco Sforza, to whose ephemeral Marchigian statelet Fabriano reluctantly belonged. Internal tumults were also a factor in this decline; these culminated in a bloody uprising in 1435 against the traditional lords of Fabriano, the Chiavelli family. Most of the Chiavelli were massacred, though a few escaped to the court of the related clan of the Da Varano at Camerino; Nello's partner in the *dogana di bestiame* of Campagna Marittima, Arcangelo Chiavelli da Camerino, was doubtless a member of this group. The property of the Chiavelli, who like the Malatesta of Rimini and other ruling families of the region were officially ecclesiastical vicars, reverted to the Church (Sassi 1955a; 1955b; 1964–65).

Nicholas visited the town twice, in the summers of 1449 and 1450; he may have come not only because Fabriano seemed a safe haven from the plague, but also because the palace was unoccupied and belonged directly to the papacy. The original decision to come to Fabriano was made impromptu, while the pope was staying in the not far distant Spoleto (Sassi 1955b, 3). The visit can be set, however, in the context of a general program of reviving the economic fortunes of minor centers in the papal states, whatever the attraction of labor, skills, and investment toward the capital, now clearly in a period of upswing (Mack 1982, 64f., 68 nn.27–32; Heydenreich 1937, 105–146; Molajoli 1968, 45–57). Nicholas's policy had, needless to say, a clear political and indeed military component at a time of often tenuous control over large areas *de iure* subject to the papacy; the consistent improvement not only of fortifications but also of public buildings and churches, from the construction of which the local economies surely benefited, made clear to the townspeople the advantages of papal rule while reminding them of the temporal power and sacred authority wielded by the popes. The reality did not match the claims made by Manetti (1734, c.929) and other panegyrists; Fabriano is perhaps typical for the early commitment shown to projects that soon withered as funds and energies were diverted elsewhere.

The projects at Fabriano have recently been well discussed by C. R. Mack (1982), 64f.; apart from the usual work on the fortifications, these included most notably the restoration of the papal palace (the former palace of the Chiavelli) and the adjacent church of S. Francesco, as well as work on the cathedral that faced the Franciscan convent across an extensive piazza (fig. 34). The Franciscan church no longer exists, while many other buildings have suffered extensive alteration or even replacement, so that only an approximate reconstruction of the quattrocento appearance of the area is possible. The piazza itself was funnel-shaped, its wider and lower end marked by an impressive medieval fountain and by the robust *palazzo del podestà*, which is pierced by a deep vault leading into the center of town, to the market square, and to mills and other industrial facilities built on and over the river. The lower end of the main square was defined on one side (to the east) by the facade of the papal palace, but beyond the palace and on the same side the edge of the square was formed by the flank of the Franciscan church, which faced toward the side of the papal palace. The pope had steps built to the church, which stood on a slight rise above the level of the piazza; presumably these steps gave access to the main entrance in the front of the church facing the papal palace (the portal is indicated in the seventeenth-century view illustrated in fig. 34), unless there was a subsidiary entrance in the flank facing the piazza. In either case the relationship of the piazza and church must have been formalized and even monumentalized.

If the steps joined the piazza and the side entrance of the church they will have penetrated a new, two-storied structure erected to flank S. Francesco, thus further defining and ennobling the piazza. This building contained shops on its lower floor (replacing earlier, less dignified premises) and an arcaded loggia above, perhaps on line with or even connected to the papal palace. Documented work on the cathedral, the major building on the other side of the square, involved only the roof, though it is at least possible that minor cosmetic work on the exterior was done. By the seventeenth century this side of the piazza was also flanked by a grand arcade. Today, the piazza is framed on both sides by nineteenth-century porticoes, obliterating all traces of the earlier buildings; it is tempting to suppose that the portico in front of the cathedral was also conceived during Nicholas's sojourn in Fabriano, but there is no evidence for this. On the other hand, it is quite likely that the impressive hospital, constructed soon after Nicholas's death a short distance from the cathedral and the Piazza Maggiore, was projected under Nicholas or at least in resonance with his interventions in the town.[72]

In general, the work at Fabriano is surely, as Giovannoni and Heydenreich argued, of great importance in the development of ideas about the regularization and monumentalization of urban spaces, while its tapering ground plan, emphasized by the erection of the arcade building, suggested to Heydenreich (1937, 141) the operation of a visual sensibility already deeply marked by the discourse of perspectivism. If so, there is clearly some relationship to the nearly contemporary reinterpretation of the spatial order of Rome, and the mediatory role of Fabrianese craftsmen becomes of potentially great, if hardly provable significance.[73]

Nicholas's first visit to Fabriano was brief. He arrived on July 24, 1449, doubtless accompanied by the orators whom the town council had voted two days before to send to greet the pope at Spoleto (Sassi 1955b, 3). The townspeople had not expected the papal visit, though two high-placed prelates, Cardinal Torquemada and the bishop of Camerino, were already in Fabriano. The news was brought at extremely short notice by a clerk of the *camera apostolica*, the bishop of Rimini Giacomo Vannucci. The latter had evidently been charged to see to the arrangements for the visit, and the town council elected a committee to assist him; meanwhile all the craftsmen in the town were bidden to stand by to await orders. The pope entered Fabriano along a hastily decorated processional way marked by doubtless rudimentary triumphal arches. He received a warm welcome, for he represented the "libertas ecclesiastica," freedom from the assorted tyrannies of petty so-called vicars; before long, the people would think differently (Sassi 1964–65). Vannucci acted during the summer as vicechamberlain (ASV, DC 26, fol. 13or [July 21, 1449]); on October 27, 1449, he was transferred from the see of Rimini to that of the far wealthier and important city of Perugia (Eubel 1914, 237). Clearly he had done his work well.

The following summer the Fabrianesi were given more notice of Nicholas's impending arrival. A letter from Pietro da Noceto, who had accompanied the pope to Fabriano the summer before, was brought from Rome with the news; the bearer was the local craftsman Niccolò di Lorenzo, who had worked for Vannucci the previous year, perhaps already with special authority, since he is identified in the documents as Niccolò *sindaco* (Müntz 1878, 161; Sassi 1955b,

1of.). He was now appointed by the commune their representative and plenipo-
tentiary for the duration of the pope's visit ("amministratore e sindacho con
pieni poteri per tutta la durata del soggiorno del papa"); from the commune's
point of view his position was much like that of Vannucci the year before
(Archivio di Stato, Fabriano, Riformanze del Comune 12, fol. 90v). There is no
mention of credentials given to him in Rome, however, and in the records of
the town council's deliberations he appears as the representative of the commune, evidently functioning as an intermediary between the two sides. This
he was well able to do; he was by trade a builder (specifically a paver, *selciatore*), but he also enjoyed sufficient public esteem in his town to take the place
of the chancellor, Angelo di Masso, in certain situations (ibid., fol. 53v ff.).[74] He
also acted as representative of the commune in various negotiations, as indicated by his identification as *sindaco* in the papal ledger of 1449. It was Niccolò, for example, who in September 1451 negotiated and signed with a builder
on behalf of the commune a contract for the reconstruction of a large section of
the town walls (ibid., fol. 111v).

Niccolò clearly played an important part in the flurry of activity at the piazza
in 1450. He was the conduit for papal payments for work on the papal palace as
on the new steps leading to the entrance of S. Francesco (ibid., fol. 168r).
Curiously the funds for the roof of the cathedral passed through the hands not
of Niccolò but of Nicholas's half-brother, Cardinal Filippo Calandrini, the new
legate of the March, perhaps because the money was sent on to Ancona to
purchase timber (ASR, TS 1450, fol. 166r [August 10, 1450]). Niccolò, on the
other hand, dealt on behalf of the commune with the Fabrianese banking firm
of the Agostini, who were charged, shortly before the pope's departure, to make
the final payments for the steps of S. Francesco on completion of the project;
already the firm had been reimbursed for 80 ducats that they had advanced for
materials and labor (*magistero*) according to the estimates of Niccolò, who had
transferred the money concerned to the appropriate recipients.[75] Clearly Niccolò's administrative role was far more important than his activity as builder.
The most remarkable proof of his standing in his hometown that summer is
the provision to him, at the pope's expense, of a jacket of scarlet cloth from
Verona (ASR, TS 1450, fol. 37r [August 31, 1450]); he must have cut a splendid
figure as, at least on special occasions, he moved between the building sites on
the piazza, the papal palace, and the bank of the Agostini.

By the end of 1451 Niccolò di Lorenzo, now in papal service, had moved to
Rome and was drawing a regular salary of 5 ducats. He was employed as a paver
(he is referred to as "selciatore nostro"; ASR, TS 1451, fols. 132r–v, 136r), but
is still identified as Niccolò da Fabriano "detto il sindaco" (ibid. 1452, fol.
153r), though not after 1452. Early in 1452, indeed, Niccolò was still acting in
Fabriano as a *factor*, but now he represented not his commune, but the provincial treasury of the March of Ancona based at Matelica; in the latter's
accounts, moreover, he appears occasionally with the title Ser, implying that
he had had legal training (ASR, Tesoreria Generale della Marca 1451, fol. 177r).
Niccolò was soon succeeded by Gaspare da Lucca, a professional administrator
who was later to handle the crusade tax under Nello, but not before he had

appointed as his deputy the chancellor of Fabriano for whom he himself had stood in in the previous year (ibid., fol. 188r [January 12, 1452]).

Niccolò perhaps took this step in view of the gathering pace of building operations at the Vatican. In 1452 he entered a partnership with a Lombard, Romano da Milano, not hitherto mentioned in the accounts: they are recorded as the "selciatori della fabrica," that is of the Vatican, though no details of their work are known (ASR, TS 1452, fol. 172r). Niccolò was the senior partner, receiving a salary of 5 ducats to Romano's 3. The partnership, however, did not survive the year, and Romano disappears from the accounts. Niccolò's salary remained at 5 ducats (ibid. 1453, fol. 200r), and he may not have flourished financially; in September 1453 he paid back four florins that he had borrowed from Francesco del Borgo during an illness from which he recovered at Tivoli (ibid., fol. 172r). Nevertheless he is recorded in 1453 as "soprastante a lavoro del palazo," and evidently had supervisory responsibilities of some importance. His position is often given as quartermaster ("sopra la munizione de la fabricha"); in this capacity he was responsible for the provision of food and drink to the workmen on special occasions such as the feast of Corpus Christi (ibid., fol. 27v). With the collapse early in September 1454 of the great tower (the "torrione di Niccolo V" in the Vatican), on which the technical role of Rossellino seems to have been of particular importance (ibid. 1452, fol. 167r–v), Niccolò received money to buy food for the men who spent their Sunday morning removing the fallen masonry and bringing out the bodies of several unfortunate laborers who had been crushed to death (ASR, SMP 1454, fol. 153v; Magnuson 1958, 62 n.19).

Niccolò's sphere of influence, the palace and the fortifications adjacent to it, appears to have been quite distinct from that of Beltramo, whose activity was concentrated on the basilica project. The question arises, however, of Niccolò's relations with the two men who carried the title of *ingegnere di palazzo*, Antonio da Firenze and Bernardo Rossellino. This is especially problematical as it is unclear whether Niccolò's activity "sopra la munizione" reflected a clearly defined and permanent official role or simply his ad hoc employment for specific tasks requiring administrative skills and the confidence of Nicholas's household staff.[76] Apart from their titles, there is no evidence in the papal ledgers for supervisory activity in the palace, let alone the basilica, on the part of Rossellino and Antonio; workers in the palace, for instance, tended to be paid directly by officials from the papal financial staff (i.e., one of Nello's associates). On the other hand, Antonio da Firenze is occasionally recorded as making payments to contractors for separate projects; for instance in 1453 he paid Beltramo's nephew Pietro for his work on S. Teodoro, presumably after checking the workmanship on that hitherto ill-fated project (ASR, TS 1453, fol. 11r; Golzio and Zander 1968, 497). In contrast, in May 1454 he is recorded as receiving funds for his part in the construction of the *tribuna*, but without any reference to general supervisory responsibilities (ASR, TS 1454, fol. 115v);[77] it is not clear if this marks a change in the organization of the project as Nello's death and the probable date of the decision to abandon the project grew closer.

Whatever Niccolò's exact status and responsibilities, he handled himself well, for in November 1454—perhaps at a time of abrupt and major changes in the

Vatican project—he received the honor of appointment to the college of *servientes armorum* (ASV, RV 430, fol. 188r). This was an honor once given to Nello, and it may be significant that Nello's death must have occurred about this time; perhaps Niccolò was being groomed to take over some at least of Nello's responsibilities. In the winding up of Nicholas's projects under Calixtus III Niccolò certainly played an important role. The workmen at the Vatican were paid off according to an assessment of what was due them prepared by Niccolò with two other men, one of whom may have been Frate Cola (Müntz 1878, 198).

Nothing is known of Niccolò's career for the next few years. His next appearance places him at the heart of the papal financial administration, again indicating some degree of continuity with Nello's regime: by 1463 he and a colleague are named as commissioners of alum, their task presumably to supervise the exploitation of the reserves of alum, a valuable substance vital in the textile industry, recently discovered at Tolfa in the Patrimonium (Gottlob 1889, 286; cf. Delumeau 1967). Niccolò was the junior partner, receiving a salary of 20 ducats, five fewer than his colleague. Later, however, for unknown reasons, the salaries of both men were reduced to 14 1/2 ducats. Niccolò's connection with the alum mines continued at least to 1469, and his name appears frequently in the ledgers of the crusade tax, which Pius II, like Nicholas before him, imposed in a vain effort to lead a united Christian resistance against the Turks (Zippel 1907, 388 n.5).[78] Niccolò did not abandon his earlier career: in June 1465 he was engaged by the officials of the new pope, Paul II, to restore the surface of the Ponte S. Angelo (Müntz 1879, 98). From the heights of his responsibilities under Nicholas V he was once more reduced to a paver.

5

The Other Rome: Sacrality and Ideology in the Holy Quarter

The Madonna and the General: Reverence and Triumph on the Esquiline Hill

It is now usual to refer the terms *abitato* and *disabitato* to two quite distinct areas lying within the Aurelianic walls of medieval to eighteenth-century Rome; one of these areas densely occupied, mainly through its proximity to the river, and the other largely abandoned to the brambles emphasized in humanist accounts of the fallen state of quattrocento Rome. The degree of abandonment of the *disabitato*, however, was doubtless always a relative matter, while the attention given by Nicholas V to the area in question may even be regarded as a modest anticipation of the concerns of late-sixteenth-century popes, whose architectural and urbanistic projects opened out the urban fabric, gave it a new scale, and brought about the realization of a suburban zone of avenues and fine houses, gardens hidden behind high walls and elaborately rusticated portals, and occasional views over the congested quarters of the city.

Fifteenth-century documents refer to the area later known as the *disabitato* as Monti; most of it lay within the administrative entity of the Rione Monti (map 1). The name referred, of course, to the hills that dominate the topography of the eastern and southeastern quarters of the Aurelianic city, notably the Quirinal, which later became the preferred seat of the popes, and the Esquiline. The history of the latter, as of Monti in general, is paradoxical. It was of enormous importance in the early development of a Christian topography of Rome. At the synod of 499 fully a third of the Roman *tituli* represented were located here; the Basilica Sicinini, later S. Maria Maggiore, became the leading Marian shrine of Rome and the closest of the canonical seven basilicas to the center of the old city (Jordan 1907, 1:281; two of the other basilicas, S. Giovanni in Laterano and S. Croce in Gerusalemme, were located in Monti, though not on the Esquiline). But the religious associations of the area did not lessen its vulnerability to changes in fortune. Settlement on the hill had depended largely on the provision of water by aqueducts; the destruction of these in the wars that followed the collapse of the Roman Empire left the Esquiline depopulated and the shrines often in decay and in some cases abandoned.

Nevertheless, the closeness of the area to the *abitato* and the availability of open space encouraged the creation of gardens and *vigne*, though these were of course very different from the elaborate pleasure gardens of the later Renaissance. Far more significant was the continued presence of numerous religious communities and institutions on the Esquiline as indeed throughout Monti (map 2); their members and households must have constituted a major element of the permanent population. The late medieval revival in the fortunes of the area was centered on the basilica of S. Maria Maggiore and was especially associated with the Colonna family. Pope Nicholas IV carried out extensive building and decoration at the basilica in the late thirteenth century; he was closely allied with the Colonna, and his building patronage constituted a public demonstration of this alliance (Gardner 1973b). In the succeeding century the basilica enjoyed the support and patronage of two great cardinals of the family, though it is remarkable that the elevation of a Colonna to the papacy as Martin V in the early fifteenth century did not bring particular benefits to the basilica and its environs, for Martin concentrated his favor on the Lateran (Müntz 1878, 2f.).[1] A fine altarpiece, however, was painted for the basilica; this celebrated its legendary foundation through a miraculous fall of snow and was presumably commissioned by Martin himself (Pope-Hennessy 1952; Davis 1951, no. 5963). In general, these were splendid days for the Colonna and their adherents, as they basked in the pope's nepotistic favor.

The succession of Eugenius IV brought a drastic change; the campaign waged by Eugenius's generals against the Colonna and its aftermath has already entered the discussion on many occasions. In 1434 Cardinal Vitelleschi, at the head of the forces of the Church, occupied and destroyed the strongholds of the Colonna in the nearby hills, notably Palestrina; the papal victory over the Colonna seemed complete (Pastor 1949, 302). The victory was celebrated with a triumphal procession; Vitelleschi, who had in fact entered the city by the Porta S. Giovanni, made a symbolic triumphal entry through the Arco di San Vito, near S. Maria Maggiore (map 2). This was the ancient Arcus Gallieni, which kept (and still keeps) its triumphal dedicatory inscription, recorded by Poggio in his *sylloge* (Valentini and Zucchetti 1953, 137). A contemporary account of Vitelleschi's entry reports that a multitude headed by the *caporioni* with their banners assembled at the arch (Petrone 1912, 31; Vitale 1791, 2:405). The scene is compared to the procession of the Assumption, which had taken place two weeks before the triumph of Vitelleschi on August 29, for the clergy came in procession and the people carried torches. On Vitelleschi's arrival at the arch from the direction of S. Giovanni, where he had revered the heads of Saints Peter and Paul, he was received by the crowd with great enthusiasm and a golden cloak was draped over him. He then rode in procession to S. Lorenzo in Damaso, where he hurled his cloak down as spoil for the populace.

The absence in this account of any explicit reference to ancient triumphal processions and the emphasis on the procession of the Assumption reflects either ignorance of or indifference to humanist ideals and preoccupations. It is surely probable, however, that the intentional reconstruction of a classical triumph, albeit with medieval (i.e., contemporary) paraphernalia and properties, was in question here, especially in view of the part played by the Arco di San Vito (fig. 35, center left; fig. 37, top left). This was not a city gate, and had not been since it had formed part of the so-called Servian wall in the early republican period of ancient Rome; later, freed of this defensive function by the expansion of the city and the certainty of security from external aggression, it was recycled as a triumphal arch (Nash 1961, 2:104). Moreover, the Romans voted Vitelleschi on this occasion the honor of an equestrian statue (the vote was never implemented), presumably on the model of ancient precedent (Esch 1971, 5).

The Arco di San Vito was not the only triumphal monument in the area: nearby stood the so-called Trophies of Marius, set up after the victory over Germanic tribes. The sculpted trophies still exist; they stand on the balustrade of the Campidoglio, where they were removed in the sixteenth century along with various other sculptures that exerted a similarly powerful symbolic force in the city (Buddensieg 1969). By the mid-fifteenth century they were regarded by those with antiquarian leanings as worth a detour to see; Giovanni Rucellai, describing his visit to them in 1450, calls them, in refreshingly unantiquarian fashion, "l'oche armate," the geese in armor (Rucellai 1960, 75). Such particular triumphal associations may have been relevant for Vitelleschi's triumph, saving the general, at least in the eyes of a more pedantic historian, from the charge of hubris, since Marius, though he later became dictator, was at the time of his triumph a general, a servant of the state.[2]

These associations of the site of Vitelleschi's triumph do not fully explain the emphasis on the Arco di San Vito. Clearly, Vitelleschi was concerned to assert his victorious presence in a part of the city closely associated with the defeated Colonna. But if the symbolic occupation of the Esquiline reflected the real and bloody conquest of the territory of the Colonna as a whole, it also served to negate or even mock other symbolic associations of the area. The notion of Rome as built in the shape of a lion was familiar in the late medieval city and was occasionally expressed in graphic form (fig. 36), implying that Rome could claim among cities the rank enjoyed by the lion among animals. The Esquiline formed the lion's raised tail, emphasis on which was of political significance, for the lion with raised tail was a heraldic symbol of the Ghibelline faction. Since the leadership of the Ghibellines of Rome was traditionally in the hands of the Colonna, heraldry and topography here coincided (Frutaz 1962, 1:44; Miglio 1981, 323–326).

During the regency in Rome of Cardinal Vitelleschi as apostolic legate, some attention was given to the Esquiline area. An example is the reform of a convent of apparently naughty nuns at S. Bibbiana, that stood near the Aurelianic wall at the apex of a straight street that led through the Arco di San Vito to one of the major intersections of the Esquiline (map 2). In February 1439 Eugenius ordered S. Bibbiana to be merged with S. Maria Maggiore, for he had heard of shameful and illicit doings at the convent; in addition, the buildings of the convent were in dire condition, and the roof of the church was allegedly about to collapse (Ferri 1907, nos. 205f.). If there was any truth in these charges, S. Bibbiana could have served as a model for Alberti, who remarked on the undesirability of a remote location for a convent, where the nuns, out of the public eye, might more easily succumb to temptation (Alberti 1966a, 1:363). It is perhaps more likely that the abbess and her convent had the wrong political connections and were the victim of machinations that had nothing to do with their moral standards; in any case, a year elapsed before the merger was carried out, suggesting that there was resistance. Eugenius further transformed the religious character of the area through the settlement of a community of Celestine monks, whose austerity was celebrated, at S. Eusebio, which was also situated beyond the Arco di San Vito, close to S. Bibbiana.[3] It is likely that here, as certainly at S. Maria Maggiore, some restoration took place under Eugenius.

Pope Eugenius never stayed in the area. Though a papal palace was available at S. Maria Maggiore, he preferred to make use of residences in the *abitato* or at the Vatican (Westfall 1974a, 7 n.20). He does not seem even to have used the Lateran palace, suggesting a consistent and no doubt politically motivated avoidance of Monti. Eugenius did not neglect the Lateran, continuing Martin's program of decoration in the basilica and presumably supporting in some way the erection of new quarters for the canons. But the accession of Nicholas V saw renewed emphasis on the Lateran, though of a relatively discreet character; much more overt were the measures, architectural and otherwise, with which he manifested his concern for other shrines of Monti, notably S. Maria Maggiore, S. Prassede, S. Pudenziana, and S. Stefano Rotondo. But Monti also included sites and buildings of particular significance for the commune and related institutions; these too attracted Nicholas's attention and concern. Indeed, I will argue that Nicholas's measures in Monti are of crucial importance in understanding his policies toward the city, and his ability to build on, but subtly manipulate, developments already in process and of markedly diverse character and even ideological connotations.

This chapter will focus, then, on two distinct sections of Monti: it will begin with a discussion of the district between the Lateran and the Campidoglio, where communal associations were especially strong and where communal measures to encourage urban development were perhaps influential in Nicholas's pontificate; it will then move to the Esquiline, tracing the possible effect of communal precedent in Nicholas's early years as pope and exploring the later complex intersections of intellectual, political, and even personal concerns that underlay Nicholas's dealings with and attitudes toward Monti and its leading citizens.

The Via Maggiore: Conflict and Convergence in a Privileged Enclave

The *Tractatus de rebus antiquis et situ Urbis Romae* is a topographical treatise produced in Rome in the early fifteenth century, though almost entirely innocent of humanist influence. In a section entitled "viae principales urbis" the anonymous author enumerates a number of important thoroughfares, most of which are not city streets, however, but extraurban roads, which may extend into the city in some cases; they are, of course, mostly the great consular roads to which I will return in chapter 6. There are two exceptions, two cases of truly urban thoroughfares. One is the Via Francisca, which the author describes as leading from the Porta Viridaria in the Borgo to the area in front of the Vatican palace, although this street, as the author relates, had disappeared to make way for a *platea* created by Pope Boniface IX in front of his palace (Esch 1969, 263). This would have been within living memory. The other urban street is the Via Sacra, for which the author is even able to provide an apposite classical reference: "According to Suetonius, the via Sacra is the one that came from the Porta Maggiore to the Colosseum, then on to the Temple of Romulus, which is now known as the Temple of Peace, and descended into the public forum . . . which I think was between SS. Cosma e Damiano and S. Adriano" (Valentini and Zucchetti 1953, 117). As Valentini and Zucchetti (ibid., n.3) point out, however, while Suetonius mentions the Via Sacra, he nowhere indicates its route. The Via Sacra that the anonymous medieval author has in mind here is not the street familiar to Suetonius and his contemporaries, but that of his own time, which he conflates with its ancient predecessor.

The medieval Via Sacra was associated, above all, with two processions, one of predominantly civic, the other of papal significance. It was the final section of the Via del Papa, the route of the *possesso* from the Vatican to the Lateran (map 2). It was also the route of the great annual procession of the Assumption, when the image of Christ was taken from the chapel of the Sancta Sanctorum on the Campo Laterano and borne in triumph to S. Maria Maggiore. The initial part of the route lay along the Via Sacra as far as the church of S. Adriano (the ancient *curia senatus*, known to late medieval Romans as S. Triana; fig. 37, lower left), where the city magistrates paid homage (Marangoni 1747, 120–125; Dell'Addolorata 1919, 275–278; Montenovesi 1942, 5).[4]

The Via Sacra, therefore, formed a fundamental topographical, ritual, and symbolic axis within the city;[5] it linked the traditional political center of the city, the Campidoglio, with S. Giovanni in Laterano as cathedral church of the pope as bishop of Rome, by way of the Colosseum, which often served as a kind of emblem of the city itself (map 2; figs. 15, 35). The importance of the route was all the greater at a time when the age-old rivalry between the two great basilicas of Rome, the Lateran and the Vatican, had not yet been definitively settled in favor of the latter. Accordingly, the name Via Sacra, emphasizing the ritual significance of the street, appears relatively rarely in late medieval usage; instead it was generally known as the Via Maggiore, the urban street par excellence, and appears as such in the documents cited below. It is tempting to see in the general use of this name the particular implication that the Via Maggiore was superior to its continuation to the northwest, the Via del Papa.

I have already noted the attention given by early-fifteenth-century popes to the Lateran. The splendor of the paintings executed by Pisanello for Martin V was admired as late as 1551 by Paolo Giovio, who also commented wrily on the vandalism of his times: "Pisanello was an excellent painter and was at the height of his fame in the time of Popes Martin, Eugenius, and Nicholas [in fact, Pisanello had succeeded Gentile da Fabriano, and he did not work for Nicholas], and painted both sides of the great nave of S. Giovanni with much ultramarine blue; so rich was it that the daubers [*pittorelli*] of our day have often taken the trouble to climb up ladders and scrape away the blue" (Giovio 1560, 59). Martin V was buried in the basilica in a tomb, still extant, that is an early example of the diffusion to Rome of the new style of sculpture developed in Florence (Golzio and Zander 1968, 233; Montini 1957, 270).

The area of the Via Maggiore was also notable for the patronage of certain high-ranking prelates, doubtless following papal example. Cardinal Branda Castiglione held S. Clemente as his titular church and commissioned Masolino and Masaccio to execute the famous frescoes there, a further example of the appearance—or even development—in Rome of the new stylistic tendencies (Golzio and Zander 1968, 207; Wohl 1980, 8–12). Eugenius IV's nephew, Pietro Barbo (later Paul II), was given S. Maria Nova as his *titulus*. Although in 1451 he was transferred by Nicholas V to S. Marco, where he was to build the famous palace, his association with his former church continued, at least in the consciousness of the Roman people; a document of December 21, 1452, gives his *titulus* as S. Marco, but adds that he is still known *vulgariter* as Cardinal of S. Maria Nova (ASR, CNC 1684, fol. 11r). This is of some importance as in the early quattrocento this church became a center of popular religious enthusiasm through its association with the holy Francesca, pious scion of a local family, who established a community of nuns nearby and contributed greatly to the current of devotional piety and moral reform that marked the Rione Monti in the fifteenth century; the church itself soon became known as S. Francesca Romana (Monachino 1968, 164, 177). Nearby were other religious foundations of importance in the life of the city, to which the discussion will return in due course.

Against this background Eugenius IV chose to make of the Lateran a center of religious reform and ascetic monastic practice within the confines of the city. This was perhaps a laudable undertaking, but it was neither tactful nor, in the long term, successful. With a bull of September 13, 1299, Pope Boniface VIII had suppressed the regular canons of the Lateran and had replaced them with fifteen secular canons chosen from noble and powerful Roman families. According to Widloecher (1929, 75), the historian of the Lateran canons, this was because secular canons were better able to defend the rights and property of the basilica from usurpers; no doubt Boniface also saw the nomination as a means to gain political support. Over the years the secular canons became markedly worldly; finally the strict Eugenius determined to reform the chapter, an intention, according to the reform bulls of February 6, 1439, and May 1, 1444, that he had long entertained (ibid., 75f.). The canons of S. Maria in Fregionaria near Lucca were invited to undertake the reform, but the pope was driven to near coercion, as the former initially declined the task. By 1434 a procurator general had been sent to Rome to look into the matter of the transfer of members of the order to Rome, but political events in the city forced the postponement of the reform until 1439, when feeling against Eugenius had died down (ibid., 76). The procurator, Pietro de Rido, was perhaps a relative of the Paduan Antonio de Rido, castellan of the Castel S. Angelo under Eugenius and favorite of the chamberlain (Paschini 1939, 149). If so, the prospect of the kind of material support that the castellan could offer may well have been reassuring to Pietro; he may also have appreciated the relaxation available in the bath house operated by Antonio's brother Niccolò in the Borgo (BAV, ACSP, Censuali 7 [1450], fol. 46r).[6]

In 1439 Pietro reappeared, now with the title of prior of S. Agostino in Forlì, as one of six procurators appointed to see to the transfer of the new canons to S. Giovanni under their newly elected prior, Don Benedetto da Piacenza (Widloecher 1929, 80). The opposition, needless to say, of the dispossessed canons and their families, who stood to lose a lucrative source of income and influence, was unremitting and occasionally violent. There was fighting in May 1440, for example, and only the tenacity of Eugenius kept the new canons from abandoning the Lateran. In 1444, indeed, a new bull was issued and new canons were in fact brought in (ibid., 85). One of these was a certain Tommaso da Verona, whose northern Italian origin was typical of the chapter at this time. Tommaso was a compatriot of the best-known contemporary member of the order, Timoteo Maffei, who three times held the office of general of the Lateran canons, and was so devoted to his order that he turned down Nicholas V's offer of the archbishopric of Milan; instead, in 1451, he went to the Badia di Fiesole, where he became closely associated with Cosimo de' Medici, whose rebuilding of the Badia is well known. He was close to the humanistic concerns of Nicholas, who was impressed by his book *In sanctam rusticitatem*, in which he defended the reading by Christians of classical poetry (Zippel 1904, 8 n.2; Cosenza 1962, 2:2066). Whether or not Tommaso da Verona was a particular contact, Timoteo must have maintained close links with developments at the Lateran, and his openness to humanist concerns may have affected the spiritual and intellectual atmosphere there, heightening the pope's concern for the canons' position in the face of opposition from groups in the city population with whom he was generally concerned to maintain good relations.

That economic concerns were at the bottom of the opposition to the reformed canons is clear from the stubborn resistance to the latter's claims to properties and revenues of the basilica. Finally Eugenius had to intervene with the appointment in September 1446 of a commission of bishops to proceed against usurpers of property rightfully belonging to the Lateran chapter (Widloecher 1929, 102). Such revenues were perhaps of particular importance at the time, as the canons were proceeding with the construction of a new convent. To judge from Biondo's report of discoveries of antiquities made in the excavations for the foundations, this was a major project, but all traces of it have disappeared. It stood to the southwest of the basilica on a site now occupied by the Lateran seminary erected by Pope Pius X (Lanciani 1902, 1:49). The chronicle of the order relates that Eugenius gave generously to the construction of the convent ("amplum et pulcherrimum monasterium"), and names the architect as Frate Cola (Widloecher 1929, 29, using a sixteenth-century copy of a lost document commissioned in 1464; ibid., 13).

The date of the design was probably 1439, but the political situation necessitated a delay probably until 1444, when work was resumed under the direction of one of the canons of the order, though still apparently following the design prepared by Frate Cola. Under Nicholas the situation was quiet, though trouble flared up from time to time and was probably always simmering under the surface. There is no record of open conflict until the Jubilee, when religious institutions in general and not least the basilica of S. Giovanni, as one of the great pilgrimage shrines, stood to profit mightily from the alms and offerings of the faithful. At S. Giovanni the canons shared the alms with the pope; they used their portion for the embellishment of the church, including the acquisition of a new organ (ibid., 106, 114).

The pilgrims did not only come to the Lateran to visit the basilica; no doubt they also strolled in the Campo and visited the other shrines and wonders in the neighborhood. No doubt, too, crowds of hawkers, hucksters, and outright footpads infested the square, and it can well be imagined that the presence of officials to keep the peace and administer justice was required. The reponsibility for the appointment of such officials, however, was a controversial matter, which had to be settled by papal edict. On the one hand, the Lateran canons claimed the right to exercise jurisdiction on the Campo and were doubtless not without influence in the Vatican, possibly through Timoteo Maffei, whose presence in Rome during the Jubilee is probable, though not documented. This claim was challenged, on the other hand, by the chief officials of the Confraternity of the Salvatore, whose chapel and major hospital adjoined the Campo. The pope found in favor of the confraternity, as is evident from the account of the latter's secretary, who noted that the *nobilis vir* Petruccio Soderini of the Rione Campitelli was appointed to administer justice on the Campo Laterano on behalf of the confraternity, in spite of the opposition of the canons regular. Soderini was appointed for the duration of the Jubilee, during the terms of office first of Cencio Porcari and Giovanni Alperini, then of Pietro Margani and Giacomo Cenci as *guardiani* of the confraternity (Adinolfi 1857a, 154).

All four of these men were important members of the patrician elite of their day; Porcari and Alperini, during whose term of office the appointment of Soderini took place, were presumably responsible for the negotiations that led to the papal ruling. If so, both were able to exploit their recent experience as civic officials and their consequent contacts with members of the papal administration. Little is known about Alperini, except that during his term as *guardianus* he also served as *conservator* (Tommasini 1887, 210). More is known about Cencio Porcari: closely related to Stefano, he was known not to sympathize with the aims of that firebrand, whose transformation of the family name into the pretentious latinization Portius he resented, according to Pietro de Godis (Lehnerdt 1907, 64).

Cencio was a locally well-known figure with extensive business interests, some of which brought him to the Vatican. Under Nicholas V, for instance, he regularly leased from the Church the pasture rights at Ostia, which were doubtless of great importance for the flocks wintering in the Roman district (ASR, TS 1453, fol. 6v);[7] it is likely that the right to exploit such sources of revenue was not simply thrown on the open market, but went to a purchaser who enjoyed the confidence of the papal officials involved. Cencio indeed had family connections in the Vatican that may have stood him in good stead, for his brother Pietro had been a canon of St. Peter's at least from 1432 (BAV, ACSP, Censuali 5 [1441], fol. 54r; Tommasini 1880, 130). Pietro too made full use of the economic opportunities available to those associated with ecclesiastical institutions, as in the case of a partnership into which he entered in 1447 with the protonotary Giorgio Cesarini, also a Vatican canon, to lease an important territorial concession from the Church (BAV, ACSP, Censuali 5 [1441], fol. 12r). The two Porcari brothers continued to be associated in various similar ventures long after the conspiracy of Stefano, in which neither was evidently suspected of the slightest complicity (though one of Stefano's leading fellow conspirators was a Vatican canon; Tommasini 1880, 130).

The social and economic tensions centered on the Lateran came to a head with the visit of the Emperor Frederick III in early 1452, as related by the prior of the Lateran chapter in a letter of March of that year (Vitale 1791, 2:143). As I have noted, Frederick's visit had in other respects too an unsettling effect on the Ghibelline-inclined elements of the local population, and was handled with great care by Nicholas. Curiously, the authorities seem not to have anticipated the uproar that occurred when the emperor went in procession to the Lateran. He was met outside the hospital by the chanting canons, fifty strong, who with raised crosses and baldachins escorted him to the entrance of the basilica. Here he dismounted in front of the *porta maior* and was about to proceed into the basilica when the former canons began a demonstration, ingeniously attempting to disrupt the course of the ceremonies by conferring on the emperor the status of canon (this perhaps pointed up the social distance between the secular canons and their successors). The prior stepped forward and in the name of the pope commanded them to desist, calling on the city magistrates who were present, including the senator and the *conservatori*, to remove those who would not leave of their own free will. The operation proceeded, apparently, relatively peacefully, except that one of the former canons who showed more spirit than the others was thrown to the ground and beaten up.

This incident, though doubtless highly embarrassing for Nicholas and the municipal authorities, did not lead to further trouble during Nicholas's pontificate. After his death, however, pressure must have mounted rapidly, and the new pope, Calixtus III, soon deemed it advisable to expel the canons regular in favor of their adversaries. The situation was reversed by Paul II, Eugenius's nephew and closely associated with centers of popular spirituality in the area. Paul also assigned the canons an annual provision of 800 ducats and gave 50 ducats in 1468 for the restoration of the organ, presumably that installed in 1450; it seems that the sound of the organ in S. Giovanni had associations that went beyond the religious and aesthetic. The brief heyday of the canons regular was soon followed by their definitive replacement, under Sixtus IV, by secular canons (Zippel 1904, 8 n.3).[8]

The concern evinced by his predecessors, notably Eugenius IV, with the spiritual enhancement of the Via Maggiore area and its shrines may well have served as a model for Nicholas's measures, notably his assignment to *tituli* in Monti of newly created cardinals, as noted in detail below. On the Caelian hill Nicholas carried out the famous restoration of S. Stefano Rotondo, where the physical restoration was associated with the replacement of the original canons with a strict order of Augustinian hermits in 1454 (ASV, RV 430, fol. 256v). The *titulus* had been given in 1448 to Cardinal Jean Rolin, whose great wealth may well have been tapped for the restoration of the church (Eubel 1914, 11). Rolin himself did not maintain a residence at S. Stefano; he lived in a palace at S. Maria in Via Lata, suggestively close to the palaces of the Colonna (Infessura 1890, 56).

The building work at S. Stefano began before the Jubilee, and from 1451 was apparently in the hands of Bernardo Rossellino. Before Rossellino's arrival, however, the reconstruction was entrusted to Frate Cola (ASV, CDG 1449/

1451, fol. 100v), who had been involved, as noted above, with a major Eugenian project at the Lateran, suggesting a programmatic consistency between the two projects. Further, the other important church on the Caelian, SS. Giovanni e Paolo, was also reformed under Nicholas, who in this case introduced a strict order of Hieronymite monks, the Gesuati (ASV, RV 431, fol. 102v; Rice 1985, 70f.). It is plausible to describe the policy of Nicholas, following from and expanding that of Eugenius, as the attempt to create a spiritual quarter, a kind of *kreuzviertel*, in the least populated area of the city.

In 1433 Eugenius issued a bull suppressing two small churches and merging their revenues with those of S. Jacopo, a church adjacent to the Colosseum; the bull was in response to a petition of the Confraternity of the Salvatore to expand the hospital that it administered at S. Jacopo, since it was so much closer to the main population centers of Rome than the confraternity's other hospital at the Lateran (Adinolfi 1857a, 154 doc. 10).[9] The documents reveal both parties' awareness of the disastrous social effects of the recent wars and the general deprivation and poverty in the city, from which women were particularly suffering.

Eugenius's bull tacitly indicates his acceptance of the traditional role played by the confraternity in the Via Maggiore and environs. In statutes of 1386 the Roman commune had granted the confraternity jurisdiction over the area, which became thereby a privileged enclave within the city, its inhabitants enjoying immunity from various taxes, criminal liabilities, and civic duties, like that of bearing arms for the city (ibid., 140–144 doc. 5).[10] They had both the right and duty, however, to ride to arms whenever their own security was threatened and to ring the bells of the four churches of the area (S. Clemente, S. Jacopo, SS. Quattro Coronati, and S. Angelo, the Lateran hospital chapel) *ad tumuldam* in case of trouble. The moral welfare of the inhabitants was to be carefully supervised, and neither prostitution nor usury was allowed.

The statutes explicitly encouraged new development in the area and were concerned with the maintenance and improvement of properties adjoining the street, which was to undergo a *reductio et renovatio*. Demolition was permitted only on condition that it formed part of a restoration campaign, and the taking of spoils was sternly prohibited; columns, planks, marble blocks, and windows are mentioned as architectural elements that should not be transported elsewhere, suggesting that some at least of the property concerned was of reasonable quality. Rents were to be controlled and owners were forbidden to stand in the way of construction or cultivation on their lots, on pain of confiscation of the latter. Such restrictions on the rights of ownership and encouragement of construction on fallow land anticipate to a degree the famous legislation of Sixtus IV, though the 1386 document does not contain a clear provision for compulsory purchase. Nor does it seek to enlarge lots and the buildings on them, as the Sistine document was to do, encouraging a grander and more exclusive generation of buildings for the benefit of a small elite, all in the name of the aesthetic quality of the city, the *decus urbis* (Müntz 1882, 182; Golzio and Zander 1968, 357; Spezzaferro 1973).

In the 1386 statutes the extent of the Via Maggiore is rather vaguely defined: one limit is the church and hospital of S. Jacopo, the other is located variously at the hospital chapel of S. Angelo or at the Campo Laterano (map 2). The intent of the framers of the document appears to have been to define the area subject to the jurisdiction of the confraternity as that extending between the latter's two hospitals. A clearer and more generous definition of the boundaries is a particularly striking innovation in a new version of the statutes issued in 1418 (Adinolfi 1857a, 144–149 doc. 6).[11] Now the confraternity laid claim to the Colosseum and the whole of the Campo Laterano, both of which lay beyond the respective hospitals that adjoined them. The document does not rehearse in detail the regulations and provisions of its predecessor, for it is made clear that they have worked; the Via Maggiore area, once a desert and a haunt of bandits, has now been returned "ad bonam condicionem" and is the home of a flourishing population.

No doubt there was some truth to this assertion; on the other hand, the attack on the random violence of the bad years before 1386 refers probably not to general lawlessness but, with specific political intent, to the overweening authority exercised by the baronial clans that had established bases in the quarter. The document remains fully within the agenda of the radical commune of the fourteenth century, which opposed the growing power of the urban patriciate, with its commercial interests, to that of the land-based feudal aristocracy. The Via Maggiore area, in particular the Colosseum, became a theater of the resolution of this conflict in favor of the patriciate, though this victory was to pale in the context of new political and economic realities as the fifteenth century progressed.

If the content of the 1418 document belongs in an older tradition, its style looks to the future. It expresses with far greater clarity than the 1386 statutes the basic principles, aims, and specific urbanistic intent of the Via Maggiore regulations. The dry and grammatically insecure Latin of the earlier document has given way to language distinguished by relative elegance and variety, perhaps indicating the influence, albeit still quite dim, of the papal chancery and the well-known humanist current within it. In fact, the author of the 1418 document was the *scribasenatus* Niccolò Signorili, whose main activity was certainly within the communal sphere but who also dedicated a book to Pope Martin V, a topographical treatise that indicates a certain community of interests with early humanist antiquarianism. Signorili had a personal concern for the Via Maggiore statutes, for he served for many years as the secretary of the Confraternity of the Salvatore and had in 1408 drafted a new edition of the latter's statutes.[12]

These contained a clause restricting membership to *nobiles viri*; the Roman patriciate, after the revolutionary stage of their struggle for power, were now closing ranks, though the question of the exclusiveness of the confraternity was to be temporarily raised again under Nicholas V, with interesting results. Nicholas certainly supported the confraternity and upheld its rights over the Via Maggiore; in general, however, the enclave of the Via Maggiore was an increasing anachronism in the Rome of the Renaissance papacy, and the 1386 statutes were finally dissolved under Julius II. It is ironic that Signorili's text of 1418, drafted in the year following Martin V's accession (though he did not actually enter Rome until 1420), proudly asserts the privileges and powers of the commune and the great confraternity associated with it in linguistic and rhetorical forms already somewhat redolent of the developing political and cultural hegemony of the papacy, which would soon absorb or even terminate those powers.

There is no doubt that the confraternity enjoyed the support of the papacy, or at least of Cardinal Trevisan, when work was begun on a new wing of the Lateran hospital, the *hospitale Salvatoris*, in the early 1440s.[13] The evidence is sparse, but there are references to donations made for the construction and roofing of the new hospital in 1440–41. The donor was Giacomo Cenci, on behalf of his parents (Egidi 1908, 372). Cenci was a leading member of the confraternity, serving as *guardianus* in 1435 and again in 1442 and 1450 (Marangoni 1747, 361); in 1447 he held the chief communal office, that of *conservator* (Tommasini 1887, 208). His own base was in the Rione Regola (Arenula), where in 1448 he appears among the *gubernatores* of the parish of S. Maria in Monticelli (map 2; see ASR, CNC 1232, fol. 76r), the church in which his father was buried (Egidi 1908, 372). He had family contacts in the Rione Monti: his mother Rita belonged to one of its leading patrician clans, the Valentini, and was buried in their family chapel in SS. Apostoli (ibid.). Cenci's wife, on the other hand, was buried in S. Maria in Aracoeli (ibid., 385).

Giacomo Cenci was perhaps directly involved with the construction of the new wing of the hospital: his presumed relative, Francesco Cenci, had played a quite major role in the building programs of Eugenius IV as a supplier of building materials and as a transport contractor (Corbo 1969, 63, 89). Though Francesco does not reappear under Nicholas, he was among those who attended Eugenius's funeral dressed in cloth provided at the expense of the Church (ASR, M 830, fol. 9r).[14] Whether or not Giacomo had links with Francesco's business, he was appointed by the confraternity in 1448 to investigate building improvements carried out by a tenant against which a neighbor had protested (the leading builder and cleric Antonello d'Albano served as a technical expert in this case; ASR, AOSS, Istromenti 24, fol. 18v). In 1452 he was appointed *commissarius* of the building works at S. Paolo fuori le Mura (ASV, RV 419, fol. 179r); his colleague on this occasion was Massimo de' Massimi, who was as deeply involved with architectural and urbanistic developments in Ponte as Cenci was at the Lateran. But Cenci too had contacts in Ponte; indeed, in 1456 he appears as *factor et procurator* of the Florentine banking firm of Francesco Baroncelli, a relatively rare case of a local patrician flourishing in the world of large-scale banking dominated by Tuscans (ACR, AU, Fondo notarile 253, fol. 192r). But he did not neglect his local roots; in the same year he was the representative of his *rione* at an assembly of the confraternity (ASR, AOSS, Istromenti 24, fol. 58r).

The records of the confraternity refer to donations of money for building materials for the new hospital in the course of the 1440s; a major donor was Luca Savelli, scion of the great baronial clan headquartered at the Theater of Marcellus, who gave 3,000 florins (Egidi 1908, 392). Since the Savelli, who were allies of the Colonna, had suffered badly in the campaigns of Vitelleschi, a political motif can be suspected.[15] In 1448 and 1449 roof timbers were given, indicating that the building was near completion (ibid., 403). And in the *catasto* of the property of the Lateran chapter of 1450 the old and new hospitals are both listed as paying the same ground rent (Lauer 1911, 513).[16]

Doubtless the hospital facilities of Rome were unable to deal adequately with the pressures to which they were subjected by the influx of pilgrims and the plague epidemic of Jubilee year. Certainly by the end of the year the decision had beeen made to expand the Lateran hospital further; on April 19, 1451, the Lateran chapter conceded to the confraternity a site "per ampliare il nostro ospedale nuovamente facto" (Curcio 1978, 36f.).[17] Giacomo Cenci, *guardianus* in 1450, must have been involved in the formulation of the project, along with his colleague Pietro Margani, whose involvement with at least one papal building project can be demonstrated (Burroughs 1982a, 98 n.21). Two of the witnesses of the 1451 contract are of interest. One was Cola Valentini, who had been *caporione* of the Rione Monti in 1447 (Tommasini 1887, 197), and was related to Cenci; his presence indicates the particular concern of the latter for the project. The other was Antonio Paciuri, a leading builder-entrepreneur of Nicholan Rome and a former colleague of Francesco Cenci on Eugenian projects (Corbo 1969, 50, 56, 62). But Paciuri was not present only as a technical expert; he was a leading citizen of his *rione*, Trastevere, where he was *caporione* in 1448, and it is likely that he belonged to the confraternity.

The new structure was to be erected to the side of the recently completed *ospedale nuovo*; the design was circumscribed by conditions laid down by the prior of the Lateran, Aurelio da Piacenza, who made the *guardiani* promise "to make the doors and windows of the said hospital . . . toward the public main road [*publica et magna via*] and not at the head of the said hospital toward the church of the Lateran" (Curcio 1978, 37).[18] What was the purpose of Aurelio's stipulations? As Curcio has noted, they seem consistent with a continuing attempt on the part of the Lateran chapter to establish authority over the Campo Laterano, whatever the letter of the Via Maggiore statutes or Nicholas's ruling on their application to the Campo in Jubilee year. There is no evidence that in less than two years Nicholas formally overturned his earlier decision. Rather the chapter perhaps exploited the hospital's need for a convenient site for its planned extension; the 1450 *catasto* of the chapter's holdings makes it clear that there was little property around the Campo that it did not own (Lauer 1911, esp. 511f.). If so, the uproar at the time of the emperor's visit may have been occasioned not only by an old grudge, but also by a new stimulus, and when the canons marched out to meet Frederick at a point near the hospital and then accompanied him across the full extent of the Campo they surely meant to demonstrate their presumed rights over the latter.

It is perhaps relevant that construction was also under way at the basilica; in a bull of January 1452 the prior was directed to begin a general restoration "magna et continua," and to use for this purpose all rents, revenues, and diverse profits of S. Giovanni (ASV, RV 419, fol. 178r). This was doubtless connected with the general program of restoration, supervised by Nello, undertaken in expectation of the emperor's visit.

The uneasy relationship in 1450–52 between two parties, the chapter and the confraternity, both evidently enjoying papal favor, contrasts with the situation evidenced by a document of September 13, 1454 (ASR, AOSS, Archivio Antico, Armadio 1, Mazzo 4, no. 37). On that day Agostino delle Celle, factor of the Lateran chapter, appeared before the senator to declare the chapter's formal approval of the privileges assigned to the Confraternity of the Salvatore by the Via Maggiore statutes. Even more extraordinary is that Agostino did this not only in the name of the chapter, but also of all "who have an interest in this and similarly in the name of the venerable hospital of the Image of Our Savior." The appearance of amity, even alliance, between the two institutions that faced each other across the Campo Laterano may simply be due, however, to the fact that in late 1454 the pope's life already seemed to be ebbing away, and the chapter hoped to gain the confraternity's support in the correctly anticipated difficult period for the canons regular that followed Nicholas's death.

If a genuine rapprochement took place, however, some credit may have been due to a major figure in mid-quattrocento Roman society, whom it is somewhat surprising to find deeply involved in affairs at the Lateran. Francesco Orsini, the prefect of the city and leading member of the powerful baronial clan based in Ponte, completed in 1451 his new palace at the point where the Via del Papa skirted the Piazza Navona (map 2). At Easter of that and the following year, Orsini made two donations, totaling 800 florins, to the confraternity. These must have been intended for the building fund, especially as Orsini also contributed 100 florins for an altar for the new hospital (Egidi 1908, 405).[19] On both occasions the money was not paid to the officials of the confraternity, but to Giacomo Cenci and one Silvestro, knight of St. John of Jerusalem. Cenci's role as middleman between Orsini and the confraternity followed the termination of his year of office as *guardianus*; his involvement seems due to personal and social factors, especially perhaps his experience of building projects, rather than to any official position. At the time, moreover, Giacomo was also a papal appointee, one of the two *commissarii* charged with oversight of the restoration of S. Paolo (ASV, RV 419, fol. 178r); his papal connections, then, may have been of importance here.

As for his colleague on the occasion, the knight Silvestro, no other documents have come to light concerning him; he was, however, a colleague of Francesco Orsini's illegitimate son Giambattista, who entered the order of St. John of Jerusalem in 1446 and rose to become prior of the order in Rome and subsequently grand master (Zippel 1921, 185F., 189–191). Silvestro may well also have been known to the pope, who reformed the order with a bull of October 1450 (ASV, RV 403, fol. 253r), a measure that surely indicates a particular interest on Nicholas's part in the Jerusalemite knights, as might be expected in view of the gathering clouds in the East. The money was paid over to the *guardiani* in a room in the hospital that was part of the residence of Pietro Stefani, who undertook to see that it was spent on the construction of the new hospital; it is not clear what Stefani's official role was or why he had rooms in the hospital. He was a man of some local eminence; he had been *guardianus* in 1445, together with the powerful Battista Leni, and he came from the Rione Monti (Marangoni 1747, 316).

Orsini's donations to the confraternity and the Lateran hospital coincided with or perhaps rather followed generosity to the basilica. By 1450 he had given to the chapter an olive grove, the annual revenue of which was to be used for the upkeep of a chapel of S. Leonardo, which Orsini had founded in S. Giovanni. The date of the foundation of this chapel is not known; it is likely that Orsini, who owed his appointment as prefect of the city to Eugenius (whose attachment to the Lateran was noted above), endowed his chapel in the context of Eugenian patronage—and politics—at the Lateran (Lauer 1911, 527).[20] In any case, it is likely that Francesco Orsini, perhaps aided and abetted by Giacomo Cenci, played a role in the improvement of relations between the confraternity and the chapter that followed the trouble of the early 1450s, and that Nicholas knew and approved of these initiatives.

At the other end of the statutorily defined Via Maggiore from the Campo Laterano and the rapidly expanding hospital stood the Colosseum (fig. 37, center). This immense and famous structure, of enormous symbolic significance to the people of the city, was associated with the confraternity not only through the proximity of the hospital of S. Jacopo. In the later medieval period more and more of the Colosseum passed into the hands of the confraternity: a large section was purchased from an aristocratic clan that had occupied the Colosseum, turned it into a fortress, and proudly become known accordingly as the Annibaldi de Coliseo; another section came to the confraternity from a member of the Colonna clan (Guidoni 1983, 377; Adinolfi 1857a, 120; Egidi 1908, 321, 438). The Colosseum, then, became something of an emblem of the rising power of the urban patriciate in Rome vis-à-vis the baronial clans, the prevalence of whose towers in the area between and around the Colosseum and the Campidoglio was noted in chapter 1. The confraternity, however, was perhaps not the only Roman institution with interests in and rights over the Colosseum, for it was the site of the annual *sacra rappresentazione* of the passion of Christ enacted by the brothers of the Confraternity of the Gonfalone. The earliest documented reference to this is an edict of Pope Innocent VIII of 1490 regulating the use of the Colosseum by the Gonfalone, and implying that this was traditional (Adinolfi 1857a, 158 doc. 12). In any case, Innocent's intervention indicates the weakness of the Confraternity of the Salvatore and its claims in the face of late-fifteenth-century papal authority. Even more striking is the obligation of the *guardiani* of 1472, under Sixtus IV, to apply to the *maestri di strada* for permission to build a minor expansion of the hospital of S. Jacopo on land that, according to the Via Maggiore statutes, still fell under the confraternity's jurisdiction (ibid., 156 doc. 11).[21]

The question of Nicholas's attitude to the confraternity's rights over the Colosseum raises the question of papal concern with the preservation of the venerable building or, alternatively, with its exploitation as a stone quarry. Eugenius had sought to put a halt to the familiar practice of subtracting stone from the Colosseum, threatening severe penalties if even the slightest stone ("minimus lapis") was taken from it. Under Nicholas, however, the demands of the various construction projects, some in the vicinity of the Colosseum, must have contributed to a change of policy; thus in the single period from September 1451 to May 1452 just one entrepreneur took no fewer than 2,522 wagon loads of stone from the Colosseum (Jordan 1907, 1:286 n.13; Lanciani 1902, 1:51; Battisti 1959, 46). No protests are recorded on the part of the confraternity, though it is *prima facie* improbable that the brothers welcomed the large-scale destruction for the benefit of papal projects of a prominent monument that lay in an area under their jurisdiction and was in great part owned by them; I have found no evidence that the confraternity itself gained financially from the demolitions. Further, large-scale quarrying and the functions of the Ospedale S. Jacopo seem hardly compatible. It is likely, however, that some of the stone went to the confraternity's own projects.

There is evidence that suggests that Nicholas did not regard the Colosseum merely as a convenient stone quarry, and even implies that the stone recorded as taken from the Colosseum in fact came from its environs, as was permitted by Eugenius's edict. An entry in Nello's ledger of March 21, 1453, records the payment to a painter, one Gianni Antonio da Roma, for six papal coats of arms painted on the Colosseum (Müntz 1878, 95 n.5). Unfortunately the document does not specify the location of these insignia, nor even whether they were painted on the interior or exterior. It is most likely that they were painted on the exterior, presumably in some carefully worked out relationship to the celebrated architectural articulation of the facade, so as to catch the eye of passers-by on the Via Maggiore/Via del Papa. The sixfold repetition of the insignia implies that they were so placed on the oval structure that travelers approaching from different directions had a view of at least one of them, or experienced them sequentially as they moved around the building.

As we have noted, however, the Confraternity of the Salvatore owned much of the Colosseum; here, according to its regular practice, it made sure that its arms, the head of Christ between two candles, were prominently displayed (they were certainly there in the fourteenth century [Guidoni 1983, 377 n.5]). And it is unlikely that Nicholas, himself a brother of the confraternity, would have ordered the painter Gianni (himself, perhaps significantly, a Roman citizen) to paint over the insignia of the confraternity; such an act would have flouted the letter and spirit of the Via Maggiore statutes, the traditional symbolism of the Colosseum, and the conciliatory and tactful policies so far adopted by Nicholas within the city. The timing of the placing of the insignia, moreover, seems too close to the Porcari conspiracy not to be connected with it in some way. If so, a gesture of reconciliation rather than provocation would have been in order, consistent with the absence of what might now be called a witch hunt in the early months of 1453 (and with the developments at Trevi as described in chapter 3). No doubt Nicholas wished to assert papal authority, but this was not all that was involved here.

In the 1517 *catasto* of the Confraternity of the Salvatore there is a long description of the new infirmary of the Lateran hospital, a building that extended from the chapel of S. Andrea toward the piazza.[22] The *catasto* states that the infirmary of the hospital was moved here in 1452 from the building previously used. The author of the document regards the period in which the infirmary opened as one in which the confraternity particularly flourished: "when by the grace of God and our Savior the hospital and the aforesaid confraternity were growing in quality and number of good persons, in wealth, and in works of piety." The religious character of the new building was enhanced by the installation at one end of the long, narrow space of altars to Saints Cosmas and Damian and to St. Michael (replacing a chapel of the archangel located in the old infirmary), and of a chapel of S. Ciriaco at the other end, so that the patients could all be in sight of the daily celebration of the Eucharist. Probably they were more appreciative of the fire kept burning in the center of the room.

There is, indeed, historical evidence of the confraternity's growth, for with a bull of January 11, 1452, Nicholas removed all restrictions on the number of brothers admitted; it may be, as Egidi suggested, that the mid-fifteenth-century *liber fraternitatis* was brought into use in response to a rapid increase in membership, while a documented inventory of the possessions of the confraternity was carried out in 1452 (Egidi 1908, 431, 453).[23] A further significant event was the enrollment in July of that year of the influential chief penitentiary, Cardinal Domenico Capranica, among the brothers; the fact that he was also archpriest of the Lateran points to a consistent pattern of reconciliation between the Lateran chapter and the confraternity. Further confirmation of this was provided by the appointment of Capranica as chaplain of the confraternity; the date of this is unknown to me, but it can hardly have been before he joined the confraternity, and he died in 1459.[24]

Nicholas in fact may have given his support of the confraternity visible expression. In the eighteenth century Marangoni, the early historian of the confraternity, saw a marble tablet set into the wall in the courtyard of the Lateran hospital (Marangoni 1747, 285). The tablet, carved in "Gothic style," bore the face of Christ between two candelabra and to either side a shield, one carved with the arms of the Roman commune and the other with those of the pope. The papal arms described by Marangoni were the crossed keys, which he points out were used as his own insignia by Nicholas V. Here, then, in close and deliberate juxtaposition, are the arms of the confraternity, the commune, and the pope. It is an association of symbols that can only have been of conciliatory significance to contemporaries. The tablet did not carry a date, but surely no more likely date can be proposed for it than 1452, when the new infirmary was opened, no doubt in the presence of Domenico Capranica, Aurelio da Piacenza and his Lateran canons, Francesco Orsini, Giacomo Cenci, the officials of the confraternity (the *guardiani* were Pietro Mellini and Ciriaco Capodiferro), the *caporione* of Monti, Pietro Stefani with the staff of the hospital, and perhaps also Nicholas V himself.

The appearance of the pope's insignia on the Colosseum, then, in association with the arms of the confraternity and perhaps also the commune was no isolated incident. Rather it called attention to a balance, perhaps recently established, of interests and claims in the Via Maggiore. It also marked a stage on the major processional route of the early Renaissance city, and it is worth noting here the attention given by Alberti, Biondo, and others to the theme of the processional or triumphal thoroughfare. It is striking that Alberti's examples of processional routes are in many cases not marked as such by any consistent architectural treatment; he refers to several marked by distinctive trees or paving (Alberti 1966a, 2:706). The Via Maggiore, certainly, was never rationalized and monumentalized in the canonical forms usually associated with the theory and practice of Renaissance town planning (and exemplified in Alberti's list, for instance, by the early Christian treatment of the routes from Rome to the basilicas of St. Peter's and S. Paolo fuori le Mura, both lined with regular buildings, in this case colonnades);[25] nevertheless it received at least symbolic enhancement of its significance and topographical structure. Any further development of this, for example through architectural means, was perhaps cut short through the definitive transfer of attention from the Lateran to the Vatican in the second half of the fifteenth century.

The display of the pope's arms at the Lateran hospital and at the Colosseum, moreover, must be seen in context with the papal building work at the Campidogli. Apart from the significance of the Via Maggiore in ecclesiastical processions, the route from the Campidoglio toward the Lateran (fig. 37) had particular municipal processional significance, for it was still marked by three ancient triumphal arches and it was taken by the magistrates and officals of the commune in order to be present at ceremonies that took place at the Lateran itself or along the route to it. Many such ceremonies must have expressed the close relationship of the commune and the confraternity, as the two leading institutions associated with the patrician elite of the city.

It is surely significant, accordingly, that in the pontificate of Nicholas references occur to a new residence of the officials of the confraternity situated in the palace of the *conservatores*, the major officers of the communal government, which had been recently rebuilt by Nicholas V. The first case known to me dates from 1452, when notarial transactions are recorded as carried out and witnessed "apud capitolium ante domum nostre residencie sub palatio novo dominorum Conservatorum" (ASR, AOSS, Istromenti 24, fol. 20v).[26] In 1452, moreover, the confraternity bought, apparently for the first time, grain storage facilities (*putei*) in the area of the Campidoglio;[27] the significance of this is difficult to assess, but it is a further indication that the patrician brethren of the confraternity may now have regarded the Campidoglio and the Lateran as two extreme points of a processional axis extending well beyond the Via Maggiore as statutorily defined, and as bracketing a theater of their ideological concerns and political aspirations.

If so, the symbolic presence of the confraternity in the area of the Roman Forum (fig. 38) brought it into association with certain other important institutions of the city. The guilds of the city had offices in the Palazzo dei Conservatori; the major guild, that of the *bovattieri*, who owed their livelihood to stock raising and related activities, had particular interests in the Forum area, as the site of the *dogana di bestiame*, the municipal office regulating and taxing the sale of beasts in the nearby livestock markets.[28] The chambers of the important guild of *speziali*, the purveyors of drugs, are documented in the Palazzo dei

Conservatori by September 1453 (cf. ACR, AU, Fondo notarile 253, fol. 42r); the church of the guild was the nearby S. Lorenzo in Miranda, so-called because of its location among the awe-inspiring ruins of the Roman Forum, and itself built in the well-preserved temple of Antoninus and Faustina. Here in 1450 a hospital was founded under the patronage of one of the most powerful men in Rome, Astorgio Agnese, titular cardinal of S. Eusebio until his death in 1451 (Grifi 1862, 60; Querini 1892, 201).[29] The Neapolitan Agnese was an experienced and tough negotiator who received his red hat from Nicholas in December 1448 (DBI, 1:439); he was no stranger to the Campidoglio as a former governor of Rome, and it was perhaps still in this capacity that he spoke out in the church of the Aracoeli in 1447 against the attempt of Stefano Porcari to arouse the passions of the assembled citizenry against papal rule on the very eve of Nicholas's accession (Infessura 1890, 45).

The foundation of the Spedale degli Speziali, a further case of collaboration between the Roman patriciate and Nicholas or his proxies in the earlier part of his pontificate, occurred in an area that economically and demographically was far from the desert it is sometimes claimed to have been; in November 1454, for example, a German baker leased a house "in a portico" to one side of S. Lorenzo (ACR, AU, Fondo notarile [Amati], fol. 60r).[30] Significantly, the house belonged to the Confraternity of the Salvatore (the transaction was carried out in the portal of the courtyard of the Lateran hospital), further exemplifying the confraternity's economic as well as symbolic interests in the area, and there was no rebuilding or improvement clause, implying that the property was in good condition by the standards of the day. Clearly, the German anticipated that there would be sufficient demand for his wares, presumably in the environs of the shop.

A short distance from S. Lorenzo on the processional route was the church of SS. Cosma e Damiano, which was connected with the confraternity in two respects: it was the station on the route of the procession of the Assumption where a delegation of the city's women came forward to pay obeisance to the image of the Savior (Marangoni 1747, 176), and, apparently since 1440, it was the guild church of the *barbieri* (Monachino 1968, 176). Since barbers performed surgical operations, they, no less than their neighbors, the druggists, were perhaps associated with the work of the confraternity's hospitals. Indeed, in the infirmary established in 1452 in the new building at the Lateran hospital there was a chapel dedicated to Saints Cosmas and Damian (ASR, AOSS, Piante e Catasti 390, no. 1010, fol. 8r). The church was also the starting point of a *palio*, presumably a horse race, run along the Via Maggiore to the Campo Laterano on the occasion of Nicholas's coronation (Cancellieri 1802, 42; did the equestrian statue of "Constantine" have a ceremonial role on such an occasion?). No doubt this event was organized by the Confraternity of the Salvatore and had the incidental function of demonstrating the latter's claims over the area traversed by the competitors.

The church of SS. Cosma e Damiano adjoined open ground, some of which, like the *vigna* leased for horticultural use in 1451, was still cultivated. In many of the *vigne* of the area, however, the major crop was building stone, and in

1451 the pope's officials bought land here for use as a quarry (ASR, CNC 482, fol. 98v; this does not necessarily imply that the area was unpopulated, only that the proceeds from quarrying exceeded those from rents from houses). Thus in 1453 we find the contractor Pietro da Castiglione quarrying travertine from the "Templum Pacis" (the basilica of Maxentius; ASR, TS 1453, fol. 161r); this Pietro may have been identical with the Pietro da Varese who worked at the nearby church of S. Teodoro, so close to Nicholas's heart, at the same time, and who was the nephew of the powerful entrepreneur Beltramo.[31]

As noted in connection with the Colosseum, the Confraternity of the Salvatore was not the only confraternity with interests in the area. On August 2, 1447, Nicholas issued a bull "pro erectione" in favor of the Confraternity of S. Bernardo alla Colonna, founded in the pontificate of Martin V. It had received at that time, evidently as a foundation relic, an image of the Madonna said to have been painted by St. Luke; the provenance of this icon from the chapel of Sancta Sanctorum makes clear the dependence of the Confraternity of S. Bernardo on that of the Salvatore.[32] It is not clear why the brethren of the new confraternity took so long to build or at least complete their church on the property donated to them in the environs of Trajan's column (from which the church took its popular name). In any case, a document of March 23, 1450, documents the reconstruction of the church, indicating that new urgency had come with Nicholas's pontificate (ASR, CNC 518, fol. 10r).[33] A leading figure in all this was perhaps the confraternity's banker, Evangelista Leni, whose brother Battista was a leading member of the Confraternity of the Salvatore and a business partner of the Medici and beneficiary of the pope's administrative and fiscal policies. The Leni brothers were *bovattieri* as well as bankers; indeed, Evangelista's donation to the Confraternity of the Salvatore for masses to be said in S. Maria della Strada for his wife Gentilesca was made in young oxen to the value of 50 florins (Egidi 1908, 399).

There is indirect evidence, further, that Domenico Capranica was associated with the Confraternity of S. Bernardo (he was among the executors of Francesco de' Foschi's will; see note 32); certainly this would be consistent with the cardinal's support of religious and caritative institutions in the city, not least in this area. It would also emphasize the probable relationship of dependence between the Confraternity of the Salvatore, whose chaplain Capranica became, and that of S. Bernardo; it was only 20 years later that the Confraternity of the Salvatore became exclusive, after a vote of its general assembly, and began to insist that the brothers give up membership in other confraternities (Egidi 1914, 453). Hitherto, apparently, it was usual for members to belong to other confraternities, implying that a relative social and institutional fluidity characterized life in Rome in mid-quattrocento, until the barriers of exclusivity went up.

Near S. Bernardo and overlooking the processional way was the headquarters of an important religious order, reformed by Nicholas V, the Knights of St. John of Jerusalem. The building occupied by the order at this time was largely transformed by later fifteenth-century construction (Ricci 1930, 157; Tomei 1942, 95), but it is possible that some repairs were carried out in connection with

Nicholas's reform and the involvement of the Orsini family, and that these were marked by visible signs or inscriptions of some kind. Here too Domenico Capranica made his influence felt; in February 1450 Nicholas responded to a supplication of the cardinal on behalf of the latter's nephew, Dionisio, who was thereby created a knight of St. John (ASV, RV 414, fol. 136v).

The dominant structure in the area of the Forum, of course, was the Senator's Palace, with its new tower erected under Nicholas at its southeastern corner to command the path up to the municipal palaces above from the Forum and the Via Maggiore (figs. 3, 39). This was the most convenient route from the medieval Senator's Palace to the church of S. Adriano, the former *curia senatus* of ancient Rome; on the way it traversed an area ennobled by the arch of Septimius Severus and by the presence of the statue of a reclining river god known as Marforio (figs. 38, 40), Pasquino's later colleague, who may already have possessed the capacity to speak to the Romans about their city and themselves.[34] This was the point where the procession of the Assumption, coming from the Lateran, turned off the axis of the papal processional way to proceed toward the church of S. Maria Maggiore. Before doing this, however, it paused to receive the homage of the city magistrates who assembled there after marching down from the Campidoglio, dressed in their robes of office (Marangoni 1747, 124).

It was perhaps at this moment, more than at any other, that the ranks, offices, and professions of the Roman people, indeed the very social and political structures of the city, became visible. The ceremony was essentially and traditionally communal; communal symbols and insignia predominated and probably, even by mid-quattrocento, there was little visible reference to the overall political reality, the temporal power of the pope. Yet above the place where the procession and the magistrates met stood the tower of Nicholas V, displaying his modest insignia in a close and still conciliatory association with the nearby insignia of commune, guilds, and confraternities. For the juxtaposition of insignia noted at the Lateran hospital and surmised at the Colosseum was surely also present on the various buildings of the Campidoglio.

The intervention, then, of Nicholas V in the Via Maggiore was of a very different kind, say, from that of Julius II in the Via Giulia. Not one single building along the length of the Via Maggiore (understood as extended to the Campidoglio) was built by Nicholas, except at the Capitol itself, and there were certainly no grand effects; yet the language of the symbols placed along the route and the attitudes and policies that lay behind them no doubt spoke as clearly to contemporaries as the more ambitious alterations of a later age. In Nicholas's policy toward the Via Sacra it seems legitimate to see a tactful yet firm response—or set of responses—to the varied and complex symbolic horizon of the area, as well as a heightened awareness of urban form, not so much seen as read.

Suburban Continuities: The Esquiline and Its Palaces
The papal palace of S. Maria Maggiore (fig. 35, center) was founded in the twelfth century by the future Clement III, bishop of Palestrina, as an official

residence for himself and his successors in office; on his accession as pope he gave the canons of S. Maria Maggiore quarters in the building (Biasiotti 1911a, 117). This dual function of the palace, as apostolic residence and canons' quarters, survived the improvements and extensions carried out by Nicholas IV, who, according to Panvinio, lived for much of his pontificate at S. Maria (Panvinio 1570, 241; cf. Lanciani 1902, 1:52, 55). Nicholas died in the palace, which was then used for the ensuing conclave. It is significant that Nicholas did not use the palace as his summer residence; soon after his accession it became his primary residence, while he spent his summers away from Rome, at Rieti or Orvieto (Ehrle and Egger 1935, 27).

In the thirteenth century Urban IV is known to have used the palace, while in the fifteenth century Martin V stayed there; his favorite residence was not far away at SS. Apostoli, near the stronghold of his kinsfolk (Müntz 1878, 2 n.3). There is no evidence that construction of note was undertaken until the accession of Nicholas V, who replaced Clement III and his own earlier namesake in at least one later account of the foundation of the palace, that of Albertini in a passage on the extensive improvements carried out by Julius II (Valentini and Zucchetti 1953, 513). The implication is that Nicholas left the palace as an almost uninhabitable shell; even taking into account the changes in fashion and standards of comfort in the intervening years, this must be an exaggeration. We know, for instance, that Pius II used the building, though not for a long sojourn (Biasiotti 1911a, 105). In the sixteenth century the airy heights of Monti attracted the popes, but their favor shifted from the Esquiline to the site of Cardinal Oliviero Carafa's residence on the Quirinal (fig. 35, far right). The Quirinal palace was especially expanded under Gregory XIII, who seems also to have carried out some reconstruction at the palace on the Esquiline. Gregory's successor, Sixtus V, gave attention both to the Quirinal and the Esquiline, the latter at the expense of the papal palace, much of which fell victim to Sixtus's grandiose urbanism (Marconi, Cipriani, and Valeriani 1974, 2:19 no. 2427; Wasserman 1963, 205f.).

The extent and nature of Nicholas V's interventions at S. Maria Maggiore are impossible to reconstruct from the few plans and views of the palace that are extant, or from building records (Lanciani 1902, 1:52f.; Castagnoli et al. 1958, 409f.; Magnuson 1958, 224). By a *motu proprio* of April 23, 1452, Nicholas gave two houses and an adjoining chapel, hitherto the property of the Vallombrosan monastery of S. Prassede, to the chapter of S. Maria Maggiore in recompense for other houses demolished in the course of work on the palace (De Angelis 1621, 70f.). This indicates that the work was on a considerable scale and that it was more than a mere restoration of existing fabric. Work is documented in 1447, 1450, and 1451 under the direction of Antonello d'Albano; curiously the Carmelite brothers of the basilica are explicitly named as *committenti*, though the funds came from the Camera Apostolica (Müntz 1879, 316). This suggests that Antonello worked on the basilica or the brothers' quarters, rather than on the papal apartments, but the documents do not distinguish the different projects. Antonello had worked at the basilica under Eugenius; his first documented appearance is in 1436, along with another contractor-builder who was to play a major role in Nicholas's projects, Antonio Paciuri (Corbo 1969, 54, 55). It is perhaps significant, further, that one of the canons, Niccolò della Valle, was a clerk of the Camera Apostolica and a member of the prominent family of the Via del Papa where their largely fifteenth-century palace still stands (Marchetti-Longhi 1919, 481); he is doubly likely, then, to have been in close contact with the chamberlain, whose involvement after 1440 in the development of the city I have noted; he was perhaps the chamberlain's contact at S. Maria, at least until Cardinal d'Estouteville, appointed archpriest in 1443, asserted himself. If so, it may be pertinent that he hailed from a part of the city well beyond the traditional Colonna sphere of influence.

Antonello d'Albano's activity at S. Maria is paralleled by that in 1447 at S. Eusebio (fig. 37, top left), where the Celestine brothers were named as *committenti*, though the Camera Apostolica made the payment (ASV, IE 414, fol. 88v). At S. Eusebio, as at S. Maria, Antonello had clearly been in charge of a Eugenian project, here connected with the introduction of the Celestine order. Later Calixtus III empowered Francesco del Borgo, the former assistant of Nello da Bologna, to wind up the project at S. Maria; though in this document, as in the other records, neither the basilica nor the palace is specified, the mention of *camerae* suggests that the latter was involved (Müntz 1879, 200; Tomei 1942, 72f.). It appears that very early in his pontificate Calixtus determined to have nothing to do with the palace of S. Maria; as we will see, Nicholas was motivated by special concerns.

Nicholas's sojourns at the palace at S. Maria were thought worthy of comment by at least one contemporary: Stefano Caffari, with the laconism characteristic of Roman diarists, recorded two such visits (Caffari 1885–86, 587, 601). The first of these is dated August 31, 1448, two weeks after the procession of the Assumption, which Nicholas would have awaited at S. Maria, as was the custom by the mid-quattrocento. It is probable that Caffari was referring to the pope's taking up residence in the palace of S. Maria, now sufficiently renovated, perhaps after a procession through the streets of the city. Caffari's second reference to a visit to the basilica is of October 25, 1450, noting that the pope went there on his return from his peregrinations in the Marche. Nicholas would certainly have returned to Rome by the Via Flaminia, entering the city through the Porta del Popolo (de' Conti 1883, 2:348); it was clearly not convenience that led him to S. Maria on this occasion, and it is probable that he wished to give thanks to the Madonna for his safe return and deliverance from plague. If so, Nicholas's practice was followed by Pius II and Julius II, both of whom stayed at the palace at S. Maria before extended and prospectively difficult journeys, in each case requiring departure from Rome through the Porta del Popolo. Thus the restoration of S. Maria for Nicholas, and perhaps also for Julius, should be related to the performance of supplicatory ritual in the basilica and to the belief in the Virgin's actual or potential intercession in the affairs of state.

On his return to Rome in August 1450, his biographer assures us, Nicholas was greeted with spontaneous outbursts of popular enthusiasm (Miglio 1975, 236). The biographer, Michele Canensi, writing soon after the event (at the latest

1452), quotes Virgil's first eclogue on the much-desired return of a different kind of shepherd: "The pine trees, the very springs, these very bushes were calling you back, Tityrus." And Canensi adds some variations of his own on the theme: "All the churches, every place, each corner, every part of the city seems to exult in an extraordinary way." Clearly the evidential value of such a text is compromised by its exaggeration and rhetorical embellishment, but if such acclamation greeted the pope in August 1450 at S. Maria there were good reasons for it, for the residents of the area owed to him particular material advantages.

Only two months after his accession, on May 23, 1447, Nicholas had issued a bull granting extensive tax relief to residents of the area bounded by the Arco di San Vito, S. Prassede, the piazza of S. Maria Maggiore, and the Via in Fontana (Appendix, no. 1). There is no evidence that this area existed as a topographical entity before Nicholas's edict, like, for example, the nearby Borgo di S. Agata. It was situated in an especially elevated part of the Esquiline hill known in antiquity as the Cispian hill, but there is no reason to suppose that this toponym or an equivalent referring to the same topographical feature was still in use (Ferri 1907, 160 no. 211, 162 no. 214). The edict of 1447 was followed by another in the following year, dated August 21, 1448, in which the fiscal privileges were extended to include immunity from the *gabella* on wine (Malatesta 1886, 179). Ten days later the pope visited the area in person, as Caffari noted.

The pope's immediate concern, however, was not to benefit the existing inhabitants of the area; he hoped to attract new settlers, as is made explicit in the first edict. To this end, in case material incentives should not be sufficient, immunity was granted from a range of less than heinous crimes, on condition that each former offender undertook to live in the area for a continuous period of not less than ten years. It might be supposed that the prospect of an influx of new neighbors of this kind would be anything but welcome to those already resident in the area; the second edict, however, was not occasioned by some papal policy conceived without consultation of the residents and executed over their heads, but by a petition on behalf of the residents themselves, who complained of the "molestatio" to which they had been subjected by communal officials, who seem to have taken a narrow view of the pope's first edict as producing only a decrease in revenue. In general, the measures taken to improve the physical environment and increase the population of a privileged enclave on the Esquiline echo the Via Maggiore statutes (rather than, as Westfall [1974a], 106, thought, unsuccessful edicts of Martin V and Eugenius IV to attract settlers to the Vatican Borgo); if so, however, a communal precedent was combined with a program of reform of religious institutions taken over, as we saw, from Eugenius.

The question arises of the pope's success in securing demographic and economic change on the Esquiline. The fragmentary evidence is not conclusive either way; many documents regarding property transactions in Monti do not specify the sites concerned in ways that allow for identification, and none that I have found refer to the evidently artificial district defined by the Nicholan edicts. It is of interest that on August 8, 1453, Nicholas allowed the canons of S. Maria to sell extensive property once belonging to the Benedictine convent of S. Bartolomeo in Suburra, which has been suppressed by Nicholas and its property and revenues made over to S. Maria, on condition that they not be alienated for any secular use (Marx 1915, 41f.; Ferri 1907, 162; Armellini 1942, 2:222). The location of the property is not specified, but the church of S. Bartolomeo was located not far from the Via in Fontana, one of the boundaries of the area identified in the 1447 edict, and it is not unlikely that property belonging to it fell within the stipulated boundaries; if so, the canons of S. Maria may have taken the opportunity to get a good price for property rising in value. Nicholas's assent to the canons' supplication, which entailed setting aside his own earlier decision, manifests a contradiction between two aims of the pope. On the one hand, Nicholas was concerned to foster economic development and social/moral improvement through the encouragement of settlement in an underpopulated district; on the other hand, he was committed to the conservation of ecclesiastical property and privilege. Ecclesiastical institutions too, however, were caught up in urban change, as Nicholas himself must have recognized, at least in this case.

Whatever the effect of the pope's interventions, independently of them development was taking place in the Rione Monti. Nomenclature in the documents points to an influx of new immigrants from the hill towns to the east of the city (map 3).[35] Such immigrants appear, it is true, in other *rioni*, but they are most common, to the virtual exclusion of immigrants from other areas, in the Rioni Monti, Trevi, and Colonna. The occasion of such large-scale and homogeneous immigration is easy to specify. Various chroniclers refer to this phenomenon in connection with the operations of Vitelleschi against the Colonna in 1436, in particular the destruction of Palestrina. According to one chronicler, Pietro di Lello Petrone, Vitelleschi was supported by considerable elements in the population of Palestrina; it is possible, then, that the immigration in this year was supervised or even encouraged officially (Petrone 1912, 25–35; cf. della Tuccia 1852, 160). It was not in the interest of the papal regime that the already volatile population of the city be joined by numerous destitute and desperate Colonna partisans from the hills, but the leavening of the pro-Colonna population of Monti, many of whom had old family links with Palestrina and the adjoining region, with kinsmen or compatriots loyal to the papal cause made sense in terms of Vitelleschi's pacification of Rome, as did the transfer of even low-level economic activity from Palestrina to the *disabitato*. Indeed, in the 1450 property *catasto* of the Lateran chapter several Palestrinesi appear renting *vigne* and other property from the chapter, a clear sign of at least moderate prosperity (Lauer 1911, 511). Once again, then, Nicholas's interventions should be seen in the context of policies undertaken, albeit with less tact, under Eugenius, whose building campaigns in Monti may have acted—not accidentally—as a stimulus to the rional economy.

Though Nicholas's interventions in Monti have at first sight the air of unilateral, direct measures, they were in fact typically carried out through the offices of and perhaps in response to the initiatives of an intermediary, in this case one who had been in place since the latter years of Eugenius. Guillaume d'Estouteville, the immensely wealthy and influential French prelate, had been created cardinal in 1439 by Eugenius, who assigned him the titular church of S. Martino in Monti, perhaps already with ulterior motives. Shortly afterward, presumably on the death of Cardinal Niccolò Albergati in 1443, d'Estouteville was appointed his successor as archpriest of S. Maria Maggiore (Eubel 1914, 98; Barbier de Montault 1889, 5; Ferri 1907, 158 no. 195). In this position, d'Estouteville was surely involved with the Eugenian restoration campaign at S. Maria; this was perhaps a difficult role for the cardinal, in view of the strong Colonna connections of the basilica and, no doubt, its clergy, who may well have resented even so potentially generous a representative of Eugenius's regime as d'Estouteville.

The cardinal's primary concerns as *committente* at the time were of a less altruistic nature; by 1450 the palace he had built at S. Apollinare was in a sufficiently finished state to elicit the admiration of that better-known palace builder, Giovanni Rucellai (Rucellai 1960, 76). But he may already have planned the donation to S. Maria of an elaborate sculpted shrine to house the remains of St. Jerome, whose life and works were of enormous importance in Renaissance religious and literary culture. In 1463 this monument, commissioned by d'Estouteville and carved by Mino da Fiesole, was set in place behind the basilica's high altar (Rice 1985, 56).

D'Estouteville took his duties as archpriest of S. Maria seriously, to judge from the frequent appearance of his name on documents registered in the archive of the chapter. On March 31, 1451, moreover, Nicholas V confirmed new statutes for the canons of S. Maria that had been issued by d'Estouteville (Ferri 1907, 163 no. 217). And the second edict concerning the development of the Cispian, that issued on August 21, 1448, in reponse to a supplication of the residents, was copied into the papal ledger with a note at the head of the document stating that the bull had been given to Cardinal d'Estouteville in S. Pudenziana (ASV, RV 4073, FOL. 196r), adjacent to S. Maria (though the bull itself was issued at the Vatican). It is possible that the house at S. Pudenziana, which the pope occasionally used, was kept open even in his absence as a kind of office from which a papal representative might deal with matters arising in the area, not least in connection with the construction work at the nearby papal palace at S. Maria.[36] The chapter of S. Maria itself is not mentioned in either of the documents concerning the Cispian; it is as if d'Estouteville appears here in the name of the local population, whose successful supplication he had perhaps helped on its way through the official channels of the curial administration.

D'Estouteville owed his red hat to Eugenius; to Nicholas he owed his transfer from the see of Angers, worth 1,700 florins, to that of Rouen, worth 12,000 (Eubel 1914, 244). The cardinal's wealth was already legendary; this considerable addition to his resources was perhaps in part intended to encourage his patronage. As Nicholas's pontificate progressed, d'Estouteville found himself as the senior member of a group of mostly rich and foreign prelates who owed both their red hats and their association with Monti to Nicholas. On December 20, 1448, six cardinals were created, all of whom received *tituli* in Monti, all but two in or near the area of the Cispian that was the subject of the contemporary legislation (ibid., 11 n.1). Astorgio Agnese received S. Eusebio, Nicolaus Cusanus received S. Pietro in Vincoli, while S. Prassede, named as one of the boundaries of the development area, was assigned to another wealthy French prelate, Alain Coetivy, whose tomb may still be seen there. The pope's half-brother, Filippo Calandrini, received S. Susanna, which was located on the Quirinal, but at no great distance from the Via in Fontana. On the distant Caelian hill, which was also part of Monti, S. Stefano Rotondo and SS. Giovanni e Paolo went to the wealthy French prelate Jean Rolin and to Latino Orsini respectively. In addition, the important church of SS. Apostoli, at the fringe of the Rione Monti toward the *abitato*, had been the *titulus* of Cardinal Bessarion. When Nicholas transferred Bessarion to the see of S. Sabina in March 1449, he was allowed to keep SS. Apostoli *in commendam*; I have noted elsewhere his concern for the church and the reform of its clergy, which we may now see as perhaps related to the roughly contemporary reform carried out by d'Estouteville at S. Maria. Some of these churches had become vacant only recently on the death of previous incumbents, as at S. Eusebio. S. Prassede, however, had been vacant since 1441 and S. Stefano and SS. Giovanni e Paolo since 1444, while another cardinal had to be moved to the see of Ostia to make way for Cusanus at S. Pietro in Vincoli.

Nicholas's campaign of restoration on the station churches of Rome is well known. It has not been noticed, however, that the churches of Monti benefited to a particular degree from this, especially those that received a titular cardinal in 1448. Thus S. Stefano and SS. Apostoli are listed by Manetti among the major basilicas (in place of the more usual S. Croce and S. Sebastiano fuori le Mura), while S. Pietro in Vincoli and S. Prassede appear among the four city churches individually named as restored by Nicholas (Magnuson 1958, 352). Canensi, writing in 1451, gives particular emphasis to S. Maria Maggiore, S. Stefano Rotondo, S. Prassede, and S. Susanna (Miglio 1975, 231), and I have noted the documentary evidence for restoration at S. Maria Maggiore, S. Pietro in Vincoli, and S. Eusebio. I have found no trace of work at S. Prassede in the papal documents, but it is likely that its restoration was paid for privately by Cardinal Coetivy, and perhaps entrusted to the equipe of Antonello d'Albano, already engaged on several projects in the area. We find, then, that Nicholas deliberately used the creation of cardinals as one of several strategies for the development of a particular quarter of the city. It is noteworthy that he never again resorted to this strategy, while he also gave up the use of edicts as direct means to promote his goals in the city; instead, as I have argued in chapter 3, he turned to more indirect and subtle strategies, at least until 1453.

The assignment of S. Susanna to his brother reflects a predilection on Nicholas's part for this church, which had been his own *titulus* during his short cardinalate. He referred to this connection himself in a bull of June 1, 1447, in which he lamented the ruinous condition of the church and the adjoining buildings (ASV, RV 406, fol. 196r). Once again, religious reform and physical reconstruction were combined, for the bull concerned the transfer of S. Susanna and its dependent churches, including a S. Agata (possibly the church in Monti to the parishioners of which Nicholas showed particular consideration),[37] to a congregation of Augustinian monks. Cardinal Calandrini, however, found S. Susanna not to his liking, and he was especially displeased by the residence attached to his church. Within three years, during which he had frequently been absent from Rome on missions, he pleaded for a new residence; in the bull granting this, Nicholas recognized his brother's claim that the condition of the buildings at S. Susanna was such that he could not be expected to live there (ASV, RV 418, fol. 173v [September 10, 1451]).

If the palace at S. Susanna was indeed as ruinous as Calandrini's supplication asserted, the contrast with the palace now assigned to him was extreme, for this was the palace of S. Lorenzo in Lucina, constructed largely by an affluent French prelate of an earlier generation, Cardinal de la Rochetaillé, and considered by Flavio Biondo to be the finest in Rome (Tomei 1942, 36). It is noteworthy that this grant of a palace attached to a titular church was made independently of the assignment of the *titulus* itself, though a month later Calandrini was in fact transferred to S. Lorenzo (Eubel 1914, 11). This did not end the cardinal's association with S. Susanna and its convent of Augustinian monks; in April 1452 the prior of S. Susanna, Fra Agostino da Siena, was named as Calandrini's procurator in connection with an exchange of properties carried out by the convent and the Confraternity of the Salvatore (ASR, AOSS, Istromenti 24, fol. 123r). It is probable that Calandrini held the church *in commendam*, just as Cardinal Albergati had held the similarly neglected and outlying church of S. Balbina (ASV, Schedario Garampi, Titoli Cardinalizi, 44). It is possible that a further prelate of importance under Nicholas also had links with the area, for on his death in 1473 Cardinal Jean Jouffroy owned a *vigna* at the Baths of Diocletian (Chambers 1976a, 41 n.140), perhaps the property later owned by Jouffroy's compatriot, Cardinal Du Bellay, and associated with the latter's nephew, the celebrated poet and author of melancholic reflections on the gulf between the glorious ancient city and the broken ruins of the present (Dickinson 1960, 51f., 101f.). In any case, Jouffroy's *vigna* is an early example of the attraction exerted on the social elite of papal Rome by the high ground and fresh breezes in the area of the Alta Semita.

Nicholas's bulls promoting settlement in the area of the Cispian refer to population decline in the "extremitates urbis"; evidently, the pope saw the situation at S. Maria as typical of a much larger area, and it is likely that the measures taken to bring new population to the Cispian were conceived as part of a wider strategy. On the other hand, the logical next step to increase population in the southern and eastern quarters of the city, the repair of the Acqua Vergine and the provision of new outlets in an area relatively remote from the river, was delayed until 1453, for reasons explored in chapter 3. The pope's urban policies and the sociopolitical framework within which these might be realized were at variance, at least for several years. To a degree, the situation can be reduced to the wary relationship between two men, Nicholas and Cardinal Prospero Colonna, both of whom had particular and personal attachments to the Rione Monti and especially to the region of the Quirinal and Esquiline hills; the investigation of these attachments reveals much about the culture and society of Nicholan Rome, while it throws light in particular on Alberti's position in and response to this complex and sometimes treacherous world, challenging us to a new reading of his treatise on architecture.

It has hitherto not been noticed in studies of Nicholas V's pontificate or of the development of Rome in the quattrocento that before his accession Nicholas had already had close links with the Esquiline. These were centered on the church of S. Pudenziana, a shrine of great antiquity dedicated to one of a greatly revered group of Roman martyr saints (the church actually stood below the hill, at the rear of S. Maria Maggiore; see fig. 35). Pudentiana and her sister Praxedis, to whom the nearby church of S. Prassede was dedicated, were the daughters of a Christian convert of senatorial rank who, according to legend, gave the apostle Peter hospitality in his house. The sisters survived the first great persecution, that in which Peter died, and collected and buried the remains of the newly slaughtered martyrs. Relics of the sisters were contained in the shrine of the Sancta Sanctorum, while both were represented on the casing of the miraculous image of the Savior in that shrine (Grisar 1908, 65). The church was officially a Camaldolese monastery; it was not yet, as it became in the sixteenth century, a titular church.

In the 1430s the evidently quite modest structures of the convent were restored and improved and became the Roman residence of Cardinal Niccolò Albergati, the great Bolognese prelate and diplomat, who proved his ability both as a negotiator on behalf of the Church and as bishop of his strife-torn and rebellious native city (Adinolfi 1857a, 2:238; de Töth 1922, 2:461). He was also known as the friend and protector of leading humanists; Alberti was one of these, as was Tommaso Parentucelli, the future Nicholas V, who lived in Albergati's household for many years and whose career in many respects followed that of his patron (as was recognized by Vespasiano da Bisticci; cf. Bisticci 1970, 1:30f.). In the biography of Albergati written by Jacopo Zeno, who enjoyed Nicholas's confidence and was created bishop of Belluno and Feltre in the year of the latter's accession, the debt of the young Parentucelli to the older man is emphasized. Indeed, Jacopo names Nicholas as the chief source of information about Albergati, and it is Nicholas whom Albergati's modern biographer, de Töth, regards as the real author of the *Vita beati Nicolai de Albergatis* (de Töth 1922, 2:457).

The house that Albergati occupied at S. Pudenziana still existed in the nineteenth century and was described by Adinolfi, who saw it, as a two-story structure with a chapel on the upper floor. It extended in front of the coenobium of the convent proper and the facade of the church, so that a kind of atrium was formed (Adinolfi 1857a, 2:101f.; cf. Morini 1859). The house fronted on the Vico Patrizio (Vicus Patritius), the ancient road that ran up the depression below the western flank of the Cispian; above it on the hill ahead was the apse of S. Maria and the rear of the papal palace. The circumstances of Albergati's choice of this house as his residence are not altogether clear. It was in easy reach, however, of two churches with which he was closely associated, S. Croce in Gerusalemme, his *titulus*, and S. Maria Maggiore, of which he was archpriest (De Angelis 1621, 35; Rice 1985, 107). In this way the clergy of

S. Maria and S. Croce were left in undisturbed occupation of the available residential quarters, while remaining under the eye of the cardinal.

Albergati could, of course, have anticipated d'Estouteville, his successor at S. Maria on his death in 1443, by taking a residence in town, but he seems not to have done this. If so, it is likely that Albergati's choice of residence was a matter of a deliberate and even programmatic decision. Poggio Bracciolini, a further humanist close to the cardinal, suggests a reason perhaps intimated by Albergati himself in conversation with Poggio: "and in Rome he had a house, which he largely had rebuilt, next to the church of S. Pudenziana; here, when he was in residence, he could live remote from the noise of the populace" (de Töth 1922, 1:459).

Poggio's echoes of Horatian disdain of the popular world of Rome may represent the humanist Albergati, but not the man of religion. The evidence suggests that Albergati had a particular reverence for St. Jerome; indeed, a portrait exists of the cardinal as St. Jerome, probably painted by Jan van Eyck or a close follower on the orders of Philip the Good, Duke of Burgundy, to serve as a diplomatic gift on the occasion of the Congress of Arras in 1435. Albergati, who was the prior of a Hieronymite monastery, perhaps selected the house at S. Pudenziana to be near the tomb of St. Jerome in the choir of S. Maria Maggiore on the hill above, but also because the semirural and rather unkempt area seemed appropriate to the residence of a scholar who, like Jerome, balanced activity in the wider world with the lonely meditations of a hermit (Rice 1985, 106–109). And the association of the Esquiline with groves of trees, to which we will return, coincided with the traditional association of Jerome himself with sacred groves (ibid., 24).[38] Finally, the modesty of the house may have exemplified a concept of *architettura povera* operative in a theme, if not the imagery, of Nicholas's private chapel, as argued in chapter 2.

Residence at the house on the Vico Patrizio did not, however, cut the cardinal off from contact with the Curia and humanist circles within it. Pietro da Noceto, for example, the future chief secretary and confidante of Nicholas V, described the importance to him of Albergati's support: "As long as the cardinal lived (and he will live in my memory for ever) I had great hopes, which completely vanished with his death" (de Töth 1922, 2:459 n.2). In this letter of November 18, 1443, to a further young humanist linked with the cardinal, Aeneas Sylvius, Pietro clearly did not anticipate the elevation to the papacy of another of his close friends, Tommaso Parentucelli. The humanists at the Curia, however, did not constitute a cohesive or harmonious group, and Albergati was not on equally good terms with all of them. Indeed, the general of the Camaldolese order, the great humanist Ambrogio Traversari, among whose friends in Rome were the brothers Stefano and Mariano Porcari, visited the house in 1432 in order to demand its return to the order (Traversari 1912, 12). No confrontation took place, for Albergati was away on a diplomatic mission in France, and the order seems to have made no further attempt to secure possession of the house, at least during Albergati's lifetime. The convent in fact never reverted to the Camaldolese community; from the sixteenth century it was occupied by Cistercian monks.

There is no direct evidence that the Camaldolese order reasserted its claims to the house after Albergati's death; it is not unlikely, however, that representations continued to be made to the ecclesiastical authorities. If so, these would have involved a further humanist of some note, the *abbreviator* Leonardo Dati, who served as the *procurator* of the Camaldolese order in Rome (ASV, OS 76, fols. 93v, 96r, 99v).[39] Dati had long experience of the Curia and was especially close to Traversari, from whom he learned Greek; he is perhaps best known as the friend and correspondent of Alberti, who sought his advice on the text of the *Della Famiglia* and involved him in the Certame Coronario, Alberti's attempt to promote the literary use of the vernacular by soliciting Italian dramas, one from the hand of Dati. Dati's literary output was large enough, if not of the highest quality. He dedicated to Nicholas his *Dialogi humilitatis*, while his poem *De elevatione boni genii* described the preparations in heaven for the arrival of Nicholas's soul. This was matched in sycophancy by his later attempt to make a reputation as a historian of pre-Roman Italy, in which guise he sought to add the Etruscan kings to the family tree of Pius II. Dati's qualities were at least appreciated by Paul II, who showed him particular favor, both before and after his accession (Zippel 1904, 23 n.1; Cosenza 1962, 2:1191).

Dati did not flourish in Nicholas's pontificate. Certain benefices that he secured during this time were granted reluctantly, in response to the intercession of others (including Carlo de' Medici, Cosimo's illegitimate son). He must have been—and considered himself—an obvious candidate for the office of apostolic secretary, but it was Calixtus III who gave him that appointment, significantly at the very beginning of his pontificate, in May 1455 (Zippel 1904, 23). The coolness of Nicholas toward Dati, which perhaps was a factor in the favor shown him by Nicholas's successor, was paralleled by that between Nicholas and another humanist who enjoyed the support of Paul II, Gaspare da Verona. Again there is a link with the Camaldolese order, with Traversari, and perhaps even with the claim to the house in the Vico Patrizio, for Gaspare was at one time a member of the Camaldolese order and entertained close links with Traversari's friend Stefano Porcari and, after the latter's execution, with his family. The status of Albergati's house, then, even after his death, may have been an issue, even if intrinsically trivial, that threw into relief the division between two humanist factions in Rome and brought some humanists into dangerous company.

There can be no doubt that Nicholas V, especially in the years that he belonged to Albergati's household, came to know the house at S. Pudenziana. It is probable, therefore, that personal associations influenced his choice of the Vico Patrizio as site of a secondary residence, whether at Albergati's house or at the palace at S. Maria. Here he could recreate, albeit on a larger scale, the cultivated and pious modesty of Albergati, in a place distinguished by its seclusion and sacred associations, yet convenient for the city. Perhaps it occurred to the humanists who gathered at the house from the 1430s into the 1450s to make a comparison with Plato's Academy or other semirustic settings for learned discourse in antiquity. Yet the house was nearer the communal center at the Campidoglio than was the Vatican, while in the immediate neighborhood were local centers of civic life, like one of the churches of the Confraternity of the Gonfalone, for example, which stood on the slope of the Cispian, below S. Maria.[40]

Nevertheless the attractiveness of the area must have been marred by the ruinous condition of much of the property, and Nicholas may well have wished his suburban residence to be surrounded by well-kept houses and gardens, whether on the Cispian or at S. Susanna. Further, it is reasonable to suppose that the retinue that followed Nicholas to the Vico Patrizio was smaller than that by which he was surrounded at the Vatican and from which he seems to have been happy to escape. The more isolated a residence, however, the greater the dependence on supplies of food, wine, firewood, etc. brought in the train of the pope. This could be avoided by the establishment in the environs of the palace of an economically active community that could function as a ready source of the basic necessities of life to the household of the pope as an occasional resident.

The palace at S. Maria, then, combined the advantages of the city with those of the country. It was double-fronted, for the main facade faced onto the Piazza di S. Maria, which was the edge and perhaps focus of the new tax-free zone, at least when the pope was in residence, while the rear of the palace looked over the Vico Patrizio and S. Pudenziana, but also over the city toward the Vatican. Probably there was an upper loggia from which the view and the cooling breezes could be enjoyed.[41] The mediating position of the palace between a relatively open landscape and a newly established—or reestablished—urban community recalls the papal palace at Pienza. No formal relationship is present; the conscious and careful planning of an ensemble that characterizes Pienza is not anticipated on the Cispian. Both papal projects seem related, moreover, to the model of a suburban residence, combining the advantages of urban and rural living, proposed by Alberti in the *De re aedificatoria* (Alberti 1966a, 1:335), or at least to the fashionable ideas about villa life that were being bandied about in curial circles (Zippel 1900, esp. 15).

A direct link with Alberti and his ideas is suggested, however, by traces in his treatise of a particular concern with the character and development of the Esquiline, including Nicholas's contribution to this. But these traces can be identified only after patient excavation in the text, especially the celebrated passages in which Alberti lays out his conception of the ideal city.

The Absence of Maecenas: Topographical and Textual Explorations in Alberti's Treatise on Architecture

In the fifth book of the *De re aedificatoria*, Alberti distinguishes two types of monarchic ruler, the King and the Tyrant, and discusses the architectural implications of this distinction in terms of a dichotomy of urban structural types (Alberti 1966a, 1:333). The distinction follows a long argument in the course of which Alberti establishes the principle that buildings reflect the social status, occupation, and interests of those that occupy them, while cities, by analogy, reflect the social composition and political stratification of their populations. In the context of prescriptions for an ideal city, buildings can be classified according to the requirements of the major societal groups that they would serve and whose needs and character they would outwardly express (ibid., 269). Alberti works with three categories, the patricians, the plebs, and these two groups together, forming the population as a whole (ibid., 271).

The patrician class itself is subject to a further tripartite division: the controlling and decision-making element, the executive element that operates in both the civil and military fields and that will succeed the former in time, and, finally, the accumulators of wealth (ibid., 269). The distinction between the first two groups is thus, at least as far as some of the members of the second group are concerned, a matter of age and experience; that between the latter two groups is of a more radical nature. It is noteworthy that Alberti, evidently wrestling with the imperfect fit between philosophical categories and his own perceptions and attitudes, divides the patrician class in exactly the way that Plato, as quoted with apparent approval by Alberti, divides the total population, on the basis of the divisions of the human soul. Thus Alberti states at one point, basing his argument on the authority of Plato, that the wealth-producing and supportive element is the whole gainfully employed population, and later in the same chapter such a group within the ruling class ("quibus aut ex agro aut mercatura facultates suppeditat") is distinguished from the rest of the economically active population only quantitatively, in terms of the volume of its economic activity (ibid., 271). On the other hand, Alberti's patrician class constitutes a model or paradigm of human society as a whole, about which it then becomes possible to theorize on an elevated level of discourse or, in Alberti's terms, without departing from *digniora* (ibid., 265). Yet, though this is a frequently expressed attitude in Alberti's writings, in practice he is not always so rigorous nor indeed so exclusive.

Certainly, Alberti does not altogether neglect consideration of the plebs. These too may be divided into various groups according to occupation (ibid., 267). Yet while Alberti quotes with gusto various such distinctions, taken from a wide range of often abstruse classical sources, he avoids advocating any divisions on his own account, nor does he base on them any fundamental features of his ideal city. Indeed, his references to caste or artisan groups in India, Egypt, or elsewhere appear to be intended mainly to support his emphasis on the multiplicity of human groups as background to the multiplicity of building types. His emphasis on this is central to his argument; he can now demonstrate the inadequacy of the at first sight correct and sufficient analysis of buildings in terms of functional categories (protection and shelter, convenience, and pleasure) that also operate as abstract historical categories (in terms of the development of buildings in line with the increasing sophistication of human beings). In its place Alberti advances an analysis predicated on the distinction of social categories. This also justifies Alberti's antihistorical bias, which is a corollary of his explicit preference to develop an argument from more lofty subject matter. The tension between this principle and Alberti's practicality and concern with the nature and functioning of quite humble things adds much interest to the book.

Prior to making the distinction between the King and the Tyrant, Alberti had also established the essential facilities (we might say the infrastructure) for any city, comprising those elements that would not be affected, in terms of their design or location, by the existence of one or another form of regime. These include the site and territory of a city and such elements as bridges, sewers, and streets, though Alberti reserves for later his detailed discussion of city walls, which were a prerequisite of the infrastructure of any fifteenth-century town and might well have been considered subject to purely military exigencies. But the value-free and technical discussion of city walls (see the brief passage in the fourth book; ibid., 265) is possible only to a limited degree, as becomes clear from Alberti's subsequent consideration of urban fortifications in cities of contrasting sociopolitical character.

The technically slanted discussion of urban infrastructure forms a kind of parenthesis in the treatment of the relationship of social structure and urban/architectural form. When at the beginning of the fifth book Alberti returns to this theme, it is in the context of a discussion of types of buildings in a city. He begins, in the familiar manner, from those of the highest social status, *a dignioribus*. Clearly it is a society's controlling element that is to be the initial subject of the discussion. Alberti begins with the distinction of two types of controlling element, each of which may comprise one or many individuals. In the ensuing argument, however, he restricts himself to consideration of forms of monarchy, though he is not entirely consistent; at one point he expresses the contrast as that between a city ruled by a tyrant and one with a free population, whatever its form of government (ibid., 333). The dichotomy of monarchic and tyrannical political structures may reflect, then, both a concern with explanatory simplicity and, perhaps, a recognition of the political reality of contemporary Italy and the nature of the most desirable potential sources of patronage.[42] It would be rash to regard the emphasis on the rule by one as reflecting the author's own political or theoretical persuasion.

The distinction between the King and the Tyrant is succinctly made. Both have enemies to guard against. The King expects intermittent attack from outside but can count on the loyalty of his subjects, while the Tyrant must continuously be on guard against both internal and external aggression. From this follow the different defense requirements, which affect the location as well as the design of palace and wall system, and indeed the very layout of the city. The problem for a tyrant is to maintain and manipulate urban structures and facilities in such a way that concerted action against his own regime is, as far as possible, discouraged. "Divide and rule" is the principle adopted, and many precedents are adduced. These are worth discussing in some detail, for they are not merely illustrative but essential to the argument.

It should be noted in advance that the solution to the Tyrant's problems here drawn from historical precedent is not necessarily tyrannical. Indeed, Alberti's treatment of his Tyrant is fundamentally ambivalent. On the one hand, the contrast between the two forms of monarchy is expressed to the disadvantage of the Tyrant, in the familiar fashion.[43] On the other hand, certain provisions recommended for the Tyrant's city appear to be of such a nature as to meet with Alberti's approval in any situation, especially where more sophisticated means of social control are adopted (Alberti 1966a, 1:335: the patricians will settle "non inviti" in the place allotted to them).

The essential characteristic of the Tyrant's city, however, is that it is fortified against its own population ("munita in suos"). Alberti quotes Euripides on the potentially irresistible strength of the populace. The *multitudo*, with which the Tyrant is here confronted, is at this point clearly understood as the plebs rather than the combined plebs and patriciate. This reference continues in the example of Cairo, a convenient application of the principle of divide and rule; in this case frequent canals have turned a large and turbulent city into many connected small cities ("plurimas pusillas iunctas urbes"). This division has been effected not only to ensure general enjoyment of the advantages brought by the Nile (presumably Alberti is thinking of hygienic advantages and transport, in the manner of the later proposals of Filarete and Leonardo; Simoncini 1974, 2:64, 66) but also to enable the easy suppression of serious popular disturbances ("graves multorum motus"), a phrase unambiguous in its reference to the plebs. The division of Cairo is compared to the dismembering of a huge statue, a *colossus*, to make it easier to transport. The source for the Cairo example is unclear: obviously it is not classical, though the comparison with the *colossus* introduces a classical note.

The case of the city of Cairo is followed by one involving a province. The transition, however, is rendered easier by the fact that the scene is still Egypt; Alberti alludes to the form of administration adopted by the Romans uniquely in Egypt, and so perhaps thought to be connected more than by mere association with the foregoing example. The Romans, writes Alberti, appointed equestrian officials to different localities rather than relying on a single senatorial proconsul to govern the whole province. It is true that under the Romans Egypt was governed in an anomalous way by a prefect who was indeed of equestrian rank, a practice adopted for precautionary reasons, since a proconsul with aspirations to govern Rome itself could easily cut off the vital grain supply from Egypt. On the other hand, the province was not divided up, as Alberti asserts, between a plethora of minor officials, even if the prefect disposed of the services of equestrian subordinates.

Alberti's source is the Greek historian Arrian's assertion that Alexander the Great, after his conquest of Egypt, divided the country among many officials, and that the Romans learned a lesson from Alexander in how to govern it (Alberti 1966a, 1:335 [V.i]). Alberti's mistake arises from an excessively literal reading of a text that was in fact not quite so germane to his thesis as he thought. The Romans, of course, were concerned to limit the potential for mischief not of the Egyptian populace but of a Roman official disposing of huge military and material resources; such a figure cannot be imagined as relying on *motus multorum* in Egypt to secure a position in Rome. If local support were to come into question, then surely only that of the upper class could be involved. The example turns out, then, to be far less closely related to the previous example than at first appeared, yet both, in different ways, point forward to what follows.

The next step of the argument is puzzling: "And they noticed that no city was immune from civil factionalism whose site was naturally divided, whether by a river, or by various hills, or if part lay on high ground and part in the plain" (ibid., 335). The discussion now returns—but as if it had never left it—to the topic of cities. The subject of the sentence must be the Romans supplied from the previous sentence, in which Alberti had referred to the division by the Romans of a rebellious province. Here, evidently, a more general statement is intended; there is no specifically Egyptian reference, except insofar as this conclusion, reached by the Romans on the basis of experience gained perhaps in Egypt but not necessarily only there, influenced their colonial policy in Egypt. It is not, however, clear how this could be, for while it might be argued that the division of Egypt (by a river, one of Alberti's three categories) contributed to this unruliness, Egypt is certainly not an *urbs*.

Nevertheless, an account can be given of Alberti's argument that preserves its consistency: the Romans applied to a troublesome province experience gained in cities; they divided it among equestrian governors to avoid the risk of a renegade proconsul; and this division was the result of administrative measures, and not of preexisting natural divisions of terrain (which tended to encourage disturbances of the kind the Romans hoped to stamp out). According to this reading, the word "nature" becomes the emphatic term in the sentence, which would then revolve around the contrast of willed and unwilled divisions. This would at least solve the problem of the apparent contradiction between the *discordia* produced or encouraged by, among other things, a river flowing through the middle of a city (and thus a bad thing) and the divisions created by the canals of Cairo, of which Alberti had written with approval in the preceding paragraph. Certainly he stressed there that the canals of Cairo had been deliberately planned in part as a precautionary control system, such as might appeal to any tyrant or indeed monarch. The problem of where Alberti thought the Romans or others had experienced undesirable results of the natural division of a city must remain open; an example close to hand, of course, which contained all three of the natural divisions cited by Alberti, was the city of Rome itself. And Rome had suffered particularly badly from civil disorder in Alberti's own day.

Planning, therefore, must take into account the natural potential of a site, but it must not accept the arbitrariness of nature. A further application of this principle provides another apparent contradiction within Alberti's text. In his discussion of the criteria pertinent to the selection of the site of a city, Alberti had recommended that for maximum *commoditas* cities should be erected on sites that were neither completely hilly nor flat, but a mixture of both (ibid., 279 [IV.ii]). Yet in the passage under review the existence of flat and hilly sections in a city is seen as contributing to tensions within it. However, as in the case of divisions by water, such topographical contrast can be exploited by a city's ruler, as long as it is contained within the context of a rational urban structure, for which Alberti advances a concentric model. This model is outlined without reference to any source, but it must be related to Herodotus's description of Babylon, to which Alberti makes explicit reference elsewhere (ibid., 2:699 [VIII.v]; cf. 1:335n), or to that of Ecbatana (ibid. 1:296 [IV.iii]). The general formal resemblance is undoubted, as is the type of source—i.e., classical authority for an exotic and nonclassical urbanistic model—but it may not be accidental that Alberti, who is generally keen to quote Herodotus by name, here neglects to. The concentric plan appears, accordingly, as the almost inevitable physical realization of Alberti's social, political, and even moral logic as developed in connection with the ideal type of the Tyrant.

This city model is divided by a wall into inner and outer concentric zones. In the central zone craftsmen ply their trades and goods are bought and sold. Alberti's actual phrase is "macellum mediasque urbis officinas et artificia," in which the only trade specifically mentioned is that of the butchers, who also appear in the quotation from Terence that Alberti adds to his own description: "illa turba fartorum, laniorum, coquorum et eiusmodi." The wealthier inhabitants will dwell, willingly separated from the rabble in the center and in a state of peaceful dependence on the Tyrant, in a spacious and elegant residential area ("in laxioribus spatiis"). There is no mention of the exercise of the respectable business of a banker or merchant *in grosso* in the city center, which is entirely given over to low-class and distasteful occupations; evidently the whole patrician class that Alberti for the moment has in mind is free of the necessity to engage in economic activity.

Nevertheless, Alberti's trenchant characterization of the avaricious market traders, the "cupidenarii circumforanei," does not necessarily reflect consistent and extreme prejudice on his part, for when elsewhere in his treatise he discusses the benefits of combining urban and rural advantages on the same site, he recommends the presence of shops and workshops even on a patrician's property (ibid., 1:433–437 [V.vi]). It is true that Alberti's consideration of architectural and urban types is at this stage entirely independent of the King-Tyrant dichotomy, but in both cases Alberti's prejudice seems to be paradoxically rather antiurban than antiplebeian or even (given the accent on money-making) antibourgeois. Nor does Alberti elsewhere neglect what on a moment's consideration appears as a fundamental problem of his concentric model, namely the necessity of access roads from the central markets to the periphery, disturbing the ideal geometry and the strict social zoning associated with it. The apparent inconsistencies, however, are a corollary of Alberti's elusive and ironic style of discourse; the concentric city, indeed, should be regarded not as an ideal city and still less as a feasible project, but as the diagrammatic demonstration of a stage in the argument, to which other considerations and aspects of reality are for the moment not pertinent.

Whatever Alberti's debt to Herodotus, the concentric city model is explicitly related to another classical example, not indeed of concentricity but of planned or at least deliberate zoning with a clear sociopolitical function. This example is extrapolated from the very brief explanation—and here we return to the Esquiline—of the derivation of the ancient Roman toponym "vicus patritius" by the second-century AD grammarian Sextus Pompeius Festus in his *De significatione verborum*:

Servius Tullius ordered the patricians [*patritii*, the senatorial class] to live in a quarter [*vicus*, which often carries connotations of rural settlement] in which, if they showed any sign of rebelliousness, they could be suppressed from higher ground. (Lindsay 1913, 247)

Festus intended this simply as the explanation of the toponym "vicus patritius," applied to the street running northwest between the Esquiline and Viminal hills, which constitute the high ground from which police action could be taken; for Alberti it is a classical anticipation of his own ideas and functions as a convenient cornerstone in his theoretical construct.

Before turning to the actual use made of Festus by Alberti, it is important to consider the general character of the sources that Alberti cites in his discussion of the Tyrant's city. The text of Festus was hailed some twenty years after Alberti's use of it by as widely read a humanist as Politian as something rare and of special interest. Knowledge of the text at mid-fifteenth century cannot have been widespread. Certainly, Biondo failed to make use of Festus in the section on the Esquiline in the *Roma instaurata* (Valentini and Zucchetti 1953, 283). Festus, then, may be regarded as a somewhat recherché author read by Alberti in a corrupt text, an author of little literary merit or indeed few pretensions. Alberti's other sources in the passage are equally recherché, to an extent that is remarkable even in the *De re aedificatoria*, where a certain pleasure is often taken in the unexpected, even perverse insertion of examples from unusual sources (see Krautheimer 1961). The Arrian quotation, noted above, is taken from a narrative otherwise almost exclusively concerned with the details of Alexander's military campaigns. The Cairo reference is as yet unexplained; it is clearly unclassical. Nor is any source named for the remark on the topographical stimulants of civil disorder. And the Herodotean motif of the concentric city reflects Alberti's general predilection for exotic, preclassical or unclassical motifs, though usually gathered from Greek sources, especially the historians Herodotus and Diodorus. The Terentian quotation, finally, with its reference to the "ignava turba fartorum, laniorum, coquorum," constitutes a vivid, contrasting and somewhat surprising accent in the section on the ideal Tyrant's city, with its rigid geometrical layout and its authoritarian character. The sudden irruption of the tang of the streets, though admittedly assimilated into elevated literary form, undermines the ostensibly articulated attitude.

Alberti's interest in Servius Tullius and in the latter's association with the Esquiline is not unprecedented in postclassical literature. Giovanni Cavallini in his *Polistoria de virtutibus*, written about 1350, states that Servius's house was on the site of S. Vito in Macello, one of the ancient diaconates of the area, though by Giovanni's time in ruins. The church stood next to the Arco di San Vito and gave the latter its medieval name. Cavallini continues: "And therefore in the area of this gate is the tail of the lion by which is signified the government of the city of Rome, since this long ago used to be exercised in this place *in the time of the said Servius Tullius*" (Valentini and Zucchetti 1953, 32; my italics). I have already noted the political resonance of the idea of Rome "in forma leonis" (fig. 36); here it is elaborated by reference to the establishment by King Servius, in the area corresponding to the lion's tail, of the site of his autocratic government of the city (from which he suppressed not bandits as Pomponius asserted without classical precedent, but the social elite of the city). If, as seems likely, the tradition of Servius's domination was associated with Ghibelline and pro-Colonna sentiment, the triumph of Vitelleschi at the Arco di San Vito, a major opening in the Servian wall, takes on new significance.

For fifteenth-century humanists the main explicit interest in the Esquiline was antiquarian and far removed from naive political symbolism. The range of classical references to the area was explored and filtered into the discussions on ancient topography and nomenclature. An obvious starting point for any humanist discussion of the early topography of Rome is Livy, who gives a detailed review of Servius Tullius's achievements, providing yet another motive for the location of his residence: "At that time he [Servius] saw to the expansion of [settlement on] the Esquiline, and so that the place might be ennobled [should gain *dignitas*] he took up residence there himself. He surrounded the city with a bank and ditches and a wall; in so doing he expanded the pomerium" (*Ab urbe condita* 1.44). The expansion of the *pomerium*, the sacred boundary of Rome, and the inclusion within it of the new urban area was a ritual act of the greatest importance. It enabled Servius to establish himself as a subsidiary cofounder of Rome. Yet he is not included among city founders enumerated by Alberti, for whom, it should be noted, the foundation of a city is essentially that of a political unit, a city-state, and entails the articulation of a constitution and of a legal system, and in particular the division of the populace into groups or classes, as Theseus, to cite one of Alberti's examples, had done at Athens.

On Livy's account, Servius would certainly seem to qualify; he is represented as "the founder of the social division [*discrimen*] in the city and of the classes [*ordines*] by which the degrees of dignity and fortune are distinguished [i.e., of social and economic worth]...for he instituted the census...then on the basis of the census he distinguished the classes, the voting units, and this order, as appropriate for peace as for war" (ibid., 1.42). Once again the notion of *dignitas* is introduced. In the former passage, the assertion that Servius aimed to confer *dignitas* on the new quarter was cryptic; the motive remained vague, the circumstances unexplained. Here *dignitas* has a clearer, more official reference; Livy suggests that Servius's distinctions were made according to objectively valid, uncontroversial criteria.

These divisions are not expressed in any topographical form, though had Servius wished to confer *dignitas* on the Esquiline, this would have been achieved by the settlement there of the *patritii*, the senatorial class. This is, of course, not what Livy says, for according to him Servius's own residence on the Esquiline sufficed to upgrade the area socially; yet an interpretation of Livy's material along the lines suggested is a minor step, if Festus's assertion is taken as the starting point. Alberti, however, makes no explicit use of Livy in this connection, which raises a puzzling aspect of the *De re aedificatoria*. Orlandi's index (Alberti 1966a) gives but one reference to Livy, which is itself remarkable; stranger still, all Alberti has admitted to taking from Livy is the name of an ancient Italian people, the Emerici (ibid., 1:275 [IV.ii]), who originated not, as did many other fabled peoples of the peninsula, in the legendary east, but in a blatant corruption of Livy's text (Livy wrote *emporia*). This single pseudo-reference to Livy, moreover, contrasts with the thirteen explicitly made to Herodotus and the eleven to Diodorus.

Alberti's neglect of Livy is certainly not due to ignorance of the text, especially as Alberti himself recommends the reading of Livy as an essential part of a humanist education in the *Della Famiglia* (Alberti 1969, 86); perhaps Alberti did not regard Livy as an author to be taken seriously by the learned and mature. He may even have objected to certain irrational aspects of the contemporary cult of Livy, notably the donation by King Alfonso of Naples to Livy's birthplace, the city of Padua, of a relic of the writer (an arm), ceremoniously handed over by the humanist Panormita (Sambin 1958). On the other hand, Livy had been recently subjected to fierce criticism by that pugnacious intellectual leveler, Lorenzo Valla (McDonald 1971, 335). Alberti may well have known of this.

Alberti's list of city founders and legislators, in defiance of Livy, does not include Servius Tullius. It is not that Alberti gives Romulus sole responsibility for the foundation of the Roman social system: "Romulus distinguished the equestrians and the senatorial class [*patritii*] from the plebs; but King Numa divided the plebs according to their occupations [*artes*]" (Alberti 1966a, 1:267 [IV.ii]). The source for Numa's division of the people into craft groups, a social stratification of no consequence in Alberti's model of the state, is Plutarch's biography of Numa.[44] The pattern asserts itself again of a Greek author preferred to a Roman, the rare to the commonplace. This does not seem, however, to resolve satisfactorily the absence of Servius from Alberti's list; it is as if Alberti was concerned that Servius's social engineering should not be seen in a positive light.

Throughout the imperial period the Esquiline was a luxurious suburban area (I have already noted the residence there of the noble sisters Pudentiana and Praxedis), though as a result of other factors than Servius's program of conferring *dignitas*. This had not been successful, partly through the circumstances of Servius's own death in a palace revolution. According to Livy, Servius's own daughter killed her father in or near the Vicus Patritius by running him down with her chariot, having seized the reins from the squeamish charioteer. The site of this parricide was henceforth a place of ill omen and was known as the Vicus Sceleratus (*Ab urbe condita* 1.48).[45]

The eventual transformation of the Esquiline into a fashionable suburban quarter came much later; it is celebrated notably by Horace: "Now the Esquiline is a healthy place; one can live there and stroll on the sunny hill[46] where once there was a sad prospect over a terrain ugly with white bones" (Satires 1.8.14). Horace, however, had his own reasons for emphasizing the degree of this transformation, which he associated with the settlement on the Esquiline of his friend and patron, Maecenas, who developed extensive pleasure grounds on the site of a former cemetery (hence Horace's white bones). The hill had never been exclusively a site of ill omen, however; I have already noted its association with sacred groves, which clearly predated Maecenas. For all Horace's frivolity and Livy's sensationalism, a major aspect of the Esquiline was always its religious associations.

Interest in the Esquiline area in the early Renaissance was not exhausted by the antiquarian concerns of a small minority, for the area was reacquiring its aristocratic character. The name "Esquiline" was somewhat confusingly applied in the fifteenth century. According to classical usage, the Esquiline hill, comprising its two summits, the Cispian and Oppian, is one of three adjacent fingers of high ground in the southeastern sector of the city (maps 1, 2; fig. 35); it is flanked by the Viminal and, nearest the *abitato*, the Quirinal. In the fifteenth century it was well known that the gardens of Maecenas had been on the Esquiline, but medieval tradition identified a tower on the Quirinal, in the area of the supposed Temple of the Sun, as the Torre Mesa or Turris Maecenatis (fig. 41); there was a tendency, accordingly, for the name Esquiline to be applied also to the Quirinal, indeed to the whole high ground of which the Esquiline proper formed part (Lanciani 1902, 1:51; Gnoli 1939, 328).

The tower was also called, until its demolition in the seventeenth century, the Frontispiece of Nero, since it was identified as the lookout point from which Nero watched Rome burn; in Suetonius's words, "Nero, dressed in that theatrical costume of his, watched the fire from the tower of Maecenas and sang of the fall of Troy" (*Vita Neronis*, chap. 38). This was quoted by Biondo, who follows the medieval tradition in his *Roma instaurata*, placing Nero's tower on the Quirinal (Valentini and Zucchetti 1953, 283). The tower had curious literary associations, in particular an apocryphal and facetious connection with an amorous escapade of Maecenas's best-known protege, Virgil. The story, which became proverbial as an example of the power of love to make even the most grave and dignified of humans ridiculous, is alluded to, for instance, in the *Historia de duobus amantibus* of Aeneas Sylvius: "Consider the poets: Virgil clung to a rope half way up the tower, since he hoped for the embraces of a little woman" (Amadei 1969, 15). Even after the demolition of the tower these associations lived on, though transferred to the nearby Torre delle Milizie.

In the mid-fifteenth century the property around the tower, the Giardino della Torre di Nerone, as it was called, belonged to Cardinal Prospero Colonna.[47] Biondo describes at some length the restorations and excavations carried out here by Cardinal Prospero; he notes the discovery of extensive marble floors and other remains (Müntz 1878, 36 n.3). Almost inevitably he calls the cardinal "alter nostri saeculi Maecenas," but the identification of Prospero Colonna with Maecenas is carried by Biondo into contexts where no direct association with the historical Maecenas is present. Thus Prospero's restoration of his titular church, S. Giorgio in Velabro, is said to be the work of a modern Maecenas (Valentini and Zucchetti 1953, 298). Such an emphasis on Maecenas is readily understandable: the latter occupied a central position in Augustan cultural life, mediating between the emperor and the poets, to whom he was both friend and generous patron. This was naturally common knowledge in the Renaissance; even so fantastic a story as that of Virgil and the tower alludes to the special relationship of Maecenas and the great poet, to which it gives a topographical context. Emphasis on Maecenas by a Flavio Biondo or his like might well constitute an implicit recommendation to contemporary patrons to behave toward the literary men of their time with the same generosity and air of equality that characterized Maecenas's dealings with Virgil or Horace.

Whether Prospero responded to Biondo's promptings is not clear. It is even possible that he himself fostered the identification with Maecenas, as the latter's successor in the gardens of "the Esquiline." Certainly, his patronage was important: apart from his support of Biondo, we may note the hospitality of Prospero and his kin fondly recalled by Ciriaco d'Ancona. This may not have been entirely disinterested, for Ciriaco made public his sympathy for republican ideas, which in Rome meant a Ghibelline, pro-Colonna stance (Angelini 1971, 14). In the cases of both Ciriaco and Biondo, Prospero seems to have associated himself quite deliberately with a current of *renovatio Romae* that could hardly avoid ideological connotations in the conditions of quattrocento Rome.

The same might be said for the cardinal's association with Alberti, whom he commissioned to raise the famous Roman ship from the depths of the lake at Nemi; the undertaking was unsuccessful, but Alberti wrote a lost pamphlet about it (Mancini 1911, 278). There is no direct evidence that Alberti took part in the excavations in the cardinal's gardens, but it is extremely unlikely that he remained aloof from the archaeological sensation of the time. There is no mention of Maecenas's pleasure grounds or of the excavations in the *De re aedificatoria*; even more curiously, Alberti not only neglects to represent Maecenas as a paradigm of a patron, he even quotes, out of context and with apparent approval, lines in which Horace expresses his disapproval of Maecenas's mania for building (Alberti 1966a, 1:103 [II.ii]). But had Prospero been elected to the papacy in 1447, as many expected, the figure cut by Maecenas in the pages of Alberti's treatise might well have been different.

While Prospero Colonna, like Maecenas before him, was doubtless a pioneer in developing an area hitherto relatively neglected, at least by the arbiters of fashion, by the middle of the fifteenth century he was not alone. The region of the Alta Semita, the ancient road along the spine of the Quirinal, was beginning to attract the attention of those who wished to posses convenient *vigne* near the *abitato*; apart from Cardinal Jouffroy, whose *vigna* at the Baths of Diocletian was noted above, Giovanni de Primis, cardinal of Metz, established a *vigna* on the Quirinal, which he used as a pleasure garden, to judge from the scandalous circumstances in which he allegedly met his end in 1449 (Chambers 1976, 32). This *vigna* later belonged to Cardinal Oliviero Carafa, who carried out extensive work there, and thus it became the nucleus of the later papal palace and of a luxurious suburban quarter whose development was to receive symbolic and monumental completion through the project for a gate at the end of the Alta Semita, now renamed the Via Pia, entrusted about 1561 by Pius IV to Michelangelo (Briganti 1962, 1–13, 59; MacDougall 1976, 32). The *laxiora spatia*, in which Alberti imagined the houses of Servius Tullius's patricians, had certainly returned.

Nicholas's emphatic support of the development of the Esquiline area has been noted. Of course, Nicholas's bulls promoted the establishment of a different class of settler, but cardinals and other luminaries of Roman social life would have been less likely to respond to the obvious topographical and other advantages of the Esquiline if the area was deformed, to use Nicholas's word, by the ruinous condition of the ecclesiastical and other buildings. Prospero Colonna was spurred by classical example; such a correspondence may have impelled Nicholas too. Canensi in 1451–52 emphasized the restoration work at S. Maria Maggiore and noted the continuity of religious worship at the site, where he claimed a temple of Cybele had stood in antiquity (Miglio 1975, 230).

Nicholas's palace at S. Maria was close to the site of the palace of Servius Tullius at San Vito. Servius was said to have coerced the patricians to move into the area, so that he could better exert control over them. Nicholas's attempts to affect population distribution in Rome directly did not involve the social elite. On the other hand, it is not unreasonable to suppose that Nicholas intended his palace at S. Maria to be a convenient reminder to residents of the area of the omnipresence of papal power and a place from which, if necessary, those residents could be kept under surveillance. Nicholas restricted the number of papal palaces in Rome to two (if S. Pudenziana is regarded as a subsidiary extension of S. Maria); one of these was close to the Orsini family chapel in St. Peter's and was well equipped with an advance bulwark at the Castel S. Angelo to monitor the traditional Orsini area; the other adjoined a basilica with traditional Colonna associations and provided a view from its loggias over the traditional Colonna quarter. Both palaces, then, had something of the function ascribed by Festus to Servius's residence, to which one of them corresponded in topographical terms. It is even possible that Albergati's decision to take the house at S. Pudenziana had not been entirely free of papal influence, and that its supervisory potential was taken over by Nicholas.

Did Alberti intend to suggest a correspondence, however covert, between Nicholas and Servius Tullius? He uses Servius's Esquiline as a model of the successfully executed reorganization of a city by a tyrant. But the Tyrant's goal is the domination and suppression of patrician opposition, rather than the reconciliation associated with Nicholas's policies. It is prima facie unlikely that the loyal *abbreviator* Alberti branded Nicholas as a tyrant by drawing a parallel between Servius and the pope. Alberti's attitude toward the figure of the Tyrant is ambivalent, however. Servius's methods are not described as tyrannical in the modern sense of the word; rather Alberti's gloss on Festus's statement emphasizes the persuasive, even corrupting effect of suburban luxury, the *laxiora spatia*. Indeed, Alberti's language betrays a realization of the gradual transformation, which was under way in Rome as in other Italian cities, of an independent patriciate into a court aristocracy. Further, Alberti offers an interesting justification, if one were required, of the coercive character of ecclesistical administration and building, by arguing the close relationship of military and ecclesiastical activity: "What about the priest [*pontifex*, which in Renaissance usage typically denotes the Pontifex Maximus or pope]? He doesn't only require a temple, but also buildings that are like armed camps, since priests and those who on their account do administrative duty perform a harsh and warlike labor [*militia*]" (Alberti 1966a, 1:359 [V.vii]). And Alberti elsewhere spells out the comparison of military and ecclesiastical buildings, since the latter are required to protect the chastity of their inmates. Even when a religious institution stands in a city, on a site where a martial aspect would be out of place, Alberti recommends that everything that might disturb the people as they go to worship, especially the women, should be kept at a distance (ibid., 361, 365 [V.vii]; 2:559 [VII.v]).

The concern with the preservation of the sanctity of places and people leads to Alberti's other quotation from Festus: "Festus asserts that the citadel [*arx*] in antiquity was dedicated to religious observance and used to be called augurial, and secret [*archanum*] and hidden rites were carried out there by virgins, far from the notice of the populace" (ibid. 1:347 [V.viii]).[48] The original *arx*, then, is also a shrine and is associated with the augurs, whose ritual acts are typically carried out on a high place from which they can scan the heavens, though Alberti does not make this point. The etymological correspondence of *arx* and *arcanum*, which is not in Festus, is for Alberti an important confirmation of the religious origin of the citadel; it is typical for him to use etymology to indicate an originary and essential function.[49] In this case, the citadel was originally used for the most sacred and hidden rituals, notably those involved in discovering the will of the gods. How then did the term *arx* come to mean merely a fortified place, with no religious connotations?

Alberti's answer is that the change in meaning of *arx* is just another example of the effects of tyrannical rule, here expressed in radical shifts in the language of the affected population, no less than in their built environment. He does not consider the possibility of a reversal of the process, the regaining by a citadel of its original ritual significance and sacrality. If he had wanted an example, the Esquiline would have served his purpose. Though the only ancient building on the Esquiline mentioned by Alberti is the fortress residence founded by Servius Tullius, dominating the houses of his potential rivals, certain contemporary authors stressed the much later shrine of the mother goddess Cybele, which was succeeded by the Christian basilica of the Mother of God. The foundation legend of the miraculous fall of snow that marked the ground plan of the church (see Davies 1951, 273–275), and which distinguishes S. Maria Maggiore (or ad Nives) from the other great basilicas that owed their origin to the acts of pious founders, perhaps reflects early embarrassment, not shared in the Renaissance, at the continuity of pagan and Christian worship. Indeed, the specific concern for christianized monuments of antiquity may be regarded as an important element of Nicholas's restoration campaign, especially as presented by Canensi (Miglio 1975, 230f.).[50]

Alberti, needless to say, expresses no interest in the christianization of Rome, any more than in patristic and scholastic literature, which he nevertheless uses. He must have been aware, however, of the difference in character between the Servian Esquiline, as he presents it, and the shrine-dotted quarter of the Christian city. The idea of a fortress residence placed on the edge of a city has been claimed as a characteristic motif of late medieval and early Renaissance city development (Mumford 1961, 386f.; Simoncini 1974, 204f.). The conscious application of such an idea, for example, may lie behind the emphasis given by Francesco Sforza to the new castle peripheral to the city of Milan, while a similar phenomenon seems to be present at Mantua or indeed the Vatican. It was an urbanistic motif that can be followed throughout the history of city design and development in early modern Europe; there are indeed numerous cases of the residence of a princely ruler and a dependent town placed in a hierarchical relationship to each other. Nicholas's conciliatory policies in Rome, as we have already seen in connection with the Vatican, could only to a degree be reconciled with his preference for peripheral residences; his concern with the development of the Esquiline and the welfare of its population should perhaps be interpreted in this light. The theoretical articulation of the peripheral princely residence appears of course in the *De re aedificatoria*, in Alberti's model of the Tyrant's city; the fact that an important topographical reference deeply embedded in Alberti's argument points to the site of Nicholas's residence implies that the cunning author was hinting at the current ideological and even political resonances of his discussion.

The Esquiline of Alberti's treatise, then, is the hill of the grim monarch Servius, not of the cultured aristocrat Maecenas. With the death of Nicholas, Servius, as it were, yielded once more to Maecenas, but the erection of the papal palace at the Quirinal gave the upper hand, definitively, to the former. For on the heights of the Quirinal the priest-kings of the city could enjoy the breezes and survey, not the flight of birds, but the dependent populace and the palaces of a loyal aristocracy laid out at their feet (fig. 41).

6

Mirror and Frame: The Surrounding Region and the Long Road

Beyond the City Walls: Urban Limits and Regional Order

The walls of a medieval city enclosed space, defended it, and manifested and guaranteed its identity. To a degree, a city was its walls, and an image of those walls, wherever it might lie on a scale from hieroglyphic schematism to representational accuracy, might stand as a sign for the city itself. Such a sign, of course, did not depend on the everyday experience of city walls as an occasional edge to fleeting and fragmentary glimpses through thronged streets and densely clustered buildings;nor even was it distilled, at least directly, from the aspect of a towered and gated ensemble as seen from some privileged external viewpoint. Rather it constituted an ideal construct, in abstraction from experience. As such it depended ultimately on transcendent paradigms, operative especially in the assimilation of real cities—both conceptually and in gradual and halting practice—to the celestial Jerusalem, though the latter's antitype, Babylon, colored the occasional denunciations of cities as sumps of confusion and vice (Gatti Perer 1983, esp. 105–115; Braunfels 1979, 45–50, 134–139; Chastel 1954; Buttafava 1963, 21–36; Gambi 1976, 218–222; Davis 1982, 19–40). It is surely only in the light of such enduring paradigms that we can account for the remarkable persistence of the model of the city as an essentially bounded and framed space, most notably in the schemata favored by Renaissance writers on urban form, but also even in the face of later transformations of settlement patterns and scale.

The ideal New Jerusalem, set around at regular intervals with uniform towers (fig. 42), was a place of order, in plan no less than in profile. Such a paradigm of the city, however, presupposes the opposition of its own bounded configuration with the world excluded by its walls and characterized by qualities suppressed or even sublimated in the ideal image of the city, though doubtless present in the often anarchic and disorderly reality. The city, accordingly, appears as a mechanism of exclusion, defined as much by what it is not as by what it is, by what lies outside its walls as much as by what these contain. The other of such a paradigm, excluded yet essential to the paradigm itself, is the random topography of a countryside determined by river and hill, firm or marshy ground, or by the primeval paths of men and beasts, seemingly as natural as the channels cut by streams in soft rock.

The walls of a city face in two directions, however; they may structure and even define the surrounding countryside as much as the surrounded city. If the model of the city as a device of exclusion seems compelling and historically prevalent, the influence of a contrary model must not be overlooked. This is the model of city and country, urban and rural space, as mirroring one another, or at least as both mirroring a further transcendent model. In ancient Rome and its colonial foundations, for instance, the sacred boundary (*pomerium*) constituted an exclusionary frame of a most emphatic kind, since it was a ritual rather than defensive perimeter; indeed, the *pomerium* of pre-Aurelianic imperial Rome was the only perimeter.[1] Where topographical conditions permitted, on the other hand, the cosmic axes (*cardo* and *decumanus*) of the typical Roman city (Rykwert 1976, 90f.; Müller 1961) were projected out into level land beyond the city walls, generating a geometrical order echoing the urban grid and making of the city and its environs a single homogeneous spatial system, or set of systems (Sereni 1974, 142–144; Dilke 1976, 133–137). Gridded cities were not uncommon in late medieval Europe, whether as relics of Roman planning or as new foundations. Nevertheless, though many rural areas retained (and still retain) the unmistakable imprint of the Roman organization of space, the so-called centuriation, which came to form the subject matter of a specific discipline and of a technical literature of surveying revived by Renaissance humanism (Dilke 1971, 126–131; Müller 1961, 15–21),[2] this geometrical order no longer provided a common matrix—at least a conceptual matrix—for city and country. Indeed, the often approximate order of medieval gridded towns frequently stood in marked and even deliberate contrast to the countryside beyond the walls. In many parts of Europe, rectilinear street patterns were associated especially with the domestication of conquered or subdued territory; the grid constituted thereby an emblem of the authority of a major city, often involving the resettlement of villagers around the official residence of the representative of their rulers (Friedman 1974, 31–47; Braunfels 1976, 132–138).

The proliferation of such centers of ideologically charged rationalism, however, should not be discounted as a mere device of oppression; it was also the fragmentary realization of a territorial order, regulated by published statutes and contrasting with the feudal relations of a countryside still dominated visually by the castles of local lords and socially by the complex systems of personal loyalty that in the Italian mercantile city-states were at least overlaid with other political and associational forms. Indeed, the desire for an ordered and orderly—not to speak of clean—physical environment existed also in the major cities, though it generally foundered on the complexities and resistances of urban society, except occasionally in limited areas, as in the configuration of important institutional complexes (Braunfels 1979, 86–130). The realization, then, of a geometrized spatial order in the settlements in subject territories was both colonial and utopic; it was also, most importantly for our purposes, a crucial symptom of a concern with regional coherence in the era of the development of city-states into territorial powers.

The restoration of the walls and gates of the city of Rome was among Nicholas V's first concerns after his accession to the throne of St. Peter. His achievements in this regard were stressed no less by Canensi in 1451–52 (Miglio 1975, 234) than by Manetti in 1455 (Magnuson 1958, 352f.), indicating a consistent policy of attention to the fortifications of Rome, in addition to and doubtless correlated with the more extensive construction carried out on the walls and gates of the Leonine City (Miglio 1975, 232; Magnuson 1958, 16–18; Pastor 1949, 166f.; Westfall 1974a, 105–110). In the period following the fall of Constantinople, little over two years before Nicholas's death, a concentration of energy and resources on fortifications was to be expected, along with the expansion of the papal fleet and similar measures. Much the same was true of the beginning of the pontificate, when the army of King Alfonso of Naples lurked menacingly in the environs of the city. Nicholas, however, was concerned to represent himself as a pope of peace and concord, as is especially clear from the assertions of Manetti and from the pope's reliance until the Porcari affair on a relatively modest and inconspicuous security force, at least in Rome (Pastor 1949, 62f.).

The defense of the city, then, was mainly entrusted to and embodied in its venerable walls, whose expressive and symbolic aspect was emphasized (Westfall 1974a, 33f.; von Moos 1974, 70–73). After all, the walls of Rome were in large part still those thrown around the ancient city by the Emperor Aurelian in the third century, though they had since been overlaid by extensive accretions (Krautheimer 1980, 6f., 237). They resonated, accordingly, the power and prestige of imperial Rome. They had Christian associations, moreover, notably in view of the late medieval tendency to assimilate Rome to the celestial city (Westfall 1974a, 84–87), as in a miniature of the 1450s showing Rome as Augustine's City of God (fig. 43; cf. Biblioteca Apostolica Vaticana 1975, 82 no. 214). On the other hand, it is likely that the walls had become infused with political symbolism in the course of the intermittent confrontation, dating at least to the thirteenth century, between the commune of Rome and the Campagna barons. Though the latter's power bases lay in the wild hill country at some distance from the walls of Rome, their towered city palaces were only too conspicuously expressive of the power they could wield in Rome, at least in certain neighborhoods. The walls, on the other hand, potentially cut the routes between the barons' city and country residences, providing both a real and symbolic bulwark against their capricious violence (Dupré-Theseider 1952, 517–611; Partner 1972, 258f.; Guidoni 1983; Tomassetti 1979, 1:106–116, 168f.). It is plausible, then, to relate Nicholas's work on the walls to his campaigns at the Campidoglio and other sites of particular significance to the elements of the population most closely associated with the commune. Many of the associations I have reviewed here may have been aroused by the image on a medal struck by Nicholas (if it is authentic) of Rome surrounded by its walls and accompanied by the motto *Roma felix* (Pastor 1949, 172 n.3).

The city walls and gates provided, as is often noted, prominent sites for the reiterated display of the papal arms, visible in several places to this day. No doubt such display was concentrated and especially conspicuous at points of particular significance in the social and ceremonial life of the city and its major institutions; that is, at points where Nicholas's insignia were most likely to be replaced or overlaid by the insignia of later rulers (ibid., 172). Canensi emphasizes, for instance, the restoration carried out by Nicholas at the basilica of S. Paolo fuori le Mura (Miglio 1975, 230), and we can be sure that no pilgrim or traveler who passed through the Porta S. Paolo, also restored by Nicholas, was left unaware of the pope's concern for the physical condition of both gate and basilica, and for the prominent commemoration of that concern. This would have been true also of the walls of the Leonine City, though the symbolic connotations there were doubtless different, since the Vatican and Borgo constituted an enclave distinct from the city proper. The Vatican and its walls spoke, of course, to the world of Christendom, in which this newly emphasized fount of authority and sacrality played its part in the struggle of opinions between a residual conciliarist movement and Nicholas's advocacy and practice of papal supremacy (Westfall 1974a, 20f.).

The symbolic dimension of the defenses of the Vatican would have been considerably heightened had the projected great gateway to the palace been constructed; as described by Manetti (Magnuson 1958, 355) this was to consist of two massive towers flanking a triumphal arch, an arrangement reminiscent of the Neapolitan Castel Nuovo or, to note an ancient precedent, the Arch of Augustus at Rimini (fig. 45; cf. Gobbi and Sica 1982, 15f.). Such an emphatic gateway would have marked a climax on the path through the city and the various architectural and topographical expressions of local loyalties. The demand for such a motif perhaps had long existed: we may note, for instance, the implications of the remark in the early fifteenth-century Roman diary of Antonio dello Schiavo that the Porta di Castello, an important gate into the Leonine City in front of which certain papal ceremonies were held, was more like a "cancello di vigna" than a city gate (dello Schiavo 1917, 1).

The manifestation of symbolic hierarchies in the physical environment, needless to say, was a particular concern of Nicholas and his advisers; one need only consider the proposed establishment of a hierarchy of urban thoroughfares, distinguished functionally and no doubt visually by their association with distinct types of commercial activity. Implicit in dello Schiavo's text, on the other hand, is a hierarchical ranking of city and *contado* similar to that implicit in most accounts of Nicholas's building campaigns, which emphasize the crucial place of these campaigns in the development of European urbanism as a matter, almost exclusively, of planning within and/or of cities. Such a hierarchy is already apparent in Manetti's review of Nicholas's architectural patronage and ambitions. Certainly, the documents indicate that Rome and the Vatican attracted the greater part of the available resources for building and restoration. Nevertheless, Nicholas's policies toward city and country (or region) should not simply be ranked hierarchically; their relationship requires study, as does the conceptual framework within which each seems to develop.

Inevitably the discussion must begin with the city walls, whose exclusionary character and symbolic values I have noted. These are most remarkably evident in the well-known plan of Rome *in forma leonis*; here the very outline of the walls of the late medieval city constitutes a shape of heraldic and even emblematic significance (fig. 36). The associations of the figure of a standing or striding lion are intensified by the natural reading of the battlements on the walls as the lion's rough and shaggy mane and hide. Clearly, in images of this kind the wall is presented as a harsh and impenetrable barrier against adversaries, though these might well not be external foes but citizen factions (allied often, it is true, with other cities and so constituting a real external threat). It is not surprising that the act of raising an ambitious new wall system and expanding the area of the city, as in late-thirteenth-century Florence, should be associated with radical political change and the seizure of power by new political and, to a point, social elements. Nothing short of a refoundation of the city is at issue here, as in the case of the ceremonies, perhaps forming a dim model for medieval practice, of the expansion of the Roman *pomerium*. In this light we can see the rational utility of the extravagant and surely in part utopic wall-building programs of medieval communes, utopic as the walls often far outstripped the capacity of the cities to expand out toward them (Fanelli 1973, 1:64–67; Braunfels 1979, 64f.; Trexler 1980, 47f.).

The erection or restoration of city walls conferred legitimacy on the authority that carried it out; this was no less true of Nicholas V than of the revolutionary guild regime of Florence. This legitimacy was partly a matter of the sacral associations or even character of the wall, watched over by divine or saintly protectors whose images might appear at the gates or in other prominent locations (Trexler 1980, 47f.). If the walls of the city-states of Tuscany, however, might bound and define a sacral space, this could not be the case at Rome, where major shrines stood beyond the walls, though linked back to the city by processional routes (the fifteenth century, for instance, preserved the memory of the porticoes that once linked the shrines of Saints Peter and Paul with the city proper; Alberti 1966a, 2:708f.). The outermost wall of Florence had been thrown around the formerly extraurban foundations of the mendicant orders or the miracle-working pilgrimage center at the SS. Annunziata. No such containment was conceivable at Rome, where the shrunken settlement huddled in a small fraction of the area of the imperial city, and the countryside of vineyards, rough pasture, and decaying ruins extended far within the walls: a more capacious wall system was out of the question. Yet the contrast with Florence should not be exaggerated, for there, too, at least from the fifteenth century, the wall became a highly porous barrier; Trexler (1980), 6f., has noted, in particular, the projection of sacrality into the *contado* and the progressive consolidation of the city region on the level of ritual.[3]

The porosity of late medieval wall systems is evident in two models of urban form, the concentric and the radial, that can be traced in contemporary discourse and practice. The successive wall circles of cities that, like Florence, underwent dramatic expansion in the twelfth and thirteenth centuries doubtless suggested the concentricity of Dante's poetic topography or, more directly, of the most distinguished city description of the early Renaissance, that of Leonardo Bruni. Bruni's *Laudatio Florentinae urbis* of c. 1403 imitates an ancient text, but, as Baron (1968), 157–159, noted, the various metaphors of concentricity that Bruni adopted from his source were employed, in a wholly original manner, to structure the visual impression of Florence and its surroundings and to clarify topographical realities producing that impression.

The concentric model in Bruni's text consists of four major zones: the inner city, which is bounded by the walls and centered on the Palazzo della Signoria; the suburban zone; a zone of villas; and a zone of castles and subject towns. All this, in Bruni's view, makes up the city; indeed, on the model of the symbolic and functional role of the citadel (Palazzo della Signoria) within the walled city, he introduces the conceit that the latter constitutes the citadel of an extended city that flows out from the walls to occupy the adjacent hills. The potentially centrifugal emphasis of the concentric model is avoided, however, by the hierarchical structuring of the formal order of the region, such that each successive inner zone is regarded as surpassing its outward neighbor (ibid., 233–240). Florence, in short, is reduced to a scheme of compelling clarity, uncomplicated, for instance, by the settlements of the poor that increasingly clustered in the outer parishes straddling the walls and occupying space in the suburban zone extolled by Bruni (Cohn 1980, 111–127). But Bruni's sense of the region and his identification of distinct topographical zones mark the text as a significant piece of topographical analysis, for all the encomiastic context and the attention drawn, in typically humanistic fashion, to its own literary and stylistic qualities. It is not surprising, then, that it was quite widely imitated in the first half of the fifteenth century, serving, for example, as Pier Candido Decembrio's model for a text on Milan and as Aeneas Sylvius's for one on Basel (Baron 1968, 152; Schmidt 1981, esp. 120–124; Goldbrunner 1983; Kugler 1983).

Bruni's concentric topographical model is valid, *mutatis mutandis*, for other cities, not least Rome. A survey of late medieval Roman property categories, for example, reveals three major types, *case*, *vigne*, and *casali*, distinguished most obviously by the amount of land involved, the functions associated with that land, and the distance from the city center (these three categories dominate, for instance, the lists of properties donated to the Confraternity of the Salvatore as recorded in the latter's anniversary lists). The *casa*, the house in the city, varied greatly in size and value, though the better Roman houses typically included a court or yard with a well, an open-fronted portico or lean-to of some kind, and a patch of garden; there might also be a portico on the front of the house (Magnuson 1958, 45f.; Broise and Maire-Vigueur 1983). *Vigne*, as the name suggests, were pieces of ground, often not large, on which vines could be grown, as well as other crops requiring intensive labor and surveillance (Prete and Fondi 1957, 153). By the mid-fifteenth century it is unlikely that most *vigne*, though doubtless already used for summer relaxation and as a refuge from the epidemics of the city, included substantial buildings, while the crops produced in the *vigne* were primarily for the subsistence of the cultivators and their kin (an exception might be the exploitation of *vigne* that contained ancient ruins as quarries for stone, lime, or even antiquities, like that in front of S. Adriano that was bought by the papal staff: ASR, TS 1451, fol. 45r). *Vigne* did not form so neat a zone as Bruni's suburban area, not least because gardens and orchards (as was doubtless the case also at Florence), extended within the walls of the city, as did some pasture (Partner 1958, 120). *Vigne*, then, were characteristic of an area surrounding the inhabited area of the city and easily accessible from it.

Beyond the *vigne* were the *casali*, often large estates centered on strongholds dominating the surrounding countryside and thoroughfares. The *casali* sometimes produced cereal crops, and the quattrocento popes applied pressure on local proprietors to turn their land to this use; the *casali*, however, were more likely to be integrated into the region's dominant pastoral economy as hayfields and meadows. In any case, as recent studies have demonstrated, they served as centers for the penetration into the Roman Campagna of urban capital and patterns of investment and exploitation. The owners or more frequently leaseholders of the estates, typically members of an entrepreneurial sector of the Roman population known, in reference to the source of their economic and political power, as *bovattieri*, regarded their land most unsentimentally as a means to generate profits, or as itself a commodity. As such, the zone of the *casali*, worked by a seasonal and seminomadic labor force, differed greatly from the inner zones, where economic dynamism in the exploitation of rents and other income from property was largely lacking (Gennaro 1967a; Maire-Vigueur 1974; Coste 1976; Brezzi 1977).

The character of the environs of Rome was transformed in the Renaissance, at least where the ground was high enough to catch summer breezes, by the development of stable and status-laden retreats, on which affectionate attention was often lavished. By the mid-fifteenth century the practice of *villeggiatura* was established, in large part because of improved security in the region, and evidence begins to appear of the architectural elaboration of the buildings on the *vigne* of the affluent. In humanistic circles literary and broadly philosophical responses to the growing taste for country pleasures, beyond but not excluding the traditional and widely popular pursuit of hunting, also appear (Coffin 1979, 16–22, 24–26; Westfall 1974a, 67). But the degree and pace of change should not be exaggerated: indeed, the classical term *villa* does not begin to supplant the vernacular *vigna* until well into the sixteenth century. Nor did the growing practice of *villeggiatura* as a genteel fashion affect the distinction of *vigne*, whether primarily for pleasure or for small-scale food production, and *casali*. As we will see, the *casali* were associated with a class or stratum within Roman society whose culture remained essentially foreign to the humanistically tinged concerns of those, often outsiders and attached to the Curia, who played a role in the development of the Roman Renaissance villa. This may be a factor in the absence in the Campagna, even in the later Renaissance, of the kind of fusion of villa and working farm that was to become characteristic of parts of the Veneto. On the other hand, the *castella* of the Florentine countryside, into which, according to Bruni, the peasants could take refuge in time of danger and which he distinguishes sharply from the villas of the next zone (Baron 1979, 240), correspond broadly to the *casali* of the Roman countryside, for all the later contrast of a desolate Campagna and a smiling, cultivated Tuscan countryside.

Concrete examples of the investment of considerable funds in the improvement of suburban properties in mid-fifteenth-century Rome are somewhat rare. Among them are the documented cases of Tommaso Spinelli's *vigna* on Monte Mario, where he received Emperor Frederick III (Dykmans 1968; Coffin 1979, 66f.), or, rather later, the still extant retreat of Cardinal Bessarion on the Via Appia (Tomei 1942, 92; Coffin 1979, 64f.). Nicholas V himself preferred to move out of the Vatican in hot weather; within the city he saw to the restoration and expansion of an old papal palace adjoining S. Maria Maggiore on the breezy heights of the Esquiline, while his building campaigns at the baths of

Viterbo (Valtieri 1972, 687; Pinzi 1887–1913, 4:107–110) and of Vicarello, on the Lake of Bracciano (Ashby 1970, 237; ASR, TS 1452, fol. 216r), may indicate a concern to provide appropriate summer resorts where his severe physical ailments, as well as other needs, could be catered to. The chamberlain, Cardinal Ludovico Trevisan, acquired a country property at Albano (map 3) and dedicated considerable resources and energy to developing it, possibly in response to the diminution of his role in the administration of the city under Nicholas (Paschini 1926, 56of.). Several humanists at the papal court referred in letters or other documents to country sojourns or retreats enjoyed by them or their friends,[4] while Alberti devoted a lengthy and well-known passage of his *De re aedificatoria* to country and suburban residences, dealing with villas as places of pleasure and recreation but also as agricultural centers (Alberti 1966a, 2:400–405 [V.xiv], 414–433 [V.xvii]), associated with strictly utilitarian structures and providing the familial autarky that he had advocated in the *Della Famiglia* (Alberti 1969, 236–243).

The penetration of urban interests, whether commercial or broadly recreational in character, into the region around Rome grew from a long history of military and political expansionism conducted especially by the medieval Roman commune; this had consistently sought to assert its control over an area, known as the Roman district or *agro Romano*, that in the early quattrocento still had, in the view of staunch supporters of the commune, an extent of over 100 miles.[5] But this outward movement, typical of medieval Italian city-states, was balanced by the converse impact of rural interests and power centers, at least into the fifteenth century, in ways that set Rome apart from other major Italian cities.

It is surely significant, then, that Manetti begins his account of Nicholas's building program with the outlying towns of the papal states that Nicholas favored with restoration and construction projects. He mentions Gualdi, Assisi, Civitavecchia, Civita Castellana, Narni, Orvieto, Spoleto, Viterbo, and Fabriano, and refers vaguely to work carried out in a host of lesser and unspecified places (Magnuson 1958, 352). Manetti's account is borne out both by that of Canensi, to a degree, and more fully by archival evidence. But Manetti's impatience to commence his description of building carried out in Rome is only too evident; indeed, Manetti seems to use the subject cities as a foil to set off the grandeur and ambitiousness of the projects for Rome.

Manetti's discussion of the city begins with the walls. He then deals with the churches of Rome; crosses the Ponte S. Angelo to undertake the famous ideal description of the replanned Borgo; and brings the account to a resounding climax with passages on the projects, again largely unexecuted, for the Vatican palace and basilica. Textual and topographical movement coincide, and the inward unfolding of always smaller, hierarchically superior zones seems a rhetorical device at least colored by the example set by Bruni and his imitators. The concentricity in Manetti's account, needless to say, is symbolic rather than real, as the Vatican is situated beyond the perimeter of the city as defined by the Aurelianic walls. In the emphasis on the triad of axial streets leading toward the Vatican as identified and emphasized in the 1452 statutes of the *maestri di strada*, we may see a related concern to center the Vatican within the city. In any case, it is likely that the Bruni text was as familiar to Nicholas and his advisers as it was to Alberti, and that the former's attitudes and policies toward the city region may have depended on a Brunian reading of its configuration, at least by the end of the pontificate. It is certainly suggestive that the concentric model of urban form plays an important role in Alberti's writings of the same period, notably in references to the seven-ringed city of Ecbatana and to Babylon (Alberti 1966A, 2:846f.),[6] where the immediate source is Herodotus, translated into Latin by Lorenzo Valla at the express behest of Nicholas V (Cochrane 1981, 149; Pastor 1949, 198).

Sanctioned though the concentric model may be by such recherché references, its shortcomings as an analytical instrument are only too apparent, most notably its static and schematic character. A further model of urban form formulated in the fifteenth century (as already in antiquity), however, provides a framework for a far more dynamic and concrete understanding of social and economic relations in their topographical expression. This is the radial model, which was given striking and well-known schematic form in the plan of the ideal city Sforzinda in Filarete's treatise of c. 1461 (fig. 44; cf. Simoncini 1974, 2:29f.). The primary spokes of Filarete's plan, however, end at the gates; the result is an image of geometrical perfection (belied, certainly, by the unresolved conflict of distinct geometries at the center) and formal absoluteness that disguises its relationship with the actual conditions of contemporary Italian cities. Prescriptive concerns have here supplanted the subtle probing of an Alberti into past and present urban realities (though certainly Alberti too was concerned to develop a basis for the formulation of norms).

The reality suggested and yet denied by Filarete's plan is that city gates, whatever their symbolic value or military function, were typically mere incidents on routes that led from a sector of the hinterland of a city into its core, especially to the markets that attracted the majority of travelers, who entered the city for the sake of trade. The gates allowed the regulation and, as stations for the collection of tolls, the fiscal exploitation of the flow of commodities into the city; this function was hardly less important than the military function, and we find at Florence that gates were the first elements of the city wall system to be built. The major routes into a city, moreover, constituted demographic corridors; immigrants to a city along one of the major radial routes would settle in the part of the city into which the road from their homeland led, where they would find a supportive and familiar community. They might bring with them, too, their customary loyalties to local lords and feudal clans, themselves often also established in the city, so that some aspects of traditional rural social patterns were transferred into urban neighborhoods (Weissman 1980, 7–9).

The connective, homogenizing quality of major routes was given statutory expression in the late medieval Tuscan communes. Already in the twelfth century laws regarding the maintenance of urban streets were extended to the roads and bridges of the subject countryside (Szabo 1975, 141; Szabo 1976, 22; Russell 1960). The division of a city into administrative units, often according to a schematized disposition of the gates, was typically projected out into roughly wedge-shaped sectors outside the walls (Guidoni 1974, 490–495). In the fourteenth and fifteenth centuries a process of consolidation and centralization occurred as more powerful city-states subjected the less powerful to their rule, and the major radial routes served as conduits for the exercise of authority. This development of territorial states, however, was slow to be reflected in changing legal forms; even at Florence it was not until the early fifteenth century that the statutes were revised to take account of the assimilation of the subject towns and Florence itself into a new political and administrative order. No doubt the recognition implicit in such statutory innovations of Florence's changing character depended, to some degree, on humanistic studies of the rise of the Roman Republic and its transformation into a territorial state, in part through the foundation of colonies (including the original city on the site of Florence). In contrast, the diminished medieval city of Rome seemed to Tuscan observers, at least, to have suffered the reverse process.[7]

Radial arrangements of major streets occur in many medieval cities, sometimes structuring the outer areas and contrasting with the residual rectilinearity of the Roman core of cities like Bologna or even Florence. The radial configuration of Rome, however, was especially evident; it was felicitously compared to a starfish by Thomas Ashby (1970), 50, who noted the paucity of circumferential connecting routes between the convergent thoroughfares. The latter, of course, were the great consular roads of antiquity, which penetrated into the city and dominated its topography, a topography that, since they preexisted much of the development of the city, they had in large part generated. The attention of scholars of early Renaissance Rome has focused on the three thoroughfares converging on the Ponte S. Angelo and officially given privileged status in the 1452 edition of the statutes of the *maestri di strada*; indeed, it is now generally accepted that this formalized a major reorientation of the topography of the city, now turned toward the peripheral Vatican.

While the general validity of this interpretation seems beyond doubt, it is important to note that the new topographical accents appearing in the city echoed the radial principle underlying the city's traditional topographical structure. Moreover, the central thoroughfare of the three, the Via del Papa, resumed the function of an ancient processional route leading from a triumphal arch near the Ponte S. Angelo at the edge of the city toward the Capitol, the symbolic center of ancient Rome (map 2). The Via Retta, on the other hand, was an ancient link between the bridges over the Tiber at the apex of the Campus Martius and the Via Lata, the prolongation within the city of the Via Flaminia. The Via del Papa itself might be regarded as a continuation of the ancient spur of the Via Cassia that brought travelers from the north into the Vatican area. The emphasis under Nicholas V on radial topographical structures, then, innovative though it may have been in some respects, is nevertheless grounded in the time-honored configuration of the city. The question arises, then, of the conditions under which comprehension of such a configuration and its paradigmatic potential for urban reform could occur. It was a configuration that was, as it were, writ large in the region, and it is to regional radial structures that the discussion will now turn.

With the increasing importance of temporal as opposed to spiritual revenues in the budget of the late medieval Church, the territories subject to the Church assumed crucial significance, as did the routes connecting them with the capital (maps 3, 4; cf. Partner 1972, 420–430; Potter 1979, 19–29).[8] In Nicholas's policies toward these territories three major concerns are evident: the assertion of sovereign rights, the provision of security for resident populations and travelers (Maire-Vigueur 1981, 121), and the consolidation of the economic base, generating tax revenues for the papal coffers and food supplies for the city of Rome. During the early years of Nicholas's pontificate priority was given to preparations for the Jubilee of 1449–50, though these must in general have been consonant with longer-term objectives. The assertion of sovereignty, certainly, was the necessary precondition for everything else, and Nicholas's prompt and, at times, harsh actions in this regard have often been noted (Pleyer 1927; Toews 1968, 277–279; Pastor 1949, 62–64); the consistency and efficiency of his administration of the papal territories is indicated by the appointment of officials to a range of posts in numerous subject communities.

The crucial role of Nello da Bologna in the solution of the problems posed by the Jubilee, including the provisioning of Rome, necessarily involved him in many aspects of the administration of many of the papal provinces, notably those, like the Patrimonium s. Petri or the March of Ancona (map 4), that were of particular agricultural importance. In the years following the Jubilee, however, Nello's involvement in the administration of the wider hinterland of Rome intensified, at the same time as his control of urban affairs was consolidated and formalized. The scope of his responsibilities indicates not merely the importance of the region at this time, but also the interrelatedness of urban and regional administration. In order to understand the latter, however, we must first review the geographical conditions and context of papal regional policies.

The lower Tiber valley, in which Rome is situated, spreads out into the plain known as the Campagna (maps 3, 4). South of the city a largely continuous range of mountains marches from near the Mediterranean coast east and north to the chain of peaks marking the center of the peninsula; this area is of less concern to the present discussion. North of the city three major zones, each extending roughly north-south, can be discerned: to the west a coastal zone of plains and low hills; in the center a series of extinct and eroded volcanic basins; and to the east the valley of the Tiber (Prete and Fondi 1957, 7, 18, 43). These three zones can be characterized by distinct ecological conditions, types of cultivation and economic activity, and settlement patterns that continued until quite recent radical technological and demographic changes. The projection of such categories onto the fifteenth century can be done, needless to say, only tentatively, though impressive archaeological and documentary studies of some aspects of the late medieval region have been carried out (Potter 1979, esp. 1–18; Barker 1973). Nevertheless, the general framework is clear.

The coastal region or Maremma is relatively dry, with high summer temperatures. Climatic and topographical features encouraged the early development of large estates and the concentration of the population into few centers (notably Civitavecchia, Tarquinia/Corneto, Tuscania/Toscanella, Montalto di Castro, and Monte Romano). Overall population density was low, and migrant labor played an important role in the agricultural economy. This was largely seasonal in character, depending on transhumance, the movement of extensive numbers of animals (mostly sheep and goats, with some cattle) from high summer pastures in the mountains to winter meadows greened by fall rains. The history of this practice can be traced into remote antiquity: Iron Age populations already employed transhumance as a rational and successful response to geographical and climatic conditions (Potter 1979, 22–24).[9]

The central section is somewhat varied in character, including some rich agricultural areas, like the productive territory around Viterbo, the capital of the Patrimonium (Serra 1972, 14, 57–60, 89), and stretches of rugged and heavily wooded terrain, divided by deep gullies and steep-sided valleys cut by streams flowing with sudden violence, in season, from the peaks and volcanic lakes. The promontories occurring at the junctions of valleys provided easily defensible sites of great importance in the aftermath of the collapse of Roman imperial power and in subsequent periods of unrest and confusion, not least in the early fifteenth century. In this zone the pattern of large estates gave way, in relative terms, to one of smaller and more intensively worked parcels of land whose proprietors generally maintained their residences in the towns; it is not long since the lines of carts bound for the towns from the countryside as the sun went down were a familiar sight in the region, and it is likely that this was already the case in the fifteenth century. The rich volcanic soil favored the cultivation, necessarily intensive, of vines and fruit trees (the nut production of the area is still celebrated), while the forests abounded with game and pannage for pigs, and the many lakes with fish and waterfowl (Potter 1979, 168f.).

The Tiber valley has in recent centuries been an area of relatively high population density and scattered settlements. In the mid-fifteenth century, though many communities are mentioned in the documents, population levels between the Tiber and the Via Flaminia may only have begun to recover from the disorder of previous decades. If the presence of major long-distance routes, including the Tiber itself, doubtless favored the rapid demographic and economic development of the communities that they connected with major centers, yet they may also have laid these same communities open to the depredations of feudal warlords and mercenary captains, such as infested central Italy in the pontificate of Eugenius IV.[10] This eastern zone of the three under review was dominated to the south by the stronghold of Castelnuovo di Porto and to the north by those of Civita Castellana and Nepi or even, to extend the zone beyond the Patrimonium, by that of Spoleto (map 4); we will note below the attention given to these places under Nicholas.

This is the overall configuration, then, of a region whose pastoral economy was crucial to the late medieval papacy and in which the northern territories, especially the Patrimonium, generated revenues that greatly exceeded those of the territories to the south of Rome (Partner 1972, 426f.). In 1448 Nello da Bologna's involvement with the pastoral economy began, an involvement that grew into one of his most significant responsibilities. In that year he took the oath of office for the *dogana* of Campagna Marittima, the province south of Rome, and the city itself (ASV, RV 407, fol. 234v; cf. ASR, TS 1450, fol. 3r; TS 1451, fol. 5r). This office involved the supervision and fiscal exploitation of transhumant flocks summering in the mountains of Campagna Marittima and beyond (especially in the territory of the kingdom of Naples) and wintering in the environs of Rome. In terms of the prevailing usage, this means that Nello and his partner, Arcangelo Chiavelli, formed a partnership to purchase the right to collect the revenues accruing from the leasing of pasturage in the winter meadows in the year of their contract (Partner 1958, 118–123). Chiavelli, a stockraiser and entrepreneur from Camerino in the March, was evidently a man of substance; in the last years of Eugenius's pontificate he had held the post of *doganiere* of the Patrimonium, and he remained in this post, as far as can be determined, until 1451 (Anzilotti 1919, 386f.; Maire-Vigueur 1981, 110; Oliva 1981, 227).[11] There seems to be no precedent, at least in the fifteenth century, for the pairing of a man like Chiavelli and a close papal collaborator and official like Nello in a major *dogana*, but the example was followed, for when in 1451 Chiavelli lost the *dogana* of the Patrimonium, he was succeeded by Nello, now in partnership with a Perugian (ASR, TS 1451, fol. 6v). And later in the same year, perhaps indicating the fluidity of the situation, Nello appears with a different associate as *doganiere* of the Patrimonium and, at the same time, of Campagna Marittima and the city, a most unusual double appointment (ASV, RV 433, fol. 204r).[12] The primary economic activity of the whole region around Rome, then, was now under unified control.

In his study of the records of the *dogana dei pascoli* of the Patrimonium in the fourteenth and fifteenth centuries, J.-C. Maire-Vigueur (1981) 46f., 111f., notes but gives insufficient emphasis to changes in the administration of the *dogana* that occurred around the middle of the fifteenth century (cf. Sereni 1974, 144F., 196f.). Previously the *dogana* had been awarded annually to one or, more rarely, two individuals whose background, as in the typical case of Arcangelo Chiavelli, was invariably in stockraising. These were men familiar, we can be sure, with the world of the annual migration of massed flocks and herds; with the difficulties of protecting the animals from the depredations of bandits and wolves; with the high passes and remote paths traversed by the flocks on their way from or into the mountains; with the topography of the coastal plains and the various territories populated in winter by multitudes of grazing beasts; with the negotiations with potential leasors of pastorage against a background of complex patterns of land ownership and control; with the assignment of the animals to different areas; and with the social world of the landlords, stockraisers, drovers, petty officials, guards, and hucksters, as it revealed itself especially in the heady atmosphere of festival at the time of the autumn count (*calla*), when the long march from the summer pastures, now completed, could be appropriately celebrated (ibid., 38, 114; cf. Pinto 1982, 63f.).

Much of the best pasturage was on land directly owned by the Church, but much was leased by the *doganieri* from feudal lords, religious institutions, or local communities to satisfy the needs of the wintering flocks and preserve the monopoly of the *dogana*; the negotiations conducted and deals struck between the *doganieri* and landowners must have frequently required considerable diplomatic skill and a sensitive balancing of interests, often with clear implications for the success of the papal administration and its fiscal exploitation of the province concerned. Indeed, there is evidence from the early 1450s of a progressive institutionalization of the practice of granting special terms to local communities needing to winter part of their own flocks on land controlled by the *dogana*; we find Viterbo and Tuscania especially favored in this respect (Maire-Vigueur 1981, 118–120).

It is not surprising, then, that the *dogana* began to be awarded, clearly as a matter of deliberate policy, to men associated with the Curia and perhaps already employed within the papal administration (as was Nello), possessed, then, of administrative experience and, at least in some cases, of legal expertise;[13] it was not enough to have a background in stockraising and sufficient capital. Maire-Vigueur dated this trend to about the middle of the fifteenth century. On the basis of documents not used by him we can be precise: in 1451 Nello da Bologna took control of the *dogana* of the Patrimonium, having learned the trade, as it were, through his association with Chiavelli in 1448 and his experiences as general organizer of the Jubilee of 1449–50, when much of his attention was focused on the Patrimonium. In 1452 the *dogana* of the Patrimonium was awarded to one Jacopo del Dottore da Bologna, significantly a compatriot of Nello (Anzilotti 1919, 387); his name suggests, as Maire-Vigueur (1981, 112) noted, a legal background. The process of integration, albeit on a personal rather than institutional level, of the *dogana* of the Patrimonium into the papal financial administration parallels developments in the city that I have connected with the formulation and implementation by Nello, acting directly on behalf of the pope, of new policies. The changes made, however, were subtle and tactful: Nello insinuated himself into existing administrative structures, taking time to become familiar with the topographical and economic features and sociopolitical dynamics of the areas with which he was concerned.

Though the revenues of the *dogana* of Campagna Marittima and Rome were less important than those of the Patrimonium, there may well have been, in Nello's eyes, considerable room for improvement. In 1452 an edition of the statutes governing the *dogana dei pascoli* of Campagna Marittima and Rome was issued by order of Nicholas V; much of this confirmed provisions contained in the statutes of the city for the area administered by the *doganieri* in question (Maire-Vigueur 1981, 106; cf. De Cupis 1911, 549–557). Nello's hand can be suspected in this, though it is not clear why an edition of the statutes of the *dogana* was needed at this time; certainly none was produced for the *dogana* of the Patrimonium, as Maire-Vigueur has shown. But it is likely that the concern evinced in the 1452 document for the ordered administration and security of the drove routes was warranted by the fact that they converged on the *agro Romano,* indeed on Rome itself, while those of the Patrimonium led to the remote Maremma.

The flocks of Campagna Marittima and beyond approached the city by way of the Aniene valley, keeping to the north side of the river until they crossed by one of three bridges in the environs of Rome (map 3; see Partner 1958, 120); these, the Ponti Mammolo, Salaro, and Nomentano, all appear to have undergone major restoration under Nicholas V.[14] The 1452 statutes stipulate the stationing of officials at all three bridges to count the animals and check that all were registered. Other officials were to be stationed at Tivoli, where the flocks descended from the high country, "in Campagna," and at the Villa S. Antimo near the border with the kingdom of Naples (Re 1880, 276f. nos. 3, 5; cf. Partner 1958, 120; Tomassetti 1879, 1:117f.). The latter two officials were doubtless charged to see that the flocks were allowed to pass without let or hindrance through the territories of various lords and communities, and perhaps also to encourage stockmen to use the winter pastures of the Church rather than those of the kingdom; the patterns of transhumance, rooted in ancient custom as they were, did not escape the impact of the political and economic rivalries of the fifteenth century (Maire-Vigueur 1981, 126f.).

In a single year, then, and equally under the direct authority of Nello, two sets of statutes were issued, one dealing with the spatial expression of the pastoral economy of the Roman hinterland and the other, that of the *maestri di strada,* clarifying the spatial expression of the economic and ceremonial life of the papal city. It is significant to find Nello involved in judicial hearings in the province of Campagna Marittima, like the quite trivial case of 1452 in which Nello, together with the senator of Rome, adjudicated the value of horses rustled by the men of Sezze from the lands of the Caetani, a powerful baronial family.[15] This indicates that Nello was concerned not only with the administration and exploitation, thorugh the two *dogane,* of the transhumance system, but also with the consistent and integrated administration of the Roman district and its wider hinterland.

The authority exercised in the Roman region by Nicholas and his officials overlapped, of course, with a plethora of other territorial rights and claims. The radial topography of the city and region alike, both structured by the great consular roads, had a marked sociopolitical dimension, for these roads connected the urban and rural properties and strongholds of the barons. Control of roads leading into Rome, therefore, indeed of whole sectors of the countryside, was a central preoccupation of the barons (Tomassetti 1979, 1:111–116), who met determined resistance in the thirteenth and especially in the fourteenth century from the Roman commune (Palermo 1979, 31). Nor could the popes of the mid-fifteenth century yet flout the feudal social structure of the Campagna and its topographical expression, as later quattrocento popes sought to do through a series of campaigns against powerful lords (Caravale and Caracciolo 1978, 6f., 88f., 143f.). The response to the situation adopted by Nicholas's predecessors was to array themselves on the side of one of the major clans, in the hope of turning an intensified factional conflict to the good of the Church. Martin V, himself a Colonna, asserted papal power by supporting his own kin and enhancing their power in city and country alike (Partner 1958, esp. 194–198). Eugenius IV reversed this policy, unleashing a merciless military campaign against the Colonna and their allies, while depending on the support of their great rivals, the Orsini (Caravale and Caracciolo 1978, 55–62). The Colonna survived Eugenius's onslaught, though with heavy loss of property and human life, and were soon able to rebound. For lesser clans, on the other hand, the protracted wars of the 1430s and 1440s sealed a process of decline that had been occurring over many years (Silvestrelli 1970, 1:302f.). The result was the relative simplification of the complex world of Campagna feudalism: by the end of Nicholas's pontificate the Orsini and Colonna had emerged with undisputed preeminence from the years of turbulence, and this, no doubt combined with the exhaustion of the various parties, provided the opportunity for Nicholas's policy of neutrality and balance.

In real terms, such a policy could only mean confirming the Colonna and Orsini in their traditional control of or claims to territory within the papal states. Clearly, however, territorial concessions, however carefully balanced, involved the risk of long-term detriment to the interests of the Church; indeed, a major concern of Nicholas's administration was the systematic restitution of properties lost to the Church or to ecclesiastical institutions through illicit alienation, which was sometimes a matter of recompense for military or other support or, in other cases, of response to economic dynamism or the mere display of strength.[16]

The exercise of ecclesiastical authority in the papal states under Nicholas was not, as is frequently implied, a matter of the consistent application of a principle of political centralization or even homogenization. The evidence suggests, rather, a topographical pattern or direction in Nicholas's policies, at least toward the Roman region. This is in part, certainly, explicable in terms of the familiar radial model of Campagna feudalism and papal responses to it and the obvious priority of security in certain areas. On the other hand, Nicholas's regional policies responded to and clarified the topographical order of a particular sector, thereby organizing or reorganizing an ancient landscape as a physical matrix of numerous interventions, in themselves often insignificant but together producing from the wreck of centuries of turbulence a coherent and compelling spatial and symbolic order. The evidence is fragmentary, to be sure, but the argument gains validity from the integrated understanding of the region that, as we saw, was operative in the papal administration of the period.

Early in 1448, Pietro Lunense, one of Nicholas's secretaries, was sent on a mission, unfortunately unspecified in the documents, to two communities subject to the Church, Montalto (di Castro) and Foligno (ASV, IE 414, fol. 97v). The date suggests that Pietro's journey was related to the preparations for the Jubilee of 1449–50, especially as regarded the welfare and security of the pilgrims, most of whom approached from the north. Both Montalto and Foligno are situated on major routes toward Rome from that quarter: Montalto was the northernmost town in papal territory on the Via Aurelia (map 3), while Foligno straddles the Via Flaminia shortly before it ascends into the mountainous territory of the March (map 4). Whatever Pietro's itinerary, it must have taken him along two of the major routes of the Patrimonium, the Aurelia and Flaminia. The other major road of the region, the Cassia, he already knew well, even if he did not take it on this occasion. For though Pietro, like Nicholas and many of his close collaborators, was of Ligurian origin, he had obtained Viterbese citizenship. Indeed, in a bull of April 1, 1447, Nicholas appointed him chancellor for life of Viterbo, the capital of the Patrimonium, where he was perhaps already building a palace (a project supported, in time, by tax privileges granted him by Nicholas) in remarkably up-to-date, if not Albertian, style. It was doubtless in this house that in May 1448, shortly after his return from Montalto and Foligno, he entertained the pope's mother and sister who had come to Viterbo to take the baths, also favored by Nicholas himself (Pinzi 1887–1913, 3:65f.). Pietro, therefore, was well placed to report to Nicholas on the state of the main routes of the Patrimonium and the adjoining areas, as on that of the towns along the roads, supplying information of evident importance for the planning of the Jubilee.[17]

Pietro Lunense's appointment as chancellor of Viterbo typifies a consistent series of papal appointments, often of ostensibly communal officials, to subject cities. Cesare da Lucca, for example, Nicholas's brother-in-law, was made governor of Spoleto, where Nicholas's mother also took up her residence (ibid., 66; Mack 1982, 65). Here considerable resources were committed to work on the walls of the town, a project that was not a tyrannical measure on the part of the pope but a response to supplications made by the commune of Spoleto, which was allowed to divert to the fortifications certain taxes otherwise destined to the *camera apostolica* (ASV, RV 411, fol. 73r [February 1450]).

Spoleto, of course, was a major strategic site on the Via Flaminia (map 4); a comparable and notable example is that of Castelnuovo di Porto, which occupied a strategic position commanding the Via Flaminia some 27 kilometers from Rome (map 3). At Castelnuovo restoration work on the walls is documented in 1453 (Mack 1982, 65), though it may well have begun earlier. The town had been held by the Colonna, but in a bull of 1448 in which Nicholas restored to the various branches of the clan the lands and properties stripped from them by Eugenius IV, Castelnuovo was the only major exception. Though the main centers of Colonna power lay to the southeast of the Roman district, they were not indifferent to the fate of Castelnuovo; indeed, on the news of Nicholas's death, Stefano Colonna rode into the town at the head of an armed band and recaptured it, as he later claimed, with the support of the inhabitants (Tomassetti 1979, 3:367; Silvestrelli 1970, 1:530–532). This is probably true; in 1448 Nicholas had appointed a committee of three prominent abbots to see to the restitution to the abbey of S. Paolo fuori le Mura of extensive lands in the area of Castelnuovo that the townspeople had evidently claimed for themselves (Trifone 1909, 68 no. 158).[18] There were obvious grievances, then, for the Colonna to exploit. In any case, Nicholas's concern to reconcile the Colonna with the papacy here took second place to his policy of securing, if only through intermediaries, territories of particular value to his government.

Nicholas consistently supported the territorial claims of the great religious institutions of Rome, especially S. Paolo. No doubt he was concerned to restore lost revenues that could finance institutional reforms and building campaigns, as was the case at S. Paolo (Miglio 1975, 230): it is likely too, however, that the restitution of abbatial estates formed part of his regional policy. Certainly, a group of properties in the area between the Via Flaminia and the Tiber were restored to the abbey of S. Paolo, perhaps a case of the consolidation of territory that may have been frequent in the period, doubtless markedly affecting the security, prosperity, and even character of the southern section of the Via Flaminia and the country through which it passed.[19]

Further north, on the other hand, the Via Flaminia could be policed from the papal strongholds at Civita Castellana, Spoleto, and Foligno.[20] At the same time as Pietro Lunense's mission a further confidante of the pope, the eminent Roman patrician Lorenzo Altieri, was dispatched into the Patrimonium to see to the restitution to the Church of Nepi and Monterosi.[21] Monterosi stood at the junction of the Via Cassia and a spur road across country to the Flaminia; Nepi, on its nearly impregnable peninsula site between deep gorges, dominated this spur road and the surrounding territory.[22] At Nepi it was the Orsini and their allies the Anguillara who raised the population against the ecclesiastical government when Eugenius attempted to reclaim it. Nicholas resorted not to force but to the expensive redemption of the original pledge of the town made by Eugenius in order to raise money for his campaigns. Further north, of course, the Cassia could be controlled from Viterbo, which remained loyal, if not always peaceful, under Nicholas (Pinzi 1887–1913, 4:96–100, 132). Here the main municipal building, the Palazzo dei Priori, was restored at Nicholas's behest, while urban improvement projects can be documented (ibid., 59, 209 n.1).

To the west, finally, conditions along the Via Aurelia were addressed by the purchase from Cardinal Ludovico Trevisan of Civitavecchia, which, for all its importance as a harbor, had become his fief. For the chamberlain had exploited the vacuum left in the area by the extirpation of the clan of the Prefetti di Vico and the later fall of their destroyer, Cardinal Vitelleschi, Trevisan's predecessor as commander of the papal forces. (In recompense for Civitavecchia the chamberlain received the distant town of Iesi; Silvestrelli 1970, 1:17.) In Civitavecchia part of the revenues of the *dogana* of the Patrimonium were used in 1451, at least, for building work on the castle (Mack 1982, 65), while unspecified construction is documented in Civitavecchia, Montalto, and Monte Romano in preparation for the descent of Emperor Frederick III into Italy in the winter of 1451–52.

This is curious. When Frederick traveled from Siena to Rome in the winter of 1452, accompanied by Aeneas Sylvius Piccolomini, whose elevation to the papacy he foretold on the way, he traveled along the Cassia, from Roman times the main route from Tuscany toward Rome (Pastor 1949, 138–160). This was expected, for preparations, possibly of a quite elaborate nature, were made in Viterbo. The emperor traveled in January perhaps partly to take advantage of the abundance of provisions for his swollen cortege, which accepted with enthusiasm the proffered fare. The work at Montalto and Monte Romano, sited on an important route linking the Aurelia and Cassia, may have been related to the contemporary administrative changes in the *dogana* of the Patrimonium, whose chief pastures were in this area and whose successful operation, including perhaps the provisioning of the emperor and his retinue, depended on the maintenance of security. In any case, the attention given to the towns of the Maremma and the provision of an appropriate processional route through Viterbo can both be counted among Nello's responsibilities in 1451; again, I note the coincidence of ceremonial and representative concerns and their spatial expression, on the one hand, and an economic policy at regional scale, on the other.

As the three great pilgrimage roads and economic arteries of the Aurelia, Cassia, and Flaminia converged on Rome, they defined the topography of a distinct region. This had already been noted in antiquity. Cicero declared in one of the *Philippics*: "There are three main routes [from Rome to Modena in north central Italy]: from the upper sea [the Adriatic] the Flaminia, from the lower sea [the Tyrrhenian] the Aurelia, and in the middle the Cassia. . . . The Cassia bisects Etruria" (Cicero 1951, 539). The convergent pattern inscribed on the landscape by these three roads was perhaps all the more striking in that each traversed and organized one of the three geographical sectors distinguished above. The succession of these sectors would have been apparent along the few thoroughfares that crossed the territory from east to west, among them the drove roads converging on the pastures of the Maremma. Nello and his staff, of course, were concerned with both north-south and east-west systems of communication, with their very different functions and associations but together structuring a complex but unitary region.

The two major and most familiar documents of Nicholas V's urbanism, the 1452 statutes of the *maestri di strada* and the account of the Borgo project transmitted by Manetti, though highly dissimilar in character and function, both describe an urban space structured by a triadic ordering principle. The arrangement of the three converging thoroughfares distinguished in the statutes is echoed by that of the three thoroughfares projected for the Borgo (Magnuson 1958, 36f.; Westfall 1974a, 69f.). In both cases, the formal configuration corresponds to and articulates topographical and functional realities, but is not fully explained by these. For in the relevant passage of the 1452 statutes routes are ignored that would, if recognized, have disturbed the schematic elegance of the system (e.g., the bifurcation of the Via de' Banchi Vecchi into the Via del Pellegrino and the Via Mercatoria). In contrast, genuinely functional criteria had been applied under Eugenius in the distinction of major and minor thoroughfares (Paschini 1939, 140f.), as was customary in late medieval Italian communes (Szabo 1976, 23), though doubtless this distinction carried aesthetic and ideological overtones.

If we can posit, then, a new degree of schematization or even aestheticization of urban space under Nicholas, the question arises of the source of this. Noting the entanglement of regional and urban policy and administration in these years, and the comprehension of regional space implicit, especially, in the management of the transhumance system, I would suggest that the formal structure articulated in the 1452 statutes mirrored the space of the region. The most obvious paradigm, with its convergent pattern of order centered, like that of the statutes, on the Vatican as fount of authority and sacrality, is the road system of the Patrimonium, sanctioned by ancient and Christian associations, and reconciling these with contemporary requirements of a highly practical nature. We should not neglect, however, the other statutes of 1452, those of the *dogana* of Campagna Marittima and Rome, in which the triadic ordering of routes into the *agro Romano* is enunciated. Moreover, the structure discerned in or imposed on the city in 1452 was soon to be mirrored across the river in the Borgo project, a crystallization of triadic structure in a utopic papal enclave framed between the city and countryside, belonging to neither but controlling both.

With Manetti's account of the Borgo the triadic motif, as Allan Ceen (1977), 74–85, has well described, entered the vocabulary first of Roman and later of European urbanism. It became the projection par excellence of absolutist ideology onto the land, directing the traveler's glance and steps ineluctably toward a monumental focus at the point where the three axes meet. This motif has its roots, I would argue, not only in the Roman republic's organization of subject territory in relation to a political and military focus, but also in an older and yet more constant world of ancient custom and contract, of landscapes traversed and structured by trackways connecting not walled and gated cities, but open grazing lands studded by the conical thatched huts of herdsmen, such as were found in the Roman Campagna even in this century (Prete and Fondi 1957, 140–148). In this world, however, regularity and even permanence lay largely in the process, the repeated performance of tasks and the exercise of skills and expertise by the seminomads who accompanied the flocks. This order was characteristic of medieval and Renaissance central Italy alike, but was apparent perhaps only to those with a direct interest in perceiving it. To outsiders, especially those with a predilection for a stable or even geometrically structured visual environment, the churning sea of animals that periodically flowed through the wide pastures and around the relics of antiquity of the Campagna or even of the city was incomprehensible and repugnant. Humanists in Rome, though their world and that of the local pastoral economy must have often intersected,[23] turned to more elevated subjects (Sereni 1961, 196f.). The references made by humanists to the rusticity of even the better-class Romans or indeed to the very decay of the city surely involved, on a deeper level, a distancing from the economic and social realities of the region (Weiss 1969, 59–89; Gaeta 1977; Miglio 1983, 252–255; Stinger 1985, 89–91). Poggio Bracciolini and his like were impelled, needless to say, by an image of ancient glory, an image that was perhaps operative also, in the sphere of concrete action, in Nicholas V's concern to move noisome industries, notably those associated with the processing of hides and other products of the transhumance system, downstream of the city. On the whole, the humanists affected to ignore the life of the city in which they lived, and it is not surprising, accordingly, that none of the panegyrists or historians of Nicholas's pontificate recorded or even mentioned the work of Nello da Bologna, the chief intermediary between the sphere of the Curia and that of the local society, and between perceptions and categories current in each.

Northern visitors to Rome, on the other hand, free from the nostalgic nationalism of the Italians, were soon to respond positively to the overgrown landscapes of forlorn ruins surrounded by grazing animals and inhabited, in some cases, by the herdsman and their dogs (see especially Dacos 1965; of course, the northerners were no more aware than contemporary Italian intellectuals of the underlying order of what they saw). For all the papal injunctions to encourage cereal cultivation, the pastoral landscape remained characteristic of the Campagna. In the seventeenth century the flocks and herds, washed by a golden Claudean light, were to take their place in canvas after canvas as painted denizens of a pastoral idyll. But this artistic vision of the Campagna was then translated, at first in distant regions, into real landscapes of charmingly disposed and deliberately decayed and fallen buildings, drifts of trees, and sweeping greenswards and lakes that effaced, in many cases, the traces of more formal and geometrical planning. Indeed, the grazing animals that unconsciously adopted picturesque poses in the carefully modulated glades and meadows of a Stowe or a Blenheim contributed now to the destruction of landscape forms and a landscape sensibility that drew from many sources, but not least from the tradition of monumental avenues and nodal points inaugurated in Manetti's Borgo. And this tradition, I would suggest, other flocks and herds, on their great marches through the rugged terrain of central Italy, had helped to bring about.

I must not overstate; the paradigm of regional economic and political geography, if I am right, was operative in the city at the level of administrative process and reform, at a remove from the consciousness or interests of cultured circles in Nicholan Rome. If I may posit the reinterpretation of urban space in terms of regional models, however, it is likely that the ceremonial and representative aspects of the regional context, more generally accessible and intelligible, played a conspicuous role. The major elements structuring the region were, as I have noted, the consular roads. These carried various associations, but of particular importance in the humanistic culture of the Renaissance, with its emphasis on the acquisition and expression of glory, was the processional or even triumphal quality assignable to these roads. The theme of the Roman triumph may well seem distinctly urban, to be sure, but the evidence that I will now present suggests that this too had in our period a marked regional dimension, and that this was significant for the development of urban spatiality and form.

The Triumphal Road: Augustus Caesar, Sigismondo Malatesta, and Nicholas V

In the opinion of humanist authors writing in the fifteenth century, the ancient triumphal route into Rome had entered the city by way of the Vatican and the Pons Triumphalis over the Tiber, thence passing across the Campus Martius before reaching its goal at the Capitol (Martindale 1979, 56–65). Flavio

Biondo, for instance, believed that physical evidence of its course was still apparent in the fabric of the city, notably in the remains of the ancient arch adjacent to the church of S. Celso, while the Vatican obelisk marked the site of the marshaling area for the processions. Such an account, needless to say, neglects the ancient Via Sacra, whose course, marked by extant triumphal arches, traversed the Roman Forum (fig. 38); indeed, scenes of triumph appeared on the arches of Titus and Constantine, while the ancient Via Sacra still retained its function as a major processional route as part of the medieval Via Maggiore, which linked the Capitol to the Lateran. The antiquarianism, then, of Biondo and other humanists was clearly influenced by contemporary usage and interests; certainly, Biondo's triumphal route corresponds in general terms to the Via del Papa of his own time and to the central role of the Vatican in the reception of important visitors to the city.

The year 1452 saw the arrival in Rome of Emperor Frederick III and his coronation by Nicholas V (fig. 12). There can be no doubt that Frederick's entrance into Rome was carefully stage-managed by Nicholas's staff, for it was of great importance, in view of the Ghibelline sympathies still current in the city, that the emperor's visit should at least appear to be consonant with Nicholas's own policies and interests (Pastor 1949, 150–152; Burroughs 1982a, 102f.). Frederick approached the city by way of the Vatican, having taken the ancient pilgrims' road from the Via Cassia over Monte Mario, from which he enjoyed the panoramic view of the rooftops of Rome. He spent the night before his formal entrance in a villa on the slope of Monte Mario belonging to Tommaso Spinelli, the Florentine banker whose central role in communal administration and papal building programs under Nicholas V has been emphasized. On the following day he was escorted by a distinguished group of officials and representatives of the Church to the Porta di Castello, where the ceremony of entrance occurred at the threshold, not of Rome, but of the Leonine City. There is no evidence that references to ancient triumphal practices were made at this time, though it is not unlikely, especially as a further conspicuous ceremony involving the emperor took place on the Ponte S. Angelo, whose ancient and Christian associations alike had been stressed under Nicholas, and which now provided the point of entry into the city proper (Mitchell 1979, 114f.).

In the ceremonial entrances of the sixteenth century, on the other hand, it was the Porta del Popolo that generally served as the privileged threshold into the city. Returning popes also used this route, as in the well-documented case of Julius II, whose devotions at the shrine of S. Maria del Popolo, adjacent to the gate, doubtless formed part of the ceremony. Julius's reverence for the Madonna del Popolo was given conspicuous physical expression in the transformation of the church into a mausoleum for his kin and court and a showpiece of new architectural and decorative ideas, including the deployment of a range of triumphal motifs.[24] The church itself, of course, had been rebuilt by Julius's uncle, Sixtus IV, and we may wonder if such a major project was not already connected with the role of the gate as a triumphal threshold into the city. Certainly the majority of pilgrims first set foot here on the sacred ground of Rome and could give thanks to the Madonna del Popolo for their safe arrival.

They could then penetrate the city along the Via Lata that, relatively broad and straight, continued the line of the Via Flaminia, passing under three triumphal arches on its way to the foot of the Capitoline hill (Spezzaferro 1973, 19, 37).[25] The Via Lata, then, had clear potential as a triumphal route, even if, like the Via Sacra, it was neglected in early humanist accounts of Roman triumphs.

At least one triumphal entrance into Rome by way of the Porta del Popolo is documented; it was a most important one, for it involved an apostle. In 1464, Pius II had the head of St. Andrew, rescued from the advancing Turks, brought to Rome. The ceremonies that marked the advent of the relic corresponded to the practices followed in more conventional receptions of distinguished personages: the head rested for a night outside the city; and on the next day, at a place marked by a shrine that stood until the nineteenth century, it was greeted by the pope and his retinue, who escorted it back into the lavishly decorated city and ultimately to the Vatican (Rubinstein 1967, 22–26). The event was of the greatest importance to Pius, and it is likely that the condition of the Via Flaminia, or at least that part of it along which the processional cortege passed, was reviewed. Little restoration may have been necessary, however, since Nicholas had already seen to the improvement of the road between the city gate and the Ponte Milvio, both of which were also restored (Lanciani 1902, 1:52; Romano 1948, 246). It is also likely that the pre-Sistine S. Maria del Popolo was among the forty station churches restored by Nicholas (Magnuson 1958, 58 with n.10).

It is significant, further, that the triumphal arrival of St. Andrew's head, like the arrival of Julius II in 1507, was associated with the repulsion of a foreign threat. Julius's concern was the impact in Italian affairs of the great European powers; Pius's the inexorable advance of the Turks. The elaborate reception of St. Andrew into the city of Saints Peter and Paul, extending the *concordia apostolorum* that underlay the special character of Rome refounded as a Christian city, was one of the stratagems employed by the politically astute Pius to remind the Christian peoples and their rulers of their duty to confront the infidel. The Via Flaminia connected the securely fortified city of Rome with the increasingly vulnerable Marchigian coast, from which Pius himself attempted to lead a seaborne military expedition against the Turks (Mitchell 1962, 255–267).

Nicholas V had not delayed to assert his concern for the expansion of Muslim power in the East, though it is true that the fall of Constantinople in 1453 injected a new sense of urgency. In addition, he was well aware of the importance of the Marchigian economy to the revenues of the Church and, quite often, to the provisioning of the city. It is not surprising, then, that Nicholas carried out a major reconstruction campaign on the Ponte Milvio (then known in the vernacular as the Ponte Molle) that carried the Flaminia, shortly after its junction with the Cassia, over the Tiber some five kilometers north of Rome (map 3; see Müntz 1878, 158; Lanciani 1902, 1:52; Pastor 1949, 172). The timber central arch was replaced by a masonry structure, and a strong tower was built at one end of the bridge. This later carried the arms of Calixtus III, Nicholas's successor, either because he completed it or because he wished, for whatever reason, to associate the bridge with his pontificate and his family, the Borgia. In any case, the bridge constituted a bulwark, perhaps largely of a symbolic kind, on the road from Rome to the east. And we can be sure that Nicholas, as was his custom, at least intended to display his insignia on the bridge, and probably did so.

Steeped as he was in the history and literature of Christian antiquity, Nicholas had good reason to focus attention on the bridge. Here and over the adjoining meadows was fought the battle in which Constantine, inspired by the vision of the cross, defeated Maxentius and gathered to himself the power to inaugurate the Christian empire (Keresztes 1981, 10–26). The bridge itself was old in Constantine's day and already carried important imperial associations, for it had been rebuilt by Augustus as part of his thorough restoration of the Via Flaminia. To mark the starting point of that great road, Augustus had adorned the Ponte Milvio with a triumphal arch (Suetonius, *Vita Augusti* 30.3–6; Kähler 1939, c.38; Scagliarini-Corlaita 1988, 66).

Though the arch had apparently disappeared without trace by the fifteenth century, it is possible that knowledge of it, transmitted by literary sources, affected the character of Nicholas's restoration and the signifying function assigned to the bridge. Certainly, by the early sixteenth century triumphal associations adhered to the bridge, which was used as the marshaling point for processional corteges, like that of Julius II in 1507 (Mitchell 1979, 114f.; cf. 129 on the return of Paul III from Nice in 1538). And it is perhaps significant that already in 1464, on his departure from Rome for Mantua, Pius II was escorted as far as the Ponte Milvio by a large crowd of Romans and clergy, who there left him to proceed with his selected companions, staff, and guards. Pius's return from his mission was explicitly likened by the pope himself to a classical triumph; he expressly mentions his entrance into Rome via the Porta del Popolo, and it is likely that he was met by the usual reception committee at the Ponte Milvio (Piccolomini 1984, 1:125f., 295f.). If so, the ceremonies that marked a ruler's departure and expressed the city's desire for his success and those that celebrated his victorious return were connected with the Ponte Milvio, giving it clear triumphal connotations, at the latest, by the third quarter of the fifteenth century.[26]

The Via Flaminia, after following the valleys of the upper Tiber and the Nera and traversing the mountainous spine of Italy, reaches the Adriatic at Fano and then follows the coast to Rimini (map 4). Just as Augustus had marked the inception of the road with a triumphal arch, so its termination at Rimini was marked by a further arch, which still exists (fig. 45). This was not constructed as a freestanding monument; rather it constituted an elaboration of a city gate, set between polygonal towers. Subsequently it served as the Porta Romana or Aurea of the medieval city, until the construction of a further wall system in the thirteenth century under the Malatesta rulers of Rimini (Gobbi and Sica 1982, 17, 47). The new wall, however, was for much of its length at no great distance from the older perimeter, and the Augustan arch remained an emphatic symbolic marker of the entrance of the Via Flaminia into the city. The original inscription on the arch is largely extant even today; it proclaims the arch's connection with the Via Flaminia, as with Augustus, the virtual re-founder of the city of Rimini (Mansuelli and Zuffa 1966, 688–690; Kähler 1939, c.411). All this would have been familiar to humanists who knew Rimini and the ancient history of the region. A further Augustan triumphal arch stood at Fano, commemorating the construction under Augustus of new city walls and marking the beginning of the short connecting road that led from the town to the Flaminia; this arch, too, was well known in the Renaissance and had prompted the impromptu but impassioned plea by Ciriaco d'Ancona to the citizens of Fano to strive, by means of the arch and its inscriptions, to understand the antiquity and true character of their city (Weiss 1969, 109). Ciriaco's visit, of 1448 or the following year, occurred when work on the Tempio Malatestiano at Rimini, which I discuss below, was already underway, shortly before the decision was made to incorporate a triumphal arch motif in the facade.

Nicholas's concern with the ecclesiastical province of the March was, at least initially, of a more practical nature. Here, as in the Patrimonium, territories were reclaimed or their occupation by feudal lords technically subject, as *vicarii*, to the Church was formalized. The March was an agriculturally rich province and a good source of fighting men; control of the province, then, and a fortiori of the Via Flaminia that linked it to Rome was of great political and economic importance for Nicholas (Toews 1968, 278f.; Pastor 1949, 61–63). It was clearly more than the mere concern to escape the plague, as certain unkind critics alleged, that impelled Nicholas on wide-ranging peregrinations in the March and adjoining ecclesiastical territories in the summers of 1449 and 1450 (Pastor 1949, 85–87). In 1449 he appeared at short notice in the strategic and economically important town of Fabriano, whose long-established paper industry may well have been of interest to the papal court and administration as a major consumer of the product. He came to Fabriano partly, no doubt, since it was free of the plague that was raging elsewhere, but it is clear that a major factor in his decision to adopt the town as a preferred summer residence, if not to visit it in the first place, was the political situation there.

Fabriano had long been ruled by the Chiavelli family, but the people had recently risen against their masters, massacring most of the Chiavelli and expelling the survivors. The goal of the Fabrianesi, as of many similar communities, was *libertas ecclesiastica*, direct rule by the Church excluding control and exploitation by local tyrants like the Chiavelli or Francesco Sforza, whose depredations had left a strong impression. As a result of the violent termination of the Chiavelli *signoria*, the city palace they had occupied and from which they had ruled the city now reverted to the Church. Nicholas found, then, in Fabriano extensive and uncontested accommodations and the fervent support of a grateful population, for whom the presence of a pope in their midst provided a guarantee of their own political aspirations. Nicholas responded by returning to Fabriano in 1450 and initiating some interesting if poorly documented building projects (see chapter 4), perhaps in the unfulfilled hope that this would not be his last visit to the town.

Among the business transacted in Fabriano in the summer of 1450 was the pressing matter of the formalization of papal policy toward the rule of the Malatesta brothers, Sigismondo and Domenico (known as Malatesta Novello), in large areas of the March and Romagna. Nominally vicars of the Church, the Malatesta and their forebears had built a strong and independent power base at the edge of the papal states and bounded to the north by territory under Venetian control or influence (Sassi 1951, 175–178; Ricci 1925, 218–220; Jones 1974, 203f.). In addition, Sigismondo had emerged as one of the most effective *condottieri* of the period, though hardly as one of the most dependable (Jones 1974, 176–179). Nicholas had already shown signs of favor to Sigismondo before 1450 (Ricci 1925, 209–216; Mitchell 1978, 74f.), and may well have preferred to enlist him as an ally, rather than attempt to dislodge him from his possessions along the Adriatic littoral; Nicholas's policy, then, was the opposite of that of Pius II, whose later campaign against and vituperation of Sigismondo are a major theme of his *Commentaries*.

When Sigismondo and his brother made their way to Fabriano in 1450, however, Sigismondo at least was under a cloud, for the allegation was now widespread in Italy that he had been responsible for and even participated in the abduction and sadistic rape of an aristocratic German lady, seized during her Jubilee pilgrimage. Nicholas had proclaimed the Jubilee and shown particular concern for the welfare and security of pilgrims; significantly, he chose to disregard the rumors, the truth of which it is impossible to determine, though the charge came back to haunt Sigismondo in his later, sadder years. Indeed, the pope conspicuously favored Sigismondo, recognizing and even extending his and his brother's vicariates and legitimizing Sigismondo's bastard sons and, as an implicit corollary, his dynastic aspirations. The rule of the Malatesta, then, was viewed by Nicholas not as a fait accompli to be reluctantly accepted, but as an important element of his policy toward the March and Romagna (Jones 1974, 202–204).

Whatever the truth of the rumors of Sigismondo's complicity in the rape of the German lady, the story was widely believed. The credibility of the story suggests beliefs not only about Sigismondo's moral character, but also about the extent of his power in the regions of central Italy through which the pilgrimage roads ran. It is even likely that Sigismondo had been charged by Nicholas to see to the security of the major routes through the areas under his control, and that his enemies, who were numerous, took advantage of this to discredit him (even though the lady was seized at Verona, far indeed from Sigismondo's territory). In any case, Sigismondo himself celebrated Holy Year in conspicuous fashion: on the church of S. Francesco in Rimini, which he had recently decided to reinterpret as a personal and dynastic monument, the date 1450 occurs with almost obsessive frequency, though the building was not officially consecrated until 1452.[27] The date appears also on numerous commemorative medals, notably those showing the building in an ideally completed state, with a grand dome rising beyond a facade organized around central superimposed arches (Pasini 1983, 82f., 140–145). The medals may have been struck later and, like the building itself, may involve a retrospective chronological reference, but in any case they mark Holy Year as a major point in Sigismondo's career and imply his and the pope's close alliance at that time.

The building history of the Tempio Malatestiano (fig. 46), as S. Francesco came to be known, is complex and not yet fully clarified. Sigismondo's original conception (1447) had evidently been the insertion of chapels into the old church, one dedicated to his own name saint, St. Sigismund (Ricci 1925, 209), another endowed by his mistress, Isotta, in remembrance of her lost child, the fruit of her affair with Sigismondo that had begun the previous year (Salmi 1951, 157; Mitchell 1978, 74). No doubt the two chapel projects were coordinated. The idea of the total transformation of the building, with Malatesta tombs in the interior and those of courtiers along the flanks, apparently developed in a series of phases between c. 1448 and 1454; the date and scope of Alberti's contribution to the project, in particular, is not documented. Mitchell (1978), 72–84, has argued that Alberti became involved only in 1453, after Sigismondo's victory at Vada (the date 1453, however, does not appear on the inscription-studded building). Sigismondo's triumphal entry into Rimini on that occasion, the apogee of his career, may not have occasioned, as Mitchell proposes, a rethinking of the project, but merely a reinterpretation of a design already making conspicuous use of triumphal imagery that, I will argue, was particularly appropriate in the conditions of 1450. There is no doubt, on the other hand, that the working out of a *concetto* of the exterior of the Tempio, which is all that can be claimed for 1450, took much time, especially with work proceeding on the interior and with Alberti himself at a distance.[28]

An early date of the *concetto* of the Tempio is circumstantially suggested by the connections of both patron and architect with the court of the humanist prince of Ferrara, Leonello d'Este, whose esteem for Sigismondo is surely indicated by the series of medals made for the latter by Leonello's chief court artist, Pisanello. The medals themselves anticipate the Tempio in their employment of the formal devices of the new visual culture in the service of individual and dynastic aspirations and authority. Both integrate into their formal vocabularies the traditional heraldic and emblematic imagery that appears with particular insistence, even by the standards of the day, on the buildings and other commissions of Sigismondo and his brother (Pasini 1983, 82f., 140–142; Mitchell 1978, 73, 77).

The connection between architectural patronage and the production of medals, however marked the difference of scale and materials, is brought into relief especially by the image of the Castel Sismondo, the castle built by Sigismondo in Rimini, in Piero della Francesca's fresco of 1451 in the Tempio (fig. 47). Here the castle appears, as if on a medal, constricted within a circular field (for the possible cosmic and political significance of this see Lavin 1984, 27–44). Mitchell has drawn attention to the emblematic quality of the fortress, which had been completed in 1446; his arguments apply a fortiori to this image, a case of a building as emblem within a building replete with emblems and itself fraught with emblematic resonances. If so, the emphasis on the castle in the view of Rimini in the Chapel of the Planets in the Tempio (constituting no less an identifying sign of the city than the Roman bridge that also appears in the view) comes into greater prominence, as does the image of the castle (presumably the Castel Sismondo) that the documents, not unambiguously, indicate was to be placed on the facade of the Tempio.[29] In a sense, then, the Tempio, for all the unprecedented audacity of its design, can be understood within a current of concerns traceable through the 1440s.

Whatever earlier meetings they might have had, it is plausible that Sigismondo and Alberti came into contact in Fabriano in 1450. No document places Alberti there in that year, but there is no more likely period for the visit to the area indicated by personal observations recorded in the *De re aedificatoria*. The campaign of demolition and reconstruction initiated by Nicholas in Fabriano, apparently involving the spatial reordering of the piazza in front of the papal palace, recalls Albertian precepts for urban open spaces and the principles behind those precepts; unfortunately, the structures around the piazza were subsequently rebuilt and Nicholas's project can no longer be securely reconstructed from the existing evidence.[30] If, in the absence of proof, we accept for a moment the hypothesis of an Albertian intervention in Fabriano, the proximity of this project and that, securely attributed to Alberti, at Rimini raises the question of the relations of one project to the other and, more significantly, of both to Nicholas's policies and interests. Indeed, the close and mutual relations that seem to have obtained between the pope and the *condottiere* imply—even without an Albertian project in Fabriano—that the conception of the Tempio Malatestiano should be interpreted in the light of papal concerns.

Clearly such a reading of the Tempio runs counter to the familiar account of the building as a direct expression of Sigismondo's personal, dynastic, and especially amatory interests, but this owes much of its force to the intemperate denunciation by Pius II of the Tempio as a "temple of heathen devil worshipers," suggesting that it was dedicated to Isotta herself (Ricci 1925, 225). But we have no reason to suppose that the original conception of the Tempio would have elicited from Nicholas a response similar to that of Pius some ten years later.

The main idea in the facade of the Tempio (fig. 46) is clearly the allusion to the triumphal arch of Augustus in Rimini, a structure that had already appeared as a sign of Rimini on seals and medals, at times associated with the Roman bridge (Pasini 1983, 94; Lavin 1984, 37). At first sight, then, the reference is local and can be subsumed within the context of Malatesta propaganda. On the other hand, the single-bay motif of the arch of Augustus is here expanded into a triple-bay arrangement recalling famous examples in Rome, notably the arch of Constantine.[31] The most appropriate site, in Alberti's opinion, for a triumphal arch was at the entrance of the forum of a city, as the center of government and of religious and ceremonial activity (Alberti 1966a, 2:717f.). The Tempio, accordingly, entered through a formal configuration immediately reminiscent of the city gate, becomes an emblem of the city itself; at the same time it serves as a kind of sacral forum, introducing the worshiper, across a space richly elaborated with references to Malatesta's concerns, to the great domed space planned to rise beyond. Here, if Alberti was true to his own principles, an austere and celestial dignity would have succeeded the various and rich visual stimuli of the nave, dominating the latter as the temple of the city god provided a dominant, culminating element in the forum aligned before it. After all, in fulfillment of a vow made by Sigismondo in his recent campaigns, the building was dedicated in 1450 to God and the city (Pasini 1983, 94; Lavin 1984, 7; Mitchell 1978, 81): these are indeed the referential poles of the Tempio.

The conception of the Tempio as a Valhalla for Sigismondo and his court and as a monument to his patronage of the new culture (represented both by the physical remains and the works of its practitioners) may have been formed at the outset. In any case, the design solution, at least for the tombs of court literati in arched niches on the exterior of the building, bears the mark of Alberti's ideas, for he excluded tombs from the interior of churches, no doubt in view of the Roman practice of burying their dead along the streets leading outward from the city gates, often in structures of considerable architectural elaboration and sheer size (Alberti 1966a, 2:666f.).[32] While the motif of the tombs set in arches may have been suggested by the Roman aqueducts or the Mausoleum of Theodoric (at nearby Ravenna) as it then was (Ricci 1925, 20, 280; Mitchell 1978, 99), the architectural treatment of the flanks of the Tempio surely establishes the idea of a street of tombs, implying a processional reading of the successive tombs and their inscriptions by persons moving along the flanks of the building before entering it.

The processional aspect is crucial here, for the Tempio was established by Sigismondo as a pilgrimage shrine, recognized as such by the pope (Ricci 1925, 221); Sigismondo's own act of obeisance before St. Sigismund, painted with remarkable verisimilitude by Piero della Francesca in the "royal antechamber" to the chapel dedicated to that saint (Lavin 1985, 63; the space is generally known as the Chapel of the Relics), eternalizes the necessarily temporally limited worship of the anticipated pilgrims, for whom it also provides a model of proud and courtly religious devotion (fig. 47). Still more important in this context is the resonance of the facade itself. With the christianization of the Empire through Constantine—and again more directly in the Holy Year of 1450, so emphatically inscribed on the Tempio—the Via Flaminia itself became a pilgrimage road, a major artery to the shrines of the martyrs in Rome (cf. Partridge and Starn 1980, 85). If the Augustan arch of Rimini had framed the ancient Via Flaminia, referring back to the road's beginning at the triumphal arch on the Ponte Milvio, so under Nicholas, whose building patronage was compared by contemporaries to that of Augustus (Stinger 1985, 247),[33] and who was, it should be emphasized, the titular lord of Rimini, the Tempio Malatestiano was established as a framing device for a Christian Via Flaminia. As such it surely recalled the inception of the road at the newly rebuilt Ponte Milvio with its associations both with the first Christian emperor and with the emperor in whose reign Christ was born.

Conspicuous on both the exterior and interior of the Tempio is the motif of the elephant. This was a traditional Malatesta heraldic motif, but it had hitherto been used only as a helmet crest. Now it flourished on buildings of Sigismondo and his brother, notably the splendid new library at Cesena, and on medals (we may assume that it appeared also on less durable objects) as a fully fleshed emblematic device, in some cases complete with motto (Baum and Arndt 1956, 1240; Pasini 1983, 137–139, 144f., and figs. 155, 157). It is likely that many of the legendary moral attributes of the elephant, on which the later emblem books would dilate, were already suggested here, since the ancient sources were well known. On the other hand, more specific references may have been involved. The use by the Malatesta of the elephant may have been suggested originally by the elephant carved on the keystone of the Arch of Augustus at Fano, a city that had long been ruled by the Malatesta (Ricci 1925, 322). Elephants in a triumphal context, as in the triumph of Pompey recorded by Pliny, were especially appropriate in the commemoration of a victory over a territory associated with elephants (Baum and Arndt 1956, 1222; Wellman 1905, cc.2255–2258). Augustus set up four obsidian elephants, evidently the team of an actual or suggested *quadriga*, in the Temple of Concord at Rome, as Pliny relates; they alluded, no doubt, to his victory over Cleopatra, Queen of Egypt, which enabled him to establish concord within the Empire.[34] And many of the coins issued under Augustus to celebrate the restoration of the road system of Italy, especially the Via Flaminia, carried images of triumphal arches surmounted by statues of elephants drawing chariots; it is possible that these were known in the fifteenth century.[35]

Ricci (1925), 315, has suggested that the black stone and high shine of the four sculpted elephants set up in Holy Year in the Chapel of St. Sigismund in the Tempio (fig. 48) allude to Augustus's four elephants of obsidian, a hard and shiny black stone. If so, the elephants corroborate my hypothesis of the connections of the Tempio with Nicholas, the new Augustus, concerned both with internal concord and with the external threat from the East, specifically from Egypt. In the 1440s, indeed, the sultan of Egypt applied pressure on the Christian kingdom of Cyprus and on Rhodes, stronghold of the hospitallers; treaties were signed, but the Egyptians may well have seemed in the long term as dangerous an enemy in the eastern Mediterranean as the Ottoman Turks, at least until the accession of Mehmet the Conqueror in 1451, in the Balkans.[36] Moreover, there is a contemporary documented case of the association of elephants with the crusade idea; on February 17, 1453, a masque in Lille designed to rouse the Burgundian aristocracy against the infidel featured the grieving figure of the Church atop an elephant automaton (Heckscher 1947, 167). The reference was perhaps both to the eastern threat and to the desired triumph over the East.

Such connotations of the design of the Tempio Malatestiano may illuminate certain curious aspects of its construction history. The extant documents indicate various sources of stone and other materials used in the project. It is well known that an especially scandalous source was the venerable abbey of S. Apollinare in Classe, near Ravenna, still famous for its Byzantine mosaics. The government of Ravenna, nominally a papal city but from 1441 ceded officially to Venice, protested to the Doge of Venice, Francesco Foscari, who in 1449 took steps to halt the depredations. Sigismondo's response, as recorded in a document of 1450, was to pay 200 golden ducats for the restoration of the abbey (Ricci 1925, 211f., 586). But this was perhaps not the end of the matter. A loose, unfortunately undated sheet discovered by Ricci in the city archive of Ravenna contains a remarkable list of grievances compiled by an unknown person about a series of losses suffered by the abbey at the hands of Sigismondo (ibid., 212, 238 n.21, 536–587); though the author's outrage peaks at the mention of marble panels stripped from the abbey's walls and carried off to Rimini in a hundred carts, the list also includes such trivial items as towels and bedding and accuses Sigismondo of rustling the abbey's flocks. The blame is directed at the holder of the *commenda* of the abbey, Cardinal Filippo Calandrini, who is effectively accused of complicity. Ricci notes that Calandrini received the *commenda* of the abbey only in 1454, after the death of the abbot who appears in the 1450 document, and supposes that the accusation against Calandrini arose from mere confusion on the part of the author, writing some time after the events (Calandrini is named as Cardinal Bishop of Porto, an appointment he received only in 1471).

It is possible, however, that Calandrini's association with the abbey predated 1454. He may, for instance, have been appointed *commendatarius* designate by his brother, who was, though Ricci fails to note the fact, Nicholas V himself (C. Gennaro in *DBI* 16 [1973]: 451f.). Nicholas had given Calandrini considerable responsibilities in the region: in 1448 he was appointed governor of Spoleto, a strategic town on the route from Rome to the March and Romagna, and in 1450 legate of the March.[37] This office, crucial in the period of Nicholas's closest concern for Fabriano and other Marchigian communities, must have brought him into frequent contact with Sigismondo or his emissaries, and there is no reason to suppose that such contacts were not of a friendly nature.

Among the towns officially consigned to Sigismondo by Nicholas in 1450 was the small and ancient port of Senigallia on the Adriatic coast of the March, at the time in sorry decline. Sigismondo had already controlled the town for some years and had set about reviving it (Caravale and Caracciolo 1978, 61). Apart from construction of fortifications, considerable rebuilding was carried out in the town itself, reordered, it seems, according to the observed traces of the gridded ancient layout (Ortolani and Alfieri 1953, 166–171). On the other hand, Sigismondo had the cathedral of Senigallia demolished to provide building stone for the Tempio Malatestiano, presumably after the decision of 1450 to expand the scale of the project (Touring Club Italiano 1962, 100; I have not found the source for this, but see no reason for its fabrication). This is exactly the type of high-handed and even irreligious act that conforms to the image of Sigismondo diffused by his enemies. It is probable, nevertheless, that he had received papal approval for removing stone from a community that had declined too far to warrant a cathedral: indeed, Sigismondo's new town occupied only a fraction of the original site. Once again, then, papal and Malatesta interests and policies appear to coincide.

No account of the sign value of the Tempio Malatestiano or of the circumstances of the formulation of its design can ignore the original and continuing function of the building. Sigismondo's elaborations and additions notwithstanding, the Tempio remained a Franciscan convent, and its official title, as we meet it in Nicholas's bulls and similar documents, continued to be S. Francesco. The other great Malatesta architectural project of the middle of the century, Malatesta Novello's splendid library at Cesena, was also built within a Franciscan convent, though it was intended as a public resource and responsibility for its administration was charged to the town government (Pasini 1983, 106–117, 160). Courtly humanism and provincial Franciscanism might seem an unnatural graft, but we know of at least one friar who moved easily between the two worlds. The dialogues of Fra Giovanni de' Cocchi on the immortality of the soul are imagined as occurring at a banquet at Sigismondo's court; the richly illuminated dedication copy of c. 1455, once a treasure of the library of S. Francesco at Rimini, contains fine ornamental borders replete with Malatesta insignia, while the frontispiece shows Fra Giovanni presenting his book to Sigismondo (ibid., 116–118, fig. 121). The Franciscan community, then, was at least not entirely external to Sigismondo's cultural policy, still less opposed to it.

Whatever the unorthodoxy of the architectural and sculptural motifs of the Tempio, it is likely that the religious orthodoxy of the friars was firmly maintained, especially as the radical Franciscans known as *fraticelli* had made inroads in the hardscrabble hill towns of the region, arousing Nicholas V's concern. In 1450 a number of *fraticelli* went to trial in Fabriano, presumably during the pope's sojourn, on charges of heresy. Some went to the stake in Fabriano itself; others were sent to Rome for further investigation and, no doubt, execution (Sassi 1955b, 15–17; Toews 1968, 279 n.61).[38] The *via dolorosa* of these unfortunates lay, we may assume, largely along the Via Flaminia, and the opportunity was surely taken to impress the people of the communities along the road with the retribution promised to the condemned men in this and the next world for their heresy. If so, the theatrical mis-en-scène of the execution of Stefano Porcari in Rome a few years later provides a comparable example of a well-staged public punishment as a deterrent to apostasy, in this case of a political nature. Nicholas's response to lapses of religious orthodoxy, however, was generally milder, and he countered the menace of the *fraticelli* in the March and elsewhere mainly by the dispatch of charismatic preachers (Zippel 1904, 32; De Angelis 1621, 142; Infessura 1890, 47).[39]

The work on the piazza at Fabriano—the same, perhaps, where the fire consumed the group of heretics—involved especially the clarification of the space in front of the papal palace and the adjoining Franciscan convent, and the formalization of the relationship of the two buildings, as far as can be determined, by the use of continuous porticoes (Mack 1982). In Rome, Nicholas associated himself with Saints Peter, Stephen, and Lawrence and with the Fathers of the Church; in Fabriano and Assisi, where his close concern for the physical condition of the greatest of all Franciscan shrines was noted by Canensi (Miglio 1975, 231), Nicholas stood at the side of St. Francis, whose authority and charisma were used as a sword against those who perhaps most faithfully followed his teaching and to legitimize the rule of the pope's Malatesta allies.

The Sense of the Region: Contemporary Conceptualizations

The foregoing argument suggests, at very least, that a reading of the Tempio Malatestiano that aspires to completeness requires a reference to Nicholas's regional concerns and policies. But we should not think of such policies as formulated in advance of artistic production that merely reflected or expressed them; they did not flow unmediated from the doctrines of papal supremacy elaborated at Nicholas's court. Rather the conception and development of the Albertian design of the Tempio proceeded contemporaneously with the establishment of Nello da Bologna at the nerve center of Nicholas's administration of Rome and its wider hinterland, with the clarification of regional, urban, and even neighborhood space over which he presided, and with the appearance of models of environmental organization crystallized in the Manettian Borgo project. We should see the creation of this extraordinary building, then, as a contributory factor in the working out of political strategies in which cultural and especially architectural programs played a major role; more narrowly it was fundamental, together perhaps with the work commenced at Fabriano, for the architectural and broadly urbanistic ideas operative in Nicholan Rome in the years following the Jubilee.

Such ideas, needless to say, are associated especially with Alberti, whose authorship of the design of the Tempio Malatestiano, even if documentation were lacking, would be assured by its complexity and ingenuity. Alberti's theoretical work on architecture and urbanism was doubtless well advanced in 1450—it may well have received a particular impetus from the hopes raised by Nicholas's accession—but there is no evidence that Alberti had yet been implicated in any of the pope's building projects, except perhaps in a limited capacity as a technical expert; nor had these projects yet acquired a specifically urbanistic dimension in terms, at least, of a unitary conception (Burroughs 1982a). Contemporaries noted that the Jubilee constituted a watershed in the availability of resources for construction (Westfall 1974a, 171; Pastor 1949, 102), and we may suppose that a quantitative change of scale also involved qualitative shifts. In any case, the direct or indirect impact of Alberti on some at least of Nicholas's projects after 1450 can be assumed and in some cases proven. The question arises, then, of the echoes in Alberti's theoretical writings of the spatial conceptions that appear to underlie Nicholas's urban and regional policies after 1450, and of the associated conception of the rhetorical and performative dimension of architectural and environmental reform. I shall return in chapter 7 to the vexed question of the date of (at least provisional) completion of Alberti's treatise and its chronological relationship to Nicholas's projects. Whatever the truth of this, however, it would be surely mistaken to suggest that Alberti either supplied paradigms to a receptive milieu or, alternatively, abstracted from a historical situation in process; the model of primacy should be replaced by that of mutuality.

Both the concentric and the radial paradigms of urban space play important roles, in different ways, in Alberti's treatise. The lofty city of Ecbatana was surrounded by no fewer than seven circles of walls, Alberti tells us, and Carthage by three (Alberti 1966a, 1:294 [IV.iii], 108 [II.iv]; he repeats Herodotus's confusion of the many-terraced ziggurat with the ancient Near Eastern city). Though he notes that multiple wall systems were not typical in antiquity, Alberti gives the conception particular emphasis, adopting it for his own purposes. He proposes, on the explicit basis of sociopolitical criteria and normative concerns, a concentric model of city form in which different social groups or classes are assigned to walled-off concentric zones, with the citadel connected to the different wall systems and ensuring easy egress from the city; this is the Tyrant's city discussed in chapter 5. The separation of the classes advocated here by Alberti is designed to inhibit the interclass feudal loyalty systems that bedeviled, as Alberti had no doubt observed, the political life of Rome and marked the physical aspect of the city and countryside. The radial model of city form is introduced in the same passage but discounted as inappropriate for the kind of social engineering that Alberti has in mind (ibid., 334–337 [V.i]).

Elsewhere in the *De re aedificatoria*, on the other hand, Alberti's conception of a hierarchical system of communication within both urban and regional space and unifying the two is unambiguously grounded in a radial spatial model. This is clearest in his lengthy discussions of roads, which he sees as generating and ensuring regional coherence across city boundaries. Alberti's classification and analysis of road types is carried out chiefly in two passages of the *De re aedificatoria*, once in the fourth book in the context of city form and infrastructure (ibid., 302f.), and again in the eighth book in the course of a discussion of the ornamentation, to use Albertian language, of secular buildings and facilities in the public realm (ibid., 2:706–711). In the former, accordingly, functional characteristics are emphasized, while in the latter Alberti dwells on ceremonial and expressive aspects of the environment, and indicates the role of streets and their architectural framing in processes of ideological mediation. In both cases, as is characteristic of the treatise, the discussion is both historical and descriptive, on the one hand, and prescriptive on the other, consistent with Alberti's conception of social or historical analysis as the comprehension of fundamental factors constituting a system not unlike a code of law (Mühlmann 1981, esp. 54–67).

Alberti's discussion of cities and their necessary and/or appropriate elements emphasizes, needless to say, the bounded quality of urban space: city walls frame a piece of territory and mark it off from the surrounding area.[40]

Nevertheless, I will argue that Alberti's analysis of street types clearly indicates the correspondence of the bounded and framed area within the walls to the area outside in terms of contiguity, structural resemblance, and the relationship of part to whole (since the region includes the city). Several commentators have noted, indeed, though without sufficient emphasis, Alberti's concern with the city region as a whole (Germann 1980, 60).[41]

I will begin with the fourth book. Here Alberti distinguishes three main types of roads: military roads, secondary roads, and those of ceremonial character. By military roads Alberti evidently means the consular roads of the Romans, which still dominated the network of long-distance thoroughfares in Italy; secondary roads branch off the main roads, may be straight or curved, and often have a semiprivate character; ceremonial roads, finally, are defined by their role in providing access to major religious or secular buildings or sites, and are assimilated by Alberti to clearly ceremonial bounded urban spaces, the fora. All three kinds of road occur both in urban and rural areas, though Alberti notes that in the case of secondary routes different terms apply to urban and rural examples. Alberti's analysis penetrates beneath the level of ancient linguistic usage, for all his concern to reintroduce the latter, in the Latin of his treatise, into contemporary discourse. The distinction, then, of major and minor routes, together forming a branching pattern around a central spine, is common to city and country, though in the latter a certain laxness is admissible: in larger urban centers, at least, major streets should be straight, in Alberti's view, while in the country curving stretches may on occasion be appropriate.

Less obvious than Alberti's distinction of major and minor roads, which corresponded to late medieval usage, is that of two kinds of major road or street, drawn essentially in terms of their character as relatively framed or unframed spaces. Ceremonial streets, which Alberti discusses at length in the eighth book of his treatise, exist as such by virtue of their relationship to a particular place to which they lead; their forum-like quality, however, which Alberti emphasizes, involves lateral framing, which may take the form of buildings, porticoes, or trees. Some secondary streets, moreover, are assimilated, to a degree, to the category of ceremonial streets, for Alberti stresses the prevalence and convenience in an urban situation of dead-end streets that anticipate the privacy and enclosed quality of the mansions to which they give access. The framed quality of these small-scale ceremonial streets, leading only to the houses of affluent private citizens, is such as to inhibit rather than, as in the case of ceremonial streets proper, facilitate and encourage the approach of the uninvited. This implies a distinction between a withdrawn and sober lifestyle, which might be characterized as bourgeois, and the magnificent display of social and political elites and their representatives.

Military roads, on the other hand, are relatively unbounded; they lead, according to Alberti's rather vague formulation, into the provinces ("in provinciam"). He recommends that such roads, as they traverse rural territory, should be raised above the level of the surrounding countryside and should not be adjacent to landscape features that might obscure the view from the road over the surrounding terrain. This is partly for security—since brigands would thereby be deprived of opportunities for easy ambush—but also for the aesthetic pleasure and restorative effects enjoyed by travelers as a series of varied landscapes unrolls before their eyes. This open quality of military roads is in marked contrast with the framed character of ceremonial roads, even when they lead outside the city (for, like military roads, ceremonial roads traverse both urban and rural space). Alberti mentions, for instance, the colonnaded processional ways that once led from Rome to the basilicas of Saints Peter and Paul, but in most of his examples the framed quality of the route is architectural only in metaphorical terms and may comprise lines or groves of trees, as in the case of the sacred way from the city of Knossos to the cave of Jupiter in the nearby mountain.

The distinction of military and ceremonial roads, however, is not absolute and appears to draw its validity from a historical or rather originary system of categories. At times, we find Alberti working with an apparently general conception of a major urban thoroughfare as framed, in accordance with the dictates of *decorum*, by uniform buildings, corresponding in height and alignment and optimally fronted by porticoes. Moreover, military roads are themselves described as partaking of some of the framed character and even of the ceremonial function of the other category. In his eighth book Alberti distinguishes regional thoroughfares that lead to a city and those that lead to the coast. In the one case the road is bounded by a harbor, in the other by a city gate (the distinction presumably plays on the similarity of the Latin words *portus* and *porta*), in both cases providing opportunities, though this is not here expressly noted by Alberti, for architectural elaboration and other eye-catching elements.

Still more remarkable is Alberti's ascription of ceremonial and monumental character to parts of major streets, at least in an urban setting, whatever their origin and function. He defines such crucial elements of the ancient city as the forum or bridges not in terms of distinct and intrinsic qualities, but as incidents on a continuum represented by a major street; such elements stand out through the relative elaboration of the architecture and the concentration of commemorative, exhortatory, or—more generally—rhetorical elements, notably triumphal arches. And as if he wanted to avoid a dichotomous opposition of forum and mere street, Alberti introduces the *trivium*, which he defines as an element midway between them. The major street of a city, then, is a concatenation of bilaterally symmetrical spaces of varying width and formality, characterized by more or less elaborate framing motifs and thresholds.

In this case, certainly, Alberti's subject is the major urban thoroughfare. Crucial in his habits of thought, as in Renaissance culture in general, is the use of analogy. There is no more familiar example of this than the assertion, which we read in Alberti as in many other writers of the period, that the house is a small city and the city a large house; here the analogy connects the discourse of architectural and urban form and values to the wider context of the microcosm (Alberti 1966a, 1:338 [V.ii], 2:764 [IX.i]). It is legitimate to stress, therefore, the correspondence of Alberti's discussion of successive spaces and experiences along an urban axis to the variety that he recommends, evidently both as an architectural and as an experiential category, in the layout of a house.[42] Similarly, the idea of marking the entrance into a dining room with giant sculpted figures flanking the portal may be related to the function of a triumphal arch as marking the entrance of a forum (ibid., 2:786f. [IX.i]). Though Alberti never spells it out, his text surely suggests an analogical relationship between a thoroughfare traversing a region toward a gate marking the entrance into a city, on the one hand, and on the other hand a road within a city that leads toward a triumphal arch marking the entrance into a forum. Indeed, Alberti himself notes that triumphal arches originated as city gates that survived the demolition of the wall systems to which they once belonged, when these became obsolete with the expansion of the city and the erection of new walls. We may regard the forum and city alike, therefore, as concentrations of devices of representative and symbolic display within a larger area. And we may note that implicit in Alberti's account of the origin of the triumphal arch is a model of historically determined concentricity suggesting Bruni's encomium of Florence, which may in its schematism have provided a negative model for Alberti.

Alberti's sense of the region and the analogical habits of mind that underlie it are most clearly evident, however, in his famous discussion of the villa. This, he maintains, constitutes a mean between the extremes of urban and rural life, combining the advantages of both and set in a suburban area that mediates between city and country. Indeed, these terms lose their contrastive aspect and begin to merge, and Alberti even notes the possibility of introducing some characteristics of rural—or at least suburban—life into the city itself (ibid., 1:432f. [V.18]). The villa has intrinsic qualities that immediately suggest analogies with larger and more complex settlement forms; it is defined by what it is both related to and distinct from, the city. It is, notably, an ornament of the thoroughfare that approaches it, traversing urban and rural space, and from which it is visible, though Alberti emphasizes the desirability of siting a villa at a distance from the nearest main road and on a higher elevation. Beyond the effect on invited guests, then, the villa contributes to the visual pleasures of passersby on their way to or from the city. The landscape of villas envisaged by Alberti as an extensive suburban zone forms, therefore, a unified region, apparent to travelers on the roads radiating from the city at its core, but experienced in a full sense only perhaps by those affluent or fortunate enough to own a villa, and able to enact in their regular routines the coherence of the region fundamental in Alberti's account.[43]

Though none of Alberti's contemporaries, finally, could match the subtlety and analytical intelligence of his ruminations on the categories of social life and their physical expressions, the theme of regional space plays an important role in the writings of at least one other author in Alberti's literary milieu. In a letter of late 1453 Flavio Biondo, the noted antiquarian and historian who had been out of favor with Nicholas V, noted that the pope was reading, apparently with approval, his recently completed work, the *Italia illustrata*: Biondo had dedicated the book to Nicholas and clearly hoped that it might bring about a revival of his fortunes. He seems to have been disappointed in his hopes, as he was soon to set about expunging references to Nicholas V and his court from his book (Nogara 1927, 217). The *Italia illustrata* was written as a sequel to the earlier *Roma instaurata*, a most important example of early humanistic antiquarian literature, which described the ancient city of Rome as it could be reconstructed from various sources (Weiss 1969, 68–70). In the later work, Biondo moved from the scale of a single city to that of the whole peninsula, which he discussed region by region. In his magisterial work on Italian Renaissance historiography, Eric Cochrane asserts that Biondo began the *Italia illustrata* after his departure from Rome in 1448 (Cochrane 1981, 40). On the other hand, as Cochrane surmises, Biondo's discussion of Lazio may have been designed as a separate study and dedicated to Cardinal Prospero Colonna. Such an account of the region surrounding Rome and its antiquities is likely to have followed directly after Biondo's study of the city itself, and may well have been under way before Biondo's temporary abandonment of Rome, at a time when he and Alberti alike enjoyed the patronage of Cardinal Colonna, as Biondo himself tells us (Weiss 1969, 108, 112–114; see note 4 above).

Biondo's text is unlikely to contain reflections of ideas current in circles close to Nicholas and possibly operative in architectural projects in the crucial years around 1450; after all, Biondo was largely absent from Rome at the time and anyway lacked the pope's support. All that can be claimed is that the expansion of Biondo's antiquarian interests from an urban to a regional dimension is likely to be related to Alberti's concerns, while it may also have contributed to the process of clarification of regional topography that I have associated, though devoid of antiquarian overtones, with the activity of Nello da Bologna. Alberti's researches, on the other hand, are crucial. He was allied, as I have demonstrated, with various figures implicated in different ways in architectural or urbanistic projects in Nicholan Rome, and there were various conduits by which his ideas could filter through to those in charge of the administration of building projects as of other sectors, or by which Alberti could learn of their concerns and interests. I posit, then, an intellectually flexible Alberti, open to varied and subtle shifts in the world around him and to material that might not, as I will argue in the following chapter, be sanctioned by classical hierarchies of values. And it is ironic that the clarification and comprehension of territorial structures that I have associated with Alberti's influence should have led already in Nicholas's pontificate to the schematization of perceived patterns in urban space, and to the articulation of a formal vocabulary amenable to—if it did not encourage—imposition in other contexts as a mystification of existing conditions, concentrating all value in a privileged spatial diagram within which a theater of power could be realized.

Connecting and Dividing:
The River Tiber and the Urban Policies of Nicholas V

The symbolic connection of the city of Rome with its river, the Tiber (map 2), has always been related to more material forms of dependence (Lombardo 1978; Palermo 1979; D'Onofrio 1980). Never was this more true than in the later medieval period, when the river constituted the main source of drinking water for the majority of the population that clustered in the low-lying and unhealthy areas adjoining its banks. As we have seen, the deliberate destruction of the aqueducts, only slowly and haltingly made good in the Renaissance period and later, made such a settlement pattern inevitable. And if the river was convenient for the drawing of water—as doubtless also for the bathing of bodies and the washing of clothes—it was equally convenient for the disposal of wastes, and as such was a major factor in the frequent outbreaks of pestilence.

Directly or indirectly, numerous Romans owed their livelihood to the river and worked in trades indissolubly linked with it. Water carriers filled their containers at the river and hawked their wares through the thirsty streets, while some of the fish sold in the markets of the city (notably at S. Angelo in Pescheria and S. Celso) came from the Tiber. The thriving tanning and leather-processing trades used the river to carry away their noisome effluents and waste, although the efficient performance of this function by the river reflected the enactment and efficacy of statutory provisions rather than the place of the Tiber in the topography of the city (Romano 1941, 5).

The river, too, so vital for the life of the citizens, was often a cause or companion of their deaths. Fatal brawls were not uncommon in the city, and it was easy to dispose of inconvenient corpses in the river. For unwanted children the river might provide a death by water, kinder than by starvation or disease; the care of young children rescued from the water was one of the original functions of the Hospital of S. Spirito in Borgo, whose site near the river was not accidental.[1] The population in general must have been frighteningly vulnerable to the savage floods of the river, and it was the most powerful and wealthy who were able to occupy the areas of high ground near the river, like Monte Giordano (map 2) or Monte Citorio, which themselves were composed of detritus heaped up by the action of the river in spate. In this way the river, acting upon the crumbling fabric of the ancient city, had contributed not only to the settlement structure of the medieval city, but even to the physical substratum of its topography (Adinolfi 1860, 1–4).

The Tiber was navigable to the city and beyond, constituting an avenue of communication of major importance. The population of Rome was dependent on the importation of basic foodstuffs by water; the continuing problems of the production of grain in the Roman hinterland are well known. Moreover, the presence of the papal court and the households of great prelates, notably certain French cardinals whose conspicuous and magnificent tastes were legendary in Rome, created a demand for the luxury goods that characterized the style of life in larger, richer, and more sophisticated cities than Rome, from whose ruling elites, of course, many of the high ecclesiastical dignitaries came. Indeed, Nicholas V himself, for all his relatively humble origins, had a particular predilection for precious materials, while his reputation as an enthusiastic tippler may well not have been founded only in malicious rumor; certainly, there is evidence that agents were sent out in search of fine wines as they were, on a different scale, in search of manuscripts.[2]

The greater part of the cargo imported into Rome, whether staples or luxury goods, came into the harbor known as the Ripa Romea or Ripa Grande, which was situated in Trastevere near the Porta Portese, as the latter's name suggests (fig. 49). Seagoing ships delivered cargo to transshipment points at or near the mouth of the Tiber, where it was loaded onto barges to be hauled upriver by teams of buffalo (Martini 1965, 233).[3] Tolls were levied on all goods imported at the harbor, where a small staff operated the office of the *dogana di ripa* on behalf of a *doganiere* who was sometimes a papal official, sometimes a tax farmer. A smaller harbor, the Porto di Ripetta, was located on the left bank in the Campo Marzio upstream of the main inhabited quarters; this received goods freighted down from the valleys of the Tiber and its tributaries, especially the Aniene (or Teverone), and points beyond. Neither harbor now exists.

The flow of goods on the river had a political dimension; as Palermo has argued in his study of the late medieval port of Rome, the Tiber offered a route into the city that was less amenable to the control of the feudal lords of the hinterland than were the various land routes (Palermo 1979, 97; cf. Delumeau 1975, 30–33). In general, it was relatively secure from the violence that characterized life in the late medieval region. The case of Eugenius IV's escape from the city is exemplary; disguised as a monk, he sought refuge from the hostile crowds that sought him through the streets of Rome on a boat that took him downstream to safety, though he was soon recognized and pelted ineffectually from the shore. This was in 1434; he was not to return until 1443 (D'Onofrio 1980, 189; Partner 1972, 409, 416). Not surprisingly, the popes maintained their own boats and guards on the river, especially after the recognition with the fall of Constantinople of a more immediate Turkish menace; clearly security of passage on the Tiber was a particular concern (Palermo 1979, 93, 182).

Manetti makes no mention in his biography of Nicholas of the latter's provisions for the improved functioning of harbors and other facilities on the river (cf. Westfall 1974a, 106). Nevertheless, the documents reveal a coherent pattern of interventions and measures undertaken toward this end. These involved administrative decisions and innovations as well as physical alterations to the installations along the river. The former, clearly, could be implemented with rapidity, at least in comparison to the pace of building campaigns, and the discussion will begin with them.

In 1447 two edicts were issued to control the activities of butchers, tanners, and those practicing associated trades in Rome (Romano 1941, 5; Re 1928, 86, 93). They were enjoined to dispose of the waste products of their activity, which were particularly unpleasant, in the river. No doubt these waste products had in the past often simply been dumped in the city streets, so that these edicts may be regarded as a step in the ongoing battle to improve environmental conditions and the circulation of persons and goods in the densely populated quarters of Rome; this it certainly was, in part. But the second edict specifically prescribed that offal and other wastes should be disposed of in the river below the Ponte S. Maria, which was at the time the southernmost bridge in the city (now the Ponte Rotto, it was damaged beyond repair by high water in the late sixteenth century; it appears intact in fig. 49). Such a regulation, if enforced, would surely have had the effect of encouraging the transfer by butchers, tanners, and others of their shops from areas such as Ponte, which had once been particularly associated with such trades, to the region near the Ponte S. Maria and the harbor. In other words, in the course of 1447 a primitive kind of zoning was perhaps proposed, involving the development of a broadly industrial area downstream of population concentrations.

It is impossible to assess the number of men or the proportion of the Roman labor force engaged in work on the river and at the harbors. In 1447 the coopers, who made containers vital for trade in bulk goods on water (they are identified as *barilai di ripa*), received their statutes as an independent guild; hitherto they had been associated with the carpenters (Rodocanachi 1894, 1:147).[4] The formation of a new guild implies that their numbers were increasing, presumably in response to an increase in waterborne trade, since the roads in 1447 were still far from secure; the timing of the official ratification of their status and statutes at least implies an interest on the part of the new papal government in the proper regulation of the coopers' activities and in the fostering of the commercial operations that required their products. The activity of the boatmen was also more carefully monitored; in 1450 Nicholas issued an edict regulating salvage activities on the river, which had evidently been marked by various abuses (ibid., 409; cf. Martini 1965, 232–235). Once again, a concern with ensuring both security and order on the river seems to have been in question.

In the month after Nicholas's accession the Roman patrician Battista di Lorenzo Martini Leni was appointed chancellor of the harbor (*camerarius ripae*) (ASV, RV 432, fol. 6v [April 5, 1447]; cf. Palermo 1979, 334). This, like most ostensibly communal appointments, was by now the prerogative of the papal government, and the appointees, though normally Roman citizens, were clearly held to be acceptable to the ecclesiastical authorities (Palermo 1979, 81). The appointment of Leni was wisely made. He was a prominent member of the citizen elite: he held the office of *guardianus* of the Confraternity of the Salvatore in 1445, acting as its ad hoc representative in negotiations conducted in 1455 (Marangoni 1747, 317; ASR, AOSS, Istromenti 25, fol. 45r); he married into the powerful family of the Porcari who were based, like his own clan, in the Rione Pigna; and his brother Evangelista was also a figure of significance in mid-fifteenth-century Rome. What is known of the brothers' business activities indicates that they were *bovattieri*, large-scale stockmen and land dealers, of the type familiar from the brilliant studies conducted by Gennaro (1967) and Maire-Vigueur (1974, 1976) on the fourteenth-century Roman socioeconomic world.[5]

Besides his position at the *dogana di ripa*, in 1447 Battista Leni also controlled the *dogana di terra di Roma*, the office that collected tolls on the goods brought into the city by land (ASV, IE 414, fol. 5v [May 17, 1447]).[6] Without doubt, therefore, he was a pivotal figure in the financial affairs of Rome in 1447, the year not only of Nicholas's accession but also of important changes in the financial administration of Rome: Roberto Martelli of the Medici bank was appointed banker to the *camera apostolica*, while Martelli's predecessor, Tommaso Spinelli, now became banker to the commune. It is probable that Leni was already involved in business transactions with the major Florentine banks; certainly in 1449 he and Roberto Martelli entered a partnership to buy the *dogana di ripa*, for which 15,000 florins were asked, although the partners were let off 3,000 of these because of the absence of the pope from the city at the time (ASV, IE 416, fol. 49r; IE 420, fol. 53v).[7] In the same year Leni held the chief magistracy of the Roman commune (Tommasini 1887, 212): clearly his local political career was not damaged by his close links, which had no real parallels in this period, to the financiers of Banchi. It is probable that his standing within both the local political and economic world of Rome and that of the Curia and the commercial operations associated with it reflected his value as an intermediary between distinct but increasingly intertwined spheres of activity.

In the aftermath of the difficulty experienced in supplying the city during Jubilee year, by 1451 the decision had apparently been made to keep the administration of the harbor and its revenues under tighter control. From 1451 until 1453 Nello da Bologna and his assistant Francesco del Borgo are recorded as *doganieri di ripa* (Palermo 1979, 335). It is improbable that they purchased the *dogana* in the usual way; there is no firm evidence of independent commercial activity carried out by either during Nicholas's pontificate.[8] In fact this must have been the moment of the foundation of the office of the *abbondanza*, dated by Palermo (1979), 194, to the mid-fifteenth century, which supervised the supply of grain into the city. Certainly in 1450 Nello da Bologna was appointed *provisor et commissarius abbundancie et gra&cie alme Urbis* (ASV, RV 433, fol. 92r), while the office of *cameriere dell'abbondanza di Roma* was awarded to Giovanni di Giordano Boccabelli, a Roman lawyer (ASR, TS 1450, fol. 27v).

Giovanni (or, as often, Gianni) di Giordano is a figure of great interest. Perhaps significantly, he came from the Rione Pigna, where he was a neighbor of the Leni brothers, though his own family was traditionally settled in Campitelli (see Tommasini 1887, 214). He had recently held important administrative positions on the Campidoglio, having been notary and chancellor of the *conservatores* in 1447 (he perhaps still held this position in 1449 when Battista Leni was *conservator*) and *camerarius* of the *camera urbis* in 1449, working under Tommaso Spinelli (ASV, RV 432, fol. 31r [May 28, 1447]; Tommasini

1887, 212). At the time of his appointment to the new or at least redefined office of the *abbondanza*, Giovanni must have seemed to the papal officials who appointed him an effective and experienced professional administrator in the financial institutions of the commune.

Giovanni also soon received judicial authority when in May 1451 he was appointed *gabellarius major* with powers to proceed against tax evaders (ASV, RV 433, fol. 174v; on the office see Lombardo 1970, 49), a post he held at least until September 1453 (Malatesta 1886, 179). In the latter year he handled, in his capacity as notary, transactions between the papal financial staff and craftsmen, all members of the equipe of Beltramo da Varese, working on the construction campaign at the Campidoglio (Müntz 1878, 150, 159 n.2). Also in 1453 we find him benefiting directly, as property owner, from his association with the *dogana di ripa*: in November the papal ledgers record 16 ducats spent on repairs to a house at the Ripa Grande owned by Giovanni and used by the *dogana* (ASR, TS 1453, fol. 11r).[9]

In conjunction with such administrative developments, and equally under the direction of Nello da Bologna, a number of construction projects were undertaken along the river; given the close involvement of Francesco del Borgo with these projects it is possible that Francesco's career as an architect, if Frommel (1984a) is right about his central role in the design of the Palazzo S. Marco, began at this time. In 1450 a large payment of 500 florins is recorded for construction at the Ripa Romea and on the Ponte S. Maria (ASR, M 830, fol. 155v);[10] further extensive work at Ripa is recorded in 1453, when the contractor involved, as perhaps he already had been in 1450, was Beltramo da Varese (ASR, TS 1450, fol. 159v), whose labor force was simultaneously committed in 1453 to the major campaigns at the Vatican and the Campidoglio. It is surely not coincidental that in 1450 the projects at the Ponte S. Maria and the harbor were recorded and financed together; this indicates, indeed, a campaign to improve the handling and distribution of goods in the city in the year of the Jubilee.

There is some evidence that the volume of trade was increasing; this is suggested, at least, by the repairs made to the Ponte S. Bartolomeo (ASR, SMP 1454, fol. 118v), one of the bridges to the Tiber Island, perhaps to improve an alternative route from Trastevere into Rome for traffic that otherwise overburdened the Ponte S. Maria; this may also be in part the background of Sixtus IV's slightly later restoration of the Ponte Sisto. By 1453, moreover, the *dogana* was occupying the building rented from Giovanni Boccabelli; this was surely supplementary to the *dogana*'s regular premises, which were presumably close by, though the building's location is specified only as in Trastevere.

At about the same time a watchtower was built at the mouth of the Fiumicino canal, not far from the ancient harbor of Porto (map. 3; D'Onofrio 1968, 258). In spite of the silt deposited by the river at its mouth and the consequent encroachment of the land on the sea, it was not until 1662 that a new tower was found necessary; it was constructed at a distance of 950 meters from that of Nicholas V, indicating the rate of sedimentation in the intervening years. But Nicholas's tower stood very close to the settlement of Porto; evidently in the preceding centuries very little sedimentation had taken place. This apparently drastic increase in the rate of sedimentation can perhaps be explained by the effects of dredging work associated with the construction of Nicholas's tower. There is no direct evidence for such operations, but it may be significant that a tower built by Martin V stood on the other branch of the river, toward Ostia (ibid., 256), suggesting that Martin's engineers improved the primary route from the sea to the river and that Nicholas's engineers reopened a secondary route that had been blocked perhaps since antiquity.

Nicholas also had construction carried out at Ostia. By April 1451 work was under way on a *casa del sale* (Müntz 1878, 158), presumably the building where salt from the important salt pans of Ostia was stored prior to shipment upstream. The building was somewhat martial in character, for it boasted a *scarpa*, evidently battering of the kind that was a characteristic feature of fortification architecture of the period and was also occasionally applied to palaces, like that of Nicholas V at the Vatican. Subsequently work is also recorded on the castle (ASR, TS 1453, fol. 69r) and on a "new bridge" at Ostia (ibid. 1451, fols. 53v, 123v; SMP 1454, fol. 8v). These projects at the Tiber's mouth should perhaps be related to work documented at Civitavecchia, the major port on the Tyrrhenian coast of the papal territories above Rome. This was purchased in 1451 from Cardinal Trevisan (Paschini 1939, 138; Pleyer 1923, 47), who had received it as a fief from Eugenius IV and apparently carried out some construction there. On July 29, 1451, the newly appointed castellan of Civitavecchia, Pietro da Sarzana (a compatriot of Nicholas V), received in Nello's chambers 200 ducats for the restoration of the castle (ASR, TS 1454, fol. 95v), and in the following year further expenses are recorded (Müntz 1878, 161); these expenses are no doubt those referred to in Nello's quittance of 1454 as made in preparation for the emperor's visit to Rome (see Appendix, no. 5).

The work on the castellated salt warehouse at Ostia was entrusted to a leading local contractor, Antonio Paciuri. Also in 1451 Paciuri was charged with the restoration of the Ponte alla Galera (Müntz 1878, 158 n.4; ASR, TS 1451, fols. 73v, 170r, 212v), a bridge that carried the Via Portuense over a tributary of the Tiber, the Galera, that flowed into the Tiber not far north of the Capo de' Rami, the point where the Fiumicino canal branched off. Paciuri, whose base was in the Rione Trastevere, had already built a business as a supplier of building materials—lime, bricks, and tile—in Eugenius's pontificate (Corbo 1969, 50, 56, 62). His business boomed under Nicholas: in November 1452, for instance, he delivered a consignment of 48,000 *mattoni* to the canons of St. Peter's (ASR, TS 1452, fol. 217r), from whom he leased a brickworks, paying his rent in wine (ibid., 1451, fol. 170v). By 1451 he was active also as a contractor; in 1454 he is recorded as paid for further projects, one of which was the clearing of obstacles from the bed of the Tiber at the Ponte Milvio (Müntz 1878, 158). We find Paciuri, then, active along the whole extent of the Tiber as an urban river; evidently he owned or had access to boats as well as his limekilns and brickworks.

Paciuri was clearly a further member of that quite large group of Roman patricians who worked closely with Nicholas's officials and derived benefit from his pontificate. Paciuri's involvement with improvements along the river is of particular significance as here his own interests and those of the papal government evidently overlapped; indeed the series of Nicholan projects along the river may well have taken place, to a degree, in response to local initiatives and concerns, such as would perhaps have been particularly the case in Trastevere, Paciuri's *rione*. Paciuri himself lived near the harbor; at least until 1447 he rented a house in the parish of S. Biagio di Corte, in the vicinity of S. Francesco a Ripa (BAV, ACSP Censuali 5 [1447], fol. 47r).[11] In 1448, the first full year of Nicholas's pontificate, Paciuri was elected *caporione* of Trastevere (Tommasini 1887, 219; the name is transcribed Antonius Pacuto), implying that he already enjoyed support in high places and was regarded both by his neighbors and the papal staff as a useful intermediary.

In 1449 Paciuri lent money to the rector of his parish, a certain Francesco da Gubbio, to enable the latter to purchase a quantity of unfortunately unspecified books worth 73 ducats from the preceptor of S. Spirito in Sassia, Pietro Capoccini (ASR, Archivio dell'Arcispedale di S. Spirito 211, fol. 97r). Paciuri must have been the intermediary between the two, since he already knew Pietro and had been engaged in a business transaction with the Hospital of S. Spirito in the previous year (ibid., fol. 71r).[12] Pietro was a member of Paciuri's class; *camerarius* of the hospital under Eugenius, he was promoted to preceptor by Nicholas V in 1447, and held the post through five pontificates (Egidi 1908, 139). Looking back on his career, Pietro Capoccini was especially proud of his success in achieving the redemption of alienated or usurped properties of the hospital (ibid.). Like Paciuri he benefited from Nicholas's pontificate; in 1450 he was leasing a house at the Campo de' Fiori (Lauer 1911, 513), perhaps to house pilgrims during Jubilee year (Pietro himself no doubt had quarters at the hospital). His status at S. Spirito was soon translated into wider recognition; in 1448 he served as the procurator of the important abbey of S. Anastasio alle tre Fontane, whose abbot, Angelo, had been active in Eugenian construction projects, including work at the castle of Civitavecchia (Adinolfi 1865, 141). On behalf of the abbey Capoccini managed the sale of a house, witnessed by Pietro Mellini, to Niccolò della Valle, a clerk of the Apostolic Chamber and canon of S. Maria Maggiore; this document places him in contact with some of the leading individuals and families of the most dynamic sector of the city at mid-fifteenth century. Capoccini's standing in the city and that of the institution he represented may have been a factor in the apparent lack of Nicholan intervention—the contrast with Sixtus IV is instructive—in the affairs and building program of S. Spirito.

Paciuri may have owed to Capoccini his developing career as a contractor, for Pietro's relative Giovanni Capoccini, who was *conservator* in 1447 (Tommasini 1887, 202), held the office of *doganiere del sale* in Rome in 1450 (ASV, RV 433, fol. 123v); it was perhaps he, therefore, who brought in Paciuri to build a new salt warehouse.[13] It is likely, then, that Paciuri's unspecified business with S. Spirito in Sassia involved construction at the hospital, while he may well also have worked on the expansion of the Lateran hospital; much later, under Pius II, he appears as contractor on the restoration of the roof of the

Lateran basilica (Müntz 1878, 293), the timbers for which he perhaps freighted downriver in his own boats. Deeply involved in communal institutions and their physical maintenance, Paciuri was the main local contractor in the Rome of Nicholas V, and it is no accident that his activity was centered on the river as a particular arena for the merging of papal and communal interests, in addition to his own.

Though the Ripa Grande was by far the more important urban harbor, certain waterborne commodities reached Rome from the north, from the upper valley of the Tiber and its tributaries, and were unloaded at the port of Ripetta (map 2). This was located in a largely uninhabited part of the Rione Campo Marzio; typically it handled heavy cargo, timber from the hills and mountains enclosing the Tiber valley, stone from the quarries of Tivoli, and grain and other agricultural produce from the March and other papal lands to the northeast (D'Onofrio 1980, 279f.). The Tiber was navigable as far as Borgo S. Leonardo, often known simply as Borghetto, where cargo was transferred onto barges and where passage dues produced considerable but not always uncontested revenues;[14] the Aniene was navigable until shortly before Tivoli. Both the Aniene and the upper Tiber were important in meeting one of the particular needs of Nicholas's pontificate, the supply of building materials. In Nicholas's time the papacy employed six boatmasters, who were doubtless used for this purpose (e.g., ASR, M 830, fol. 3v); in addition the contractor Beltramo da Varese owned a boat in which he brought stone to the Vatican for use in the *tribuna* project, while Paciuri seems also to have been active in this way. Since building materials are generally bulky and heavy by nature, it is not surprising to find references, even in the pages of Manetti, to dredging operations on at least the Aniene (Magnuson 1958, 359); I have already noted the task assigned to Paciuri of freeing the bed of the river from obstacles at the Ponte Milvio.

The pope's particular concern for the smooth transit of building materials on the rivers is documented, for example, by a bull of July 11, 1451, addressed to a certain Nicolaus de Civitate Castelli, *scriptor et familiaris papae*, ordering him to supervise the transport downstream of fir beams for the repair of the roofs at St. Peter's and S. Paolo fuori le Mura (Müntz 1878, 109 n.2). The problem was not so much the passage of the timber, presumably lashed together to make a raft, as the transport from the forest to the transshipment point on the Tiber, at or near Borgo S. Leonardo. This area, which was of importance for other building materials, including brick and mortar, was owned by the hospital of S. Spirito in Sassia, to which it had been given in 1392 by Boniface IX (De Angelis 1962, 638). If, as is likely, Borgo S. Leonardo was of importance under Nicholas V as a source of such materials, the relationship I have noted between Antonio Paciuri and the hospital's administrator takes on a new significance, and the former's economic interests can now be seen to extend the length of the Tiber as a navigable river.

Though I have found no direct evidence of improvements made to the port facilities, proably quite primitive, at Ripetta, it is clear that the surrounding area became under Nicholas a center of demographic and economic growth that may well have been in part a result of papal policy. Thus in 1453 the pope granted the church of S. Marina in Ripetta, said to be deserted and "profanata," to a congregation of Illyrian Hieronymite hermits, who renamed it S. Girolamo degli Illirici (Lanciani 1902, 1:56; Maroni-Lumbroso and Martini 1963, 154f.; for the area in general see Paschini 1925). A hospice was attached, where recently arrived Illyrians, many of them refugees from the Turkish advance in the Balkans, could be accommodated. No doubt these immigrants, after crossing the Adriatic from their homeland and traversing the Appennines, reached Rome by way of the Tiber valley; it would be natural for them to settle in the northern quarters of the city. Some of them may have worked on Nicholas's building projects; certainly Illyrians appear prominently in building records in many Italian cities of the time (Marchini 1969b, 212f.; Rotondi 1950, 1:209f.; cf. Anselmi 1976 on Slavic immigration in general at this time), and an Illyrian, Paolo da Ragusa, supplied bricks to the Vatican, apparently from his own kilns, in 1451 (ASR, TS 1451, fol. 184v). A further national community traditionally involved in building, indeed to a far greater extent, may also already have begun to settle in the Campo Marzio; certainly under Sixtus IV the national church of the Lombards was formally established on the Via del Corso (it is now SS. Ambrogio e Carlo; Drago and Salerno 1967, 5), and it is likely that this reflected an existing settlement pattern.

It was not only the immigrants into the northern quarters of Rome who had interests in the building trades. The Roman citizen Giuliano Sercoberti of the Rione Ponte, for example, operated a limekiln, while he was also the owner of hostelries. In 1452 he was *caporione* (Tommasini 1887, 206), a position that must have involved him in the improvements carried out in the Canale di Ponte, in the heart of his *rione*, at that time. In February of the same year he opened a *hospitium* near the Mausoleum of Augustus (the "mons Augustorum") in the vicinity of the Ripetta harbor; since the site was owned by the *camera apostolica*, Giuliano received permission for his development in a papal letter (ASV, RV 424, fol. 124r).[15] It is likely that this hostelry, the size and precise function of which are not recorded, was connected with the settlement of Illyrians around the Ripetta and the pope's evident encouragement of this. If so, the pattern asserts itself once again of a convergence of papal and local patrician interests, while Giuliano may well be identified as an early real estate developer, if not speculator, in an area that was particularly ripe for such activity.

There can have been no more conspicuous sign of Nicholas's particular concern for the river as thoroughfare than the attention lavished on bridges; I have noted the restoration of the Ponte S. Maria and the Ponte S. Bartolomeo in Trastevere, and that of the Ponte alla Galera and an unspecified bridge at Ostia at or near the river's mouth. In addition, bridges over the Aniene were repaired, perhaps in conjunction with dredging work, while the Ponte Milvio was largely rebuilt. Some of the bridges were equipped with defensible towers, which would have been a natural location for Nicholas's insignia. But the most important construction project along the river was surely the restoration of the Ponte S. Angelo and the adjacent embankment walls; it is a project that leads the argument from the economic life of Nicholan Rome to the symbolism inherent in the urbanistic interventions carried out in Nicholas's pontificate.

In the sacralization of the imperial city of Rome that is a recurrent theme of patristic authors, the Tiber plays a vital role. As Pietri (1961) has shown, in the eyes of the Christian apologists for the city the apostles Peter and Paul, taking the place of the original founding pair, refounded Rome. Even the placing of their tombs was providential, one upstream of the city on the right bank and the other downstream on the left bank. Prudentius's verse is not untypical: "The Tiber is sacred from each bank as it flows between the sanctified sepulchers" (quoted in ibid., 319). The tombs of the apostles, along with all the other shrines distributed throughout the city, guaranteed the unity of the city, a unity that was inscribed in the liturgy of the stations and acted out in the pilgrimage rituals (Magnuson 1958, 58 n.10; Kirsch 1926, esp. 244).

Such notional unity as the river provided was physically effected through the bridges of Rome. Until Sixtus IV's reconstruction of the ancient bridge that was thenceforth known as the Ponte Sisto, the Ponte S. Angelo was the only bridge over the Tiber between the Ponte Milvio and the Island; it was a vital hinge between the city and the Borgo (D'Onofrio 1980, 256–268; Burroughs 1982a, 1982b). In the nomenclature of the building accounts kept by Nicholas's staff, however, the bridge's immediate local function is uppermost; it is typically identified as the "ponte del castello" (e.g. Müntz 1878, 152), indicating that the bridge and the Castel S. Angelo were regarded as elements of a single complex. Originally, indeed, they were, and in the fifteenth century it was well known that both structures had been built by the Emperor Hadrian, the bridge to give access from the city to his mausoleum.

The work carried out by Nicholas's craftsmen on the Ponte S. Angelo was on a considerable scale and continued from 1447 to 1453. In 1450 a Lombard paver was paid for surfacing the carriageway (Müntz 1878, 152), suggesting that the brunt of the construction work had already been completed, though major repairs to one of the piers of the bridge are documented in the following year (Tomei 1942, 108).[16] The bridge had certainly needed repair, as is emphatically demonstrated by passages of the *De re aedificatoria* in which Alberti laments the sorry condition of the bridge and expresses pessimism about its capacity to survive much longer.

At least one of Alberti's references to the bridge must surely predate any restoration carried out by Nicholas and proudly celebrated by the display of the papal insignia. Alberti writes: "I dare to assert that the bridge of Hadrian, of all the works that men have made, is the most powerful [*validissimum*], though repeated floods have brought it to the point that I doubt it can resist much longer" (Alberti 1966a, 2:948f. [X.x]). He goes on to describe the effects of floodwater and the debris carried by the river in spate and dashed against the masonry of the bridge. It is a passage closely if not at first obviously related to Alberti's meditations, frequent in his social and ethical writings, on the role of fortune in human affairs, but whatever its architectural or extraarchitectural reference, it is prima facie unlikely that such a passage could postdate the thoroughgoing restoration of a bridge.

In the second passage Alberti gives details, mostly entirely hypothetical, of the ancient superstructure of the bridge. He envisages a glittering structure, surmounted by a magnificent, colonnaded portico, carrying a roof clad in bronze:

Some [bridges] are even roofed. An example at Rome is the most outstanding of all bridges, that of Hadrian, assuredly a work worthy to be remembered; indeed I used to look with admiration even, so to speak, on its corpse. For there had once stood on that bridge a roof raised up on 42 marble columns and a system of architraves. The covering was of bronze, and the architectural details were extraordinarily fine. (Ibid., 710f. [VIII.vi])

Alberti's choice of tenses suggests that the bridge's condition had improved since he had studied its cadaveral remains, as he puts it; certainly, if the Ponte S. Angelo as restored by Nicholas could not be compared with Alberti's vision of it, there was no bridge in existence that could. It is possible, then, that this second passage postdates the work carried out under Nicholas. And there is some evidence that Alberti's ideal reconstruction of the bridge in the pages of his treatise was related to a graphic working out of his ideas about its original appearance. For Vasari possessed a drawing, now lost, that he considered to be by the hand of Alberti himself, showing the bridge surmounted, as in the second passage cited above, by a colonnade (Vasari 1906, 2:546).[17]

Vasari's attributions are in general highly questionable. Since, however, there is no reason to doubt that such a drawing once existed, three possible scenarios can be proposed. The drawing may, as Vasari asserts, have been done by Alberti, perhaps in connection with the work on his book; an anonymous later architect may have worked up a drawing on the basis of the description in Alberti's book, most probably after its publication in 1485, so that Vasari may at least have correctly identified the drawing as of fifteenth-century date; or Vasari, in his eagerness to add an Alberti drawing to his comprehensive collection, was simply taken in by a drawing by a contemporary passed off as Alberti's, incidentally documenting the continuing interest in the theme of the porticoed bridge in the sixteenth century, most splendidly exemplified in Palladio's designs for the Rialto bridge (Zorzi 1967, 187).

In any case, in both the passages cited, Alberti reveals his deep admiration for the Pons Aelius as one of the great public monuments of ancient Rome and as a particular triumph of Roman engineering; it is this passionate concern for the bridge that justifies the supposition that Alberti indeed made or commissioned an elaborate graphic reconstruction of the bridge, and that Vasari possessed either this or a copy from it. If so, it is probable that Alberti's concern with the bridge was related to the attention given to the bridge under Nicholas, though it is important to note that not all this attention should be simply subsumed under the heading of papal patronage.

The restoration of the bridge under Nicholas was associated with the remarkable series of interventions on the city side of the bridge that produced a piazza, arguably the first realized new piazza of the Renaissance. Hitherto, my discussion of Nicholas's interventions in Ponte has concentrated on the relationship of the newly created or reinterpreted space to the venerable route that led through it; at the Ponte S. Angelo, however, the axis of the Via del Papa and of the *possesso* crossed the axis of the Tiber, an intersection that is of crucial importance in understanding the Nicholan interventions in the area.

It is a remarkable aspect of Nicholas's new piazza that it was open on one side to the river, which was, of course, also visible from the bridge itself. This openness to the river was, if anything, enhanced by the measures taken in commemoration of the terrible and tragic incident of 1450: some two hundred pilgrims had suffocated or plunged to their death in the river when a large crowd returning from the Vatican found its movement forward over the bridge blocked and succumbed to panic. It was a particularly unfortunate event in Jubilee year, and it made a great impact on contemporaries, not least because it formed a climax in a series of catastrophes that had afflicted the people of Rome (Burroughs 1982a).

Nicholas responded quickly to the crisis. Twin chapels were erected to mark the site of the tragedy, one dedicated, for obvious reasons, to the Holy Innocents, the other to the Magdalene, no doubt in reference to the cult of the Magdalene in the nearby church of S. Celso, but also, as argued in chapter 3, in reference to Nicholas's emphasis on penitential behavior, with which the Magdalene was especially associated; the chapels, octagonal and of no great size, flanked the entrance of the bridge from the piazza.

Two points are of interest here: on the one hand, the chapels visually dramatized the point of juncture—or division—of the piazza and bridge, and shaped the open side of the former; on the other hand, the chapels gave emphasis to Christian, specifically penitential associations of the bridge, to which its ancient associations now yielded. If Alberti's hypothetical reconstruction of the bridge had predated Nicholas's restoration, the erection of the two chapels now precluded any actual reconstruction of the superstructure of the bridge along the lines he envisioned. The reference to the fallen state of the bridge, almost as an emblem of the irredeemably fallen state of the city, may after all, then, refer to the bridge as it was after 1450, and include a veiled criticism of the character of the Nicholan *renovatio*. The incident on the bridge, however, directly induced the pope to order the demolition of buildings adjoining the bridge approach on the side toward the city; this was the first step of a process that involved many people, among whom Alberti surely played a significant role, in the reordering of the adjacent area.

It is particularly interesting, then, that no sooner were the two chapels built than a ceremony took place on the bridge that temporarily denied or at least obscured its religious associations. In January 1452 the emperor Frederick III, after his coronation at the hands of Nicholas V at the Vatican, made his way through the Borgo, accompanied by the pope, until their formal leave-taking at the church of S. Maria in Traspadina. Frederick then proceeded to the Ponte S. Angelo, where he celebrated his enhanced authority and sacrality by conferring knighthood on a number of men, many of whom were members of his traveling entourage, while some were representatives of the local aristocracy (Pastor 1949, 156f.).

There is no doubt that the location of this ceremony was carefully chosen by Nicholas's staff, who were concerned about the disruptive potential of the emperor's visit in a city still marked by Ghibelline sentiment. Nello, whose overall responsibility for the arrangements for the emperor's visit is documented, may have regarded the bridge as an appropriately neutral zone for the ceremony, a space suspended between the city and the Borgo, though symbolically, at least, divided from the former by the two chapels, and overlooked by the guns of the Castel S. Angelo and the papal arms. The citizens of Rome interested in viewing the spectacle presumably assembled in Nicholas's new piazza, the creation of which indeed surely made the use of the bridge for the ceremony possible; their view of the ceremony, as in a contemporary representation on a marriage chest (fig. 12), would have been across the water to the bridge.

The idea of a piazza open to a river was not new in 1450–52. In his biography of Filippo Brunelleschi, Antonio Manetti (1976), 123, describes his hero's proposal to rebuild the great Florentine church of S. Spirito on the same site, but reoriented to face in the opposite direction from its predecessor, toward the Arno river. As Manetti puts it, the facade of the new church would be visible to fishermen coming up the river; we may add that it would also have been visible from at least one of the bridges over the Arno. Nothing came of the scheme, though it was not perhaps entirely without precedent; after all, the church of Ognissanti, on the opposite side of the river, faced an open space that ran down to the river (Davidsohn 1973, 530; the space was presumably connected with the industrial activity of the Umiliati monks of the church), while to the north of the Ponte alle Grazie at the other end of the town an open space surrounded a circular building that appears quite prominently on early representations of Florence. This was the fourteenth-century mausoleum erected by a member of the Alberti clan, whose family palaces stood nearby (Paatz and Paatz 1952, 3–5); it is mentioned by Leon Battista in a late dialogue (Alberti 1966B, 2:187).[18]

Such probable Florentine resonances of a water-bounded piazza corroborate my suggestion that the piazza project—at least insofar as this exceeded the mere demolition of obstacles to passage over and from the bridge—originated in the Tuscan community of Ponte, and that Alberti played a central role. But Alberti's role, whatever it was, was perhaps mediated through the good offices of one of the most powerful men in Rome and the most prominent resident of the Canale di Ponte, Tommaso Spinelli. I have suggested that Spinelli was a moving force behind the improvements in Ponte, where he maintained his business premises and, no doubt, his urban residence. It is unlikely that the emperor, who had spent the night prior to his ceremonial entry into Rome at Spinelli's villa on Monte Mario, and who had no doubt met him in his capacity as banker to the city when he was entertained on the Campidoglio by the communal magistrates and city notables, passed through Ponte without greeting Spinelli at his house.

For the various elites of Rome, including the proud Tuscans, the contact with the visiting emperor perhaps served to reinforce their sense of their own social status. In any case, the bridge and bridge approach regained something of the grand imperial ceremonial connotations that Nicholas's chapels had obscured, though we have no way of knowing whether these connotations were temporarily given physical expression through built structures and decorations of some kind.

Whatever the interest of the Tuscan community in the improvement of their quarter, the symbolic dimension of the Piazza del Ponte is best sought in a Roman context. The Tiber was notoriously dangerous and unpredictable, indeed it had something of the character both of the smooth-flowing and navigable *publicus fluvius* of Roman law, and of the seasonal torrent swollen by sudden rains or melting snows.[19] Reinforcement of the banks was necessary, so that the impressive bridges of antiquity were only the most conspicuous elements of a whole system of constructions through which the river flowed; Alberti (1966a), 2:955, notes in the tenth book of the *De re aedificatoria*: "At Rome we can see that the Tiber along much of its length is confined by masonry structures." The intermittently wild river, then, had been made to surrender to Roman domination through the genius of the ancient engineers and builders; a natural force had become a product of rational human agency. The large-scale restoration of these embankments under Nicholas, therefore, though clearly its primary function was economic and as such was related, for instance, to Brunelleschi's projects for the improvement of river transport at Florence (Prager and Scaglia 1970, 111–123), had connotations of a specifically Roman nature.

In 1422 the city was beset by a terrible flood. Unlike most of the occasions when the Tiber burst its banks, this flooding was the result of deliberate human agency, or at least so some believed. Infessura (1890), 24, reports that the *condottiere* Braccio da Montone "gave orders for the destruction of the retaining wall [?(*marmore*)] of the lake of Pedelupo, and did this with the intention of flooding Rome, and in this he succeeded" (cf. D'Onofrio 1980, 189 n.15). It is the strategy employed, with signal lack of success, by Brunelleschi at the siege of Lucca, where he attempted to flood the town with the waters of the Serchio river (Prager and Scaglia 1970, 128); Alberti (1966a), 2:952f., characteristically, cites what seems to be an exotic ancient example of such a stratagem, the siege of Stymphalus by Iphicrates, in this case foiled through divine intervention.

Braccio's act clearly made a considerable impression on the people of Rome; after all, Infessura wrote several years after the event. This was surely not just a matter of the later fame of an exercise of strategic cunning, or even the memory of discomfort and worse on the part of those who had been in Rome at the time; Braccio placed himself in a tradition of those whose power over men conferred on them—and was even legitimized by—power over nature. In his famous speech on the Lex Vespasiana, for instance, Cola di Rienzo had enumerated the powers given to the Emperor Vespasian by the Roman people: ". . . he could unmake and remake the cities; he could destroy the beds of the rivers, and move them elsewhere" (Ghisalberti 1928, 10; cf. Alberti 1966a, 2:878f., on the associations of Hercules with triumph over water).

Through his public works and especially the reconstruction of bridges, Nicholas V both controlled the river and displayed this control, especially at the Ponte S. Angelo, the only urban bridge of ceremonial importance. And it is probable that many passersby on the Via del Papa, on reaching the new piazza and the restored bridge, associated the water flowing at the foot of the castle, newly expanded with towers and impressive outworks, with the familiar motif of a castle moat, carrying obvious connotations of strength and defensibility. More important, perhaps, were the ancient connotations of the site, which were surely apparent to the educated elite at a time of developing antiquarian enthusiasm and research. For Hadrian, doubtless in emulation of Augustus Caesar, had erected his massive mausoleum to command the adjacent river; in addition, Hadrian's mausoleum was sited in such a way that the final stage of a procession to reach it passed over the waters of the Tiber. The river of imperial Rome, then, had been both an infrastructural element of great importance and an ideologically charged amenity, enhancing the most monumental tombs of the city.

I have found no explicit reference in mid-quattrocento writings to the topographical context of the imperial mausolea. A passage in Alberti, however, once again culled from a recherché source, suggestively asserts the representative value of such a situation. Though Alberti refers to a distant and remote historical situation, the possibility of a reference, albeit covert, to contemporary circumstances cannot be ruled out; certainly Alberti's text implies his prescriptive approval of the practice described. Alberti quotes the Greek author Xenophon: "The kings of Sparta had the special right, in respect of their high rank [dignitatis gratia], to have a pool of water in front of their residence, in line with the main portal" (Alberti 1966a, 2:880f. [X.ii]). He then points out the importance of water in the liturgical practices of his time, while he notes that these belong to a most ancient tradition of ritual.

Though Alberti apparently refers in this passage to an artificial pool rather than a river, the passage suggests a coherent and ideal vision of the aesthetic and ideological role of bodies of water as a central motif of the reformed city all'antica; it seems related to his emphasis on bridges as conspicuous monumental structures and to his recommendation that a city be divided by watercourses. Much of the tenth book of the De re aedificatoria, indeed, is devoted to a discussion of the various uses of water and problems posed by water in both urban and nonurban environments; in the course of this Alberti notes the aesthetic and enlivening effect of an abundance of water in an urban setting, and dwells on the desirability of fountains, bathing establishments, and irrigated gardens. In general terms he sums up: "An abundance of water makes the face and spirit of a city purer and cleaner" (ibid., 926f.).

Alberti laments, moreover, the disfiguring disorder of the Tiber as he knew it, its broad stream obscured by the floating mills familiar in views of the city up to the nineteenth century. Alberti had read, once again in a Greek author, this time Procopius, that the ancient Romans had used the aqueducts to power the wheels of their grain mills, and that it was only with the destruction of the aqueducts that mills on the river became necessary (ibid.). The mills appear, then, as an emblem of the decline of Rome.

In addition, Alberti's disdain for the prominence of mills on the river that had once been a major amenity of the ancient city is surely related to his prejudice against commerce, at least when commercial activity interfered with the dignity and splendor of the monumental zone and spaces of a city. In general, then, the *De re aedificatoria* expresses as a central theme a conception of the representative role and character of the river flowing through, and constituting a conspicuous element of, the ideal *all'antica* city, which in this context is particularly closely identified with the actual city of Rome. Such a conception is remote indeed from the provisions actually taken by Nicholas regarding the river, even if, as is likely, the ceremonial use of the bridge during the emperor's visit found favor with him. But the image of the Tiber in Alberti's treatise is a matter not only of antiquarian and architectural concerns, but also of ethical principles; indeed, the emphasis on the river and the Ponte S. Angelo itself acts as a bridge between two different kinds of discourse in Alberti's oeuvre.

The River and the City: Ethics and Authoriality

Alberti's remarkable praise of the Ponte S. Angelo forms part, as I have attempted to show, of a general concern with the the the theme of the river or of water in general in the ideal urban environment. Though Alberti's social and ethical concerns, discussed in a variety of writings throughout his long career, are at best only implied in the *De re aedificatoria*, they are not absent. In this case, the emphasis of the tenth book is remarkably closely related to a major theme of Alberti's late dialogue, *De iciarchia*, written in Florence in the late 1460s.

The *De iciarchia* purports to record the conversations of Alberti and his friends and the advice given to the young men of the Alberti family. The dialogue is set in the city of Florence shortly after a terrible flood of the Arno river, and the river provides not only a major element of the mise-en-scène but also an introductory motif that continues to well up, more or less explicitly and emphatically, in the thematic and language of the work. This begins with an encounter between Leon Battista and two of his friends near the Alberti palace, at a point where the swollen river is clearly visible and naturally forms the opening subject of their conversations (Alberti 1966b, 187). Grayson, editor of the standard text of the dialogue, suggests that the immediate stimulus for the *De iciarchia* was a particularly severe flood that struck Florence in 1465 (ibid., 442); this may well be so, though the resonances of the theme of the flood in Alberti's earlier writings should not be neglected.

To a degree the *De iciarchia* constitutes a reversal of the thought, or at least the posture, of the *De re aedificatoria*. The proposals for an improved and enhanced urban environment that constitute a central, though not uncontested, motif of the earlier work give way to the recommendation of withdrawal from public life and concentration on individual and family welfare. On the other hand, the emphasis is not very different from that of many passages of the *Della Famiglia* of the 1430s, while throughout his life Alberti showed a deeply skeptical ambivalence about the motives and moral values of those engaged in politics and wielding authority. In the context of Medicean Florence, indeed, an attitude of political quietism might well seem advisable.

The *De iciarchia*, however, may mark its own relationship to the *De re aedificatoria* in a covert but telling way: one of the chief interlocutors of the *De iciarchia*, Niccolò Cerretani, is a man of importance in the political life of Florence. Since he had several times held the office of naval prefect, at the beginning of the dialogue he is challenged by his companion, a member of the prominent Niccolini family, to devise a way that the Arno could be made navigable for galleys all the way to Florence (ibid., 187). The spectacle of the river in spate induces consideration of the taming of the river for the benefit of the city; it is the great theme of the tenth book of the *De re aedificatoria*.

Cerretani and his companion turn to Alberti, and one asks him what he thinks; his response is simply to suggest that they all withdraw to talk at the fireside away from the roughness and roar of the water. The theme of withdrawal is further emphasized when Alberti notes, somewhat sarcastically, that the fullness of the water, which his interlocutor had suggested might be artificially maintained for the sake of shipping, had broken the embankments and was coursing through the lower-lying areas.

When the discussion resumes in the safe recesses of the palace, Alberti turns it not to the utilitarian aspect of river control, but to the moral lessons suggested by the metaphor of a river in spate. A man should control the flow of passions within his soul; by so doing he will avoid the emotions of greed, ambition, anger, and audacity that damage social relations, and often, if not inevitably, lead to tyrannical behavior on the part of those in authority.

In particular, Alberti condemns the exportation of urban luxury to the country, the expenditure on villas and their furnishings, which he regards as an unfortunate emulation by the Florentines of the lifestyle of the court of Rome ("a imitazione dei massimi prelati" ibid., 202). He goes on to extend the metaphor of flood to the villa, which he describes as "colluvione di gente sviata." For obvious reasons Alberti would not be expected to vent his spleen on the conspicuous consumption of the Medici and their associates, yet his choice of a negative paradigm is revealing. In the *De re aedificatoria* Alberti argues for restrained and decorous living and its expression in the built environment; in particular, as he already had in the *Della Famiglia*, he envisages a nonostentatious though comfortable villa life and suggests the kind of architecture that should frame it (Alberti 1966a, 1:400–433 [V.xiv]).[20] In this way he had contributed to a wider cultural movement, the investment of surplus capital by social elites in increasingly pretentious rural or quasi-rural retreats, not least in the world of papal Rome. The trenchancy of his remarks in the *De iciarchia* implies that he wished to disown this contribution, and even, if only in passing, to indicate his dissatisfaction with the architectural and other patronage characteristic of the court of Rome, though he had himself, as theorist and even architect, been centrally involved in this.

In the *De iciarchia* the soul and its passions are discussed in terms taken from the urban environment (Alberti 1966b, 2:206f.); in the passages on the Ponte S.

Angelo/Pons Aelius in the *De re aedificatoria*, however, the direction of the metaphoric borrowing is reversed. The bridge once stood tall in the water, raising its splendid superstructure on its many columns, and now resists to the point of its own imminent dissolution the ravages of the river; Alberti's language suggests a degree of empathy, a sense of the bridge as possessed or at least emblematic of the strength, endurance, and general *virtus* of the civilization of ancient Rome itself. It is significant, finally, that Alberti refers to the bridge of his day as reduced, no less than the city of which it had formed a particularly magnificent element, to a corpse; this is no mere literary cliché.

Under Nicholas the river was treated as a central infrastructural element and amenity, guaranteeing the unity of the city on the level of the exchange of goods and circulation of traffic, but also in terms of the convergence of papal and communal Rome. At the Ponte S. Angelo the Tiber served as much as a connector as a divider, associated as it was with signs of various kinds that emphasized the majesty of the popes yet welcomed the Roman citizen or pilgrim into the papal enclave. The use of the bridge in 1452 for the ceremonial dubbing of knights following the coronation of the emperor, which itself symbolically joined distinct spheres of contrasting sacral and political character and affiliations within the city, perhaps enhanced the conciliatory and unificatory aspect of the bridge and river. But the execution of Stefano Porcari at the Castel S. Angelo in 1453 gave a new symbolic dimension not only to the bridge and piazza, but also to the river itself; no less than the bridge the river became a barrier and other associations were thereby obscured. In particular, the fateful chasm between the pope and the city elite, which was to be a central motif of the life of the city and region into the sixteenth century, was now topographically expressed. And the role of the river as unificatory stage around which monumental architecture, mirrored in the water, rose in majestic pomp was to be characteristic of the urbanism of absolutism (Oechslin 1984, 5of., 76f.; Blunt 1978, 120). In Rome, indeed, already in the pontificate of Alexander VI, a project was articulated to reduce the *publicus fluvius*, in the vicinity of the Ponte S. Angelo, to the most conspicuous element of a papal garden, an environment devoted to courtly pleasures and the projection of monarchic ideology and dynastic ambition (D'Onofrio 1980, 256).

The theme of the river and of flowing water, whether managed or unmanaged, whether beneficial or harmful, courses through the oeuvre of Alberti, not least the *De re aedificatoria*, as it does through the history of Rome and through the concerns of Nicholas V's administration. Indeed, many of Alberti's best-known practical interventions in Rome and its vicinity—the raising of the Roman ships at Lake Nemi, the repair of the Acqua Vergine, the possible consultation on the repair of the Ponte S. Angelo and the involvement with the layout of the adjoining piazza—involved work with various bodies or currents of water. They also involved, needless to say, close contact with powerful figures in the political world of the day, men whose control of water-as-negative and provision of water-as-positive could contribute to the realization of specific agendas or to the general goal of self-promotion and representation. The *De re aedificatoria*, however, is a subtle and cunning work, written by a master of dissimulation; echoes of the contemporary political and even social world are exceedingly difficult to identify.

My discussions, nevertheless, have indicated traces in Alberti's text of guarded references to construction projects and urban development in Nicholan Rome; they have also, perhaps more tellingly, drawn attention to the absence of references to certain personages and events. In particular I have argued that Alberti eschewed possible, indeed natural references to Cardinal Prospero Colonna and his *alter ego* Maecenas, and that he did so in the context of the ambivalent position occupied by the cardinal throughout much of Nicholas's pontificate. On the other hand, Alberti's only reference to Maecenas in connection with architecture (the only other mention of him [Alberti 1966a, 2:980–983] comes in the context of ant infestation and methods of removing it!) identifies him as an example of a reprehensible building patron excessively interested in grand and expensive constructions; if this has a contemporary resonance, it should surely be taken as a criticism, not of Prospero, but rather of Nicholas himself. The Albertian ambivalence about architecture, the necessary and challenging art that can so easily become a vehicle of and an incentive for hubristic display, may well have been particularly exercised by Nicholas's role as a patron and instigator of architectural and urbanistic interventions. Ironically, as we have seen, Nicholas himself shared some of this ambivalence, at least at one time.

It is often assumed, of course, that Alberti and Nicholas were in contact; hypotheses of Alberti's "authorship" of the projects for the Borgo or the Vatican either assert or entail this (Grayson 1960, 152; Westfall 1974a, 169f.; Krautheimer 1970, 268–270 n.28; Borsi 1975, 316 n.1).[21] There is only one source for even one meeting between the two men; it is as frequently cited as it is highly problematical. It relates that Alberti presented his books on architecture to Pope Nicholas V and that he successfully advised Nicholas to call off the project of rebuilding the west end of St. Peter's. In other words, Alberti appears as a critic of Nicholas's most ambitious and, perhaps, controversial project, one that nevertheless constitutes a central achievement in Manetti's account of the pope's building programs.

The information in question is contained in a schematic chronicle, the *De temporibus suis*, written by Mattia Palmieri, a Pisan humanist active in Florence and Rome, whose entry on Nicholas, Alberti, and the papal building works is introduced by the reference to the coronation of Frederick III of 1452. Consequently it is generally assumed that the presentation of Alberti's treatise to Nicholas occurred in 1452, soon after Rossellino's arrival in Rome and about the time of the beginning of work on the St. Peter's *tribuna* project; acceptance of this has led to extensive debates on whether or not Alberti had completed his book in 1452 or continued to work on it after its presentation to Nicholas. As Westfall correctly notes, however, Palmieri's chronicle, if its evidential value is accepted, does not require the assignment of the date 1452 to anything except the emperor's visit.[22]

If Alberti found papal favor in 1452, he may well have owed this to the good offices of men such as the bankers Tommaso Spinelli and Roberto Martelli, who were deeply implicated in the financing of the pope's building programs and who, at least in the case of Spinelli, played an important role in the ceremonies welcoming the emperor. On the other hand, the pope's attitude to Prospero Colonna, his kin, and perhaps those associated with him underwent a change, as argued in chapter 3, following the conspiracy of Stefano Porcari. If, then, Alberti was still, like Flavio Biondo, associated in the pope's eyes with the Colonna, the presentation of the treatise should more plausibly be dated in the year or so after the execution of Porcari in January 1453. For much of that year, however, the news of the fall of Constantinople, which reached Rome on July 8, gave the pope other and more pressing concerns than Alberti's theories or even the building programs, though these were not markedly cut back until 1454, the year, perhaps not coincidentally, of Nello da Bologna's death.[23] A date in late 1453 or early 1454 seems particularly likely, therefore, for the presentation of the treatise. If so, this was already in its final form; at least, the text seems to reflect no changes made in the atmosphere of post-Nicholan Rome, when Prospero Colonna's standing in the city was particularly high.

But what of the assertion that Alberti's advice stopped the papal project? At first sight it seems preposterous; the political circumstances at the end of Nicholas's pontificate are surely far more likely to have curtailed expensive building campaigns, except those directly concerned with the improvement of the defenses of the Vatican. It is likely that Palmieri, who was probably writing many years after the events described, indeed after Alberti's death in 1472, relied on accounts of the matter that perhaps derived from Alberti himself, who in his old age, as we have seen, was especially opposed to conspicuous and, as he saw it, typically curial building campaigns. But the question also arises of Mattia Palmieri's relations with the author whose chronicle, abandoned at the year 1448, he continued. This was the remarkably similarly named Matteo Palmieri, a Florentine humanist of some importance, whose chronicle had proved to be extremely popular thanks to its clever and easily legible diagrammatic layout of the main facts of successive years (Scaramella 1906, xxvi).

It is not clear why the Florentine Palmieri gave up this enterprise in 1448; he continued to produce his more expansive chronicle of Florentine history, the *Annales*, until 1474, the year before his death (ibid., xxi). In the *Annales* he has little enough to say about Nicholas V and nothing about the building campaigns, perhaps because his major concern is with events in Florence. It is surely of significance, however, that Matteo Palmieri was in close contact with Leonardo Dati, who made a copy of his friend's chronicle in 1448, the year it ended (ibid., xxiv). Dati, as we have seen, was one of the group of humanists, associated with Ambrogio Traversari and including Gaspare da Verona and Flavio Biondo, as well as Matteo Palmieri himself (Varese 1955, 351), who enjoyed a marked lack of success under Nicholas, at a time when the skills and expertise of the humanists were much in demand; I have also noted Dati's close links to Alberti. It might even seem that Palmieri's concentration on specifically Florentine matters, or at least those of direct pertinence to Florence, during a time when events in Rome may well have seemed of particular interest and when the Jubilee was less than two years away, involved a deliberate silence. It is, once again, a case of a missing witness.

The question of Alberti's role in the conception and formulation of Nicholas's architectural and broadly urbanistic projects can probably never be solved satisfactorily. Tafuri (1987) has argued cogently that Alberti's ethical and intellectual position necessarily placed him in opposition to Nicholas's projects. This argument presupposes, however, acceptance of Manetti's account as accurately representing Nicholas's architectural visions and his urban policies throughout his pontificate; as we have seen, this view cannot withstand the evidence. In any case, moreover, Alberti's authorial performance in the *De re aedificatoria* is surely that of a master courtier, indeed dissimulator. It is worth giving attention, then, to the proposal of C. R. Mack (1982), esp. 63, that the Vatican project went through three stages, one of consolidation and restoration, one of partial reconstruction, which was begun in 1452, and a third project that is echoed in Manetti's account.[24] If Alberti produced or at least contributed to such a third project, presumably in the context of the abandonment of the second project in circumstances indicated by Mattia Palmieri, his concept was surely related to the project for the Tempio Malatestiano that I have argued was created, at least in broad terms, in 1450 in the context of papal policies in the ecclesiastical territories more distant from Rome and less susceptible to direct papal control. It involved the fusion of a new celebrative and commemorative architecture with an existing, in some ways outmoded building, and as such provided a paradigm for the discussions about St. Peter's, if not for specific solutions.

A serious fault in this scenario is the coincidence, pointed out by Urban (1963), 136–149, between Manetti's Vatican basilica and the evidence of the actual construction. If so, Manetti recorded not the third, the "Albertian project," but the second, which surely has no features that require us to link it with Alberti. And though Rossellino, the recently appointed *ingegnere del palazzo*, is recorded by Manetti as the architect of Nicholas's Vatican projects, we may suspect, like most students of these problems, the unrecorded involvement of more influential figures.

Alberti is not the only candidate. It is certain that Nello da Bologna played a major role in the formation and management of the Vatican *cantiere*; it would be consistent with his administrative style if the design of 1452 resulted from a collaborative situation, not from the work of a single author, as Manetti represents it. No doubt Rossellino was involved, perhaps with particular responsibility for architectural ornament (though his assignment to the ill-fated *torrione* project implies that his position in the *cantiere* was weak, even before that building collapsed). And Nello's assistant Francesco del Borgo may have played a significant role, drawing both on his studies of classical mathematics and engineering and on his own administrative experience at the Ripa Grande, which involved, as I noted, a number of construction projects; if so, the river led to the basilica. But with Nello's death in 1454, Francesco's star may have waned precipitously, while Manetti, concerned to transmit a magnificent image of the pope's building campaigns, chose to represent them as carried out under the unified direction of the new—and Florentine—Hiram of Tyre, Rossellino. Francesco, as we saw, found employment with Cardinal Barbo, becoming papal architect on the latter's accession as Paul II; it is important that Paul not only expanded the Palazzo S. Marco, but also had work resumed on Nicholas's project for the west end of St. Peter's. Francesco perhaps oversaw both projects, owing his leading role in the former to his involvement under Nicholas in the the latter, the boldest construction project of the century, to which he now returned.

Alberti, on the other hand, played no discernible role in the Nicholan restoration projects carried out in Rome in preparation for the Jubilee and the emperor's visit, with the probable exception of some technical consultations and his involvement with the replanning of the Piazza S. Celso of 1451–52 thanks to the mediation of well-placed friends. His one documented major architectural commission was for the partial rebuilding of a church in remote Rimini, in which he was able to experiment in the application of a rich *all'antica* vocabulary and the realization on a limited scale of his ideas about urban space and monumentalism. If an Alberti design for St. Peter's was ever entertained, it was later, probably in 1454, when, after a period of crisis and agony, Nicholas was able to engineer a treaty among the reciprocally suspicious and often hostile Italian powers, when Alberti could point to the Tempio, now in an advanced state of realization, as a paradigm for a more splendid basilica than any dreamed up by Nello's committee, and when Cardinal Colonna had been fully restored to favor. This may have been the basis for Palmieri's story about the end of Nicholas's St. Peter's project.

Alberti conducted the work at Rimini at a distance, doubtless with little concern for the place itself and its inhabitants. Rome, however, was another matter. Here he had studied the ancient fabric of the city with deep reverence and had become associated with some of the leading figures of its elite society, both curial and aristocratic. His proposals for urban transformation in accordance with principles extrapolated from ancient writings and practice coexist, as we saw in the particular and emblematic case of the Ponte S. Angelo and its reconstruction, in a condition, not of committed opposition to, but doubtless of tension with papal architectural patronage and its ideological resonances; to this extent Tafuri's argument holds.

The ideal *all'antica* city of the *De re aedificatoria* illustrates general principles; it does not constitute a physical model in the manner of Filarete's slightly later ideal city (fig. 44). Alberti conceives of the city as a place both expressive and productive of public and private morality and *virtù*. An aspect of that *virtù* is the active engagement of a free patriciate, mindful of the cultural and ethical values of antiquity, in framing the setting of the rituals and processes of their lives. Ironically, Alberti's general position accords best with the atmosphere and policies of the earlier part of Nicholas's pontificate, a period of reconciliation and collaboration between Nicholas and the local social elite, indeed of Westfall's "concordat." By the time Alberti's moment came, if it came, the pope's life was ebbing. Soon Nicholas's main concern was no longer the actual improvement of the city and the enhancement of its shrines, but his own place in the history of his office and his faith; we recall his commitment to the discipline of history, to collective memory, and his conviction of the efficacy of historical representation. No longer did he seek to improve and clarify the existing city; now he commissioned Manetti to set against it a utopic and monumental double, an imaginary place that belongs more in the realm of the fulsome rhetoric of the Renaissance papal court than in that of the myriad exchanges and compromises of which the development of any city, as opposed to an artificial enclave, is necessarily composed.

Notes

Note on Currency
In mid-fifteenth-century Rome various currency systems were used simultaneously, giving rise to a variety of scholarly opinions about the value of particular coins at a given time. The papal florin was a gold coin modeled on the famous Florentine coin. With the increasing prestige and widespread use of the Venetian ducat during the fifteenth century, the ducat tended to replace the florin at Rome as elsewhere as the major currency of account (by the sixteenth century the *scudo d'oro* was taking its place); generally florins and ducats were equivalent in value. In 1439, however, Eugenius IV carried out a reform of the currency, issuing a new coin, the *ducato papale*, worth 70 *bolognini*, at a higher value than the *ducato* (or *fiorino*) *romano*, at 68 *bolognini*. By 1451 the papal ducat had stabilized at 72 *bolognini*; in ledgers of Nicholas's pontificate it is referred to as the *ducato d'oro de Camera* (Oliva 1981, 232 n.28). The term *fiorino di camera* that occasionally occurs in these account books apparently does not refer to a separate coin, though by the pontificate of Paul II the *fiorino di camera* had established itself as a separate coin, and was worth 72 *bolognini* or *baiocchi*, slightly less than the *fiorino papale* at the time. The ledgers clearly often refer to gold currency as a money of account; no doubt in actual transactions considerable use was made of silver coinage, i.e., of the *grosso*. Under Nicholas V an attempt was made to stabilize and rationalize the relationship between the *grosso* and the gold coinage (the ducat was to be worth 10 *grossi*), but this was unsuccessful, perhaps because of the crisis of silver production caused by the loss of Venetian mines in modern Yugoslavia to the Turks (the Venetian *grosso* had already suffered a drastic reduction in weight during the wars with Milan of 1426–54). See Muntoni (1972), xxiii–xxvii, 51–53; Spufford (1988), 358–359.

Introduction
1. These remarks draw especially on McClung (1983); Cosgrove (1984); Rowntree and Conkey (1980); Pred (1984). I am grateful to Meg Conkey for the last two references.

2. See the brief but apposite discussion in McClung (1983), 116–119, of what he calls "natural artifacts." The arrival of Aeneas in Latium is the subject of an interesting discussion in Herendeen (1986), 54–58.

3. On the building legislation of Rome see Re (1920); Scaccia-Scarafoni (1927); Magnuson (1958), 34–41; Westfall (1973), 77–84. Stephen Tobriner is preparing a major study on this subject.

4. An exemplary study of these issues is Connors (1980), esp. 81–83, 90–92, on the process by which major institutional complexes of the later sixteenth and early seventeenth centuries developed in topographical contexts to which at first they adapted themselves, but which they ended by dominating. The bibliography of the development of papal Rome is of course vast, but the names of Krautheimer (1980, 1986), Frommel (1973), Tafuri (1984, 1987), and Guidoni (1972, 1981) nevertheless stand out. These scholars, in turn, built on the work of Tomei (1942) and Giovannoni (1935, 1946). Of great importance to this study, in addition, is the postwar current of social historical investigation represented especially by the numerous publications of Corbo, Brezzi, Esch, Lombardo, and Maire-Vigueur.

5. Tafuri's recent study (1987), briefly discussed below, integrates the social historical and architectural historical traditions; it came to my notice after the present work was substantially complete.

6. On Pasquino there is an excellent chapter in Dickinson (1960), 155–163. See also Silenzi and Silenzi (1968); Marucci (1983). There is agreement that pasquinades as such do not occur until the early cinquecento, but that the tradition of satirical verse in Rome goes back at least to the time of Martin V, though it is not well documented for the earlier period (see the examples of attacks on Nicholas collected in Silenzi and Silenzi 1968, 231f.). Any connection of this with Marforio or other statues is, at present, purely speculative.

7. See the remarks of Flavio Biondo in *Roma instaurata* (Basel 1559), 222, cited by Marchant (1973), 63. The book was composed in 1444–46, according to Weiss (1969), 68.

8. Clearly, Renaissance representations of cities continued to have iconological or even emblematic import, as is clear for example from the work of Schulz (1978). The significance of the mode(s) of representation in early modern city views is a theme of Marin (1973), esp. 257–290; it is also beautifully discussed in a forthcoming article by J. G. Turner (paper delivered at the annual conference of the Society of Architectural Historians, 1987).

9. The dating of Alberti's treatise is a vexed question; see chapter 7.

10. Among many possible examples see Alberti (1966a), 1:146f.(II.x), on the practice of tile makers, and 1:216f. (III.x), on the *periti* who know about wall building.

11. Note especially the study of Urban (1963) on Nicholas's building project at St. Peter's, which judiciously correlates the archival and documentary evidence with that of Manetti's text, though even here the former is interpreted in the light of the latter.

12. On the Florentine material see Bec (1967); the most successful of the relatively few studies of the Roman situation that attempt to work along the same lines, though using very different documentation, is Esch (1973). Note also the work of Massimo Miglio (see bibliography), who has in recent years given increasing attention to material from more popular milieus.

13. Millar (1977) contributed a radical rethinking of the relation of center and periphery in the Roman Empire; he was able to show that the emperors and their staffs to a great extent responded to initiatives and problems arising locally, rather than instituting and then implementing a coherent, a priori policy; Warnke's work on medieval architectural campaigns (1976) is explicitly influenced by Millar's work.

14. Westfall (1974a), esp. 36–39. The notion of the "book of nature" and kindred ideas proved particularly durable, and indeed underwent something of a revival in the later Renaissance with the rise of the fashion for emblems: see Harms (1973).

15. The passage is partially quoted and discussed at length by Westfall (1974a), 33f. The full text is still only accessible in Manetti 1734, cc.949–950.

16. See, for example, Heydenreich (1937), which attempts to group the projects of Fabriano, Rome, and Pienza as realizations of a common perspectival vision of urban space. A critique of such notions is offered by Burroughs (1982b).

17. Manetti (1734), c.353: "molem ipsam extrinsecus [Nicholas] crebris propugnaculis corrobavit, ac tectoriis dealbavit." See D'Onofrio (1978), 254.

18. It is appropriate here to cite a suggestive passage in Giovannoni's discussion (1935, 37f.) of the remaining vernacular residential architecture of the fifteenth century in Rome: "Tutte codeste, pur modeste, opere architettoniche non sono mute ed anonime...ma narrano con le iscrizioni e con gli stemmi le proprie vicende, parlano amichevolmente al popolo del loro tempo..."

19. The recent outpouring of books on Ruskin is a phenomenon of great interest. For Ruskin's own critique of Renaissance classicism see, e.g., *The Stones of Venice* (London 1851), 36–39.

20. The public rituals of Renaissance Rome are the subject of the unpublished research of Richard Ingersoll, to whom I am grateful for sharing his work with me.

1 Urban Pattern and Symbolic Landscapes

1. Aeneas Sylvius (Pope Pius II) quoted by Pastor (1949), 193; Decembrio cited in Borsa (1893), 376f. There was particular interest in Nicholas's architectural program in Counter-Reformation Rome: Lewine (1965), 225 n.129. This was surely not, as Lewine suggests, merely a matter of the adventitious impact of Vasari's recently published life of Alberti.

2. On the *possesso* of Nicholas V, see Pastor (1949), 30–32, quoting from the account of Aeneas Sylvius, who had carried the cross in front of the pope. On the *possesso* in general see Schimmelpfennig (1974).

3. The famous frescoes of Masolino and Masaccio in S. Clemente must, in addition, be regarded as related to the embellishment of the Lateran (Wohl 1980, 7–12).

4. In a fresco in Nicholas's chapel Fra Angelico shows St. Peter ordaining St. Stephen in a building that clearly evokes St. Peter's basilica (Stinger 1985, 173) and in which St. Peter stands at the altar, the marker of his own tomb (fig. 20).

5. Already in 1452 alterations to the liturgy of major ceremonies were made to accommodate the physical frailty of the pope (Wasner 1968, 153).

6. Nello's name appears in many documents published by Müntz (1878), though Müntz was not aware of his crucial role and missed the most important documents relating to his activity (see chapter 4 below).

7. Infessura (1890), 36–38. The execution took place on the Campo, doubtless partly through its proximity to the scene of the crime but also perhaps through its traditional association with communal acts of judicial retribution (Herklotz 1985, 8). The ceremony during which the malefactors were stripped of their clerical rank occurred in S. Maria in Aracoeli, the church most closely associated with the commune, while they waited for their execution in an elevated cage in the Campo de' Fiori, the traditional site of public executions. Their punishment, then, was distributed throughout the city.

8. Westfall (1974a), 95, describes the building campaign at the Senator's Palace, noting that Nicholas planned a tower at each end of the side facing the Forum. He assumes that Nicholas's arms on the walled-up arcades of the Tabularium indicate that this work was done for Nicholas and, more controversially, that this and the work on the towers formed parts of a unified project, though he admits (ibid., n.46) that the work on the towers may have been undertaken sequentially, as the documents suggest. The eastern tower, the only one of the two to be completed, always projected more distinctly from the building to which it was attached. It is possible, then, that an original design with a single tower was replaced by one that framed the rear of the building; in other words, that an emphasis on the architectural celebration of a processional axis gave way to that on the formal symmetry and overall aesthetic character of the building itself (in actuality, the building when seen from the west remained something of a jumble of elements). If so, the former design echoed the thirteenth-century (?) emphasis on the steps to the side of the Senator's Palace through the placement of an obelisk in line with them (Krautheimer 1982, 286). For representations of the palace as four-towered at the corners see the Dupérac view (fig. 3), and note the phrase of Fichard, who visited Rome in 1536, "oblunga quadrataque forma est." This is cited by Thies (1982), 85, though he insists on the irregularity of the building and the absence of a tower at the southeastern corner: evidently, Thies's perceptions do not correspond to those of the sixteenth, to say nothing of the fifteenth century!

9. See the important analysis of Ceen (1977), esp. 3–12, of the particular sequential character of urban space in Rome. I would argue that Ceen's comments can be applied to urban conditions of the period in general, and that his contrast of sequential and triumphal axial throughfares is overdrawn.

10. I am grateful to Richard Ingersoll for sharing with me his research on processions and processional routes in Renaissance Rome. On the agreements often signed by popes, including Nicholas, and the commune, see Westfall (1974a), 74f.

11. The basic study of the Via Maggiore is still Adinolfi (1857a). It is remarkable that Guidoni (1983), 373, mentions the Via Maggiore only once, and then almost in passing, though he emphasizes the importance of the church of S. Francesca Romana (S. Maria Nuova) in the policies of Gregory XI (1370–78).

12. See Lanciani (1902) 1:193–195; Gnoli (1939), 323. The area was often designated as a *campo* (e.g., Campo Turclani/Torrecchiano), perhaps because of the quite extensive open space where animals were bought and sold in fenced corrals as regulated in the fourteenth-century city statutes (Re 1880, 164; Malatesta 1886, 100, 112).

13. On the distribution of baronial strongpoints in early fourteenth-century Rome see Guidoni (1983), 325–327, and on the decline especially of the Annibaldi, ibid., 347–360. Guidoni interprets the change in the Via Maggiore area in terms of the ascendancy of the Colonna; however, the baronial caste in general was challenged by the legislation for the Via Maggiore (see chapter 6 below).

14. Broise and Maire-Vigueur (1983), 101–103, emphasize the documentary importance of the property records of the major confraternities. These are not,however, discussed in the passage (ibid., 141f.) on public space and the sense of community. The archives of the fourteenth-century Roman confraternities are finally receiving the attention they deserve; see the synthesizing remarks of A. Esposito in Brezzi and Lee (1984), 69–80.

15. On the confraternity see Maroni-Lumbroso and Martini (1963), 394–399; Maire-Vigueur (1974), 94–97; Guidoni (1983), 369, 377. The major studies are still those of Egidi (1908, 1914). Paola Pavan is at work on a major study of the confraternity and its records; see Pavan (1978, 1984).

16. Guidoni (1983), 377 n.5, notes the gradual acquisition by the confraternity of much of the Colosseum. See also chapter 6 below.

17. The statutes remained in force until 1510 (Guidoni 1983, 377). For Nicholas's creation of the confraternity "domina e custode del Coliseo" see Grisar (1908), 18. This must have been interpreted by contemporaries as a gesture of support for the confraternity and its claims.

18. The standard works on the chapel are Grisar (1908); Dell'Addolorata (1919); Cempanari and Amodei (1963). See also Rohault de Fleury (1877), 380–390.

19. Perosa (1960), 71: "Item si dice che in detta cappella non si puo dire messa se none per la persona del papa, et ch'egli e piu che cento anni che non vi si disse mai messa, ne per lo papa ne per altri, salvo che il passato papa Nichola quinto vi fece dire messa a uno suo cappellano l'anno 1448." (For the legend of St. Peter, see ibid., 70.) See also Caffari (1886), 609: on Friday, May 24 (in 1447 according to Caffari's editor, Coletti), Nicholas himself was present at a mass in the chapel "quod nunquam fuit auditum." This was in the context of several processions and similar rituals noted by Caffari. It is possible that restoration work on the chapel was carried out under Nicholas, though it is not documented: according to Grisar (1908), 24, the arms of Calixtus III appear on the building; if so it is likely that they mark the completion of work initiated under Nicholas, as seems to have been the case at the Ponte Milvio (see chapter 6 below).

20. Grisar (1908), 39–54. The decoration of the icon is largely medieval, though there is some fifteenth-century work of high quality (ibid., 47). For the ritual importance of the icon in the ceremonies marking the establishment of the papal state see ibid., 39–40.

21. On the procession see Marangoni (1747), 117–124; Dell'Addolorata (1919), 270; Montenovesi (1942). It was banned in the sixteenth century (Grisar 1908, 44). I am grateful to Richard Ingersoll for sharing with me his unpublished study of the procession.

22. For Everso's will see Adinolfi (1857a), 135–137. It seems that Everso's association with the hospital was related to his alliance with the Colonna (Curcio 1978, 30).

23. Curcio (1978), 30, notes that a special sale of five palaces occurred shortly before, presumably to raise funds for, the building of the new wing of the hospital in 1450.

24. For references to sales of property due to shortage of "pecuniae manuales" see, e.g., ASR, AOSS, Istromenti 25, fol. 2r (vineyard); fol. 11r (*domus studii*); fol. 45r (*casale*). One of many cases of payment in installments is at Egidi (1908), 369.

25. Egidi records a quilt valued at 37 florins (1908, 351) and two beds valued at nearly 50 florins (ibid., 378). Half a house, a mere *domuncula*, could be valued at as little as 36 florins (ibid., 414). On the generally poor quality of housing in early quattrocento Rome see Corbo (1967); Broise and Maire-Vigueur (1983), 106.

26. This is occasionally made explicit; for example on February 4, 1454, the *guardiani* sold a *vigna* donated to the confraternity because "guardiani non habent de presenti pecunias manuales pro subventione dicte vinee propter alias necessitates hospitalis" (ASR, AOSS, Istromenti 25, fol. 2r).

27. For an example of a large pledge of property in Nicholas's pontificate see ASR, CNC 482, fol. 184r: on September 4, 1451, Jacopo Luzi promised a dowry of 14,000 florins and pledged half a *casale*. On aristocratic marriage usage in general see Gnoli (1938), 20f.

28. On the Capranica estate at Cave see Tomassetti (1979), 3:613. Broise and Maire-Vigueur (1983), 131, have emphasized the rural paradigm of the organization of urban space in medieval Rome. They do not posit a deliberate allusion to rural models, such as castles, in urban architecture.

29. See Tomei (1942), 49, 60f.; Magnuson (1958), 227–229. More recently, C. W. Westfall has devoted an important article to quattrocento palace architecture (Westfall 1974b): he also places a radical shift at midcentury, but sees this as a formal phenomenon and ascribes it purely to the influence of the design of Nicholas's Vatican palace, which in turn marks, in his view, a direct expression of political ideas in architectural form. It is an argument consistent with Westfall's thoroughgoing idealism and his tendency to maintain "trickle-down" theories of cultural process.

30. The Caetani palace is described and its resemblance to the slightly earlier palace of Nicholas V noted by Michele da Prato in a letter of November 15, 1453 (Caetani 1926, 34). It is not mentioned by Westfall.

31. Tomei (1942), 61, gives the date 1451 for the completion of the remodeling; the college was founded in 1456. A full, more up-to-date discussion of the building is in Westfall (1974b), 103f.

32. There is a useful survey of window types in use in quattrocento Rome in Golzio and Zander (1968), 103f., though they do not mention inscriptions, insignia, etc., associated with windows. On the fashion for guelph windows in Rome see Tomei (1942), 49f., 53, emphasizing the role of the Val d'Aosta and Piemonte in the process of diffusion from France. Westfall (1974b), 106, points specifically to the possible role in this of the papal palace at Avignon. Giovannoni (1935 [article first published in 1913]), 32, on the other hand, saw the guelph window as derived from vernacular practice: "puo dirsi la pietrificazione del telaio in legno della finestra medioevale." Inscriptions on guelph windows occur conspicuously at the Palazzo S. Marco (Palazzo Venezia) (Magnuson 1958, 216; Frommel 1984, 115, 139, suggesting that the model was the windows on the Nicholan Palazzo dei Conservatori) and at the Vatican palace, though the earliest extant examples there carry the monogram of Leo X (Pietrangeli 1984, 214f.). For the celebrated inscription *HAVE ROMA* on the windows (some of which were guelph windows) of 1468 in the Casa dei Manili at the Piazza dei Giudei see Giovannoni (1935), 33.

33. Two brothers of the Rione Trevi, Angelo and Francesco Papazzuri, perhaps on the occasion of the former's marriage, commissioned two Illyrian craftsmen to build an addition to their palace situated "iuxta montem," no doubt the Quirinal. The work was to be "ad similitudinem domorum rev. domini Cardinalis de Columpna" (ASR, CNC 418, fol. 287r). The marriage contract was signed on August 21, 1447 (ibid., fol. 277r). For the letter of March 29, 1462, of Guido de' Nerli to Mantua see Chambers (1976), 43 doc. 3. It should be noted that scholarly emphasis on the indigenous character of fifteenth-century

Roman architecture is relatively new; Giovannoni (1935), 29, for instance, had argued that the "decline of the fourteenth century" interrupted local architectural traditions, and that building in the succeeding century only reflected what was going on elsewhere, especially in Lombardy and Tuscany, where the majority of builders came from.

34. On the almost canonical use of the octagonal pier at Rome see, e.g., Broise and Maire-Vigueur (1983), 159. Frommel (1984), 146f., assumes that the use, even with an admitted high degree of sophistication, of octagonal piers at the Palazzetto S. Marco reflects merely the conservatism of the auteur-architect, Francesco del Borgo, posited by Frommel; this betrays a remarkably narrow view of architectural historical explanation.

35. Tomei (1942), 51, followed by Broise and Maire-Vigueur (1983), 158, denies that the *cortile* was a regular element of Roman palace architecture until the later quattrocento; instead, Roman palaces consisted, in his view, of a line of rooms. However, such early Roman palaces as the Palazzi del Governo Vecchio, Sforza-Cesarini, and dell'Orologio contained spaces that should surely be described as courtyards, and their example suggests that an enclosure existed also behind the Palazzo Capranica, surrounded by service buildings (Magnuson 1958, 228f.). Such enclosures, especially in grander palaces, should surely not be distinguished—at least in functional terms, which is what is at issue here—from Florentine *cortili* as sharply as they are by Tomei. Broise and Maire-Vigueur (1983), 146, 150, indeed, see the linear palace type as mediating between street and courtyard. On the Florentine courtyard type see the overstated but valuable arguments of Hersey (1976), esp. 164–191.

36. A case of a courtyard used for a notarial transaction is that recorded in Caetani (1930), 5:9 no. 2690 (July 29, 1450). Such use of courtyards was doubtless typical, when they existed. In this respect, the cloister yards of conventual establishments and secular palace courtyards overlapped functionally; Caffari (1885), 574, for instance, records a betrothal transaction carried out in the cloister of S. Maria sopra Minerva.

37. The crucial phrase is "ut quasi non publicum expeditumque iter, sed potius obiectae domus aditum praebeant (minutiores viae)" (Alberti 1966a, 1:309 [IV. vi]). The example given is Babylon, albeit in antiquity, though elsewhere Alberti praises the Islamic house, closed to the exterior (ibid., 1:341 [V.ii]). Note also his comments on the fragmentation of Cairo into distinct neighborhoods (ibid., 1:335 [V.i]).

38. Alberti 1966a, 1:339 [V.ii]: "Porticum quidem et vestibulum non servorum magis, uti Diodorus putat, quam universorum civium gratia positum arbitramur." Alberti clearly implies that Diodorus's words are valid for his own day. On the other hand, porticoes would presumably retain their high status if adorned with images of famous deeds, as Alberti recommends (ibid., 2:803 [IX.vi]).

39. ASR, CNC 482, fol. 53v; cf. ibid., fols. 88v, 141v. Examples of arbitration from the same period from four other notarial protocols are CNC 1085, fol. 1r; CNC 1232, fol. 151; CNC 1684, fol. 111; ACR, Archivio Urbano, Fondo notarile 253, fol. 2r. A case of an eminent arbitrator is that involving the Milanese ambassador Nicodemo Tranchedini, called to adjudicate a dispute between Cardinal Pietro Barbo and a commune near Todi (ASR, CNC 1684, fol. 111 [December 21, 1452]). The tribunal was held in Tranchedini's own house.

40. ASR, CNC 481, fol. 454 (April 13, 1454). Similarly, an arbitration was held by a judge enthroned "in quodam sede" in the sala of Marino Orsini, Archbishop of Taranto (ibid. 1684, fol. 1r [April 21, 1451]).

41. Note Westfall's observation of the theatral character of the loggia specifically of the Medici palace, which, significantly, was an interior structure, mediating between *cortile* and garden.

42. "Veteres aut porticum aedibus aut sessionem apponebant, utramque non semper lineis rectis, sed insinuatis in theatri modum" (Alberti 1966a, 2:795 [IX.iii]).

43. Mellini was procurator of the Vatican chapter throughout Nicholas's pontificate: BAV, ACSP, Censuali 5 and 6 passim, see esp. 6 (1452), fol. 49r (Mellini represents the chapter in the litigation on the rights to the estate of S. Pietro in Formis). He is once named as "procurator et notarius curie Romane" (ASR, CNC 482, fol. 200r). He had clients in baronial circles; in 1451 he represented Jacoba de' Conti, wife of Orsino Orsini, in a case arbitrated by Archbishop Marino Orsini (!) (Coppi 1864, 335 n.184, citing ASR, CNC 1684, fol. 1r). He appears often as witness in transactions carried out for the nuns of the important convent of S. Lorenzo in Panisperna, including the sale of houses on the Piazza of S. Maria Rotonda (ASR, CNC 482, fol. 135r). And he was procurator and *depositarius* of Angelo, Abbot of S. Anastasio alle Tre Fontane, the close associate of Cardinal Ludovico Trevisan (see chapter 3) (ASR, CNC 1684, fol. 14v; sale of a house in Viterbo). In December 1452 Mellini appeared as a witness in the "camera paramenti" of the cardinal's palace (ASR, CNC 1684, fol. 10v).

44. Contrast transactions enacted up to 1451 "in domo Petri Milini" (e.g., ASR, CNC 1684, fols. 3v, 31r, 53r). Curiously, these documents seldom mention Mellini himself; evidently the notary, Giorgio de Signo, was a protégé of his. One of de Signo's transactions, enacted in Mellini's house in 1451, involved the builder Paolo Pisanelli, who undertook to work with marble "pro intagliando" in the house of Paolo Mezzatesta; Pisanelli perhaps also worked for the Mellini, though no direct evidence has yet come to light.

45. On the later elaboration of the Mellini houses by Pietro and his descendants see Tomei (1942), 270; under Sixtus IV Pietro restored the fine tower that still stands on the Via dell'Anima.

46. On the house signs of the Vatican chapter see Pecchiai (1952). The holdings of the Confraternity of the Salvatore were more uniformly marked with the sign of the Savior (Guidoni 1983, 377). In 1456 a carpenter was hired to add a second story to a building facing the Piazza Mercatelli and to display on the house the figure of the Savior to make clear the ownership of the house, which was rented for life to Pietro Juliani, one of the confraternity's staunchest members (ASR, AOSS, Istromenti 25, fol. 50v). A further interesting case implies that house signs occasionally were considered emblematic of the occupants; in July 1448 a house passed from the knight Sbardellato to Jacopo Vannucci, bishop of Rimini, and the sign changed from the paw of a lion to a bishop's miter though the landlord continued to be the chapter of St. Peter's (BAV, ACSP, Censuali 5 [1447f.], fol. 12r).

47. The church acquired by the confraternity was S. Lucia Vecchia in Ponte; the confraternity expanded rapidly, and a revision of its statutes was needed already in 1456.

48. On the general phenomenon of towers, see Tomei (1942), 51. Westfall (1974a), 105, notes evidence that towers were thought to be relics of ancient palaces; this was a rationalization that was apparently not widely adopted in the fifteenth century.

49. "Non tamen proximam abhinc ad annos CC aetatem laudo, quam habuit communis *quidem morbus turrium astruendarum* etiam minutis in oppidis: nemo pater familias turre potuisse carere visus est; hinc passim silvae surgebant turrium" (Alberti 1966a, 2:699 [VIII.v]). Alberti stresses the sociopolitical inappropriateness of such towers (ibid., 2:809 [IX.iv]). See the general discussion of von Moos (1974), 80f.

50. On the triumphal arch see Alberti (1966a), 2:717f. [VIII.iv]. The historical paintings that Alberti recommends for porticoes (ibid., 802f.) imply an assimilation of the portico to the triumphal arch, the most conspicuous surviving ancient site of images of historical events, as also of the house to the city.

51. The *locus classicus* is Alberti (1966a), 1:65 [I.ix]. Von Moos (1974), 24, notes the relation, which he restricts to Tuscany, of residential and civic towers.

52. This is often noted; e.g., Hay (1977), 41: "Nicholas began the process of putting his name with his insignia." For contemporary attention to Nicholas's arms (in this case in a noteworthy context) see Infessura's statement on the Trevi fountain ("Rifece e adornò la

fonte di Trevi, secondo che si dimostrava per le lettere et armi sue inpiù luoghi"), while in the next century Vasari was struck by the juxtaposition in the same place of the arms of the pope and commune (Müntz 1878, 156f. nn.3–4). Müntz also notes the conspicuous presence of Nicholas's arms on the city walls (ibid., 159). The fullest account of Nicholan inscriptions is unfortunately unpublished (Marchant 1973); Marchant counts 17 documented inscriptions from Nicholan Rome (ibid., 65–67: 5 were on the city walls, 5 on restored churches, and the rest at the Vatican) and argues for a quantitatively distinct phase under Nicholas in the papal employment of architectural epigraphy. It was also a qualitative shift; see the discussion of the innovative type of certain Nicholan epigraphic texts in Kajanto (1982), 60–63. On the early Renaissance use of inscriptions in the city see the general discussion of Petrucci (1983), 17–28. It is interesting that not all the inscriptions were meant to be seen: Nicholas's arms are stamped on tiles used in the restoration of the Pantheon, suggesting that a quasi-magical association of the great building and the pope was in question, though there were doubtless also visible reminders of Nicholas's role in the project (Marchant 1973, 79).

53. Nicholas gave particular attention to the Ponte S. Maria (Ponte Rotto) and the harbor facilities at Ripa (Castagnoli et al. 1958, 359). See the discussion in chapter 7 below.

54. Krautheimer (1982), 58, emphasizes the original association of S. Stefano Rotondo and the Lateran. The twelfth-century restoration of the church, moreover, was connected with a renewed emphasis on the Lateran (ibid., 325).

55. Here, of course, the discussion is indebted to Foucault (1972), esp. 22–25. In contrast note Westfall's use of Nicholas's Jubilee Bull and other edicts (Westfall 1974a, 17–34).

2 Interior Architectures: Discordance and Resolution in the Frescoes of Nicholas's Private Chapel

1. The chapel was created within a corner tower in the existing palace structure, on the floor above Nicholas's bedroom; hence Fra Angelico could go to work while the building of the new *ala di Niccolò V* was in progress (Westfall 1974a, 132). The *studiolo* is thought to have been one of two adjoining rooms.

2. For negative assessments of the frescoes see Gori-Montanelli (1959), 170 ("le architetture tendono a tornare verso quell'eccessiva oggettivazione che aveva caratterizzato le sue cose giovanili"); Beck (1981), 66f., singling out for criticism the scene of St. Lawrence distributing alms. Even Pope-Hennessy (1974), 32, has reservations, especially about the treatment of the architecture.

3. Krautheimer (1941), 364f., proposed that the later fifteenth-century restoration of a group of churches according to "neo-Early Christian" principles, as then understood, was dependent on formal ideas current under Nicholas V and exemplified in a hypothetical project of no later than 1451 for the restoration of St. Peter's. Magnuson (1958), 203, introduced Fra Angelico's backgrounds into the discussion, noting the serious discrepancies between the architecture represented and what is known of Nicholas's St. Peter's project, though he accepts general stylistic cross-influences. Krautheimer (1977), 292–295, returns to the issue, arguing against Magnuson that the backgrounds constitute a rather direct reflection of a Nicholan St. Peter's project, though he also notes the Brunelleschian echoes in Fra Angelico's work.

4. See Vespasiano da Bisticci (1970), 1:43: ". . . istava la casa del vescovado come istanno le più case de' preti, che sono male a ordine; giunto maestro Tomaso a Bologna, il cardinale cominciò a ragionare collui dello edificare quella casa del vescovado, e dette la comesione a maestro Tomaso, che facessi lui. In brevissimo tempo fece riedificare la casa del vescovado tutta di novo."

5. Michele Canensi (writing in 1451–52) in Miglio (1975), 231: "Nuper autem Assisium profectus nihil Beatitudinis Tuae potius fuit quam ecclesiam illam Beati Francisci collustrare totam undique ac tamquam in omni etiam architectura et aedificio summus auctor excellentissimusque magister universam circumspicere." He goes on to imply

that Nicholas was directly concerned—surely an exaggeration—with the rebuilding of the basilica. Curiously, neither Magnuson nor Westfall cite this passage.

6. As late as March 1455, two years after the fall of Constantinople, Arras tapestries were still being acquired for the dying pope (Müntz 1879, 320).

7. Manetti (1734), c.923. It is a long passage, but note especially: "pontificalibus praeterea mitris... mira quadam... gemmarum... copia exornatis, omnes Ecclesiasticas pontificalesque caerimonias praeter consuetum et usitatum morem mirabiliter condiebat." (On the importance and symbolic resonance of precious stones in Paul II's tiara see the discussion in Miglio [1975], 121–153, esp. 143, citing a passage of Canensi's encomium of Paul that seems to echo this passage, which Miglio does not cite.) Manetti then refers to the psychological effect of Nicholas's stage management of the liturgy: "unde ubicumque illa tam speciosa et tam digna officia intuebantur homines, tanta admiratione, tantoque stupore simul atque devotione capiebantur, ut adumbratam quandam triumphantis Ecclesiae in hac nostra militanti imaginem recognoscerent..." The illocutionary aspect of Nicholas's sacred buildings is emphasized by Battisti (1960), though without giving due attention to the minor arts. The contamination of architecture by the minor arts—embroidery, tapestry work, the arts of goldsmiths and gem cutters and the like—is even suggested in the consecration liturgy, with its reference to the walls of Jerusalem as made of precious stones (Stookey 1969, 37).

8. The presence of architectural metaphor in Italian paintings can be traced back at least to Giotto (Bongiorno 1968; Hausherr 1968, esp. 102). For the notion of disguised symbolism, of which architectural metaphor is a variety, see the classic account of Panofsky (1964a), 1:140–144.

9. For the idea that the figures in the fresco of the ordination of Lawrence represent leading members of Nicholas's court, mostly cardinals, see Orlandi (1964), 100. This is too literalistic, but points in the right direction. On Nicholas's concern with history, see the discussion below.

10. Documentary evidence indicates that the windows of the *studiolo* contained images of the two saints, while Stephen, at least, appeared in the glass of the chapel (Gilbert 1978, 251f., with further references).

11. On Nicholas's restoration of S. Stefano see chapter 1. It is likely that this church, like the Lateran and like SS. Apostoli (see chapter 1), had or was thought to have Constantinian associations; it is all the more likely, then, that Nicholas had Constantinian precedent in mind when he chose the imagery for his private chapel, for a passage of the *Liber pontificalis*, which Nicholas surely knew, informs us that Constantine gave to the basilica of St. Peter's four brass candlesticks, ten feet in height, overlaid with silver, with representations of the acts of the apostles (Kessler 1979, 109). According to Kessler this was a much-noticed case of the use of such imagery.

12. Nicholas's arms were displayed on the building, but it was especially associated with the powerful Cardinal Guillaume d'Estouteville, who in 1448 was charged to proceed against unlawful usurpation and alienation of the church's property (ASV, RV 408, fol. 61v). If d'Estouteville was successful, it is likely that some of the regained wealth went to the restoration of the building.

13. It is perhaps significant that the chapel was rebuilt in the thirteenth century by Nicholas's namesake, Nicholas III (Krautheimer 1980, 209). Some aspects of Nicholas's restoration campaigns may have been modeled on work undertaken by his namesake, as on that of Nicholas IV (see chapter 5). The arms of Nicholas's successor, Calixtus III, appear on the Sancta Sanctorum, perhaps replacing those of Nicholas V (Grisar 1908, 24; cf. Panvinio 1570, 187f.).

14. The provost of the church from 1448 was Gemignano Inghirami, a prominent local citizen with close ties to the Medici and to Nicholas V; at his death in 1460 he was succeeded by Carlo de' Medici, who had been provost designate since at least 1448 (Borsook 1975, 4f.). For Carlo's penchant for magnificence and lavish display see Rochon

(1963), esp. 138 with n.440. Carlo's own artistic interests are suggested by the extant portrait of him by Mantegna, which he presumably commissioned (Borsook 1975, 56; Gilbert 1968, 282 n.5). Gilbert incorrectly asserts that Carlo had no ties with Prato before 1460. It is likely, rather, that he acted as an unofficial Medicean envoy in Prato, whose townspeople were difficult subjects and whose good will it was in the interests of the Medici to cultivate, as suggested by Fubini (1977), 155 no. 52. Certainly, Cosimo's constant concern with the decoration of the church, beginning even before 1434, is documented (Borsook 1975, 4, 58; Marchini 1957, 62f.), while a cupola remarkably similar to that of the Old Sacristy of S. Lorenzo, the burial place of Cosimo's father, appears prominently in the skyline of Jerusalem in a fresco in the church, executed in the 1440s, of the stoning of St. Stephen (Salmi 1935, 118f., fig. 20; Marchini 1969a, 51–56). This may be a motif, then, with political resonances, presenting Medicean Florence as physical counterpart to the heavenly Jerusalem.

15. For Tommaso da Sarzana (Parentucelli) as *scriptor penitentiariae* see Göller (1907), 122 no. 24 (January 27, 1435). In 1440 Cardinal Albergati, Nicholas V's friend and mentor as grand penitentiary, received from the pope power to absolve penitent former supporters of the Council of Basel: (ibid., 276f.). The penitentiary, then, was centrally involved in the suppression of conciliarism. Nicholas showed his concern for the *penitentiaria* by appointing to the office the powerful Roman cleric Domenico Capranica (Göller 1911, 71 no. 3, January 29, 1449). He also admitted the *scriptores* of the *penitentiaria* to the status of *familiares* (ibid., 71 no. 4, August 2, 1449). In 1458 Nicholas's brother, Filippo Calandrini, was appointed grand penitentiary; he had probably already been associated with the office (ibid., 9).

16. On Nicholas's mother's almsgiving see Pastor (1949), 20 n.3, and on that of Bessarion, ibid., 71. These were surely not unrelated to that of Nicholas.

17. Antonio Agli dedicated to Nicholas his *Vitae sanctorum* (Miglio 1965, 16; Pastor 1949, 206 n.4; Vespasiano da Bisticci 1970, 296). Jacopo Zeno dedicated his *Vitae pontificum*, modeled on the *Liber pontificalis*, to Paul II, but his hagiographic work began under Nicholas, his close friend, who received the dedication of Zeno's biography of their mentor, Cardinal Albergati (Miglio 1975, 17f.; de Töth 1922, 2:457; Stinger 1985, 190). Zeno began his account with St. Peter. On the study of the early Church as a significant aspect of Roman humanism see Billanovich (1958), 103–137.

18. This is a paraphrase of Westfall (1974a), 132, who devotes only one sentence to the themes of the chapel.

19. Manetti, from whom a translation of the whole Bible was commissioned, completed little more than the Psalms. Even this aroused objections to which Manetti felt obliged to reply in an extensive apology begun in Rome and completed in Naples by 1456 (De Pretis 1975).

20. Kirschbaum and Braunfels (1968–72), 8: c.398, note the diffusion since the eleventh century of the *Vita fabulosa* with events from the early life of St. Stephen. One of these involves the capture and subsequent abandonment by the devil of the infant Stephen, who is then suckled by a hind until rescued by a passing bishop. If, as is likely, this legend was known by Rome, the parallel with Romulus may have proved irresistible, though no evidence of such associations in a Roman context had yet come to light. The scene of the saint suckled by a hind appears in a fresco at Prato (ibid., c.400).

21. Westfall (1974a), 33, notes similar language to that used by Manetti in the text of Canensi of 1451–52.

22. Cullman (1958–59), 164–168, notes the prevalence of such views in the Gospel of St. John, which he suggests was written after the destruction of the temple.

23. On the patristic tradition of the contrast of David and Solomon as that of king and tyrant see Simon (1951), 140, who quotes, e.g., the *Recognitiones* once attributed to Clement of Alexandria: "ubi vero tyranni sibi magis quaesivere quam reges tunc etiam in loco, qui eius orationis causa fuerat praedestinatus, templum pro ambitione regia

construxere, et sic per ordinem regibus impiis invicem succedentibus, ad majoris impietatis etiam populus declinavit." Simon connects the *Recognitiones* to a movement in which opposition to the temple on religious grounds is coordinated with an antimonarchical political stance.

24. After noting Demosthenes' praise of earlier generations of Athenians for investment in public rather than private building programs, Alberti continues: "Sed ne hi [the Athenians] quidem laudandi Lacedaemoniis videbantur, si forte urbem fabro magis quam rerum gloria excoluissent; se autem laudantes, qui civitatem haberent virtute cultam magis quam structura." Temples are among the public buildings mentioned by Demosthenes; the opposition of *virtus* and *structura*, then, enunciated by Alberti, though without direct theological overtones, resonates with the critique of monumental architecture of the tradition of opinion represented by Stephen. Elsewhere Alberti makes an unfavorable comparison of the simplicity of the primitive Church and that of his day (Alberti 1966a, 2:628f. [VII.xiii]). Grayson (1960), 164, discusses this in connection with arguments for an earlier dating of Alberti's treatise, on the grounds that Alberti would not have indulged in such criticism in the pontificate of the first humanist pope; according to Grayson, "it is not necessary to assume that he must have abandoned [such views] immediately Nicholas V was elected in 1447." It seems that, unbeknown to Alberti, this was Nicholas's view also, at the time of the commissioning of the chapel frescoes.

25. The narrative of Acts 6:2–6 states simply that the apostles appointed and ordained the deacons; Peter is not singled out. The choice of a basilica resembling that of the Vatican as setting for the ceremony follows quite naturally from the desire to emphasize Peter's role in the ordination, and to express the ideological aspect of this. See the discussion in Greco (1980), 20, of the political, even "propagandistic," nature of the frescoes, though Greco does not come to terms with the implications of the private, intimate character of the chapel. It is interesting, further, that St. Peter was prominent in the decoration of Nicholas's bedroom (the room beneath the chapel); a bust of the saint holding a key and a book can still be seen in the vault (Westfall 1974a, 132).

26. Greco (1980), 36, gives a more positive evaluation of the distinction of foreground and background: "le storie, la basilica, Roma, rimangono al di là della cornice della porta. Il santo per andare dai poveri deve varcare la soglia della storia e ottemperare atemporalmente alle pagine del vangelo." Greco is at least surely correct in seeking to discover meaning in the compositional oddness of the painting.

27. See Paul's formulation in Ephesians 2:19–20: "estis cives sanctorum et domestici: superaedificati super fundamentum apostolorum et prophetarum, ipso summo angulari lapide Christo Iesu" (cited and discussed by Sauer 1924, 103 n.1). Augustine found the metaphor congenial, as in his sermon on Psalm 39: "Unde struitur templum? De hominibus qui entrant in templum. Lapides vivi qui sunt nisi fideles dei? Iunctura lapidum viventium charitas est. Tantum autem valet iunctura charitatis ut, quamvis multi lapides vivi in structuram templi Dei conveniunt, unus lapis ex omnibus fiat" (ibid., 37). Durandus's summation of this tradition was perhaps of particular significance in Nicholan Rome in view of his connections with the Dominican convent at S. Maria sopra Minerva, where he was buried in 1296 in a still extant tomb (ibid., 30) and which at mid-fifteenth century was especially associated with Cardinal Torquemada, the leading proponent of theories of papal supremacy (see Westfall 1974a, 20f.).

28. Manetti (Magnuson 1965, 362) claims that Nicholas's building projects surpass those of Solomon just as the New surpasses the Old Law. These remarks do not meet the radical objections of a Stephen, and indicate that Manetti was probably unaware of concerns on the part of the pope that, though doubtless intensified by the events of 1453, predated that year.

29. One of Nicholas's two reasons, enunciated—according to Manetti (1734), cc.949–950—on his deathbed in 1455 to justify his building campaign was the provision of adequate defenses for the Church (see Westfall 1974a, 129).

30. Manetti (Magnuson 1958, 361) mentions the fortifications of Egyptian Thebes, the walls of Babylon, the Mausoleum of Halicarnassus, the pyramids of Egypt, the temple built by Hadrian at Cyzicus, and the Roman Capitol. The first two, however, are said to have been so magnificent that even Nicholas's buildings could not have surpassed them.

31. Note also the implications of Prudentius's hymn to St. Lawrence: "Refrixit ex illo die [of Lawrence's martyrdom] cultus deorum turpium/ Plebs in sacellis rarior/ Christi ad tribunal curritur/ Mors illa sancti Martyris/ Mors vera templorum fuit" (Sollerio et al. 1735, 5–12).

32. The Stephen cycle in Prato does not include the scene of the expulsion from the city. Eleen (1977), 263, notes that in Acts cycles studied by her the scene of the laying down of the executioners' clothes precedes that of the stoning, as a separate event, and is more typical than the scene of the expulsion. Clearly, the choice of episodes in Nicholas's Stephen cycle was not the only one possible (even given strict fidelity to the biblical text) to match the available fresco fields.

33. Examples include the fourteenth-century version by Bernardo Daddi in S. Croce, Florence, the fifteenth-century version by Filippo Lippi in Prato, and the sixteenth-century versions by Raphael in the Sistine Chapel tapestries and by Giulio Romano for the altarpiece of S. Stefano, Genoa (on the latter and its antecedents see Hartt 1958, 1:55f.; on Raphael's version, Shearman 1972, 57f.).

34. The correct depiction of the vision perhaps marks Fra Angelico's concern with fidelity to the text: Kirschbaum and Braunfels (1968–72), 8: c.398, suggest that the introduction of the vision into the martyrdom scene was standard in the period concerned. On Augustine's picture see Migne (1844–64), 38: c.1434 ("Pictura Stephani lapidationem et Sauli conversionem exhibens. Dulcissima pictura est haec, ubi videtis S. Stephani lapides . . ."), and on the connection of the vision and Stephen's martyrdom see ibid., c.1437.

35. The peripheral position of the saint has Byzantine and Byzantine-influenced precedents; see Eleen (1977), figs. 47–52.

36. The principle of continuing a scene across a corner, albeit to a further fresco surface, is found in Lippi's fresco of the stoning of St. Stephen at Prato (Borsook 1975, 21). A later parallel to what is proposed here is the probable placement of Raphael's portrait of Julius II across physical space from but in dramatic and ritual relationship to the icon of the Madonna on the high altar; see the argument of Partridge and Starn (1980), 96f. Certain points of contact between the Prato and the Vatican St. Stephen cycles, for all their differences (see Borsook 1975, 19, on the more popular character of the former) should be noted. In particular, the intrusive rocky terrain of the Prato cycle—more emphatic than that in the St. John cycle where it would be expected in view of the association of the Baptist with the wilderness—may allude to the allegory of the stones. And the dance of Salome, which ends the St. John cycle, occurs in a palatial hall, while the discovery of the relics of St. Stephen, the final scene of the Stephen cycle, takes place in a basilican interior that seems to rhyme with the actual space of the church (Borsook 1975, 23). Implicit in this contrast, in my view, is the opposition of the Old and New Law, the Earthly and Heavenly Jerusalem, and of an unredeemed and a redeemed monumental architecture.

37. Vasari (1906), 2:516: "Papa Niccola . . . gli fece fare la capella del palazzo, dove il papa ode la messa, con un Deposto di Croce ed alcune storie di San Lorenzo, bellissime." For a definitive rejection of an identification of this lost work with a painting in Washington see Pope-Hennessy (1974), 232. On Vasari's painting, a Martyrdom of St. Stephen, which is also lost, see Greco (1980), 19.

38. In 1455 King Alfonso of Naples acquired tapestries woven after models provided by Rogier van der Weyden; these included a *Deposition*, now lost, the design of which echoed Fra Angelico's S. Trinita altarpiece, as appears from a painting in Naples apparently based on the tapestry (Padoan Rizzo 1981, 15–17).

39. Giovanni Rucellai, Palla Strozzi's son-in-law, remained in close contact with Palla after the latter's exile. In 1448, however, Piero di Cosimo de' Medici stood as godfather to Giovanni's son, Bernardo, who was later to marry into the Medici family (Kent and Perosa 1981, 29; could Nicholas have played a role in this?). In 1453 Giovanni's eldest son was betrothed to a girl from the firmly pro-Medici Pitti family. In 1455 (!), however, Giovanni's public advancement ceased (ibid., 30). On the general question of the links between the Strozzi, the Rucellai, and Nicholas see ibid., 51–53.

40. The *Deposition* by Colantonio in S. Domenico Maggiore in Naples is thought by Padoan Rizzo (1981), 16, to be modeled on the S. Trinita altarpiece, though she entertains the possibility that it may rather echo the lost Vatican painting; it seems to me far more likely that a model for a king's tapestry (the apparent model for the Naples painting) should be sought in a pope's chapel, rather than in a bourgeois chapel. Colantonio's painting, though its format is such as to limit the landscape component relative to the S. Trinita painting, contains a view of Jerusalem in the top left corner, the place nearest, in a putative Vatican altarpiece, to the kneeling St. Stephen. It is of note that Fra Angelico in his representation of the Deposition harked back to a Byzantine tradition (Kessler 1979, 271; Eleen 1977, 263). In the medieval West, there had been a tendency for the landscape to disappear.

41. St. Augustine, in Migne (1844–64), 38: c.1425: "Quando Adam de paradiso ejectus est, . . . contra humanum genus clausum est coelum: post passionem Christi latro [the Good Thief] primus intravit, postea Stephanus apertum vidit." Stephen was, however, universally regarded as the first martyr. Stephen's last words were "Domine, ne statuas illis hoc peccatum" (Acts 7:60), a close echo of Christ's, and St. Stephen's day is the day following Christmas.

42. In the St. Stephen's day mass one of the readings is Matthew 23:34–39, which includes the following lines, uttered by Christ: "Jerusalem, ierusalem que occidis prophetas et lapidas eos qui ad te missi sunt . . . ecce relinquetur vobis domus vestra deserta" (Lippe 1899, 1:22). The "house" appears to refer both to the temple and the city, and the destruction of both to be foretold.

43. Westfall (1974a), 22–27, esp. 25, has given particular emphasis to Nicholas's concern for the sacraments, not least that of the Eucharist.

44. In the western manuscript tradition, at least, Saul is shown typically seated to the left, directing the men stoning Stephen (Eleen 1977, 263; Kessler 1979, 271).

45. There are remarkable parallels in Netherlandish painting, at least: Purtle (1982), 146f. (developing an observation of Panofsky), notes that the Virgin in one painting is seen "as a larger and more substantial 'column' than the one present at her side."

46. It is worth noting that Wickhoff (1893), 50, describes the subject of the *Disputa* as the heavens opened; it is the vision, in other words, of St. Stephen. Stridbeck (1963), 14f., notes an "archaistic tendency" in Raphael's tapestry designs for the Sistine Chapel (if Stridbeck is right, it is surely relevant that the subject of the tapestries was the acts of the Apostles!). Pastor (1950), 542, has suggested that Nicholas's chapel decorations spurred Julius to have his own rooms frescoed.

47. Barry Wind has emphasized, rather, the relationship of this image to Melozzo da Forlì's painting of Sixtus IV as founder of the Vatican Library (personal communication). Sixtus appears here as himself, however, not as a distant predecessor, while the markedly hieratic character of Melozzo's imagery may itself reflect the power of Fra Angelico's example. Fehl (1973), 378f., argues, in my view unsuccessfully, that this is not a portrait of Julius II.

48. Pastor (1950), 574, calls the disputants "less advanced believers." The suggestion that they are heretics goes back to Passavant (1872), 82; see also Kelber (1964), 24. There is a full discussion of the question of Bramante's "portrait" in Wolff-Metternich (1975),

185–189, 195f. Wolff-Metternich rejects the identification on two main grounds: the *Disputa/School of Athens* figure is too unlike the portrait of Bramante on a medal by Caradosso; and there is no reason for such a portrait to appear in the Stanza and some reason—for the sake of *decorum*—why it should not. The Caradosso image is clearly highly idealized and stylized, however, while the question arises why Vasari chose not to use it, especially as he was quite familiar with Caradosso's work, as Wolff-Metternich (ibid., 179) admits. My argument indicates that the presence of Bramante could have significance, albeit ambiguous. For a further reason for Bramante's presence here see Pfeiffer (1975), 66, 94f. On Bramante's controversiality see Ackerman (1974).

49. An attractive suggestion is that the building represents the Church militant; see, e.g., Chastel (1961), 475f. This may also have been a theme of Nicholas's chapel (Greco 1980, 20).

50. On the possible allusion to St. Peter's through the motif of the building site see Chastel (1961), 476; Gutman (1958), 32. Frommel (1984b), 127, identifies the building under construction tentatively as the Vatican Logge. This is surely too specific: the structure may indeed vaguely recall elements of the Vatican, but the important point is that a large-scale building campaign is under way on an obviously monumental structure. See also the fuller discussion in Frommel (1981).

51. The identification of St. Lawrence is generally accepted. That of St. Stephen is opposed only, as far as I have been able to ascertain, by Gutman (1958), 30, in the course of an original but not widely accepted iconographical reading of the fresco. See especially the remarks of Pfeiffer (1975), 64f., who also identifies the figure of Pope Sixtus II in the fresco.

52. Gombrich's general position is that "every gesture and every expression of the Stanza is charged with significance" in that all "contribute to the celebration of the exalted theme." In other words, it is idle to seek other kinds of significance, for the artistic amplification of the given material occurs in such a way that the "visual realization of [the] idea" is "infused with Raphael's own kind of harmony and beauty" (Gombrich 1978, 100f.). This is a highly classicizing view of classicism, which is clearly opposed to my attention to fissures beneath the apparent unity and harmony of a work such as the *Disputa* (afforded to it largely by the architectural metaphor of the enclosing apse). It is interesting in this context that even so committed a proponent of the notion of classicism as Freedberg (1979), 72, proposes "faulting"—albeit on a formal level—as a major characteristic of Raphael's paintings of a few years later. Things that happen "on a formal level," of course, tend to have reverberations on other levels too.

53. The strongest assertion of this is that of Frommel (1984b), 122f. Frommel's argument rests largely on his attribution to Bramante of Uffizi 287A (on this drawing see Bruschi 1969, 874) and his observation of the resemblance between the program indicated there to that described by Manetti. The general relationship of Julius's and Nicholas's architectural patronage is uncontroversial; see Ackerman (1954), 143f.

54. Note, e.g., the stance of Raffaele Maffei, cited with further bibliography by Stinger (1985), 234. Maffei was himself, as Stinger points out, a leading patristic scholar, and so is likely to have been especially familiar with the issues that I have sought to connect with the Fra Angelico frescoes. He was, further, the son of a well-informed and well-connected figure in Nicholan Rome, Gerardo Maffei, who was equally at home in curial and city circles (see chapter 3 below). The elder Maffei, a business associate and perhaps friend of Alberti and Bessarion, may well have been aware of discordant voices during Nicholas's pontificate.

55. Prodi notes especially the remarks "de moderanda temporali ecclesiae ditione" in a text presented by Zaccaria Ferrario to Adrian VI: according to Prodi, the whole argument turns on the idea that the Christian should have his permanent abode on the earth.

3 Far and Near Perspectives: Urban Ordering and Neighborhood Change in Nicholan Rome

1. The emblematic quality of the regular quadrilateral plan of Nicholas's castle is corroborated by the similar form proposed, according to Manetti, for the Borgo fortifications (Westfall 1974a, 109); the infeasibility of the Borgo plan seems to indicate its particular symbolic value.

2. The documentation for the campaign at S. Maria della Febbre (entered in the ledgers of Nicholas's staff inextricably combined with entries concerning the work on the Vatican basilica) is in Müntz (1878), 124. On the wider context of the project see Burroughs (1982a), 115–118.

3. For contemporary descriptions of Porcari's execution see Pelaez (1893), 68 (Paolo dello Mastro); ASM, ASD 40, 282 (Nicodemo Tranchedini).

4. The projection through real space of the fictive gaze of an angel is paralleled, e.g., in annunciation representations, as in the Arena Chapel or in S. Clemente, Rome, or even in urban space, as in the relationship of a figure of an angel atop the campanile of S. Marco, Venice, to the basilica placed under the protection of the Virgin (Braunfels 1976, 81).

5. Under Julius II a three-bay loggia was built high up on the central tower, facing out over the bridge; it is often represented as a temple front, as in the Cock engraving after Heemskerck of the Sack of Rome, with Pope Clement framed between the loggia's columns (D'Onofrio 1978, fig. 143; on the loggia see ibid., 269). It is as if the pediment has returned to its ancient apotropaic role.

6. The concept of panopticism is central in the classic discussion of Foucault (1979), 200–209. Foucault does not bring Renaissance perspective into his discussion; this step is taken in a forthcoming study by Donald Preziosi, whom I thank for sharing with me his work on panopticism. Alberti's image of the *paterfamilias* as spider occurs in the third book of the *Della Famiglia* (Alberti 1969, 263): "Voi vedete el ragno quanto egli nella sua rete abbia le cordicine tutte per modo sparse in razzi che ciascuna di quelle, benchè sia in lungo spazio stesa, pure suo principio e quasi radice e nascimento si vede cominciato e uscito dal mezzo, in quale luogo lo industrissimo animale osserva sua sedia e abitacolo; e ivi, poichè così dimora, tessuto e ordinato il suo lavoro, sta desto e diligente, tale che, per minima ed estremissima cordicina quale si fosse tocca, subito la sente, subito s'apresenta e a tutto subito provede. Così faccia il padre della famiglia." A related but less striking passage is at ibid., 232, where Alberti recommends that the whole family should live under one roof "per vedervi in mezzo padre di tutti ogni dì sera acerchiato, amato, riverito, padrone e maestro di tutta la gioventù. . . " Note the image of the circle centered on the master of the house, here associated not so much even with benign surveillance as with mutual affection; one thinks of the devices of centering evident in Alberti's discussion in the *De re aedificatoria* of the city as marked by contrasting political regimes (on this see chapters 5 and 6 below).

7. On the symbolic value attached by medieval Romans to the topography of their city see the somewhat hypothetical remarks of Guidoni (1972). The sixteenth-century *trivium* converging at the piazza at the Ponte S. Angelo is exhaustively discussed by Günther (1984; see also Günther 1985).

8. The inventory was published by Zippel (1912), 175–180; see also Borgatti (1930), 157–163. It is mentioned by D'Onofrio (1978), 248 n.1, 254, as carried out for Eugenius II [sic], though D'Onofrio himself gives the date as April 12, 1447, a full month after Nicholas's election on March 6.

9. On August 1, 1447, Giacomo de' Nobili da Noceto was appointed castellan (ASV, RV 432, fol. 119r). According to a contemporary letter (Stefano Caccia, cited by Pastor [1958], 840 n.3), this was the brother of Pietro da Noceto, Nicholas's chief secretary and key adviser (see chapter 5 below). A probable relative, if not brother, of the two men was Federigo da Noceto, castellan of an important stronghold in the Patrimonium, the *rocca*

at Nepi (ASR, M 830, fol. 152v). On the same page we find references to disbursements made by Pietro da Noceto to Beltramo da Varese as contractor for the work on the Castel S. Angelo. Nicholas, therefore, was evidently maintaining very close control over the project.

10. Contemporary references to the apartments include those of Manetti (Magnuson 1958, 353); Pietro de Godis (Lehnerdt 1907, 64); and Canensi (Miglio 1975, 232). Canensi lays less stress on the apartments than the others, but mentions work in progress at the castle ("magis in dies augmentas ac munis"). It is likely, then, that the apartments were not yet fully completed in 1451–52, the year of Canensi's text, and may well have been planned in conjunction with the improvements made in the environs of the castle around that time.

11. There is no direct evidence for Nicholas's concern for the view from the castle, though Manetti notes the view from the new Vatican palace—at least from the projected benediction loggia—toward the Ponte S. Angelo (Magnuson 1958, 355). An evident desideratum was eye contact from the pilgrims' route before it traversed the castle's defenses, to the pope's window of appearance.

12. No actual processions are documented here under Nicholas V, but it is likely that they occurred. It is relevant that the celebrated preacher Roberto da Lecce, "that strange, violent character" who made flamboyant use of theatrical display to reach his audiences, came to Rome early in Nicholas's pontificate and is known to have organized processions there during attacks of plague, including one in which a number of boys marched from S. Maria in Aracoeli to S. Maria Maggiore, flogging each other and crying for mercy (Moorman 1968, 572). Contemporaries who commented on Roberto's activities included Infessura (1890), 47, and Caffari (1885), 575. D'Estouteville, the archpriest of S. Maria Maggiore, supported Roberto and made him chaplain of the altar of St. Jerome, though it is not clear when (Zippel 1904, 32 n.2). It is probable that this happened during Nicholas's pontificate, at the time of Roberto's celebrated processions.

13. There is an excellent discussion of the three streets, their varying topographical functions, and the varying political implications of plans for their improvement in Spezzaferro (1973), 36f., 41–43. On the course of the Via del Papa and its ceremonial function see Schimmelpfennig (1974), 231–237.

14. The work in Ponte was clearly an anticipation of the *gettito* (or *tassa delle ruine*) institutionalized later in the century (Re 1920, 39f., 45, 60). On the contrast of Rome and the Tuscan cities see chapters 1 and 6.

15. Massimo is regularly referred to in the documents as Massimo di Lello Cecco, but his surname occurs, e.g., in the record of his donation on behalf of his brother in the anniversary list of the Confraternity of the Salvatore (Egidi 1908, 424). He was a merchant with a *spetiaria* at the Piazza della Rotonda, and occasionally supplied the papal household (ASR, TS 1450, fol. 6v). On his house see Wurm (1965), 7f. Massimo was *caporione* in 1447; in 1454 he achieved the highest civic office, that of *conservatore* (Tommasini 1887, 207). For his work, with Andrea Santacroce, on the revision of the statutes of the notaries' guild see Paschini (1939), 141. Their draft was presented by August 30, 1446.

16. Massimo's involvement with building continued after his term of office; in January 1452 he was one of four men appointed papal commissioners of building at the Lateran and S. Paolo fuori le Mura (ASV, RV 419, fols. 178r, 179r). Massimo was attached to S. Paolo. He also acted as an intermediary between the craftsmen working on the restoration of the palaces on the Campidoglio and the papal staff (ASR, TS 1451, fol. 70r; Corbo 1966, 205); the most important craftsman involved was Paolo Romano, who also did the octagonal chapels at the Ponte S. Angelo.

17. In 1448 Massimo served as *depositarius* and agent of the monastery of S. Anastasio alle Tre Fontane; this is important as the abbot, a certain Angelo, was a close associate of the chamberlain and oversaw building projects on his behalf, notably the preparation of

structures for the conclaves of 1447 (ASR, TS 1450, fol. 132r) and 1455 (Paschini 1939, 172; ASV, IE 427, fol. 81v). The association of Abbot Angelo and the chamberlain is documented, e.g., in a letter of Nello da Bologna to the *priori* of Siena of June 27, 1448: the abbot "e andato affare comp. allo R. mon. S. Lor. Cam. quale andato nello reame" (ASS, Concistoro 1962, no. 6). In other words, he accompanied the chamberlain on a diplomatic mission to the court of Naples. In 1450 he appears as a *familiaris* of the chamberlain's at an official ceremony in the Vatican, witnessing the swearing in of a clerk of the *camera* (ASV, RV 435, fol. 11v). In 1445 Angelo had supervised repairs at the castle of Civitavecchia (ASV, IE 1445–47, fol. 132r). For Massimo's involvement with S. Anastasio see Adinolfi (1865), 143 doc. 10. He was succeeded as *depositarius* by Pietro Mellini, his near neighbor (ASR, CNC 1684, fol. 14v [January 16, 1453]). Nicholas's favor extended to other members of the Massimi family; Paolo de' Massimi was appointed supervisor of the city mint in December 1451 (ASV, RV 433, fol. 210v), indicating that Paolo, like his brother Massimo, was close to Tommaso Spinelli, banker to the city and a major figure in Nicholan Rome. Significant evidence of Massimo's standing is that his career did not suffer after the execution of his other brother Giacomo for complicity in the Porcarian conspiracy (ASV, RV 425, fol. 57v). In 1454, indeed, Massimo served as *conservatore* (see note 15 above).

18. The family palace remodeled by Tommaso in the 1450s was situated in the Borgo S. Croce, close to the family palace of the Alberti family. Spinelli's change of office (he was succeeded in 1447 by Roberto Martelli of the Medici bank as *depositarius* of the *camera apostolica*) may not have been a demotion, at a time of increasing papal control of communal finances. In addition, in about 1448 Spinelli established an independent bank (he had previously managed the Rome branch of the "Boncomei" company, perhaps the Borromei or the old Pisan firm of the Buonconti; see Herlihy 1958, 170f., 176; E. Cristiani in *DBI* 15 [1972]: 189f.). Spinelli's bank is referred to frequently in the protocols of Gerardo Maffei, perhaps the leading lawyer of the Florentine community (ASF, Not. antecos. M34, unnumbered). For Spinelli's villa see Dykmans (1968), 560–566, and for his chapel in S. Celso, Burroughs (1982a), 110. Westfall (1974a), 77 n.43, erroneously states that Spinelli died in 1453, and that the communal and cameral treasuries were merged in 1453 under "Jacobo di Mozzo." Giacomo di Rodolfo Mozzi indeed succeeded Spinelli as *depositarius urbis* (ASV, RV 434, fols. 19v–20r); the Medici bank, represented by Roberto Martelli, remained in control of the cameral treasury (De Roover 1963, 198, 211). Mozzi was the head of the Rome branch of the Pazzi bank (ASF, Not. antecos. M34 [G. Maffei], unnumbered [e.g., January 16, 1448: Mozzi is involved in a transaction in Spinelli's bank in Ponte]). In 1455 Nicholas paid for Arras tapestries acquired by Spinelli (Müntz 1879, 320).

19. Parronchi (1972), 229f. (March 12, 1447; April 9, 1450). The lawyer involved was Gerardo Maffei, whose own house was not far away at Monte Giordano (ASF, Not. antecos. M34, unnumbered [July 22, 1445; October 20, 1448]). This suggests a particularly close relationship between Alberti and Spinelli, for there seems to be no other reason for the use of Spinelli's premises on this occasion.

20. For Spinelli's contributions for the street improvement see ASR, TS 1453, fol. 8v. For Spinelli's involvement as financier with Nicholas's building campaign at St. Peter's see Müntz (1878), 122, 124. Spinelli's architectural patronage in Rome (including a chapel in S. Celso) and his close relations with prominent Roman families of Ponte, notably the Bonadies and Dello Mastro, are documented and discussed in Burroughs (1982a). It is likely that Spinelli had something to do with the visit of Giovanni Bonadies to Florence in 1452 on behalf of the Confraternity of the Salvatore to research hospital design there; see chapter 5 note 22 below.

21. The question of the disposition of the piazza, ambiguous in Manetti's account, is well discussed in Westfall (1974a), 112–115. On the symbolism of the obelisk see ibid., 115, 126, though Westfall does not emphasize the obelisk's prospective function as a

spatial marker (a function that it already had, in my opinion, in its position next to S. Maria della Febbre).

22. On Manetti see Tateo (1971), 79f.; De Pretis (1975), 15; Onofri (1979), 31f., with further bibliography. His appointment as secretary to Nicholas was made in 1451 (Hofmann 1914, 2:113) though he did not take up the appointment until 1453 (Wittschier 1968, 25) or even 1454 (Onofri 1979, 30). Nicholas commissioned from Manetti a translation of the Bible, which the latter, a leading Hebraist among contemporary humanists, was uniquely qulified to attempt (Stinger 1985, 211).

23. On Nicholas's response to the Porcarian conspiracy see Pastor (1949), 223–235. On the flight from Rome of the humanist Paride Avogadro see Carini (1892), 12.

24. Paschini (1940), 227, quoting the Milanese ambassador's letter of February 28, 1468. Paul left the Vatican "per levarsi dalle mani degli Orsini e stare fra i Colonnesi. Ma per quello che si vede, c'è pericolo per tutto."

25. Niccolò Amidani da Cremona was appointed apostolic notary and created bishop of Piacenza in 1448 (ASV, RV 432, fol. 125v). In May 1449 he became governor *in temporalibus* of the city of Rome in the pope's absence (ASV, RV 433, fol. 12r). In January 1453, evidently in connection with the Porcari affair, followed his formal appointment as vice-chamberlain and governor of Rome (Westfall 1974a, 73). He had effectively discharged the former function since at least March 1448 (ASV, RV 435, fol. 303r). In this capacity he occupied a *camera* in the Vatican palace, but by April 27, 1448, he was established in a house in Ponte "apud cecham" (ASV, RV 435, fol. 19v). One of his aides (a *scutifer*) was in 1453 renting a house in the parish of S. Salvatore in Lauro (BAV, ACSP, Censuali 6 [1453], fol. 17v). In 1453 Amidani was created archbishop of Milan (Cazzani 1955, 225). Francesco di Mariano, known as "della Zecca," was master of the mint under Nicholas, though appointed already by Eugenius. He was a Florentine who took Roman citizenship and settled in Ponte; in May 1451 he leased from the Confraternity of the Salvatore a house and garden (ASR, AOSS Istromenti 24, fol. 98v). This adjoined other property belonging to Francesco, who was perhaps consolidating his holdings. Eugenius had moved the mint to the Vatican, but under Nicholas the "palazzo della zecca," the restoration of which was complete by 1453, was in the Via Mercatoria; the building was sold to Rodrigo Borgia in 1457 (Monaco 1962, 43). It was quite elaborate, with woodwork by Niccolò da Firenze (ASR, TS 1453, fols. 33r, 93r), who was also responsible for the inlay work for Nicholas's *studiolo* (Müntz 1878, 86). Calvi is mentioned as *soldano* by 1450 in Fabriano; evidently he was acting as Nicholas's bodyguard (ASV, OS 76, fol. 41r). Nicholas also made him governor of Frascati (Ilari 1965, 47 nn.5, 6). His house stood opposite the church of S. Cecilia in Turre Campi, on the site of the Oratory (ASV, RV 425, fol. 57v). Pietro da Noceto's house is mentioned by Magnuson (1958), 298; see also Zippel (1930), 376 no. 3. Pietro himself had been secretary to Cardinal Domenico Capranica and was well known in humanist circles in Rome (Pinzi 1913, 66 n.2). In addition, Berardo Eroli da Narnia, Bishop of Spoleto and vicar *in spiritualibus* in Rome, lived in the Rione S. Eustachio on the Via del Papa (Adinolfi 1865, 145–147). He was a celebrated legist, praised by Pius II (Strnad 1966, 173f.), and was in charge of the chancery, at first without a formal appointment, from 1451 at latest (Hofmann 1914, 2:72; Zippel 1904, 35 n.4).

26. On Monte Giordano see Pecchiai (1963), 5–12; Westfall (1974a), 88f.; Krautheimer (1980), 253. The Orsini palace had already been an important cultural center in the lifetime of Cardinal Giordano Orsini. According to Pietrangeli (1978), 62, the church of S. Salvatore in Lauro was reconstructed in 1449 and given to the Venetian canons of S. Giorgio in Alga, known as Celestini. On Latino Orsini's career see Katterbach (1931), 25.

27. On the function and location of the Tor di Nona see Cametti (1916), 411; Pietrangeli (1978), 54–56; Gnoli (1939), 329 (noting that at this time it was leased by the papal administration from the Confraternity of the Salvatore). It was extensively used under Nicholas for legal hearings, in one of which a German witness is identified as warder of the *soldano*'s prisons, which were evidently in or attached to the tower (ASF, Not. ante-

cos. M34 [Maffei], unnumbered [February 13, 1449]). The new piazza, then, may have been regarded as connecting the shrine of the Magdalene at S. Celso (later also in one of the octagonal chapels) with the judicial center of the Tor di Nona; penitence and retribution were topographically linked.

28. Pietro da Noceto's appeal to the Venetian Senate is in the Archivio di Stato, Venezia, Deliberazioni del Senato 19, fol. 92r (November 10, 1451); the Senate saw no objection to Pietro's plan to invest considerable funds in Venice, but denied his request for noble status and a seat in the Council. Giacomo de' Massimi's plea to Latino Orsini is in Pastor (1949), 228. Latino was the candidate of Venice at the conclave of 1455 (ibid., 321).

29. The sale is mentioned, not without relish, by Pietro de Godis (Lehnerdt 1907, 59: "Et Jacobus ille, ut haberet pecuniam pro armis et sociis, hiis diebus vendiderat pro mille ducatis domum unam Jacopo Calvo soldano papae . . . "). On Giacomo's part in the conspiracy see Pastor (1949), 227; ASV, RV 424, fol. 216r. On his relationship to Paolo and Massimo de' Massimi see ASV, RV 425, fol. 57v. I have found no other information about him except for his appearance as arbitrator in a case involving a "strenuus miles" from Trevi and a merchant of the Rione Monti, in ASR, CNC 482, fol. 141v (June 23, 1451). It is not surprising to find Giacomo with connections in the more Ghibelline district of Rome, as well as in the district associated with his own family.

30. The conspirator was Pietro da Monterotondo, who is mentioned in Stefano Caccia's account of the conspiracy (Wolkan 1918, 3:123): "Petrus autem de Monterotundo, cui papa ducentos aureos in annos singulos, ut familie sue curam haberet . . .". It is true, however, that Pietro, a doctor who was in papal employ, was not a citizen (ASV, RV 424, fol. 216r). A better if less certain example is that of Renzo Marini of Ponte, known as Godente, who in a bull of February 1, 1449, was granted confirmation of an accord reached between the *camera apostolica* and him concerning a house in Ponte. The house, in which Marini had lived for many years, had come into the possession of the *camera*; in 1450 Marini paid 8 ducats rent, but since this was to cover the period up to December 1450 at the rate of one ducat a year, Marini had enjoyed a long period of free accommodation (ASR, TS 1450, fol. 70v). Marini was given permission to stay in the house, which had apparently gained in value through its proximity to Nicholas's new mint, since, as he pointed out in a petition, the prospects of his daughters to secure good matches depended on the circumstances of their father. For the case of Angelo di Masso's daughters, see note 61.

31. For Orsini's investment in the palace on Monte Giordano see Westfall (1974a), 88f. He took his house in Parione, then, for other reasons than concern for an appropriate residence. On his death he left the house in Parione, not to the members of his clan, but to the chapter of St. Peter's, who let it to Massimo de' Massimi (BAV, ACSP, Censuali 7 [1441], fol. 54 [January 15, 1440]). On Francesco Condulmer see Westfall (1974a), 72; he died in October 1453 and was succeeded by Berardo Eroli (see note 25 above).

32. The chief secondary source on Trevisan (in older literature erroneously referred to as Scarampo) is Paschini's monograph of 1939. This is not cited by Westfall, though it is an excellent source for the period 1440–47. This omission may explain Westfall's lack of attention to Trevisan, and his emphasis on the role of Astorgio Agnese, created governor of Rome in 1442 and vice-chamberlain in 1444 (Westfall 1974a, 74 n.26). But Agnese was clearly subordinate to Trevisan, whose role is documented, e.g., in the quittance granted him by Nicholas soon after the latter's accession (Paschini 1939, 146).

33. Schiacchi's nomination was made by the chamberlain on July 31, 1441; it was confirmed by Eugenius on August 3. On the street-cleaning and other preparations on the eve of the procession of the Assumption see Dell'Addolorata (1919), 274 n.1; Schiacchi may have been in charge of comparable provisions. Alessandro Schiacchi was doubtless related to the *bullator* Giacomo de Schiaccis (Baumgarten 1907, 340). Giacomo died in 1450 and was succeeded in office by Frate Cola Jacobelli, one of Nicholas's major building entrepreneurs. A further member of the Schiacchi family, the doctor of law Fulgen-

zio, was made a papal *cubicularius* in 1452 (ASV, RV 435, fol. 40r). Unless Alessandro had died, it is surprising, in view of such links with the Vatican, that he does not appear among Nicholas's men. He and members of his family appear as clients of the notary Pietro Pantaleoni, along with several patricians associated with Nicholas's building campaigns (Renzo Petroni, Giacomo Cenci, Domenico Salviati; ASR, CNC 1232, fol. 51r, "tabula omnium contractum" [sic]).

34. Westfall does not refer to the *barigellus ad custodiam stratarum* who appears in a document of January 23, 1451, in which payment for his services is authorized (ASR, M 830, fol. 182r). It is interesting that payment, to be made by Spinelli, was authorized by the chamberlain; probably the *bargello*'s term of office coincided with the absence from Rome of the *soldano* Calvi, who accompanied Nicholas to Fabriano in 1450 (see note 25 above).

35. For what follows see Paschini (1939), 139–141. The provisions, in Paschini's view, were published sometime before their formal approval by the *conservatori* and some cardinals on July 20, 1446, and confirmation by the pope on August 28.

36. It was possible for a house to be "posta in Campo de' Fiori appresso ad S. Lorenzo in Damaso . . . et confina con la strada maestra [Via del Pellegrino?]" (Lauer 1911, 513 [Catasto de' beni del Laterano 1450, fol. 7r, cf. fols. 7v, 9r]). (Note here the vernacular use of the name Campo de' Fiori; the document, however, belongs in an ecclesiastical context.) It is impossible to ascertain exactly the extent of the parish, but in the other direction it reached the Via del Papa and included the Piazza di Parione (BAV, ACSP Censuali 5 [1447], fol. 40v). On the general history of the Campo in the fifteenth century see Valtieri (1984).

37. A local banker resident in the area was Angelo Scaputi, who with his brothers leased a house there in 1441 (BAV, ACSP Censuali 5 [1441], fol. 40r). In 1450 the lease was held by Gaspare Scaputi (Egidi 1908, 425). Angelo was quite eminent in local affairs; he was *guardianus* of the Confraternity of the Salvatore in 1441 (Marangoni 1747, 316). In 1443 he was buried in a chapel that he had endowed in the church of S. Barbara (Egidi 1908, 374). The connection of Gaspare with banking is proved by *protestationes* against him in 1461 by the officials of the Confraternity of the Salvatore; he was accused of refusing to pay back funds deposited with him by Niccolò Gaetani in 1456 (ibid., 425; see also ASR, CNC 1684, fol. 7r). The family also had curial connections; a Giacomo Scaputi was a *scriptor penitentiarum* who in 1461 applied for permission to marry and was given three years to find another job (Hofmann 1914, 1:217 n.5). It is likely that he owed his original position to the chamberlain. A further family doing business, perhaps involving banking, at the Campo was the Porcari; in 1452 a notarial instrument was drawn up and witnessed in front of the *banchum* of Cola Porcari (ASR, AOSS Istromenti 24, fol. 138v).

38. In 1448 two aged Roman ladies, in an agreement signed in the premises of a Florentine merchant on the Campo, leased a property used as a tavern to another Florentine (ASR, CNC 1232, fol. 45r). The involvement of the Florentines and the proximity to the Jubilee of 1449 suggest that this tavern was more than a rough hangout for horse copers. Further evidence of upgrading is Everso di Anguillara's purchase of property at the square (Sora 1907, 117 n.13). In 1443 the Vatican chapter let a large house situated "in capite Campi Florum in parrocchia S. Laurentii" to a goldsmith from Tivoli, with a rebuilding requirement more stringent than usual, and at a high rent (21 florins a year when the pope was in residence; BAV, ACSP Censuali 5 [1441], fol. 51v). The leasor undertook to build "unam portam magnam," presumably on the Campo, and to keep the area around his building clean. Official recognition of the status of the Campo—and perhaps of its changing character—came with Paul II's establishment of the office of the *grascia* there (Zippel 1904, 98).

39. The key document is published by Cugnoni (1885), 582f. In 1457 the canons of S. Maria Rotonda, opposing the intent of the current *maestri di strada* to rid the piazza of stalls, cited the chamberlain's inspection of the place in the pontificate of Eugenius IV,

and his ruling about the permitted type and location of stalls, benches, etc. ("certam formam dedit quomodo et qualiter bancos tecta et tabulata tenere possent . . . "); see also Paschini (1939), 140f. Note that the 1457 document describes the context of the chamberlain's visit: "D. Ludovicus ... Camerarius *dum plateas urbis reformare proposuisset,* inter alia publica plateam Ecclesiae [S. Maria Rotonda] visitavit" (Cugnoni 1885, 582; my italics).

40. The passage is from Biondo's *Roma instaurata,* c.63, which gives a date of 1444 for the improvements. On the surroundings of the Pantheon Biondo writes: "Et cum ipsa insignis ecclesia . . . celsas quibus attollitur columnas habuisset sordidissimis diversorum quaestuum tabernis a quibus obsidebantur occultatas, emundatae nunc in circuitu bases et capita denudatae mirabilis aedificii pulchritudinem ostendunt. . . . Acceduntque decori stratae tiburtino lapide subiecta templo area et quae ad aetatis nostrae campum Martium [evidently he means the *rione*] ducit via."

41. See the claim on behalf of Lorenzo (or, in the archival record, Renzo) in his descendant Marcantonio Altieri's *Li Nuptiali* of c. 1511 (Gennaro 1967a, 27 n.33). This is confirmed, e.g., by ASR, M 830, fol. 161r (February 3, 1452); Müntz 1878, 145 (Lorenzo received 25 ducats for work on the building). As Marcantonio points out, Lorenzo had held various important offices under both Eugenius and Nicholas and was a key figure mediating between the patriciate and the papacy (see chapter 6 note 21). For his burial in S. Maria Rotonda, though he had buried his wife in the Altieri family chapel in S. Maria in Aracoeli, see Niutta (1986), 398.

42. The Massimi were one of the major clans associated with the church of S. Lorenzo in Damaso; for their family chapel, in which Massimo's father Paolo was buried in 1461 and Massimo himself between 1462 and 1468, see Wurm (1965), 7; Egidi (1908), 190, 424. On the occasion of his father's death Massimo gave 50 florins to the Confraternity of the Salvatore for the celebration of anniversary masses. On Giacomo de' Massimi see note 29, and for Massimo's apparent enjoyment of continuing papal favor after 1453 see notes 15, 17. It is interesting that a kinsman of Stefano Porcari, Domenico Antonio Porcari, held office as *maestro di strada* in the early part of 1453 (Tommasini 1887, 213). Domenico was married to Giovanna della Valle, daughter of Paolo and sister of the lawyer and humanist Lello and the doctor Filippo; evidently he belonged to the circle of Massimo de' Massimi on the Via del Papa (see chapter 4 below). In fact Massimo witnessed the sale of a *vigna* to the della Valle brothers in 1445 (ASR, CNC 712, fol. 4v).

43. D'Estouteville's palace at S. Apollinare (later the Palazzo Altemps) was well known in the later quattrocento (Armellini 1942, 2:346). It was admired in 1450 by Giovanni Rucellai when it must have been new (Rucellai 1960, 76). I have found no documentation of building or decoration, though there is circumstantial evidence as to its builder and perhaps architect: in March 1451 Antonio da Firenze, presumably the papal architect (on his position see chapter 4 below), took a house at the sign of a galley in the parish of S. Apollinare (BAV, ACSP Censuali 6, fol. 18v; Censuali 7, fol. 81r); he was surely motivated by contacts of some kind with the parish's most prominent resident. The cardinal's earlier house is so far known only through one reference: "quietanza pro Boncomeis [whose agent in Rome at this time was Tommaso Spinelli] actum in domibus habitationis dicti domini (Guill. Andevagensis) in platea Parionis sitis, in camera paramentorum" (ASF, Not. antecos. M34 [Gerardo Maffei], unnumbered [December 5, 1447]). Although d'Estouteville was already a powerful member of the sacred college before Nicholas's accession, he received clear support and favor from Nicholas, as well as significant responsibilities. In 1448 Nicholas charged him to restore to the abbey of S. Lorenzo fuori le Mura all illegally alienated properties (the prior's complaint had specified that *commendatarii* and abbots had been among the culprits; ASV, RV 408, fol. 61v). On d'Estouteville's role at S. Maria Maggiore see chapter 5. In 1453 Nicholas granted him a *vigna* confiscated from Stefano Porcari (ASV, RL 502, fol. 192r; Calixtus III's confirmation of Nicholas's dispensation). On this *vigna* see Eubel (1914), 38; Westfall (1974a), 67 n.6. It was near the Ponte S. Maria (Ponte Rotto), in an area distinguished by several

Nicholan projects. Also in 1453 Nicholas gave d'Estouteville the bishopric of Rouen, worth 12,600 florins (Eubel 1914, 249).

44. The Mellini property was partly on the site of the later Pamphili palace, built for Innocent X, whose niece married a Mellini (Cecchelli 1946, 40). A further house with a surviving fifteenth-century tower faced onto the present Via dell'Anima from the other side, near the family burial church, S. Agnese in Agone (Gnoli 1939, 169; Tomei 1942, 270). Pietro Mellini acted in 1453 as notary of the *studium Romanum* (the university; Tommasini 1887, 207). His work as notary helped cement neighborhood bonds; he drew up the will of Matteo Muti, who was buried in S. Pantaleo in the Piazza di Parione in 1466 (Egidi 1908, 441). Pietro never held high communal office, as far as can be determined, but he was prominent in the Confraternity of the Salvatore, serving as *guardianus* in 1452, the year the statutes of the *maestri di strada* were issued (Marangoni 1747, 317). Pietro must have known his way around the Vatican; throughout Nicholas's pontificate he was the agent of the Vatican chapter (BAV, ACSP Censuali 5 and 6 passim). He is once named as *procurator et notarius curiae Romanae* (ASR, CNC 482, fol. 200r). Obviously he moved in the same circles as Gerardo Maffei and Tommaso Spinelli. He had business links, at least, with the Orsini, and in 1451 represented the wife of Orsino Orsini in a case arbitrated by the Archbishop of Taranto, another Orsini (ASR, CNC 1604, fol. 11; cf. Coppi 1864, 335 n.184). In 1453 Pietro served as agent for the abbey of S. Anastasio alle Tre Fontane (ASR, CNC 1684, fol. 14v [January 16, 1453]). As such he formalized and perhaps arranged the purchase from the abbey of a house in the Via del Papa by his neighbor Niccolò della Valle, a canon of S. Maria Maggiore (Adinolfi 1865, 137 [May 22, 1448]). The della Valle too had good connections with the Vatican under Nicholas; Lorenzo della Valle appears in 1452, for instance, as a *scriptor* and *familiaris papae* (ASV, RV 424, fol. 1v). The family, then, was in good position to benefit from development in their quarter and, partly with the help of Pietro Mellini, consolidated their holdings along the Via del Papa (Marchetti-Longhi 1919, 481). Needless to say, Mellini must have been close to the chamberlain; in December 1452, for example, he appeared as a witness to a transaction drawn up in the "camera paramentorum" of the chamberlain's palace at S. Lorenzo (ASR, CNC 1684, fol. 10v). For Mellini's building work on his residence see chapter 1. Finally, at the end of the 1468 manuscript of the city statutes appear the words "expliciunt statuta urbis et populi romani propria [manu] nobilis et egregii civis domini Petri Milini civis Romae" (Re 1880, 238; Lanciani 1902, 1:112 n.1).

45. Clause 29 of the 1452 statutes reads "che nullo possa gittare stabio ne letame in Nagoni" (Re 1920, 97). The area of the piazza had long been of concern to the commune, but in 1452 the injunction not to throw refuse "in Agone" was amplified, as Re points out, with an explicit reference to the purpose of the clause: "accio che li edifici et theatri antiqui, quelli che vi sonno, non siano occupati" (ibid., 17). But Mellini would have benefited more than anyone from the implementation of this.

46. Valeriano Muti was made governor of Orvieto in 1448 (ASV, RV 432, fol. 206r). For acquisitions of property by members of the Muti family in the 1450s, including Francesco's purchase of a house on the Piazza Navona, see ASR, CNC 1164, fols. 85r, 102r, 105v. Francesco's house, which he bought on September 27, 1453, cost him 100 ducats; on July 15, 1454, Paola Muti left 200 ducats to found a chapel in the church of S. Pantaleo. Her son, Matteo di Lorenzo, was wealthy enough by 1464 to buy a house from the Confraternity of the Salvatore for 4,000 florins (Egidi 1908, 438). On the other hand, a branch of the family, resident in the Colonna area, had a history of noncooperation with the papacy; in 1435 a Paolo Muti was fined for his part in an attempted coup against the papal government, and his son Muzio was resident in the Rione Monti in 1458 (Ameyden 1914, 90f.). In 1451 a Stefano di Paolo Muti was resident in the Rione Trevi (ASR, CNC 482, fol. 127v). In a less extreme way such divergences parallel those in the Porcari family.

47. Neither the fountain of the Maddalena nor the hospital itself is mentioned by West-fall. Spezzaferro (1973), 34f. with n. 59, acutely notes the work at the Maddalena in 1447 and the association of the institution with the Confraternity of the Gonfalone, though he does not recognize the importance of this in the context of Nicholas's policies toward the Roman patriciate and its institutions. The pertinent document is published by Müntz (1878), 157 (August 4, 1447): "duc. 25 di com. di N.S. e quali sono per fattura di una fontana fatta alla Maddalena, dove stanno i poveri lazari." The money was disbursed through Giorgio Cesarini, a prominent member of a leading patrician family, whose palace in the area of the "turris argentina" abutted the Via del Papa and was extensively added to in the fifteenth century (Marchetti-Longhi 1972). Cesarini's involvement here is surely related to his office in the penitentiary, of which he had been in charge in 1443 (Ferri 1907, no. 208). Cesarini's praise of Nicholas V's performance in the same office is recorded by Canensi (Miglio 1975, 217f.); in turn, after his accession Nicholas showed particular favor to the penitentiary and its personnel (ASV, RV 409, fol. 275v [*scriptores* of the penitentiary are made *familiares*]). Cesarini was a Vatican canon and was involved in 1453 with the restoration of a house for himself or the canons in general "in capite platee iuxta scaleas [of St. Peter's]" (ASV, RV 430, fol. 80r). His involvement in building projects was germane to his office as this was viewed by Nicholas; for a papal bull expressly linking penance with support for public works projects, as well as those of more predictable type, see Pastor (1949), 75 n.2. Cesarini was otherwise a confidante of Nicholas and in 1451 was sent as Nicholas's ambassador to the court of Naples (ASV, RV 418, fol. 12r). For similar missions see Sora (1907), 72 (to Norcia); ASV, RV 429, fol. 158r (mission of May 1454 to arrange a truce between Spoleto, Norcia, and Cassiano). Also in 1454 Cesarini appears as Bessarion's *procurator generalis* and vicar (ASR, CNC 482, fol. 291r [December 28, 1454]). He was also well connected in Parione, acting as an executor of the will of Valeriano Muti on July 3, 1452 (ASR, CNC 1164, fol. 72r). Cesarini, then, apparently moved in the same circles in both the Orsini and Colonna areas as Alberti, Gerardo Maffei, and Spinelli.

48. In a document of that year Domenico Capranica, vicar general in the March, was charged to take action against heresy, and to see to the reform of monasteries and the absolution and rehabilitation of the lapsed. He was to encourage the display of penitence in the building or restoration of churches, hospitals, and even bridges (ASV, RV 406, fol. 29r). The date is given only as 1447. On January 29, 1449, Nicholas appointed Capranica as grand penitentiary (Göller 1911, 71 no. 3).

49. "Item, che ancora siano tenuti una volta el mese andare a vedere la fonte de Treio et avere cura d'essa, che non sia occupata ne guasta la forma et la chiavica..." (Re 1920, 90; see Magnuson 1958, 38). The magistrates are also to maintain all other fountains (none are specified) in and around Rome. In the statutes of 1410, but copied and apparently still valid in 1480, the same general prescription occurs, but there is no mention of Trevi (Scaccia-Scarafoni 1927, 278 n.20).

50. Nicholas provided 200 ducats "per le forme di Treio," while the total amount expended on "fabriche extraordinarie fuora di palazo" in 1453 was 25,021 ducats. The entry in Nello's ledger (ASR, TS 1453, fol. 143r) is published in Müntz (1878), 157: "1453, 18 giugno. duc. 200 d.c. cont. a Pietro di Giuliano di Cholona di chomandamento di Nello e quali N.S. dona per la forma de l'acqua di Treio, e duc. 200 papali lo dette il prefatto N.S. piu di sono de suo propri de quali non [ho] fatto scrittura." Evidently, then, Nicholas made a further, somewhat irregular subvention, for reasons that will become clear in my discussion. According to Orlandi (in Alberti 1966a, 2:927) the most difficult part of the restoration was the work on the underground conduits.

51. Alberti gives instructions "si forte transfosso monte aqua in oppidum ducenda sit." See Mancini (1911), 279, who connects the passages in the *De re aedificatoria* with Alberti's discussions of instruments developed to survey a city in technical writings such as the *Descriptio urbis Romae* or the *Ludi matematici*. See also Borsi (1975), 22f.

52. The total sum was 445 ducats and 12 bolognini, all disbursed in 1453. The builder was Francesco da Bologna, *maestro di legname*; 650 chestnut planks were supplied by a Viterbese merchant, while the tiles came from the brickworks of Beltramo da Varese.

53. Pius II formally transferred the church to the *fratres minores* (Coccia 1973, 378). This is doubtless connected with Bessarion's appointment as protector of the order on the death of Cardinal Domenico Capranica in 1458. It is probable that Bessarion's links with the Minorites extended back to 1450, and had some bearing on the choice of SS. Apostoli for the consecration festivities.

54. Perotti was one of the more able humanists associated with Nicholas's translation program; he received 500 ducats (compare the expenditure on SS. Apostoli!) for his version of Polybius, while he also translated some Plutarch (Reynolds 1954). His role, then, illustrates the pope's interest in ancient history that I emphasized in chapter 2. Perotti's position in Bessarion's household is documented in a notarial deed of November 1455 in which he is identified as "magister domus reverendissimi domini cardinalis Niceni" and is responsible for letting property belonging to the cardinal (ASR, CNC 483, fol. 185r). The transaction was carried out in the Piazza SS. Apostoli in front of the main portal of the cardinal's palace; one of the witnesses was Gerardo Maffei, the Volterran lawyer (see following note), and another was Giorgio Cesarini (see note 47), who can perhaps be seen as a human link between Nicholas's two fountain restoration projects, that at the beginning of his pontificate at the Maddalena, and that near the end in Trevi.

55. A copy of the document is BAV, Cod. Vat. Lat 5560 ("Volaterrano G. Notizie storiche della basilica dei SS. XII Apostoli scritte nel 1454"). The author is referred to simply as "Il Volaterrano" by Armellini (1942), 1:309f., and by Zocca (1959), 9, who otherwise give reliable accounts of the text. On the title page Maffei refers to himself as a protonotary and as Bessarion's vicar. Details of his curial career are given by Paschini (1953), 338 (who, however, completely misses his role at SS. Apostoli); he became a notary of the *camera apostolica* in 1436 and was given the rank of *scriptor et familiaris papae* in 1444. This indicates that Maffei, like Spinelli and many of the leading patricians of Ponte and Parione, came to prominence during the period of ascendancy of Cardinal Trevisan.

56. In fact, the church was founded by the Byzantine general Narses and dedicated to the apostles Philip and James. On this and the later misconceptions about the church's foundation and claims for its importance see Santilli (1925), 1–9. Like Maffei, Manetti counted SS. Apostoli as one of the principal basilicas of the city (see following note).

57. Canensi mentions S. Paolo, S. Giovanni in Laterano, S. Maria Maggiore, S. Maria Rotonda, S. Stefano Rotondo, S. Susanna, S. Prassede, and the Vatican. Certainly Canensi himself notes that his list is not exhaustive, but it is surely likely that he would have mentioned substantial restoration on as important a church as SS. Apostoli. Manetti (Magnuson 1958, 353), on the other hand, claims that Nicholas restored all the station churches, of which he specifically mentions S. Maria in Trastevere, S. Prassede, S. Teodoro, S. Pietro in Vincoli. He also cites the seven principal basilicas of Rome, including S. Stefano Rotondo and SS. Apostoli instead of the more usual S. Croce and S. Sebastiano.

58. Spezzaferro (1973), 34, insists on the pertinence of Nicholas's attention to the Trevi fountain to his policy toward the Colonna clan and their allies. He does not, however, note the chronological disjunction between Nicholas's pro-Colonna legislation and the restoration projects most clearly associated with their quarter of the city.

59. Already in the month after his accession Nicholas issued a bull (April 24, 1447) restoring the strategic town of Palestrina to the Colonna and giving permission for it to be rebuilt. The right to refortify came in 1452, as did that of minting coinage; both these concessions seem related to the visit of Frederick III and the concern to placate Ghibelline sentiment in Rome, especially among supporters of the Colonna. A further symptomatic case is that of Velletri; on August 13, 1448, Nicholas at the instigation of Cardinal Prospero Colonna obliged the townspeople of Velletri to pay 1,000 ducats to

obtain absolution for acts of violence against the Colonna (Tomassetti 1979, 2:428). On January 26, 1448, Nicholas confirmed Martin V's division of territories between the various branches of the family, presumably to avert discord within the clan. Though the bull gave Frascati to Prospero Colonna, in fact it continued to be administered by papal governors, one of whom was Jacopo Calvi, the *soldano* (see note 25 above; Ilari 1965, 47 nn.5, 6). There were, then, effective limits to Nicholas's restoration to the Colonna of the powers and lands they had held when their kinsman Martin V was pope.

60. On the execution of di Massa and the confiscation of his property see Appendix, nos. 4, 5. He had not had the house long, if it was the same property that he bought for 325 ducats on October 1, 1446, from the *guardiani* of the Confraternity of the Salvatore (ASR, CNC 712, fol. 18v). It was a substantial house in the Rione Trevi, with garden and porticoes; Stefano Porcari was among the witnesses. For the sale of the house by Nicholas's staff to Antonio Colonna see ASR, TS 1453, fol. 10r (October 9, 1453): "Da Messer Antonio Cholonna principe de' Salerno adi 9 dottobre d.600 de camera e quali a fatti buoni per lui Piero e Giovanni de' Medici [i.e., Roberto Martelli]...sono per una chasa possta a cholonna che N.S. vende ad detto principe piu mexi sono la quale fu de messer Agniolo de Masto e detti d.600 si spendono in reparazione de la chiesa de Santo Apostolo de com. de N.S." The original document of sale (dated February 1, 1453) is cited in the papal confirmation(ASV, RV 424, fol. 225r). This states that the house is in the Rione Trevi. Antonio Colonna's purchase of the house may have helped him to a position of prominence in the city, for he was *praefectus urbi* under Pius II (*EI* 10:851).

61. The source is Pietro de Godis. Though Angelo and at least one son died for their part in the conspiracy (Pastor 1949, 521), the family was not destroyed; Angelo's two daughters were granted a house (not in Trevi but in Pigna) and a *vigna* (ASV, RV 424, fol. 258r). This is pehaps a further case of Nicholas's charity to distressed gentlefolk (cf. note 30 above).

62. One of the men is named as Gaspare di Antonio Zacchia "arciprete volterrano"; he is also a papal acolyte. Gerardo Maffei was also in contact with Alberti's humanist friend Leonardo Dati, whose position as procurator of the Camaldolese order he officially guaranteed (ASV, OS 76, fol. 99v [July 3, 1454]). The ties between Bessarion and Pietro Barbo are illustrated from an unexpected quarter in documents relating to the career of the Florentine stonemason Bernardo di Lorenzo (not Bernardo Rossellino!) (Corbo 1971). Bernardo worked on the Palazzo S. Marco (later Palazzo Venezia) and rented a house in the *contrada* of the SS. Apostoli in 1455. He had been resident in Rome since 1447, however, when he was enrolled in the Roman masons' guild. He had perhaps been associated with the shadowy Antonio da Firenze, apparently the leading craftsman at the Vatican until the arrival of the other Florentine Bernardo (Rossellino) in 1451.

63. On Perotti see note 54. The Ptolemy manuscript has since the sixteenth century been among the noted treasures of the Vatican Library, and was exhibited in the fifth centenary exhibition (Biblioteca Apostolica Vaticana 1975, 61 no. 159).

4 Middlemen: Lines of Contact, Mutual Advantage, and Command

1. Müntz, needless to say, published documents that mention Nello, but he was unaware of the quittances in Nello's favor and other crucial documents published here for the first time (see Appendix). Neither Westfall nor Mack mentions Nello; Pastor noted occasional references to a Nello in contemporary documents, but without realizing their significance (e.g., Pastor 1949, 192 n.1). None of the authors in Esch (1981), a collection of essays on mid-quattrocento Roman fiscal institutions and economic structures, seems aware of Nello's role, though at least one cites a document that underscores his importance (see Ait 1981, 89).

2. This assertion is based on a review of the reports of the Venetian and Milanese ambassadors in Rome. Pastor, who was well acquainted with the diplomatic correspondence of the period, notes no references to the building campaigns, with one single exception

(Pastor 1949, 192 n.1). The author of this dispatch, however, was Nicodemo Tranchedini, who was not an admirer of Nicholas's building works (see Miglio 1975, 105 n.55).

3. Certain humanists referred to Nicholas's building works, as noted by Pastor (1949), 192–194. But I have found no mention of Nello in the correspondence, for instance, of Poggio Braccolini, Aliotti, or Bussi, or in the writings of Mafeo Vegio.

4. Several Bolognesi, who may also have been associated with Albergati's household, played important administrative roles under Nicholas. A Giovanni Destro was in charge of "la munizione" (on this see the discussion of Niccolò da Fabriano's career below), and Giacomo del Dottore was *doganiere* of the Patrimonium in 1453 and otherwise held important positions in Nicholas's financial administration; see chapter 5 below. Particularly interesting is the case of Aristotile Fioravanti, who was brought to Rome to convey particularly large pieces of stone to the Vatican and perhaps to move the Vatican obelisk (Müntz 1878, 83, 168; Müntz 1879, 24; Mack 1982, 69 n.62, with full bibliography).

5. See, e.g., ASV, IE 414, fol. 84v (referring to a *mandatum* of August 11, 1447). A *factor* typically belonged to the household or institution that he represented (cf. Niccolò da Fabriano, whose career is discussed below). A *factor* was generally of quite low status; see, e.g., Chambers (1976b), 105 n.58.

6. The document cites a letter of the vice-chamberlain Niccolò Amidani of February 28, 1449, in which Nello is referred to as *scutifer*. See also Appendix, no. 2. Other high curial officals, like the chamberlain, had shieldbearers, who were evidently considered necessary elements of a late medieval court (BAV, ACSP, Censuali 6 [1452], fol. 17v). It is as if Nello's career marks the transition, familiar in studies of the extended period, from feudal household to early modern administration. Nello is still referred to as *scutifer* in a document of February 20, 1453 (ASV, RV 424, fol. 216r).

7. Thus during the Jubilee of 1450 Nello controlled the household operations centered in the sites of the pope's successive sojourns in the provinces (ASV, RV 435, fol. 218v). A much earlier document refers to Nello's labors "circa nostri palacii statum" (Appendix, no. 2 [March 15, 1448]). Shortly afterward a quittance was issued in Nello's favor to grant papal confirmation to an investigation of his accounts from the day of the coronation (ASV, RV 409, fol. 5v [April 22, 1449]).

8. The inventory of the volumes in ASR, Archivio Camerale 1, no. 13 (Tesoreria Segreta), indicates annual registers from 1450 to 1455. Müntz (1878), 21 n.30, saw the earlier volumes, but reported that they were in very bad condition; I saw the 1447 volume and found it illegible. Mack (1982), 67 n.7, reviews the extant archival sources and mentions the 1447 volume, which he seems to have been able to use, though it is not clear to what extent the information that he gives supplements that already provided by Müntz. He does not mention volumes for 1448 and 1449, though he states (ibid., 60) that the records of the Vatican treasury under Nicholas are unbroken. The loss of the Tesoreria Segreta volumes from 1447–49 is in part made good by the information provided in the volume of cameral mandates, kept by the chamberlain's staff and covering the period from 1447 to 1450 (ASR, M 830). The name Tesoreria Segreta is neither original nor accurate.

9. There are several references in ASR, M 830, e.g. fol. 109r: "Nello de Bolonia familiari 16 flor. pro cannis tribus damaschini albi traditis pro una planeta et biretis pro d[omino] n[ostro] p[apa]." See the quittance of 1454 (Appendix, no. 5) "for the purchase of vestments, ornaments and gold, silver, jewels, pearls, and other precious stones, and for the labor and skill of the craftsmen and workmen involved."

10. In Müntz's view the evidence suggests that this began in 1447; if so, Nello's inventory should be set in the context of preparations for the campaign of construction (Müntz 1878, 151–154). The payments of June 1449 and June 1450, both of 1,000 florins, are recorded at ASR, M 830, fol. 152v.

11. The castellan, appointed on August 1, 1447, was Giacomo de' Nobili da Noceto (ASV, RV 432, fol. 119r). He is identified as Pietro's brother by Stefano Caccia, quoted by Pastor (1958), 840 n.3. Pietro played a similar role with regard to payments to another

probable relative, the castellan of Nepi, Federigo da Noceto (ASR, M 830, fol. 152v). The latter payments concerned work on the castle of Nepi.

12. In August 1448 Nello received a quittance on the basis of an examination of his financial records (carried out by Giacomo Vannucci and Niccolò della Valle on July 29, 1448; ASV, RV 407, fol. 179r), suggesting that he already held a significant position in the household administration. I have not discovered the text of the quittance, which is referred to in a further quittance of the following April (ASV, RV 409, fol. 5v [April 29, 1449]). It is important that on March 15, 1448, Nello already appears with a regular salary of 25 florins, and though he does not yet have a title, reference is made to his "curis variis circa nostri palacii statum" (BAV, Cod. Vat. Lat. 8035, fols. 181r–182v).

13. Thus on September 23, 1449, the treasurer of the province of the March sent a messenger to S. Severino "ad Nellum de Bononia commissarium cum certis scriptis camere" (ASR, Tesoreria provinciale della Marca, Busta 6, Registro 17, fol. 132r). On the following day a further messenger was sent to Nello, who was now thought to be at Fabriano, to deliver to him the "liber clavium" of the provincial treasury. By September 26 the messenger (the *caballarius* Cristoforo da Fermo) had returned, for he was dispatched once more to Fabriano with letters for the pope. This time he certainly made contact with Nello, who sent him on with letters "ad magnificos dominos Camerinenses" (ibid., fol. 132v). This correspondence was "de facto talearum," indicating Nello's close concern with the fiscal structures and economic processes of a province rich in agricultural produce (on this see Anselmi 1976, 203f.); and on the revenues from the *tracta grani* of the March see the accounts of the provincial treasury for 1449–50, e.g. ASR, Tesoreria Generale della Marca, Busta 6, Registro 1, fol. 92r–v). Among the leading citizens of Camerino was an old associate of Nello's, Arcangelo Chiavelli, a member of the Fabrianese seigneurial family that had fled thither to the court of the related Da Varano family (see chapter 6 below). This may be a factor in Nicholas's ruling in favor of the Chiavelli family in certain disputes with the citizens of Fabriano (Sassi 1955a, 100f.). It was to be many years before the question of rights over these properties, which included industrial premises in the town, was finally settled.

14. The career of Niccolò di Lorenzo da Fabriano is discussed below, as are those of Jacopo Vannucci and Antonio Fatati. Gaspare Pellegrini da Lucca served as clerk to the provincial treasury of the March, and went on to play a key role in preparations for defense against the Turks in 1453 and 1454 (see note 37). On Calandrini's role in the March see chapter 6.

15. By May 1450 Nello appears as "commessario e fameglio" of the pope in the records of the chamberlain's office (ASR, M 830, e.g. fol. 155r–v). But the use of this title is not yet standard (cf. ibid., fols. 159v, 161r). On the title page of the ledger kept by Nello in 1450 to record papal expenditure and revenues, he is referred to merely as *fameglio* (ASR, TS 1450, fol. 1v). In the following year, however, the title *commessario* is used (ibid. 1451, fol. 1v). For a reference to "la signoria di miser Nello da Bolognia e fameglio e commessario della santita di n.s. papa Nicola," see Ait (1981), 89; Ait does not comment on Nello's role.

16. Nello's quittance of July 23, 1451, is referred to in the quittances of 1453 and 1454 (Appendix, nos. 4, 5). I have not found the text.

17. For Nello's "licentia corrigendi pistores urbis" see ASV, RV 414, fol. 120r. The bakers are alleged to have committed "multas et diversas fraudes" to the great detriment of the pilgrims. Naturally it was not the latter but the papal coffers that benefited from the fines levied by Nello (and collected by Gianni Boccabelli; ASR, TS 1451, fol. 71r). There is perhaps reason for some cynicism about the tardiness of the judicial process.

18. See Appendix, no. 3. The key passage reads: "We have granted to you responsibility and full power of ruling, administering, and governing our household, as well as of founding, raising, and restoring churches and other sacred places both in the city and in other

cities and communities subject to the Church, as well as, in order to carry out all these tasks, of exacting and receiving revenues and income due to the Church."

19. Nello traveled with Pietro da Sarzana, former *doganiere* in the Patrimonium (ASV, RV 432, fol. 5r [April 5, 1447]). Nello was reappointed *commissarius generalis* in the following September (RV 407, fol. 287r). The records of the trip to Florence are in ASR, TS 1451, fols. 29v–34v. The two men were in Florence during April and May 1451; in Rome the Sienese Luca Amadei deputized for Nello, taking over responsibility for the bookkeeping for that year (ASR, TS 1451, fol. 1r; ASV, DC 27, fol. 27r, a quittance for his activities in 1451).

20. In 1451 Gottifredo, a papal *cubicularius*, handled several payments to builders, and in August he is even referred to as the pope's chamberlain (ASV, TS 1451, fols. 7v, 10v). The earliest reference is of August 9, 1451. On Francesco del Borgo see chapter 6.

21. Amadei's surname is known from correspondence between the papal court and the Sienese government, which he perhaps informally represented; the earliest letter known to me is that of September 30, 1448 (ASS, Concistoro 1962, no. 99).

22. See, e.g., the remarks of Bowsky (1981), 294–297. Bowsky's remarks are addressed specifically to the situation before the mid-fourteenth-century fall of the Nine, but he himself notes (ibid., 303) that "many aspects of their [the Nine's] style of administration continued almost uninterrupted." In the sphere of urbanism, the configuration of the Campo (ibid., 286), which in 1349 was so paved that "its shell-like surface was separated into nine equal parts, pointing to the Palazzo Comunale," may have played a paradigmatic role in the development of the idea of the trident of streets converging on the Ponte S. Angelo, as discussed in chapter 3 above.

23. Mack (1982), 67 n.2, calculates that Rossellino left Florence for Rome in August 1451, though his name first appears in the papal ledgers in December. On March 26, 1452, he received the sum of 30 ducats "per resto de suo provisione fino adi ultimo del presente mese de marzo dachordo collui e co Nello" (ASR, TS 1452, fol. 109v).

24. The architectural aspects of this have been discussed in full, notably by Urban (1963), whose discussion is restricted to the basilica. Manetti, followed by Westfall and others, emphasized the unity of the work at the Vatican, on the basis of the Solomonic paradigm (see chapter 2 above). It is important, however, that at least administratively the work on the *tribuna* and on S. Maria della Febbre and that on the palace complex were separate.

25. In April 1451 Nello purchased "per se proprio" six silver panels (*quadri d'ariento*) from Niccolò Amidani; he paid the money into Spinelli's bank, if not perhaps, in view of the eminence of the vice-chamberlain Amidani and the value of the objects concerned, to Spinelli himself (ASR, TS 1451, fol. 78v [April 19, 1451]). Amidani is identified in the document as vice-treasurer; on his career see the discussion below.

26. The emperor's entourage was large; of the over 300 men dubbed on the Ponte S. Angelo in 1452 all but a few had traveled with Frederick. Among them was the latter's brother, Prince Albrecht, who stayed in a house rented for him from the Roman patrician Pietro Astalli, who received 50 florins for his service (ASR, M 830, fol. 190v). Once again, Nello exploited his good relations with the patriciate. Pietro himself is named as *gonfaloniere* of the city in a document of September 4, 1454 (ASR, CNC 482, fol. 184r).

27. On Porcinari see Vitale (1791), 2:31 (citing a letter of Girolamo Aliotti to Tortelli of November 17, 1451). His appointment is recorded at ASV, RV 433, fol. 57v. This is dated December 18, 1448, near enough to the beginning of Nicholas's pontificate to suggest that the pope was directly involved in his selection. It is not clear if Porcinari's term of office in 1451–52 was a reappointment, or if he was able only then to take up an earlier appointment.

28. Caccia's letter is partly published by Tommasini (1880), 65f., and in full in Wolkan (1918), 3:117–125. For Porcari's capture see Wolkan, 122f.: "Captus est igitur Porcar-

ius...hora quasi septima noctis, ante quam apparitionis dies illucesceret, indeque ad palatium ductus in camera nobilis Nelli aliquandiu custoditus est. Ibi plerisque ex iis, qui eum custodiebant, interrogantibus, sponte multa confessus est et illud maxime, quod nulli parcere sed omnes ferro, igne vel aquis extinguere decreverat, ut sic tandem victor evaderet. Post paululum temporis Nellus et alii quidam pontificem adeunt et captum Porcarium iam in palatio esse significant, quod papa audiens humanamque et fortune conditionem considerans, vices eius doluit. Interrogatus vero papa, quid de eo fieri juberet, nihil alius respondisse fertur nisi, quod de eo agerent, quod eis videretur. Intelligens hoc Nellus illum saltem in custodia tenendum, donec plenior deliberatio super eo haberetur, ad castrum sancti angeli perduci jussit et castellano presentavit."

29. Michele is frequently mentioned in the Mandati Camerali, e.g. ASR, M 830, fol. 165v (here he appears both as *procurator fiscalis* and as *in terra Gualdi s. d. n. pape commissarius*; the importance of the position of *procurator fiscalis*, which formed part of the court of the auditor of the apostolic chamber, is emphasized by Partner 1958, 136). Manetti (Magnuson 1958, 352) mentions extensive work on the main church of Gualdi. This does not seem to be documented. On the other hand, Müntz (1878), 162, notes documentation of repairs to the *rocca* in 1449; also in 1449 Cesare da Lucca, treasurer of Perugia and the Duchy of Spoleto, reached an agreement with the commune of Gualdi according to which funds generated by the local judicial system should be applied to restoration of the walls (ASV, RV 410, fol. 154, recording the papal confirmation of the agreement). The attention given to Gualdi in 1449 is partly explicable through the town's place on the pope's itinerary of that summer, when a lawyer called Giovanni Mazzancolli was appointed papal commissioner in Gualdi to arrange the renting of accommodation for members of the papal entourage (ASV, DC 26, fol. 130r). He was working under the vice-treasurer, the bishop of Perugia, Giacomo Vannucci, in whose house in Fabriano he was sworn in as secretary in 1449 (ASV, RV 435, fol. 107r).

30. Michele received the commission through a *motu proprio* of April 19, 1452 (ASV, RV 422, fol. 195r). There is perhaps a connection with the concession to the chamberlain on November 23, 1452, of the charge to reform S. Lorenzo (i.e., S. Lorenzo in Damaso, since the *titulus* is mentioned) and its dependent churches in the city (ibid., fol. 301r).

31. This question occupies much space in the dispatches of the Florentine ambassador in Rome, Donato Donati, who does not mention Nello (ASF, Dieci di Balia, Carteggio responsivo 22). The abbey was concerned to withdraw its investments in the Florentine Monte. Donati's dispatches are briefly considered by Westfall (1974a), 77 n.44, though I do not share his reading of the documents. Nello's involvement is indicated, though not with certainty, by a transaction drawn up by Gerardo Maffei da Volterra on July 1, 1447 (ASF, Not. antecos. M34, unpaginated). For papal involvement in the campaign to consolidate the abbey's holdings in the Tiber valley, see chapter 6 below.

32. On Berardo Eroli, bishop of Spoleto, see chapter 3. He was created vicar *in spirituali-bus in Urbe* in 1449 (Hofmann 1914, 2:72). On the death of the vice-chancellor Francesco Condulmer he was appointed temporary head of chancery (*regens cancellarii*) on November 2, 1453, though this was a mere formalization of his earlier activity. He was an eminent jurist, esteemed, e.g., by Pius II, who made him cardinal (Strnad 1966, 173f.).

33. The quittance applies to the period from January 1, 1451, to January 1, 1452. Amadei's successful discharge of his responsibilities during 1451 must have led to his promotion on January 23, 1452: "tibi rem familiarem nostram ac palatii nostri apostolici fabricam et aliarum que circa ea fuerint...cum plena potestate gerendi, faciendi et disponendi...committimus" (ASV, RV 433, fol. 218v). In 1454 he was appointed treasurer of the province of the Patrimonium (RV 434, fol. 71v [May 25, 1454]).

34. A papal brief, dated January 18, 1451, granting the castle of Acquapuzza to Caetani states that Nello acted as intermediary in the transfer of the property (Caetani 1930, 18 no. 2111). See also the letter of Cardinal Ludovico Trevisan, the chamberlain, to Onorato

Caetani on September 15, 1452: "Havete fatto bene a mandare le troitte al vescovo di Perusa e a Nello, ma ce ne dole che tanto speso voy le mandate a noi" (Caetani 1926, 21 no. 825).

35. The statutes are preserved in a seventeenth-century copy (BAV, Cod. Vat. Lat. 8886). See also chapter 6 below. In 1452 Nello purchased vellum from the shop in Rome of a Florentine paper dealer "per fare statuti" (ASR, TS 1452, fol. 34r [December 31, 1452]). The statutes concerned were presumably those of the *dogana*.

36. ASR, SMP 1454, fol. 5: Beltramo pays 20 ducats for two of his men "per pena gli mise Nello." Note also ibid., fol. 4r: "Da Mo. Giovanni da Castiglioni che lavorava con Giuliano di Ser Ruberto adi 28 de Marzo duc.6 de cam. contati per mano di Janni Jacobo equali sono pertanti ne condanno misser Nello de uno pezzo de muro avea fato senza calchina."

37. The first ledger of this tax is preserved in fragmentary condition; Gottlob (1889), 42, publishes the title page that records the role of Francesco del Borgo, identified as "fameglio de la S. de N. S. e per la pref. Sta. Sua in nome de Nello da Bologna suo commessario e depositario." It is possible that the use of the term *depositarius* indicates that Nello was advancing some of the moneys involved; in other words, that he was farming the tax. For the activity of Pellegrini see ASV, RV 430, fol. 111 (August 7, 1454: Pellegrini is appointed "commissarius ad recipiendum 14,000 ducatos . . . pro armandis galeis contra Theucros"). The galleys were fitted out at Venice (ASV, DC 27, fol. 124v). On March 31, 1454, Pellegrini had been appointed *dohanerius generalis* of the March with the specific task of supervising the storage facilities for salt, the production of which was an important part of the provincial economy (ASV, RV 430, fol. 64r).

38. Francesco del Borgo was particularly concerned with the work at S. Maria Maggiore, and on July 16, 1455, he was paid over 30 ducats to pay off workmen and cover repairs (Müntz 1878, 200).

39. As in Donato Donati's dispatch of December 13, 1451, in which he claims that Nicholas is refusing to give audience even to cardinals and that all communication with him is through Pietro da Noceto and Giacomo Vannucci (ASF, Dieci di Balia, Carteggio responsivo 22, fol. 100r). See also Pastor (1949), 305–308.

40. In 1454 Paciuri was paid for work on the "ponte di Terrione" (ASR, TS 1454, fol. 142v). It is not clear what this was, but Turrione was an area in the Borgo, and the Porta di Turrione was the later Porta dei Cavalleggeri, next to the church of S. Spirito in Sassia (Tomassetti 1979, 2:474). Nicholas certainly had work carried out at the Porta di Turrione, though it was not complete at his death (Calixtus III ordered that moneys from tolls levied at the gate should be used for the construction, which was entrusted to Giuliano di Ser Roberto); this must have been Paciuri's project. For more on Paciuri's career see chapter 7 below.

41. Barone's position is known from a document granting a canonicate in Arezzo to his former assistant (ASV, RL 445, fol. 273v), which refers to the funeral of Francesco Barone "prepositus S. Salvatoris de Urbe tam basilice principis apostolorum et aliarum ecclesiarum de dicta urbe quam palatii apostolici finestrarum vitrearum fabrice magister." The date of this reference is not certain; it is entered at the foot of the document in a different hand from that of the scribe who copied the document into the register. The previous document is dated April 18, 1451, so that it is possible that the document mentioning Barone is of the same year. There is no external evidence that supports an earlier or later date.

42. The *censuali*, ledgers recording income from property and other sources as well as expenditures, of the chapter of St. Peter's regularly begin by naming the members of the commission of canons and *beneficiati* appointed for the term in question. See, e.g., BAV, ACSP, Censuali 5, fol. 1r–v (March 6, 1447); Antonello is one of the *beneficiati* named as *camerarii*.

43. Various entries concerning the house appear in the *censuali* of the Vatican chapter from 1439 to 1447. The latest entry recording Antonello as tenant is crossed out and replaced with the statement "pro emptione castri s.Petri in Formis vendita fuit dicto Antonello pro ducatis 58 bol.54" (BAV, ACSP, Censuali 5 [1447], fol. 44v).

44. The estate is discussed by De Cupis (1911), 73; Tomassetti (1979), 2:384. For the history under Nicholas see ASV, RV 427, fol. 267v (papal confirmation of the sale of property by the chapter to raise funds to buy S. Pietro in Formis and part of Attigliano); BAV, ACSP, Censuali 6 (1452), fol. 49r (records the chapter's *procura* of 1450); ibid., fol. 52r (payment in March 1452 "pro una commissione et pro citatione et relatione litis S. Petri in Formis"; Pietro Mellini represented the chapter).

45. Antonio Margani is named as a canon of St. Peter's at ASV, RV 413, fol. 251v (January 21, 1450). Pietro guaranteed the work of Paolo Romano and his father on the Ponte S. Angelo (Müntz 1878, 153f.). He was *conservator* in 1448 and *guardianus* of the Confraternity of the Salvatore in 1450 and 1459 (Tommasini 1887, 214; Marangoni 1747, 317), and was surely not himself a contractor, as suggested by Mack (1982), 66.

46. The church is the later S. Caterina dei Funari. The appointment may have been of some importance; according to Armellini (1942), 2:567, "qui risiedeva il primicerio della scuola dei cantori."

47. Another family member, Giovan Angelo Cesarini, a *cubicularius* of Eugenius IV and a medical doctor, rented a house from the Vatican chapter in the same parish (S. Niccolò de' Calcarari) as Antonello (Marchetti-Longhi 1919, 472 n.2). Giovan Angelo, in contrast to Giorgio Cesarini, fades into obscurity under Nicholas.

48. In 1325 John XXII conferred on Bishop Tignosi, his vicar in Rome, the following responsibilities: ". . . administrationem officii altariatus basilicae principis apostolorum de urbe, quod helemosinaria consuevit alias nuncupari, necnon curam atque custodiam palatii et viridarii nostri dictae basilicae" (Ehrle and Egger 1935, 55 n.2). This combination of the two posts was common into the fifteenth century, but Santi seems to have had no connection, except perhaps via Antonello, with the building campaigns of Nicholas. But Santi must have played an important role in the programs of charity that were dear to Nicholas's heart (Pastor 1958, 380).

49. ASV, RV 406, fol. 50v: "cum itaque . . . basilica predicta reparacione non modica in spiritualibus et temporalibus indigere noscatur nos ad illius directionem conservationem et augmentum te generalem vicarium facimus." The ambiguity of the term *reparacio* is perhaps deliberate. Alberti's reference in the *De re aedificatoria* to the parlous condition of the basilica and his recommendations for strengthening it are well known, and may have arisen through consultation with Fatati (Alberti 1966a, 2:998).

50. Antonello was paid in 1451 for his work at S. Teodoro (the same payments were also for S. Maria Maggiore): ASR, TS 1451 fols. 3r, 52r, 81v. Pietro da Varese was paid in 1453 for his vault (the date 1453 is still visible in the capstone).

51. In 1470 and 1471 the three "presidentes fabrice tribune" (one of them Giovanni Destro da Bologna, who had worked for Nicholas) received payment "per le mani di messer Antonello," suggesting that Antonello's responsibilities were financial and administrative (Bertolotti 1885, 2).

52. Various items are left to churches and religious orders, but Cola is the only cleric to whom a bequest is made as an individual. Cola seems to be identified here as a mendicant: in a document of 1453 he appears as a *conversus* of the Cistercian abbey of S. Maria Formosa, perhaps only through the traditional association of the *bullatores* with this institution (Baumgarten 1907, 33).

53. Marchetti-Longhi (1919), 481, tentatively identifying the tower documented as belonging to the compound with the extant tower of the later house of Johannes Burchardus. The della Valle family may have used Cola's professional services; in 1448, after Paolo's death, his brother Niccolò purchased from the abbey of S. Anastasio ad Aquam

Salviam property adjoining that already held by the family in the Via del Papa (Adinolfi 1865, 137f. no. 10). On the condition of the house see ibid., 138: "considerate etiam quod propter canalia que domum circumdant muri in bona parte marcidi et putridi facti, et muri debilitati etiam in aliqua parte sussistunt, ut ex eorum inspectione apparet eviden-ter." Clearly a builder, if not architect, was urgently required.

54. Widloecher (1929), 109f., suggesting that the building was ready for use by the canons by 1445. The chronicle cited by Widloecher states that 12,000 ducats were spent by Eugenius on the project; no contribution from Nicholas is mentioned. "Frater Nico-laus murator" is not only mentioned as architect (the term *disegnare* is used), but his role is also distinguished from that of the supervisor of the project, one of the Augusti-nian friars, who may have taken over only after Cola's departure.

55. For the cases of Bramante and Sebastiano del Piombo, who held the office, and Celli-ni, who declined it, see Baumgarten (1907), 342f. Nicholas's *bullator* on his travels in 1450 was Nicholaus de la Furona, who took the oath of office in Fabriano on June 17, 1450 (Hofmann 1904, 2:86; ASV, RV 435, fol. 107v). I have found no other reference to de la Furona.

56. Cola's predecessor in office was Giacomo Schiacchi. On his residence see ASR, CNC 1232, fol. 58r (May 3, 1448): Giacomo acts as procurator for a monastery; the transaction takes place "in palatio principis apostolorum in loco ubi de presenti retinetur bulla, in quo loco dictus Jacobus residentiam facit." On his family (to whom, as a matter of fact, Nicholas showed favor) see Baumgarten (1907), 3371–341. A further *bullator* was sacked during Nicholas's pontificate; it must be supposed, then, that Cola's appointment was carefully considered.

57. Giacomo Calvi da Milano was created governor of Frascati, perhaps a delicate post as Frascati was one of the Colonna fiefs that Nicholas had undertaken in 1448 to return to Cardinal Prospero Colonna and his clan (Ilari 1965, 47). Calvi held office also in the papal court; he was a *scriptor* and papal *familiaris* (ASV, RL 472, fol. 169v).

58. Calvi's activity as procurator is evident in ASV, RL11 472, fol. 169v (November 24, 1453). For Beltramo see ASV, IE 417, fol. 47v (February 13, 1450): he acted on behalf of a certain Giovanni Conti, a Milanese cleric, whose payment of a toll (*annata*) to the apos-tolic chamber he handled. The relationship between Beltramo and Conti may have been connected with the former's professional activity, since a locally important family of sculptors called Conti is attested in Milan in the fifteenth century, and in 1452 an *armaiolo* named Gaspare di Giovanni del Conte was active in Milan (Motta 1914, 205 no. 59).

59. Westfall (1974a), 73–75, esp. 75 n.33, discusses the office of *vicecamerarius* and that of *gubernator urbis*, often held concurrently. On the basis of ASV, RV 433, fol. 12r (May 2, 1449), he states that in early May 1449 Amidani was named governor *in temporalibus* in the pope's absence from Rome; my notes on the same document indicate that Amida-ni was now appointed *gubernator urbis*, and was already *vicecamerarius* and gov-ernor of Rome in the pope's absence. He had been created apostolic notary at the end of 1447 and bishop of Piacenza early in the following year; he apparently took over as vice-chamberlain on the promotion of Astorgio Agnese to the rank of cardinal in Decem-ber 1448 (Cazzani 1955, 225; E. Labande in *DBI* 2 [1960]: 792; ASV, RV 432, fol. 125v). For his part in the audit of Nello da Bologna's books, for which he appointed a commis-sion (Niccolò della Valle and Giacomo Vannucci), see ASV, RV 407, fol. 179r (July 29, 1448).

60. Pietro was working at the same time at the nearby S. Teodoro (Golzio and Zander 1968, 545). A Pietro Lombardo was running a quarry at S. Triana (S. Adriano at the rear of the Capitol) in 1452; this may be the same man (ASR, TS 1450, fol. 218r).

61. The craftsman was a Lombard, Antonio da Milano. The importance of the gate was partly economic, given the revenues that accrued from the *gabella del Borgo* that was collected at the gates and amounted to over 600 ducats in 1454 (ASR, SMP 1454, fol. 111r;

Bauer 1927, 353). It produced less revenue than many of the city *gabelle*, though its importance increased under Calixtus when the latter were reduced (Malatesta 1886, 145 no. 145). In Sixtus IV's time, however, the income from the gate was merely enough to be a perk for the captain of the guard. For Nicholas's expenses on the fortifications by 1450 see Lanciani (1902), 1:52; by October 1451 Beltramo had received 2,000 ducats (ASR, TS 1451, fol. 107v).

62. It is interesting that on June 26, 1452 Spinelli took a house in the Borgo perhaps to facilitate his dealings with the contractors on the *tribuna*: BAV, ACSP Censuali 6, fol. 7r ("a Tom. de Spinellis pro parte pensionis domus cum signo canonici de par. S. Gregorii de Cortina duc.6"). This church was located on the Cortina, the piazza in front of the atrium of St. Peter's (Gnoli 1939, 89).

63. The total expenditure on "fabriche di palazo o nela nave di s. Pietro" came to 21,015 ducats. Bertolotti (1861), 15, estimates that Beltramo received in all between 25,000 and 30,000 ducats.

64. The list of local contractors and craftsmen working in Nicholas's projects published by Mack (1982), 66, does not include Giuliano, though the circumstantial evidence indicates that he was of considerable importance.

65. Other consignments are recorded in ASR, TS 1453, fols. 138r, 164r, 187r, 190r, etc. On one occasion, in October 1453, Pietro da Varese received on behalf of his uncle 1,600 ducats for tiles "per mattoni deba dare al palazo" (ibid., fol. 11r).

66. De Godis also notes that after the suppression of the conspiracy Amidani preached a sermon at the Capitol "de malis moribus seditione factione et ingratitudine Stephani." The culmination of Amidani's ecclesiastical career was his appointment as bishop of Milan in March 1453; it has been suggested that this had much to do with the importance of his brother Vincenzo at the court of the new ruler of Milan, Francesco Sforza, though Niccolò Amidani's evident standing at the court of Nicholas V and his role in the Porcari affair must have been at least as significant (Cazzani 1955, 225; DBI 2:792). In 1450 Vincenzo had been Sforza's emissary in Rome; his first dispatch, of March of that year, concerned the still unconfirmed news, transmitted by the chamberlain, of the pact between Naples and Venice (ASM, ASD 40, no. 1). In November Vincenzo Amidani was joined by the career diplomat and humanist Nicodemo Tranchedini, perhaps in preparation for Vincenzo's return to Milan where he became in 1451 the secretary of Sforza's secret council. One of Nicodemo's early dispatches reveals that he had lodgings at the time some three miles from Vincenzo, who was staying with his brother (ibid., no. 6 [November 4, 1450]). Niccolò Amidani lived at the palace of the mint, the building later elaborated by Rodrigo Borgia and now known as the Cancelleria Vecchia (ASV, RV 435, fol. 19v; on the building see chapter 3). If Nicodemo's lodgings, then, were within the walls of Rome, there are few places where they can have been. The most likely direction for a long, if hardly three-mile hike lay toward the Lateran, perhaps to the environs of the church of S. Clemente that had enjoyed the patronage of the eminent Lombard prelate Branda Castiglione, who founded there a chapel of St. Ambrose, the patron saint of Milan (Golzio and Zander 1968, 207f.). By 1452, not surprisingly, Tranchedini had moved, though his new lodgings, like those of Amidani, were much closer to the palace of the chamberlain than to the Vatican (ASR, CNC 1684, fol. 11r). Tranchedini's choice of lodgings may not be unrelated to his evident coolness, for all his humanist sympathies, toward Nicholas V or at least toward the building campaigns (Miglio 1975, 105 n.55; Pastor 1958, 623). Clearly there was a range of attitudes within the Lombard community toward the papal regime, though there is evidence of a degree of solidarity among the Lombards on the level of practical concerns.

67. Sbrandellato's position and salary are recorded in the cameral ledgers (e.g., ASR, M 830, fol. 7v: the "strenuus conestabilis" Sbrandellato is named as "ad custodiam palatii deputatus"). He is sometimes referred to as Sbardellato. Della Tuccia's account of his role in the affair is confirmed by a letter of Tranchedini to Francesco Sforza of January 13,

1453, in which he says that Porcari was taken by Amidani and Sbardellato (ASM, ASD 40, no. 282). In October Tranchedini identifies the latter as a partisan of Sforza (ibid., no. 383). His mention of him in the earlier dispatch, therefore, may not have been simply for the sake of accuracy.

68. For a photograph of the house see Golzio and Zander (1968), plate 48.2. There is some controversy about the date of the house: Mack (1982), 69 n.51, claims that the design is derivative from aspects of the work at Pienza in 1458–64; Valtieri (1972), 686–694, on the other hand, dates the house to c. 1451. The documents indicate unequivocally that construction took place during Nicholas's pontificate, and there was no more likely opportunity for Lunense to commission expensive architecture (he was certainly closer to Nicholas than to Pius or any other pope).

69. Della Tuccia seems to place the pope's visit in October and November 1454, but there is no trace of this in the extant communal ledgers. Since these are missing from January to July 1453, a papal visit can be posited in that time. A visit in early 1453 may well have fueled rumors in Rome about a planned withdrawal from Rome in the aftermath of the Porcarian conspiracy. On architecture at Viterbo in Nicholas's time see Valtieri (1972), 686–694. She argues that the baths were designed by Rossellino, a claim rejected by Mack (1982), 69 n.51.

70. On April 24, 1455, in line with Calixtus III's general policy of discontinuing Nicholas's projects, the chamberlain wrote to the treasurer of the Patrimonium ordering him to see to the selection of three experts in architecture to measure the work in Viterbo of the *providus vir* Stephanus Beltrandi de Doxis de Lombardia. One of the assessors was to be chosen by the treasurer, Giovanni Rustici, one by the government of Viterbo, and one by Stefano himself. Golzio and Zander (1968), 546, give his name as Stefano di Bissone da Como.

71. Golzio and Zander (1968), 512f., state that Beltramo worked at the castles of Arquata, Cassia, and Monteleone. They provide neither an exact date nor a source.

72. This is the hospital of S. Maria del Buon Gesù, unifying in one building three preexisting institutions; according to Molajoli (1968), 114–118, it was built in 1456 in response to the appeal of S. Giacomo della Marca. The construction of such a major caritative structure is, however, entirely consistent with Nicholas's general policies, while the pope made use of the persuasive skills of S. Giacomo della Marca, one of the leading preachers of the day and later canonized. The rapidity with which the townspeople became disillusioned with the pope's initiatives may explain the traditional association of the hospital with a prominent local holy man. See Mack (1982), 68 n.198.

73. Heydenreich relates spatial conceptions that he finds expressed in the reinterpretation of the piazza of Fabriano to the reordering of the Borgo as described by Manetti, and he notes Manetti's own emphasis on the Fabriano projects: "dum itaque Pontifex Fabriani commemoretur nova aedificandi cogitatio, ad quod propria natura trahebatur, animum suum irrepsit" (Manetti 1734, c.929). The suggestion of an emphasis on a *nova cogitatio aedificandi* at Fabriano is ignored by Westfall (1974a, 170f.), who hardly mentions Fabriano. Westfall otherwise relies heavily on Manetti, but insists (ibid., 171) that the ideas expressed in Manetti's account arose from a constellation of political and intellectual concerns formulated in the papal court at the very beginning of the pontificate.

74. This section of the documents (headed "introitus et exitus") is written by Niccolò in his own hand "in nome del cancellario." Niccolò seems to have been concerned only with the accounts of the commune; he did not, as far as I have been able to ascertain, take over from Angelo the responsibility for the minutes of the council's meetings or for framing official correspondence. On June 10, 1451, Niccolò was appointed by the council as one of the *procuratores* or *sindachi* of the commune to represent Fabriano in the arbitration of a boundary dispute (ibid., fol. 102r).

75. ASR, TS 1450, fols. 167v–168v, records payments for the "lavoro della piaza e della schala" and the "schala del palazo di Fabriano" (it is not clear what this was; it might

have been the stair to the church if it ran up to the latter's entrance facing the palace). There is also mention of payment to Niccolò di Lorenzo to buy tools "per conciare il muro dela piaza di San Francesco e per le stalle." This was perhaps a project to close off the stables from the improved piazza. For Niccolò's role in connection with the Agostini bank see esp. ibid., fol. 168r (September 18, 1450): payment to Filippo d'Agostino "che gli paghassi per bisogna dela detta fabricha per magistero e chalcina de quello che bisognasse sichondo che desse loro Niccolo fattore facendosi il dovere del comune."

76. Niccolò seems to have succeeded a certain Giovanni Destro da Bologna, who is mentioned in the accounts merely as "gharzone sopra la fabricha" in 1449, though in 1450–51 he has the title held by Niccolò in the following years (Müntz 1878, 112).

77. This document states: "Mo Antonio de Fiurenze capo de la fabricha di palazo de dare adi 23 Maggio d.50 de papa contati allui per parte di pianelo deba fare per la trebuna di S. Pietro." This may still mean that Beltramo was in charge of the overall construction. Antonio, on the other hand, may have had close links with d'Estouteville, and perhaps worked especially on projects, like the construction at S. Maria Maggiore, with which the cardinal was involved (see chapter 3 note 43).

78. Niccolò evidently kept records of the revenues from alum; on the death in 1484 of a clerk of the *camera apostolica*, Antonio da Forlì, a number of volumes were found that Antonio, against all the regulations, had been keeping in his quarters, perhaps only out of an excessive devotion to duty. An inventory was made of the volumes, the earliest of which was dated 1462; one of them, unfortunately undated, was listed as "unus liber Nicolai de Fabriano de materia aluminum" (Göller 1924, 227).

5 The Other Rome: Sacrality and Ideology in the Holy Quarter

1. Müntz accepts the legend that a medal commemorating Martin's restoration of churches was issued by Martin himself; in fact this and other medals of similar purported antiquity were struck in the later sixteenth century by Giorgio Paladino (Martinori 1918, 21).

2. The "trophies" in fact had no connection with Marius; they were Domitianic reliefs that originally formed part of a grandiose fountain in one of the splendid gardens that existed in the area in antiquity (Coarelli 1974, 210). They were moved to the Campidoglio in 1590.

3. Eugenius's introduction of the Celestines at S. Eusebio is mentioned in the bull of confirmation issued by Nicholas V (ASV, RV 406, fol. 54v). The statement of Urban (1961), 274, that Sixtus IV gave the church to this order is therefore incorrect.

4. S. Adriano appears variously in medieval nomenclature and was sometimes referred to as "in Via Sacra," perhaps because it was a station not only on the procession of the Assumption, but also on that of the *possesso* (Armellini 1942, 1:202f.; 2:1227).

5. Note the stimulating if not convincing hypothesis of Guidoni (1972), 3, according to which the Via Maggiore/Via del Papa formed a *decumanus* in late imperial Rome, and was interpreted in a Christian sense as the bar of a cross organizing the topography of the Christian city. On the ritual use of the street see chapter 1 above and Schimmelpfennig (1974).

6. The history of the bath house is a minor example of the changing of the guard under Nicholas: by October 1, 1447, it had been leased to one Carlo Spini.

7. In 1444 Cencio is recorded as proprietor of the estate La Marmorea outside the Porta Latina, i.e., in the direction of Ostia (ASR, AOSS, Istromenti 24, fol. 10v). On the transhumance economy of the Roman region see chapter 6 below.

8. Zippel's assertion that Nicholas suppressed the canons regular is incorrect; the document in question (he cites Giorgi, *Vita Nicolai Quinti*, 155) in fact records the bull of May 1, 1454, by which Nicholas suppressed the canons of S. Stefano Rotondo.

9. No details have come to light regarding building work carried out at S. Jacopo at this time. The hospital, which was sited on the side of the Colosseum toward S. Clemente, survived into the sixteenth century (Adinolfi 1857a, 155).

10. The statutes are described as issued by the "conservatores officium Senatus exercentes" and their scope is specified as "super balya et libertatem morantium in via maiore urbis, de regione montium, pro honore civitatis inclite alme urbis, et reductione ac renovatione dicte vie, rue, strade." The statutes have only relatively recently received due attention; see Spezzaferro (1973), 22 (advancing the hypothesis that they were intended as an instrument of papal policy toward the Lateran; nothing in the text of either version bears this out); Guidoni (1983), 377 (denying that they were an exceptional measure, and interpreting the Via Maggiore area as a familiar type of feudal enclave, in this case under the control of the Colonna; this seems a mistaken assessment of both the commune and the confraternity); Pavan (1984), 85f.

11. The document was issued by the *conservatores*, and though mention is made of the pope, Urban VI, this is only in connection with the dating of the document, which clearly stems from a strongly communal milieu. Unlike the earlier document, the proem mentions the *caporioni*, with the representative of Monti at the head of the list, not just because the Via Maggiore was in Monti, but also because of the latter's traditional precedence (Re 1889, esp. 375; Valentini and Zucchetti 1953, 151–153).

12. On Signorili see Valentini and Zucchetti (1953), 151–169; Weiss (1969), 62, 126; Pavan (1984), 86. He dedicated to Martin V his *Descriptio Urbis Romae eiusque excellentiae*, and as a leading citizen of Monti (*caporione* in 1425) may well have played some role in the restoration projects at the Lateran under Martin. For his role in the confraternity see Egidi (1908), 312; Egidi (1914), 458. Among other things, he drafted the first *liber anniversariorum*.

13. Earlier papal support for the confraternity had come from Martin V, who had ordered that the official stewardship of the image of the Savior in the Sancta Sanctorum should pass from the *ostiarii*, representatives of old aristocratic families, to the confraternity; see now Curcio (1978), 29. Curcio, not unreasonably, suspects political intent here—that Martin sided with the urban patriciate against members of his own class—but it is possible that his main concern was the adequate supervision of the greatest collection of relics in Rome.

14. There is a curious reference to him in the lists of municipal office holders kept by Marco Guidi, the *scribasenatus*, where he is listed among those "qui non habuerunt officia in tempore Nicolai V" (Tommasini 1887, 210).

15. The gift is all the more remarkable as the Savelli were in financial straits in the mid-quattrocento (De Pinto 1907, 179). Perhaps accordingly they sought papal favor, and a Battista Savelli appears as *maresciallus* in a list of March 4, 1447 (Bourgin 1904, 216).

16. The *catasto* was drawn up by the *factor* of the Lateran chapter—he was also a canon—Agostino delle Celle. It was he who handled the property transactions with the confraternity documented below. Curcio (1978), 30, suggests that the project of the new wing should be dated c. 1450 and that it was related to the preparations for the Jubilee; the evidence adduced here indicates that the project was older and had nothing to do with the Jubilee, though the decision to further expand the hospital may have had.

17. Rohault de Fleury (1877), 247, and subsequent authors date the work on the addition only to 1460–62, following Count Everso's donation of 1462. It seems more likely that work began in the latter years of Nicholas's pontificate, but was interrupted and needed the impetus of the donation to be restarted.

18. There is a puzzle here: the new infirmary, as clearly indicated on the plan published by Curcio (ibid., 35, fig. B), does not adjoin the Via Maggiore; its long side faces the Campo (perhaps the road to S. Giovanni in Fonte, the baptistery, passed in front of this and was merely a paved section of the Campo), while one of its short sides adjoins the *ospedale nuovo* at its eastern end and the other faces roughly in the direction of the

baptistery (or, in the terms of the document, also toward the "church"—evidently the Lateran basilica—and the *platea* or piazza of the Lateran, which is here more restrictively defined than is usual in references to the Campo). It is unclear, then, how any aperture in the infirmary could face the Via Maggiore. A possible solution may lie in the existence in the part of the *ospedale nuovo* abutting the infirmary of a chapel of St. Michael Archangel, with a subsidiary dedication to Saints Cosmas and Damian. A chapel dedicated to the archangel is mentioned in the 1386 statutes of the Via Maggiore; this is clearly an antecedent of the one in the infirmary (does the chapel of S. Andrea marked on Curcio's plan occupy the same space?). It is possible that the chapel of S. Michele was regarded as part of the new building; that the new construction project involved elaboration of the chapel, including a conspicuous portal, which the Lateran canons did not want to confront them across the Campo. The emphasis on a chapel dedicated to the archangel makes sense in the context of Nicholan Rome; see the discussion of the angel of the Castel S. Angelo in chapter 3 above. And the dedication to Saints Cosmas and Damian, patron saints of doctors (*medici*) in general and the Florentine Medici in particular (Pope-Hennessy 1974, 24–26, 199–201; Kirschbaum and Braunfels 1968–72, 7: cc.344, 348–352), may echo both the function of the hospital and—in 1451—the preeminence of the Medici bank in the city, and even the alliance of the bank with Battista Leni, a leading *bovattiere* and member of the confraternity.

19. Further support for the hospital came in these years from the *condottiere* and baron Everso di Anguillara (Marangoni 1747, 291). It is perhaps relevant that Everso's wife was an Orsini, and that as late as 1448 he lent military support to Rinaldo Orsini, besieged in Piombino by Alfonso of Naples. Everso had been a staunch ally of Vitelleschi in the fighting in the Patrimonium; his and Francesco Orsini's involvement with the Lateran look like elements of a consistent policy to establish anti-Colonna centers at both ends of the Via del Papa. In Nicholas's later years he conceived and began to realize the project of carving an independent state in the Patrimonium, in spite of the pope's evident alarm. This brought him into conflict with the Orsini and alliance with the Colonna, a volte face not untypical in the period. (On Everso see *DBI* 1 [1960]:302f.)

20. Orsini's main loyalties were of course to the Vatican: on his donation of 200 ducats to the chapter in 1444 see BAV, ACSP, Censuali 5 (1444), fol. 7r, and on the Orsini chapel in St. Peter's see ASV, RV 407, fol. 102v; Egidi (1908), 405.

21. The eighteenth-century index of the archive of the confraternity records "scritte diverse," which I could not locate, supposedly proving the claims of the confraternity over the Colosseum (ASR, AOSS Rubricellone vol. 1, ad voc. Colosseo). This implies that these claims had been challenged, though perhaps only after the loss of jurisdiction over the Via Maggiore in 1510 (Maroni-Lumbroso and Martini 1963, 296). There is evidence that the church of S. Maria Nova (S. Francesca Romana) had such claims, and a sixteenth-century antiquarian, Flaminio Vacca, reported assertions of some of the clergy that Eugenius had had walls built out from the church to enclose the Colosseum (i.e., from the other side from the hospital of S. Jacopo). The pope's purpose was to "levare l'occasione del gran male che in quel luogo si faceva." After many years in the church's possession, the Colosseum became a public monument when the Romans, objecting that "così degna memoria non doveva stare occulta," proceeded "a furor di popolo" to throw down Eugenius's walls. (See Müntz 1878, 35 n.1; Di Macco 1977, 50). If there is any truth in this (Müntz didn't believe it), Eugenius's nephew, Pietro Barbo, cardinal of S. Maria Nova, would certainly have been involved.

22. ASR, AOSS, Piante e Catasti 390, no. 1010, esp. fol. 8r: "Quia primum crescente per gratiam dei et salvatoris nostri hospitali et societate prefata in qualitate et numero personarum bonorum copia et in operibus pietatis infirmaria olim facta et antiqua, ubi erat capelle sancti Angeli ad aliam infirmariam novam translata fuit A.D. 1452 pontificatu Nicolai V, apud ecclesiam sancti Andree in via Sacra versus plateam Lateranensem ex opposito formarum et aquaeductus maioris Urbis. . . . Habet ea infirmaria capellas duas, unam in capite apud ecclesiam sancti Andree sub vocabulo sancti Cyriachi, aliam in

pede versus Lateranum sub vocabulo s. Michaelis archangeli et ss. Cosme et Damiani ubi singulis diebus per capellanos hospitalis prefati ante oculos infirmorum ad illorum consolationem misse celebrantur. . . . In medio autem infirmarie eiusdem foculare est magnum cum camino et igne continuo et caldaria cum aqua calida semper parata . . ." (This document is cited by Pavan 1978, 61 n.178, who does not publish it, preferring the "more complete" text of the statutes in the version of 1419.) In the period under review the confraternity was seriously looking into up-to-date principles of hospital design; in 1452 Giovanni Bonadies brought from Florence an "Ordo hospitalis Florentiae" (ibid., 58), perhaps derived from the great fourteenth-century hospital of S. Maria Nuova rather than from Brunelleschi's Spedale degli Innocenti. On Bonadies and his circle see Burroughs (1982a) and chapter 3 above.

23. Pavan (1978), 45, notes the midcentury change of character of the confraternity, without relating it to specific political factors: "dopo la metà del secolo . . . qualcosa va mutando nella vita e nello spirito del sodalizio . . . Si comincia ad avvertire il bisogno di un ripensamento, di ripercorrere le tappe della propria storia, di riaffermare la propria vocazione ed identità." And she notes the "fioritura di libri sociali" (containing especially lists of members) beginning in 1452 (see ibid., 45 n.57).

24. On Capranica and the Lateran see Egidi (1908), 455; Lauer (1911), 447; ASR, AOSS Rubricellone vol. 1, entry on Domenico Capranica. In his will of 1458 he transferred the college founded in his palace (see chapter 3 above) to the confraternity; an example that was followed by Stefano Nardini with the college that he founded (Curcio 1978, 30 n.24).

25. The name "porticus S. Petri" survived into the fifteenth century as a synonym for the Borgo. Thus on May 3, 1447, a German rented from the Confraternity of the Salvatore a "casalenum situm in portico seu burgo sancti Petri" (ASR, AOSS, Istromenti 26, fol. 20v). Incidentally the document reveals the confraternity's quite extensive property interests in the Borgo.

26. The transaction in question was witnessed by the secretary of the confraternity, Giovanni Vallati, who appears quite frequently in documents concerning the confraternity drawn up at the Campidoglio, not the Lateran. Vallati may well have helped engineer this, as his house was near the Campidoglio, in the Via del Portico d'Ottavia in the Rione S. Angelo (Pietrangeli 1976, 28). Another member of the family, Angelo di Giovanni, perhaps Giovanni's brother, was appointed secretary of the conservatores in June 1453 (ASV, RV 434, fol. 28v; Angelo's father is described as dead in the document). The roles played by the two Vallati in the commune and the confraternity underscore the intimate connection between the two institutions.

27. The putei were located on the side of the Capitoline hill overlooking the hospital of S. Maria delle Grazie, and were part-owned with Giacomo Margani of the Rione Campitelli (ASR, AOSS, Istromenti 24, fol. 135r). I have found no earlier reference to such facilities, and in this case the confraternity was not extending existing facilities, since the putei in question were entirely surrounded by the property of other owners. It is likely, then, that the confraternity was in this and no doubt other ways engaged in establishing a new focus of its activities, doubtless in conjunction with Nicholas's restoration of the municipal palaces on the hill.

28. The association of the bovattieri with the city administration was long and sanctioned by statute: De Cupis (1911), 55, cites the city statutes of 1365: "nobilis ars bobacteriorum semper sit in sua robore et firmitate pro pace et dignitate urbis." See the fundamental discussion of Gennaro (1967a), 155–160. For the portico (lovium) in the Palace of the Conservatori occupied by the consuls of the bovattieri see BAV, ACSP Censuali 5 (1441f.), fol. 56v. This is the building before its restoration by Nicholas, but there is no reason to suppose that the Nicholan building, with its generous portico, did not continue to shelter the guild officials. On the location of the dogana di bestiame see Tomassetti (1979), 1:119. The important livestock market of the Campo Turchiano

was held in the environs of S. Lorenzo in Miranda (Amadei 1969, 15–18; Malatesta 1886, 100, 112).

29. A hospital of some kind was in existence before 1450, as is clear from the mention of "pauperibus confluentibus hospitali" in 1448 (ASV, RV 407, fol. 213r). For the reorganization of 1450 see Monachino (1968), 45. Clearly the hospital was caught up in the activity occasioned by the Jubilee.

30. The grain wells purchased by the Confraternity of the Salvatore (see note 27) adjoined wells owned by S. Lorenzo, presumably S. Lorenzo in Miranda, as the nearest major church dedicated to St. Lawrence.

31. A Pietro Lombardo is also mentioned as quarrying in the area (ASR, TS 1452, fol. 218r; 1453, fol. 10r). Golzio and Zander (1968), 545, assume the identity of Pietro Lombardo and Pietro da Castiglione.

32. I found the reference to Nicholas's bull in Giuseppe Garampi, "Miscellanea chronologica," unpublished manuscript in the Archivio Segreto Vaticano, ad ann., August 22, 1447. On the confraternity see Maroni-Lumbroso and Martini (1963), 70–72; it was founded by Francesco de' Foschi della Berta, who endowed it with extensive property in the district around the church. However, a will of one Francesco de' Foschi, recorded in ASR, CNC 518, fol. 46v, is dated 1450. Francesco is named as rector of S. Bernardo.

33. In the document the *guardianus* of the confraternity, Giordano Carboni of the Rione Monti, appears as procurator of the rector of the church. In 1453 Carboni, his brother, and his uncle went to court against no less a figure than Cardinal d'Estouteville over the rights to some land that the Carboni had held for some time; the pope's *vicar in spiritualibus*, Berardo Eroli, ruled that the land belonged to S. Martino ai Monti, d'Estouteville's *titulus*, and should revert to it. This looks like further evidence of a policy against the alienation of ecclesiastical property under Nicholas.

34. For Marforio's original position see, e.g., Gnoli (1939), 154; Dickinson (1960), 159f. Without giving details, Dickinson notes that the sixteenth century continued the medieval tradition of anticlerical satire in Rome (ibid., 163). The name Marforio was variously explained, but a frequent etymology derived it from the Foro di Marte (actually the Forum of Augustus that contained the Temple of Mars Ultor), which stood nearby (Silenzi and Silenzi 1968, 20). In the *Mirabilia*, Marforio was even explained as "Martis filius" (Gnoli 1939, 155). Given these traditional associations with the ancient war god, Marforio may well have served as a mascot for rebellious, antipapal elements in the population. I certainly cannot share the opinion of Siebenhüner (1954), 104f., that even in the later sixteenth century Marforio's transfer to the Campidoglio was a matter only of aesthetic concern, since he was moved merely to serve as fountain decoration.

35. See, e.g., the preponderance of toponyms associated with the Colonna hill territories among the leaseholders listed in the Lateran *catasti* of the fourteenth and fifteenth centuries (Lauer 1911, 511–520). I have found no such *catasto* of property belonging to the chapter of S. Maria Maggiore. An interesting and perhaps locally important figure in Monti under Nicholas was Cristoforo Ruggieri, a notary with excellent connections at the papal court, where he was a *scriptor* by 1436 and was appointed *bullarum apostolicarum taxator* and *electionarius* in 1448 (ASV, RV 432, fol. 188v; von Hofmann 1914, 22 [in 1457 he was one of only eight papal acolytes]). In 1453 he went to court before the *auditor sacri palatii* to secure his right to a benefice at the parish church of S. Salvatore in Velletri; in the document he is named as *familiaris* of the pope, a status that he had evidently achieved since 1448 (ASV, RV 426, fol. 265r). Though his family was based in the Rione Pigna, where a Jacopo Ruggieri was *caporione* in 1449 (Tommasini 1887, 207), Cristoforo owned property in Monti (a house and a taverna near the Arco di San Vito), which he left to the chapter of S. Maria in his will of 1461 (Ferri 1907, 163 no. 229). He may have acquired this property before or after Nicholas's pontificate, but a connection between Cristoforo and the Cispian district under Nicholas can be demonstrated, for on

May 31, 1448, he drew up the deed—it is the only documented case I have found of his exercising his profession—recording the gift of land by Cola and Antonio Rubei da Alatri to the basilica (Ferri 1907, 161 no. 213; De Angelis 1621, 126). Cristoforo, then, had close contacts both with the Cispian and the hill country with which it was associated, and it is possible that his investment at San Vito was an early response to Nicholas's edicts and helped Cristoforo reinforce his position in the inner circles of the papal court. In contrast Niccolò della Valle, a canon of S. Maria, far from supporting Nicholas's policies for the Cispian, bought a house on the Via del Papa in May 1448 (Marchetti-Longhi 1919, 481). Ruggieri, in other words, seems not to represent a coherent pattern, but took advantage of a situation in his own way and on his own initiative.

36. The acting vice-treasurer, Giacomo Vannucci, certainly had an office at S. Pudenziana in 1448. On September 29 he conducted negotiations there with a deputation from S. Severino in the March (ASF, Not. antecos. M34 [Gerardo Maffei], unnumbered). On November 11 he swore in Francesco Orsini as prefect of the city (ASV, RV 434, fol. 162v); for Orsini's involvement with Monti see above.

37. This church is S. Agata in Suburra. The problem here was that the church was so ruinous and the revenue accruing to it so small that none of the seven canons of the church (theoretically a *titulus*) were resident there or carried out their duties. The parishioners had on their own initiative chosen as rector a certain Bartolomeo da Vercelli, and now petitioned the pope to suppress the canons and confirm the appointment of Bartolomeo. Berardo Eroli, the vicar *in spiritualibus*, and two abbots were delegated to review the matter (ASV, RL 472, fol. 94r [Feb. 15, 1452]). On June 6, 1453, S. Agata was given *in commendam* to d'Estouteville, reinforcing his links with the Rione Monti (ASV, RV 426, fol. 29r). Presumably Nicholas expected d'Estouteville to undertake the restoration of the church.

38. Jacobus de Varagine derived the name Hieronymus from *nemus*, meaning "grove." Rice suggests that this may lie behind the persistence of wooded landscapes in paintings of St. Jerome.

39. Note especially the last of these records, dated July 3, 1454: "ven. vir Leonardus de Datis proc. generalis ord. Camaldul. ut Ser Gherardus de Vulterris fidem fecit." It is not clear why Gerardo was needed to vouch for Dati in this instance; the incident suggests that Dati was little known or even little trusted in curial circles.

40. This was S. Alberto all'Esquilino (Ruggieri 1866, 11). The confraternity was originally founded by two canons of S. Maria, but was then moved to S. Alberto under the influence of St. Bonaventure. It kept a chapel at S. Alberto until 1748 (Biasiotti 1911a, 25). There is no evidence that Nicholas directly supported the confraternity, though it may well have benefited indirectly from the Cispian edicts. Ruggieri, 235, cites a bull of Gregory XIII reviewing the privileges granted by various popes to the confraternity; while Eugenius IV and Sixtus IV appear among its benefactors, Nicholas does not (perhaps as a result of his association with the Confraternity of the Salvatore).

41. The view of the palace, already partly demolished, in the Salone Sistino of the Vatican library shows such a loggia. Magnuson (1958), 224, denies that a loggia existed, on the basis of nineteenth-century photographs of the remains and sixteenth-century representations. It is entirely possible that a timber loggia was constructed under Nicholas, and that the restorations carried out by Julius II comprised the conversion of existing elements into more durable materials. The absence of a loggia would be surprising in view of contemporary patterns of residential building in Rome (see chapter 1 above) and the site and function of the palace.

42. By 1452, the traditional date of the presentation of the *De re aedificatoria* to Nicholas (but see chapter 7 below), Alberti had been closely associated with the building projects of two "tyrants," Leonello d'Este and Sigismondo Malatesta (Borsi 1975, 19–26, 127–130).

43. See, e.g., the distinction made by Thomas Aquinas between two states of *dominium*, the "officium gubernandi et dirigendi liberos" and the "subiectio servilis" (*Summa Theologia* 1:96.4). Thomas does not use the term *tyrannus*.

44. Alberti does not expressly cite Plutarch in this passage, but his use of Plutarch here is assumed by Orlandi and Portoghesi (Alberti 1966a, 1:267n). Alberti certainly knew Plutarch's *Life of Numa*, which is the explicit source of his assertion that Numa was born on the day of the foundation of Rome (ibid., 293 [IV.iii]).

45. The daughter did not act alone; the patricians, provoked by Servius's redistribution of land, plotted against him. This is perhaps a further aspect of Alberti's neglect of Livy; the latter represents Servius's "tyranny," if it should be called that, as directed against a small and pampered elite and conducted for the benefit of the population as a whole.

46. *Agger* ("hill") can refer more specifically to the earthen rampart and mound that protected this part of Rome (Coarelli 1974, 21).

47. Prospero had purchased the land, which constituted his own property, unlike the palace which was part of the patrimonium of the Colonna kinship group (Rodocanachi 1922, 240).

48. This passage and those cited above reveal an almost obsessive abhorrence of the contagion that certain places and practices associated with chastity may suffer; nevertheless, typically, Alberti also recommends the public and conspicuous placement of cult centers. Moralism and monumentalism collide in Alberti's thinking on this matter.

49. Compare "salam, quae a saltando dictam puto, quod in ea nuptiarum et convivarum alacritas celebratur" (Alberti 1966a, 1:338 [V.viii]).

50. Note also that Pier Candido Decembrio in his preface to his translation of Appian, which he dedicates to Nicholas, compares the latter's building campaigns with the restitution of ancient texts; he mentions the palace "Petri basilicae contiguam," the "molem Hadriani," and the "deorum templum ab Agrippa conditum." In other words, Nicholas restored both pagan and Christian buildings erected in antiquity. See Giorgi (1742), 208, appendix 5.

6 Mirror and Frame: The Surrounding Region and the Long Road

1. On the *pomerium* of ancient Rome and some municipalities (on which the evidence is not decisive) see von Blumenthal (1952): cc.1867–1876, with discussion of apparent medieval survivals (ibid., c.1876). Of Renaissance authors, Alberti (1966a, 2:716f. [VIII.vi]), discusses the *pomerium* as the ritual urban space that those who had enlarged the Empire had the right to expand (the source is Tacitus, *Annales* 13.23.2). Significantly, the reference occurs in Alberti's passage on the triumphal arch; in his view the first such arches were city gates deprived of their original function by the expansion of the *pomerium*.

2. Dilke, 134, finds no evidence that Renaissance intellectuals perceived the *Corpus agrimensorum* as a key to the comprehension of the Italian landscape. On a more practical level, the study of this literature is a case of the Renaissance development of scientific disciplines on the basis of ancient technical sources (Oestreich 1971, 320f.).

3. In the Patrimonium a comparable case is that of S. Maria della Quercia near Viterbo. The elaboration of this shrine as a major pilgrimage center occurs in the 1460s, but the original miracle dates from 1447 or soon after and so may be connected to Nicholas's attention to Viterbo (Silvestrelli 1970, 2:661). More generally, Guidoni (1981), 192, has noted the regional dimension of the movement of the Bianchi, which broke down, at least temporarily, both topographical and social barriers.

4. Poggio Bracciolini was especially fond of his country retreat (Bacci 1959, 24f.). For Poggio's sojourns in summer residences of the Colonna family in the early fifteenth century see Coffin (1979), 25, and for those, rather later, of Flavio Biondo, see Biondo (1531), 91r, 100r, 102v. Biondo describes visits made to ancient sites in the area in the

company of Cardinal Prospero and describes Colonna properties clearly on the basis of personal experience. Both Poggio and Biondo were interested in the traces of ancient villas in the hills near Rome (Walser 1914, 143; Biondo 1531, 93v, 108r, 109r).

5. The Roman commune was engaged in warfare against both Tivoli and Viterbo by the twelfth century, and in the thirteenth century against Viterbo (Partner 1972, 178–182, 250f.). In the statutes of Rome of 1363, the district extended from Terracina to Montalto, and in the early fifteenth century Signorili claimed communal rights, inherited from the *praefectus urbi*, over an area some 100 miles in extent (Tomassetti 1979, 1:93–95). In 1580 the district was limited to 40 miles, probably reflecting earlier practice.

6. "Deiocem illum Medorumque regem non laudo, qui Ecbatanam urbem septeno incinxit muro, distinxitque coloribus." See also ibid., 1:108f. [II.iii]. Alberti's criticism is apparently directed at the extravagant use of contrasting, bright colors for the walls. In his discussion of the Tyrant's city Alberti writes with apparent approval of the rational use of a concentric wall system to achieve specific sociopolitical ends.

7. Chittolini (1979), 294f., 328 n. 10, makes this point in connection with innovative features of the editions of the statutes of Florence issued in 1408–9 and 1415. He claims that the steps taken at Florence were not matched at the time by any other city of central or northern Italy. Goldbrunner (1983), 320, sees Bruni's *Laudatio* as an important index of a new consciousness of the developing nation-state. On the contrast of Roman decline and the rise of Florence see Villani (cited by Miglio 1983, 252).

8. Potter's remarks on quattrocento revival (at least for the Patrimonium), supported by evidence reviewed here, are in contrast with the views of Brezzi (1977), esp. 160. Early-fifteenth-century papal concern with the region is evident in Martin V's bull of 1425 (Tomassetti 1979, 1:122).

9. The traditional, indeed ancient character of the regional pastoral economy needs to be stressed in view of claims (e.g., Brezzi 1977, 157) that fifteenth-century pastoralism was a mark of economic decadence relative to fourteenth-century conditions.

10. Sereni (1974), 237–240, indicates that malaria, which may also have been an important factor in demographic fluctuations, was not rife until the later Renaissance. For the orthodox opposing viewpoint see, e.g., Tomassetti (1979), 1:131–133.

11. All these authors transcribe the name, in its Latin form, as de Clavellis; no other instances of this family name are known to me. Their discussions, including Oliva's careful description of the ledger of the *dogana di bestiame* in 1451, suffer from a lack of historical contextualization. It is possible that the *doganiere* should be identified with the Arcangelo di Antonio Chiavelli who appears in a notarial transaction of 1422 in Camerino naming a procurator to sell his property in Fabriano, presumably after deciding to settle in Camerino (Sassi 1955b, 41 n.49). A further member of the family enjoyed Nicholas's favor (or that of his staff): in 1454 Gentile Chiavelli, "in legibus licentiatus," appears as *podestà* of the strategic papal city of Narni (ASV, RV 434, fol. 77v). As for Arcangelo, I have found no trace of him after 1451, but he may have been already advanced in years. Apart from his activity as *doganiere* in two areas (but in each case involved with the exploitation of winter grazing, indicating his expertise in this economic sector), he does not appear in connection with any other papal or communal office; it is probable, then, that he came to the *dogane* from and because of a background in stock-raising. The contrast between his situation and that of Nello and other successors in office suggests that he bought the *dogana dei pascoli*, even if the relevant ledger suggests he was a papal official, as Oliva (1981), 227, notes.

12. The partner, Bartolomeo di Matteo da Perugia, had been the treasurer of the *dogana* of Campagna Marittima and Rome in 1450. His background, clearly, was not entrepreneurial but administrative. His appointment was missed by both Anzilotti and Maire-Vigueur.

13. Maire-Vigueur (1981), 111f., on the new type of official: "Il faut certainement rattacher le changement que l'on constate alors dans le recruitement des Douaniers aux transformations qui affectent tout le gouvernement de l'Église, avec l'appel de plus en plus frequent à des curialistes originaires de toute l'Italie pour remplir des charges administratives dans les provinces de l'État Pontifical." This describes exactly the reforming spirit of the administration of Nello.

14. It is clear from Theiner (1882), 3:367 no. 314, that Nicholas undertook a general restoration of the bridges in and around the city. The Ponte Nomentano carried Nicholas's arms and an inscription (Müntz 1878, 158). Müntz found no documentation of repairs under Nicholas, perhaps because they were carried out early in the pontificate or were merged in more general expenses. According to Pastor (1949), 171, Nicholas consistently restored bridges in the neighborhood of Rome. The bridges themselves were badly damaged in the nineteenth century, and little about their construction history can be learned from their present condition (Ashby 1970, 96). Nicholas certainly appointed custodians for the bridges (e.g., ASV, RV 432, fol. 181v.; RV 433, fol. 13r); doubtless their responsibilities included maintenance and even repair. It is likely, too, that restoration of the bridges accompanied the dredging operations mentioned by Manetti (Magnuson 1958, 359).

15. The case is known since it involved Onorato Caetani, Lord of Sermoneta and friend of Cardinal Trevisan, much of whose correspondence survives (Caetani 1930, 75 no. 2369). The case involved the exchange, overseen if not ordered by Nello, of a castle for a large quantity of grain supplied by Onorato in 1450 (ibid., 18 no. 2111). Nello is named as *commissarius in hac parte*; he may have held a particular commission in Campagna Marittima, then, separate both from his Jubilee commission and from his earlier tenure as *doganiere*.

16. On April 21, 1452, Michele da Prato, an experienced financial administrator and papal representative, was appointed procurator for the redemption of all illegally alienated properties of every kind of ecclesiastical institution in Rome(ASV, RV 422, fol. 195). This looks like the institutionalization of an existing practice. Caravale and Caracciolo (1978), 65–70, note Nicholas's general acceptance of the status quo, and attribute to him a policy of working with de facto rulers of territories subject to the Church, while he relied on revenues from areas that he directly controlled. This account seems at variance with those of Pleyer (1927) or Toews (1968). But Nicholas clearly chose with care the occasions on which he challenged incumbent holders of authority.

17. Pietro was married to the sister of Nicholas's chief secretary, Pietro da Noceto, who in turn was related to Cesare da Lucca, who held important administrative posts in the papal states under Nicholas V and was married to Nicholas's sister (Pinzi 1887–1913, 3:66 n.2). A further relative of Pietro da Noceto holding an important post in the Patrimonium was Federigo da Noceto, documented as castellan of Nepi in 1450 (ASR, M 830, fol. 152v). Finally, Giacomo da Noceto was appointed castellan of the Castel S. Angelo with a staff of 60 in 1447 (ASV, RV 432, fol. 119r; the family name was de' Nobili, as appears in many of the cited documents). Pietro Lunense, then, was a key member of a group of men, associated by provenance and kinship, who were given important roles in the maintenance of security in Rome and the sector to the north and northeast.

18. It is interesting to note that the document was drafted by Flavio Biondo, evidently not long before he abandoned Rome and Nicholas's court for some years. The abbot of S. Anastasio, one of three appointed to the committee, was a figure of some importance and a close associate of Cardinal Trevisan. Like the latter he was inconspicuous under Nicholas. In 1445 he had been in charge of restoration work on the castle of Civitavecchia (Corbo 1969, 163). In 1448 he accompanied Trevisan on a mission to Naples (ASS, Conc. 1962, fol. 67r), and in 1455 he received 400 ducats from Trevisan, as chamberlain, to pay the craftsmen making ready for the upcoming conclave (Paschini 1939, 172).

19. The document cited above (Trifone 1909, no. 158) mentions lands in the vicinity of Leprignano, Castiglione, Vaccariccia, Riano, and Scorano. In addition, Civitella, which occupied a strategic position between the Via Flaminia and the Tiber, was redeemed by the monks of S. Paolo from certain of Eugenius's captains, to whom it had been granted in 1434. In 1446 Eugenius had revoked the grant, but without effect. In 1447 Nicholas absolved the abbey of S. Paolo from taxes to enable the chapter to raise the 2,000 ducats required for the redemption of the property (Tomassetti 1979, 3:397; Silvestrelli 1970, 2:524). It is significant that Civitella, like Castelnuovo, had been in Colonna hands before Eugenius's campaigns. Further north Nazzano, where there was a ferry on the Tiber and a papal timber depot with a resident agent (at least in 1452; ASR, TS 1452, fol. 86r), was confiscated by Nicholas after the incumbent feudatory, Giacomo Savelli, had approved if not engineered the murder of a representative of the abbey of S. Paolo. Nicholas granted the property to S. Paolo, but on his death the Savelli reoccupied the place, though they were soon dislodged by Calixtus III (Tomassetti 1979, 3:400; Silvestrelli 1970, 2:522–523).

20. Civita Castellana was for a time governed by the same official as Nepi, but received in 1452 its own governor (ASV, RV 433, fol. 250v). A treasurer was also appointed (ibid., fol. 252r). We can discount, therefore, Silvestrelli's (1970, 2:497) presumption that Calixtus III's revocation of the Savelli vicariate in the town indicates that the Savelli had regained from Nicholas the rights taken from them by Eugenius. Foligno was also directly administered, at least from July 1451, when Cesare da Lucca (see note 17) was appointed governor (ASV, RV 433, fol. 182r). He may have held the post contemporaneously with that at Spoleto, in which case he would surely have been especially concerned with the condition of the Via Flaminia, which linked the two towns. The construction projects undertaken at the castle of Spoleto under Nicholas are listed by Mack (1982), 65.

21. In the 1420s Lorenzo Altieri had a flourishing shipping business in Rome (Lombardo 1978, xxxii-xxxv, 31). According to his son, he held important missions under Eugenius: among other things, he reformed the tax system of Tuscania and Viterbo (De' Rossi 1882, 86, appendix). Under Nicholas he was in 1448 *doganiere* of the salt tax of Rome and of the March of Ancona (ASR, M 830, fol. 85r). His son asserts that Lorenzo played an important role, which he does not specify, in the recuperation of the March from Francesco Sforza; this is echoed by his descendant Marcantonio Altieri in his *Li Nuptiali* of 1511 (Altieri 1878, 23). The unspecified other duties entrusted to Altieri by Nicholas were probably, then, of a diplomatic nature, perhaps involving fiscal questions.

22. Nepi was sold by the Orsini to Antonio Colonna and his brothers (who included Prospero) in 1427. Eugenius took it from the Colonna and pledged it to the Orsini and Everso dell'Anguillara in 1435, though the latter soon withdrew. When Lorenzo Altieri was sent to redeem the town in 1448, all infeudation was prohibited for the future (Tomassetti 1979, 3:193–194; Silvestrelli 1970, 2:558). In December 1450 a governor was appointed; this was Giovanni Mancini, who was also made governor of Civita Castellana (ASV, RV 433, fol. 121v). Control of Nepi was doubtless actually in the hands of the castellan, also appointed in 1450, Federigo da Noceto, probably a relative of Pietro da Noceto who received his salary on his behalf (see note 17).

23. A possible case of intersection, at least on an economic level, is the partnership documented in 1449–51 between the Medici bank and the leading Roman *bovattiere* Battista Leni in the *dogana* of the harbor of Rome (ASV, IE 416, fol. 49r; IE 420, fol. 53v). The association is reminiscent of that of Nello and Chiavelli in the *dogana* of winter pasturage of the region. Leni was very eminent in his own community and served as *conservator* in 1449 (Tommasini 1887, 217). In 1447 he had been appointed *camerarius ripae Tiberis* (ASV, RV 432, fol. 6v; Palermo 1979, 334). This was effectively a papal appointment; evidently Battista, like Lorenzo Altieri, enjoyed the confidence both of papal administrators and his own social peers. Further examples of patricians operating

in the communal and curial worlds include Massimo de' Massimi (Burroughs 1982a) and Andrea Santacroce (Aliano 1981), whose literary interests are documented.

24. Julius added a choir, designed by Bramante, to the rear of the high altar; the choir contained two Serliana windows surmounting and echoing the triumphal motifs of the two elaborate wall tombs situated beneath them. (On this see Partridge and Starn 1980, 91, and on the architecture of the church Bruschi 1969, 911–921; Bentivoglio and Valtieri 1976, 35–44.) Triumphal motifs, however, had appeared in the church in the fifteenth century, notably in the altar tabernacle carved by Andrea Bregno for the high altar (Bentivoglio and Valtieri, 27f.). In 1464 this was carried in procession to implore divine aid against the Turks.

25. In antiquity three arches crossed the street, the *arcus novus* erected by Diocletian (it stood at S. Maria in Via Lata and was demolished in 1491); the arch of Claudius that carried the Aqua Virgo over the street; and the Arco di Portogallo, which survived until 1662 near the entrance of the Via della Vite (Coarelli 1974, 236).

26. That the Ponte Milvio had other symbolic functions usually associated with city gates is documented by the macabre case of the display on the bridge of the quartered remains of an executed criminal (Infessura 1890, 43). The other quarters were displayed at the Campo de' Fiori and two other symbolic thresholds of the city, the Porta S. Giovanni and Monte Mario (I am grateful to Richard Ingersoll for this reference).

27. Ricci (1925), 216, 220, notes twelve instances of this date and draws attention to the alteration of the date in the inscription in the Chapel of Isotta from 1446 (the year of the beginning of Sigismondo and Isotta's relationship) to 1450 as a response to a supposed "congiuntura di voci accusatrici" (ibid., 51). For Ricci the date 1450 is that of Sigismondo's solemn vow to rebuild the church (ibid., 220). Mitchell (1978), 76, postpones the date of such a decision to 1453, and explains the stress on 1450 by reference to the placing of the figures of elephants in the Chapel of St. Sigismund in that year. Neither scholar recognizes the importance of Nicholas V's Jubilee, or even entertains the possibility of its relevance.

28. Mitchell's main arguments for dating Alberti's intervention in 1453 are as follows: (1) details of the facade design were still being worked out in 1453 and 1454; (2) Basinio da Parma's epic poem *Hesperis* emphasizes Sigismondo's triumphal return to Rimini in 1453 after his victory at Vada, and his subsequent decision to rebuild the church of S. Francesco; (3) the physical fabric of the Tempio bears evidence of successive design changes. Mitchell posits a de' Pasti scheme for a redesign in toto of the interior after Sigismondo's 1448 victory at Piombino (Mitchell, following Basinio, sees Piombino and Vada as the two great achievements of Malatesta the warrior). This plan was radically revised in 1453 in conjunction with Alberti's design for the exterior, and Mitchell notes a stronger *all'antica* style asserting itself in the interior. Finally, as Sigismondo's fortunes waned, a more modest project for interior and exterior alike was adopted.

There are clear problems with this account: (1) The prominence of the date 1450 is not satisfactorily explained. Mitchell stresses the ceremonial installation of the four elephant figures in the Chapel of St. Sigismund in that year and argues that this constituted an act of foundation, consistently (ibid., 76, 80) referring to this as an occasion, in the singular. But, as we learn from Mitchell himself (ibid., 75), the elephants were set up on two occasions, on October 15 and 23, 1450. Mitchell is correct to draw attention to the ritual celebration of these two occasions, but if this is to carry the significance attributed to it by Mitchell, it is surely curious that the installation of the first pair of elephants was not delayed by a week so that all four could be set up and blessed at the same time. It is more likely that the date gave significance to the elephants, rather than vice versa, and that the elephants were set up as they were delivered by the workshop involved (significantly, on different days of the week). (2) The V[oto] F[ecit] of the facade inscription is connected by Mitchell with a vow made by Sigismondo after the battle of Piombino, which was followed by the de' Pasti project of 1448. He even suggests (ibid.,

75) that de' Pasti's medal of the Tempio also alludes to this vow retrospectively. But both the Tempio facade and the medal carry the date 1450, while neither 1448 nor 1453, the dates of Sigismondo's victories, appear on the Tempio, and I know of no medals that specifically commemorate either victory. (3) Basinio's epic of Malatesta's career hints at a refoundation of S. Francesco after the triumph of 1453, but it is no more than a hint. On the other hand, Basinio himself did not arrive in Rimini until late 1449, and he may have owed his initial fortunes there as much to his relationship with a noble Riminese widow, whom he married in 1451, as to Sigismondo's patronage. Certainly, he maintained contact with literary circles around Nicholas V; he had tried to obtain Nicholas's patronage in 1449, and in 1453/54 he wrote a verse epistle to Nicholas apparently declining an offer to translate Homer for the pope; it is likely that such an offer came in response to supplications from Basinio. In 1453 Basinio became a Riminese citizen and acquired property, giving him perhaps the economic and personal security to refuse Nicholas's offer, and to turn to the composition of the *Hesperis*. It is likely, then, that Basinio himself played an important role in the festivities and celebrations after Vada; if so, he had good reason to stress the events of 1453 and to neglect those of 1448 or even of 1450. (On Basinio's career see A. Campana in *DBI* 7 [1965]: 89–98; Pächt 1951, 91f.) (4) Mitchell (1978), 82, 99, associates Alberti with the iconographical program of the interior (that is, the sculptural decoration of Mitchell's 1453/54 project), and relates this, in the light of his elaborate neoplatonist reading of it, to Alberti's demand in the *De re aedificatoria* that the design of sacred buildings should be suffused with philosophy. Alberti's concern in this passage, however (Alberti 1966a, 2:610, but see Portoghesi's cautious remark [ibid., n.2], limiting the sense of Alberti's words), seems to be that architectural values should be paramount, and that all ornamentation should satisfy this demand. The complex iconography of the Tempio reliefs, especially as elucidated by Mitchell, seems particularly foreign to Alberti's taste and practice as designer.

29. The "castellum" projected for the facade has been interpreted as an image of the *rocca* (the Castel Sismondo) or as some sort of supporting device (Ricci 1925, 257, citing a document of December 17, 1454). Ricci inclines to the former hypothesis, as do I (cf. Mitchell 1978, 82). On Malatesta medals bearing the image of the *rocca* see, e.g., Pasini (1983), 144, 155; Mitchell (1978), 73; Lavin (1984), 31f., suggesting that della Francesca's representation of the castle in a medal-like format in the Tempio preceded the medals and influenced their design. The Roman bridge in Rimini had always had a representative as well as functional aspect, and appears on medieval seals of Rimini together with the Augustan arch as a sign of the city (Lavin 1984, 37; Scagliarini Corlaita 1988, 54). On the Malatesta enthusiasm for heraldic insignia see Pasini (1983), 133–140.

30. Mack (1982), 64, has collected the evidence and concluded that a two-story structure with a loggia above a row of shops was projected, though never completed, while the church of S. Francesco behind it was restored. For the hypothesis that Alberti was involved in the early 1450s with a number of Malatesta projects (in Cesena and Fano as well as Rimini) see Pasini (1983), 95, admitting that such involvement may well have been merely a matter of giving advice.

31. The superimposed arches of the central bay, however, may suggest not the Arch of Constantine but the so-called Arch of Augustus at Perugia (Ricci 1925, 280). Constantinian reflections may still be present, nevertheless, given the apparent relationship of the facade of the Tempio to the three equal bays of the Basilica of Constantine (usually known at the time as the Temple of Peace) in Rome (Mitchell 1978, 82).

32. Orlandi and Portoghesi (Alberti 1966a, 2:671 n.6) note the relevance of this to the Tempio. In a passage on funerary inscriptions (ibid., 2:694–695), Alberti recommends the use of inscriptions that address and attract the attention of the passerby.

33. Mitchell (1978), 81, calls the marble exterior casing of the Tempio an "impresa veramente augustea," implying that this was the view of contemporaries, or at least of Basinio. Mitchell here associates the Augustan allusions with Sigismondo, not Nicholas, as may well have been the case after the former's victory at Vada in 1453.

34. On the images of elephant *bigae* perched atop arches on Augustan coins see Pensa (1988), 24–26. Pensa suggests that the viaduct-like appearance of some of the arches represented was meant to indicate the Via Flaminia. Elephants may also have been associated with arches set up by Augustus in commemoration of the victory at Actium in the Roman Forum and at Brindisi, the point of debarcation for the East (Scagliarini Corlaita 1988, 68). It would have been easy for Renaissance antiquarians to conflate the function and type of the two sets of arches, especially as those commemorating the victory of Actium had entirely disappeared, except in representations on coins.

35. On the resonances of the Roman triumphal use of elephants in the Renaissance see Martindale (1979), 147f. Martindale is unaware of evidence for interest in the 1450s in triumphal elephants, and is accordingly surprised at the presence of elephants in Mantegna's painting of Caesar's triumph. The fullest account of the Roman use of elephants in triumphal contexts is that of Wellmann (1905). See also Heckscher (1947), 160, on the association of the *gens Caesar* with elephants.

36. See Setton (1975), 318–320, 376f., 497f.; and Setton (1976), 109. For Nicholas's own expression of concern with the policies and ambitions of Sultan Jakmak of Egypt see Tomassetti (1857–72), 5:103–106.

37. On February 26, 1450, Nicholas had appointed Cardinal Bessarion legate for Bologna, Romagna, and the March (Pastor 1949, 69); Calandrini's appointment as legate of the March came, presumably, later in the year, perhaps after his appointment, also in 1450, as bishop of Bologna (C. Gennaro in *DBI* 16 [1973]: 450). It is not clear why these overlapping appointments should have been made, although they seem to emphasize Nicholas's concern for the city and provinces concerned, since both Calandrini and Bessarion must be counted among his closest collaborators. The need for strong and reliable government in Romagna and the March was intensified by the pressure exerted by Venice on the region; Thomson (1980), 126f., notes that Ravenna's passing under Venetian control in 1441 may already have provoked a clash between Venice and the papacy, anticipating the open conflict during the succession struggle for Milan (1450–52) and Venice's support of Malatesta against the papacy in the 1460s (see also Stinger 1985, 101f.). All this suggests that the depredations at S. Apollinare had far-reaching implications within the context of papal-Venetian relations, and were not merely a case of Malatesta arrogance and unscrupulousness.

38. Nicholas's severity is mentioned in the draft of the *Italia illustrata* prepared by Flavio Biondo for presentation to the pope (Nogara 1927, 223). Evidently Biondo believed that Nicholas would welcome the commemoration of his resolute handling of the problem of the heresy in the March. Needless to say, Manetti makes no mention of the matter.

39. For the activity of S. Giacomo della Marca in and outside Italy under Nicholas see R. Lioi in *BS* 7 (1965): 392, and Moorman (1968), 455; in this case, Nicholas followed his predecessors' policies. Giacomo referred to these campaigns in a dialogue written soon after 1450, in which he describes actions taken in 1449 against the Fraticelli and claims to have found a bell inscribed with the name of the heresiarch Gabriel "Bishop of the Church of Philadelphia and Minister General of the Order of Friars Minor."

40. Alberti (1966a), 1:284–303 [IV.ii–iv], discusses various aspects of city walls, which he clearly regards as essential elements of the infrastructure of any city. There is a further discussion, significantly, in which Alberti dwells on the *maiestas* projected by wall systems of various kinds, like that of Babylon (ibid., 2:538f. [VII.2]). He emphasizes the desirability of ringing the city, between the wall and the sacral boundary, the *pomerium*, with a wide-open space consecrated (the choice of words is far from casual) to "public liberty": "intra pomeria et pro muris velim patulam circumscribi viam sacrarique publicae libertati" (ibid., 540f.).

41. Cantone (1978), 31, remarks that in a discussion ostensibly of the maintenance of buildings (in the tenth book of the *De re aedificatoria*), Alberti deals with the ecological

aspects of the city and its environs. But Cantone overemphasizes the concentricity of Alberti's model, which she thinks implies a sharp break of city and country (ibid., 41f.). I would emphasize this passage from the opening of the seventh book: "Regionem urbis atque aream vehementer honestabit copia aedificiorum aptissimis locis distributa et collocata. Platonis ager et area probabatur distincta classibus xii, et in singulis singula templa sacellave constituebat" (Alberti 1966a, 2:532f.). Alberti clearly refers here to a political and sacral division of territory that cuts across distinctions of urban and rural space.

42. Alberti (1966a), 1:66–69: "condimentum quidem gratiae est omni in re varietas." This is Alberti's recommendation for the layout of a house so long as bilateral symmetry (and hence organicity) is observed. The metaphorical application of human physical characteristics to buildings is explicit (cf. ibid., 2:810–813 [IX.v]). On the successive distinct spaces in a house see ibid., 792f. [IX.2].

43. Alberti (1966a) 1:414f. [V.xvii]: "Faciles ad se ex agro porrigit aditus; venientem hospitem honestissimis excipiet spatiis; spectabitur, spectabitque urbem oppida mare fusamque planitiem, et nota collium montiumque capita, ortorum delitias, piscationum venationumque illecebras sub oculis habebit expositas." On the ancient sources of this passage and its echoes in Palladio's thought see Forssman (1965), 149–162.

7 Epilogue: The River, the Book, and the Basilica

1. For the "pesca macabra" (the repeated discovery of children's corpses in the nets of fishermen that induced Pope Innocent III to found the hospital) see De Angelis (1962), 399–401. The appearance of the fishermen before the pope was illustrated in the fresco cycle commissioned by Sixtus IV in the hospital.

2. Stefano da Reggio, a papal familiar, was in Naples in 1449 spending the remarkable sum of 1,500 florins on wine "pro ipso domino nostro" (ASR, M 830, fol. 108r). Other missions conducted by Stefano indicate that he was a military man (ibid., fols. 120r, 147r). Father Leonard Boyle has told me that Nicholas's wine cellar occupied a room adjacent to the library. At least toward the end of his life it appears that Nicholas had an alcohol problem (Infessura 1890, 58, in connection with the execution of Angelo Roncone, which the pope allegedly could not remember ordering the day after Roncone went to the block). See also Pastor (1949), 526f. n.3. Pastor (ibid., 20) insists that Nicholas had good taste in wine, but drank sparingly and only on the occasion of formal banquets and the like.

3. The *alaggio* (towing franchise) was traditionally a monopoly of the cardinal bishop of Ostia, until abolished in 1567. There was a Torre Buffalara near the Ponte Galera, perhaps used for surveillance of the towpath and the buffalo teams that labored along it at the point where they crossed the Galera river (Ashby 1914, 54). The *alaggio* and the work force associated with it are discussed by Martini (1965), 232–235.

4. The existence of the 1447 statutes is attested only by the preamble to a summary revision of them published in 1571. In the sixteenth century the *barilai* held the church of S. Maria in Capella, situated near the Ripa Grande; probably they received this at the same time as their statutes, perhaps in connection with Nicholas's campaign of restoration of the city's churches.

5. Among other things, Evangelista was prominent in the confraternity of S. Maria delle Grazie, which administered the hospital of that name (ASR, CNC 481, fol. 359v [November 22, 1447], which names Evangelista as *socius* of the *guardiani*). For further information on Battista see chapter 6, note 23. Some of the brothers' business transactions, involving landholdings (*casali*) in the Roman district, are recorded by the notary Antonio Finagrani (ASR, CNC 712, e.g. fols. 2r, 3v). It is significant that, quite unusually, donations made by the brothers to the Confraternity of the Salvatore were generally in kind, specifically in draught animals. Thus for masses for his father Lorenzo in the church of SS. Quadraginta ad Pellipariam (evidently the traditional name of the church still corres-

ponded to the character of the area or at least the major parishioners), Battista gave four young oxen, still not broken in to the plough, at a value of "approximately" 60 florins (Egidi 1908, 378; cf. ibid., 387). Evangelista gave oxen for the masses for his wife Gentilesca, perhaps an Altieri or related to that family, in S. Maria della Strada (ibid., 399). The compound of the Leni family, which stood on the site of the present archaeological zone of the Largo Argentina, is discussed by Marchetti-Longhi (1972), 32. Both brothers sometimes appear with the surname Martini; for the simultaneous use of the names Martini and Leni see, e.g., Egidi (1908), 387. Battista's wife was Leonarda Porcari; apparently balancing her loyalties to both her families, she provided for masses to be said for her both in the church of the Minerva, traditionally associated with the Porcari family, and at SS. Quadraginta (ibid., 413). She desired burial in the former.

6. Battista, named as "dohanerius urbis," was recorded as transferring to the Camera 3,000 florins, part of the income received from the *dogana*. He may, then, have held office already under Eugenius, and have been an important participant in the negotiations leading to the "concordat" of 1446 (see chapters 1 and 3 above).

7. Such business relations may have encouraged or even reflected relations in other spheres; Valentini and Zucchetti (1953), 251, in their introduction to Biondo's *Roma instaurata*, mention Battista and Giorgio Cesarini (who was a near neighbor in Pigna; see Marchetti-Longhi 1972) as followers of the humanist tendency and members of the Curia. Clearly Battista was no *curialis* in the strict sense, though he was a vital figure in Nicholas's administration.

8. There is a possible exception, the reference at ASR, TS 1450, fol. 6r, to a Francesco del Borgo, identified as a merchant, who supplies nails (*bulette*) to the papal household. This is the only reference so far discovered to commercial activity on the part of Nello's assistant, if this is he. If so, his involvement in the world of the building trades lends support to Frommel's (1984a) suggestion that he was the architect of the Palazzo Venezia.

9. In contrast to some of his associates under Nicholas, Boccabelli found favor with Calixtus III, and on September 28, 1455, was created *scutifer honoris* in the presence of, among others, Gaspare da Verona (ASV, RV 435, fol. 128r).

10. D'Onofrio (1980), 144 n.8, 145, notes that only paving was involved on the bridge, and suggests that Nicholas merely improved on the repairs carried out by Martin V after the great flood of 1422.

11. As usual a rebuilding clause was involved, though the rent, at 6 florins, was quite high. Paciuri does not appear as a tenant after 1447; perhaps he bought the house (note the case of Antonello d'Albano discussed in chapter 4 above).

12. The page carries the heading "pacta celebrata inter preceptorem et Antonium Paciaro de Transtiberim (sic)." The rest of the document was never copied into the hospital's ledger; whatever the reason for this, the association of Paciuri and Capoccini is proven.

13. In 1445 Giovanni Capoccini had received fine vestments at papal expense; clearly he enjoyed papal support. Under Paul II, however, his son was to be cut down in street fighting, while Giovanni himself was among those arrested in a sweep of actual or potential troublemakers. See Miglio in *DBI* 18 (1975): 598–599; Miglio uses the form Capocci of the family's name, but notes that it was usually written de Capoccinis in Latin.

14. In 1459 Pius II resorted to excommunication against Francesco Orsini of Gallese, who had usurped the hospital's rights to the tolls of Borgo S. Leonardo (De Angelis 1962, 279f.). Francesco had perhaps taken advantage of the unsettled conditions at the end of Nicholas's pontificate.

15. Sercoberti's other property is listed in the bull (which is, interestingly, a *motu proprio*, perhaps indicating the particular favor enjoyed by Sercoberti). His term as *caporione* of Ponte coincided with the publication of the new statutes of the *maestri di strada*, in

which emphasis is laid on the three streets converging in Ponte at the *trivium pontis*, where improvement work was currently in progress. This may be enough to explain dispensations in Sercoberti's favor.

16. D'Onofrio (1980), 258f., notes the date 1451 in a Nicholan inscription on the south face of the bridge, but sees this as marking the beginning, rather than the completion of repair work. This is surely incorrect, but is required to support D'Onofrio's argument about Alberti's direct involvement in the restoration of the bridge (see following note). It is important to note that the work on the bridge was associated with work on the nearby embankments, as reported, e.g., by Infessura (1890), 49: Nicholas "fece . . . uno muro a canto fiume, ad Torre de Nona." More generally see Cametti (1916), 411–414.

17. Spezzaferro (1973), 524, connects with Alberti a group of drawings of bridges, apparently copied from a fifteenth-century original, in a manuscript in Leningrad. D'Onofrio (1980), 268, relates these to Vasari's supposed Alberti drawing, and suggests that the travertine bases, later used for the statues of angels, were part of the Nicholan restoration and were intended to carry a superstructure designed by Alberti himself. The main problem with this is that the platforms are too far apart to carry a colonnade of the kind envisaged by Alberti. On the problem of how such a superstructure could be reconciled with Nicholas's chapels see below.

18. The chapel marked the site of a miracle-working image of the Madonna on the first pier of the Ponte alle Grazie to the left at the northern end; hence the chapel was known as S. Maria delle Grazie, and gave its name to the bridge. The chapel was built with funds bequeathed in 1374 by Jacopo di Caroccio degli Alberti, who prepared with his own hands a wooden model (at the scale of 1:8) and a drawing of the building; evidently he was the designer. The building was a domed octagon with a canopy over the entrance, and Jacopo was buried inside it. According to Francesco Sacchetti it resembled the holy sepulcher in Jerusalem. In 1456 it became a parish church, and in 1458 a priest's house was built.

19. Herendeen (1986), 23, notes the expression of the distinction in such diverse sources as the *Timaeus* and the *Institutions of Justinian*. He also notes the Virgilian motif of the Tiber as the promoter of social harmony and reasonable behavior (ibid., 54–58): "The three components of the river's primary public roles emerge: the river is the *genius loci*, it is associated with a heroic, moral or civic *virtu*, and its banks provide [Aeneas] with a site for founding a city or nation."

20. Alberti deals with both the modest country house and the aristocratic country residence, but in general he counsels moderation. Thus on the rural houses of the affluent and the poor he writes (400f.): "In utroque aliud tenuiores aliud opulentiores cives exigunt: namque tenuiores quidem cohabitandi modum ex necessitate metiuntur, lautiores vix ex societate finiunt libidini terminos. At nos quae in quibusque bene consulti moderatio comprobet referamus." In general he attacks the behavior of the affluent in very strong terms.

21. These authors accept the year 1452 as the date of a presentation to Nicholas of a manuscript version of the treatise on architecture, though there is considerable uncertainty about just how much of the text as we now have it was presented to the pope in that year. There is one major dissenter from the opinion that Alberti and Nicholas were close; unfortunately, Manfredo Tafuri's brilliant and iconoclastic discussion of this point came into my hands when this chapter was substantially complete (Tafuri 1987, 68–72). Tafuri argues that Alberti could at best have been involved only reluctantly and as a "dissimulator" in Nicholas's projects. To a great extent Tafuri is right, though he neglects the many social, institutional, and other forms of mediation between Nicholas and Alberti, whose opposition is presented in overly dramatic and even subjective terms (see my discussion of Tafuri's argument in the introduction).

22. The passage in question is discussed at length and published in translation by Westfall (1974a), 169f.; see also Urban (1963), 133f., 160. (The full text appears in Palmieri

1748.) The passage concerning Alberti reads in Westfall's translation: "The pope, wanting to make the Basilica of the Blessed Peter a greater adornment, laid deep foundations and erected a wall of thirteen *braccia*, but he stopped this great work, which could be compared to that of any of the ancients, by the distinguished advice of Leon Battista, and then an untimely death cut short this enterprise. Leon Battista Alberti, a scholar endowed with sharp and penetrating intelligence and an excellent education, and well versed in doctrine, presented these learned books on architecture, which he had written, to the pope." It is of some interest that Mattia Palmieri served as executor of Alberti's will in 1472; the reference under that year in Palmieri's chronicle to Alberti's death is the only evidence for the date of the latter (Grayson 1960, 154).

23. For the chronology of the work on the basilica see Urban (1963), 133: "Der Chorneubau, in den Quellen 'Tribuna (grande) di S. Piero' genannt, wird in den Rechnungsbelegen seit Juni 1452 erwähnt. Die finanziellen Aufwendungen steigern sich im Laufe des Jahres 1453, nehmen im darauffolgenden ab und hören Ende 1454 auf." Urban declines, however, to accept the result of his own review of the documents, and continues: "Nikolaus V. starb im März 1455. Man wird annehmen dürfen, dass die Bauarbeiten durch seinen Tod unterbrochen wurden und das Nachlassen der Rechnungsbelegen mehr auf einen Erhaltungszufall beruht." Westfall (1974a), 170, on the other hand, sees "no significant change in the project" in 1452, and emphasizes the importance in Palmieri's account of Frederick III's visit; he is right on the latter, wrong on the former point.

24. Urban (1963) gives the fullest account of the hitherto prevailing position that there were two plans, one a reconstruction program associated with preparations for the Jubilee, and the second reflecting the crucial role of Alberti at Nicholas's "Musenhof" (ibid., 156) in and after 1452.

Appendix of Documents

1. May 23, 1447
ASV, RV 407, fols. 196r–198r

Nicholas V's first edict granting privileges to existing and future inhabitants of part of the Rione Monti, as long as they remain for ten years

(In margin: "datum fuit presens bulla R.mo d. card. de Estoutevilla in sca. Potentiana de mandato d. n. p.")

Nicolaus papa V . . . pro felici directione status urbis, et illius conservatione salubri nostros potissime dirigimus cogitatus, et ad inhabitandum ipsius loca urbis utriusque sexus personas per privilegiorum et libertatum media provocamus. Accepimus siquidem quod propter nimiam habitationum distantiam, ac habitatorum inopiam nec non diversarum impositionum et gabellarum onera, aliasque varias causas, plurimum presertim in ipsius Urbis extremitatibus, ubi personarum copia sive frequentia non habetur, constituti se ab inde plerumque trasferunt sibi alibi habitacula querentes, unde fit dicte Urbis regiones, et precipue Regio Montium in huiusmodi extremitatibus, habitatoribus destitute fuerunt ac destituantur in dies, in dedecus Urbis at desolationem Regionum earundem. Nos super hiis quantum possumus et prout nobis ex debito pastorali tenemur officio salubriter providere volentes, auctoritate Apostolica presentium serie statuimus, et ordinamus quod ex nunc in antea perpetuis futuris temporibus, omnes et singuli in Regione Montium huiusmodi, videlicet ab arcu Sancti Viti in Macello usque ad Plateam Sancte Marie Maioris inclusive, at etiam ab ipso arcu usque ad viam que in Fontana nuncupatur versus Sanctam Praxedem, nec non viis illi adiacentibus suum incolatum ducentes, et ibidem pro tempore commemorari volentes, et se ad hoc disponentes suasque lares illic foventes cum eorum familia, ab solutione cuiuscumque gabelle, salvo si populum Romanum aliquod pro exercitu contra eorum inimicos et dicti Urbis invasores aut hostiles incursus subsidium communiter colligi contigerat, prorsus et omnino liberi exempti sint et immunes, eosque et quoslibet eorum cum huiusmodi familia a dicta solutione realiter absolvimus, liberos exemptos absolutos et immunes esse volumus: pariter et censemus quodque ad emendum sal aliquod ultra quam voluerint sive pro eorum usu et necessitate egerint, dummodo in loco ad hoc per Cam. Rom. deputato id emerint et receperint, nullatenus nec teneantur nec ad id compelli possint inviti; ac quod de eorum propriis vel quos pro tempore excolere sive coltivare contigerit vineis vinum colligere et ad domos suas et sine cuiusvis in portis dicte Urbis absque solutione dicte gabelle ducere, nec non si quod de vino huiusmodi ultra eorum in huiusmodi domibus necessitatem ipsius superfuerit illud in domibus platea via in fontana aut vicis suprascriptis dumtaxat vendere libere et expedite volueri[n]t, nec non quod omnes et singuli tam in pref. Urbi quam alibi et in terris ecclesiae commorantes qui pro pecuniariis aut aliis quibusvis penis preter quam occasione homicidii sive lese maiestatis criminis condemnati fuerint in parte Regionum huiusmodi habitare volentes, dummodo inibi ad minus per decennium continuo habitare velint et ad hoc se obligaverint ac propterea sufficientem cautionem prestiterint, a premissis condemnationibus liberi ac ab omni conturbatione securi existant mandantes, auctoritate predicta condemnationes huiusmodi tam de dicta Urbis quam terrarum ubi huiusmodi condemnationes forsan facte fuerint officialium libris et codicillis in quibus scripte sive notate reperiantur prorsus cassari atque deleri mandantes, insuper universis et singulis eiusdem Urbis gabellariis et officialibus aliisque quorum pro tempore interfuerit distinctius inhibentes eiusdem ne deinceps predicte partis regionis habitatores, aut eorum familie seu eorum aliquem preter et contra statutum et ordinationem et voluntatem et libertatem in huiusmodi quomodocumque molestare vel inquietare aut occasione alicuius gabelle solutionis aliis quam et promissum est aliquod petere vel exigere audeant seu presumant, non obstantibus statutis et consuetudinibus dicte Urbis.Datum Rome apud S.Petrum, A.D. 1447, 10 Kal. Junii, P.A. 1. Poggius.

(Nicholas's second edict, of August 21, 1448, is not published here, as it essentially only confirms the earlier bull, with emphatic directions to the city's fiscal officers to respect the tax immunities granted therein. In addition, it grants immunity from the wine tax. For the text see BAV, Cod. Vat. Lat. 8035, fols. 181r–182v, and for a brief description, Ferri 1907, 162 no. 214.)

2. March 15, 1448
ASV, RV 407, fol. 288v

Nicholas establishes Nello's salary at 25 florins per month, but without formally defining his role

Nicolaus...dilecto filio nobili viro Nello civi Bononiensi scutifero et familiari nostro...grata tue devotionis fidelia quoque et prompta familiaritatis obsequia, que nobis et apostolice sedi hactenus impendisti et adhuc solicitis studiis impendere non desistis, non indigne merentur ut circa statum tuum prospere dirigendum (qd pro tuorum exigentia meritorum sic salubriter provideatur) ut bene meritis tuis talis compensatio fiat quod exinde de nobis et sede predicta valeris merito contentari. hinc est quod nos considerantes te in continuis solicitudinibus et laboribus, curisque variis circa nostri palacii statum prospere et utiliter dirigendum intentum et diligentem, ac attendentes quod unicuique sui laboris praemia condigna debentur, idcirco in tuorum laborum recompensam tibi provisionem 25 flor. auri de cam. singulis mensibus et pro dictis nostris et dicte sedis serviciis...persolvendam constituimus et ordinamus...concedentes quod pecunias inantea a die dat. praesentium computando pro huiusmodi tue pensione debeas ex quibuscumque pecuniis ad manus tuas undecumque proventibus et ad nos vel dictam cameram spectantibus usque ad integram dicte provisionis satisfactionem tibi valeas retineri.

1447, 16 Kal. April., anno primo pontificatus [i.e., March 15, 1448; the secretary here uses the reckoning *ab incarnatione Dei*, as was customary in Florence]

3. July 23, 1451
ASV, RV 416, fol. 158r

Nello's commission

Nicolaus etc. dilecto filio nobili viro Nello Bartholomei civi Bononiensi familiari nostro salutem etc.

Suffragantia tibi ex laudabilibus tuis operibus merita probitatis et fidei quibus experientia teste apud nos clarere dinosceris, non indigne exposcunt ut sedes apostolica, cui tantopere fideliter et prudenter ad hanc usque diem gratam servitia impendisti, ea tibi pro sua equitate concedat per que tue heredumque et successorumque tuorum indemnitati valeat salubriter provideri. Dudum siquidem, postquam ad apicem summi apostolatus fuimus divina miseratione assumpti, tibi, quem iamdiu antea propter eximie tue circumspectionis industriam compertum habueramus in agendis rebus providum et fidelem, nonnullarum ecclesiarum ac aliorum locorum edificiorumque diversorum fundationem, constructionem et reparationem, ornamentorumque et iocalium cappelle et domus nostrarum emptionem, aliarum quoque diversarum rerum negociorumque expeditionem et executionem, unacum rei familiaris nostre cura, vive vocis oraculo per nos specialiter tibi facto, prout locorum rerum et ipsorum necessitas ac beneplacitum et voluntas nostra exegerunt, commisimus absque aliquarum literarum super nostris huiusmodi beneplacitis et mandatis confectione pro quibus efficaciter peragendis, plures et diversas pecuniarum summas camere apostolice debitas, quas a diversis personis et locis interpelatis [sic] temporibus exegisti recepistique, exposuisse fideliter comprobaris.

Nos igitur...motu proprio...te nostrum generalem commissarium negociorumque gestorem usque ad nostrum beneplacitum facimus, constituimus et etiam ordinamus, tibique rem nostram familiarem regendi, administrandi, gubernandi; ecclesias quoque et alia pia atque sana loca tam alme urbis ipsiusque edificia quam aliarum civitatum terrarum locorum R.E. subiectorum, prout tibi opportunum videbitur, fundandi, erigendi et reparandi; nec non pro iis omnibus peragendis et exequendis fructus, redditus et proventus eidem camere apostolice debitos exigendi, recipiendi et recuperandi; ac alios ad tuas manus provenientes retinendi, de receptis quoque exactis et retentis quitandi et finiendi; eosque in usum, utilitatem et necessitatem premissorum omnium prout discretioni tue videbitur oportunum, ac iuxta commissionem per nos vive vocis oraculo tibi factam seu in posterum faciendam, convertendi disponendi et distribuendi motu et scientia similibus auctoritate prefata facultatem concedimus ac eciam plenariam potestatem. Per hoc autem te penitus eximere non intendimus quominus cum dicta camera imposterum de receptis expositisque pecuniis tenearis reddere rationem...

Datum Romae apud S.P., anno dni 1451, 8 Kal. Aug., P.A.5.

4. February 20, 1453
ASV, RV 424, fol. 216r

General quittance for Nello da Bologna

Nello Bartholomei civi Bononiensi...conceditur generalis quietantia...
...presertim de omnibus per te receptis solutis habitis et expositis in Anno Jubilei proxime exacto tam pro annona sive abundantia grani frumenti farine quam aliter quomodocumque et qualitercumque ordinarie et extraordinarie computatis in...salariis officialium et personarum ad ipsam annonam deputatorum, necnon amissione frugum sine proditione et dannis in emendis et conducendis victualibus prout nobis facta existit plena fides, et similiter de pecuniis oblationum ecclesiarum Urbis prefati anni...Item de quibuscumque pecuniarum summis que etiam ad te pervenerunt de gabellis tam per terram quam per mare seu penis et maleficiis per curiam capitolii exactis aut ratione camerariatus [?] salarie grosse et minute dohane pecudum dicte Urbis ac etiam Patrimonii b.Petri in Tuscia salis et focatici, neque de quibuscumque expensis in adventu carissimi...Frederici...imperatoris, tam in provisionibus personarum familie eiusdem imperatoris et equorum [sic], quam etiam eorum victu vestitu habitationibus fabricis et reparationibus domorum stabulorum...utensilium ad eorum necessitatem paratorum, necnon de omnibus aliis expensis similiter per te et personas a te deputatas pro reparatione et refectione ecclesiarum, menium, capitolii, portarum, domus conservatorum dicte Urbis tam intra quam extra ac aliorum murorum in Civita Vetula, Montalto, Monte Romano, Ostia, Tiberina et aliis quibuscumque locis, ac pari modo de expensis factis in provisionibus officialibus et custodibus [i.e., officialium et custodum?] portarum et aliarum quarundam personarum ac vestibus rosati et paonacii urbis eiusdem officialibus in adventu dicti Imperatoris assignatis; seu pro detegendo tractatu factione et conspiratione quondam Stephani de Porcariis eiusque in ea parte complicum fautorum atque sequacium ac quibuscumque bonis tam ipsius Stephani quam iniquitatis filiorum Nicolai Galli, Jacobi Lelli Cecchi, Angeli de Masso, Francisci Gabadeo, Baptiste et Nicolai Sciarre tunc civium Romanorum ac Petri de Monterotundo habitatoris dicte Urbis et quorumcumque aliorum sequacium fautorum et conspiratorum eiusdem camere prefate urbis confiscatis venditis et de mandato nostro donatis...

10 Kal. Marcii. PA 6. De Curia.

5. January 12, 1454
ASV, RV 429, fols. 144v–146v

*Nicholas V reviews Nello's activity as commissarius generalis and confirms both the
quittances granted to him in the past and his present powers and responsibilities*

Nicolaus etc. dil. fil. nobili viro Nello Bartholomei civi Bononiensi familiari et generali
commissario nostro... Attendentes igitur quod, postquam tibi nonnullarum ecclesiarum et aliorum locarum diversorumque edificiorum in alma urbe et extra edifica-
tionem ac reparationem et quamplurium rerum negotiorumque executionem una cum
rei familiaris et palatii nostri cura tibi commiseramus, tu qui plures et diversas pecuniarum summas tunc camere apostolice debitas pro predictis expediendis et exequendis
a diversis personis receperas ac de receptis et expositis post redditum per te calculum
et communem quitationem et liberationem per quasdam sub dat. octavo kal. Augusti
pontificatus nostri anno quinto fueras consecutus primo et deinde sub dat. decimo kal.
Martii pont. eiusdem anno sexto per alias nostras letteras, per quas te etiam generalem
commissarium nostrum ac negotiorum gestorem usque ad nostrum beneplacitum
fecimus tibique rem nostram familiarem regendi administrandi et gubernandi, necnon
ecclesias et alia pia atque prophana loca et edificia tam alme urbis quam aliarum civitatum terrarum et locorum Romane ecclesie subiectorum prout tibi opportunum videretur
fundandi erigendi et reparandi et pro hiis peragendis fructus et proventus camere prefate
debitos exigendi et recipiendi illasque pro huiusmodi exequendis exponendi et distribuendi facultatem et plenariam potestatem concessimus, tu tam ante dat. litterarum
predictarum quam post multa atque diversa de mandato et voluntate nostris bene lauda-
biliter fideliter et prudenter gesseras administraveris et exposueras prout in libro
rationum tuarum plenius continetur... motu proprio... absolvimus et liberamus, de-
cernentes te aut personas ad ea tuo nomine deputatas ad ulteriorem rationem redden-
dum de gestis... predictis etiam si ad plenum liquidata non essent usque in diem dat.
posteriarum litterarum predictarum amplius non teneri et presertim pro receptis et expositis in anno Jubilei pro annona ac aliis quomodocumque et qualitercumque ordinarie
etextraordinarie computatis etiam salariis officialium et personarum ad ipsam annonam
deputatorum necnon amissione frugum ac damnis in emendis et conducendis victualibus, et similiter de pecuniis oblationum ecclesiarum urbis dum [*sic*] Jubilei huiusmodi
aliorumque locorum que ad manus tuas quomodolicet pervenerant, seu de gabellis per
terram et mare aut penis exactis ac pro salaria grossa et minuta doana pascuorum et
tractarum grani urbis et patrimonii salis et focatici, et de quibuscumque expensis in
adventu imperatoris pro reparatione ecclesiarum menium urbis, capitolii, portarum,
domus conservatorum necnon murorum in Civitate Vetula, Monte Alto, Monteromano,
Ostia et aliis locis, necnon pro expensis factis in vestibus donatis officialibus et nonnullis civibus dicte urbis, provisionibus quoque officialium et custodum portarum, ac pro
detegendo tractatu et conspiratione quondam Stephani de Porcariis, ipsius quoque
Stephani ac suorum complicum confiscatis bonis venditis et donatis... confirmamus et
approbamus...

Cum autem post redditam per te rationem gestorum et administratorum huiusmodi
necnon commutationes... quas denuo ratificamus... tu ex similibus commissione
voluntate et mandato nostris iniunctum tibi gerendarum rerum nostrarum onus atque
ministerium exigendo plures et diversas alias pecuniarum summas tam de proventibus
salis dicte urbis quam aliarum salariarum aliquorum locorum... necnon de pretiis et
venditionibus bonorum rebellium... confiscatorum ac ipsas pecuniarum summas iuxta
voluntatem et mandatum nostrum tam pro premissis quam etiam pro eiusdem palatii
nostri et pro tribune basilica principis apostolorum de urbe et dicte urbis et burgi sancti
Petri sive civitatis leonine murorum fabricis et refectione, necnon reparatione aqueduc-
tus fontis trivii, eiusdem domus conservatorum, pontis milvii et pro nonnullis aliis rebus structuris atque operibus publicis et privatis, necnon pro paramentis ornamentis ac
auro argento gemmis margaritis sive perlis et aliis lapidibus pretiosis emendis ipsoque

ornamentorum opere et artificiorum eorum magistris et operariis, tum etiam pro emptione domorum et ypotecarum que demolite fuerunt iuxta ecclesiam ss.Celso et Juliani ac pontem s.Petri dicte urbis earunque emendo et pro capellis inibi denuo erectis, per te et personas alias tuo nomine datas solutas atque expositas . . . suscepisti.

prid. Id. Jan., pont. anno septimo
Domenicus de Luca.

Bibliography

Unpublished Sources

Archivio di Stato, Rome [ASR]

Archivio Camerale 1
Mandati Camerali 830 [cited as M 830] (1447–1452)
Tesoreria Segreta [TS], Registri 1284–1287 (1450–1453)[1]
Spese Minute del Palazzo [SMP], Registro 1469 (1454)[1]
Conti della Depositeria Generale [CDG], Registri 1756–1757 (1448–1451)

Tesoreria provinciale della Marca
Busta 6, Registro 18 (1448–1450)
Busta 7, Registro 19 (1450–1451)

Collegio dei Notari Capitolini [CNC]

481, 482, 483	Petrus de Caputgallis
518	Antonius de Leys
712	Antonius de Finagranis
1085	
1164	Johannes Nicolai
1232	Pantaleo de Pantaleonibus
1641	Marianus Scalibastri
1684	Gregorius de Signo
1725	Domenicus de Taglientibus

Archivio dell'Ospedale del SSmo. Salvatore [AOSS]
Istromenti 24 (1443–1453)
Istromenti 25 (1454–1457)
Rubricellone di tutti li libri e scritture, 2 vols., 1745 [AOSS, nos. 990, 991]
Piante e Catasti 390, no. 1010: Catasto dell'Ospedale 1517[2]
Archivio Antico

Archivio dell'Arcispedale di S. Spirito in Sassia
Atti notarili 210, 211

Archivio Capitolino, Rome [ACR]

Archivio Urbano [AU], Fondo notarile
252, 253 Giovanni Amati

---

1. Volumes of the TS and the SMP are cited in text and notes by date rather than volume number in accordance with the practice of Müntz to facilitate collation with his publications.

2. Other extant *catasti* were unavailable to me during the period of research.

Archivio Segreto Vaticano [ASV]
Introitus et Exitus [IE] 414–428 (1447–1455)
Diversa Cameralia [DC] 26, 27
Obligationes et Solutiones [OS] 76 (1447–1455)
Registri Vaticani [RV] 403–435
Registri Laterani [RL] 445, 472
Fondo dell'Archivio di Stato 2494 (Libri servitiorum minutiorum tres, 1447–1455)

Biblioteca Apostolica Vaticana [BAV]

Archivio Capitolare della Basilica di S. Pietro [ACSP], Arm. 41, 42
Censuali della basilica Vaticana
no. 5 (mainly 1441–1448)
no. 6 (mainly 1450–1453)
no. 7 (1454, 1455, also later material)

Archivio di Stato, Florence [ASF]
Notarile antecosimiano M34, protocol of Gerardo Maffei da Volterra, 1444–1451, un-
paginated (citations by date of documents)
Dieci di Balìa, Carteggio Responsivo 22 (dispatches of ambassadors)

Archivio di Stato, Milan [ASM]
Archivio Sforzesco Ducale [ASD] 40, 41 (1450–1455)

Archivio di Stato, Siena [ASS]
Concistoro 1960–1967 (1447–1450)

Archivio di Stato, Fabriano
Riformanze comunali, vols. 10, 11, 12

Archivio di Stato, Venice
Deliberazioni del Senato, vol. 17.

Published Sources

Abbreviations

AB	Art Bulletin
ASRSP	Archivio. Società Romana di Storia Patria
BHR	Bibliothèque d'Humanisme et Renaissance
BS	Bibliotheca Sanctorum (13 vols., 1961–70, Rome)
DBI	Dizionario Biografico degli Italiani
EI	Enciclopedia italiana di scienze, lettere ed arti (35 vols., 1949–51, Milan and Rome)
IMU	Italia Medioevale ed Umanistica
JSAH	Journal of the Society of Architectural Historians
JWCI	Journal of the Warburg and Courtauld Institutes
MAH	Mélanges d'Archéologie et d'Histoire
MEFR-M	Mélanges de l'Ecole française à Rome. Moyen Age—Temps moderns
MH	Medievalia et Humanistica
MKIF	Mitteilungen des kunsthistorischen Instituts in Florenz

PW	*Paulys Realenzyklopädie der klassischen Altertumswissenschaft*, ed. G. Wissowa et al. (1893ff., Stuttgart)
QFIAB	*Quellen und Forschungen in italienischen Archiven und Bibliotheken*
RIS	*Rerum Italicarum Scriptores: Raccolta degli storici italiani dal 500 al 1500*, ed. L. Muratori (1748ff.)
RIS²	*Rerum Italicarum Scriptores*, second series, general editors G. Carducci and V. Fiorini
RJK	*Römisches Jahrbuch für Kunstgeschichte*
SR	*Studi Romani*
ZK	*Zeitschrift für Kunstgeschichte*

Ackerman, James S. 1954. *The Cortile del Belvedere*. Studi e documenti per la storia del Palazzo Vaticano, 3. Rome.

Ackerman, James S. 1974. "Notes on Bramante's bad reputation." In *Studi Bramanteschi. Atti del Congresso Internazionale Milano—Urbino—Roma 1970*, 339–350. Rome.

Ackerman, J. S. 1982. "The planning of Renaissance Rome, 1450–1580." In Ramsey (1982), 3–17.

Adinolfi, Pasquale. 1857a. *Laterano e Via Maggiore. Saggio della topografia di Roma nell'età di mezzo*. Rome.

Adinolfi, Pasquale. 1857b. *Roma nell'età di mezzo*. 2 vols. Rome.

Adinolfi, Pasquale. 1859. *Il Portico di S. Pietro ossia il Borgo nell'età di mezzo*. Rome.

Adinolfi, Pasquale. 1860. *Il Canale di Ponte*. Narni.

Adinolfi, Pasquale. 1865. *Via Sacra o del Papa tra il Cerchio di Alessandro ed il Teatro di Pompeo*. Rome.

Ait, Ivana. 1981. "La dogana di S. Eustachio nel XV secolo." In Esch (1981), 81–148.

Alati, B. da. 1950. *Gli ospedali di Roma a le bolle pontificie*. Viterbo.

Alberti, Leone Battista. 1966a. *L'architettura [De re aedificatoria]*, ed. G. Orlandi and P. Portoghesi. 2 vols. Milan.

Alberti, Leone Battista. 1966b. *Opere volgari*, ed. C. Grayson, vol. 2. Bari.

Alberti, Leone Battista. 1969. *I libri della famiglia*, ed. R. Romano and A. Tenenti. Turin.

Aleandri, Vittorio E. 1911. "Artisti e artieri lombardi a Vitorchiano nei secoli XV–XVI." *Archivio Storico Lombardo* 15: 102–208.

Altieri, Marcantonio. 1878. *Li nuptiali*, ed. E. Narducci. Rome.

Amadei, Emma. 1969. *Le torri di Roma*. 3d ed. Rome.

Amayden, T. 1910, 1914. *Le storie delle famiglie romane*, ed. C. A. Bertini. 2 vols. Rome.

Angelini, P. 1971. "Poésie et politique chez les Colonna: une *canzone* de Cyriacque d'Ancône." *Revue des Études italiennes*, n.s. 17:14–50.

Anselmi, S. 1976. "Piovi, perticari e buoi da lavoro nell'agricoltura Marchigiana del XV secolo." *Quaderni storici* 31:203ff.

Anzilotti, A. 1919. "Cenni sulle finanze del Patrimonio di S. Pietro in Tuscia nel secolo XV." *ASRSP* 43:349–399.

Apollonj, Bruno. 1937. *Fabbriche civili nel quartiere del Rinascimento in Roma*. I monumenti d'Italia, 12. Rome.

Arasse, Daniel. 1977. "'Fervebat pietate populus': art, dévotion et société autour de la glorification de S. Bernardin de Sienne." *MEFR-M* 1:117–187.

Arasse, Daniel, ed. 1982. *Symboles de la Renaissance, i, Art et langage*. Paris.

Argan, Gian Carlo. 1946. "The architecture of Brunelleschi and the origins of perspective theory in the fifteenth century." *JWCI* 9:96–121.

Armellini, Mariano. 1882. "Un censimento della città di Roma sotto il pontificato di Leone X." *Gli Studi in Italia*, 4/5: 7–143.

Armellini, Mariano. 1942. *Le chiese di Roma dal secolo IV al XIX*, ed. C. Cecchelli. 2 vols. Rome.

Ashby, Thomas, ed. 1914. *La Campagna romana al tempo di Paolo III: Una mappa della Campagna romana del 1547 di Eufrosino della Volpaia*. Rome.

Ashby, Thomas. 1970. *The Roman Campagna in classical times*, rev. ed. with an introduction by J. B. Ward-Perkins. New York.

Bacci, Domenico. 1959. *Poggio Bracciolini nella luce dei suoi tempi*. Florence.

Bandmann, G. 1981. *Mittelalterliche Architektur als Bedeutungsträger*. 7th ed. Berlin.

Baracconi, G. 1971. *I rioni di Roma*. Rome.

Barbier de Montault, X. 1889. *Oeuvres complètes, i (Inventaires de Rome)*. Poitiers.

Barker, Graham. 1973. "The economy of medieval Tuscania: The archaeological evidence." *Papers of the British School at Rome* 41:155–177.

Baron, Hans. 1968a. "Imitation, rhetoric and quattrocento thought in Bruni's *Laudatio*." In *From Petrarch to Leonardo Bruni: Studies in humanistic and political literature*, 151–171. Chicago.

Baron, Hans. 1968b. "Leonardo Bruni: 'Professional rhetorician' or 'civic humanist'?" *Past and Present* 36:21–37.

Barroero, Liliana, ed. 1982. *Guide rionali di Roma. Rione I, Monti*. 2 parts. Rome.

Battisti, Eugenio. 1959. *I comaschi a Roma nel primo Rinascimento*. Arte e artisti dei laghi lombardi, 1. Como.

Battisti, Eugenio. 1960. "Roma apocalittica e Re Salomone." In *Rinascimento e Barocco*, 72–95. Turin.

Battisti, Eugenio. 1962. *L'Antirinascimento*. Milan.

Battisti, Eugenio. 1981. *Filippo Brunelleschi*. New York.

Bauer, Clemens. 1927. "Studi per la storia delle finanze papali durante il pontificato di Sisto IV." *ASRSP* 50:353ff.

Bauer, Clemens. 1928. "Epochen der Papstfinanz." *Historische Zeitschrift* 138:457–503.

Baum, J., and K. Arndt. 1956. "Elefant." In *Reallexikon für deutsche Kunstgeschichte* 4:1240ff.

Baumgarten, P. M. 1907. *Aus Kanzlei und Kammer. Eröterung zur Kurialen Hof- und Verwaltungsgeschichte im XIII, XIV und XV Jahrhundert (bullatores, taxatores domorum, cursores)*. Freiburg-im-Breisgau.

Bec, Christian. 1967. *Les marchands écrivains: affaires et humanisme à Florence, 1375–1434*. Paris.

Beck, James. 1981. *Italian Renaissance painting*. New York.

Becker, Marvin. 1968. "The Florentine territorial state and civic humanism in the early Renaissance." In N. Rubinstein, ed., *Florentine studies*, 109–139. Evanston.

Bentivoglio, E., and S. Valtieri. 1976. *Santa Maria del Popolo*. Rome.

Bering, K. 1984a. *Baupropaganda und Bildprogrammatik der Frührenaissance in Florenz, Rom und Pienza*. Frankfurt-am-Main.

Bering, K. 1984b. *Fra Angelico: Mittelalterlicher Mystiker oder Maler der Renaissance*. 1984.

Bertolotti, A. 1861. *Artisti lombardi a Roma.* Milan.

Bertolotti, A. 1885. *Artisti bolognesi, ferraresi ed alcuni altri del già Stato Pontificio in Roma nei secoli XV–XVII.* Bologna.

Bertolotti, A. 1900. "Giunte agli artisti lombardi in Roma." *Archivio Storico Lombardo* ser. 4, 10:98ff.

Biagetti, Biagio. 1932–33. "Una nuova ipotesi intorno alla studio e alla capella di Niccolò V nel palazzo Vaticano." *Pontificia Accademia Romana di Archeologia: Memorie* 3:205–214.

Biasiotti, G. 1911a. *La Basilica esquilina di S. Maria Maggiore e il Palazzo Apostolico.* Rome.

Biasiotti, G. 1911b. *Le diaconie cardinalizie e la diaconia S. Viti in Macello.* Rome.

Biblioteca Apostolica Vaticana. 1975. *Quinto Centenario della Biblioteca Apostolica Vaticana, 1475–1975: Catalogo della mostra.* Vatican City.

Billanovich, G. 1958. "Gli umanisti e le cronache medioevali. Il *liber pontificalis*, le *decade* di Tito Livio e il primo umanesimo a Roma." *IMU* 1:103–137.

Biondo, Flavio. 1531. *Opera.* Basel.

Bisticci, Vespasiano da. 1970. *Le vite. Edizione critica,* ed. Aulo Greco, vol. 1. Florence.

Black, Anthony. 1979. *Monarchy and community.* Cambridge.

Blumenthal, W. von. 1952. "Pomerium." In *PW* 21.1: cc.1867–1876.

Blunt, Anthony, ed. 1978. *Baroque and rococo architecture and decoration.* New York.

Bongiorno, L. M. 1968. "The theme of the Old and the New Law in the Arena Chapel." *Art Bulletin* 50:11–28.

Borgatti, Mariano. 1938. *Il Castel San Angelo.* Rome.

Borsa, Mario. 1893. "Pier Candido Decembrio e l'umanesimo in Lombardia." *Archivio Storico Lombardo* ser. 2, 20:5–75, 358–441.

Borsi, Franco. 1975. *Leon Battista Alberti.* Milan.

Borsi, Franco, ed. 1980. *Filippo Brunelleschi: la sua opera e il suo tempo.* 2 vols. Florence.

Borsook, Eve. 1975. "Fra Filippo Lippi and the murals for Prato cathedral." *Mitteilungen des kunsthistorischen Instituts in Florenz* 19:1–148.

Bourgin, Georges. 1904. "La *famiglia* pontificia sotto Eugenio IV." *ASRSP* 27:203–224.

Bowsky, W. M. 1981. *A medieval Italian commune: Siena under the Nine, 1287–1355.* Berkeley and Los Angeles.

Bracciolini, Poggio. 1964. *Epistolarium.* In *Opera Omnia,* ed. T. Tonelli, vol. 3. Turin.

Bracelli, Jacopo. 1969. *L'epistolario di Jacopo Bracelli,* ed. Giovanna Balbi. Genoa.

Braudel, Fernand. 1972. *The Mediterranean and the Mediterranean world in the age of Philip II.* 2 vols. London.

Braudel, Fernand. 1981. *Civilization and capitalism, 15th–18th century.* 3 vols. New York.

Braunfels, Wolfgang. 1976. *Abendländische Stadtbaukunst: Herrschaftsform und Baugestalt.* Cologne.

Braunfels, Wolfgang. 1979. *Mittelalterliche Stadtbaukunst in der Toskana.* 4th ed. Berlin.

Brezzi, Paolo. 1977. "Il sistema agrario nel territorio romano alla fine del medio evo." *SR* 25:153–168.

Brezzi, Paolo, and Egmont Lee, ed. 1984. *Sources of social history: Private acts of the late middle ages.* Toronto.

Brezzi, Paolo, and Maristella Lorch, ed. 1984. *Umanesimo a Roma nel Quattrocento.* Rome and New York.

Briganti, E. 1962. *Il palazzo del Quirinale.* Rome.

Broise, Henri, and Jean-Claude Maire-Vigueur. 1983. "Strutture famigliari, spazio domestico e architettura civile a Roma alla fine del medioevo." In *Storia dell'arte italiana,* 3.5: 99–160. Turin.

Brunel, Georges, et al. 1981. *Les fondations nationales dans la Rome pontificale.* Collections de l'École Française de Rome, 52. Rome.

Bruschi, Arnaldo. 1969. *Bramante architetto.* Bari.

Buck, August, and B. Guthmüller, ed. 1984. *La città italiana del Rinascimento fra utopia e realtà.* Venice.

Buddensieg, Tilman. 1969. "Zum Statuenprogramm im Kapitolsplan Pauls III." *ZK* 32:177–228.

Burroughs, Charles. 1982a. "Below the angel: An urbanistic project in the Rome of Pope Nicholas V." *JWCI* 45:94–124.

Burroughs, Charles. 1982b. "A planned myth and a myth of planning: Nicholas V and Rome." In Ramsey (1982), 197–207.

Burroughs, Charles. 1983. "Cubes and context" (review of Goldthwaite 1980). *Art History* 6:359–363.

Buttafava, C. 1963. *Visioni di città nelle opere d'arte del medioevo e del rinascimento.* Milan.

Caetani, Gaetano, ed. 1926. *Documenti dell'Archivio Caetani: Epistolarium Honorati Caetani. Lettere familiari del Cardinale Scarampo e corrispondenza della Guerra Angioina 1450–1467.* San Casciano Val di Pesa.

Caetani, Gaetano, ed. 1929, 1930. *Documenti dell'Archivio Caetani: Regesta Chartarum,* vols. 4, 5. San Casciano Val di Pesa.

Caffari, Stefano. 1885, 1886. "Dai diari di Stefano Caffari," ed. S. Coletti. *ASRSP* 8:553–575; 9:583–611.

Cametti, A. 1916. "La torre di Nona e la contrada circostante dal medio evo al secolo XVII." *ASRSP* 39:409–466.

Campana, A. 1959. "Giannozzo Manetti, Ciriaco d'Ancona e l'Arco di Traiano ad Ancona." *IMU* 2:483–504.

Cancellieri, F. 1802. *Storia de' solenni possessi de' sommi pontefici.* Rome.

Canezza, A. 1933. *Gli arcispedali di Roma.* Rome.

Cantone, G. 1978. *La città di marmo da Alberti a Serlio: La storia tra progettazione e restauro.* Rome.

Cappelli, L. 1970. *Riti, ceremonie, feste e vita di popolo nella Roma dei papi.* Bologna.

Caravale, M., and A. Caracciolo. 1978. *Lo stato pontificio da Martino V a Pio IX.* Turin.

Carini, I. 1892. "Tre lettere di Paride Avogadro relative alla congiura di Stefano Porcari." *Il Muratori* 1:12ff.

Carrier, E. H. 1980. *Water and grass: A study in the pastoral economy of southern Europe.* New York (reprint of 1932 edition).

Castagnoli, F., C. Cecchelli, G. Giovannoni, and M. Zocca. 1958. *Topografia e urbanistica di Roma.* Bologna.

Castelli, S. 1975. *Iscrizioni sulle case ascolane del '500.* Ascoli Piceno.

Cazzani, E. 1955. *Vescovi di Milano.* Milan.

Cecchelli, Carlo. 1946. *I Margani, i Capocci, i Sanguigni, i Mellini.* Le grande famiglie romane, 4. Rome.

Ceen, Allan. 1977. "The Quartiere de' Banchi: Urban planning in Rome in the first half of the Cinquecento." Ph.D. dissertation, University of Pennsylvania, Philadelphia.

Celletti, M. C. 1966. "S. Maria Maddalena." In *BS* 8:1078.

Cempanari, A., and T. Amodei. 1963. *La Scala Sancta*. Le chiese di Roma illustrate, 72. Rome.

Cenciarini, A. C., and M. Giaccaglia. 1982. *Rocche e castelli del Lazio*. Rome.

Cerioni, L. 1970. *La diplomazia Sforzesca della 2 metà del XV secolo e suoi cifri segreti, i*. Fonti e Studi, 7. Rome.

Certeau, Michel de. 1984. *The practice of everyday life*. Berkeley and Los Angeles.

Chambers, David. 1976a. "The housing problems of Cardinal Francesco Gonzaga." *JWCI* 39:21–58.

Chambers, David. 1976b. "Studium Urbis and Gabella Studii: The University of Rome in the fifteenth century." In C. Clough, ed., *Essays in honor of P. O. Kristeller*, 68–110. Manchester.

Chastel, André. 1961. *Art et humanisme à Florence au temps de Laurent le Magnifique: Études sur la Renaissance et l'umanisme platonicien*. 2d ed. Paris.

Chastel, André. 1964. "Une épisode de la symbolique urbaine au XVᵉ siècle: Florence et Rome, cités de Dieu." In *Urbanisme et architecture: Études écrites et publiées en l'honneur de Pierre Lavedan*, 75–80. Paris.

Chittolini, Giorgio. 1979. *La formazione dello stato regionale*. Turin.

Ciampi, Ignazio. 1872. *Cronache e statuti della città di Viterbo*. Florence.

Ciapponi, L. A. 1968. "Il 'De Architectura' di Vitruvio nel primo umanesimo." *IMU* 3:59–99.

Cicero, M. Tullius. 1951. *Philippics*, ed. W. C. A. Ker. Cambridge, Mass.

Coarelli, F. 1974. *Guida archeologica di Roma*. Milan.

Coccia, A. 1973. "Il Cardinale Bessarione e la Basilica dei SS. Apostoli in Roma." *Miscellanea Francescana* 73:371–386.

Cochrane, Eric. 1981. *Historians and historiography in the Italian Renaissance*. Chicago.

Coffin, David. 1979. *The villa in the life of Renaissance Rome*. Princeton.

Cohn, Samuel. 1980. *The laboring classes in Renaissance Florence*. New York.

Collectio bullarum brevium. 1750. *Collectio bullarum brevium aliorumque diplomatum sacrosanctae basilicae Vaticanae*, vol. 2 (Urban V to Paul III). Rome.

Comba, R., G. Piccinni, and G. Pinto, ed. 1984. *Strutture familiari, epidemia, migrazioni nell'Italia medievale*. Naples.

Connors, Joseph. 1980. *Borromini and the Roman Oratory*. Cambridge, Mass.

Contardi, B., ed. 1987. *L'angelo e la città*. 2 vols. Rome.

Coppi, A. 1864. "Documenti storici del medio evo relativi a Roma ed all'agro romano." *Dissertazioni della Pontificia Accademia Romana di Archeologia* ser. 1, 15:173–368.

Corbo, Anna-Maria. 1966. "L'attività di Paolo di Mariano a Roma." *Commentari* 17:195–226.

Corbo, Anna-Maria. 1967. "I contratti di locazione e il restauro delle case a Roma nei primi anni del secolo XV." *Commentari* 18: 233–251.

Corbo, Anna-Maria. 1969. *Artisti e artigiani in Roma al tempo di Martino V e di Eugenio IV*. Rome.

Corbo, Anna-Maria. 1971. "Bernardo di Lorenzo da Firenze a Palazzo Venezia." *Commentari* 22:92–96.

Corbo, Anna-Maria. 1984. "Relazione descrittiva degli archivi notarili Romani dei secoli XIV–XV nell'Archivio di Stato e nell'Archivio Capitolino." In Brezzi and Lee (1984), 49–68.

Corboz, André. 1964–65. "Marquéterie, théatre et urbanisme dans l'Italie du XVe siécle." *Architecture Formes + Fonctions* 11:93–100.

Cosenza, Mario. 1962. *A biographical and bibliographical dictionary of the Italian humanists and the world of classical scholarship in Italy 1300–1800.* 4 vols. Boston.

Cosgrove, Denis. 1984. *Social formation and symbolic landscape.* London.

Coste, Jean. 1976. "La topographie mediévale de la Campagna romaine et l'histoire socio-économique: Pistes de recherche." *MEFR-M* 88:621–674.

Cozzi, L. 1968. *Le porte di Roma.* Rome.

Cugnoni. 1885. "Diritti del Capitolo di S. Maria della Rotonda nell'età di mezzo." *ASRSP* 8:577–590.

Cullman, O. 1958–59. "L'opposition contre le Temple de Jerusalem, motif commun de la théologie joannique et du monde ambiant." *New Testament Studies* 5:157–173.

Curcio, Giovanna. 1978. "L'ospedale di S. Giovanni in Laterano: Funzione urbana di una istituzione ospedaliera, i." *Storia dell'Arte* 32:23–40.

Dacos, Nicole. 1965. Review of E. Mandowsky and C. Mitchell, *Pirro Ligorio's Roman antiquities* (London 1963). In *Revue Belge de Philologie et d'Histoire* 43:200–205.

Damisch, Hubert. 1979. "The column and the wall." In J. Rykwert, ed., *A.D. Profile 21: Leonis Baptiste Alberti* (*Architectural Design* 39, nos. 5–6). London.

Davidsohn, R. 1973. *Storia di Firenze,* vol. 7. Florence.

Davies, Martin. 1951. *National Gallery, London. Catalogue of the early Italian schools.* London.

De Angelis, Paolo. 1621. *Historia basilicae S. Mariae maioris de Urbe a Libero papa I usque ad Paulum V pontificem maximum.* Rome.

De Angelis, Pietro. 1958. *L'Arcispedale del Salvatore ad Sancta Sanctorum a S. Giovanni in Laterano.* Rome.

De Angelis, Pietro. 1962. *L'Ospedale di S. Spirito in Sassia, ii (1301–1500).* Rome.

De' Conti, Sigismondo. 1883. *Le storie de' suoi tempi dal 1475 al 1510.* 2 vols. Rome.

De Cupis, C. 1911. *Vicende dell'agricoltura e della pastorizia nell'Agro Romano: l'Annona di Roma.* Rome.

De Fusco, R. 1984. *L'architettura del Quattrocento.* Turin.

Dehio, Georg. 1880. "Die Bauprojekte Nikolaus' V und Leon Battista Alberti." *Repertorium für Kunstwissenschaft* 3:241–257.

Dell'Addolorata, S. 1919. *Sancta Sanctorum.* Grottaferrata.

Delumeau, Jean. 1957, 1959. *Vie économique et sociale de Rome dans la seconde moitié du XVIe siècle.* 2 vols. Paris.

Delumeau, Jean. 1967. *L'alum de Rome.* Paris.

Delumeau, Jean. 1979. *Vita economica e sociale di Roma nel Cinquecento.* Florence.

De Pretis, A. 1975. "Le teorie umanistiche del tradurre e l'*Apologeticus* di Giannozzo Manetti." *BHR* 37:15–32.

De Roover, Raymond. 1963. *The rise and decline of the Medici bank, 1347–1494.* 2d ed. Cambridge, Mass.

De' Rossi, G. B. 1857–1915. *Inscriptiones Christianae Urbis Romae septimo saeculo antiquiores.* 2 vols. Rome.

De' Rossi, G. B. 1881. "Della famiglia, del nome e della casa dei Porcari nel rione Pigna." *Studi e Documenti di Storia e Diritto* 2:98–103.

De' Rossi, G. B. 1882. "Note di topografia Romana." *Studi e Documenti di Storia e Diritto* 3:86ff.

de Tóth, L. 1922. *Il beato Niccolò Albergati e suoi tempi.* 2 vols. Acquapendente.

De Tummulillis, Angelo. 1890. *Il "Notabilia temporum" di Angelo de Tummulillis da Sant'Elia,* ed. C. Corvisieri. Fonti per la storia d'Italia, 8. Rome.

Deuchler, F. 1980. "Siena und Jerusalem: Imagination und Realität in Duccios neuem Stadtbild." In H. von Kühnel, ed. *Europäische Sachkultur des Mittelalters,* 13–20. Vienna.

Dickinson, Gladys. 1960. *Du Bellay in Rome.* Leiden.

Dilke, O. A. W. 1971. *The Roman land surveyors: An introduction to the agrimensores.* Newton Abbott.

Di Macco, M. 1977. *Il Colosseo: Funzione simbolica, storica, urbana.* Rome.

D'Onofrio, Carlo. 1967. *Gli obelischi di Roma.* Rome.

D'Onofrio, Carlo. 1968. *Il Tevere e Roma.* Rome.

D'Onofrio, Carlo. 1978. *Castel S.Angelo e Borgo. Tra Roma e papato.* Rome.

D'Onofrio, Carlo. 1980. *Il Tevere: L'Isola tiberina, le inondazioni, i molini, i porti, le rive, i muraglioni, i ponti di Roma.* Rome.

D'Onofrio, Carlo, and Carlo Pietrangeli. 1971. *Abbazie del Lazio.* Rome.

Drago, G., and L. Salerno. 1967. *SS. Ambrogio e Carlo al Corso e l'Arciconfraternità dei Lombardi in Roma.* Rome.

Dunston, A. J. 1973. "Pope Paul II and the humanists." *Journal of Religious History* 7:287–306.

Dupré-Theseider, E. 1952. *Roma dal comune di popolo alla signoria pontificia (1252–1377).* Bologna.

Dussler, Luitpold. 1966. *Raffael: Kritisches Verzeichnis der Gemälde, Wandbilder und Bildteppiche.* Munich.

Dykmans, M. 1968. "Du Monte Mario à l'escalier de Saint-Pierre de Rome." *MAH* 80:547–594.

Egidi, Pietro. 1908, 1914. *Necrologi e libri affini della provincia Romana.* 2 vols. Fonti per la Storia d'Italia 44, 45. Rome.

Ehrle, Franz, and Hermann Egger, ed. 1911. *Römische Veduten. Handzeichnungen aus dem XV–XVIII Jahrhundert,* vol 1. Vienna and Leipzig.

Einem, Herbert von. 1971. "Das Program der Stanza della Segnatura im Vatikan." *Rheinisch-Westfälische Akademie der Wissenschaften: Geisteswissenschaften: Vorträge G. 169.* Opladen.

Eleen, L. 1977. "Acts illustration in Italy and Byzantium." *Dumbarton Oaks Papers* 31:255–277.

Esch, Arnold. 1969. "Spolien: Zur Wiederverwendung antiker Baustücke und Skulpturen im mittelalterlichen Italien." *Archiv für Kulturgeschichte* 51:1–64.

Esch, Arnold. 1971. "Dal Medioevo al Rinascimento: Uomini a Roma dal 1356 al 1450." *ASRSP* 94:1–10.

Esch, Arnold. 1972. "Florentiner in Rom um 1400. Namensverzeichnis der ersten Quattrocento-Generation." *QFIAB* 53:476–525.

Esch, Arnold. 1973. "Die Zeugenaussagen im Heiligsprechungsverfahren für S. Francesca Romana als Quelle zur Sozialgeschichte Roms im frühen Quattrocento." *QFIAB* 54:93–151.

Esch, Arnold, ed. 1981. *Aspetti della vita economica e culturale a Roma nel Quattrocento.* Rome.

Esposito Aliano, Anna. 1981. "Famiglia, mercanzia e libri nel testamento di Andrea San-tacroce (1471)." In Esch (1981), 197–220.

Eubel, Conrad. 1914. *Hierarchia Catholica Medii Aevi, ii (1431–1503)*. Munster.

Fagiolo, M., and M. L. Madonna, ed. 1985. *Roma 1300–1875: La città degli anni santi. Atlante*. Milan.

Falco, G. 1926. *I comuni della Campagna e della Marittima nel medioevo*. Rome.

Fallani, Giovanni. 1984. *Vita e opere di Fra Giovanni Angelico*. Florence.

Fanelli, G. 1973. *Firenze, architettura e città*. 2 vols. Florence.

Fasolo, F. 1941. "San Teodoro al Palatino." *Palladio* 5:112–119.

Fehl, Philipp. 1973. "Raphael and the throne of St. Gregory." *Art Bulletin* 55:378–79.

Ferri, G. 1907. "Le carte dell'Archivio Liberiano dal secolo X al XV." *ASRSP* 30:119–168.

Flasche, Hans. 1949. "Similitudo templi: Zur Geschichte einer Metapher." *Deutsche Vierteljahrschrift für Literatur und Geistesgeschichte* 23:81–125.

Fontana, V. 1973. *Artisti e committenti nella Roma del Quattrocento: Leon Battista Alberti e la sua opera mediatrice*. Rome.

Forcella, Vincenzo. 1869–84. *Iscrizioni delle chiese e d'altri edifici di Roma dal secolo XI fino ai nostri giorni*. 14 vols. Rome.

Forssman, E. 1965. *Palladios Lehrgebäude: Studien über den Zusammenhang von Architektur und Architekturtheorie bei Andrea Palladio*. Stockholm.

Foucault, Michel. 1971. *The order of things: An archaeology of the human sciences*. New York.

Foucault, Michel. 1979. *Discipline and punish: The birth of the prison*. New York.

Franceschini, G. 1973. *I Malatesta*. Varese.

Freddi, R. 1974. *Edifici rurali nella pianura romana*. Rome.

Freedberg, Sidney J. 1979. *Painting in Italy 1500–1600*, rev. ed. New York.

Friedman, David. 1974. "Le Terre Nuove Fiorentine." *Archeologia Medioevale* 1:31–47.

Frommel, Christoph L. 1973. *Der römische Palastbau der Hochrenaissance*. 3 vols. Tübingen.

Frommel, Christoph L. 1981. "Eine Darstellung der 'Loggien' in Raffaels Disputa." In *Festschrift für Eduard Trier*, 103–127. Berlin.

Frommel, Christoph L. 1982. *Der Palazzo Venezia in Rom*. Opladen.

Frommel, Christoph L. 1984a. "Francesco del Borgo: Architekt Pius' II und Pauls II, ii. Palazzo Venezia, Palazzetto Venezia und San Marco." *RJB* 22:71–163.

Frommel, Christoph L. 1984b. "Il Palazzo Vaticano sotto Giulio II e Leone X: strutture e funzioni." In C. Pietrangeli, ed., *Raffaello in Vaticano*, 118–135. Milan.

Frutaz, Amato P. 1962. *Le piante di Roma*. 3 vols. Rome.

Fryde, E. B. 1983. *Humanism and Renaissance historiography*. London.

Fubini, R., ed. 1977. *Lorenzo de' Medici, Lettere i (1460–1474)*. Florence.

Fumi, L. 1883. "Il governo di Stefano Porcari in Orvieto." *Studi e Documenti di Storia e Diritto* 4:33ff.

Gadol, Joan. 1969. *Leon Battista Alberti: Universal man of the early Renaissance*. Chicago.

Gaeta, F. 1977. "Sull'idea di Roma nell'umanesimo e nel rinascimento: Appunti e spunti per una ricerca." *SR* 25:169–186.

Gambi, L. 1976. "La città da immagine simbolica a proiezione urbanistica." In *Storia d'Italia* 6:217–228. Turin.

Gardner, Julian. 1973a. "Nicholas III's Oratory of the Sancta Sanctorum and its decoration." *Burlington Magazine* 115:283–294.

Gardner, Julian. 1973b. "Pope Nicholas IV and the decoration of S. Maria Maggiore." *ZK* 36:1–50.

Gasparinetti, A. 1943. *Stampatori veneziani e mercanti fabrianesi.* Urbino.

Gatti Perer, M. L., ed. 1983. *La dimora di Dio con gli uomini: immagini della Gerusalemme celeste dal III al XIV secolo.* Milan.

Geertz, Clifford. 1973. "Thick description: Toward an interpretive theory of culture." In *The interpretation of culture.* New York.

Gennaro, Claudia. 1967a. "Mercatanti e bovattieri nella Roma della seconda metà del Trecento." *Bulletino dell'Istituto Storico Italiano* 78:155–187.

Gennaro, Claudia. 1967b. "La Pax Romana del 1511." *ASRSP* 90:17–60.

Germann, Georg. 1976. "Krumme Strassen: Strassenbautheorie der Frühneuzeit." *Zeitschrift für Stadtgeschichte, Stadtsoziologie und Denkmalspflege* 3:10–25.

Germann, Georg. 1980. *Einführung in die Geschichte der Architekturtheorie.* Darmstadt.

Ghisalberti, A., ed. 1928. *La vita anonima di Cola di Rienzo.* Rome.

Gilbert, Creighton. 1968. "The Renaissance portrait." *Burlington Magazine* 110:278–285.

Gilbert, Creighton. 1975. "Fra Angelico's fresco cycles in Rome: Their number and dates." *ZK* 38:245–265.

Giorgi, D. 1742. *Vita Nicolai Quinti.* Rome.

Giovannoni, Gustavo. 1935. "Case del Quattrocento in Roma." In *Saggi sulla architettura del Rinascimento,* 2d ed., 27–47. Milan.

Giovannoni, Gustavo. 1946. *Il quartiere romano del Rinascimento.* Rome.

Giovio, Paolo. 1560. *Lettere vulgari.* Rome.

Gnoli, Domenico. 1938. *La Roma di Leone X.* Milan.

Gnoli, Umberto. 1934. "S. Maria Maddalena." In *EI* 22:298.

Gnoli, Umberto. 1939. *Topografia e toponomastica di Roma medioevale e moderna.* Rome (reprinted 1984).

Gnoli, Umberto. 1942. *Alberghi e osterie di Roma medievale e moderna,* rev. ed. Spoleto.

Gobbi, G., and P. Sica. 1982. *Rimini. La città nella storia d'Italia.* Bari.

Goldbrunner, H. 1983. "'Laudatio urbis': Zu neueren Untersuchungen über das humanistische Städtelob." *QFIAB* 64:312–328.

Goldthwaite, Richard. 1980. *The building of Renaissance Florence: An economic and social history.* Baltimore and London.

Göller, Emil. 1907, 1911. *Die päpstliche Pönientiarie von ihrem Ursprung bis zu ihrer Umgestaltung unter Pius V.* 2 vols. Rome.

Göller, Emil. 1924. "Untersuchungen über das Inventar des Finanzarchivs der Renaissancepäpste." In *Miscellanea F. Ehrle* 5:227–272. Rome.

Gollob, A. 1965. "Pisanellos Fresken im Lateran und der Codex Vallard." In *Arte lombarda, studi in onore di N. Fasola,* 51–60. Milan.

Golzio, Vincenzo, and Giorgio Zander. 1968. *L'Arte a Roma nel secolo XV.* Bologna.

Gombrich, Ernst H. 1976. "From the revival of letters to the reform of the arts: Niccolò Niccoli and Filippo Brunelleschi." In *The heritage of Apelles: Studies in the art of the Renaissance,* 93–110. Ithaca.

Gombrich, Ernst H. 1978. "Raphael's Stanza della Segnatura and the nature of its symbolism." In *Symbolic images: Studies in the art of the Renaissance ii*, 2d ed., 85–101. London.

Gori-Montanelli, Lorenzo. 1959. *Architettura e paesaggio nella pittura toscana*. Florence.

Gottlob, Adolf. 1889. *Aus der Camera Apostolica des 15 Jahrhunderts*. Innsbruck.

Gragg, F. A., and L. C. Gabel, ed. 1959. *Memoirs of a Renaissance pope: The Commentaries of Pius II*. New York.

Grayson, Cecil. 1957. *Alberti and the Tempio Malatestiano: An autograph letter from Leon Battista Alberti to Matteo de' Pasti*. New York.

Grayson, Cecil. 1960. "The composition of L. B. Alberti's *Decem libri de re aedificatoria*." *Münchner Jahrbuch der bildenden Kunst* 11:152–161.

Greco, Aulo. 1980. *La cappella di Niccolò V del Beato Angelico*. Rome.

Greco, A., M. Monaco, and G. Carettoni, ed. 1969. *Aspetti dell' Umanesimo a Roma*. Rome.

Grenier, A. 1905. "La transhumance des troupeaux en l'Italie et son role dans l'histoire romaine." *MAH* 25:293–328.

Grifi, P. 1862. *Opere pie a Roma*. Rome.

Grisar, H. 1908. *Die römische Kapelle Sancta Sanctorum und ihr Schatz*. Freiburg-im-Breisgau.

Guasco, L. 1946. *L'Archivio Storico Capitolino*. Rome.

Guidoni, Enrico. 1972. "Il significato urbanistico di Roma tra antichità e medioevo." *Palladio*, n.s. 22:3–32.

Guidoni, Enrico. 1974. "L'architettura delle città medievali: Rapporto su una metodologia di ricerca (1964–74)." *MEFR-M* 86: 481–525.

Guidoni, Enrico. 1981. "Trasformazioni urbanistiche e teoria della città nell'età brunelleschiana." In Borsi (1981), 65–77.

Guidoni, Enrico. 1983. "Roma e l'urbanistica del Trecento." In *Storia dell'arte italiana*, 2.1: 309–84. Turin.

Günther, Hubertus. 1984. "Das Trivium vor Ponte S. Angelo. Ein Beitrag zur römischen Urbanistik der Hochrenaissance." *RJK* 21:165–252.

Günther, Hubertus. 1985. "Die Strassenplanung unter den Medici-Päpsten in Rom (1513–1534)." *Jahrbuch des Zentralinstituts für Kunstgeschichte* 1:237–294.

Gutman, H. 1958. "Zur Ikonologie der Fresken Raffaels in der Stanza della Segnatura." *Zeitschrift für Kunstgeschichte* 21:27–39.

Harms, J. 1973. "'Mundus imago Dei est.' Zum Entstehungsprozess zweier Emblembücher Jean Jacques Boissards." *Deutsche Vierteljahrshrift* 67:223–244.

Hartt, Frederick. 1973. *Giulio Romano*. 2 vols. New Haven.

Hausherr, Reiner. 1968. "Templum Salamonis und Ecclesia Christi: Zu einem Bildvergleich der Bible moralisée." *Zeitschrift für Kunstgeschichte* 31:101–121.

Hay, Denys. 1977. *The Church in Italy in the fifteenth century*. Cambridge.

Hay, Denys, and John Law. 1989. *Italy in the age of the Renaissance, 1380–1530*. London and New York.

Heckscher, William S. 1947. "Bernini's elephant and obelisk." *Art Bulletin* 29:154–182 (also in idem, *Art and literature: Studies in relationship* [Durham, N.C., and Baden-Baden, 1985], original pagination).

Herendeen, W. H. 1986. *From landscape to literature: The river and the myth of geography*. Pittsburgh.

Herklotz, Ingo. 1985. "Der Campus Lateranensis im Mittelalter." *RJB* 22:1–43.

Herlihy, David. 1858. *Pisa in the early Renaissance: A study of urban growth*. Port Washington, N. Y., and London.

Hersey, George L. 1973. *The Aragonese arch at Naples, 1443–1475*. New Haven.

Hersey, George L. 1976. *Pythagorean palaces: Magic and architecture in the Italian Renaissance*. Ithaca.

Heydenreich, Ludwig H. 1937. "Pius II als Bauherr von Pienza." *ZK* 6:105–146.

Heydenreich, Ludwig H. 1965. "Der Palazzo Baronale der Colonna in Palestrina." In *Festschrift für Walter Friedländer*, 85–91. Berlin.

Heydenreich, Ludwig H., and W. Lotz. 1974. *Architecture in Italy 1400–1600*. Harmondsworth.

Hofmann, W. von. 1914. *Forschungen zur Geschichte der kurialen Behörden vom Schisma bis zur Reformation*. 2 vols. Rome.

Houston, J. M. 1964. *The western Mediterranean world: An introduction to its regional landscapes*. London.

Hughes, Diane O. 1974. "Towards historical ethnography: Notarial records and family history in the middle ages." *Historical Methods Newsletter* 7:61–74.

Hyman, Isabelle. 1975. "Notes and speculations on S. Lorenzo, Palazzo Medici, and an urban project by Brunelleschi." *Journal of the Society of Architectural Historians* 35:98–120.

Ilari, A. 1965. *Frascati fra Medioevo e Rinascimento*. Rome.

Imhof, A. E. 1984. *Die verlorenen Welten: Alltagsbewältigung durch unsere Vorfahren*. Munich.

Infessura, Stefano. 1890. *Diario della città di Roma di Stefano scribasenato*, ed. O. Tommasini. Fonti per la storia d'Italia, 5. Rome.

Jones, Philip J. 1965. "Communes and despots: The city state in late medieval Italy." *Transactions of the Royal Historical Society* ser. 5, 15:71–96.

Jones, Philip J. 1974. *The Malatesta of Rimini and the papal state*. Cambridge.

Jones, Philip J., ed. 1978. *Studi Malatestiani*. Rimini.

Jordan, H. 1907. *Topographie der Stadt Rom im Altertum*. 3 vols. Berlin.

Jouvel, Pierre. 1977. *Le culte des saints dans les Basiliques du Latran et du Vatican au 12e siècle*. Rome.

Kähler, H. 1939. "Triumphbogen (Ehrenbogen)." In *PW* 2d series, 13:373–493.

Kajanto, I. 1982. *Papal epigraphy in Renaissance Rome*. Annales Academiae Scientiarum Fennicae, 203. Helsinki.

Kelber, W. 1964. *Raphael von Urbino. Leben und Werke, ii (Die römischen Werke)*. Stuttgart.

Kennedy, R. 1964. "The contribution of Martin V to the rebuilding of Rome, 1420–1431." In L. Gabel, ed., *The Renaissance reconsidered: A Symposium*, 13–52. Smith College Studies in History 44. Northampton, Mass.

Kent, Francis W. 1972. "The Rucellai family and its loggia." *JWCI* 35:397–401.

Kent, Francis W. 1977. *Household and lineage in Renaissance Florence: The family life of the Capponi, Ginori, and Rucellai*. Princeton.

Kent, Francis W., and Alessandro Perosa, ed. 1981. *Giovanni Rucellai e il suo Zibaldone, ii: A Florentine patrician and his palace*. Studies of the Warburg Institute, 24.2. London.

Keresztes, P. 1981. *Constantine: A great Christian monarch and apostle*. Amsterdam.

Kessler, Herbert. 1979. "Scenes from the *Acts of the Apostles* on some Early Christian ivories." *Gesta* 18:109–120.

Kirsch, J. 1926. *Die Stationskirchen des Missale Romanum.* Freiburg-im-Breisgau.

Kirschbaum, E., and W. Braunfels, ed. 1968–72. *Lexikon der christlichen Ikonographie.* 8 vols. Freiburg-im-Breisgau.

Klein, Robert. 1979. "Utopian urban planning." In *Form and meaning: Essays on the Renaissance and modern art,* 89–101. New York.

Klijn, A. 1957–58. "Stephen's speech—Acts 7, 2–55." *New Testament Studies* 4:25–31.

Kohl, B., R. Witt, and E. Wells, ed. 1978. *The Earthly Republic: Italian humanists on government and society.* Philadelphia.

Kolsky, Stephen. 1987. "Culture and politics in Renaissance Rome: Marco Antonio Altieri's *Roman Weddings." Renaissance Quarterly* 40:49–90.

Krautheimer, Richard. 1941. "S. Pietro in Vincoli and the tripartite transept in the Early Christian basilica." *Proceedings of the American Philosophical Society* 83:353–429.

Krautheimer, Richard. 1948. "The tragic and comic scene of the Renaissance: The Baltimore and Urbino panels." *Gazette des Beaux Arts* 6:327–346.

Krautheimer, Richard. 1961. "Alberti's Templum Etruscum." *Münchner Jahrbuch der bildenden Kunst* 12:65–71.

Krautheimer, Richard. 1970. *Lorenzo Ghiberti.* 2d ed. Princeton.

Krautheimer, Richard. 1977. "Fra Angelico and—perhaps—Alberti." In I. Lavin and J. Plummer, ed., *Studies in late medieval and Renaissance painting in honor of Millard Meiss,* 1290–296. New York.

Krautheimer, Richard. 1980. *Rome: Profile of a city, 312–1308.* Princeton.

Krautheimer, Richard. 1986. *Rome of Alexander VII.* Princeton.

Krautheimer, Richard, Wolfgang Frankl, and Spencer Corbett, ed. 1959. *Corpus Basilicarum Christianarum Romae Romae. The Early Christian basilicas of Rome, IV–IX centuries,* vol. 2. Vatican City.

Krinsky, Carole H. 1970. "Representations of the Temple of Jerusalem before 1500." *JWCI* 33:1–19.

Kristeller, Paul Otto. 1963, 1967. *Iter italicum.* 2 vols. London.

Kugler, H. 1983. "Stadt und Land im humanistischen Denken." In H. Lutz, ed., *Humanismus und Ökonomie,* 159–182. Weinheim.

Lanciani, R. 1902. *Storia degli scavi di Roma,* vol. 1. Rome.

La Roncière, Charles M. de. 1976. *Florence, centre économique sociale au XIVe siècle: Le marché des denrées de première necessité à Florence et dans la campagna et les conditions de vie des salariés, 1320–1380.* Aix-en-Provence.

Lauer, P. 1911. *Le palais du Latran.* Paris.

Lavin, Marilyn A. 1984. *Piero della Francesca a Rimini. L'affresco nel Tempio Malatestiano.* Bologna.

Lehnerdt, Max, ed. 1907. *Horatii Romani Porcaria seu de coniuratione Stephani Porcarii carmen. Accedit Petrus de Godis Vicentini de coniuratione Porcaria dialogus.* Leipzig.

Lewine, Milton. 1965. "Vignola's church of S. Anna de' Palafrenieri, Rome." *Art Bulletin* 47:199–229.

Lindsay, W. M., ed. 1913. *Sexti Pompei Festi De Verborum Significatione quae supersunt, cum Pauli Epitome.* Leipzig.

Lioi, Renato. 1970. "Biografi e biografie di S. Giacomo della Marca." *Picenum Seraphicum* 7:211–213.

Lippe, R., ed. 1899. *Missale Romanum.* 2 vols. London.

Litta, P., and L. Passerini. 1819–1899. *Famiglie celebri italiane.* 11 vols. Milan and Turin.

Lodolini, A. 1932. *L'Archivio di Stato in Roma e l'Archivio del Regno d'Italia*. Rome.

Lodolini, A. 1960. *L'Archivio di Stato di Roma: Epitome di una guida degli archivi dell'amministrazione centrale dello Stato Pontificio*. Rome.

Lodolini, A. 1964–65. "I libri di conti di Antonio Fatati tesoriere generale della Marca (1449–1453) nell'Archivio di Stato di Roma." *Atti e Memorie della Deputazione di Storia Patria per le Marche* ser. 8, 4:137–176.

Lombardo, Maria-Luisa. 1970. *La Camera Urbis: Premessa per uno studio sulla organizazzione amministrativa della città di Roma durante il pontificato di Martino V*. Rome.

Lombardo, Maria-Luisa. 1978. *La Dogana di Ripa e Ripetta nel sistema dell'ordinamento tributario a Roma dal Medioevo al secolo XV*. Rome.

Lombardo, Maria-Luisa. 1984. "Nobili, mercanti e popolo minuto negli atti dei notai romani del XIV e XV secolo." In Brezzi and Lee (1984), Appendix, 291–310.

Lowe, David M. 1982. *History of bourgeois perception*. Chicago.

MacAloon, J. J., ed. 1984. *Rite, drama, festival, spectacle: Rehearsals toward a theory of cultural performance*. Philadelphia.

McClung, William A. 1983. *The architecture of paradise: Survivals of Eden and Jerusalem*. Berkeley and Los Angeles.

McDonald, A. 1971. *Titus Livius*. Washington, D.C.

MacDougall, Elizabeth B. 1960. "Michelangelo and the Porta Pia." *JSAH* 14:97–108.

MacDougall, Elizabeth B. 1962. Review of Magnuson (1958), in *AB* 44:67–75.

Mack, Charles R. 1982. "Bernardo Rossellino, L. B. Alberti, and the Rome of Pope Nicholas V." *Southeastern College Art Conference Review* 10:60–69.

Mack, Charles R. 1983. "Building a Florentine palace: The Palazzo Spinelli." *MKIF* 27:261–284.

Magnuson, Torgil. 1958. *Studies in Roman quattrocento architecture*. Stockholm.

Maire-Vigueur, Jean-Claude. 1974. "Les 'casali' des églises romaines à la fin du Moyen Age, 1348–1428." *MEFR-M* 86:63–136.

Maire-Vigueur, Jean-Claude. 1976. "Classe dominante et classes dirigéantes de Rome à la fin du Moyen Age." In *Storia della Città* 1:4–26.

Maire-Vigueur, Jean-Claude. 1981. *Les pâturages de l'Église et la Douane du Bétail dans la province du Patrimonio (XIVᵉ–XVᵉ siècle)*. Rome.

Malatesta, S., ed. 1886. *Statuti delle gabelle di Roma*. Rome.

Malmstrom, Ronald. 1973. "S. Maria in Aracoeli." Ph.D. dissertation, New York University.

Mancini, Girolamo. 1911. *La vita di Leon Battista Alberti*. 2d ed. Florence.

Manetti, Antonio di Tuccio. 1976. *Vita di Filippo Brunelleschi*, ed. G. Tanturli. Milan.

Manetti, Giannozzo. 1734. "Vita Nicolai summi pontificis." In *RIS* 2.2: cc.907–60. Milan. (Cc.929–940 reprinted in Magnuson 1958, Appendix, 351–362.)

Mansuelli, G. A., ed. 1988. *Studi sull'arco onorario romano*. Rome.

Mansuelli, G. A., and M. Zuffa. 1966. "Rimini." In *Enciclopedia d'arte antica* 6:688–690. Rome.

Marangoni, G. 1747. *Istoria dell'antichissimo Oratorio o Capella di S. Lorenzo nel Patriarchio Lateranense. . . .* Rome.

Marchant, H. J. 1973. "Papal inscriptions in Rome, 1417–1527." M. Phil. thesis, Warburg Institute, London University.

Marchetti-Longhi, G. 1919. "Le contrade medioevali della zona in Circo Flaminio: Il Calcarario." *ASRSP* 42:401–535.

Marchetti-Longhi, G. 1920–22. "Circus Flaminius. Note di topografia di Roma." *Atti della R.Accademia dei Lincei* ser. 5, 16:623–770.

Marchetti-Longhi, G. 1972. "Le trasformazioni medioevali dell'Area Sacra Argentina." *ASRSP* 95:5–33.

Marchini, G. 1957. *Il duomo di Prato.* Milan.

Marchini, G. 1969a. *Due secoli di pittura murale a Prato: mostra di affreschi, sinopie e graffiti dei secoli XIV e XV.* Prato.

Marchini, G. 1969b. "Per Giorgio da Sebenico." *Commentari* 19:212ff.

Marconi, P., A. Cipriani, and E. Valeriani. 1974. *I disegni d'architettura dell'Archivio storico dell'Accademia di San Luca.* 2 vols. Rome.

Mardersteig, Giovanni. 1959. "Leon Battista Alberti e la rinascità del carattere lapidario romano nel Quattrocento." *IMU* 2:285–307.

Marin, Louis. 1973. *Utopiques: Jeux d'espace.* Paris.

Maroni-Lumbroso, M., and A. Martini. 1963. *Le confraternità Romane nelle loro chiese.* Rome.

Martindale, Andrew. 1979. *The Triumphs of Caesar by Andrea Mantegna in the collection of Her Majesty the Queen at Hampton Court.* London.

Martines, Lauro. 1979. *Power and imagination: City-states in Renaissance Italy.* New York.

Martini, Antonio. 1965. *Arti, mestieri e fede nella Roma dei papi.* Bologna.

Martinori, E. 1917, 1918. *Annali della Zecca di Roma,* fasc. 1, 2. Rome.

Martinori, E. 1929. *Via Flaminia.* Rome.

Martinori, E. 1930. *Via Cassia.* Rome.

Marucci, V., et al., ed. 1983. *Pasquinate romane del Cinquecento.* Salerno.

Marx, J. 1915. "Quatre documents relatifs à Guillaume d'Estouteville." *MAH* 35:41–55.

Mastro, Paolo di Benedetto di Cola dello. 1912. "Il Memoriale 1422–1484," ed. F. Isoldi. In *RIS²* 24.2, Appendix, 83–119. Città di Castello.

Mazzocco, A. 1975. "Petrarca, Poggio, and Biondo: Humanism's foremost interpreters of Roman ruins." In A. Scaglione, ed. *Francis Petrarch, six centuries later: A symposium,* 354–363. Chapel Hill, N.C.

Miglio, Massimo. 1974. "'Viva la libertà et populo de Roma.' Oratoria e politica a Roma: Stefano Porcari." *ASRSP* 97:5–37.

Miglio, Massimo. 1975. *Storiografia pontificia del Quattrocento.* Bologna.

Miglio, Massimo. 1981. "Et rerum facta est pulcherrima Roma.' Attualità della tradizione e proposte di innovazione." In *Aspetti della società italiana nel periodo del papato avignonese. Atti del XIX Convegno di Studi,* 323–326. Todi.

Miglio, Massimo. 1982. "Il leone e la lupa. Dal simbolo al pasticcio alla francese." *SR* 30:177–186.

Miglio, Massimo. 1983. "L'immagine dell'onore antico." *SR* 31: 252–264.

Miglio, Massimo, ed. 1986. *Un pontificato ed una città: Sisto IV (1471–1484). Atti del convegno, Roma, 3–7 Dicembre, 1984.* Vatican City.

Migne, Jacques Paul, ed. 1844–64. *Patrologiae Cursus Completus. Series latina.* 221 vols. Paris.

Milanesi, Gaetano. 1854. *Documenti per la storia dell'arte senese,* vol. 2. Siena.

Milanesi, Gaetano. 1901. *Nuovi documenti per la storia dell'arte toscana dal XII al XV secolo.* Florence.

Millar, Fergus. 1977. *The emperor in the Roman world.* Ithaca.

Mitchell, Bonner. 1979. *Italian civic pageantry in the High Renaissance*. Florence.

Mitchell, Charles. 1978. "Il Tempio Malatestiano." In Jones (1978), 5–103.

Mitchell, Rosamund. 1962. *The laurels and the tiara: Pope Pius II, 1458–1464*. London.

Möhler, Ludwig. 1923. *Kardinal Bessarion als Theologe, Humanist und Staatsmann, i. Darstellung*. Paderborn.

Molajoli, Bruno. 1968. *Guida artistica di Fabriano*. 2d ed. Fabriano.

Monachino, Vicenzo. 1968. *La carità Cristiana a Roma*. Rome.

Monaco, M. 1962. *La Zecca Vecchia in Banchi*. Rome.

Montel, Pierre. 1971. "Un 'casale' de la Campagna romaine de la fin du XIVe siècle au debut du XVIIe: Le domaine de Porto d'après les archives du Chapitre de Saint-Pierre." *MEFR* 83:31–87.

Montenovesi, O. 1942. "Un codice di scuola fiamminga nell'Archivio di Stato di Roma." *Accademia e Biblioteche d'Italia* 16:282–290.

Montini, Renzo. 1957. *Le tombe dei papi*. Rome.

Moorman, J. 1968. *A history of the Franciscan Order from its origins to the year 1517*. 1968.

Morelli, G. 1937. *Le corporazioni romane di arti e mestieri dal XIII al XIX secolo*. Rome.

Morini, E. 1859. *Dell'abbazia ed oratorio che ebbe in Roma il beato Niccolò Albergati de' Cartusiani*. Rome.

Moroni, G. 1840–79. *Dizionario di erudizione storico-ecclesiastica da S. Pietro fino ai giorni nostri*. 103 vols. Venice.

Morpurgo-Castelnuovo, M. 1929. "Il Cardinale Domenico Capranica." *ASRSP* 52:89–97.

Mostra. 1955. *Mostra delle opere del Beato Angelico nel quinto centenario della morte (1455–1955)*. Florence.

Motta, E. 1914. "Armaiuoli Milanesi nel periodo Visconteo-Sforzesco." *Archivio Storico Lombardo* 11:187–388.

Mühlmann, Hans. 1981. "*Asthetische Theorie der Renaissance: Leon Battista Alberti*. Bonn.

Müller, Werner. 1961. *Die heilige Stadt: Roma quadrata, himmlisches Jerusalem und die Mythe vom Weltnabel*. Stuttgart.

Mumford, Lewis. 1961. *The city in history: Its origins, its transformations, and its prospects*. New York.

Muntoni, Francesco. 1972. *Le monete dei papi e degli stati pontifici*, vol. 1. Rome.

Müntz, Eugène. 1878, 1879, 1882. *Les arts à la cour des papes pendant le XVe et le XVIe siècle: Recueil de documents inédits*. (Bibliothèque des Écoles francaises d'Athènes et Rome, vols. 4 [Martin V a Pie II, 1417–1464]; 9 [Paul II, 1464–1471]; 27 [Sixte IV, 1471–1484]). Paris.

Müntz, E., and A. Frothingham. 1883. "Il tesoro della basilica di San Pietro in Vaticano." *ASRSP* 6:1–137.

Nash, Ernest. 1961. *A pictorial dictionary of Ancient Rome*. 2 vols. New York.

Niutta, Francesca. 1986. "Temi e personnagi nell'epigrafia sistina." In Miglio (1986), 381–408.

Nogara, B., ed. 1927. *Scritti inediti e vari di Biondo Flavio*. Studi e Testi, 48. Rome.

Oechslin, Werner. 1984. *Festarchitektur. Der Architekt als Inszenierungskünstler*. Stuttgart.

Oestreich, G. 1971. "Die antike Literatur als Vorbild der praktischen Wissenschaften im 16 und 17 Jahrhundert." In R. R. Bolgar, ed., *Classical influences in European culture, A.D. 1500–1700*, 315–324. Cambridge.

Oliva, Annamaria. 1981. "La dogana dei pascoli nel patrimonio di S. Pietro in Tuscia nel 1450–51." In Esch (1981), 221–258.

Oliver, Paul. 1975. *Shelter, sign and symbol*. London.

O'Malley, J. W. 1979. *Praise and blame in Renaissance Rome: Rhetoric, doctrine, and reform in the sacred orators of the papal court, c. 1450–1521*. Durham, N.C.

Ong, Walter. 1956. "System, space, and intellect in Renaissance symbolism." *BHR* 30:222–239.

Onians, John B. 1980. "The last judgement of Renaissance architecture." *Royal Society of Arts, London. Journal* 128:701–720.

Onofri, Laura. 1979. "Sacralità, immaginazione e proposte politiche: La Vita di Niccolò V di Giannozzo Manetti." *Humanistica Lovaniensia* 27:27–77.

Orlandi, Stefano. 1964. *Beato Angelico*. Florence.

Ortolani, M., and N. Alfieri. 1953. "Sena Gallica." *Rendiconti dell'Accademia dei Lincei* ser. 8, 8:152–180.

Ortona, E. G. 1982. "Santo Stefano Rotondo e il restauro del Rossellino." *Bollettino d'Arte* 67:99–106.

Paatz, W., and E. Paatz. 1952, 1955. *Die Kirchen von Florenz: Ein kunstgeschichtliches Handbuch*, vols. 2, 3. Frankfurt-am-Main.

Pächt, O. 1951. "Giovanni Battista da Fano's illustrations of Basinio's *Epos Hesperis*." *Studi Romagnoli* 2:91–111.

Padoan Rizzo, A. 1981. "Nota breve su Colantonio, van der Weyden e l'Angelico." *Antichità viva* 20.5: 15–17.

Pagliucchi, P. 1906. *I castellani del Castel S. Angelo, i. I castellani militari, 1367–1464*. Rome.

Palermino, R. 1980. "The Roman academy, the catacombs, and the conspiracy of 1468." *Archivum historiae pontificiae* 17:117–155.

Palermo, L. 1979. *Il porto di Roma nel XIV e XV secolo: Strutture socio-economiche e sociali*. Rome.

Palmieri, Matteo. 1906–15. "Liber de temporibus (AD 1–1448)," ed. G. Scaramella. *RIS²* 26.1. Città di Castello.

Palmieri, Mattia. 1748. "Opus de temporibus suis," ed. G. Tartini. *RIS* 1: cc.239–278. Florence.

Panofsky, Erwin. 1964a. *Early Netherlandish painting, its origins and character*. Cambridge, Mass.

Panofsky, Erwin. 1964b. "Die Perspektive als 'symbolische Form'" (1927). In *Aufsätze zu Grundfragen der Kunstgeschichte*, 99–167. Berlin.

Panvinio, Onofrio. 1570. *De praecipuis urbis Romae sanctioribusque basilicis, quas vulgo septem ecclesias vocant liber*. Rome.

Parronchi, A. 1972. "Otto piccoli documenti per la biografia dell'Alberti." *Rinascimento* 72:229–235.

Partner, Peter. 1958. *The Papal State under Martin V*. London.

Partner, Peter. 1960. "The 'budget' of the Roman Church in the Renaissance period." In E. F. Jacob, ed., *Renaissance Studies*, 256–278. London.

Partner, Peter. 1972. *The lands of St. Peter*. Oxford.

Partner, Peter. 1976. *Renaissance R.O.M.E 1500–1559: A portrait of a society*. Berkeley and Los Angeles.

Partridge, Loren, and R. Starn. 1980. *A Renaissance likeness: Art and culture in Raphael's "Julius II."* Berkeley and Los Angeles.

Paschini, Pio. 1925. "Da Ripetta a Piazza del Popolo: nota di edilizia cinquecentesca." *Roma* 3:211ff.

Paschini, Pio. 1926. "Villeggiature di un cardinale del quattrocento (Lodovico camerlengo)." *Roma* 4:560–563.

Paschini, Pio. 1933. "Una pagina di storia di Albano del Quattrocento." *Rendiconti. Atti della Pontificia Accademia di Archeologia* 9:45–52.

Paschini, Pio. 1938. "Umanisti intorno a un cardinale." *La Rinascità* 1:52–73.

Paschini, Pio. 1939. *Lodovico Cardinale Camerlengo*. Rome.

Paschini, Pio. 1940. *Roma nel Rinascimento*. Bologna.

Paschini, Pio. 1953. "Una famiglia di curiali: I Maffei di Volterra." *Rivista di Storia della Chiesa in Italia* 9:337–376.

Pasini, P. G. 1978. "Rimini nel Quattrocento." In Jones (1978), 117–158.

Pasini, P. G. 1983. *I Malatesta e l'arte*. Bologna.

Passavant, G. 1872. *Raphael of Urbino and his father Giovanni Santi*. London.

Pastor, Ludwig von. 1936, 1949, 1950. *History of the popes, from the close of the middle ages*, ed. and trans. F. I. Antrobus. 5th ed., vols. 1, 2, 6. St. Louis, Mo.

Pastor, Ludwig von. 1958. *Storia dei papi*, rev. ed., vol. 1. Rome.

Pavan, Paola. 1978. "Gli statuti della società dei Raccomandati del Salvatore." *ASRSP* 101:35–96.

Pavan, Paola. 1984. "La confraternità del Salvatore nella società romana del Tre-Quattrocento." *Ricerche per la storia religiosa di Roma* 5:81–90.

Pavan, Paola. 1986. "Permanenze di schemi e modelli del passato di una società in mutamento." In Miglio (1986), 305–316.

Pearce, Stella. 1957. "Costumi tedeschi e borgognoni in Italia in 1452." *Commentari* 8:244–247.

Pecchiai, P. 1951. "Banchi e botteghe dinanzi alla Basilica Vaticana nei secoli XIV, XV, XVI." *Archivi* ser. 2, 18:81–123.

Pecchiai, P. 1952. "I segni sulle case di Roma nel medio evo." *Archivi* ser. 2, 19:25–48.

Pecchiai, P. 1963. *Il Palazzo Taverna a Monte Giordano*. Rome.

Pelaez, M. 1893. "Il memoriale di Paolo di Benedetto di Cola dello Mastro dello rione Ponte." *ASRSP* 16:41–130.

Pensa, Marina. 1988. "Genesi e sviluppo dell'arco onorario nella documentazione numismatica." In Mansuelli (1988).

Pericoli Ridolfini, C. 1960. *Le case romane con facciate graffite e dipinte*. Rome.

Peti, P. 1981. *Il parato di Niccolò V*. Florence.

Petrone, Paolo di Lello. 1912. *La Mesticanza di Paolo di Lello Petrone, 1434–1447*, ed. F. Isoldi. *RIS*[2] 24.2: 1–64. Città di Castello.

Petrucci, Armando. 1983. "La scrittura fra ideologia e rappresentazione." In *Storia dell'arte italiana*, 3.2. Turin.

Pfeiffer, H. 1975. *Zur Ikonographie von Raffaels Disputa: Egidio da Viterbo und die christlich-platonische Konzeption der Stanza della Segnatura*. Rome.

Piccinato, Luigi. 1978. *Urbanistica medioevale*. Bari.

Piccolomini, Aeneas Sylvius. 1985. *Commentari*, ed. A. van Heck. 2 vols. (*Studi e testi* 312–313). Vatican City.

Pietrangeli, Carlo, ed. 1976. *Guide rionali di Roma. Rione XI, S. Angelo*. Rome.

Pietrangeli, Carlo, ed. 1978, 1981. *Guide rionali di Roma. Rione V, Ponte*, parts 1, 3. Rome.

Pietrangeli, Carlo, ed. 1984. *Raffaello in Vaticano*. Milan.

Pietri, C. 1961. "Concordia apostolorum et renovatio urbis." *MAH* 73:275–322.

Pinto, G. 1982. *La Toscana nel tardo medio evo: Ambiente, economia rurale, società*. Florence.

Pinto, John. 1986. *The Trevi fountain*. New Haven.

Pinzi, C. 1887–1913. *Storia della città di Viterbo*. 4 vols. Rome.

Platina, Bartolomeo (de Sacchis). 1913. *Platynae historici liber di vita Christi et omnium pontificum*, ed. Giacinto Gaida. *RIS*² 3.1. Bologna.

Pleyer, Kleo. 1927. *Die Politik Nikolaus' V*. Stuttgart.

Pope-Hennessy, John. 1952. "The S. Maria Maggiore altarpiece." *Burlington Magazine* 94:31–32.

Pope-Hennessy, John. 1974. *Fra Angelico*. London.

Potter, Tim. 1979. *The changing landscape of Southern Etruria*. New York.

Prager, P., and G. Scaglia. 1970. *Brunelleschi: Studies of his technology and inventions*. Cambridge, Mass.

Pratesi, L. 1987. *I cortili di Roma*. Rome.

Pred, Alan. 1984. "Place as historically contingent process: Structuration and the time-geography of becoming places." *Annals of the Association of American Geographers* 74:279–297.

Prete, M. R., and M. Fondi. 1957. *La casa rurale nel Lazio settentrionale e nell'Agro Romano*. Ricerche sulla dimora rurale in Italia, 16. Florence.

Preyer, Brenda. 1981. "The Rucellai palace." In Kent and Perosa (1981), 179–183.

Preziosi, Donald. 1979. *The semiotics of the built environment: An introduction to architectonic analysis*. Bloomington.

Prodi, Paolo. 1982. *Il sovrano pontefice, un corpo e due anime: La monarchia papale nella prima età moderna*. Bologna.

Proia, A., and P. Romano. 1933–41. *Roma nel Cinquecento*. 13 vols. Rome.

Purtle, Carol. 1982. *The Marian paintings of Jan van Eyck*. Princeton.

Querini, Q. 1892. *La beneficenza romana*. Rome.

Ragon, Michel. 1983. *The space of death: A study of funerary architecture, decoration, and urbanism*. Charlottesville.

Ramsey, Paul, ed. 1982. *Rome in the Renaissance: The city and the myth*. Binghamton, New York.

Re, Camillo, ed. 1880. *Statuti della città di Roma*. Rome.

Re, C. 1889. "Le regioni di Roma nel medio evo." *Studi e Documenti di Storia e Diritto* 7:349ff.

Re, Emilio. 1920. "I Maestri di Strada." *ASRSP* 43:5–102.

Re, Emilio. 1923. "Maestri di Strada del 1452." *ASRSP* 46:407–409.

Re, Emilio. 1928. "Bandi Romani." *ASRSP* 51:79–101.

Réau, L. 1956. *Iconographie de l'art chrétien*, vol. 2. Paris.

Redig de Campos, D. 1950. "Relazione: Pitture murali, palazzo Vaticano." *Atti della Pontificia Accademia Romana di Archeologia ser. 3, Rendiconti* 23–24:338ff.

Reynolds, B. 1954. "Bruni and Perotti present a Greek historian." *BHR* 16:108–118.

Ricci, Corrado. 1925. *Il Tempio Malatestiano*. Milan.

Ricci, Corrado. 1930. "Il Foro di Augusto e la casa dei Cavalieri di Rodi." *Capitolium* 6:157–189.

Rice, Eugene. 1985. *St. Jerome in the Renaissance*. Baltimore.

Richter, M. 1937. "Die 'Terra Murata' im Florentinischen Gebiet." *MKIF* 5:351–386.

Robathan, D. M. 1970. "Flavio Biondo's 'Roma Instaurata.'" *MH*, n.s. 1:203–216.

Rochon, A. 1963. *La jeunesse de Laurent des Medicis 1449–1478*. Paris.

Rodenwaldt, G. 1939. *Korkyra: Archäische Bauten und Bildwerke, i, Die Bildwerke des Artemistempels*. Berlin.

Rodocanachi, E. 1894. *Les corporations ouvrières a Rome depuis la chute de l'Empire romain*. 2 vols. Paris.

Rodocanachi, E. 1922. *Histoire de Rome de 1354 à 1471: L'antagonisme entre les romains et la Sainte Siège*. Paris.

Rohault de Fleury, G. 1948. *Le Latran au moyen age*. Paris.

Romano, Mario. 1948. *Pellegrini e viaggiatori nell'economia di Roma dal secolo XIV al XVII*. Milan.

Romano, Pietro. 1938. *Il quartiere del Rinascimento*. Rome.

Romano, Pietro. 1941. *Ponte*, vol. 1. Rome.

Rossi, L. 1950. *Niccolò V e le potenze d'Italia*. Pavia.

Rotondi, Pasquale. 1950. *Il Palazzo Ducale in Urbino*. 2 vols. Urbino.

Rowntree, Lester, and Margaret Conkey. 1980. "Symbolism and the cultural landscape." *Annals of the Association of American Geographers* 70:459–474.

Rubinstein, Ruth O. 1967. "Pius II's Piazza S. Pietro and St. Andrew's head." In D. Fraser, H. Hibbard, and M. Lewine, ed., *Essays presented to Rudolf Wittkower on his 65th birthday, i. Essays in the history of architecture*, 22–33. London.

Rucellai, Giovanni. 1960. "Il Zibaldone quaresimale." In A. Perosa, ed., *Giovanni Rucellai e il suo zibaldone, i*. London.

Ruggieri, E. 1866. *L'arciconfraternità del Gonfalone*. Rome.

Russell, J. C. 1960. "The metropolitan city regions of the middle ages." *Journal of Regional Studies* 2:55–70.

Rykwert, Joseph. 1976. *The idea of a town: The anthropology of urban form in Rome, Italy, and the ancient world*. Princeton.

Saalman, Howard. 1966. "Tommaso Spinelli, Michelozzo, Manetti and Rossellino." *JSAH* 25:151–164.

Salerno, L., L. Spezzaferro, and M. Tafuri. 1973. *Via Giulia, un'utopia urbanistica del '500*. Rome.

Salmi, R. 1935. "Paolo Uccello, Piero della Francesca e gli affreschi del Duomo di Prato." *Bollettino d'Arte* 28:1–27.

Sambin, P. 1958. "Il Panormita e il dono d'una reliquia di Livio." *IMU* 1:276–282.

Sansi, A. 1884. *Storia del Comune di Spoleto dal secolo XII al XVII*. 2 vols. Foligno.

Santilli, F. 1925. *La Basilica dei SS. Apostoli*. Rome.

Sassi, Romualdo. 1951. "Sigismondo Pandolfo Malatesta a Fabriano." *Studi Romagnoli* 2:169–186.

Sassi, Romualdo. 1955a. *Documenti chiavelleschi*. Ancona.

Sassi, Romualdo. 1955b. *Documenti sul soggiorno a Fabriano di Niccolò V e della sua corte nel 1449 e 1450*. Ancona.

Sassi, Romualdo. 1964–65. "Moti revoluzionari e agitazioni politiche in Fabriano nella seconda metà del '400." *Atti e Memoria. Deputazione di Storia Patria per le Marche* ser. 8, 4: 283–352.

Sauer, J. 1924. *Symbolik des Kirchengebäudes und seiner Ausstattung in der Auffassung des Mittelalters.* 2d ed. Freiburg-im-Breisgau.

Scaccia-Scarafoni, C. 1927. "L'antico statuto dei 'magistri stratarum' e altri documenti relativi a quella magistratura." *ASRSP* 50:239–308.

Scagliarini Corlaita, Daniela. 1988. "La situazione urbanistica degli archi onorari nella prima età imperiale." In Mansuelli (1988).

Scaramella, G. 1906. Introduction to Palmieri (1906–15).

Schiavo, Antonio di Pietro dello. 1917. *Il diario romano di Antonio di Pietro dello Schiavo, 1402–1417,* ed. F. Isoldi. *RIS²* 24.5. Città di Castello.

Schimmelpfennig, B. 1974. "Die Kronung des Papstes im Mittelalter dargestellt am Beispiel der Kronung Pius' II." *QFIAB* 54:192–270.

Schmidt, P. G. 1981. "Mittelalterliches und humanistisches Städtelob." In *Die Rezeption der Antike: Wolfenbütteler Abhandlungen zur Renaissanceforschung* 1:119–128. Hamburg.

Schulz, Jürgen. 1978. "Jacopo de' Barbari's view of Venice: Map making, city views, and moralized geography before the year 1500." *Art Bulletin* 60:425–474.

Sedlmayr, Hans. 1948. *Architektur als abbildende Kunst.* Vienna.

Segni, C., C. Thoenes, and L. Mortari. 1966. *SS. Celso e Giuliano.* Rome.

Serafini, C. 1910. *Le monete e le bolle pontificie del Medagliere Vaticano,* vol. 1. Milan.

Sereni, Emilio. 1970. "Agricoltura e mondo rurale." In *Storia d'Italia, i (I caratteri originali),* 135–252. Turin.

Sereni, Emilio. 1974. *Storia del paesaggio italiano.* 2d ed. Bari.

Serra, Joselita Raspi. 1972. *La Tuscia romana. Un territorio come esperienza d'arte.* Rome.

Serra, Joselita Raspi. 1987. *Economia e territorio: il patrimonio Beati Petri nella Tuscia.* Naples.

Setton, Kenneth M., ed. 1975. *A history of the crusades,* vol. 3. *The fourteenth and fifteenth centuries,* ed. H. H. Hazard. Madison.

Setton, Kenneth M. 1976. *The papacy and the Levant (1204–1571),* vol. 1. *The fifteenth century.* Philadelphia.

Sforza, G. 1884. *Ricerche su Niccolò V.* Lucca.

Shearman, John. 1965. "Raphael's unexecuted projects for the Stanze." In G. Kauffman and W. Sauerländer, ed., *Walter Friedländer zum 90 Geburtstag,* 158–180. Berlin.

Shearman, John. 1972. *Raphael's cartoons in the collection of Her Majesty the Queen and the Tapestries for the Sistine Chapel.* London.

Siebenhüner, H. 1954. *Das Kapitol in Rom: Idee und Gestalt.* Munich.

Siegel, Jerrold E. 1966. "'Civic humanism' or Ciceronian rhetoric? The culture of Petrarch and Bruni." *Past and Present* 34:3–48.

Silenzi, F., and R. Silenzi. 1968. *Pasquino, quattro secoli di satira romana.* Florence.

Silvestrelli, G. 1970. *Città, castelli e terre della regione romana: Ricerche di storia medievale e moderna sino all'anno 1800.* Rev. ed., 2 vols. Rome.

Simon, M. 1951. "St. Stephen and the Jerusalem Temple." *Journal of Ecclesiastical History* 2:127–142.

Simoncini, G. 1974. *Città e società nel Rinascimento.* 2 vols. Turin.

Simonelli, P. 1973. *La famiglia Capranica nei secoli XV–XVII.* Rome.

Simpson, W. 1966. "Cardinal Giordano Orsini as a prince of the Church and patron of the arts: A contemporary panegyric and two descriptions of the lost frescoes in Monte Giordano." *JWCI* 29: 135–159.

Sinding-Larsen, S. 1975. "A Tale of Two Cities: Florentine and Roman visual context for fifteenth century palaces." *Institutum Romanum Norvegiae. Acta* 6:163–212.

Sollerio, J. B., ed. 1735. *Acta Sanctorum XXV, Mensis Augusti*, vol. 2. Antwerp.

Sora, V. 1907. "I conti di Anguillara dalla loro origine al 1465." *ASRSP* 30:53–118.

Spezzaferro, Luigi. 1973. "La politica urbanistica dei papi e le origini di via Giulia." In Salerno et al. (1973), 15–64.

Sprengel, U. 1971. *Die Wanderherdschaft im mittel- und süditalienischen Raum*. Marburg.

Spufford, Peter. 1988. *Money and its uses in medieval Europe*. Cambridge.

Stilgoe, John. 1982. *The common landscape of America, 1580–1850*. New Haven.

Stinger, Charles L. 1977. *Humanism and the Church Fathers: Ambrogio Traversari (11386–1439) and Christian antiquity in the Italian Renaissance*. Albany.

Stinger, Charles L. 1981. "Roma triumphans: Triumphs in the thought and ceremonies of Renaissance Rome." *MH*, n.s. 10:189–201.

Stinger, Charles L. 1985. *The Renaissance in Rome*. Bloomington, Indiana.

Stookey, L. H. 1969. "The Gothic cathedral and the Heavenly Jerusalem: Liturgical and theological sources." *Gesta* 7:35–38.

Stridbeck, C. G. 1963. *Raphael studies, ii: Raphael and tradition*. Uppsala.

Strnad, A. 1966. "Francesco Todeschini-Piccolomini: Politik und Mäzenatentum im Quattrocento." *Römische Historische Mitteilungen* 8/9: 101–425.

Szabo, Thomas. 1975. "La rete stradale del contado di Siena. Legislazione statutaria e amministrazione comunale nel Duecento." *MEFR-M* 87:141–186.

Szabo, Thomas. 1976. "Die Bedeutung der Kommunen für den Ausbau des mittelalterlichen Strassennetzes in Italien." *Storia della Città* 3:21–27.

Tafuri, Manfredo. 1976. *Architecture and utopia: Design and capitalist development*. Cambridge, Mass.

Tafuri, Manfredo. 1984. "'Roma instaurata': Strategie urbane e politiche pontificie nella Roma del primo '500." In S. Ray et al., ed., *Raffaello architetto*, 59–106. Milan.

Tafuri, Manfredo. 1987. "'Cives esse non licere': The Rome of Nicholas V and Leon Battista Alberti: Elements towards a historical revision." *Harvard Architectural Review* 6:61–75.

Tateo, F. 1971. *I centri culturali dell'umanesimo italiano*. Bari.

Theiner, A., ed. 1882. *Codex diplomaticus dominii temporalis S. Sedis*. 3 vols. Rome.

Thies, Harmen. 1982. *Michelangelo: Das Kapitol*. Munich.

Thomson, J. A. K. 1980. *Popes and princes: Politics and polity in the late medieval Church*. London.

Toews, J. B. 1968. "Formative forces in the pontificate of Nicholas V." *Catholic Historical Review* 54:261–284.

Tomassetti, Aloysius, ed. 1860. *Bullarium Magnum Romanum*, vol. 5. Aosta.

Tomassetti, Giuseppe. 1979. *La Campagna Romana antica, medioevale e moderna*, ed. L. Chiumenti and F. Bilancia. 4 vols. Florence.

Tomei, Pietro. 1942. *L'architettura a Roma nel Quattrocento*. Rome.

Tommasini, O. 1880. "Documenti relativi a Stefano Porcari." *ASRSP* 3:63–134.

Tommasini, O. 1887. "Il registro degli officiali del comune di Roma esemplato dallo scribasenato Marco Guidi." *Atti della R. Accademia dei Lincei, ser. 4, Memorie Scienze morali, storiche e filologiche* 3:169–222.

Torselli, G. 1972. *Castelli e ville del Lazio*. 2d ed. Rome.

Touring Club Italiano. 1962. *Guida d'Italia del Touring Club Italiano. Marche.* Milan.

Touring Club Italiano. 1965. *Guida d'Italia del Touring Club Italiano. Roma e dintorni.* Milan.

Traversari, Ambrogio. 1912. *Hodoeporicon*, ed. A. Dini. Florence.

Trexler, Richard. 1973. "Ritual behavior in Renaissance Florence: The setting." *MH*, n.s. 4:125–144.

Trexler, Richard. 1980. *Public life in Renaissance Florence.* New York.

Trifone, B. 1909. "Le carte del monastero di S. Paolo fuori le Mura dal secolo XI al XV, ii." *ASRSP* 32:29–106.

Tuccia, Nichola della. 1852. *Cronaca de' principali fatti d'Italia 1417–1468*, ed. F. Orioli. Rome.

Turner, Victor, and Edith Turner. 1978. *Image and pilgrimage in Christian culture: Anthropological perspectives.* New York.

Ullman, B. L. 1933. "Poggio's mss. of Livy, alleged and real." *Classical Philology* 28:282–283.

Urban, Günther. 1961. "Die Kirchenbaukunst des Quattrocento in Rom." *RJB* 9:73–297.

Urban, Günther. 1963. "Zum Neubau-Projekt von St. Peter unter Papst Nikolaus V." In H. M. von Erffa and E. Herget, ed., *Festschrift für Harald Keller*, 131–173. Darmstadt.

Urban, Günther. 1965. "Der Tempietto in Vicovaro und Domenico da Capo d'Istria." In *Festschrift Herbert von Einem*, 266–291. Berlin.

Urlichs, C. 1871. *Codex Urbis Romae topographicus.* Würzburg.

Vagnetti, Luigi. 1969. "La 'Descriptio urbis Romae,' uno scritto poco noto di Leon Battista Alberti." *Quaderno. Università degli Studi di Genova, Facoltà di Architettura* 1:25–78.

Vagnetti, Luigi. 1974. "Lo studio di Roma negli scritti Albertiani." In *Convegno internazionale indotto nel V centenario di Leon Battista Alberti*, 73–140. Rome.

Valentini, R., and G. Zucchetti, ed. 1940, 1946, 1953. *Codice topografico della città di Roma*, vols. 1, 3, 4. Rome.

Valtieri, Simonetta. 1972. "Rinascimento a Viterbo: Bernardo Rossellino." *L'Architettura: Cronache e Storia* 17:686–94.

Valtieri, Simonetta. 1984. "La zona di Campo de' Fiori prima e dopo gli interventi di Sisto IV." *L'Architettura: Cronache e Storia* 30:346–372, 648–660.

Varanelli Simi, Emma. 1983. "La Stanza della Segnatura e la semantica del 'templum' petriana e paolina." *Storia dell'Arte* 49: 169–178.

Varese, C., ed. 1955. *Prosatori volgari del Quattrocento.* La letteratura italiana. Storia e testi, 14. Milan and Naples.

Vasari, Giorgio. 1906. *Le vite de' più eccellenti architetti, pittori, et scultori italiani, da Cimabue inso a' tempi nostri*, ed. G. Milanesi. Rev. ed., 9 vols. Florence.

Vignati, B. 1959. "Alcune osservazioni sul 'De rebus memorabilibus basilicae sancti Petri.'" In S. Corvi, ed., *Studi su Mafeo Vegio*, 58–69. Lodi.

Visconti, P. 1847. *Dizionario storico delle città e famiglie nobili dello Stato pontificio.* Rome.

Vitale, P. 1791. *Storia diplomatica de' senatori di Roma dalla decadenza dell'Impero romano fino a' nostri giorni.* 2 vols. Rome.

von Moos, Stanislaus. 1974. *Turm und Bollwerk: Beiträge zu einer politischen Ikonographie der italienischen Renaissance-architektur.* Zurich and Freiburg-im-Breisgau.

Wackernagel, M. 1981. *The world of the Florentine Renaissance artist*, ed. A. Luchs. Princeton.

Walser, E. 1914. *Poggius Florentinus. Leben und Werke*. Leipzig and Berlin.

Walsh, K. 1975. "Zum Patrimonium Beati Petri im Mittelalter." *Römische Historische Mitteilungen* 17:193–211.

Warnke, Martin. 1976. *Bau und Überbau: Zur Soziologie der mittelalterliche Architektur nach den Schriftquellen*. Frankfurt am Main.

Wasner, F. 1968. "Tor der Geschichte: Beiträge zum päpstlichen Zeremonienwesen im 15 Jahrhundert." *Archivum historiae pontificiae* 6:142–153.

Wasserman, J. 1963. "The Quirinal palace in Rome." *AB* 45:205ff.

Weil, Mark. 1974. *The history and decoration of the Ponte S. Angelo*. University Park, Pa., and London.

Weisbach, W. 1913. "Eine Darstellung der letzten deutschen Kaiserkronung in Rom." *Zeitschrift für bildende Kunst*, n.s. 23:255–266.

Weiss, Roberto. 1958. *Un umanista veneziano, Papa Paolo II*. Venice and Rome.

Weiss, Roberto. 1969. *The Renaissance discovery of classical antiquity*. Oxford.

Weissman, Ronald. 1982. *Ritual brotherhood in Renaissance Florence*. New York and London.

Wellmann, Max. 1905. "Elefant." In *PW* 5.2: 2248–2257.

Westfall, Carroll W. 1969. "Society, beauty and the humanist architect in Alberti's 'De re aedificatoria.'" *Studies in the Renaissance* 16:61–79.

Westfall, Carroll W. 1973. "Biblical typology in the Vita Nicolai V by Giannozzo Manetti." In J. Ijsewijn and E. Kessler, ed., *Acta Conventus Neolatini Lovaniensis*, 701–109. Munich.

Westfall, Carroll W. 1974a. *In This Most Perfect Paradise: Alberti, Nicholas V, and the invention of conscious urban planning in Rome, 1447–1455*. University Park, Pa., and London.

Westfall, Carroll W. 1974b. "Alberti and the Vatican palace type." *JSAH* 55:101–121.

Westfall, Carroll W. 1978. "Chivalric decoration: The Palazzo Ducale in Urbino as a political statement." In H. A. Millon and L. Nochlin, ed., *Art and architecture in the service of politics*, 20–45. Cambridge, Mass.

Wickhoff, Franz. 1893. "Die Bibliothek Julius' II." *Jahrbuch der königlichen preussischen Kunstsammlungen* 14:49–64.

Widloecher, Nicola. 1929. *La congregazione dei canonici regolari lateranensi. Periodo di formazione, 1402–1483*. Gubbio.

Wilpert, J. 1929. *Die römischen Mosaiken und Malereien der kirchlichen Bauten vom IV bis XIII Jahrhundert*. 2 vols. Freiburg-im-Breisgau.

Wittschier, H., ed. 1908. *Giannozzo Manetti: Das Corpus der Orationes*. Cologne.

Wohl, Helmut. 1980. *The paintings of Domenico Veneziano: A study in Florentine art of the early Renaissance*. New York.

Wolff, Philippe. 1977. "Pouvoir et investissements urbains en Europe occidentale et centrale du XIIe au XVIIe siècle." *Revue historique* 257:277–311.

Wolff-Metternich, Franz Graf von. 1975. *Bramante und St. Peter*. Munich.

Wolkan, Rudolf, ed. 1909. *Der Briefwechsel des Eneas Silvius Piccolomini*. Fontes Rerum Austriacarum, 2 Abt.: Diplomataria et acta, 67–68. 2 vols. Vienna.

Würm, H. 1965. *Der Palazzo Massimo alle Colonne*. Berlin.

Zabughin, V. 1919–20. *Giulio Pomponio Leto*. 2 vols. Rome.

Zangheri, R. 1983. "La formazione della campagna nell'Europa occidentale." *Storia della Città* 28:5–10.

Zippel, Giuseppe. 1900. *Un umanista in villa: Lettere di Gaspare Veronese a Giovanni Tortelli*. Pistoia.

Zippel, Giuseppe, ed. 1904. *Le vite di Paolo II di Gaspare Veronese e Michele Canensi*. *RIS*² 3.16. Città di Castello.

Zippel, Giuseppe. 1907. "L'allume di Tolfa e il suo commercio." *ASRSP* 30:5–52.

Zippel, Giuseppe. 1912. "Documenti per la storia di Castel S. Angelo." *ASRSP* 35:151–218.

Zippel, Giuseppe. 1921. "Ricordi Romani dei Cavallieri di Rodi." *ASRSP* 44:169–205.

Zippel, Giuseppe. 1930. "Il Palazzo del Governo Vecchio in Roma." *Capitolium* 6:365f.

Zöbl, D. 1982. *Die Transhumanz (Wanderschafhaltung) der europäischen Mittelmeerländer in historischer, geographischer und volkskündlicher Sicht*. Berlin.

Zocca, Emma. 1959. *La basilica dei SS. Apostoli in Roma*. Rome.

Zocca, Mario. 1943. "Sistemazioni urbanistiche del Rinascimento in Lazio." *Palladio* 7:40–50.

Zorn, W. 1939. "Giannozzo Manetti: Seine Stellung in der Renaissance." Ph.D. dissertation, Freiburg-im-Breisgau.

Zorzi, Gian Giorgio. 1967. *Le chiese e le ponti di Andrea Palladio*. Milan.

Zorzi, Ludovico. 1977. *Il teatro e la città: saggi sulla scena italiana*. Turin.

Zoubov, V. 1958. "Leon Battista Alberti et les auteurs du moyen age." *Medieval and Renaissance Studies* 4:255–266.

Index

Aurelian (emperor), 13, 47, 140, 187
Aurelio da Piacenza, 152, 156
Avignon, 250
Avogadro, Paride, 263

Babylon, 67, 175, 185, 193, 257, 292
Bagnaia, 80
Bankers and financiers
  Roman, 88, 159, 226, 265
  Romans partnered with Tuscans, 121,
    151, 159, 226, 282, 289
  Tuscan, 23, 41–42, 81, 97, 128–129
Barbo, Pietro. *See* Paul II (pope)
Barone, Francesco, 117, 275
Baronial class, 28, 34, 108, 150, 154, 187,
  199–200, 224, 281
Bartolomeo da Vercelli, 285
Bartolomeo di Matteo da Perugia, 287
Basel, 190
Basinio da Parma, 290–291
Baths and bathing establishments
  Vicarello, 192
  Viterbo, 133, 192, 201
Belluno, 168
Beltrami da Compione, Benedetto, 125
Beltramo di Martino da Varese, 102,
  106–107, 112, 125–134, 138, 227,
  230, 261, 269, 278–279
Benedetto da Piacenza, 145
Bentivoglio, Sante, 95
Bernardo di Lorenzo da Firenze (*not* Ros-
  sellino), 270
Bessarion, Cardinal Johannes, 94–95, 97,
  120, 166, 259, 268–270, 292
Bianchi movement, 286
Biondo, Flavio, 6, 14, 88, 157, 167, 177,
  180, 206, 221–222, 242, 247, 266,
  286, 288, 292
Bisticci, Vespasiano da, 97, 168
Blenheim Palace, 205
Boccabelli, Giovanni (Gianni) di Giorda-
  no, 226–227, 272, 294
Bologna, 94–95, 100, 194, 198, 292
  bishops' palace, 52
  university, 95
Bonadies family, 37, 42–43, 262
  Giovanni, 262–283
Boniface VIII (pope), 145
Boniface IX (pope), 143, 230
Borghetto. *See* Borgo S. Leonardo
Borgia, Cardinal Rodrigo. *See* Alexander
  VI (pope)
Borgo. *See* Rome: districts and enclaves
Borgo S. Leonardo, 230, 294

Bovattieri. See Guilds and professional
  associations; Trades and professions
Bracciano, Lake of, 192
Braccio da Montone, 236
Bracciolini, Poggio, 63, 93, 141, 169, 204,
  271, 286–287
Bramante, Donato, 69, 123, 258–259,
  277, 290
Brambles, as emblem of decay of Rome,
  140
Bregno, Andrea, 290
Brindisi, 292
Brunelleschi, Filippo, 45, 52, 56, 235–
  236, 253, 283
Bruni, Leonardo, 2, 189–192, 287
Buffaloes, 23, 224, 293. *See also Alaggio*
Building legislation. *See* Statutes: *maes-
  tri di strada*
Bullatores, 123, 276
Buonarroti, Michelangelo, 181
Burchardus (Burckard), Johannes, 276
Bussi, Giovanni Andrea, 271

Caccia, Stefano da Novara, 109, 131–
  132, 260, 264, 271
Caetani family, 34, 199, 250
  Onorato, 108, 110–112, 274, 288
Caffari, Stefano, 162–163, 261
Cairo, 174–175, 177, 251
Calandrini, Cardinal Filippo, 103, 137,
  166–167, 215, 255, 292
Calixtus III (pope), 139, 148, 162, 170,
  207, 249, 254, 275, 278–279, 289, 294
Calla, 197
Calvi, Giacomo, 85–86, 126, 263–265,
  277
Camerino, 134, 136, 272, 287
Canals, in urban infrastructure, 174–175
Canensi, Michele, 95, 121, 162–163,
  182, 186–187, 253–255, 261, 269
Canonization proceedings, 95
Capoccini
  Giovanni, 229, 294
  Pietro, 229
Capo de' Rami, 228
Capodiferro, Ciriaco, 156
Capranica
  Cardinal Angelo, 34
  Cardinal Domenico, 34, 38, 91–92, 115,
    132, 156, 159–160, 255, 263, 269, 283
  Dionisio, 160
Caradosso, Cristoforo Foppa, 259
Carafa, Cardinal Oliviero, 161
Carboni, Giordano, 284
Carmagnola, Domenico da, 100

Naples, 131, 197, 199, 255, 257, 268, 288, 293
  Castel Nuovo, 188
  S. Domenico Maggiore, 258
Nardini, Stefano, 85, 283
Narni, 192, 287
Narses (Byzantine general), 269
National communities in Rome, 25. *See also* Immigration
  Florentine and other Tuscan, 41–42, 79, 81, 85, 125, 235–236, 265
  French, 34
  Illyrian, 231, 250
  Lombard, 115, 124–134, 231, 251, 278
Navicella, 119
Navy (papal), 187, 224
Nazzano, 289
Nello di Bartolomeo da Bologna, 22–23, 25, 48, 78, 80, 84, 94, 96–97, 99–113, 120, 126, 128, 130–134, 138–139, 195–199, 203, 205, 222, 226, 228, 235, 242–243, 262, 271–275, 288, 298–301
Nemi, 181, 240
Neoplatonism, 14, 291
Nepi, 196, 202, 261, 289
Nero (emperor), 180
Niccolini family, 239
Niccolò da Firenze, 263
Niccolò di Lorenzo da Fabriano, 100, 134–139, 271, 279–280
Nicholas III (pope), 254
Nicholas IV (pope), 140, 161, 254
Nicholas V (pope)
  aesthetic taste, 52, 78, 84, 112, 224, 254
  architectural patronage, 20, 46, 52, 55, 69, 71, 75, 92, 99, 102, 106, 111, 113, 124–139, 161–162, 192–233, 286–288, 295–296
  concern for liturgy, 54, 73
  consolidation of fortifications of Rome, 10, 74, 111, 116, 128, 186, 256
  contemporary criticism of, 75, 92, 129, 278
  coronation (*see* Ceremonies)
  deathbed speech (so-called testament), 9–11, 58, 256
  early career, 50, 56, 65, 100, 167, 255
  edicts concerning Rome, 85, 163–167, 225, 297–298
  ill health and its effects, 27, 112
  insignia deployed in city, 12, 45–48, 78, 93–94, 96, 155–157, 187, 231, 252–254, 295
  investigation of relics, 53, 94

  as patron of literary studies, 56, 75, 84, 146, 193, 221, 242, 255, 286, 291
  policy toward baronial aristocracy, 95–96, 167, 182, 200, 242, 269
  policy toward Lateran, 27–29, 31, 53, 147–148
  policy toward Roman political class, 15, 29–30, 33, 54, 75, 82, 87, 91, 107, 111, 116, 147, 150–151, 155, 158, 244, 285
  policy toward subject territories, 195–205, 210, 216, 243, 288–289, 292
  poor relief and policy toward poorer classes, 33, 55, 86, 91, 111, 121, 255, 270, 276
  portraits, 55, 57, 63, 69
  private chapel, 17, 47, 50, 102, 254 (*see also* Fra Angelico)
  program of church restoration, 46, 52, 92, 95, 101, 104–105, 110, 116, 166, 183
  project for Vatican basilica and palace, 106, 110–111, 128–131
  regulation of commerce, 85
  studiolo, 39, 50, 53, 117, 253, 263
  travels in papal state, 103, 123, 134–137, 209
  and urban development, 42, 45, 49, 72, 77, 80, 82, 89, 91, 111, 113, 143, 163–171, 182–184, 187–188, 192, 222, 230–238
Nicolaus de Civitate Castelli, 230
Nikolaus von Kues. *See* Cusanus, Cardinal Nicolaus
Noah's Ark, as paradigm of Renaissance architecture, 62
Nobili
  Giacomo, 86, 260, 271, 288
  Pietro da Noceto, 85–86, 102, 125–126, 132, 136, 260, 263, 271, 275, 288
Nolli, Giovanni Battista, 5
Notaries. *See* Guilds and professional associations; Trades and professions
Numa Pompilius (King of Rome), 179, 286

Octagonal piers, architectural motif, 35
Organs, 146, 148
Orsini family, 26, 49, 73, 83, 95, 160, 200, 289
  Cardinal Giordano, 34, 86, 263
  Cardinal Latino, 34, 85–86, 89, 166, 263–264
  Francesco, 88, 153–154, 156, 282, 285
  Francesco (of Gallese), 294